...550 (cinq...)
...Arthur
...Signé...
C.

...Juillet
Franck
..., boulevard

— Étude
le Tribunal Civil
...soussigné.
...donné
C... demeurant
lieu où était
...Service

...immédiatement. Est ce
que j'ai bien fait?
Je vous rapporterai le
traité écrit en français
et l'argent.
Voulez-vous avoir la bonté
de m'informer, quand
il faut absolument
que je rentre.
J'ai beaucoup de reconnaissance
et amitié pour vous, mais

...Lubomirski a pris
...ant la Philharmo-
...Varsovie avec l'orchestre
...saisons. Mon grand
Fitelberg (un compos-
chef d'orchestre génial)
...directeur; il com...
...on concert à Berlin.
...au revoir, mon cher
Monsieur Astruc, j'attends
votre réponse, dites, si je
dois venir maintenant à
Paris. Avec mes meilleurs
sentiments et amitiés, votre tout
dévoué Arthur Rubinstein

mille amitiés
reconnaissantes de
votre
Arthur Rubinstein

Beaucoup de choses à Mad.
Astruc.

fait la même chose
devant le roi qui était
charmant.
Mr Boosey veut m'engager
avec Destinn pour l'hiver
prochain — je le verrai encore.
Je suis ici au Victoria-
Hôtel!
Avec mille amitiés
Arthur.

TÉLÉGRAMME.

La remise est gratuite.
Le facteur doit délivrer un récépissé à souche lorsqu'il est chargé de recouvrer une taxe.

Indications de service.

...Labastrue Astruc
39 bd ...
Paris

L'État n'est soumis à aucune responsabilité... la voie télégraphique...

Pour Paris ...

...COMMERCIAL

Succes... triomphe
Chicago critiques newyork
predisposes changeront ecrirai
Arthur

MY YOUNG YEARS

ARTHUR RUBINSTEIN

MY YOUNG YEARS

Jonathan Cape Thirty Bedford Square London

JONATHAN CAPE LTD
30 BEDFORD SQUARE, LONDON WCI

ISBN 0 224 00926 5

PRINTED IN GREAT BRITAIN
BY LOWE AND BRYDONE (PRINTERS) LTD,
THETFORD, NORFOLK
BOUND BY G AND J KITCAT LTD, LONDON

Contents

*To Nela, for forty years my wife
and friend, who encouraged me to
write this book and has showed
such beautiful understanding of my
adventurous young years.*

Illustrations

Front-page review in *Le Figaro*—December 14, 1904

Photograph of Arthur from "Musica"—Noël, 1905

News story from *Musical America*—January 6, 1906

Review from *Musical America*—January 13, 1906

Fragment of a review from the *Detroit News*—February 8, 1906

Review from *Kurjer Warszawski*—November 24, 1912
(with translation)

Program for a concert in Glasgow—November 18, 1915

between pp. 336–7

Photograph of Arthur inscribed by him to Mr. Gabriel Astruc—
Paris, February 2, 1905

Photograph of Arthur during his first tour in the United States, 1906

Photograph of Arthur inscribed by him to panine Zofji—
Warsaw, June 25, 1909

left to right—Arthur, Mrs. William Knabe, Mr. Knabe, and
their daughter in the Bois de Boulogne—Paris, 1906

Arthur in Paris wearing his first pearl stick-pin given
by George Brocheton—1909

Arthur in Warsaw 1910 with Antek Moszkowski

from left to right—Arthur, Juljusz Wolfsohn, Leo Sirota

left to right—Fitelberg, Szymanowski, and Arthur

left to right—Karol Szymanowski, Paul Kochanski,
G. Fitelberg

between pp. 368–9

Portrait of Arthur by Kramsztyk done in 1914 in Paris

Photograph of Arthur in Prague in 1914

Arthur, 3rd from right, at a banquet given by
    the Friends of the Philharmonic of Valencia
    after the concert

Arthur photographed in Madrid dressed in a
    torero's "traje de luz" (with cape draped to hide the fact
    that the trousers would not close!)

Magazine photograph of "Arturo" when he was giving
    a series of concerts in Madrid

Photograph of Arthur inscribed by him to
    the Philharmonic Society of Bilbao—1916

Foreword

I have never kept a diary, and even if I had, it would have been lost with all the rest of my belongings in the two world wars. But, it is my good fortune to be endowed with an uncanny memory which allows me to trace my whole long life almost day by day.

These few words should serve as an apology for confiding to my readers a primitive but truthful account of the struggles, the mistakes, the adventures, and of the miraculous beauty and happiness of my young years.

One

CHILDHOOD
IN POLAND

1

My life was saved by my Aunt Salomea. A seventh child, eight years after the last-born, I was utterly unwanted by my parents, and if it hadn't been for the enthusiastic persuasion of Aunt Salomea Meyer, my intrusion into this valley of suffering might have been prevented.

My parents lived in Lodz, a city under Russian rule. Situated near Warsaw, it was the youngest but nevertheless the second largest town in Poland. Toward the middle of the nineteenth century, Tsar Nicholas I, in order to establish a rational wool and cotton industry, invited German master weavers from Silesia to settle in this tiny place called Lódź, Polish word for "boat"—an anachronism, as there was no river around. Hundreds of artisans poured into the city, set up their tools, built fine plants, and rapidly developed a flourishing industry. Attracted by this new promise of wealth, Jews from all over the country invaded the young town. They quickly learned the German methods of wool weaving, and soon started to emulate their masters. A sharp rivalry ensued between these two groups, factories spread like mushrooms, houses, hotels, theaters, churches, synagogues sprang up in no time. Having the whole of Russia and a great part of Asia for a market, Lodz became, after Moscow, the biggest industrial center of the Empire.

The native Poles showed little interest in this great opportunity. Business did not attract them; their favorite occupations were agriculture, science, and art. But thousands of peasants came to work in the plants. And so, paradoxically, Lodz appeared to be a foreign town right in the heart of Poland.

My Grandfather Heyman was one of the first to try his luck in the new city; he met with success, and raised a family of eight daughters and two sons, my mother being the oldest. My father came from Pułtusk, a city up north, set up a little plant to make handwoven cloth, and married my mother. They had six children in quick succession, three daughters and three sons, and then—eight years later, on the 28th of January, 1887 —I rang the bell at the gate of life as a belated and rather unwanted guest. My mother had a very hard time letting me in, I was told, but nothing could deter me from making a brilliant entrance into this vale of tears. My name was to be Leo, for some sentimental reason, I suppose, but my brother Ignacy, then eight, protested vehemently: "His name," he cried, "must be Arthur. Since Arthur X [a neighbor's son] plays the violin so nicely, the baby may also become a great musician!"

And so Arthur I was called. In Polish it is spelled Artur.*

We lived in a spacious, sunny apartment in a nice house on the main street, Plotrkowska ulica. My physical care was entrusted to a wet nurse called Thecla who was devoted to me, but later on, I heard, she was caught thieving and was put into prison. I was frightened that possibly I had swallowed some of her vice along with her milk, though the future proved my apprehensions unwarranted. I have never stolen—yet!

My first musical impressions were formed by the lugubrious and plaintive shrieks of factory sirens, hundreds of them waking the workers at six in the morning when the city was still dark. Soon I was offered more pleasant musical fare when gypsies would appear in the courtyard of our house, singing and dancing with their little dressed-up monkeys, while the so-called orchestra man played many quaint instruments. There was also the singsong of Jewish old-clothes peddlers, of Russian ice cream sellers, and Polish peasant women chanting the praises of their eggs, vegetables, and fruit. I loved all these noises, and while nothing would induce me to utter a single word, I was always willing to sing—to imitate with my voice—any sound I heard, thus creating quite a sensation at home. This sensation soon degenerated into a sport, everyone trying to teach me some songs. In this manner I learned to recognize people by their tunes.

"Who gave you this cake?" my mother would ask me. "Ah, ah, ah, ah," I sang. "Oh, I see, it was Aunt Lucia." She would nod with satisfaction. There is a kind of cooky called *mazurki* in Polish, and in order to get some I would sing a well-known mazurka. I went on playing the role of a human parrot for about two years, when an important event took place which changed my life. My parents bought an upright piano on which my two elder sisters, Jadwiga and Hela, began to take lessons. I was so overwhelmed by the appearance of this divine instrument that from then on the drawing room became my paradise. Yelling and crying being my only defenses, I employed these weapons freely when anyone attempted to remove me from there.

As it happened, my eldest sister, then engaged to be married, took piano lessons to add an extra polish to her education. Every word said, every remark made by the obese Madame Kijanska, Jadwiga's teacher,

* In later years, my manager Sol Hurok used the *h*-less "Artur" for my publicity, but I sign "Arthur" in countries where it is common practice, "Arturo" in Spain and Italy, and "Artur" in the Slav countries.

found me the most attentive listener—and what a delight it was when she slapped my sister's hands for playing a wrong note! Sometimes when my sister was practicing and made a mistake, I was the one who did the slapping. Half in fun, half in earnest, I learned to know the keys by their names, and with my back to the piano I would call the notes of any chord, even the most dissonant one. From then on it became "mere child's play" to master the intricacies of the keyboard, and I was soon able to play first with one hand, later with both, any tune that caught my ear. At times I would play pieces for four hands with Madame Kijanska in place of my sister, and at the right moment I would solemnly stop to turn the page, pretending that I was actually reading the music.

All this, of course, could not fail to impress my family—none of whom, I must now admit, including grandparents, uncles, and aunts, had the slightest musical gift. They seemed amused at first, but later they were rather bewildered to discover such a strong evidence of talent in me. My father had a predilection for the violin; he found it more human, more distinguished than the piano. The success of a number of child prodigies also had impressed him. He presented me with a small fiddle, which I promptly smashed to pieces. And was spanked in return. He made another attempt to convince me of the superiority of the noble stringed instrument, but it definitely failed. My instinctive need was for polyphony, harmony, not this single thin tone of a violin, so often out of tune, always dependent on an accompanist!

It is astonishing—I find so many years later—what a clear picture I have of these early days. I can still draw the disposition of our apartment; I remember vividly the mornings, the tremendous uproar, when my brothers and sisters had to dash to school, invariably late; my mother and a servant used to prepare heaps of sandwiches for them. They would always be shouting and running, quarreling and forgetting things—it was like an army going to war—and then: complete silence; I was left alone with my piano.

By the time I was three and a half years old my fixation was so obvious that my family decided to do something about this talent of mine. Uncle Nathan Follman (who had a good knowledge of the German language) wrote to Joseph Joachim, the most famous violinist of his time and the director of the Imperial and Royal Academy of Music in Berlin, giving him all the details about me, and asking his advice about how to take care of such gifts. Professor Joachim replied very kindly. Nothing should be done until I was six, he answered, but then it would be advisable to place me in the hands of a good teacher. When he added, "If you can manage to bring the child to Berlin, I shall be pleased to see him," it caused quite a stir in the family . . . the great Joachim showing interest in little Arthur!

Many plans were weighed and considered, and finally there was a decision to go to Berlin. My sister Jadwiga's betrothed was a brilliant young wool agent named Maurycy Landau (a tall-dark-and-handsome type who had found his way to her heart, in no small measure by lavishing expensive toys on me), and my parents wanted their eldest daughter to have her trousseau made in the German capital. Here was the perfect opportunity; my mother and sister could take me along.

We left a few days later. All I remember of that journey was the Russian-German frontier, which we reached in the middle of the night. A sinister bell startled us from sleep, and my mother hushed me anxiously. Then after a brief silence, three bearded Russian gendarmes, armed with pistols and long sabers, spurs clinking on their high boots, entered the compartment and asked rudely for our passports. Russia and Turkey were then the only countries in Europe requiring such documents. I was terrified, certain that we were about to be taken to the gallows—a nervous fear that has never left me whenever I cross a Russian frontier.

In Berlin we stayed with my Aunt Salomea Meyer, who was my godmother and made me feel very much at home. My only recollections of the big city were the tramways and elevators, the sidewalks paved with a mosaic of black and white stones, the neatness of the streets and houses, and, above all, the absence of the familiar chimneys and sirens of the factories. I have a photograph of myself, aged four, taken with my pretty little cousin Fanny Meyer, which always brings back the memory of this first visit to Berlin.

One morning I was taken to Professor Joachim, who was expecting us in his studio. The great master was about sixty, tall, rather heavyset, with his face almost hidden by a gray, artistic mane, a round beard, a thick mustache, whiskers, and very bushy eyebrows. Even his huge ears were richly adorned with hair. At first his hollow, cavernous voice scared me, but his kindness and the sweet expression of his eyes reassured me instantly. Joseph Joachim paid little attention to my sister's elaborate account of my talents. He planned to find out for himself, and being suspicious of infant prodigies he began to examine me thoroughly, like a doctor with a patient.

First, he asked me to call out the notes of many tricky chords he struck on the piano, and then I had to prove my perfect ear in other ways. And finally, I remember, he made me play back the beautiful second theme of Schubert's *Unfinished* Symphony after he had hummed it. I had to find the right harmonies, and later transpose the tune into another tonality.

When I had performed all this satisfactorily, Professor Joachim picked me up from the floor, kissed me, and gave me a big piece of chocolate. Later he told my mother and Jadwiga: "This boy may become a very great musician—he certainly has the talent for it. Let him hear some good singing, but do not force music on him. When the time comes for serious study, bring him to me, and I shall be glad to supervise his artistic education."

Thanking the master for his great kindness, we left feeling happy. A fortnight later, when Jadwiga's trousseau was ready, we returned to Lodz, where a warm reception awaited us. The family was thrilled to learn that a great future was in store for me; the whole city was impressed by Joachim's opinion, and even the press published enthusiastic accounts of our visit to Berlin.

The fuss people made about such unimportant matters, like my playing tunes, or guessing chords, seemed absurd to me, when such courageous feats as jumping three stairs, or running more quickly than other little boys, made no impression at all.

When Jadwiga was married, she had a beautiful Jewish wedding at home. A small band of four or five players had been hired for the ball after the ceremony, and as they began to play, I became so excited at the musical noise they produced that I climbed on a chair and, assuming the role of conductor, started to gesticulate wildly. It wasn't long before I fell to the floor, ending up with a big bump on my head and a bloody nose. Apparently I was not destined to become a conductor.

2

My father bought a house and we occupied half of the second floor, while my grandparents Heyman took the other half. Being neighbors intensified greatly our contact with the rest of mother's large family, who were strict Orthodox Jews. Following the tradition that the children gather around the patriarch every Friday, we began to observe the Sabbath with great solemnity in our house.

My own life in these surroundings took a new turn with the appearance of a lovely and sweet little girl, Noemi, a cousin who was exactly my age. The adopted child of Aunt Frandzia, one of my mother's three childless sisters, she lived right next door to us.

Noemi looked like an angel painted by Raphael with her round face, crowned by golden curls, her blue eyes shining with an unearthly expression, and her lovely, soft skin. She had a kind and sweet disposition, and we loved each other so passionately that we were inseparable. The fact that she had lost her own mother at birth and that her father, my Uncle Paul Heyman, had married again, made me feel that I had to look after her.

Aunt Frandzia adored the child, and since her husband was quite well off she made life very pleasant for Noemi, and indirectly for me, too. A beautiful nursery, consisting of two big sunny rooms filled with all sorts of toys, was our daily playground. A governess watched over our games and took us for walks; we had our meals together alternately at my aunt's or at my own house. Noemi—I called her Nemutka—particularly liked playing husband and wife with me. She would obey me blindly, leaving the choicest morsels of food for me, and easily bursting into tears whenever she saw me in trouble. My piano playing made her gasp with admiration. I think we were probably the happiest children in the world.

The next two years were like a dream—the days of a completely happy, carefree childhood. When we grew tired of our games, Noemi and I would listen to fairy tales read to us by her governess, but soon we began to invent our own stories, and as this passion grew, life itself appeared to us as a continuous fairy tale. I am happy to say I have never changed this feeling toward life. . . .

Lodz was the most unhealthy and unhygienic city imaginable: there were no parks or squares, avenues or playgrounds for children. The air was so infected with gas from the chemical plants, and the black smoke from the chimneys which hid the sky was so thick, that our daily walks were, from a health standpoint, nothing but a ritual. At night Lodz was still worse. Lacking a modern system of sewage, the city had to remove its excrement in small iron tanks, driven by horses, which filled the streets with an unbearable odor.

But we saw all these flaws with quite different eyes, Noemi and I; we loved Lodz! The factories were castles with glorious towers, the Russian policemen were ogres, and people in the streets princes and princesses in disguise!

At home I used to illustrate on the piano our stories or little scenes from our daily lives. My greatest success was an imitation of grandmother's quarrels with cook. Tremolo in the bass would announce the coming storm, followed by the two voices fighting each other in a constant crescendo, and, finally, an abrupt chord brought the drama to an end.

One night my parents took me to the Opera, where *Aïda* was being played by an itinerant Italian company. I was much impressed by the singers and the scenery, but at the first forte of the trombones, I started to scream with terror and had to be taken home in a hurry. I could not bear the sound of trombones for a long time after that night. I had far better luck with the first concert I was taken to, and later I heard the Polish pianist Józef Śliwiński, but was too small to appreciate him.

About that time a little boy prodigy came to town for a concert and had a great success. He was the violinist Bronislaw Hubermann, then ten years old. I was delighted by his playing, and my parents invited him to visit us. At home, we played for each other, and he was charming to me. We were friends until he died.

The most important event for me in those days, however, was when a small symphony orchestra visited Lodz, conducted by a Dutchman, Julius Kwast. They performed the first suite of Grieg's *Peer Gynt*, which thrilled me so much that when we returned home I was able to play almost all of it—to the amazement of the family. Mr. Kwast was invited to our house, heard me play, and thought it was time for me to take piano lessons. His advice was promptly followed.

My first teacher was a Mrs. Pawlowska, a typical exponent of the old school, whose chief effort was to make me keep my elbows close to my body and to play scales without dropping the coin she placed on my hand. After three months of vain struggle, she had to admit her defeat, and my lessons were entrusted to Mr. Adolf Prechner, a strange, slightly demonic person with a pockmarked face and a thick yellowish mustache. He would always either speak too softly or shout at the top of his voice, but he knew his job. I made good progress in a short time, and was soon able to play pieces of Mozart, Mendelssohn, and Bach.

One morning my father entered my room with a terrifying expression on his face, waving a newspaper in his hand. He addressed me in a tragic voice, saying, "Arthur, do you know who has died?" I burst into tears, frightened by this question. "Anton Rubinstein," he murmured. "Now your future is ruined!" Apparently he had planned to send me to this great man, whose name I happened to share. He had been the director of the Imperial Conservatory in St. Petersburg—and now his premature death had shattered my father's plans and hopes. However, I failed to appreciate at that time the full impact of this loss. Only now can I realize how different my career might have been if Anton Rubinstein had lived a few years longer.

One day a committee from some institution came to see my parents asking if I could take part in a concert to raise money for their charities. This was a great decision for them to make. I was not yet eight, and Mr. Prechner had to be consulted. When he agreed to the idea, we started immediately to prepare a program for my debut as a concert pianist.

The date was fixed for December 14, 1894. The morning of that day the whole house was in a great state of excitement, but I remained calm and happy. I had just received a nice present from Noemi and had tried on my beautiful black velvet suit with a white lace collar, which made me feel very important. The concert went splendidly. A young lady played the Mendelssohn concerto for violin, a man sang a few songs, and then it was my turn. Having seen a huge box of chocolates in the artists' room, I performed my Mozart sonata and two pieces of Schubert and Mendelssohn in the happiest mood, and was rewarded with a warm ovation from an audience consisting mainly of my family, their friends, and the musical Jews and Germans of Lodz. Noemi was proud of me, and that filled me with joy.

A fortnight later I was sent to school—a Russian school it had to be, as no Polish schools were permitted. We were taught to rattle off the official titles of the Tsar and his family: "His Imperial Majesty, the Autocrat of all the Russias, King of Poland, Grand Duke of Finland, etc.," and then sing the Russian national anthem. I hated it, and resented the imposition of such a completely foreign element on me. We spoke Polish at home, I was a Pole. It is curious to note how much this alien atmosphere at school made me realize how I loved Poland. In the afternoon I had Polish lessons with my sister Frania which were a source of great pleasure to me.

My life went on for a year in a routine, monotonous way until, one evening, quite suddenly, I was taken to Jadwiga's home to spend the night. I had not seen Noemi for two days. She was ill, I was told. I had thought something was wrong, but my questions had been answered evasively: "You must keep away from her," they told me. "She is not well," and their faces were grave and tense. The next few days were an agony; people behaved strangely; they whispered in my presence, eluded me. I felt like a dog left behind by his master. Then, one afternoon, Jadwiga came home in tears. When she saw me, she broke down completely and I knew at once. I guessed everything: Nemutka was no more, my little Nemutka was dead!

Jadwiga said in a strangled voice: "Noemi has left for a long journey," to which I nodded, with a silly, credulous smile. I could not bear to be told . . . I would not listen . . . I wanted to be left alone.

There is a Polish word, *zal*, a beautiful word, impossible to translate. It means sadness, nostalgia, regret, being hurt, and yet it is something else. It feels like a howling inside you, so unbearable that it breaks your heart.

Next morning, my father took me for a walk. At his first words, "You know, Arthur . . . ," I cut him short, and said quickly, "Yes, I know, I know, Papa. She has left, but she will come back." My childhood was over;

I was a boy now. Only years later could I talk about this and listen to the details of the abominable scarlet fever which took her away from me. My sweet little Nemutka—she is certainly an angel now if there are any!

I went through a bad time. I became irritable and disobedient, refusing food, avoiding people at home, and starting fights with boys at school. Nobody could persuade me to play the piano for pleasure. I would just practice my daily scales, but lazily, without conviction. The only thing I liked was to play cards with my sick grandfather, who distracted me by teaching me the most intricate games. I could not be reconciled to the loss of my little friend; there was a rage in me, a grudge, a resentment against something, or someone—I could not say what. One night, wide awake, I suddenly knew. Yes, it is God, this God of my grandfather, who prayed to Him so fervently, assuring me that God knows everything, is everywhere, perceives our most secret thoughts, protects us, and is never wrong. Well, then, I thought bitterly, how could He do such an unjust and terrible thing as this? He must have been distracted, or inattentive, but for God, they say, such a thing would be impossible. A frantic desire took hold of me. I had to find out if He really existed, if He knew my doubts—yes, I must risk that, even if it cost me my life. And the little boy I was, sitting upright in my bed, holding my breath in mortal fear, thought these horrible words: God is a Fool! I expected his immediate appearance, a deadly blow, or at least thunder, but nothing materialized. I repeated the dreadful insult aloud now, but still nothing! Night after night I went through the same scene, which was very hard on my nerves. In addition, I was unhappy at school, where we were made to absorb everything too mechanically, never putting our heart in our work. But I did succeed in learning Russian and German, which was spoken all around me. With my own Polish, it made three languages.

During those years the political situation in Russia was full of unrest and disorder. The discontented working classes listened eagerly to the socialistic theories explained to them by the so-called *inteligentzia*, mostly students of universities and high schools. As it became more and more difficult to cope with this propaganda, the revolutionary movement being well organized, the Russian secret police resorted to their famous system of "provocation." One of their men would mix with a crowd at some legal, peaceful meeting—a procession or a celebration. Whereupon the *agent provocateur* would shout something offensive about the Tsar and the government, or fire a shot—a signal for the police to intervene, beating up the people and arresting the leaders. These actions were the original "pogroms."

I had the misfortune to witness such a scene. After leaving school one day, some boys and I stopped to watch the funeral of a worker, a political agitator, I suppose. Hundreds of co-workers were following the hearse quietly, when suddenly a loud cry was heard. Masses of gendarmes, rushing up out of nowhere, entered the dense crowd with drawn sabers, slashing people. Terrified, we ran to the next portal for safety and from there continued to observe the scene. The mourners tried to disperse, picking up their wounded, but when the police attacked them again, they grew angry and turned against the aggressors. Then something dreadful happened. From a side street, waving their *nahajkas*, a detachment of Cossacks appeared. (We called them Cossacks, but they were really Mongols sent from Siberia.) Mounted on their small Arab horses, their caps pulled over one ear, they charged the crowd in a furious assault, beating everyone unmercifully, and when the victims, shrieking desperately, ran for their lives, the infuriated Cossacks attacked innocent bystanders, mostly old Jews in their long coats, trampling and hurting them cruelly. Then they started to break shop windows . . . there was blood all over the place . . . and we could see the heartbreaking expressions on the faces of the victims. We went home long after it was over, death in our hearts, our eyes filled forever with the horror of it all.

One night my dear old Grandfather Heyman died. He had been ill for a long time and passed quietly away in his sleep. I was roused by cries and laments. Next morning the whole family arrived, all in mourning, tears in their eyes, speaking in hushed voices, rushing in and out, making arrangements for the funeral. As for myself, I pretended once again not to understand what had happened, and would not let anyone explain. I hated death; in fact, I was so terribly afraid of it I used to inquire among my school friends who belonged to different creeds as to which religion seemed to offer the best care for dead bodies. I did not want to be buried. I wished to lie in a transparent coffin on a high catafalque in an airy mausoleum.

My parents became increasingly worried about my brooding and my aversion to the school. I even neglected the piano, and Mr. Prechner complained about my inattentiveness and laziness. The only thing I liked was reading, and I would consume anything I could put my hands on; the novels of Sienkiewicz, Jules Verne, fairy tales, history, and biographies of famous men were my favorites. But not poetry; to me poetry was sham music, a sort of "music's poor relation." I felt ashamed to hear its form, cadence, and rhythm used for exalted words instead of sounds. If one of the young girls in our family started declaiming poetry (a fashion in those days) I would have nervous laughing spells and would have to leave the room.

My parents decided I should go to Warsaw.

3

I was glad to leave Lodz. Preparations were made in a hurry, and one morning Mother and I left for Warsaw. The distance is only three hours by train, but I was stunned by the contrast between the two cities. You leave no man's land and plunge into the heart of Poland—that constant battlefield of Europe. By simple bad luck, the ancient Poles selected the wrong neighborhood, an utterly defenseless space between those two formidable threats to peace, Russia and Germany.

Poland is a flat country of plains and forests, cut by a few rivers, with the Vistula as its chief artery, and bordered in the south by a fine range of mountains. It has nothing sensational to boast of. The cities then were unpretentious and old-fashioned, always having a hard time recovering from wars and revolutions; the villages were humble and primitive, roads were bad, people were poor.

I love my country of birth, and my love has nothing to do with patriotism or chauvinism. My story will show how little of my life I spent at home. But anything Polish exerts an irresistible charm on me, and often makes me feel homesick. The source of this charm may be a sort of authenticity. The seasons, for example, are authentic; there is no mistake about them, they are what a symphony ought to be: four perfect movements in intimate harmony with one another. There is no confusion about them, they live their short lives to the full expression of their individual beauty, they evoke deep emotions by their very nature. The great Polish writer Wladyslaw Reymont shows in his Nobel-prize novel *Chlopi* (*Peasants*) how completely the lives of the peasants, their passions and hopes, joys and sorrows, are regulated by the character of each of the seasons. I have a marked preference for the Polish autumn, with its soft and melancholic twilights, when the country, painted in every shade of gold, brown, and yellow, becomes the natural setting for some of Chopin's loveliest nocturnes.

And those forests which seem to be specially made for fairy tales! And the fields, when the wheat in all its gold moves softly in the wind! I have never been able to look at them without a lump in my throat. Even the people had the stamp of authenticity marked on them: a nobleman, a peasant, a Jew, a priest, a lady, a whore, a worker, a student—all of them showed their unmistakable identities. The peasants keep up the tradition of their colorful regional costumes.

The country, when I was born, was actually only one-third of the Polish territory. In a wicked alliance, three shrewd rulers—the Prussian King Frederick, "the Great," the notorious Empress Catherine II of Russia, also called "the Great," and the Austrian Empress Maria Theresia— divided Poland into three parts: the Northeast, with Warsaw its capital, became the sham kingdom of Poland, the Russian Tsar usurping the title of its king; the Northwest became the German "Ostmarken" with Poznań for its capital; and the South was called by the Austrians the Province of Galicia, with Lwów as the seat of a provincial Parliament, and containing Kraków, the historic Polish capital.

I was quite excited to see the real color of my country for the first time. We stayed at the Hotel d'Angleterre, a historic place, where Napoleon had spent a night during the Russian campaign, and where I was enchanted by the stately candle-lit rooms with their fine old furniture and heavy mirrors.

Near the hotel was the famous Saxon Garden, which had been built by August the Strong, King of Poland. The magnificient palaces of the aristocracy and the ancient royal castle gave Warsaw an air of great nobility. The streets were crowded with gay, exuberant people—nothing can deter the Poles from enjoying life. And the women looked particularly attractive, vivacious, and elegant. There was something so irresistibly exhilarating in the atmosphere of this town that I lost my heart to it completely! Here, the presence of Russian policemen particularly offended me. I hated to see Russian translations above the Polish inscriptions, but what enraged me most were the monuments that had been erected in prominent places, commemorating Russian victories or honoring Polish traitors. Apropos, I remember an amusing anecdote. It seemed that a newly appointed governor of a Polish town gathered all the important citizens and speaking with great eloquence urged them to contribute generously to a fund for a statue in honor of a Russian general who had quelled the last Polish revolution. "You owe it to him," he concluded, "to belong once again to Mother Russia and to our little Father, the Tsar." The men, nodding gloomily, began to pledge their subscriptions—some, five rubles, others ten rubles. The governor was exultant—this was good work indeed, which would be appreciated in St. Petersburg. "I thank you, gentlemen," he said. "And now my aides will proceed to collect the money."

"Money? Who is talking about money?" replied a Polish elder. "We were planning to go to jail instead. Five rubles would be the equivalent of ten days, ten rubles fifteen days, and so on. . . ."

My mother had made an appointment with the great pianist Alexander Michalowski, who was first professor of the Warsaw Conservatory. The music room where he received us looked just like a pantheon, bedecked with dozens of laurel wreaths tied with multicolored silk ribbons—his concert trophies—and this, I soon discovered, was the fashionable way for Polish artists to display them. But so much dust had settled on the leaves that it made it uncomfortable to play, and I couldn't stop coughing and sneezing. Nevertheless, Professor Michalowski was encouraging, saying that he thought I was still too young for him to take on right away, but that in about a year, he would be glad to hear me again. For the present he advised me to go to Professor Rózycki, who had published many exercises and studies for the piano. So my mother made arrangements with Rózycki, who took me on without even troubling himself to hear me play. "My distinguished colleague's reports are sufficient," he declared.

I was left in the care of one of our relatives—a widow, Mrs. Glass, who lived with her daughter Isabella, a very pretty young girl. Their apartment, on the third floor in the second courtyard of an old, shabby house, was anything but attractive. A hired upright piano was brought to the dark and stuffy room assigned to me, and there I was supposed to spend the next few years of my life. When my mother left, I felt terribly lonely, but within a few days Warsaw had worked its charms on me.

At last I was able to play with Polish boys of my age in the enchanting Saxon Garden, which was a new source of pleasure to me. Private lessons—in Polish—interested me intensely, and I found that Mrs. Glass had some books on Polish history that were prohibited. I read them all with passion, as well as the epic trilogy of Sienkiewicz. One of his short stories, "Hania," even inspired me to compose an opera, which I started to work on enthusiastically. While all this was very stimulating, my piano lessons with Mr. Rózycki were not. He was a big, fat, old man, lazy and flabby, with a long gray beard, and the first time we met he received me rather indifferently, making me play a Mozart sonata, at which, to my astonishment, he fell soundly asleep. Awakened by the last chord, he muttered something vague and ordered me to buy some exercises he had published and practice them three hours a day, whereupon he dismissed me. And we went through the same routine in the lessons that followed.

I neglected this boring homework and would read instead music that interested me. The daily routine was often interrupted when one or another of my uncles from Lodz would come to town. They would take me to a restaurant, and then to the Opera. They were very odd, these uncles of mine—each one quite a character. Uncle Paul Heyman, Noemi's father, was the best-dressed man in Lodz, emulating the style of the Prince of Wales (later King Edward VII). He bought his clothes and his hats in London, he had his hair and beard trimmed in the Edwardian fashion, and he loved to be photographed in the posture of his royal model, often carrying a horse whip, despite the fact that he had never mounted a horse. He had yet another idiosyncrasy: Uncle Paul was, as we would say, a "face-slapper"—in French the phrase is: "Il avait la main leste." If anyone opposed him in business, he would simply resort to this persuasive argument, although in reality he was the kindest of men. His younger brother, Jacob, was quite different. A confirmed bachelor, he led a gay life; he was a real *noceur*, haunting all the night spots. He liked to invite me for breakfast, which usually consisted of coffee, rolls, and *pressed caviar*, and he would sing naughty music-hall tunes for me.

Another uncle of mine, Boleslaw Sznek, had given me, for my birthday, two small clay busts of Beethoven and Mozart, and being a great opera lover, he said solemnly: "Arthur, remember, there are three geniuses of music—Beethoven, Mozart, and Battistini!" I was earnestly convinced of this for several years, particularly after I heard this Italian baritone in the *Demon* of Anton Rubinstein, and in Verdi's *Traviata*, and he thrilled me immensely. Along with Caruso, he had the finest male voice I have ever heard.

At my lessons Professor Rózycki continued to sleep as peacefully as ever, a practice which slowed my progress considerably. From time to time Mrs. Glass would give me an envelope containing the fee for the lessons, which I was to deliver to the Professor. On one occasion, when I rang the bell to his apartment, a young boy of about thirteen opened the door instead of the usual maid. "Did the cavalier [the term with which boys addressed each other in the third person] bring the money?" he asked in a rude voice. "No," I answered meekly. "Then there is no lesson," he shouted, and slammed the door.

This was a great shock to me. It was the first humiliation of my life and I was so hurt that I sat on the stairs and cried for a long time. I wrote a letter to my parents, describing the scene and telling them about the sleeping sickness of the professor.

A short time later, my mother arrived to take me home. In their final interview Mr. Rózycki told her he did not think I had a great future as a pianist. I was too inattentive during my lessons, he said. The boy who

had offended me was his son, Ludomir Rózycki, who later became a well-
known composer of operas, ballets, and other works. I have never played
a note of his music.

This time my return to Lodz was less triumphant. I sensed an air of
disappointment and disapproval around me; I became convinced I was an
utter failure, and the smoke and smell of the town, the rushing, gesticulating people in the streets, and the lack of trees contributed to my depression.

After my grandfather's death, my parents took over the tradition of
the Sabbath ritual—not in the same religious spirit, but in a purely sociable
and cordial way. Dinner would be served for about twenty of the closest
members of the family, and the rest would join us later. The food was
excellent: my mother was an artist at preparing carp and pike in the
Jewish manner, and her way of cooking chicken, duck, and goose was un-
equaled! I enjoyed those Friday evenings immensely, not only for their
culinary appeal, though I did not underrate that, but for their lovable and
charming spirit. At dinner, discussions would start up, at first calmly, then
becoming louder and louder, until everybody would shout at the same
time. But no one minded; it was an outlet for natural vitality. Uncle Follman, who was a witty storyteller, never failed to produce some new yarns.
Uncle Paul, the "face-slapper," would give us details of his latest exploits.
Sometimes I would be asked to play, and until late into the night, a succession of hot, light tea with lemon was served, accompanied by the most
delicious homemade cookies.

These Friday evenings went on as usual until on one evening I realized the mood had changed The men spoke in low voices, my mother
was in a dreadful state of nerves, and I was sent to bed early. My father
remained calm and silent, but his behavior was strange—and he alarmed
me most of them all.

One morning the bomb blew up. I had just been practicing in the
drawing room when a big, tall cousin of my mother's came in with his hat
on, shouting at the top of his voice. My mother tried to stop him, but only
succeeded in enraging him more; he insulted my father, threatening him
with legal action in such a rude manner that I could not bear it. Finally
I leaped at him and bit his hand so savagely that I drew blood, whereupon he shrieked, hit me on the head, and left. Then my mother told me
everything. An economic crisis had developed in Lodz; the big factories
with their thousands of workmen, and their modern machinery, had
succeeded in destroying all the handloom plants. My father was one of the
first victims—and he was completely ruined. Our cousin was afraid of losing a sum of money he had lent my father some time before, but he was
mistaken, Mother said: we would pay back every penny borrowed, even

if we had to starve. And father kept his word, selling our house, the factory, some of the furniture, silver, and other valuables. Later I saw this cousin one day smiling at me, and I cut him dead.

My father was an interesting person with an analytic, highly philosophic mind. Brought up in a very Orthodox way, he had been sent to a *hayder* (Hebrew school), where he studied the Talmud, but his passion for knowledge was not satisfied, and he managed to learn French and German in order to read the great philosophers. While he was still young, both his parents had been killed on the same day by Russian shells during the Polish revolution of 1863; so, like many others, he had come to Lodz looking for opportunities. There he met my mother, and in order to marry her he had to become a businessman, in textiles, of course.

He was well over forty when I was born. Of medium height, he stood very straight and had small eyes, a long, sharp nose, a fine brow, a short and pointed chin. I cannot remember a gray hair on his head. He was not handsome, but had exquisite charm, a disarming smile, and distinguished manners. He loathed business and money; his only pleasure was reading, with a glass of tea with lemon at his side. He was very proud of his prodigious visual memory: he had only to look at a number, a date, or a name, and it remained engraved in his mind. This gift degenerated later into a slightly pedantic mania. He liked to torture us with this sort of thing:

"Children, what happened seven years ago this date?"

Dead silence.

"Well, well, can't you remember?" he would insist.

Nothing.

"Bismarck had his famous row with Emperor William II." He would smile triumphantly.

In this way every major or minor event of the last century would be brought into constant review. He loved his family in a detached and discreet manner, seldom interfering with us and rarely losing his temper, although when he did, it was terrifying.

My mother was completely different; she possessed an excess of vitality and lived entirely in the present, particularly in the present of her family—every member of it. Poor Mama, I knew her when she was always low in spirits or ill. She had been good-looking and healthy in her youth, but later she developed a sort of chronic bronchitis that gave her the most violent attacks of coughing I have ever heard; they used to frighten me to death. Never giving a thought to herself, she would worry about everyone else from morning until night. If things seemed to run smoothly, my mother would sigh and wail with pain, pretending not to be able to move. But the minute she heard that someone else in the family was not well, she would jump up, her body bursting with energy, and dash to the patient, where she would assume full control of the situation. Only then did she feel well and happy! The whole family worshiped her, whereas they found my father too self-centered. They were unable to understand his aloofness. But he was deeply devoted to Mother, despite their many violent quarrels.

At the time of our financial breakdown, my two eldest sisters were already married. Jadwiga had three children; Helena was the bride of Dr. Adolf Landau, Maurycy's older brother, a very respectable, nice man. Frania, the youngest girl, was engaged. My eldest brother, Stanislav, who was an unpretentious young man with a heart of gold, worked in a bank, and I was very fond of him. David, my second brother, was studying electrical engineering in Berlin. The youngest, Ignacy, the brother who gave me my first name, was the black sheep of the family, but he was the most intelligent of them all. He had been dismissed from school because of his socialistic activities, and when he joined the revolutionary party he got into real trouble, which caused us all great anxiety.

The family broke up: my parents took a spare room at the Follmans', my brother Stanislav and Frania found lodging in some other aunt's flat, and I was taken by Jadwiga to a summer resort on the river Pilica, called Inowlodz. When I was younger, we used to spent part of the summer in a dreadful little village, so near Lodz that I had no feeling of getting really away from the smoke and the sirens. But Inowlodz turned out to be a delightful place. Jadzia's villa was close to the river, overlooking the fields and woods beyond. We managed through luck to get a piano on which I could work quite well, and I joined a class given by a serious young student from Warsaw. I also made friends with some charming children, and we all enjoyed our vacation, bathing in the river before lunch, then having lessons, ending with the piano; in the afternoons we would make nice excursions into the woods or go to a party at some villa. Twice a week we had dancing lessons, which opened up a new world to me. There I fell in love for the first time in my life. Mania was the girl's name—a slim, rather tall girl of twelve. Two raven-black plaits fell to her waist; she had lovely legs and the eyes of a Persian princess. And when she danced with me I was in such heaven that I could hardly speak to her out of simple emotion.

She was aware of my passion for her. Sometimes she would kiss me— the little boy who played the piano so well. Then I would scratch her and run away in rage. I could not tolerate being treated as anything less than her lover. When Jadwiga allowed me to hire a very old and quiet horse to ride, I would mount my Rosinante and set off in the morning to attract the attention of my beloved one, trying to look like a Spanish conquistador. And I would find my Mania flirting with some old boy of sixteen; furthermore, he was red-haired. I hated him!

When autumn came, it was time for us to return to town. There I found life in Lodz not too cheerful. My father had taken a job as accountant in one of my uncle's factories. He looked as serene as ever, still devoting all his spare time to reading, and he showed no sign of depression. But my poor mother did; the last year had had a disastrous effect on her. She was more irritable, and her coughing spells were quite alarming. Ignacy had been arrested, because the police had found some revolutionary propaganda in his room. We did not even know where they had taken him.

My own life became completely disorganized. I had to sleep on the couch in the Follmans' drawing room, and I had no piano, no lessons of any sort, and nothing to do. But nevertheless I was happy, very happy indeed, thanks to a miraculous circumstance. It developed that Mania Szer, my first love, lived in the house just across the street! So my days were occupied by my simply standing at the window and watching like a dog for any sign, any movement, visible in the apartment across. Whenever I caught a glimpse of her hand moving a curtain, or of her plaits as she turned her back, my heart would start to feel like a military drum.

One morning my mother and I had to make a sinister call, to see the chief of the Okhrana, the Russian secret police, on behalf of my brother. He received us, all smiles and kindness, and spoke in a soft and pleasant voice, but his eyes had the cold, cruel look of a leopard. I played the piano for him because he liked music, and then my mother started to cry. Finally he offered the information that Ignacy was in a prison in Warsaw, that money, cigarettes, and food could be sent to him, and that if he behaved well, he might be released after a while. As a matter of fact, after two months, they did let Ignacy come home. He was a little pale, a little meek, very sad to have given us so much anxiety, but we felt he had lost none of his revolutionary ideas, and would not give up his dangerous activities. After some weeks he was arrested again and was sent to Siberia for five years.

At that time there were endless discussions and consultations about the problem of my future. I was ten years old now, and it was time that something definite be done about me. Warsaw had proved to be a failure. St. Petersburg, after Anton Rubinstein's death, was out of the question. There was, naturally, Vienna, with the famous Professor Theodor Leschetitzky, but we had no connections there, and so, finally, the idea of Berlin came up again.

Two

GROWING UP
IN BERLIN

4

The great decision was taken that in a few days my mother and I would leave for Berlin. This time I felt a heartache at the thought of my departure, in first place the thought of not seeing Mania again. It had been easy to go to the enchanting city of Warsaw, so near home, but now it was entirely different; it was like leaving a sinking ship with one's people on it. My heart went out to Father. He was quiet as usual, never showing any emotion; he even continued to test our memory:

"What happened today five years ago?"

Consternation.

"Arthur spilled his hot chocolate on Aunt Rozia."

But he was unhappy. My father was terribly fond of me, and I knew what our separation meant to him. And he was right; life did separate us from that moment on.

And so my mother and I left for Berlin again. We were cordially received by Aunt Salomea, her husband, Siegfried Meyer, and their four children, and stayed with them for some time. And a very strenuous time it was for me, with an appointment every day with some famous piano teacher. I had to play for Professor Ehrlich, Professor Jedliczka, Scharwenka, and others, less well known. One of these visits I remember clearly. I was to be presented to the Hofmanns, father and son; my mother had a letter of introduction to them, and I was thrilled to meet the famous Josef Hofmann. He was a Pole from Kraków, only twenty-two, but already a celebrity. In Russia he was acclaimed as the only heir of the still-mourned Anton Rubinstein, his teacher; and the United States of America considered him as the only rival of their beloved Paderewski. It is easy to guess how scared I was to play for him. We were received with the usual Polish politeness, especially by the older Hofmann, himself a piano teacher. *He* was the one, too, who listened attentively to my performance. Young Josef remained completely detached, although when the musical business was over and we were ready to go, he did make us stay, to our astonishment, and began to show me, with an almost childish pride, all sorts of little gadgets he owned. Some were presents given him by Thomas Edison, the great inventor, and while I was duly impressed by this fact, I was slightly disappointed by this indifference to music.

Unfortunately, Ferruccio Busoni was away on a concert tour, which proved to be a heavy blow to my career. He was the one person who might have oriented my talent in a better direction—a man with a broad view, both artistically and culturally, a genuinely great human being. Slightly discouraged by the general lack of interest in me and by the obviously expensive lessons the famous teachers offered, my mother decided to take me once again to Joseph Joachim. Despite the fact that he was himself a violinist, who might be less interested in a young pianist, she wanted his advice. To our amazement he received us with the same noble cordiality as he had shown before. "Play a little Mozart for me, mein Junge," he said in his deep but soft bass voice, and I played the A minor Rondo to his evident satisfaction. Then he left the room and returned with a bar of Lindt's bitter chocolate. Afterward when Professor Joachim took my mother into another room for a conference about my future, the most important decision of my life was made! This great man took it upon himself to direct my cultural and musical education, and my mother was overcome with gratitude. In a matter of only a few days he succeeded in persuading three of his friends to put up most of the money, and he committed himself to contributing the fourth share to the fund. What a generous gesture for a great artist, who was not at all rich himself, to make in behalf of a young foreigner with merely a promising talent! His three friends were well-known bankers: Robert Mendelssohn, an amateur cellist, great-nephew of the famous composer Felix; Robert Warschauer, an utterly unmusical man whose wife worshiped Joachim; and Martin Levy, a retired businessman who made a hobby of composing string quartets which, though well written, hadn't much originality. He was the only one of the three who took a personal interest in me. At his dinner parties he used to gather the most aristocratic names in feudal Prussia and the diplomatic corps of Berlin, and would often invite me and have me perform for his guests.

One important stipulation that Professor Joachim made was that my mother had to promise not to exploit me as a child prodigy. He insisted that I should get a full education until I was artistically mature. And I state here with pride that my parents kept this promise in full!

My new life started right away. Heinrich Barth, the senior piano professor of the Imperial and Royal Academy of Music, accepted me, on Joachim's recommendation. Moreover, he agreed to teach me without any remuneration, and to take charge of all money matters on my behalf—such as gathering the contributions of the four subscribers and paying from the fund all my living expenses, other lessons, and so on. Things looked pretty good at that moment, and my near future seemed assured and in excellent hands.

The question of my schooling was a very important one, and Joachim, Barth, and my mother had many discussions about it. Finally, they agreed not to send me to a *Realgymnasium,* deciding instead that it would be better for me to be tutored at home. It was not easy to find the right person for such a task, which entailed preparing me for yearly examinations at the *Gymnasium* and following the school's full curriculum.

Eventually they found a Dr. Theodor Altmann, a man who would assume the great responsibility for my education all by himself, and I was taken by Professor Barth to my first lesson at nine o'clock one morning. The lessons were to be for two hours every day.

So this was the unforgettable day when I met Theodor Altmann! He appeared to me to be tall (I was still small, of course), a heavyset, rather fat man around forty, with a huge, round face, his nose ridden by a steel-rimmed pince-nez held by a black ribbon. His hair was cropped in the German fashion; but a warm and intelligent twinkle in his eye made me love him right away.

At this point I must express my heart's gratitude to this wonderful man. My dear, dear Theodor Altmann—you began by giving me lessons like any normal teacher. We would start with German history, geography, Latin, and, oh, the dreaded and hated mathematics. You were brilliant at introducing all these different subjects to me, and I was eager to absorb every word you said. You used precise, clear terms to express your thought, and it was delightful and exciting to listen to you.

As to mathematics—my lack of interest in it was a real calamity! You used to get angry, even going to complain to Professor Barth—but to no avail. The great Pythagoras and Euclid and the sublime science of algebra were a deadly bore to me! "Why do you make me verify their great theories?" I would protest in despair. "I give them full credit!" After a few stormy lessons, though, I saw through an unmistakable twinkle in your eye a sympathy and a secret understanding of my ordeal. You knew well that my ignorance of higher mathematics was not going to paralyze the real course of my future. From that point on, thanks to you, life became a constant joy in learning. You revealed to me the philosophers of all time— Plato and Socrates, Aristotle, and later Kant and Schopenhauer. We read Nietzsche's *Also Sprach Zarathustra* together, and I was impressed by the beauty of his prose—less by the trend of his thought, although his first book, *The Birth of Tragedy,* where he points so clearly to the distinction between music and the other fine arts, found me completely in accord.

When it came to history, you abandoned very soon the dryness of the textbook, and took me on a journey over centuries of human experience, showing me the results of its frailty upon our own time, and the greed for power, the wickedness of men.

The next moment, you would open my eyes to the beauty of living in all its incessant variety, to the infinite possibilities of life, and at the same time foster my courage for facing it.

The books you gave me to read became my best friends forever; thanks to you I made the acquaintance of Goethe, Heine, Kleist, Balzac, Maupassant, Dostoevsky, Gogol, Tolstoy. At the age of eleven I was deeply stirred by them. Yes, you treated me like a grownup, and you listened with indulgence and apparent interest to my interjections or opinions—tolerating even my sharply expressed criticisms.

Thank you for all this, my dear Theodor Altmann, from the bottom of my heart.

5

My mother had to go home to take care of the rest of the family, so she went on a feverish hunt to find a place and the kind of people to whom she could entrust me. It was a difficult task. Most *Familienpensions*, as the Germans call them, were afraid to take a pianist because they didn't want the nuisance of his practicing, and they shied away from the responsibility of having a youngster my age. Mama never told me how she did it, but she found finally what she thought was the right place and person.

Frau Johanna Rosentower, a woman in her sixties, was the widow of a well-to-do businessman. She had been born in Poland and still spoke the language in a rather halting way. Her husband had left her a modest income, a large, elegant apartment, three daughters, and a son who had left for London and had never been heard of since. The only way for her to keep the apartment and continue to live in comfort was to rent rooms to young girls who used to flock to Berlin mostly to learn German. Actually, she had turned her home into a pension for young girls. And it was here that I would spend the next three years. But I must say I felt like Achilles —the only boy, surrounded by females!

After my mother's departure, I was left in the hands of Mrs. Rosentower. Her daughters were completely unlike one another; Marie, the eldest, was a long, thin creature with very black hair and a nose like the beak of a bird of prey, quite devoid of charm, although she was a good sort. She was doomed to become an old maid. Her sister Elsa, in her middle twenties, was rather beautiful—tall, with a proud bearing and a fine nose and mouth (I liked her very much). The youngest of the three, Alice, was ugly—with muddy-colored red hair, a red, swollen nose, forever running, short unshapely legs, and a disagreeable character to match. The three of them made up a musical trio. Marie was the pianist, Elsa the violinist, and Alice tried to play the cello. Elsa hoped at one point to have a career; the other two were strictly amateurs. Right away I was adopted by the whole family, and felt quite happy in this feminine atmosphere.

As to my musical education, Herr Barth, my professor, and henceforth my tutor, decided to give me two lessons a week privately, not at the Academy, where he was not able to spend more than half an hour on each lesson, but at his home, where lessons would often run as long as an hour and a half. In addition, I had to take preparatory lessons from an ex-pupil of his, Miguel Capllonch, a native of the Isle of Mallorca. As a special privilege, I was allowed to take theory, harmony, and ensemble playing at the Kaiserliche und Königliche Hochschule (German for Imperial and Royal Academy), because Joseph Joachim, who was still president, made it all possible for me. Also, from time to time, he would have me assist as an accompanist at his violin classes—a great opportunity for me to become familiar with the whole violin literature.

Professor Barth was a formidable personality. He was more than six feet tall and heavily built, but still quite quick on his feet. His grayish hair showed just a touch of baldness. A long Brahmsian beard, the color of salt and pepper, and a bushy mustache covered a rather weak mouth and chin; but his gold-rimmed glasses gave him a look of uncompromising severity.

I was terrified by him. Nobody before had inspired so much fear in me as this sixty-year-old man! But I soon realized I was not the only one to suffer when I saw many of his pupils in tears after their lessons with him. There was a sort of naïve honesty and integrity in his approach to teaching; for example, he had a number of American girls as students, the kind who had been sent to Berlin to improve their German, to visit museums, to go to the Opera, and, maybe, to take some piano lessons with a famous professor just for the fun of showing off. But no—Professor Barth would not see things that way; *his* pupils had to work hard and do their best. "I am not going to help you steal your father's money!" he would shout at them, "and if you continue spending your time in theaters and going to dances instead of practicing your piano, I won't stand for it. Your father will hear from me!" You can imagine how drawn and pale the poor girls looked after a few weeks of this treatment. They would submit to the drudgery of practicing scales for hours on end.

My case was different, of course. To begin with, I was too young for the theater and for dances, and there was no money to be stolen from my father. Besides, I possessed a natural gift for playing the piano which you might even call talent, and I was shrewdly aware that Barth felt some respect for it. After some time I noticed that he actually became fond of me. A tender look in his eyes and a shy, boyish smile would appear now and then in his usually sad, stern face, especially after a satisfactory performance. But God help me if I arrived unprepared for a lesson! I would begin, and as soon as I hit wrong notes, I would notice with horror how his long beard rose bit by bit into a horizontal position, which meant that he was drawing up his lower lip and biting it with rage—and then hell would break loose! He would jump to his feet, shout insults at me, bang his fists on the piano, and disappear for a while. After calming down, he would dismiss me sullenly, without a word.

My other teacher, Capllonch, was a quite different kind of fellow. Still young, around thirty, he was a typical Latin, gay—with laughing blue eyes, a soft blond mustache, and a sunny disposition toward music. When he performed the classics, there was none of that frowning look, designed to show "depth of feeling," so prevalent among Germans and so much in favor with the critics. Music was a pure joy to him—and he knew how to share it with me. We would play with gusto a Schumann symphony arranged for four hands, or one or two Beethoven quartets, then eat some good chocolates, which he always had on hand, and for a happy finale, Capllonch would play some Spanish popular music . . . I loved it!

Unfortunately this idyll did not last long. Professor Barth noticed my liking for the Mallorquino, and became so jealous that he managed to invent some reason to dismiss my dear Capllonch. He immediately called upon another old pupil of his, an elderly spinster, Miss Clara Hempel, to prepare me for his lessons in *his* way—which meant "to stop the nonsense of finding joy in music," to make me take my work seriously, to play relentless scales . . . in short, to drown me in drudgery.

I would easily get discouraged as I watched my fingers run up and down the keyboard, as though they were cleaning some huge teeth; there was no incentive to it. Why don't you make me like it? I thought, remembering my famous protest when I was four and my father had tried to force me to swallow an unpalatable soup. Nor was I happy with the repertory that Barth selected for me, consisting mainly of programs out of his own youth that had long since become dated. He fed me on early Mendelssohn, on not the best Schumann, and now and then he conceded an easy sonata of Beethoven, and, to my relief, a fine prelude and fugue of Bach. Thus my life marched on. . . .

It was then nearly the end of the nineteenth century, and the city of Berlin was undergoing a political evolution. The Prussians (and Berlin was *their* capital) were still drunk with their spectacular victory over the French in 1870, as a result of which war the Kingdom of Prussia had become the dominating state in a powerful Empire—the awe-inspiring and fateful Germany we now all know too well. William, the senile king of Prussia, was the first Emperor of Germany with Berlin as his capital, while the other German sovereignties were turned, unwittingly, into mere satellites.

The old Monarch's reign did not last long, and his son Frederick, a war hero and a fine man, outlived him by only three months. Thus the throne became ready for William II, the fateful one, whose pettiness and relentless ambition were to break the long, peaceful stretch of the Victorian era and plunge the world into an endless turmoil of tragic events.

I arrived in Berlin not long after the dismissal of Bismarck, the chancellor of the new Reich. William II couldn't bear the memory of having been merely a minor officer in the war. He wanted all this glory to reflect on him alone. He would let the world know of what caliber he was made! With the great Bismarck gone, his hands were entirely free. For a start, he had to have a powerful navy, capable of beating the hated British "Rule Britannia," and it was a cousin of my uncle Siegfried Meyer, the great naval constructor Ballin, a Jew, who helped him build it. On the Kaiser's orders, the army became the supreme caste of the Empire. Five or six crack regiments of the guard were stationed in Berlin alone, and when at every turn I would run into officers in full uniform, I could feel their arrogance.

The Kaiser kept us Berliners in constant awe, calculating his every move for its sensational effect. He was the first to use this technique, later so well perfected by Stalin, Hitler, and their ilk. One day he would be making a triple alliance with Austria and Italy—an axis he believed to be a menace to the rest of Europe. Another time, because he was so obviously jealous of the great colonial possessions of France and England, he succeeded through sheer threat in annexing two major colonies, in west and east Africa. He was perpetually on the move, appearing unexpectedly in politically sensitive spots. I remember well his much-publicized visit to Turkey and how he entered some Turkish capital on horseback in Oriental garb, hoping to win over the whole Moslem world.

In Berlin itself, we had one big parade after another; "Sedan Day," in memory of the battle, became the most important holiday of the realm. The Kaiser, flanked by his five strapping sons, would march in pomp to the Zeughaus, the war museum, displaying trophies captured in recent wars. But he never paid homage to fallen soldiers. I remember two characteristics that were always noticed: his left arm, from birth shorter than the other, a disfigurement he tried desperately to conceal, and his famous mustache, angular and sharply pointed upward, which he wore with obvious satisfaction. Half of Germany's male population adopted it enthusiastically.

It was interesting to watch the rapid development of Berlin from the capital of a small kingdom to a world metropolis. A long and wide avenue, continuing the well-known Unter den Linden through the Brandenburger Tor, was cut through the Tiergarten and reached the outskirts of the city. New houses, new streets, appeared everywhere. Charlottenburg, once a modest suburb, grew into an important commercial and artistic center, with fine theaters, cafés, and restaurants. Kurfürstendamm became the Champs-Élysées of Berlin. The population seemed to grow by the thousands from one day to the next. Even the old Academy of Music, a modest but noble building, was found inadequate by the Ministry of Culture and replaced by a modern, prisonlike structure.

The artistic and cultural life of the metropolis, around 1900, was of the highest order. There were good theaters aplenty; both the Opera and the Royal Schauspielhaus, devoted to classical drama, were supported by the Kaiser's private purse and were provided with very good singers and actors. The Opera orchestra, conducted by Felix Weingartner, gave subscription concerts, a highlight of the season.

But my heart was in another theater, the Deutsches Theater, whose director, Otto Brahm, presented the dramas of Gerhart Hauptmann, the greatest German playwright of the time, and excellent performances of Ibsen, Björnson, Tolstoy, and many other less well known authors. I loved his actors and actresses, and I remember particularly Max Reinhardt, then a minor actor, who was soon to leave the Deutsches and become one of the revolutionary geniuses of the theater.

Of course, the musical life in Berlin fascinated me more than anything else. The capital of Germany was fast becoming the world's most important center for musicians who wanted to be heard and judged. The impresario Hermann Wolff brought the greatest singers, pianists, violinists, and cellists to Berlin—and it was *he* who put at the head of the Berlin Philharmonic Orchestra the greatest of all conductors, Arthur Nikisch! The Philharmonic concerts under Nikisch became the center of my musical experience and development. I simply lived for and with them. Every Sunday morning, at eleven, I would be standing in front of the box office of the "Philharmonie," anxiety written all over my face, trying to catch the eye of the omnipotent Hermann Wolff. Sometimes it turned into agony when he wasn't there—but, thank heaven, I always managed to get in one way or another to this *öffentliche Generalprobe.* The actual concert took place the next evening, on Monday, before the elite of Berlin society, a very elegant public, but less musical and enthusiastic than the Sunday morning crowd. Nevertheless, I was enchanted when occasionally some nice person would invite me to his box on Mondays.

What a wonderful, unforgettable life of music opened up to me! Nikisch's magic baton introduced me to all the Beethoven and Mozart symphonies. His performances of works by Tchaikovski, Rimsky-Korsakov, César Franck, and the young Richard Strauss, then considered modern, were revelations to the sensitive ears of the boy I was. Never since have I heard music played like that. Nikisch was a smallish man with a shapely figure and a fine head. He was always elegantly clad, and stood motionless and erect while conducting; his baton alone dominated the orchestra with short but rhythmically precise strokes. From time to time he would raise his left hand to emphasize a phrase, pointing his little finger, a diamond ring shining on it, at one or another player. That ring on this beautiful white hand was the delight of his Berlin admirers. Such an irresistible charm and power emanated from this little man that women fell in love with him, and I, too, I must confess, lived completely under his spell.

And the soloists of his concerts! I heard Eugen D'Albert play Beethoven's Fourth Concerto with a nobility and tenderness which has remained in my mind as the model performance of this work. Ferruccio Busoni, with his handsome, pale, Christ-like face, and his diabolical technical prowess, was by far the most interesting pianist alive. When he played Bach, his uncanny touch could produce at one moment the sonorities of an organ, at another those of a harpsichord, an ideal combination. His temperament and his complete mastery were such that his performances of Liszt's works were unsurpassed, and he managed to make them sound even more important than they actually were. When he played the famous *Campanella*, it became a breathtaking experience, although his Beethoven and Chopin, I must admit, left me entirely cold. To my amazement, he would approach Beethoven's last sonatas in a sarcastic mood, taking great liberties with tempi and rhythm, while his Chopin, always technically brilliant, lacked the warmth and tenderness so important in his works. All told, Busoni remains a towering personality, a shining example to all musicians for the noble way in which he pursued his career so uncompromisingly, for the high standard he set for his own compositions, and for his general culture, so rare among artists.

The Belgian violinist Eugène Ysaye was my idol. Accustomed as I was to the ascetic restraint and nobility of Joachim, who seldom used a vibrato, the exuberance and sensuousness of this Belgian lion simply overwhelmed me. But more of him later, when the First World War brought us into a closer personal contact.

There was also another major contribution to my musical development. Joachim, with his ever-alert interest in me, decided to allow me to assist at the rehearsals of his famous quartet, which took place in his private apartment. I was very proud of this opportunity to listen to the interruptions and remarks of the old master, so instructive, interesting, and useful to me. One day—I blush when I think of it—something unexpected happened to me. The four gentlemen who formed the quartet—Joachim, Halíř, Wirth, and Hausmann—were rehearsing the last quartet of Beethoven for about two hours. It was a hot day, and I was sitting right in the sun in such an uncomfortable position that I dozed off and they had a hard time waking me. Professor Joachim took it with his usual kindness, but I felt ashamed for quite a while.

As for my social life in those days, I was beginning to be known in musical circles as "the talented little Rubinstein"—a protégé of Joachim's. As a result, many of Berlin's music lovers became interested in me and began inviting me to their houses. I remember particularly liking the Landau family. The banker Wilhelm Landau (no connection with my two brothers-in-law of the same name) was married to the daughter of a banker from Lodz, and both of them were greatly interested in the arts. Mrs. Landau liked to speak Polish with me, and her husband enjoyed my playing. They used to ask me to their formal dinners, and Mrs. Rosentower, being incurably impressed by wealth, allowed me to attend. I did like the lavish food, but always had to pay with a short concert—a kind of exploitation that was very much in vogue at the time, but fortunately rarely occurs today.

It was at one of these dinner parties that I met Lotte Hahn, Mr. Landau's sister. She was a beautiful and enchanting lady of about thirty-five and a very fine pianist, well equipped for a brilliant career, if it hadn't been for her wealth, her husband, and children.

Lotte Hahn was well aware of my admiration for her (I was constantly blushing, and shy, in her presence) but she treated me in a sweet, motherly way. She became concerned that I was leading such a "lonely life," deprived of the company of boys my own age, living surrounded by girls, away from home; and so she decided to do something about it. Her eldest son, Kurt, who was thirteen and a tall, handsome boy, blessed with the most honest blue eyes, became, thanks to her, my friend. One day he invited me to join his *Lesekränzchen*, a sort of reading circle that met every Saturday at seven p.m. when Kurt and a few of his school friends would get together to read classical drama, dividing up the roles. The boys' parents would take turns having the get-togethers at their houses and offering tasty little suppers for the boys, while I had to join as an honorary member, having neither home nor supper to offer! Altmann was delighted with the idea, and I simply loved it. We read *Faust* by Goethe, much of Shakespeare in the perfect translation by Schlegel and Tieck, the best of Kleist, Schiller, and Lessing; we even read the whole *Oresteia* of Aeschylus and Sophocles' *Oedipus Rex*—though no Aristophanes, nor any of the moderns. Mrs. Hahn sent Kurt and me to some of these plays at the Schauspielhaus, where I was lucky enough to see a cycle of Shakespeare's King dramas beautifully performed.

Conceived as an autonomous body, our little circle was managed quite professionally. We would all vote on who should get what roles, always accepting the results as final. No recriminations were tolerated, and so it developed that each one of us became a distinct dramatic prototype. Kurt played, of course, noble heroes to perfection; he couldn't be anything else. Then we had Franz Pariser, a fellow with a quivering voice and laughing eyes, for the comical roles; the frail, sweet-voiced Paul Heinitz, to his great dismay, was always condemned to play feminine parts. Hugo Perls, presently an art dealer in New York, played fathers most convincingly; at that stage, he was wearing braces on his teeth, an advantage that impressed us, making us conscious of his importance. To my delight I was always elected to play the villains. How I loved to murder my way through to the throne as Richard III, what a chance for grimaces the part of Mephistopheles offered, and how delightful it was to lower my voice into a poisonous whisper as Iago!

I always admired the restraint and discipline my young colleagues showed, never praising or applauding this or that performance, simply nodding politely in appreciation. Sometimes, after a lively supper, some of the parents would ask me to play the piano, and I welcomed the opportunity to repay in a small way their hospitality.

The tacitly accepted director of our reading group was Richard Fuchs, a remarkably intelligent fellow. At fourteen, he spoke like an old professor, deadly serious, always to the point; later he became a famous lawyer.

Lotte Hahn also enjoyed playing chamber music, and it was she who introduced Brahms to me, when one afternoon she played two of his piano quartets, the A major and the C minor, with a good ensemble. It is impossible to describe my enthusiasm as I heard this music. Noticing my emotion, she made me stay on after the others had left, and played some of Brahms's piano pieces for me, which made me love and understand him even better.

From that day on, Brahms became my obsession. I had to know everything he had written; instead of working on the pieces for my piano lessons, I would read with ecstasy anything of Brahms which fell into my hands. I would buy his music on credit; I would have stolen money to get it! When anybody wanted to give me a present, it had to be some arrangement for two hands of a symphony, or a volume of songs, or some chamber music by the beloved master. My poor Altmann, who was, I suspect, living solely on the money he was earning for my lessons, would ruin himself buying some of these expensive arrangements for me. I would force dear old Miss Hempel to spend entire lessons playing Brahms's symphonies for four hands. I shall never forget Professor Barth's astonishment when I told him I wanted to learn the D minor Piano Concerto, Opus 15. "What, what?" he exclaimed. "You are mad, my boy—that is a formidable work, much too difficult for you!" Well, I discovered then that real love knows no obstacles. A week later I played the concerto, to Barth's amazed satisfaction.

My social life expanded rapidly and in many directions. Being a born extrovert, I found no difficulty in making contacts with different kinds of people—people who lived in different worlds. One day Joseph Joachim introduced me to the Engelmanns, who were a most interesting family; Professor Engelmann was the dean of the Physiological Institute of the Berlin University, and his wife was a well-known pianist, Emma Brandes, one of Clara Schumann's best pupils. She had abandoned her career after her marriage, but I often had the chance to hear her play and to perform with her on two pianos. They had a few children; the youngest, Hans, a big blond boy of my age, grew quite fond of me, and so in a short time I became practically a member of the household.

The Engelmanns lived in the institute itself and occupied its entire front. The huge music room, flanked by two smaller rooms that were filled with books, made the two Bechstein concert grands look quite small. Hans had a playroom all to himself, where he had set up his perfect little electric train all over the place, and we loved to play with it. He also introduced me to the Karl May adventure stories, which I swallowed up greedily, and reciprocated with Jules Verne. I might add that the Engelmanns had come to Berlin from Utrecht, in Holland, where the Professor held a similar position and where Brahms had been their guest on several occasions. Brahms's B flat String Quartet is dedicated to Professor Wilhelm Engelmann, a true *titre de gloire*, I would say.

I felt happy in their company, personally and musically. I remember with pleasure the cozy meals in their house, the big lamp over the dining table, the excellent Dutch cheese, the strong coffee, and particularly the intellectual tone of the conversations, so different from the usual cheap gossip. There I met a Swiss painter, a Mr. Phillips, a charming and talented man who later painted my portrait and is best known for his sensitive engraving of Robert Schumann.

Still another family played a part in my early years in Berlin: Professor Dr. Georg Salomon, his wife, and his sons Richard and Fritz. Professor Salomon was the Rosentowers' family doctor, and his title of professor was purely honorary. He was the kindest of men—soft-spoken, rosy-cheeked, a passionate devotee of music, and quite a good pianist himself. Called one day because I had some minor stomach disturbance, he immediately became attached to me, and I soon found a heartwarming atmosphere in his home. His family was the prototype of the upper-class German Jews . . . less Jewish than the Polish Jews, more patriotic than the Germans themselves. They found and took their place in the community, were highly respected for their integrity and honorability, contributing with everything in their power to the welfare of their fellow citizens. It had to take a raving-mad sadist like Hitler to destroy such an invaluable asset of the German people.

Professor Salomon loved to play pieces for four hands with me. One day when I came down with a rather high temperature, and Frau Rosentower had called him in, he looked me over, felt my pulse briefly, and said with a smile, "It's nothing, just the measles." Whereupon he asked me, with much interest, "What tempo do you take for the F major Organ Toccata of Bach?" showing me the music he already had with him. Then, after Mrs. Rosentower had left, he dragged me out of bed, sat me down at my upright piano, and, by Jove, we threw ourselves, with relish, into a performance of the Toccata to the astonishment of everyone. Often, when I had been invited to his house, after a nice dinner, the whole family would beg me to play a few Mozart concertos, which I had to sight-read, and it was touching to see all four of them listening, with tears in their sweet eyes.

Life at the Rosentowers' was dull. The daughters of the house were practically invisible. Now and then I would hear the sound of Elsa's violin, or I would be startled by a nasty screech of Alice's cello. The ever-dignified Mrs. Rosentower herself liked to pace the rooms in slow motion, nodding her head at every step like a pigeon. But one morning things brightened. The arrival of a new contingent of "paying guests" was announced, and the next day I was overjoyed to find three new young ladies admitted into the inner circle of the Rosentower household. Two of them were from America—one from Boston, the other from Philadelphia —and they were given the best room of the place, right off the entrance hall; the third one, I regret to say, got my own room, and I was relegated to a smaller one which had scarcely space enough for my piano. Since I was already lazy, and stubborn about practicing, the new arrangement proved disastrous. I hardly touched my own piano, but I did play a lot on the grand piano in the drawing room, which was situated right across the hall from the Americans, hoping to attract their attention.

I had always felt a secret need for an audience, and this need became obvious now, because one of the young ladies had awakened my interest. Miss Bertha Drew, a not too dark brunette, with soft, shiny hair, brown eyes, and very white skin, was quite lovely to look at. She had the most ravishing smile I had ever seen. As she smiled, her lips would part slowly over a perfect set of teeth, two dimples would appear in her cheeks, and her eyes would half-close. It was irresistible! And I swear it was natural. She dressed simply, with excellent taste, and never used a trace of makeup.

I soon found out, to my delight, that she was sensitive to music. She was a graduate of Radcliffe College and a proud New Englander, and she would tell me marvelous things about the musical life in Boston, about its Symphony Hall, and its famous orchestra. Some years later, I found out for myself that every word she said was true.

It is not surprising that I tried to attract her attention. And, one morning, to my joy, it succeeded. She entered the drawing room silently, as I was playing, sat down, and listened intently to the music. From then on, she was my daily audience and companion. One can imagine the fervor with which I introduced her to Brahms, to the great Schumann of the Fantasy, the *Kreisleriana*, and the *Symphonic Études*, and to the few pieces of Chopin I was studying then. But, more often than not, I indulged my passion for playing transcriptions of songs, excerpts from symphonies and operas—all of which delighted my listener, but proved detrimental to my technical progress. Professor Barth's beard was so often in a horizontal position that his lessons became sheer agony! However, Miss Drew was a good influence in those days. We would take long walks together in the Tiergarten, and she would lecture me, remind me of my talent and my obligation to it and of the brilliant future that was in store for me. I loved our cozy little tea parties in her room, which the two girls had transformed into a charming living room, giving it an American look, "like back home," as they said. A miniature flag of stars and stripes was pinned to the wall, flanked by their school pennant; there were flowers on the tables and photos of their parents, and of themselves in their graduation robes and caps. They always kept the place meticulously clean.

All this sounds too good to be true. But there was another side to
the picture. As I became more and more attached to Miss Drew, I tried
to ignore that she had other things to do, that she had in fact been sent
to Berlin to improve her German, to visit museums, to go to parties, to
the theater, and, also, to meet people. I, of course, was supposed to be
immersed in my work—the long morning hours with Altmann, two hours
of practicing (?), lessons and other chores at the Hochschule, Miss
Hempel, and, twice a week, the dreaded Professor Barth. Add to that my
social activities, the *Kränzchen*, and a few concerts I had to attend, how
and when was I to find the time for Miss Drew? It proved to be a major
problem.

I began neglecting many of my obligations, finding it hard to concentrate on my work. When Miss Drew happened to be taken out for
dinner or to a theater, and I had to stay home, life seemed sad and uninteresting. Obviously, Mrs. Rosentower noticed the change in me, but
chose to overlook it.

At about that time a brilliant young violinist from Vienna came to
town and conquered Berlin with three magnificent concerts. The entire
household was in ecstasy. Our Miss Elsa had fallen desperately in love
with him. I don't know how, but she found a way of meeting this artist—
whose name was Fritz Kreisler. His personal reputation was not too good
at that time. Rumor had it that he was a gambler, was given to drinking,
and was rather loose with his morals. But he played divinely, with a tone
of velvet, a hair-raising technique, a unique dash and charm. He had fine
stage manners, too. To me, strange as it may seem, Kreisler suggested
always an ideal (unattainable even in dreams) café player; whenever he
approached a Bach or Beethoven concerto in his most immaculate way,
I couldn't help thinking he was performing a valse by Johann Strauss. It
was too chic. He was definitely at his best in the small, elegant pieces that
he wrote himself and which nobody has equaled since.

Elsa's love so permeated the whole atmosphere of the household that
the Rosentower ladies lived in a state bordering on hysteria. They spoke
to each other in whispers, inquired every minute whether there was any
mail, and behaved, generally, like lunatics. This state of affairs finally
reached a climax when one day Mrs. Rosentower requested all the boarders
in her pension to go out for dinner: she was going to have some guests
that night, strictly *en famille*, and needed absolute privacy. I was to be
served in my room. Naturally our curiosity was aroused, and we decided
to find out what was going on. I, as the only one allowed to stay, was
made the spy, but it wasn't an easy job to discover the identity of the
mythical guests. I did manage to get to the bottom of the whole affair.
Mr. Fritz Kreisler was to be the one and only guest! The dinner party

was simply a conspiracy to ensnare the great violinist for Elsa. As history knows, nothing came of it. Many years later Kreisler married a woman with a strong character who knew how to cure him of gambling and drinking, and who helped him greatly in his career—but I can't help thinking that Elsa would have made him a more attractive wife. The only memory of this sad story was a present Kreisler gave Elsa—a little golden violin brooch with the initials F.K. engraved on the back of it. Poor Elsa wore it always on her heart.

At that time I was attending more and more concerts. The famous Hermann Wolff had a list of musicians and students whom he could draw on to fill the concert hall, which was rarely sold out, and I was on this list, entitling me often to tickets. But one night, I had the privilege of getting a ticket to hear D'Albert in a recital that was sold out at the Beethoven Hall. He played beautifully, especially the F major Toccata of Bach, which he had arranged, and the "Appassionata." At the end of the program, seeing me applauding and shouting "Bravo," Mr. Wolff caught my arm and said, "Come on, I shall introduce you to the master." The artists' room was full of people, and we had a hard time pushing our way through the crowd to the sweating but happy pianist. After a few words of praise, Hermann Wolff presented me to the great man.

"This is the young Rubinstein," he said.

D'Albert asked, with a touch of irony, "By name, or by talent?" And Wolff answered, seriously, "By both."

The startled pianist glanced at me, smiled, and exclaimed: "Prove it, young man. Let us go on the stage. I want to hear you play!" Before I knew it, I was sitting at the piano, playing the two rhapsodies from Opus 79 by Brahms. At first only D'Albert, some of his friends, among them Engelbert Humperdinck, the composer of *Hansel and Gretel*, and a few other interested people were listening. But soon some of the audience, still busy getting their coats and hats, hearing music coming from the hall, rushed back in hopes of another encore. Puzzled by the sight of a young boy playing for D'Albert, they stayed and listened. When I stopped, the burst of applause from this unexpected audience made me feel as though I had just finished a concert of my own.

D'Albert embraced me, saying, "Yes, you are a true Rubinstein." I left in a daze. On the way home, and in a happy mood, Mr. Wolff told me the following sad little story.

It seems that Ossip Gabrilówitsch, a brilliant young pianist (who was to become the conductor of the Detroit Symphony Orchestra, and son-in-law of Mark Twain) was having a hard time getting any real recognition from the difficult Berlin public. Being ambitious, he worked hard to prepare a fine program for his next concert, and Mr. Wolff through extra publicity succeeded in filling the hall.

"And then our young Gabrilówitsch steps out on the stage, looking the conquering hero, in fine fettle, in the best of spirits. But, lo, while taking his bow, his eyes fall on a man sitting in the last row: Ferruccio Busoni, the awe-inspiring master of them all! Ossip's heart dropped to the floor. He began playing like a debutante, and, what made it worse, the audience noticed. The only hope remained in the encores. With Busoni gone, he might recover his senses. But, to his despair, while he was attacking his encore he saw Busoni coming up to the platform. Agonized, he glanced at him—and . . . it wasn't Busoni at all, just someone who looked like him. . . ."

Mr. Wolff told me this story with gusto, emphasizing the contrast in the way I had just reacted with D'Albert. "You will get far, if you work," he added.

Everyone was waiting for me at home, anxious because of the late hour, but after my tale of the event they were all triumphant.

6

Shortly after the incident with D'Albert, Joachim decided to present me in public. He planned a concert in the great hall of the Hochschule, with me playing the A major Concerto of Mozart, while he conducted.

This was exciting news. Professor Barth had still other plans in mind that seemed pleasant: he wanted me to play the same concerto first, as a sort of rehearsal, at a symphony concert in Potsdam, with Professor Kulemkampff, my harmony teacher, conducting. I liked Potsdam, the German Versailles, with its fine palaces, especially Frederick the Great's Sans-Souci, which he had built for himself and where he used to give his famous concerts, playing the flute like a professional virtuoso.

And so, one winter evening, Professor Barth and I took a train for Potsdam, and all through the one-hour-long trip, Barth, like a boxing trainer, gave me his last-minute instructions: "When you come out on the platform, make a deep bow to the public, then a shorter one to the orchestra. Fix your piano stool so as to gain perfect control of movement. Don't look at the public. Concentrate on what you are going to play before giving the conductor the sign to begin." And that was not all. "Watch your pedal, don't make faces, don't sing while you are playing, never change your fingering—it might get you into trouble" . . . and more. . . .

I was terrified. The concert suddenly seemed a lion's den where, at the first wrong move, I would be torn to pieces.

But things turned out quite differently. I was received with loud applause, partly because of my youth, but also because of my friends (the Rosentower crowd and a few others had come to my Potsdam debut), I was heartened, and, trying hard to follow at least some of Barth's instructions, I gave a not too bad performance of the Concerto, though it was a little dry and scholarly.

There was a terrific ovation, with cries for an encore. Professor Barth was so nervous that he remained backstage, but now calm, and satisfied, he told me to play "The Duet," a song without words by Mendelssohn. By this time I was completely relaxed and drunk with my victory, and I ignored all his warnings, began my piece, smiled at my friends, and thought about everything but the music. Suddenly, bang, there was a catastrophe. My mind became a blank: I couldn't remember a single note. All I knew was that the piece was in A flat, and so, without stopping, my heart frozen, I began to improvise. I developed a theme in A flat, all right, but it had nothing to do with Mendelssohn. After a few modulations, I invented a second subject, in minor, for contrast, elaborated it for a while, and returned to the romantic A flat. The coda was a delicate arpeggio, played pianissimo with soft pedal.

Naturally, and for a good reason, the audience did not know the piece, and I was received with the same enthusiasm as before. It was lucky, but I hardly dared to take a bow, and I was shaking with fear when I returned backstage to be slaughtered. Well, I shall never get over my amazement when I saw Professor Barth, instead of raising the ax, come happily toward me, shake my hands, and exclaim, his eyes shining, "Teufelsjunge, you are a rascal—but a genius! I couldn't have pulled that trick in a thousand years."

Two weeks later I played the same Mozart Concerto at the Hochschule with Professor Joachim. This time I felt like a veteran. I could follow Barth's formula for correct concert behavior with ease, and without restraint. In fact, I suddenly found it really good, and I would recommend it to every pianist. And the Concerto came off much better than in

Potsdam, because I played with more warmth and freedom, while Joachim accompanied beautifully. When we took our bow, he kissed me on both cheeks in front of the audience. This was a memorable day for me.

I welcomed the stimulus that these concerts gave me, and life became more attractive; I began working better and concentrating more on my lessons. The next year, it was decided, I would give a concert all by myself, featuring two concertos with the Berlin Philharmonic Orchestra and some solo pieces in between . . . a formidable affair. But it thrilled me, and it was then that I discovered something characteristic in my nature—the capacity to work well only if there was something special to work for, like a concert, or, later, my recordings. I also realized, after my concerts, the truth of the old saying: "There is nothing more successful than success." A subtle change took place in the general atmosphere around me. I noticed that my favorite dishes would appear more frequently on the Rosentower dining table, Professor Barth's beard would rest more peacefully on his chest, and even Alice would treat her cello more gently. My sentimental gain: Miss Drew was giving me more of her time, and her smile became more tender.

It was about this time that I first heard Jacques Thibaud, whose performance of the G minor Concerto by Bruch I shall never forget. He managed to turn this pretty, unpretentious piece into a masterpiece, playing the second theme of the first movement with such tenderness that it brought tears to my eyes. I rushed to the artists' room to meet and to thank him, and this already famous, elegant, and attractive young man was kind enough to invite me, a twelve-year-old boy, to lunch. We later became close friends, and our friendship lasted until his tragic end in an air accident in 1953.

Other artists impressed me very much, too—the Walküre-like Teresa Careño, playing the Tchaikovski Concerto with the strength and dash of two men; the French pianist Edouard Risler, a wonderful interpreter of Beethoven sonatas; Busoni, giving a smashing performance of a Liszt concerto as if it were child's play; Gabrilówitsch, tender and romantic in the Schumann Concerto; Artur Schnabel, fresh from Vienna, where he had studied with Leschetitzky, making his debut at a Nikisch concert. Musicians liked his playing, but both the critics and the public found him stiff and conceited. It took him ten years to win over the reluctant Berliners.

My own musical life was enriched by Emma Engelmann's growing interest in me. She was a fat little lady, in her fifties, and although she always looked as though she were being squeezed to death by one of those old-fashioned corsets, she was terribly active, always running instead of walking. She had a round face with a pair of vivid, sharp eyes. And what a wonderful pianist she was! She played with complete simplicity and an inner intensity—none of the power of a Careño, but also none of the "emoting" of so many women pianists. We used to play much of Brahms and Schumann for each other, and because she had had direct personal contact with them, she was able to share things with me that few people knew about these masters.

Her stories about Brahms's rudeness and wit amused me in particular. For instance, I loved the one about how a great wine connoisseur invited the composer to dinner. "This is the Brahms of my cellar," he said to his guests, producing a dust-covered bottle and pouring some into the master's glass. Brahms looked first at the color of the wine, then sniffed its bouquet, finally took a sip, and put the glass down without saying a word. "Don't you like it?" asked the host. "Hmm," Brahms muttered. "Better bring your Beethoven!"

Mrs. Engelmann's friendship with Brahms became a precious source of information about his way of playing the piano and the different tempi he used in his works. She told me his comments about her playing of some of his compositions, and that way I learned a lot about the Handel Variations, the F minor Sonata, Opus 5, his piano pieces, and chamber music. Her description of his playing was most instructive. He performed, she said, in broad lines, paying little attention to detail. Sometimes, when not in the mood, he would play abominably, striking wrong notes by the dozen, banging and messing up whole passages. There was no lack of emotion, but he would shun sentimentality. Joachim also told me other fascinating things; he knew, of course, everything about Brahms worth knowing.

As to Schumann, she revealed many interesting details about the musical relationship between him and his wife. Emma Engelmann (née Brandes) had been a favorite pupil of Clara's, and I began to be suspicious about how much the great Clara had imposed her personal "interpretation" on her husband's work. Clara Schumann outlived her husband by many years, continuing her career as a concert pianist. And therein lay the danger. The continuous contact with exacting audiences and the frequent repeating of the same programs were apt to introduce changes, even distortions, into the early conceptions of the works. And Clara was a forceful woman. I couldn't help feeling her influence in many of Schumann's piano compositions. His brusque changes of mood, the frequent assembling of disconnected short pieces into one work, and especially, the exaggerated use of rhythmical staccato passages betray Clara's personal touch because they were all characteristic of her musical nature. Of course I never dared say a word about any of this to Mrs. Engelmann, who played Schumann beautifully; I shall never forget her noble, tender, and poetic performance of the A minor Concerto.

My lessons with Mr. Altmann grew more and more exciting; often, at the end of our long "séances," one or two of his friends would come to see him, and he let me stay and listen to their fascinating conversation. One of them was Dr. Alfred Kerr, the dreaded dramatic critic of *Der Tag*, who had a style very much his own, made up of short, chopped sentences, each word a revolver shot. He looked striking, too—like a dandy of the 1830's, with a monocle stuck in his left eye and a black cravat tied twice around his neck, hiding his starched white *Vatermörder* collar.

Maximilian Harden was another frequent visitor who also had a reputation for inspiring dread, but for quite different reasons. He had been born Max Witkowski in Posen, of Jewish parents, later adopting the pseudonym of Harden when he came to Berlin. Here he published a political weekly called the *Zukunft*, which rose from complete obscurity to a unique position in the German press owing to the fact that Harden told his readers the truth and nothing but the truth. As everybody knows, this takes some courage. Shortly after I had met him he engaged in an unheard-of political adventure; he attacked the camarilla of the Kaiser, which caused a scandal in Germany. It was becoming obvious that the Emperor was losing much of his popularity. His provocative political moves, which threatened the peace, were beginning to be much criticized: people were getting tired of military displays, of the insolence of Prussian Junkers, and of the arrogance of the military.

The Socialist leader August Bebel, a friend of the great Frenchman Jaurès and a splendid orator, was gaining more and more support in the country. As the Socialist party became a power to be reckoned with, the Kaiser, in an effort to minimize the threat and to deflect the growing dissatisfaction of the people, decided to take strong measures against the province of Poznań, the ancient cradle of Poland, which had lived under German rule since the Partition. There was nothing new about his tactics. For a long time, great efforts had been made to Germanize this all-Polish province. By official decree, it had to be called Ostmarken; the Polish population was continuously harassed by petty and vexing measures which merely succeeded in turning its natural antagonism into hatred.

The Kaiser felt it was time for something drastic to be done, in order to break the resistance of the Poles. The Prussian Diet passed a bill to expropriate Polish landed property by helping German settlers and encouraging them to buy large estates at ridiculously low prices, fixed arbitrarily by Colonizing Commissions. The Kaiser ordered a royal castle to be built in the very center of the city of Posen, a hideous structure in Neo-Gothic style, something between a fortress and a prison, dishonoring the ancient capital.

But the Poles took up the challenge. True enough, they did have one natural asset: their high birth rate. Being fervent Catholics, they produced many more children than their oppressors or any other European country—the Germans used to call them, derisively, "Polnische Karnickel" (slang for Polish rabbits). But that wasn't all—overnight, these carefree, free-spending, light-hearted people turned into first-rate economists. In order to fight the German offensive, clergy, peasants, and landowners pooled their money, opening banks and other organizations of credit, and thus, well armed, succeeded in buying, often under assumed German names, twice as much land as they had been losing to the settlers. The whole province became divided into two fanatically hostile groups; you could live with one or the other, but never mix with both.

My own reaction to the Emperor's whole abominable scheme can be easily imagined. I was a Polish patriot, proud of my country's indomitable spirit; I was deeply hurt by the injustice done to it. And I began to loathe the Kaiser!

7

My life in Berlin moved now more or less in the same rhythm. The summers of 1898 and 1899 were interrupted by short vacations in Lodz. My family, glad to see me in good health and making good progress, gorged me with all my favorite dishes and sent me back to Berlin with blessings and tears. I saw nothing of Mania Szer on either occasion.

The last time I had returned from Lodz, Professor Barth infringed on the remaining two weeks of my vacation by making me play with him every day practically the whole of the available literature for two pianos. He wanted to improve my sight-reading. At first I was indignant, but, now, after all these years, I am able to appreciate, with deep gratitude, how nobly he sacrificed so much of his own free time. He became more human, and more friendly, too. He would often keep me for lunch after our performances, and gradually I came to know him better. Barth had been orphaned at the age of nine and adopted by a couple named Steinmann. Herr Steinmann had been a piano teacher—an extremely severe one.

Barth's own pianistic career had been quite successful, especially in Germany and England; I doubt, however, that he played anywhere else. But his concert career was short-lived. When he was still young, he accepted a professorship at the Academy of Berlin and was appointed by the Empress Frederick (the daughter of Queen Victoria of England and mother of William II) as a Kaiserlicher und Königlicher Hofpianist of her own court. Being an admirer of Bismarck, Barth did not care much for the present Kaiser.

Barth's private life, I discovered, was rather depressing. After Mr. Steinmann's death, he took care of his widow and she came to Berlin to live with him. Barth's own sister, who had spent her youth separated from her brother, joined him, and became his housekeeper. One must admit that life between an ill-tempered, dissatisfied old woman, who was confined to a wheelchair, and a tall, spindly old maid with an eternally worried expression on her face must have been difficult and sordid for such a misanthropic man. They condemned him to remain a bachelor.

With all that I didn't forget my Aunt Salomea and her family. They lived a half-hour's bus drive from my own neighborhood, and I used to visit them sometimes on Sundays. My Uncle Meyer was a good Jew, but the kind of conformist who follows accepted religious teachings without so much as a thought. On the other hand, he was an ardent patriot. Germany's most recent victories, the ensuing parades, celebrations, and other demonstrations of the empire's growing power, were making him drunk with pride. I would find him usually lying on a sofa, a malodorous cigar in his mouth, reading and rereading the memoirs of Bismarck, of Field Marshal von Moltke, and of others instrumental in the Prussian victories. He never spoke of his personal affairs, and I never found out what business he was actually in.

The Meyers had four children. The youngest, Fanny, my own age, was the nicest of them all, quite pretty, and intelligent. She became an actress of promise, but after her marriage in Switzerland she retired from the stage.

In the Meyers' household once again I found myself in the familiar atmosphere of my own family in Lodz, but with a German setting. The food was excellent, prepared Lodz style, and filled me with nostalgia for home. Uncle Siegfried always seemed happy with his family, despite his Teutonic leanings.

.   .   .

Two major events interrupted my well-established curriculum vitae: one was the arrival of a young pianist from Australia who immediately became another protégé of Joachim; the other, my mother's return to Berlin in order to arrange for the religious preparation for my bar mitzvah, which would take place after my thirteenth birthday.

Both events upset me. Fritz Müller, a German-Australian, proved to be a boy of great promise, both as a pianist and as a composer. Exactly my age, with a winning personality and considerable talent, he struck me as a dangerous rival. It happened that Nellie Melba, the famous Australian prima donna, was making her first appearance in Berlin, and Joachim, who had heard and met her in London, felt it his duty to receive her in his own city with all due honors. Melba, still in her prime, was something of a siren, too, so it was no wonder that the old master became infatuated with her. He wouldn't miss a single one of the singer's appearances and even went so far as to take part in her last concert. All Berlin was talking about it, and I heard quite a few malicious comments about the whole affair. And it was Melba who brought young Müller to Berlin. She had heard him in Melbourne and, impressed by his gifts, decided to make him continue his studies in the German capital. To make the enamored master take him on was easy, and so it happened that another young pianist had the luck of becoming a protégé of Professor Joachim.

A curious kind of friendship developed between Fritz Müller and myself. We genuinely appreciated each other's talent, but there was a good dose of jealousy, too. Each of us would try to impress the other with his special pianistic facilities; Fritz would scare me with his rapid staccato octaves while I would retaliate with my brilliant trills. I must confess this exchange did me a lot of good, forcing me to concentrate more seriously on my finger technique.

The other event proved to be of a more disturbing nature. I had to attend a school of the Reformed Jewish synagogue to learn some Hebrew, in order to be prepared for my bar mitzvah, and I found this an unexpected moral attack on me, hard to reconcile with my past and present religious background. My parents, and especially my father, were never Orthodox Jews. My mother liked to go to temple simply in order to be seen. Only the Sabbath was upheld, more a pretext, as I have indicated, to bring the family together on Friday nights for a happy reunion. We had been brought up in the Polish language. We were little concerned about Jewish laws or dogma, although we were always proud of our race. Still, I do remember having been derisively critical of the Polish Orthodox Jews, with their long black coats and their sidelocks and beards and their singsong. My father had taken me, once or twice, to a synagogue, but only for musical reasons—to hear a famous cantor perform—and on these occasions there was a curious mixture of Jewish worshipers and Christians who were enthusiastic about the singer. During the past couple of years in Berlin, I had been even further removed from any religious activities. The Rosentowers were, I think, atheists at heart, Professor Barth an unavowed anti-Semite, and my friends and acquaintances hardly ever spoke of religion. And Altmann? Well, Altmann was certainly the one who, by opening my mind to the world of philosophy, closed it tightly to blind faith. But I had to be obedient, and so, for three or four weeks, I was forced to listen to the bored and monotonous voice of a man who tried to explain to about fifty of us the intricacies of the Hebrew language and the biblical interpretation of our existence.

When the great day arrived, my mother was exultant. We drove to the synagogue, accompanied by Aunt Salomea and her daughters. At the temple, the ladies had to go upstairs to their assigned places, separated from the men, and I was left alone, given a long white shawl with a fringe to wear, told to keep my hat on, and to watch for the moment when the rabbi, who was praying at the altar, would call me. My turn came, and I was led to a table on the platform, where the rabbi, accompanied by his assistants, addressed me with some phrases in Hebrew, whereupon he unrolled the sacred scroll and indicated a few lines of the Bible I was to read. I acquitted myself quite well. After a few more exchanges in Hebrew between the rabbi and others, the ceremony was over. The Meyers and my mother took me to an excellent kosher restaurant, and I received the traditional presents. My mother gave me the tephillin, to be used, presumably, when I would say daily prayers. The Meyers presented me with a silver watch which I found more useful.

On January 28, I was thirteen years old. This is becoming serious, I thought. I am a grownup now. Well, anyhow, I was pleased with my birthday presents. Bertha Drew gave me the piano score of the *Meistersinger* in the unsurpassed arrangement by Karl Tausig; my dear Altmann sent the four symphonies of Brahms for piano alone, a very expensive work. And many other things, some useful, some pleasant, were showered on me.

Mrs. Rosentower gave a party to celebrate the occasion. It was a good party. We all played games, and I did a few imitations of famous musicians, my specialty, and finished by playing some of my favorite repertoire: excerpts from operas, symphonies, even operettas—anything but legitimate piano music.

Miss Drew was in great form; she had drunk an unprecedented two cherry brandies, which went to her head a little, then danced a few steps to my tunes and sang some American songs—all with great charm.

The guests left, delighted with the party, and we were all about to retire when a strange thing happened: Miss Drew and I continued to talk for a while. Finally, I said "good night," as usual, and she suddenly put her arms around me and kissed me on the mouth! It was such an incredible shock to me that my heart stopped and I ran off to my room, not out of shyness or modesty—but because I was simply overcome with emotion. She loves me, she loves me, was all I could think of. We had been close friends for quite a while now, and sometimes I would hold her hand a little longer than necessary, but I would never have dared to do more.

The next morning, after a sleepless night, I was trembling at the blissful thought of seeing her again. She arrived late for breakfast, a little pale, but perfectly composed, declared she had never enjoyed herself more than last night, and gave me one of her serene, bedimpled smiles. For all my admiration of her composure, I was deeply disappointed. Nothing seemed to have changed, and yet . . . that kiss? But days passed, and nothing happened. Oh, yes, I forgot, something disagreeable did happen; for some reason of her own, Mrs. Rosentower put me out of my room and set up a cot for me at night in the main drawing room. It was a pretty disheartening thing not to have a place of one's own, and I was furious. This and Miss Drew's incomprehensible behavior kept me brooding for a few days.

Melancholy being alien to my nature, I felt I had to do something to fight it off. So, one morning, I knocked bravely at Miss Drew's door, entered the room, and without allowing her to utter a word, burst into an impassioned lament about my loneliness, playing it up a little about being pushed around and having no decent place to sleep—in other words, thoroughly making a nuisance of myself.

She was quite upset. "Have I done something to you?" she asked. "Have I offended you?"

"Oh, no," I shouted, and covered her hand with kisses. "It's simply that I have seen too little of you lately! You go out practically every night and come home so late that I am hardly able to see you at all. Ah, if you would only promise me to come and kiss me good night, no matter how late it is, I would feel so much happier."

I was a little ashamed, knowing that this was the kind of thing a child demands of his mother—but Miss Drew didn't seem to mind, and gave me her promise.

So it all turned out for the best, even the fact that I was relegated to the drawing room, as it was situated right across from Miss Drew's and at a good distance from the others.

A new life, rather a new night life, began for me. Miss Drew would often go to the Opera, especially when they gave *Tristan* or the *Meister-*

singer, and both are very long. She was frequently escorted by a young minister of the American church in Berlin, and, of course, I was not jealous of him. On the contrary, I was happy she was in such safe hands. And so I would wait for her for hours, sometimes reading, sometimes sleeping, marking time. But I always heard her come in, on tiptoe, closing the doors inaudibly. The first time, when she sat down on my cot, I was so overcome by the emotion that had been accumulating for so long that I kissed her with all my passion and tenderness, and she seemed to respond. After that, she would come to my room regularly, always with utmost precautions, moving silently through the dark hall. I would whisper some tender, loving words, and she would kiss my mouth, and smile. At one of our clandestine meetings I even proposed that she wait for me for ten years so that we could get married. Another of her sweet smiles and a kiss acknowledged my generous offer.

Then, one day, we met our nemesis.

Mrs. Rosentower called Miss Drew and me to her room one morning and declared that she could not tolerate this kind of thing going on in her house.

"Aren't you ashamed, trying to debauch a young boy his age!" she cried. "This is the most outrageous thing that has ever happened to me."

Miss Drew, ashen pale and terrified, stammered in reply that she had acted simply out of compassion for me, so far away from my family, and all she really wanted was to give me some of the maternal warmth I had been so long deprived of. Whereupon Mrs. Rosentower raised her voice: "Then why do you kiss him in secret?" she screamed. "And not only that, but I have found out that you kiss him on the mouth, a most indecent thing to do!"

Poor Miss Drew jumped at that, and now thoroughly indignant but with tears in her eyes, answered: "How dare you speak to me like that, and accuse me of debauchery and indecency? Why, back home in America, families and friends kiss on the mouth and don't attach the slightest significance to it!"

I was stunned, not only by this horrible scene, but even more by Miss Drew's violent insistence on her maternal feelings toward me. And I, little fool, had thought it was love!

Miss Drew stayed on for a few days because her parents were due to arrive. Our meetings at meals became quite ludicrous; we kissed awkwardly in front of everybody, blushing all the time under the half-ironic, half-malicious smiles of the sisters, one of whom had been, obviously, the informer.

Still hot with indignation, my friend went to Professor Barth to complain about the treatment to which she had been subjected, and he, to my great astonishment, took her side. I was to discover much later that he, too, had a keen eye for pretty girls. Her parents finally arrived, and Miss Drew left to stay with them at a hotel. They very kindly invited me to lunch with them one day and treated me like one of the family. Their daughter's dramatic account of the happenings at the Rosentowers' had little effect on them. "These Germans," the father said, "have no notion of manners."

The day they were leaving for Boston I went to see them off, with some flowers and a little composition for my dear friend. At the station, Miss Drew introduced me to her fiancé, the young minister! And I hadn't been jealous of him, ha, ha. She was married shortly after, in America, and I saw them here and there, during my American tours. We remained friends until her death. . . . Recently her son, who was devoted to his mother, was generous enough to give me the diary she kept in Berlin. And there I was secretly delighted to discover, as I read with a lump in my throat, that she had indeed felt a light stir of love for me in the depths of her heart in those young days. . . .

8

After Miss Drew had gone, life with the Rosentowers became intolerable. I felt suddenly like a complete stranger among them, frequently quarreling with one or another member of the family and resenting acutely my lack of privacy. One day this situation came to a climax when out of utter fury I smashed the piano stool in the drawing room to pieces. I expected to receive a severe punishment, but, instead, the ladies, scared by such an outburst of violence, retreated to their rooms, and I, the victor, was served dinner in the dining room all by myself.

Barth, too, noticed the change and, having been highly critical of the Rosentowers' handling of the affair with Miss Drew, decided to take me away from this female stronghold. It turned out to be quite an ordeal for him to find the right place and the right people for me; either they were too old or I was too young; sometimes they were allergic to piano playing, or hadn't adequate rooms. In short, it took a long time before he found what he thought was the ideal couple. I was introduced to them at his home before my lesson, and they looked, as one would call them now, upper middle class. The wife was in her middle thirties, the husband considerably older. She seemed much the more interesting with her pretty figure, good features, and kind, smiling eyes. In fact, she was really quite attractive. They looked me over like a piece of goods, talked about the weather, just to hear my voice, and, after going into some details, decided in my favor, mainly, I thought, because of the personality of the K.K. Hofpianist and Professor of the K.K. Academy of Music.

Mr. and Mrs. Winter lived not far from my various teachers, and, to my joy, near the zoo. They had no children; there was only a maid around—that was all. What a change after the constant ado at the Rosen-towers'. I was given a nice, not too small, room, separated from the Winters by a small corridor. The Professor managed to get the piano manufacturer, Mr. Bechstein, to send me a small grand for my present establishment, and my new life started under happy auspices. All my friends were delighted, including the Meyers, and it became clear now that they had all been disturbed for some time at my living in the un-wholesome atmosphere of women, as they said. And so Fritz Müller, Hans Engelmann, Kurt Hahn, and other members of the *Lesekränzchen* visited me more often and with more pleasure.

It was high time for me to start serious work for my forthcoming concert with orchestra at the Beethoven Saal. My program was to consist of: Mozart's Concerto in A Major, soli; Schumann's *Papillons;* a nocturne and the Scherzo in B Minor by Chopin; and, after intermission, the Concerto in G Minor of Saint-Saëns.

I loved this program; the Mozart was becoming a part of my heart, and the solo pieces were well chosen. This Saint-Saëns was a welcome novelty, and I attacked it with great energy, and, I must admit, it served me for many years as a first-rate war horse! It has everything—dash and elegance, dazzling brilliance and temperament; it is good music, too, if not devoid of a certain banality. But I am convinced that an interpreter of talent can ennoble any piece he plays, if he is a re-creator and not a mere performer.

In December 1900, just before Christmas, when the concert finally took place, my nerves were on edge, and Professor Barth's worried face was pitiful to see. The rehearsal with the orchestra had gone very well, and the musicians seemed impressed, and so, pulling myself together, honestly I did my best. Every piece was a success, and after the final Saint-Saëns, the audience jumped from their seats, started to yell, and stamped their feet. I really must say it was a triumph for me. Joachim, the composer Max Bruch, and a great pianist, Leopold Godowsky, were there, and the house was full. After my four encores, they all came on the stage to congratulate me, and Professor Joachim embraced me. Hermann Wolff began to look at me as somebody of importance. My sister Jadzia and my oldest brother Staś had arrived from Lodz for the event. The next day, according to the accounts in the papers, I was considered a coming star, and two of the most important critics (I even remember their names: Leopold Schmidt of the *Berliner Tageblatt* and Otto Lessman from the *Musik Zeitung*) declared that I was ideal in Mozart, for whom I seem to have the deepest understanding. "Er ist unter den begnadeten ein Auserwählten," one of them said, a phrase that I shall never forget. Professor Barth wrote Miss Drew about my success and Joachim's satisfaction—a letter I still have in my possession.

As a result of this memorable concert a lot of changes took place. Barth and Altmann became resigned to the fact that my allergy to mathematics would always be a stumbling block to my academic career and let me give up the exams at the *Realgymnasium*. Instead, I was to take private lessons in French and English with two different teachers, each twice a week. It was Joachim's suggestion; he thought languages were the most important asset to concert artists. And how right he was. Also, thanks to him, I got two engagements as soloist with orchestra in Hamburg and Dresden. I have wonderful recollections of both occasions, mixed with some less pleasant ones. Hamburg was the second most important city in Germany, so it was an honor to play with the Hamburg Philharmonic. The Dresden engagement was even more flattering because the concert was in commemoration of a Mozart anniversary. Joachim played one night, and I had to play the next evening—the last Mozart Concerto in B flat. In both cities, the respective conductors invited me to stay in their homes.

The Hamburg concert was a great success; I played the Saint-Saëns Concerto which never failed me. I was even forced to give an encore, a rare honor, and I was immediately engaged again for the next season. My sister and brother had come up from Berlin, and after the concert, just as we were ready to go home, my sister, whom I had introduced to Mr. Richard Barth, the conductor (no relation to Heinrich), expressed the wish to take me out to dinner that night. My host told her it would be difficult to find any restaurant open so late, but my sister insisted, and so he gave in. As it was raining hard, quite a sizable concert crowd was waiting in the street for the rain to stop, and watched us with curiosity. There was no cab in sight. My brother went to find one, and my sister and I had to wait in the street for three-quarters of an hour until he returned. When we got in we asked the driver for a good place to eat, and he answered that at that hour we could get only something cold at the railway station. It proved a sad end to a perfect day.

My conductor and host in Dresden was the famous Alois Schmitt, the Czerny of that epoch, who had published innumerable volumes of études and exercises for the piano. He was around seventy-five but still full of energy, and he conducted very well. It was a joy to play the beautiful Mozart Concerto with him. The Dresden public was very fond of Schmitt and gave us both an ovation.

Just before this concert I received a telephone call from my brother-in-law, Maurycy Landau. He had come especially to Dresden for my concert, he said, so he wanted a ticket and hoped I would have supper with him afterward. But this time there was to be a banquet at a club given by the concert committee, to which Joachim, Schmitt, and I were, of course, invited. The situation was difficult, but my brother-in-law insisted on my asking Mr. Schmitt for a ticket for the concert and an invitation to the supper. My host was slightly taken aback, but even though it was the last minute, he managed to get Maurycy a seat in the president's box and a card for the supper. After the concert, the committee, the guests, and the artists assembled in the hall leading to the dining room and waited what seemed an endless time for the signal to sit down for supper. When Mr. Schmitt came up to tell me that we must start without waiting for my brother-in-law, I was astonished. "Did he say anything to the president when he was in his box about being late for the banquet?" I asked.

"That's the trouble—he did not come to the concert at all . . . something must have happened to him. But don't worry, we'll find out tomorrow morning, first thing."

I had my own secret misgivings, and how right I was. Next morning, after a hurried breakfast, my host called for a cab, and we drove to my brother-in-law's hotel, where I rushed up to his room, leaving Mr. Schmitt waiting downstairs. I found dear Maurycy in bed, furious at being wakened; he told me that he had met some friends who took him to a club for a card game and he completely forgot about the concert and the party and got home at three in the morning.

I returned to the old gentleman and invented a lovely story about how my poor brother-in-law had been taken ill just as he was dressing for the concert, and how, being alone, he had no way of communicating with anyone. I shall never know how much Mr. Schmitt believed, but he gallantly offered any help Maurycy might need, which was, of course, politely refused.

Happily back from my concerts, I settled again at the Winters'. Mr. Winter often had business out of town and was away a great deal. His wife seemed to be a good wife and housekeeper—but there was a strong romantic streak in her personality. She would go into ecstasy about the music I played, about the books I was reading, and she was desperately curious to know all about my life. I wasn't a bit unhappy in this atmosphere; on the contrary, I liked it. Spending whole days alone with each other brought us, naturally, into a great intimacy, which gave her the opportunity to tell me everything about herself, while I would confide to her all my young troubles, dreams, and hopes.

One morning I received exciting news from Mrs. Engelmann: Her Royal Highness, the Dowager Grand Duchess of Mecklenburg-Schwerin, an old patron of hers, had expressed the desire to have me play at her palace in Schwerin. Barth was delighted with this invitation, and I was thrilled; it was my first contact with royalty.

In the beginning of this century, things artistic, especially in music, were much the same as in Mozart's time. All of Europe, except France and Switzerland, was ruled by sovereign princes (Germany alone had dozens of them). Operas, orchestras, and repertory theaters were in the hands of these titled people who provided the money and, of course, had absolute authority over everything. When a pianist was to their liking, they would appoint him Hofpianist, a pianist of the court. They were also generous with orders and medals . . . which reminds me of a good story. Alfred Reisenauer, a pupil of Liszt's, had given a concert at the palace of some German princeling. The next day, the *Hofmarschall* came to his hotel on behalf of the grand duke and offered him the choice of either one thousand marks or the Order of the Bear or the Falcon, or something like that. "What would they charge for such a medal in shops?" asked the artist. "Oh, I think twenty marks," replied the courtier. "Well," said Reisenauer, "I will accept the medal and nine hundred and eighty marks."

For obvious reasons, most members of the royal families were related to one another, being forced to marry only royal blood. Therefore, it was obviously important, particularly for a musician, to gain the patronage of one of these rulers, because a letter of recommendation from one could open many doors that would further his career. For example, this very Grand Duchess of Mecklenburg-Schwerin was the mother of the Prince Consort of Holland, the husband of Queen Wilhelmina, a very valuable relation indeed. The Crown Prince of Denmark was then the greatest "catch" of all, as he was at once the brother of the Dowager Empress of Russia, of Queen Alexandra of England, and of the King of Greece.

So, then, on a rainy morning, I took the train for Schwerin. As I arrived in this small, provincial town of only about twenty thousand inhabitants, I was astonished, realizing that it was the capital of a Grand Duchy. A court carriage took me to the hotel, a most antiquated hostelry without any modern comfort. A letter from the *Hofmarschall* informed me to be ready at two forty-five . . . the carriage would be waiting for me. The concert was to start at three o'clock; I was to wear full dress, white tie. I was terrified. I was still wearing short trousers. I didn't own such clothes; nor was it easy, at that hotel, to get ready on time. There was no bathroom, no hot water, and I had great difficulty finding a tailor to press my clothes, so I arrived at the palace ten minutes late. Half a dozen footmen in livery showed me the way to the great ballroom, where I found an astonishing assembly of about fifty persons, mostly old ladies in court dresses, *décolletés*. All the men, without exception, were in tails and wore all their decorations. It was a sight worthy of the famous Hollywood productions of imaginary European court scenes.

My entrance made one of the ladies jump to her feet and leave. The *Hofmarschall* greeted me reproachfully: "You are late, young man. Please go to the adjacent room where Her Royal Highness will receive you in private audience."

Quite abashed, I entered the room indicated and saw there the lady who had just left the ballroom. Thinking she was just a lady-in-waiting to H.R.H., I gave her a polite but indifferent nod . . . and discovered that she was Her Royal Highness when she approached me and said, "I am the Grand Duchess Marie. You are the pianist, aren't you?"

I yearned to answer: "No, I am the plumber," but instead I made a deep bow, kissed her hand, and muttered some words of excuse. She smiled and returned to the ballroom, where she led me to the grand piano and asked me to play. When everybody was seated, I gave a program of about an hour, performing some Bach, Mozart, and Brahms. The audience waited for the Duchess to give the signal for applause, and clapped politely for a short while. The concert was over. The *Hofmarschall* escorted me to Her Royal Highness, who was seated on a higher chair than the others. She thanked me very graciously and said a few kind words about my playing. Then she rose from her semithrone and the others shot up from their seats and stood to attention like soldiers. Footmen appeared carrying trays with coffee, and I was offered some, too, in a delicate cup of Meissen china, which I found difficult to balance in my hand, still shaky from the exertion. At that moment, the *Hofmarschall* came to tell me that Her Royal Highness the Grand Duchess of Oldenburg wished to congratulate me, so we walked up to a tall, attractive young princess who was wearing a lovely pink silk gown. I made a deep bow, with a click of my heels, and, oh! my cup of coffee spilled down the front of the beautiful dress! The Grand Duchess just muttered: "Ach," gave me a murderous

look, and left abruptly; I was hoping the floor would open up and engulf me, when the Grand Duchess Marie came over smilingly to console
me, asking me to return that evening for an intimate supper in her private
apartment. Naturally, her gesture restored me completely.

I soon realized that the poor Duchess of Oldenburg didn't enjoy a
great popularity among those present. The supper turned out to be charming. Only one footman showed me the way to the private rooms on the
second floor of the palace, where I found Her Royal Highness, changed
into a simple gown, two nice ladies-in-waiting, and the ever-present
Hofmarschall sitting around a cheerful fireplace. The supper was quite
informal, and I was made to feel so much at ease that I risked telling them
some choice Jewish stories and treating them to my repertoire of imitations, and I daresay I had more success with them than during my afternoon concert.

A few days later, after I was back in Berlin, Mrs. Engelmann told me
she had received a letter from the Grand Duchess expressing her great
satisfaction with my visit and hoping to hear me again in Schwerin, this
time with orchestra, at a gala concert in honor of her birthday on January 29. I received this invitation with mixed feelings; my own birthday
was on January 28, and this flattering engagement would make me miss
the usual celebration, with my friends, and all the presents and favorite
dishes. Instead, I had to rehearse with the orchestra on that very day in
Schwerin, although I must admit I was pleased to be playing for the first
time a new work I had just learned—Chopin's *Fantasia on Polish Themes*.
And so I left, happy after all, for this gala to find the little capital this
time all beflagged, in a festive mood; even a *dowager* Grand Duchess's
birthday was a holiday in her loyal state. Queen Wilhelmina and her Consort arrived from Holland for the occasion, the reigning Grand Duke
came back from the Riviera, where he used to spend his winters and his
subjects' money, and a few other royal personages were present. I was
annoyed when all of them appeared at rehearsal (obviously having nothing
else to do) because it made us performers very nervous; the conductor
hardly dared to stop the orchestra when something was wrong, and as a
result, we gave a poor performance of the beautiful piece later at the
concert. Fortunately, our audience was not musical enough to know the
difference, and they applauded politely when they saw the royal persons
doing so. After the concert, a state banquet was served in the big ballroom
of the main palace of the reigning Grand Duke. The orchestra had to play
during the dinner and later for the ball. Sitting at the *Hofmarschall's* table,
quite overcome by the luxury of it all, I felt a pang of jealousy in my
heart when the time came for the toasts, as I thought about my own lost
little birthday. Suddenly, on an impulse, I whispered to the *Hofmarschall*,

"Isn't it a strange coincidence? Today is *my* birthday, too, but, please, don't tell anybody." I knew, of course, that he would find it amusing news for the Grand Duchess and tell her, so at once there was a great fuss made over me. I was much toasted, and received some charming presents after all. I am still a little ashamed of this exhibition, particularly as the Grand Duchess Marie continued to send me telegrams of good wishes for "our" birthdays up until the First World War.

9

Little by little my musical relationship with Professor Barth continued to deteriorate; it became increasingly hard for me to put my heart into working on the pieces that I felt were insignificant or frankly disliked. For instance, with a Beethoven sonata, I might love the first movement, but not the second one, such as in the Sonata, Opus 90, so beautiful and promising in the initial movement and, in my opinion, disappointing in the second, with its overrepetitious rondo form, weakening the great effect of the first. Practically no Chopin was given me except some études, and these only as practical studies for the fingers, not as the works of art they are. Barth still neglected Bach too much; three preludes and fugues from the *Well-Tempered Clavichord* and the great Fantasia and Fugue in G Minor in Liszt's arrangement were the only Bach I studied in six years! But he continued to give me lots of the minor Mendelssohns, Schumanns, Schuberts, and never the real great works by these masters. Once he wanted me to study a concerto by Adolph von Henselt, a lengthy, difficult piece, reminiscent of Chopin, but lacking his genius. I remember on that occasion I protested, but the Professor was adamant, and so, one day, losing my temper, I tore this music to shreds and scared my tormentor so much that he finally gave in. What irritated me most was that none of the things he made me learn were practical enough for concert programs; either they were too long, finishing in a sad mood, like Schumann's *Davidsbündler*, for example, or they were simply antiquated and ineffective.

I was distressed to realize that under these circumstances I was really leading a "double life" musically—the one, the discouraging one, in my lessons with Barth; the other, the one I loved, hearing, playing, and learning all the beautiful music, whether it was symphonic, operatic, or whatever. Nikisch's concerts excited me more and more; he introduced the little-known Russians—Rimsky-Korsakov, Borodin, Moussorgsky. He was the first to play the Symphony of César Franck, and he introduced me to Richard Strauss's *Till Eulenspiegel* and *Death and Transfiguration* and many other great novelties. Barth's partisan spirit was such that he pronounced all this music bad; for him music finished with Brahms, and Wagner was so much the Antichrist that I had to hear his operas in secret!

My lessons in theory and harmony were also disappointing. My teachers tired me with eternal canons and other boring exercises, never inspiring me to greater efforts. I used to compose quite a lot in those days, and Fritz Müller and I would compete, each writing a piano piece or a song which we used to submit to each other's criticism. I soon realized, though, to my great sorrow, that I was not born to be a composer! I would imitate Brahms, I would try to imitate Beethoven, later even Chopin, and, true, I was able to turn out a pleasant-sounding little piece for piano, or a singable song, but it was not *me*—there was no urgency in creating, no real need for it. Fortunately, I saw the light pretty early. I became aware of the masses of unnecessary music published that filled the shelves of music shops and were never performed, for the simple reason that they were artificially fabricated and not written by the grace of genius. I used to say, in a jocular mood: "My only superiority over my namesake, the great Anton Rubinstein, is that I don't publish my compositions."

Fritz Müller tried to encourage me to compose, but I think he did it out of kindness; he himself impressed me sometimes as having the right stuff in him, but the future proved I was mistaken.

My manifold musical disillusionments were in part compensated for by my intellectual life, thanks to Dr. Altmann. He found me new means for stimulating my thought by enabling me to hear interesting lectures by prominent men, great writers, historians, philosophers, and scientists. It was fascinating for a boy of fourteen to participate in such feasts of the intellect. I had the privilege of hearing Professor Wilamowitz-Moellendorff talk about Greece, the famous old historian Mommsen about Roman history, a great Nietzsche commentator whose name I forget, and many others, exposing ideas which, convincing or not, *taught me to think*—and that is a wonderful gift of heaven.

One morning, Altmann handed me a ticket for the world premiere of a new play by Gerhart Hauptmann. A Hauptmann premiere was considered *the* main dramatic event in Germany, so it was no wonder that I was eager and happy. It turned out to be a beautiful evening; the drama

Rose Bernd moved me very much, the acting was perfect, and to see so many well-known people in the audience provided great interest. I was especially flattered when the critic Alfred Kerr treated me to a cup of coffee during intermission and discussed with me, barely adolescent, the merits of the play.

After the show, I found Dr. Altmann in the street waiting for me, eager to question me about every phase of the evening. Very much later I learned that he could afford only that one ticket, and had wanted to let me have it rather than to use it himself. . . .

The theatrical life of Berlin received a new, invigorating shot with the rise of Max Reinhardt, former actor of the Deutsches Theater. It started with an original show, kind of a literary cabaret called *Schall und Rauch*, which was made up of sketches of a high intellectual caliber all about political, artistic, or everyday events. The novel touch was to introduce into the audience, sitting in one of the boxes, a "Serenissimus," the imaginary figure of a degenerate, be-monocled aristocrat, created by the famous satirical weekly *Simplicissimus*, whose idiotic comments on current topics were a favorite feature. Reinhardt found just the right actor for this role, whose loud remarks to his companion in the box or to the public at large would provoke fits of laughter. The show was the hit of the season, and I enjoyed it with relish. But this proved to be only a springboard for Reinhardt's imagination and energy. He soon transformed his "cabaret" into legitimate theater, producing, one after another, plays that made history. I still consider myself lucky to have been introduced to his work then, to have seen his actors, many of whom he had lured away from the Deutsches Theater, because I feel it enabled me to witness firsthand the fabulous ascent of this genius of the theater. I shall never forget the plays I have seen, thanks to him.

Reinhardt was the first to introduce Strindberg to Germany with *Miss Julie* and *Rausch* (*Intoxication*, in English). After this, he revealed to the Berliners a strange young playwright, Frank Wedekind, with two fascinating dramas: *Spring's Awakening*, a play about adolescent love, and *Erdgeist*, now called *Lulu*, which much later served as libretto for Alban Berg's opera. *Lulu* was certainly the most daring and scandalous thing seen on a stage, but it had strength and conviction. The most successful play of all was Maksim Gorki's *The Lower Depths*—the heartbreaking tale of the down and out who were crammed together in a pestilential, cheap dormitory, and who found even there happiness brought to them by the sunny and generous nature of an old beggar. It gave me the first hint of the real meaning of happiness.

The Lower Depths ran for a year, and Reinhardt himself played the beggar Luka. Yet, all these events only whetted his appetite for bigger things. In no time, he succeeded in taking over Brahm's Deutsches Theater and another much larger one on the Quai, and he built a new one, the Kammerspiele—a lovely intimate theater, paneled with mahogany wood, blessed with perfect acoustics and the most comfortable seats. Now, a complete master of this intricate theatrical network, he was able to fulfill his great dreams. He chose his largest house for the famous Shakespeare productions which were among the most perfect I have seen. *The Merchant of Venice, Midsummer Night's Dream, Twelfth Night, Romeo and Juliet, Hamlet* remain treasured memories. When it came to scenery Reinhardt was a great innovator, creating the turning stage so that the curtain never came down and there was no break in the action, no lengthy intermissions, no distraction from the drama.

In addition, he discovered a fabulous young actor, a German of Italian descent, Alexander Moissi, who possessed the most beautiful speaking voice I have ever heard—it sounded like music—and had an immense talent for acting. His Hamlet and his Romeo were unique experiences. There was also an actress, Gertrud Eysoldt, whom I shall never forget. She was a unique Lulu, and later the perfect Salomé in Oscar Wilde's play, which had to be given at a private performance for invited guests, because it was banned by the censors for its religious implications. I was present on that magnificent occasion, and so was Richard Strauss, who, immediately, decided to write an opera based on this work without changing a word of its text.

I am writing about these things because they provided such great stimulus to my young mind. I began reading voraciously anything of quality I could put my hands on; I read in their original languages masses of German, French, English, Russian, and Polish literature. It was not always easy for me to find enough time because Mr. Winter was rather stern about late hours; my light had to be out at eleven p.m., so when I was determined to read on until three or four in the morning, I would erect on my night table a wall made up of three tall volumes of music, and bury a tiny candle there, leaving just a slit of an opening for my book, while the rest of the room was plunged in darkness.

My passion for reading began interfering with my homework, especially with Professor Barth's lessons. Instead of the prescribed two hours of practice every morning, I would lock my door, put my *Anna Karenina* in Russian or some Sienkiewicz in Polish on the music stand, place some chocolates on my right and some cherries on my left, and start playing a few mechanical exercises with my left hand alone, as I reached for chocolates with my free hand and turned the pages of my novel! After an hour of this complicated arrangement I would change, my right hand playing and the left hand picking the cherries. . . . The household thought I had never worked better, but the result was disastrous, of course, and I was always having to make feverish last-minute preparations for my lessons.

In spite of all these maneuvers I managed, miraculously, not to discourage Barth too much. After one not too bad lesson he suddenly pulled a cigarette out of his case and offered it to me. "Smoke it," he said. "You will like it." Bursting with pride, I lit it, but at the first draw I got tears in my eyes, started coughing, and with all that smoke up my nose, was a miserable sight. The Professor laughed heartily, presented me with a little box of cigarettes, saying, "You will learn how to smoke soon enough," and gave me some advice. I showed off proudly to my friends how privileged I was being allowed to smoke in public, but I hated the cigarettes more and more, and, after a week, stopped smoking them for the rest of my life. I was thirty when I learned to smoke cigars—and these I still smoke with untiring pleasure.

The inauguration of a large and beautiful building called Filharmonja, entirely devoted to music, with a big, aristocratic hall for symphonic concerts and a smaller one for chamber music, made Warsaw a proud city that year. It was a young Polish conductor, Emil Mlynarski, who initiated this great project and was the driving power behind its realization. The rich citizens of Warsaw responded so to his energy and enthusiasm that they also enabled him to create a great symphony orchestra—the Warsaw Filharmonja, which was as fine as any other of its kind in Europe. The gala opening concert had Emil Mlynarski as conductor and Paderewski as soloist. A few months later the manager of the new Filharmonja—Mr. Alexander Reichmann—having heard of my promising debut in Berlin, wanted me as soloist in one of the symphony concerts. I was overjoyed by this offer, and Professor Barth gave his permission without difficulty, stressing only that I was to bring back to him the money I would earn. My family came from Lodz for the event, and stayed with my Aunt and Uncle Wiesel, so the first day I was entirely drowned in family. The next day I had my rehearsal at the new, beautiful concert hall with Mr. Mlynarski, one of the most attractive men I had ever met. He had strangely nonchalant ways, a soft melodious voice, courteous, aristocratic manners, and he appeared to be a rather too soft character for an orchestra conductor. But the minute he walked up to his podium and took the baton in his hand, his whole attitude changed. Erect and quiet, he held his orchestra under complete control with a minimum of gestures, giving the soloist a wonderful feeling of security. I played, of course, the Saint-Saëns, the piece that never failed me, and again it proved triumphant. The concert was a great success, and I was proud to see my parents happy.

Two nights later an interesting event occurred when I was invited to a party in honor of Grieg and Mascagni, who were conducting in Warsaw at that time. The party was given by Mr. Louis Grossman, the Steinway and Bechstein agent, and he wanted me to come and play for the two great masters. They seemed to like my playing very much, but later in the evening, when a Polish soprano sang the great aria of the opera *Halka* by Poland's best operatic composer, Moniuszko, I saw Mascagni burst into tears, and Grieg, too, had to wipe his eyes. This was the only time I was ever to meet these two composers. Grieg died shortly after that, and Mascagni became a Fascist later on.

I played in another concert at the Filharmonja—this time, a mixed recital, made up of a singer (a soprano), a violinist, and myself, for the benefit of a Jewish hospital. I received no fee, but I was presented with a silver (!) laurel wreath after my solo piece, the beautiful *Wanderer Fantasie* of Schubert. When I returned to the artists' room I found a young man waiting for me, who was very striking-looking. He had a pale, expressive face, delicate nose, and longish hair that was artificially curled; and he was dressed in a way which suggested the fashion of Chopin's day—a black, tightly fitted frock coat, gray trousers, a double-breasted black velvet waistcoat, and patent leather shoes. I noticed his beautiful hands with fine, long fingers when he grabbed both my hands and showered me with the most flattering compliments. "You are the greatest piano talent I have ever heard," he cried. This is the kind of talk that displeases me always, because I hate exaggerations, especially about my playing. He noticed my reaction immediately, so he quickly introduced himself, saying that he had just won a gold medal for composition at his graduation from the Warsaw Conservatory. He then insisted that I come the next day to his home, but as it was my last day in Warsaw, I promised to come only for a short moment in the morning, in spite of having many important engagements. My family had organized a recital in Lodz, and I had to prepare a program, practice it a little, and get ready for my return to Berlin, right after this last concert.

I kept my promise and went to visit my new acquaintance, Frederic Harman, expecting that he would be living in a music student's usual modest quarters, but to my surprise, I found myself in a most luxurious apartment; the door was opened by a butler who ushered me ceremoniously into a vast salon where two grand concert pianos were standing side by side. A young girl of about seventeen received me with a smile and some compliments about my concert, then asked me to excuse her brother for being a little late. Her rather arrogant self-assurance made me feel shy, and my shyness turned into panic when I saw the butler emerging from another room with a huge tray. "Oh, no, no," I cried, "I couldn't possibly eat anything now. I have a luncheon engagement in half an hour!"

At that, she burst into shrill, silvery laughter. The butler was just passing through the salon, taking a shortcut from Frederic's room with the breakfast tray. I tried to laugh, too, but it sounded artificial.

Frederic finally appeared, fresh from bed, apologized charmingly for keeping me waiting, and immediately began to demonstrate the fine quality of the two pianos. I was impressed again by his ease and elegance, and even by the lovely tone he produced on both instruments. Unfortunately, I had to leave, being expected for luncheon with my parents at the Wiesels. So, both brother and sister saw me off most cordially.

The next night I gave my concert in the old Sala Vogla—the hall where I had heard orchestral music for the first time in my life. The house was full, but I had the feeling that I was playing just for my family. Wherever I looked, I saw some aunt, a cousin, or an uncle of mine. In the front row sat my parents, my sisters and brothers, and two brothers-in-law! With such a public, a success was easy to achieve, so the concert became, naturally, a triumph! Afterward, the whole family had supper at home, and we drank tea and ate fruit until very late hours.

The next day I returned to Berlin. At the station, where the whole family flocked again to bid me goodbye, my father took me aside and told me that I had made a profit of seven hundred rubles at my concert, but that he couldn't give it to me just then, what with his heavy expenses —the trip to Warsaw, the receptions, etc. "Tell Professor Barth that I shall send him the money in a few days," he added. As a matter of fact, my father could have kept the money without mentioning it to me; I was still a minor, and he didn't have to account to anybody. The train was about to leave, so I was much kissed by everybody present and found myself, finally, exhausted but happy, in my compartment.

Professor Barth had never talked to me about money matters. Acting as my tutor, he had assumed all the responsibility for my affairs, as I have mentioned before, and was collecting the fees due me for my concerts in Hamburg and Dresden (I never knew how much these were) and in Warsaw, where I did know I had earned three hundred rubles (about $150), which I was to take back to him. At that point I was getting a weekly allowance of two marks (fifty cents), and Mr. Winter was instructed to provide me with cash for bus fares and other necessary expenses. So, as a matter of fact, I really had no idea about my financial situation. The one thing I didn't like—in fact resented bitterly—was that Professor Barth made me write letters of thanks to my benefactors at the end of every year—and this has always been a thorn in my heart.

Mr. and Mrs. Winter were delighted to see me back, and Barth was quite satisfied with the financial as well as the artistic success of my Polish appearances, and so I plunged again into my old routine. Then only two weeks after my return from Lodz, the Professor asked me suddenly, at a lesson: "Did you hear from your father about the money?" and I answered: "No, I have had no letter from home yet." A few days later, he repeated the question, this time with a certain sharpness in his voice: "It is strange, isn't it, that we have no news about this money?" I answered a little nervously: "My father is very casual, but I feel sure he will send it any day now," and I left in a miserable state of mind.

At the next lesson, I had no sooner entered the music room when Barth jumped up in a rage and shouted at me: "I still haven't received the money; this is an outrage, and I am beginning to think the worst of your father!"

This was too much for me. I picked up my music and ran for the door, screaming. "You can't insult my father . . . you'll never see me again . . . I am leaving for Lodz!" And I dashed home, crying on the way. Back in my room, I immediately started a letter to my father, telling him the whole story, and asking him how I might come home. At that, the front door rang, and the Professor was shown in, breathless after climbing three floors. He shouted at me: "I want you to repeat to your father every word I have said. Don't hold anything back from him." I said, calmly, "I have already done exactly that and shall wait for his instructions."

He left without a word, and I finished my letter and rushed down to mail it.

I waited six agonizing days for the answer before it arrived. I didn't even recognize the handwriting because my father hated writing letters so much that he always just added a few words to the ones my mother sent me (alas, I have inherited this trait from him). But this time he wrote himself. His first phrase, I remember, was: "It was fortunate that I got your letter without your mother's seeing it, so she doesn't know anything about this." Then followed a quiet explanation of why he was so late in sending the money to the Professor. "I had to wait for the various accounts of the expenses for the concert," he wrote, "and, of course, I should have let you know, but I hate writing, and thought there was nothing for you to worry about." He added that he had just sent the money and asked me to apologize to the Professor for this long delay!

I was stunned, and deeply hurt. I felt that my father had let me down when I needed him for the first time in my life! How could he fail to understand the great importance of my decision to return home? I thought, with bitterness, that this was the traditional Jewish way of treating children: ignoring their feelings, never giving them credit for any constructive thought—whereas they, the parents, were of course infallible, always knowing what was best for us!

The day I received my father's letter was one of the crucial turning points in my life. I felt alone, thoroughly alone. After some time of brooding, I came to the conclusion that I still loved my parents and my family but that the moral and physical chain which linked me to them was broken forever. In these hard days of decisions, I made up a motto for myself: "Nie dam sie." The Polish is not easy to translate. It loses impact, but it means vaguely: "I shall never submit." I have stuck to this motto all through my life.

Professor Barth received the money, and it was he who apologized both to my father and to me. Things seemed to be back in order again, but a subtle change did take place in our relations. I continued working for his lessons, but more half-heartedly than ever, while I threw myself more and more into the world of Theodor Altmann. And this proved fatal to me. One day, Professor Barth announced cold-bloodedly that he had decided to find me another teacher; he thought Altmann inadequate for me, neglecting serious studies for unnecessary ones, robbing me of much of the time needed for my piano and musical work, and having, in general, a bad influence on my morale (!). My impassioned protestations were to no avail; his mind was made up—he had already dismissed Dr. Altmann. This was the second hard blow in quick succession! At our farewell, both Dr. Altmann and I had lumps in our throats, and later, in the street, I had to cry it out. Altmann left Berlin for a time, and I have never seen him again. He never wrote to me, and I didn't know where to write him.

10

My good friends in Berlin were becoming alarmed about me; I had lost weight and looked so pale and sad that they felt they ought to do something. So it was Professor Salomon and his wife who asked me to spend my summer vacation with them and their two sons in a villa they had rented in a small village in Pomerania, a charming place, they said, right on the border of a lake. I accepted eagerly, and for me, it proved to be more than that—it was a great experience. It was actually the first time in my life that I came into close contact with nature, real wild nature.

It was entirely different from the crowded place near Lodz where I had been taken by my parents or one of my sisters. Here we were practically alone, with only four or five houses around, and great spaces between, and we were at a fair distance from a delightful little old town, Lychen, with its medieval gate and tower, lovely old houses, and quaint inhabitants, who spoke the northern dialect which sounds like Danish. And so we had the lake and the surrounding deep forests all to ourselves. Behind our villa we had a garden with wild flowers exuding wonderful aromas at night. A nice, roomy rowboat was at our disposal. I learned to row right away, and this was heaven! I also liked to take walks by myself. A forest had always held a strange fascination for me—a mysterious world of its own, the heart of all the fairy tales I so loved. Sitting under an old tree, I had the impression that every other tree, every branch, had something to tell me. I felt surrounded by a rich, powerful life. . . . It is strange, but, by contrast, I feel quite alone in a crowded café on the Champs-Élysées in Paris. . . .

When I returned at the end of summer I was ready for adult clothes, and I got a dark blue jacket, waistcoat, and long pants. I started to shave, too, all of which gave me a moral lift. And that was not all. One night, coming back from a concert, I was waiting for my bus when a vulgar, fat prostitute with a huge bosom sidled up to me and whispered: "Kommst du, Kleiner?"—Will you come with me, little one? I felt a sudden violent shock, something like a hemorrhage, which made me almost faint with weakness. Panic-stricken, I started running and ran all the way home. But back in my room, I simply realized that I had become a man.

From that night on I felt a great change taking place in me. I became restless, incapable of paying attention to anything for long. I became nervous and jumpy—in short, I wasn't happy. But I discovered soon enough the focus of my hate . . . I was jealous of Mr. Winter! The growing intimacy between his wife and me made me suddenly conscious of her as a woman, and I couldn't stand it any more when he kissed or patted her, or ventured some playful gestures. And with time it grew worse, although she did not notice. Finally, I decided that I had to rid myself of this complex, and one morning I devised a Machiavellian plan. When she brought a glass of milk to my room where I was practicing, I said very calmly, "Dear Mrs. Winter, I am terribly sorry, but I shall have to leave your home as soon as possible." She almost dropped the glass. "What is the matter—have we done something wrong?" she cried. "No, no, nothing of the kind. I just cannot tell you why, but I must leave," I said. She wouldn't take this for an answer. "You must tell me why—or is Professor Barth behind this?" she persisted, almost in tears.

"No, it is entirely my own decision, and I wish I could tell you my reason, but it is utterly impossible. Only, please," I added, "don't tell Mr. Winter about it—this must remain between us."

She left the room. For the next three or four days she tried to persuade me to change my mind or tell her what it was all about, but I remained adamant. One morning she became frantic. "I won't let you go unless you tell me what is making you do this to me!"

The right moment had come. I knew I had nothing to lose. If she allows me to leave, I thought, I shall at least be rid of this whole nightmare, but if she permits me to stay, she has lost. . . . In a low voice, almost a whisper, I said, "If you force me, I shall tell you, but you must promise not to get angry with me?" She nodded, smiling. "Why should I, Arthur, dear? You know how fond I am of you." "Well, you see," I finally stuttered out, "I feel about you in a way I shouldn't . . . and I cannot take it any longer, living so close to you." A long, stunned silence. And then, in an artificially light tone, she said, "This is sheer nonsense, my dear. You will get over it in no time—you really don't have to leave us for such a silly thing!" But I knew—I had won.

That same night she came down the dark corridor leading to my room, dressed in a flimsy dressing gown, to wish me a good night's rest. I put my hand shyly on her round, solid breasts, and she let me. Then we kissed. Thus began my first real love affair.

And it was a complicated affair, too. One must not forget that I was still involved with my many different lessons, that I had a considerable amount of homework to do, not to speak of my practice, which was becoming imperative in view of two important concerts in Hamburg and Berlin. I had long since had to give up my association with the *Kränzchen* because of my concerts and the traveling they entailed. Quite obviously in the midst of these activities there wasn't much time for a love affair.

Mrs. Winter—I began to call her Henny—was very sentimental, and she loved to tell me stories about her past. I, too, was an inveterate talker, and for some time had found her a good listener. At first our constant talk had not interfered too much with my work, but now it was different. Henny, having but few chores to do around the place, was free most of the time. When her husband was not off on a trip, he used to appear only at meals, take naps in the afternoon before returning to his job, and retire early. No wonder Henny was constantly in my room. And we were rather careless.

Professor Barth, who was aware of my growing-up pains, now became alarmed at my unhealthy look; he questioned me about my eating and sleeping habits, but couldn't get a satisfactory answer out of me. As a matter of fact, I had needed more sleep of late, and the food at the Winters had never been very tasty or fortifying. I was fed mainly on *Kartoffelpuffer,* a German kind of potato pancake which I disliked, and I would often buy myself a rye bread to eat in the street. But Barth didn't know of all that.

One day he startled me by saying he must see Mrs. Winter, and that I should transmit to her this message. I was terrified. Did he know something? Or was he guessing? He arrived the next afternoon with a stern face, saying he had to see her alone. I spent a dreadful half-hour in my room waiting for him to leave. After his departure, I dashed to Henny for news and found her laughing. She laughed tears, then told me the story: Barth had begun by complaining about my work. "Der Junge is lazy, he is never well prepared for his lesson, but what makes it worse, he gets easily exhausted and even his memory often fails him. He looks ill and worried. Haven't you noticed it?"

"I answered him," she said, " 'No. Here at home he seems quite normal, but perhaps he has too much work?' " "Nonsense," Barth went on. "There must be something else." And, suddenly blushing, he added, "I suppose, Mrs. Winter, that you have never known about certain things young people do—but, please, look up in your dictionary . . . the word is 'onanism.' . . ." Whereupon he got up and left in a hurry.

Poor Professor! I felt sorry for him. He was so completely unsophisticated, and, in a way, inexperienced. It was this same characteristic that showed in his choice of my concert programs. His suggestions for my first recital in Berlin and my second appearance with the Hamburg Philharmonic Orchestra were wrong—I felt it in my bones. And, unfortunately, I was right. The Hamburg audience who had applauded enthusiastically a promising young boy, still wearing short trousers, for his brilliant performance of the Saint-Saëns Concerto was disappointed to hear, one year later, a pale and thin adolescent playing the Mozart Concerto in a dry and unconvincing way. And I had to agree with them. There was some polite clapping, I was called out once, and that was that.

The Hamburg Barth (Richard), with whom I was staying again, was quite incensed about his namesake. "You ought to leave him," he cried. "You are not the first young talent he has tried to ruin . . . I know of others." There was much truth in what he said, a truth I had felt myself for some time. A musical depression took hold of me, quite apart from my laziness about practicing. My work with Barth grew more and more stale, and now not even my private musical life was able to lift me from this apathy. My unfortunate Berlin recital only confirmed my misgivings. The E minor Sonata of Beethoven, Opus 90, had been exactly the wrong opening for me. I had too little understanding of its second movement. Then came the *Davidsbündler*. I loved this piece—in spite of its length—but Barth had prodded me to exasperation about this or that unimportant detail, and succeeded in extinguishing my last spark of enthusiasm. The rest of the program went even worse. I played the second volume of the Brahms-Paganini Variations in a much too fast tempo; I was nervous and discouraged by then, and hit many wrong notes. The final Liszt Rhapsody didn't go well, either. I knew the concert was a failure. There was applause but it came mainly from my many friends in the hall, and later, in the artists' room, their words of praise sounded like condolences.

The reviews were not bad, but there was no warmth in them, mirroring exactly my performance. Barth, of course, blamed my laziness, saying, "Mein Junge, wenn du nur arbeiten wolltest, könntest du ja alle in den Dreck spielen!" (My boy, if you would only start to work, you could play them all into the mud). This phrase struck me; it kept ringing in my ears for the rest of my life.

Professor Joachim, fortunately, had been prevented from coming to my concert, but he must have heard about it from Emma Engelmann in not too harsh terms. She was full of indulgence and tried to console me by saying that lives of artists have their ups and downs and that I shouldn't take my momentary setback too much to my heart. The Winters, especially Henny, insisted that my concert had been a major triumph! What an irony.

As time heals most disappointments, I regained some of my *joie de vivre*, determined, more than ever, not to surrender. But, a month later, a terrible experience was in store for me.

I received a letter from my mother saying that she had "good news for you; your father and I have decided that I should come to Berlin and live with you. Your sister Frania's marriage makes it possible for me. You have reached an age when a boy needs most his mother. It is hard for me, as you can imagine, to leave my home, your father, and the rest of the family, but we consider it absolutely necessary for me to be with you. Money is no problem, as the amount Professor Barth is collecting from your supporters will be sufficient for both of us."

I was flabbergasted by this letter; the prospect of living with my mother on money coming from strangers was unbearable! I had suffered so much these last years from this humiliating situation that I could hardly endure it myself any longer. My most fervent wish was to free myself, to stand on my own feet as soon as possible. Now my parents' plan would make me even more dependent, thwarting any hope of liberation for a long, long time.

I wrote back an imploring letter, trying to couch my objections in the most delicate terms. I hated to hurt my mother's feelings. But I was absolutely determined to reject this arrangement. I even went so far as to pretend that my sponsors were getting tired of supporting me for so many years, and I added, with a dose of bitterness, that two of them, Mr. Warschauer and the Mendelssohns, had never even invited me home, thus showing their complete indifference for me as a person.

My letter fell on deaf ears. My parents still lived with the old-fashioned, patriarchal conception that children have no voice in plans for their future, that they are expected to obey blindly. And so my mother ignored all my objections. She would be arriving, she wrote, in two weeks. She would stay for a short time with Aunt Salka, until she had found an apartment for us both and made the necessary arrangements with Professor Barth. I was furious. "How can they?" I cried, "How can they disregard so completely my own wishes, my own feelings?" My indignation mounted to such a point that I decided to do anything in my power to stop her. My first move was to confide to Professor Joachim, who listened in silence to my impassioned flow of accusations, griefs, and protests, and, after a little pause, answered with a sad smile, "My boy, it must be terribly painful for you to go against your mother's wishes—but I do understand your reasons. I went through similar difficulties in my youth. I shall try to dissuade her, and I hope I shall succeed."

Barth's reaction betrayed his unmistakable Prussian origin. "I can always refuse to deliver the money," he said with a grin, and made me regret having spoken to him. Max Bruch, Mr. Martin Levy, the Engelmanns, the Salomons, Lotte Hahn, all were sympathetic; they all saw that it would be fatal for me to have to live with my mother under such circumstances.

My mother arrived in Berlin on a gray, cold morning in March 1902. Because of my lessons, I wasn't able to meet her at the station, and the Meyers took care of her, bringing her to their home. When I went to greet her in the late afternoon, after all my work was done, she received me with shouts of joy and the usual maternal outpouring but, right away, became concerned about my looks. "You look pale and tired and you must have lost weight," she cried. "Probably you don't get enough food; they have starved you, I can see that." And she continued, "But all this will change now, my poor child. I shall fatten you on your chicken soup with noodles and beans which you like so much, and on fine boiled beef, and you will look different in no time." I was touched by this long-missed motherly solicitude, which made me feel more miserable, like a traitor! Yet, I couldn't help being amazed at her taking me so entirely for granted, at ignoring my objections to her coming and treating me like an irresponsible child. What gave me an extra chill was the sight of the baggage she had brought with her. I saw, to my horror, pillows and covers, forks and knives, and dishes, and what not—enough for a stay of years.

The day of my mother's arrival was the beginning of an agonizing torture for her and for me; it lasted two months, and that time shall remain in my memory as one of the most unhappy periods of my life.

At first, after she had talked with Joachim and Barth, I found her just a little astonished at their noncommittal, evasive response to her propositions. "These Germans," she commented. "They don't seem to understand how much a child needs its mother!" But later on, during her discussions with my tutors and supporters, she became so aware of the wall of opposition that she felt surrounded by a conspiracy against her. Then, only then, did it begin to dawn on her mind that *I* must be the one who was behind all this hostility toward her, that *I* must have persuaded them to act as they did! When she asked me bluntly, I did not deny it. When my mother looked at me, a hurt expression on her face, it was clear I wasn't the irresponsible little boy to her any more—I had become the enemy.

And yet, she was so determined to stay she wouldn't give up. Beside her strong conviction that I needed her for my own good there was also, I felt, the frustrating thought of having to go back home, defeated. And so, she started fighting it out with me, with me alone. It was a sordid, pathetic business. She had disliked the Winters from the beginning, especially Henny, and hated visiting me there. Her uncanny mother's instinct sensed something unusual; she wouldn't say anything, but I knew she felt it. Henny was very polite with her, but her manner was forced and artificial.

As my lessons prevented me from visiting my mother at the Meyers', who lived so far away, we were reduced to meeting at odd places, such as on a bench in the Tiergarten, or in the zoo, or in some café, or we would simply walk up and down a street. It was pitiful! She would beg, cry, scream at me with rage, but I was stubborn—I wouldn't give in, I wouldn't and couldn't face living with her on someone else's largesse. It did break my heart, though, seeing her in such a state.

I loved my parents very much, but I loved them in a special way. I was devoted to my mother—but there was hardly any contact between us. She was utterly unmusical, which separated us already on a very important ground, and she had little understanding of anything I stood for. And yet, I knew she was a perfect wife and mother in her own way; the rest of the family worshiped her like a saint. With my father, it was a different thing; he was unmusical, too, but he tried, he inquired—and he was a fine philosopher; a little Talmudic, perhaps, but with an open mind for new ideas. He was a failure in business, because he was too honest, and too indifferent toward money. What I liked best about him was his universality; he would pay scant attention to his own affairs or his family's, but, instead, his passionate interest would be aroused by some piece of literature or a remote item in an encyclopedia.

As I look back, I suppose that the main reason for the estrangement from my family lay in the fact that my parents sent me to live among strangers, who made a strong impact on my mind and my character at an age when I was most vulnerable. And so, caught between the sterile, interminable quarrels with my mother and Barth's ever-threatening beard, my life became intolerable.

11

One day, Professor Joachim called me to his room at the Academy. "Mein Junge," he said, "I am sorry to hear that you are still having difficulties with your mother. But I have a good plan for you. At the last Beethoven Festival in Bonn, we played trios with your famous compatriot Paderewski, who is not only a fine musician but a noble gentleman. As we are on friendly terms, I have written to him about you, asked him if he could receive you at his Swiss villa, hear you play, and give me his opinion about you. He has just wired that he will be glad to, but that you must come right away, as he will be leaving soon for a cure. So here is my proposition: you will leave day after tomorrow without saying a word to your mother, and spend a week in Switzerland. In the meantime, I shall inform her that you have gone to Paderewski, because you couldn't bear any longer the strain of the last months. I shall leave open the matter of just how long you will be away. I doubt that she will decide to follow you to Switzerland, since she won't even know your whereabouts."

My heart stopped with joy—I almost kissed him. He was offering me not only the escape from my ordeals but the anticipation of seeing a new, beautiful country and meeting this fabulous man, then at the peak of his fame.

Mr. Levy generously provided the money for my trip . . . enough to live lavishly for a week. But Professor Barth received the news with misgivings. "I can't stop you, if Professor Joachim wishes you to go," he said. "But when will you start to work in earnest?" And he was right; I was apprehensive, too, about playing for the great Paderewski, after having neglected the piano so much lately.

Professor Barth was very kind and took me to the station. After recommending various places I should visit and handing me a letter of introduction to a friend of his, a professor in Lausanne, he asked me in a low voice: "Shall I expect you for a lesson a week from today?" I nodded in the affirmative. "Na," he answered skeptically, "that remains to be seen."

After the train left, I took a long breath, a delicious feeling of freedom penetrating my whole body—even if it was to last for only a few days!

It was a night train, but I couldn't sleep as I sat at the window of my second-class compartment, watching the passing landscape or ruminating on the nightmare I had endured, or thinking of my coming performance for Paderewski.

In the early morning (it was the middle of May), after crossing a very long tunnel, the train burst suddenly into the sun, and I couldn't help cry out with joy at my first vision, which assaulted me like an electric shock, of those high mountains covered with snow, and below, the dark blue, majestic Lac Leman, surrounded by bright, green meadows, interspersed with large squares of wild flowers of an intense yellow—a shade I had never seen before. And the endless grapevines growing on the harmoniously sloping hills! I was overwhelmed by the beauty of it.

Two hours later, when we reached Lausanne, I chose a modest-looking hotel right opposite the railway station, ate a hearty breakfast, and had three cups of an excellent coffee. Then I took a long bath, tidied up, and, finally feeling better after my sleepless night, I gathered my courage and went down to the telephone. The porter wouldn't believe me. "What? You want to speak to Mr. Paderewski? What do you want of him?" I had to explain, and he agreed to call. A butler answered, in French: Yes, Mr. Paderewski knew of my arrival, and asked me to take, at a certain hour, a train to Morges, a short trip from Lausanne. There, at the station, a carriage would be waiting for me to take me to Mr. Paderewski's villa.

I followed his instructions, and the carriage deposited me an hour later, at eleven a.m., at the gate of Riond Bosson. When I rang the bell, the gate opened automatically, and a ferocious-looking dog started to bark furiously, baring his teeth at me, ready to tear me to pieces; fortunately, he was chained to his hut.

At the end of the entrance garden stood the house, built of wood and bricks, which, as architecture, was not interesting; it was neither a villa nor a château, reminding me rather of a comfortable, large *pension de famille* at a summer resort. The door was opened by a smiling butler who showed me into an enormous square hall, two stories high, with a gallery surrounding it on all three sides which led to rooms on the first floor. A big billiard table stood in the center of the hall. The butler took my coat and hat and told me to wait for the *maître* in the "salon," to which he opened a door opposite the entrance. He treated me with a little too much familiarity, and I felt shy because of my poor French. So I was glad to get rid of him, and entered the very impressive salon. I was struck first by the two concert grands with their keyboards facing each other, lined up along two bay windows. A double glass door in the center, opening on a large veranda, could be reached by the narrow passage between the pianos. On the walls hung three portraits of the master, the famous one by Burne-Jones, another one by Alma-Tadema, and the third by a French painter whose name I forgot. Both pianos were covered with flowers and framed photographs of kings and queens, Spanish infantas, and prominent aristocrats. I noticed also one or two prominent Americans, but, to my astonishment, no Poles.

Trembling with excitement and anticipation, I took up a strategic position between the two Steinways and waited, remaining standing. After a quarter of an hour, which seemed an eternity, a side door opened and a very old lady entered the room. Seeing me standing there, she came close to me and asked with a quivering voice, "Are you the young man who has come to play for the master?" I nodded. "Oh," she continued, "I feel sorry for you. Who on earth will listen to any pianist after having heard the master!" After pronouncing this shattering "sentence," she vanished.

By then I began to feel slightly sick and terribly tired. Another lady, this time a much younger one, came in, and I knew right away it was Mrs. Paderewska, having seen pictures of her. Despite her heavy frame I thought she looked handsome with her dark velvet eyes and beautiful white skin. I was just about to address her politely when she passed, holding a bunch of keys in her hand, the whole length of the salon and disappeared into another room without even looking at me. This was quite a shock! My feelings were hurt, and now I was frankly scared. The two keyboards, with their opened lids, seemed to be showing me their teeth like the dog in the garden. I was really on the verge of running away, when—a miracle happened: the center door went wide open and there appeared the Sun— yes, the Sun. It was Paderewski, the still young Paderewski in his middle forties, dressed in a white suit, white shirt, and a white lavallière tie; a shock of golden hair, a mustache of the same color, and a little bush of hair between his mouth and his chin gave him the look of a lion. But it was his smile and his charm which made him appear so incredibly sunny.

He rushed up to me with short, quick steps, and with a few warm words of apology he put me instantly at ease and made me forget all my miseries. "I have heard nice things about you from Professor Joachim, whom I admire and respect," he said. "And I am also delighted that you are a Pole," he added, with a kind tap on my arm. "Now—play something you like to play."

And then I made a big mistake—a mistake made by many young pianists on similar occasions, as I have since discovered. Instead of playing a piece I could perform with ease, showing my gifts to the best advantage, I chose the second volume of the Brahms-Paganini Variations, which I had not yet completely mastered, just for the sake of impressing him with the difficult passages. And I was punished for it, because I missed many of them, tired and nervous as I was.

When I finished, I bowed my head in shame. This is the end, I thought. He will show me the door. But no, on the contrary, he became even kinder, warmer. "My dear young man," he said, "don't be disheartened by a few wrong notes. I knew you were not doing your best, but I could see how talented you are!"

Aha, I thought. He is saying this out of respect for Joachim, and I got up, ready to leave. "You are not going, are you?" he said. "I hope you will stay for lunch?" and without waiting for an answer, he put his arm on my shoulder and led me to the dining room. By then, I had fallen completely under his spell. Madame Paderewska, who was already waiting for us, did not mention having seen me before when I kissed her hand.

We were three at the table; the old lady didn't come down. I was told she was my hostess's aunt, had her meals in her room, but got up at five in the morning to feed Madame Paderewska's prize chickens. Her age was biblical—something like ninety-five! Our table conversation was very animated. Mr. Paderewski was a fine *causeur* who talked in a high-pitched voice, like the speaking voice of a tenor, with a slight defect when pronouncing the letter *s*, so that one heard "sh" or "th" with a tiny hiss. And the effect was charming. I could well understand his fame as one of the great public speakers of the time, and he spoke with ease in five languages. I would have enjoyed the luncheon even more if it hadn't been for Madame Paderewska's loud remarks about my "proper" table manners. I thought it was bad taste to comment on my behavior to my face, and I noticed with satisfaction Mr. Paderewski's frown of disapproval.

After lunch, interrupting my effusive thanks, he escorted me to the front hall, picked from a stand a fine Malacca cane tipped with an ivory knob, and said, in a most engaging manner, "My young friend, as my carriage is not available at present to take you to the station, you will have to walk—but it is only a short distance and this cane will help you and you can keep it as a memento of your visit. Take the first train to Lausanne, pack your things in a hurry, and come back right away; we have guests for dinner and you will have to change. I hope you can stay with us until our departure for Aix-les-Bains in five days." All this was said as though I were a close relative, and I was so touched I couldn't utter a word, but he guessed my feelings and smiled.

I left, singing and whistling, and ran rather than walked to the depot. I was back in Morges in less than two hours, and took a station cab to Riond Bosson. Marcellin, the butler, showed me to my room on the second floor, which was spacious and comfortable and had a loggia, with a perfect view of Mont Blanc. I changed into my dark suit and black shoes (the only dress clothes I owned) and went down to join the hosts. The guests were already there: three middle-aged American couples and a Swiss gentleman, to whom I was introduced although I did not hear their names. The conversation was in English, a language I could understand but did not yet dare to speak.

The dinner was excellent, and most elegantly served. I remember that it was my first taste of a langouste, the southern species of lobster, and of pink champagne, of which our host was particularly fond.

After the coffee had been served in the salon Mr. Paderewski said some flattering things about me to his guests and asked me to play. And this time I was in the right mood. After I had played with all my heart my favorite pieces by Brahms, two rhapsodies and an intermezzo, and an impromptu of Chopin, Paderewski jumped to his feet and embraced me, saying, "I knew right away that you had great talent. I shall write Professor Joachim about this performance." His guests spoke to me in a very complimentary way, but I had the impression that they wouldn't dare praise too much a pianist in Paderewski's presence; they seemed rather cold. After they had all left, the great man escorted me up to my room, made himself comfortable in a low seat, and began questioning me in a fatherly way about my family, about Poland, the circumstances which brought me to Joachim—in short, about my life in general. I don't know whether it was because of his charm or his genuine interest, or because of my guilt over the last weeks in Berlin, but I felt an urge to tell him everything, to empty my heart.

Although I could see in his eyes that he didn't condone me when I unfolded the sad story about my mother, he showed a great understanding, not unlike the kind Joachim had expressed. "Artists have a hard road ahead of them before they find themselves," he said in an introspective tone. "Physicians, lawyers, engineers have their careers drawn out clearly, while we poor artists live with constant doubts."

He got up from his chair, walked up and down the room for a while, smoking a cigarette, sat down again, and began telling me the heartbreaking story of his own life. As it is a matter of public knowledge by now, I shall not elaborate on it, but I must tell about his only son. The poor boy had been born with a terrible deformity of the head and complete paralysis of the limbs. His mother died in childbirth, so the little orphan was left in the care of his grandfather and later of his future stepmother. Highly intelligent and of an angelic disposition, he was worshiped by his father. "I saw too little of him," Paderewski said, "being constantly on concert tours, and we were together in this home for only the last few years, and then—" He paused. "He died a few months ago." His voice broke, and I was almost crying. "Marcellin," he continued after a while, "you know—my butler—was his nurse and looked after him with the devotion of a mother, so now we treat him like a member of the family. He is my valet, secretary, and friend."

Exhausted from his emotion, the master bade me good night, but before leaving, he added, "Don't take your young worries too much to heart—you see there are harder things in an artist's life."

I remained deeply impressed by his long story. So this is the famous, happy, rich, great Paderewski? I thought with amazement, realizing that I had been in the presence of one of the most unhappy human beings I had ever met.

The next day I saw little of him. He sent me a message through Marcellin, suggesting that I visit Professor Budde, Barth's friend in Lausanne. My letter of introduction to the Professor was received with great cordiality, and the old gentleman was charming and introduced me to his family, who made me stay for lunch. His youngest son, slightly older than I, took me on a tour of the lake, showing me many beautiful spots, and I returned to Morges by boat late in the evening, enchanted with my day's experiences.

The last three days in Riond Bosson were most interesting. In the morning, after breakfast, I would settle down with a good book in the hall, listening all the while to the master practicing in his room upstairs. He was working on the Handel Variations of Brahms, repeating certain difficult passages slowly a hundred times. I noticed that his playing was greatly handicapped by some technical defects, especially in the articulation of his fingers, which resulted in an unbalanced sense of rhythm. After a short lunch, he used to continue practicing until seven o'clock, when he would call me to go out with him to the garden, where we would find

Marcellin for a game of bowling. We tried hard, but were invariably beaten by the butler, who would always win the stakes his master put up. Dinner was always rich and served with champagne, and after coffee we would play a little billiards. Paderewski loved these games, telling me that they were what kept him fit. Later on in the evening he liked to sit down at the card table and play a one-handed rubber of bridge, dealing the hands with consummate attention and playing them out, obeying strictly the bridge laws. At the time I found it funny, but now I must admit it is a more instructive game than solitaire.

On the last evening, he sat down at one of the pianos in the salon and played for me for about two hours, showing me all sorts of pianistic difficulties, pointing out brilliant fingerings, tricky pedaling, and other interesting sidelights. From time to time he enchanted me by a beautifully played phrase, or a lovely production of tone, which could be even moving, but he discouraged me a little by an exaggerated rubato and frequently broken chords. I became aware that my musical nature was far apart from his.

When my stay in Riond Bosson was coming to an end, Paderewski suggested that I accompany them by train to Geneva—"which you must see," he exclaimed. "It is one of the most beautiful cities." The trip from Morges to Geneva was short; when the train stopped, I took leave of my great compatriot, kissed Madame Paderewska's hand, and thanked them for everything. Seeing me still standing on the platform with my bag, he opened the window of their compartment and called out, "If you have nothing better on your mind for your summer vacations, come and spend them with us!" Before I could answer the train moved on.

Alone at the station, I suddenly remembered that it was the next day I was expected to be back in Berlin—and I remembered at the same time Barth's skepticism about my turning up on time. Rapidly studying train schedules, I found out the best thing for me would be to leave in half an hour. "No Geneva this time," I said loudly to myself, and made for my train. The next morning, early, I arrived in the German capital, exhausted from sitting up in the train the whole night, preoccupied with thoughts about my mother. At the apartment, Henny greeted me exuberantly, shouting, "She is gone, she is gone!" I was so shocked I was speechless. Something broke in me—I felt suddenly so desperately sorry for my poor mother I was on the verge of begging her to come back. It took me a long time to calm down and face the new situation. Professor Barth was visibly gratified by my return, but showed little curiosity about my impression of Paderewski and his opinion about me. And so, once more, I had to take up my old routine, but this time with even less conviction and less heart in my work.

12

Professor Joachim was delighted with the letter Paderewski had written him. "The boy has an authentic talent, without any doubt," he wrote, "and I predict a brilliant future for him." He also added some kind remarks about me as a person, and reiterated his invitation for the summer. "You see, everything worked out as we hoped," Joachim commented. "Your mother finally came over to our point of view and left you in peace, and this opportunity to spend a whole summer in the atmosphere of a really noble and great man would do you a lot of good." I listened to him, still under the shock of Mother's departure and saddened by a reproachful letter from Aunt Salka, yet I knew I was right.

The kind, old Mr. Martin Levy invited me to have lunch and talk about the whole situation. Impressed and flattered by Paderewski's interest in me, and thus reassured in his own confidence in my future, he thought the time had come for me to leave Barth—who (it was *his* expression) was "killing my enthusiasm for music. . . . Frau Engelmann," he added, "is of the same opinion, and Joachim, without saying so openly, would have nothing against it." My answer was, "But it's absolutely impossible. I couldn't suddenly leave a man who has shown me such devotion, taking no money and giving me so much of his precious time for so many years— I feel it would break his heart."

Mr. Levy found me too sentimental. but came out with another suggestion. "My daughter is married to a professor of bacteriology at the University of Marburg, a beautiful little town, very much like Heidelberg. I have rented a villa there for the summer to be near my daughter and my grandchildren. Will you join me? I can arrange through Joachim to extend your vacation for two or three weeks. And you can leave for Switzerland directly from Marburg."

The idea enchanted me, but I was afraid of Barth's reaction. And I was right. He became quite incensed when he heard of all this, but what enraged him most was that Paderewski had invited me through Professor Joachim, ignoring his own rights to decisions over my destiny. "Unless he writes to me I shall not let you go," he said, and it sounded like an ultimatum. When Mr. Levy heard this, he entered into a diplomatic exchange of letters with Paderewski and got him to send a telegram to Barth asking for his permission "to let your talented pupil spend the summer as our guest."

So Barth dropped his objections, and I prepared happily for a long, enjoyable summer.

Mr. Levy's villa, built on a hill overlooking the town and facing an old castle on the opposite hill, was a spacious, comfortable place. Everything was in good taste; paneled walls in light wood, pleasant furniture, bathrooms with all the modern gadgets, and even a fine Bechstein grand. My host had brought some of the servants from his Berlin residence, and they were to serve just the two of us! No wonder that I recovered my good humor quickly. Mr. Levy's daughter was a young, dark-eyed woman, of great charm, endowed with a well-trained singing voice. I used to accompany her to Schubert and Brahms songs, and we soon became good friends. Her husband, a well-known scientist, assistant of Professor William Jenner, looked his role, being supremely respectable, devoid of any sense of humor, and completely unmusical. And the food at Mr. Levy's villa was tasty and luxurious; he was a real connoisseur. I am afraid that it was this visit at his house that really marked the beginning of my long career as a gourmet. *Truite au bleu*, foie gras, crawfish in dill, duck *à la rouennais*, and many other such culinary masterpieces were new to my ignorant palate, and I enjoyed being initiated to these exquisite tastes.

This easy existence went on for three weeks; then it was time for me to leave for Switzerland. I must admit I was not a little apprehensive over this second visit to the Paderewskis! First of all, my farewell with Barth left me with an uncomfortable feeling of a moral obligation to him. He had said, with a pathetic ring in his voice, "Now, of course, you are going to study with Paderewski?" And I answered, with conviction, "No, never—I am invited by him just as a guest and compatriot." He smiled sadly, unconvinced, and I had left with a pang in my heart.

Mr. Levy and his whole family saw me off at the station. This time I traveled in comfort, my generous patron having provided me with a compartment in a sleeping car.

The atmosphere of Riond Bosson had changed considerably since my first visit. The house was full of guests, Marcellin informed me, taking my bags to a small room this time. "The *maître*," he said, "is hard at work, preparing programs for his coming tours and composing a piano sonata; he appears only at meals." It meant I was not going to see him before lunchtime. Madame was invisible, too, which I regretted less. In order to kill time, I went down to the hall, took my favorite seat, and read the papers. It was not long before Paderewski began working. He played long passages from his Sonata, many of which were familiar to me, since I had heard them often the time before.

The Lesekränzchen
from left to right
1st row Franz Pariser, Kurt Hahn, unidentified
2nd row Richard Fuchs, Arthur... Paul Hain... Hugo Perls

Exterior of the building
of the Rosentower apartment

interior — the living room

A gong rang, announcing lunch, and right away, coming from the garden or down the stairs, the house guests began to gather. They seemed a heterogeneous lot, as if they had nothing in common with one another. Madame Paderewska appeared presently and greeted me quite cordially without taking the trouble of introducing me to anyone. Finally, at least twenty minutes late, Paderewski entered the hall. I found him changed, too. There was no sun in him this time; he looked preoccupied and nervous. But his charm still worked. He took my arm and presented me to his guests, one by one, saying some nice things about me. I was not wrong, calling them heterogeneous; there was a couple, Mr. and Mrs. Alfred Nossig, both from Lwów in Poland; he had written the libretto for Paderewski's opera *Manru* and was an active Zionist, which belied the current gossip among Jews about the great pianist's anti-Semitism. Mrs. Nossig was a woman in her thirties, rather good-looking, a little too fat, with a sparkle in her eyes, while her husband was an elderly, bearded, and bespectacled little man, very intelligent but shy and gauche in manner.

The other guests were three gentlemen of the same profession, all of them concert impresarios, but they seemed to belong to three different worlds: Monsieur Chevrier, an old Frenchman, in elegant dark clothes and stiff collar, had been helpful in promoting our host's first concerts in Paris, had since retired, and, still a bachelor, was always a welcome guest at Riond Bosson; the second impresario was a typical Englishman with an Edwardian beard, a Mr. Addlington, Paderewski's most active agent, who had accompanied him on all his tours in England, Australia, and New Zealand, and who was completely disdainful of the Continent and foreign languages, having an enviable faith in his own infallibility; the third, Jaczewski, was a strange type, a Pole, though born and bred in Kiev and imbued with the Russian way of thinking. He could have been a prototype in some comedy: he wore a large black patch over one eye, while the other, very alert, was bursting with malice. His heavy-footed wit, his mania for making fun of everybody and everything, soon made him unpopular among us, and his insistence on the superiority of everything Russian was frankly irritating. Paderewski had engaged Jaczewski as manager of his coming tour in Russia—the tour which was keeping him so preoccupied; he hadn't played there since his early youth, and now the Russians were forcing him to accept their invitation to return. Obviously, this patriotic Pole hated having to play for the invaders of his country.

The Paderewskis always had guests for dinner—sometimes neighbors, mostly Poles living in exile. The pianist Sigismund Stojowski and his mother were daily visitors. Madame Stojowska, an affected old lady, used to amuse us with her airs, acting as if she were entering the court of Louis

XV. Paderewski enjoyed teasing her, and once he taught the overpolite Monsieur Chevrier to address her with an elegant phrase in Polish, and the innocent Frenchman, clicking his heels and kissing her hand, repeated the well-learned words: "Jak sie miewa stara krowa?" (How is the old cow today?). The poor woman, all in frills, locks, and laces, almost fainted with horror.

Madame Paderewska's birthday was feted with a gala dinner, after which some of the guests, including myself, improvised a charade in her honor. I shall always remember the end of this gay evening, however, as one of the most disagreeable incidents of my life. When the guests rose to leave, Madame Paderewska, not wanting the party to break up, asked me to play something. She caught me completely unprepared. Everybody was talking, laughing, and drinking, and it would be an anticlimax, I felt. I declined, pretending a violent headache.

"Aha," exclaimed Madame, "this is a good occasion to try out a new medicine for migraines I have just received." She sent a maid for it, and handing me a pill out of an ominous-looking bottle, she added, "Take one now, and tomorrow morning, before your breakfast, you must take two more." I promised, and retired to my room. Next morning, going down to the dining room with the bottle in hand, I found Mrs. Nossig alone, sipping her coffee. Confessing to her my little lie the night before, I asked her about taking the medicine now when I didn't need it. "Of course you musn't take these pills," she answered. "They might even upset your stomach." I was delighted.

Later in the day, as I was reading the paper in the hall, I noticed Madame Paderewska, clad in a dressing gown, shouting from the gallery, "Have you taken the pills?" And, scared to death by the tone of her voice, I answered a cowardly, "No, Madame, I was feeling much better, so Mrs. Nossig told me not to use them." Mrs. Paderewska retired to her room, without saying a word.

When the gong assembled us in the hall, we waited, as usual, for the master of the house, who finally appeared, with a deep frown on his brow and an angry expression on his face. He walked straight up to Mrs. Nossig and shouted at her, "So you are suspecting my wife of trying to poison our guests?" The poor woman looked at me in dismay, burst into tears, and fled, promptly followed by her husband, who couldn't possibly understand what had happened. I tried in vain to explain the whole matter to Paderewski, but he kept his angry mood all through the luncheon. Nobody spoke except Jaczewski, whose inopportune stories were completely ignored, and I was deeply disturbed, realizing what a strong influence Madame Paderewska had on her husband. He did apologize a little later to Mrs. Nossig, but their previously cordial relations became forced, and the Nossigs left after a week or so.

Another incident confirmed my feelings. Mr. Charles Steinway, then the head of the famous piano firm, which had introduced Paderewski to the United States, announced his presence in Geneva and was invited for lunch the next day in Riond Bosson. All of us were immediately impressed by his simplicity of manner. Seated between the host and the hostess, he started a lively conversation about musical matters. At one point, the guest of honor asked Paderewski which piano he would consider second to the Steinway. "Certainly an Erard," he replied. "How can you say such a thing?" the American exclaimed, raising his hands. "Erard is an anti-quated instrument. It still has some mechanical advantages, but its tone is like a harpsichord!" Paderewski replied a little sharply, "I am quite able to produce a fine sonority on it." "But you can't compare it with a Bechstein, either in tone or in action," Mr. Steinway cried impatiently. "I cannot imagine any pianist preferring an Erard to a Bechstein." Paderewski answered calmly, smiling ironically, "I happen to be a pianist and can assure you that you are mistaken." The piano manufacturer laughed, completely unconvinced. At that, Madame Paderewska, who fol-lowed this argument with growing irritation, said suddenly, choking with rage, "I cannot tolerate anybody permitting himself to speak insolently to the master!" Mr. Steinway instantly rose from his chair and left the room, and there was a moment of general consternation. Paderewski ran after his guest, hoping to bring him back, but he failed. His guest of honor left a few minutes later for Geneva.

More often than not, the master would play to me long excerpts from his Sonata, which I began to know and to like. I must admit he played his own compositions with perfect taste, without distorting phrases, as he did in other works. One afternoon, when he asked me to play some pieces for him that I had studied lately, I had the incredible impudence of begging him not to give me lessons, as it would hurt the feelings of Professor Barth. Any less distinguished artist would have taken this as an insult, but Paderewski, though puzzled for just a moment, praised me with a smile of understanding for my loyalty.

My long summer vacation came to an end, and even my lazy nature began to feel the need of some serious work; I had been practicing at Riond Bosson half-heartedly on an upright piano in a small pavilion in the garden. I found it far more interesting to listen to the master working on his sonata. I saw little of him during the last days of my stay; he was completely absorbed by Mr. Jaczewski and his preparations for the Russian tour, and he would practice all day long. But he did come down to see me off, kissed me on both cheeks in the Polish manner, and wished me Godspeed. I had thanked Madame Paderewska for everything the night before, and she waved goodbye from the gallery. As I left Riond Bosson, my heart was filled with gratitude.

Berlin looked cold and gray after dazzlingly colorful Switzerland. The autumnal rains had a depressing effect on my usually cheerful disposition, as I resumed my round of lessons with their long waits for buses. Professor Barth was visibly gratified by my punctual return, especially when he learned that I had not studied with Paderewski. He had moved during my absence into a new apartment, a sunny and friendly place on the fashionable Tauenzien Strasse. Having lost his old stepmother the spring before, he now lived alone with his sister, who looked after him with more care; there were vases with fresh tulips on the tables, and I found, with astonishment, that a large bust of Anton Rubinstein had been placed in the music room as the main ornament. The Professor himself had become more human, more relaxed, and as a result our relationship grew warmer and closer. He even went so far as to invite me to a lobster luncheon, having heard how much I loved the dish, so one day we went to an expensive restaurant specializing in seafood and enjoyed a regal meal of it. During the lunch our conversation revolved mainly around topics of little interest, but here and there some disquieting elements crept into the otherwise pleasant talk.

The best thing for me, the Professor proposed in an off-handed way, would be if he adopted me, which would facilitate many things for my future. He also insinuated that he had some vague plan to get me a professorship at the Academy of Music eventually. Both suggestions were not only disturbing but wholly unacceptable; in spite of my recent wicked behavior, I was deeply attached to my parents and would never have considered any change in our relationship. As to teaching at the Hochschule, I felt quite incapable of settling down at my young age to the thankless task of giving lessons to more or less gifted pupils. My dream was to go out into the world, to broaden my horizon, to give concerts— but certainly not to be pinned down to the pedantic and boring life of a piano teacher. But I didn't say anything. I was afraid to commit myself, and, above all, I wanted to enjoy my lobster in peace. (The aftermath of this culinary feast was typical of the Barthian pedantry. "And now, mein Junge," he said, when we were out in the street, "we must digest properly this heavy dish—let us climb up the Siegessäule!" I thought at first he was joking. But no—he meant it, all right, and I had to climb the interminable spiral stairs of this victory column with him.)

For the moment I was interested in languages, particularly Latin, which fascinated me. My allergy to mathematics remained unchanged. I continued to read with passion, and I was absorbing all the music within my reach—but my great outlet was the theater, and, of course, concerts.

I felt rather frustrated that there were no public appearances in view, fearing that my career, which had started so happily, was already doomed.

One day I was just window-shopping when I felt someone touch my arm. Turning around, I recognized Frederic Harman, the young composer from Warsaw. I was delighted to see him again.

"How are you? When did you arrive? Are you passing through town, or going to stay for a while?" I asked in Polish, and he spoke at the same time, "I had no idea you were still in Berlin! How wonderful to see you! We must get together!"

When we had answered each other he told me he was going to appear in a concert as composer, conductor, pianist; he had written a symphony in three movements, he was going to play his Fantasia for piano and orchestra, for which he had won a medal at the Warsaw Conservatory, and accompany a German soprano in some songs he had written. I was impressed by his ambitious program, and terribly curious to hear his compositions. The concert was to take place the beginning of December—a month off.

We arranged to meet the next day at his place, which I was pleased to discover was in a *pension de famille* not far from the Winters'. There Frederic had a combination studio-living room and alcove on the ground floor, the rest of the pension occupying the main part of an elegant new house. It was run by an elderly lady from Poland, the widow of a Warsaw lawyer, whom Harman had known. The guests were mainly writers and painters, musicians, and some ladies of means. Harman's apartment, which I liked right away, was very attractive. A fireplace with burning, crackling logs, a grand Bechstein piano, books and music scattered all over the place, and a sofa, with a coffee table and soft chairs, gave one a warm and comfortable feeling.

We had tea, and then he went to the piano and played some of his compositions. The symphony, which he called a little pretentiously *Per aspera ad astra*, was a highly romantic work, leaning heavily on Tchaikovski, whom he worshiped. Nevertheless, there was some genuine and inspired material in it; the themes sounded natural and fluent, and Frederic played with ease and clarity and a communicative enthusiasm.

His Fantasia for piano and orchestra was less ambitious. The piece had a strong Polish character with nothing of the somber mood of the symphony, and it sounded rather like Paderewski—light but charming.

It is not easy to describe this long first visit; all I can say is that there was something irresistible about it. Frederic's intelligence and vitality, his interesting compositions so well played, the pleasure of speaking Polish with him, and the warm comfort of his room left the immature boy I still was entirely defenseless. He made me stay for dinner that night, a *table d'hôte* affair served in a large dining room on the first floor of the pension. The food was excellent, and Frederic and I had a small table all to ourselves from which I could observe the other diners. By the end of the meal I knew everything about most of them, thanks to Frederic's amusing and often malicious comments. Later he introduced me to the more interesting people, among them two painters who had talent, he said: one was a German, a voluble talker; the other, a Swede who never opened his mouth. I met a lady, too, a very attractive young woman, just divorced from a famous playwright. Her makeup, her slim figure, and her deep melodious voice intrigued me, and she and Frederic seemed to be on the best of terms.

From that day on, for me Berlin changed character; it became a new city. All my old preoccupations receded because I simply stopped thinking about them. My life centered now in Frederic, whom I managed to see daily; I was helping him prepare for his concert and taking an active part in his life. With a large allowance from home, he could afford to have me often for meals at his place, or invite me to theaters and concerts, or take me to expensive restaurants. In other words, he made me conscious of a way of living I had not known. His conversation was a constant delight, whether we talked about music, literature, art, or people; his brilliant mind made everything he said sound most interesting, and he spoke five languages fluently.

Music was, of course, the basis of our friendship; we would discuss with passion composers, performers, conductors, and we would rush to the piano to prove this or that point. I made him love Brahms, whom he did not know sufficiently, and he, in turn, presented me with a gift from God—the revelation of the real authentic Chopin. I cannot stress enough the great debt I owe him for that, and I beg my readers not to underestimate this declaration.

Chopin was of course well known to me. I had heard much of his music in concerts and in private, but in Germany his music was often treated as *Salon Musik*, as they often called it, and the few times I had heard Paderewski I remained unconvinced by his often arbitrary exaggerations of tempo and expression. And so I ended up adopting the generally accepted opinion of Chopin as the young, sick, romantic figure who wrote sentimental music for the piano, elegant and difficult, unable to express anything but melancholy.

Frederic Harman felt a passion for Chopin. He was not a great pianist, he was even handicapped by a lack of memory and some technical defects, but his Chopin sounded right because he possessed the true accent for this music; a mazurka had the earthy Polish rhythm, a polonaise the dignity and strength, a scherzo or a ballade the great passion inherent in them, a valse the charm and elegance. Yes, indeed, I became conscious of hearing Chopin's music as it should sound! And I drew to a great extent my own inspiration for the Polish master from Frederic's deep and intuitive understanding of his genius.

But quite apart from our endless musical and intellectual discussions, I loved to listen to my friend's vivid descriptions of Warsaw, of life in Poland, of his family, and of his own experiences. He had a rare gift of communication, of making me visualize every incident, every personality he evoked. I was so fascinated by his stories that everybody and everything around me appeared pale in comparison with the world he opened up to me. My innate love for Poland was a great factor in this interest of mine. Frederic told me about his difficulties with his father, who didn't believe in his talent, and consequently how important his forthcoming concert was. But he spoke with love of his mother, who did understand his ambitions, and who was very musical herself. One day he announced that his mother and younger sister would be coming for the great event.

As the day approached, I became intensely involved, begging my friends to buy tickets for the concert, promoting Frederic and boasting of our friendship. My young musical comrades, like Fritz Müller and many others, were interested, and promised to come to the concert, but the older generation was somewhat reluctant. The German prejudice toward non-Germanic music was evident everywhere. Barth tried to discourage me by saying he had heard adverse opinions about Harman, without divulging his source. The Winters disapproved of my constant absences and my growing detachment from them, and the frequent late nights disquieted them more and more; her jealousy and his sense of responsibility met on a common ground. But, all said, and to my great satisfaction, my lessons and my studies were improving simply because I had found a new interest in music and life in general.

Two days before the concert, Harman's mother and sister arrived in Berlin and took an apartment at the pension. I was introduced to them that same day at tea. The sister was the girl with the silvery laughter I had met in Warsaw, but she looked now more mature and more serious, and much more attractive. She was small, which I liked; I noticed her black, intelligent eyes and the way her white teeth glittered

when she opened her full red lips. I was particularly struck by her dainti-
ness. Her mother was a tall brunette, vivacious of manner, with a touch
of coquetry. Both ladies greeted me like one of the family, evidently because of Frederic's flattering accounts of me and of our friendship. They
made me stay for dinner, and then were eager to hear me play. And I
played for them everything I could think of—a mixed salad of music: a
Bach fugue followed by the overture to the *Meistersinger*, one or two
pieces by Brahms, bits of Frederic's symphony, and other things. I wanted
desperately to please them, realizing by that time that I was falling in
love with Harman's sister. Both mother and daughter were extremely
musical, made me play on and on, and seemed delighted with me. By
the end of the evening, when it was time to leave, they made me
promise to spend all my free moments with them during their stay in
Berlin. And I would gladly have killed anyone who tried to prevent me.

I found it frustrating to miss any of the rehearsals for Frederic's
concert, especially the last one; my morning chores didn't allow me to
assist at them, but I was burning with curiosity to hear the sound of his
orchestrations, for the reactions of the musicians, and for his own impressions. On the afternoon of the great day, my homework done, I
dashed to the pension, where I found the Harman family having tea with
Josef Hofmann, the great pianist, an old acquaintance of theirs. He
pretended to remember me, but I could see that he didn't, which was
quite natural considering that it had been more than five years since
that casual visit. This time he made a much better impression on me,
showing some interest in Frederic and his concert. I also liked his dry,
sarcastic humor, although he used it mainly against his fellow musicians
and pianists.

We all went to the concert that night in a nervous mood; I sat on
pins throughout with sheer excitement. From the purely musical standpoint,
my chief interest was concentrated on the sound of the orchestration
and on Frederic's performance as a pianist and conductor. The symphony disappointed me in many ways; the instrumentation was heavy
and gauche, and the whole work too reminiscent of Tchaikovski; but
the specifically Polish, naïve freshness was his own—the characteristic
that was to be found in all his compositions. Frederic conducted the
symphony with insecurity, thus preventing the natural flow of the music,
which I attributed to a momentary nervousness, but when the same
defect appeared in his piano performance of the Fantasy, I became concerned. I was suddenly aware of a serious gap in his whole musical structure. Still, he accompanied the German singer of his songs beautifully.
The concert ended without incident; one could even call it a success, a
fair success; the public was attracted by Frederic's personality and ap-

plauded him quite warmly. He himself seemed enchanted with the warm applause, and his mother and sister were enthusiastic.

Josef Hofmann, I discovered, was mainly impressed by Frederic's triple role as a performer. After the concert, Hofmann and I had supper with the Harmans at a good restaurant, where we toasted Frederic with champagne on his successful debut.

As to the public, opinions about his concert were divided, so naturally I was apprehensive about the next morning's press notices. But the Berlin papers published long accounts of the concert, and in general they were friendly. They liked best Harman's songs and praised his playing, although they had little to say about his works for orchestra.

I spent all my free hours the next several days with the Harmans. Basia, Frederic's sister, was quite a dangerous little siren, and she succeeded in tantalizing me more and more. All of a sudden for no apparent reason, she would burst into uncontrollable laughter, and keep us all on edge. We did become good friends, though, in a funny sort of way; when she was in a playful mood, she would let me kiss her and I would play her game without daring to tell her that I was in love. Josef Hofmann, too, was a frequent guest of the ladies and, I soon noticed, was a dangerous rival. Jealous as I was, I was relieved to see that Basia didn't seem to respond to his advances; on the contrary, she liked to ask *me* to play rather than listen to the great Josef Hofmann. I learned later that he had even asked her to marry him.

Basia's and her mother's departure depressed me terribly, and if it hadn't been for Frederic I would have felt utterly despondent. So, I saw more of him than ever. He had hoped for some material results from his concert, but Hermann Wolff, who had organized it, showed little interest, put him off with vague excuses, and had no plans for the future.

Frederic's main concern was still his father. In the course of our long conversations he told me a lot more about his family and his life in Warsaw. Some of it sounded like a novel.

His father was the head of a high-level import-export business. His grandfather had been one of Warsaw's most important bankers and a man of high distinction, and there had never been any love between father and son—an incompatibility of which Frederic felt he was the victim. "My father has treated me indifferently since my early childhood," he told me. "He never believed in my talent. He was opposed to my plans for a musical career and made my life miserable. It was my mother who made it possible for me to study music and to be able to finish the Warsaw Conservatory with a gold medal for composition. And it was she who encouraged me to continue my work. The Berlin concert was, as I told you, to prove to my father that I had a right to a career."

In his frequent angry outbursts against his father, Frederic liked to make veiled allusions about not being his son at all; he told me about his mother's love affair with a well-known pianist, a notorious Don Juan, and he loved to see himself in the role of an illegitimate child. It all sounded so fantastic to me. I would listen to his biased talk with a dose of skepticism.

Henny disliked the turn my friendship with Harman had taken. I did speak to her of my love for Basia, and she listened with great understanding, but I had still to learn something about women and their reactions. Soon after, Henny complained to her husband about my constant absences and about neglecting my work because of my infatuation with the Harman family, and Mr. Winter decided immediately to see my Professor and tell him the whole thing. Barth, who was heavily prejudiced by gossip about Frederic and had heard how I had worked for his concert, was enraged by Mr. Winter's story, and at my next lesson, he ordered me to break off with Harman. "His influence," he said, "is dangerous for you, both from a musical and moral point of view, and I will not tolerate it." After a long lecture about my expending so much time on an unworthy person, he dismissed me without the lesson.

I was so stunned that I was not even angry. This is too absurd; nobody can keep me from pursuing a true friendship, I decided. And as soon as I got home, I gave Henny a piece of my mind about her treachery, whereupon, to make up with me, she promised to help me arrange meetings in the future with Frederic. And so I was still able to see him at either his or my place.

13

Somehow, I had become utterly tired of Berlin. All my thoughts were now turned toward Warsaw, and my love for Basia was not the only reason. I felt a general discouragement with my life. Even a new, rather interesting experience did not ease my depression. Dr. Max Friedländer, a famous musicologist at the Berlin University, and his wife, an ex-pupil of Leschetitzky's, had been inviting me often to their musical parties, where I had the opportunity to play chamber music with fine artists like the violinists Karl Flesch and Bronislaw Hubermann. One day Mrs. Friedländer asked me to give her piano lessons. I was extremely flattered at her request and proud to earn money as a teacher for the first time in my life.

Unfortunately, my pupil turned out to be a little hysterical; she would burst into tears at the slightest critical remark, then apologize, kissing my hands, and it all turned into a nightmare. Everything else became a nuisance to me, too, I was so sick and tired of Berlin. And as my love for Basia grew from day to day, poor Frederic had to listen to my endless prattle.

One day I couldn't stand it any longer and I wrote a passionate love letter to Basia. A real romantic outburst! I promised her I would throw the whole world at her feet—I was going to surpass Liszt and Anton Rubinstein, not to speak of Busoni and D'Albert—I would kiss her to death—I would love her until the end of my life. She, only she, could give me the will and the strength for all of this; without her there was no sense in anything.

After sending off this inflamed declaration I spent a week in dread suspense, waiting for her answer.

Frederic tried to take my mind off his sister, but to no avail. Theaters and good restaurants ceased to be attarctive, but he did begin to arouse my interest in spiritualism. He took me a few times to some rich friends of his, where after a good dinner we would settle down to a spiritualistic séance, and I would demand that the "spirits" make contact for me with Basia.

Another distraction was the young divorcée of his pension. She was infatuated with Frederic, and would send him letters accompanied by flowers and candies, fastening her burning eyes on him during meals and using all the known devices of vamps. Immune to her charms, Frederic tried instead to use his influence with her to promote *me*. The lady, endowed with an uncommon flexibility of morals, didn't see any harm in this substitution and turned to me for love. This amorous intermezzo, however flattering, only added one more disturbance to my already complicated existence. Henny resented perfumed envelopes addressed to me by someone she didn't know, and even Professor Barth was aware of strange aromas emanating from my pocket. "You stink of patchouli," he would say, and I guessed this was the only term he knew for any scent.

But there were also pleasant moments, such as small gatherings for tea in the divorcée's cozy living room, when Josef Hofmann, Frederic, and I would hang around the piano, playing this or that music. It was on such occasions that I could appreciate Hofmann's particular gifts, such as his memory or his complete control of the left hand; he could perform a whole Beethoven sonata playing the part of the left hand alone, while I played the right hand—ever so much easier. He also introduced me to some modern Russians, especially Nikolai Medtner, whose first sonata I liked very much. At that time he startled us also with a strange habit: he would bring with him a concerto he was in the midst of composing and continue quietly working on it while we would be talking aloud and sipping our tea—a real feat of serene concentration.

After more than two weeks had passed and there was still no word from Basia I became so exasperated by her silence that I wrote in quick succession two more incendiary love letters (my first one seemed tame in comparison with them). I assured her that life was not worth living without her, suggesting somberly the possibility of a suicide. . . . Another week—nothing.

But then, one afternoon, Frederic read a letter he had received from his sister, who was writing, she said, on behalf of their father. The Harmans were planning to give a big supper party and a dance for about two hundred guests and wanted it to be preceded by a concert. "Would Arthur," she wrote, "come to Warsaw and play an hour of music, and Father could easily arrange for him a public concert as well. He could stay a fortnight at our house and exploit other possibilities." She added that her father was willing to pay a fee of three hundred rubles ($150) and traveling expenses and that he could obtain for me a similar amount for a public appearance.

All this sounded like a typical business letter written by a secretary. But there was a postscript! "Namów Artura"—Persuade Arthur—and these two words were to change the whole course of my life.

I was determined to go. Basia's two postscript words were an order—the long-expected answer to my letters. It took all my courage to face Professor Barth to ask him for his permission. I felt sure he would refuse. But I underestimated his respect for money. The minute he heard about the two fees his irreconcilable attitude changed. "I will let you go if you promise to bring the full amount back minus a small allowance for your private expenses. But you must be back in two weeks."

I packed my bag in an ecstatic mood. Frederic provided me with my railway ticket and sleeper and took me to the station, giving me on the way some additional information about the whole household at home and coaching me for my first interview with his father. "He is very shrewd," he said. "He will try to prove that I am not as talented as you might think, but at the same time he will scrutinize you for your sincerity in believing in me." I did my best to reassure him on that point, thanked him for everything, gave him a friendly hug and kiss, and the train started moving toward Warsaw. At last the moment had arrived which I had so passionately desired.

I reached the Polish capital next morning at seven a.m., feeling a little shy about arousing the Harman family at such an early hour. The door was opened by the same elegant butler I remembered from my previous visit, wearing a black and yellow striped waistcoat. Helped by a younger valet, he took my bags and coat and hat, and announced that Mr. Harman wanted me to have breakfast with him, so would I please wait for him in the dining room? The ladies were still asleep, he added. I was not a little afraid, I must confess, to have to face the dreaded Papa alone.

After a few minutes, Frederic's father entered the room. I was startled by his looks. He was completely bald, with a thick gray mustache covering his mouth, and I noticed right away how the left side of his face was paralyzed and sagged as a result of his recent stroke. He wore eyeglasses, with one glass dull in order to cover the eye that had gone blind. He greeted me cordially, telling me of the favorable impression I had made on his wife and his daughter, and assured me of his pleasure at the prospect of having me play at their party. When these amenities were over, we settled down to a breakfast in the Polish fashion, consisting of tea, an assortment of rolls and breads, sausage, cheese, and eggs.

Right away, and all through the meal, our conversation concentrated on Frederic, with Mr. Harman talking. He spoke exactly as his son had predicted. "I am worried about him," Mr. Harman said. "He has such a poor memory and a lack of rhythm. It might be very difficult for him to make a career as a pianist." And then he asked, "Do you really think he has talent as a composer?" Suppressing my own secret doubts, I tried to outline most eloquently the positive aspect of Frederic's talent, such as his subtle comprehension of Chopin, his remarkable sight-reading, the Polish element in his compositions, and his potential as a conductor.

Mr. Harman seemed impressed by my arguments. "I am glad to hear all that from such a talented young man," he said. "I only hope you are right." And he left.

The butler took me to Frederic's rooms, which I was to occupy during my stay, consisting of a comfortable bedroom and a living room with an excellent Bechstein piano and a fine library of books and music. As I entered the room I heard the well-known silvery laughter, and there was Basia, lovely to look at, with her usual mixture of arrogance and sweetness of manners. She extended both hands to me, was most cordial in her welcome, but didn't say a word about my letters! So I, of course, did not mention them, either.

We talked about the party, my program, and the choice of the piano, and, finally, she gave me some information about the guests. I followed our talk only half-heartedly, observing her all the time for a hint of some response to my love, but all I could see was the same expression of friendliness touched with irony.

Suddenly, she added: "There will be also a very interesting man, a painter, at the party. I will introduce you to him—try to please him." I felt as though I had received a blow, a slap! Yes, I knew right away, he was the man she was in love with!

My heart was broken—but I still loved her! My only hope remained in my music: I knew she liked my playing, and my music might plead for me.

I answered coldly: "Yes, I shall certainly try to please your friend," and walked into the bedroom to unpack my bags.

Mrs. Harman appeared only at lunchtime, greeting me with an embrace, and her husband also came home from his office. During the entire meal, the talk centered on the party and the preparations for it. I hardly opened my mouth, and went back to my room right after, where I worked on my program until it was time to dress; I was determined to play my best that evening.

The guests began arriving at nine p.m., and it was well past ten o'clock when I started my concert. Never before had I played with such a passion and abandon as on that night; I poured all my despair and perhaps some hope into my performance, and I knew it was a success. After my last piece, the B flat minor Scherzo of Chopin, which I had prepared for this occasion only a few days before my departure, I was actually besieged by my listeners; some ladies had tears in their eyes. My hosts were enchanted, and Mrs. Harman kissed me effusively.

When I looked around for Basia, I saw her talking with great intensity to a man in his middle thirties. He was very elegant in his tails, wore a red carnation in his buttonhole, a monocle in his eye, and had the classic look of a seducer—the blue-black neatly cut hair, the short mustache (after the English fashion), a large mouth with very red lips, and the nervous nostrils of a race horse—all the characteristics!

Basia, feeling herself observed, came to rescue me from my admirers and took me straight up to him. "This is the gentleman I was telling you about," she said, as if I didn't know. "He is a great artist, and I want you two to become friends." He had a sarcastic little smile on his face as he complimented me on my playing, and I noticed then that he was lame, but he had a way of making even this infirmity an added attraction. I suddenly knew by an unfailing instinct that it was not a matter of a simple flirtation between them but that he was actually Basia's lover.

I left them brusquely and went to the dining room, where I found a huge table filled with food and drinks. I asked for a wodka and drank five or six of them in succession, then I took to wine—red or white, or champagne—I drank indiscriminately anything I could get. It was my silly notion that this might be the most pleasant way of committing suicide. But, by some miracle, I remained completely sober, and more and more conscious of my miserable state of mind.

The party lasted until early morning; Poles are not easily beaten when it comes to dancing and drinking, and they know how to maintain their innate courteousness and elegant comportment.

I had thought this ominous night was to be my first introduction to "Warsaw Society"; I was to discover later, however, that this term didn't apply exactly to the guests of the Harmans. They just formed an incongruous set of people of different classes: there were some men of the highest aristocracy, but they came without their wives, unless the wife happened to be an ex-actress, or a wealthy Jewish heiress; there was a sprinkling of lawyers and doctors, all, of course, with wives, and just a few members of the business world. The overwhelming majority consisted of poets, writers, artists, and musicians—a lively, interesting, and attractive crowd. I have never found, in later years, a more enchanting mixture of people than I did that night when I first glimpsed this so-called Warsaw Society, better termed Harman Society.

14

The day after the party was the historic date of the worst hangover of my life! My head was bursting, my stomach felt burned to ashes, and I was incapable of getting up out of bed the whole day. My hosts, fortunately, showed a thorough understanding of my miserable state and treated me naturally, without exaggerated sympathy.

After dinner, at which I wasn't able to eat anything, Mrs. Harman and Basia made me accompany them in some songs. The mother had a pleasant voice and sang with the right feeling, but had some technical flaws, while the daughter was still a beginner who showed promise. Mr. Harman did not appear at dinner, and his absence was explained to me by his wife: "My husband has a mistress, a lovely ballet dancer, so he spends all his evenings with her; he dines at home only on special occasions." This approach to marital life was a novelty for me, I confess, and I began to understand better Frederic's often cynical remarks when he talked of his family.

Before retiring that night I followed Basia to her room. "This painter whom you introduced me to is your lover, isn't he?" I asked her point-blank. She blushed a bit, glanced at me angrily, biting her lips, then, completely composed, she answered: "Yes, he *is* my lover—and you, if you really care so much for me, you must help me! I shall pretend to be taking you out to go sightseeing, while, in fact, I shall join my lover, and you do what you want by yourself. Then we will meet later in some café. Please do it for me . . . please!"

My first instinct was to slap her. But at the same time I found myself blushing, out of rage and shame, and after a long silence I said: "Well, I was expecting such a blow. It's not that I am jealous—I have no right to that—you never promised me anything—but it is something worse. I know I shall never be able to feel a love so pure and strong for anyone else. Yes, I shall help you out . . . I shall be the perfect 'confidant' whom you can trust!" And I left the room.

I felt neither resentment nor hatred. It was more important, it went even deeper: overnight I seemed to have become an adult, without any illusions, and though I was aware of my lonely situation, I was hardened enough by it to be able to pretend indifference. Basia's cold egoism was contagious. One thing I know for certain as I think back on that night: nothing, in later years, had such an impact on my character. From the love-lorn "Werther" I was when I arrived, I had turned into a cynical bad-boy.

There was the still-attractive mother, vivacious and charming, who spoke English, French, and German fluently. She had a fine flair for art and literature and was always open-minded about anything interesting. Being extremely sociable, she liked to give small tea parties, in the English manner, for young writers, actors, and musicians.

Dinner parties were more formal with the ill-humored master of the house present, but the best affairs were the almost daily late suppers, after the theater or a concert, when interesting people would be invited on the spur of the moment, and lively conversation would go on for hours. The food was invariably excellent; it was a time when servants and cooks were on hand until the last member of a household retired— a way of living hard to imagine nowadays!

Frederic's mother had one obsession: singing. She was always eager to sing, and I soon became her favorite accompanist. Sometimes it annoyed me because her voice was not very good and her performance amateurish, but I am grateful that she made known to me so many beautiful songs, especially those drawn from Polish, Russian, and French literature which I had not known before. She would sing Chopin, Moniuszko, Pankiewicz, Zarzycki, Wieniawski—some of them enchanting pieces—then a lot of Tchaikovski, Moussorgsky, Borodin, and Rimsky-Korsakov; and of the French the best of Fauré, Duparc, Chausson, and some others. A great revelation was Mahler's *Lieder eines fahrenden Gesellen*, which moved me deeply. I, in turn, introduced her to my beloved Schubert, Schumann, and Brahms—those unsurpassed masters of song.

Thus, the two weeks of my stay in Warsaw passed like one day. For some reason the proposed public concert did not take place, but nevertheless Basia's father paid the fee he had promised, pretending that my appearance was only postponed. He would be coming to Berlin soon, he said, and had some plans for the near future involving Frederic and me. I was kissed effusively by everybody at my departure, as though I were a member of the family, and Basia took me to the station in their carriage. She gave me a tender kiss and a hug, but right after I heard the mocking silvery laughter which, this time, cut deeply into my heart.

15

My parents were never informed about my Warsaw adventure. I had kept them in the dark, fearing some counteraction on their part, but nothing of the sort happened. When they found out that I had been in Warsaw, they thought Professor Barth was behind it, yet I did feel they were hurt not to have had word from me.

I got back to Berlin on time, to find Henny delighted to see me and Frederic dying of curiosity to hear every detail of the fortnight I had spent at his house.

I told him everything, and he laughed tears as I imitated the manners and voices of some of the guests, all of whom he knew so well, but then he turned suddenly serious and wanted to hear all about his father's reactions to my talk and my account of his Berlin concert. He was relieved when he heard of the plans for the two of us (he seemed to have had something to do with initiating them). And I told him tersely about Basia and my broken heart, but I did not give away her secret.

Professor Barth received me coldly, asking me immediately for the money, which I handed him in its entirety. His attitude softened right away, and he kept me on for a while, setting forth rash ideas for my future. "For a year or so," he said, "there might be a chance for you of getting a post in the Academy of Music as a preparatory teacher for some older professor, possibly myself!" I remained silent, showing neither acquiescence nor refusal, although his repeated assumptions about my future irritated me. Then he went on: "There are no concerts in view for the next season, my boy. Your last appearance showed that you did not work enough."

For the next two or three weeks I followed the same old routine again—lesson after lesson, secret meetings with Frederic, now and then a good play or a concert, although the season was coming to an end. Spring was in the air, and my friends were as nice to me as ever, perhaps even more so, as if they were aware of how detached I had become from Berlin, and that consequently they might be losing me.

One morning Mr. Harman arrived. Frederic sent me a note with the news and invited me for dinner on his father's behalf. We dined at Dressel's, Unter den Linden, Berlin's best restaurant at that time, and the old man tried to be charming, offering us a "de luxe" meal; and it was only when we reached the dessert that he began to outline his plan to hire the Warsaw Philharmonic Orchestra for a concert in Warsaw itself, of course, no later than a fortnight hence; it was to be a gala to end the season. The program, which Frederic would conduct, was to consist of a major orchestral work, and two piano concertos—which I was to play—and he thought one of the concertos should be Frederic's Fantasia (which by the way, I knew already quite well). In addition, he invited me with an unusual warmth to stay with them in Warsaw and to spend the whole summer with the family in Zakopane, a famous resort in the Polish Tatra Mountains, where they had rented a villa. His invitation did not astonish me too much; I rather anticipated something of the sort, both because the Harmans had listened with sympathy to my bitter complaints about Barth and the anti-Semitic atmosphere in Berlin and because Frederic's father saw me as an excellent promoter of his son in musical and practical matters. Besides, I was pleased to discover that the old man actually liked me.

I listened to his plan as impassively as I could manage, but it created turmoil in my mind. Needless to say that I wanted desperately to say yes right away! But there were many terrible "buts" in the way. Primo: Professor Barth, who I knew for certain would refuse to let me go this time, and this might lead to a complete break. Secondo: the question of money; the Professor had never given me any accounting of the money he held for me—concert fees as well as the yearly amount from my benefactors— and it took courage to demand it from a man who had given me, without any remuneration, so much of his time for so many years, not to speak of his really deep concern and devotion for me. It was also clear that if I accepted the Harman proposition I would burn all my bridges behind me; in other words, I would be entirely on my own, without financial help from anyone, without a plan for my future, risking a precarious and dangerous life. But, alas, this very danger attracted me. I felt adventure in my blood . . . I promised I would give my answer after I had consulted the Professor, but whatever the outcome—my decision was made. I would leave!

I had a lesson in the afternoon the next day at which I played a prelude and fugue of Bach rather well. The Professor was pleased, which made my broaching the Warsaw proposition even more difficult. But it had to be done, and so, taking my courage in both hands, with my heart beating wildly, I put forth the whole plan, trying my best to present it in rosy colors. "I have hopes for a brilliant career in Poland which might lead to some important engagements in Russia," I said. "I need it to lift my morale. You know quite well how this last year has discouraged me, but I feel sure of recovering my confidence if I am allowed to stand on my own feet." And I added quickly: "I intend to work hard on a large repertoire this summer."

Barth's reaction was much worse than I feared. He listened without interrupting me, with an angry look in his eyes and sweat showing on his forehead. His beard rose higher than ever—in fact, I was terrified to see him so disturbed. And then his answer came. In a soft voice at first, trying to appear calm, he brought up all his objections.

"You are not ready for that sort of life," he started, "and lazy as you are, living in luxury without any supervision would ruin your future completely. I had planned a decent position for you at the Academy, where in time if you worked hard you might have been granted a full professorship!" And suddenly, infuriated, he shouted at me: "You will end up in the gutter, you ungrateful boy, I predict it, and"—now he jumped to his feet and screamed—"if you leave, you'd better not come back. And don't count on your benefactors. I shall inform them that you are leaving against my will!"

This was too much for me. I was so hurt that tears sprang to my eyes, but I held them back; I felt an uncontrollable urge instead to tell him everything I had had on my mind all these years, and I forgot my usual terror. I was determined to tell him the truth at last.

It was one of the worst and most cruel things I have ever done. Completely self-possessed, I said: "Herr Professor, I am sad to realize that you know nothing about me, and that you do not understand my real character. Your plan for my future seems to follow exactly the pattern of your own life—and that is something I refuse to accept! I would rather live one full and blissful week and then die, or land in a gutter, as you say, than to lead a long life like yours. I see you working all day long, without pleasure, giving lessons, mostly to untalented pupils, never traveling, never enjoying yourself. I know that you supported, nobly, your stepmother, and now your sister, and neither of you dared to marry because you were dependent on each other. Even in your musical outlook, you are hemmed in by prejudice and lack of curiosity and interest. You took me away from Dr. Altmann because he represented all that makes living meaningful. No, Herr Professor, I don't want to stay in Berlin any more. I don't want to be supported by anyone any more. I wish to be independent, but, believe me, that I am deeply grateful to you for all you have done for me and much, much more so for the love you have shown me." I burst into tears, and grabbed his hand to kiss it, but he withdrew it violently and said with rage: "Well, go if you must, but I shall keep the money I hold for you for a later day because now you would spend it stupidly in no time at all!" To which I answered, choking with pride: "I do not want this money, and I shall never ask for it. Please give it to some needy musician on my behalf!"

And that was all. I left, completely exhausted and remorseful. This day remains in my memory as one I am deeply ashamed of.

I couldn't utter a word when I got home, and Henny was quite upset, seeing me so depressed; but I begged her to leave me alone, promising to tell her everything when I calmed down. Then half an hour later the bell rang, and Professor Barth announced to the maid that he was there to see Mrs. Winter and did not wish to see me! So poor Henny had to listen to his bitter outburst. "I should have killed him," he said, "for what he dared to tell me—I was just too stunned to react!" He repeated to her his nice vision of me in the gutter and ended by declaring that he was giving up, that the Winters shouldn't interfere with my departure, and that he didn't want to see me again.

My last days in Berlin were among the gloomiest I had spent there. There was a difficult visit to Professor Joachim, who, as usual, showed a complete understanding. "I saw it coming, my boy," he said, "and I wish you all the luck in the world. You will face hard times as we all did in our youth, but I believe in you and your talent." In a broken voice I thanked the noble artist and great gentleman.

Most of my friends showed a good deal of sympathy and offered to help, though, I am afraid, having heard only my side of the story, they were apt to be unjust toward the poor Professor. Mrs. Friedländer went so far as to go to him and make a scene about his "malicious and cruel behavior"!

I sent my three sponsors flowery letters of thanks and informed them of my decision to take my future into my own hands.

And that was enough of Berlin for me. In 1903 an important page of my life had turned!

Three

ON MY OWN

16

After I had gone through many tearful farewells with Henny and other friends and had made empty promises that I might return the next winter, I was finally ready to leave for Warsaw, in the company of Frederic and his father. This time, my arrival was like a homecoming. Everybody, including the servants, gave me a cordial welcome. Frederic's living room was turned into a cozy bedroom for me. In no time I was back under the spell of the exciting atmosphere of this house. I couldn't put my finger on the actual reason for it, but I was attracted beyond words by the whole setup of this household, what with the strange combination of the unloved and detestable father, who could be also very nice at times, the mother with her passion for singing and her inexhaustible sociability and hospitality, and the two lovely daughters (the married one was a daily guest now)—not to speak of Frederic, who threw all the weight of his irresistible personality into the bargain. Undoubtedly, their luxurious way of living, the exquisite cuisine, the theater parties followed by gay suppers in good company, had much to do with my infatuation, I must admit. A few days of this life so intoxicated me that I forgot Berlin, Barth, and all the recent worries, and I began to enjoy to the fullest my new freedom.

Frederic and I plunged enthusiastically into the preparation for our concert. I played the D minor Brahms Concerto for him, showing him the symphonic character of the ensemble of piano and orchestra, indicating the right tempi, and giving him some hints for conducting this beautiful work. His Fantasia presented no difficulty to me because I knew it so well by now. In addition to these two works, Frederic was planning to conduct the *Romeo and Juliet* Overture of Tchaikovski, a composition he adored. I was looking forward to this concert. We had three rehearsals, and we needed them badly, for my friend had much to learn; his rhythm was still uncertain and his memory faulty. At one of the rehearsals I saw Emil Mlynarski wringing his hands in dismay. "It will be a disaster," he murmured. "He doesn't know how to hold his baton properly!"

And yet, somehow, the concert went well, and it was a success for both of us; there was a good attendance. I received a large fee and an engagement for a solo concert in the Conservatory Hall. My sisters Jadzia and Hela were present at both events, but they attacked me angrily for my reprehensible behavior toward my family, whom I again had left in complete ignorance of my plans. They soon changed their minds, though, when they found out that I was staying with such a rich and important family. And this new attitude offended me even more. I preferred their indignation, and so I saw as little as possible of them.

Warsaw was an enchanting city in the year 1904! The Poles called it proudly "the Paris of the East," and I found they were entitled to the boast. You couldn't say it was a beautiful city; architecturally it was uninteresting, but there was something special in the air, an undefined charm emanating from the streets and parks, from the houses and palaces, from the theaters, restaurants, and cafés. The Warsaw natives are a special variety of Poles. Endowed with an indomitable spirit and courage, an inexhaustible vitality, and a passion for pleasure, they create an atmosphere of gaiety and excitement which envelops you right away. Of course, they have their faults, too—such as their very sharp and often too malicious sense of humor, and their insatiable curiosity linked with an utter lack of discretion. They are individualists, not unlike the Parisians—ever ready to criticize everybody and everything.

But the women, the Warsaw women, deserve a special chapter! Let me state here and now that, in my humble opinion, they are the most attractive species of the weaker sex in the world! Add to the feminine grace and chic of the Parisienne the famous *charme slave*, mix Nordic beauty with Italian fire and exuberance, and you can imagine a typical Varsovienne.

Frederic was fond of his city and its people. He knew that the memories of my early days in the Polish capital were not of the best, owing, naturally, to my young age and to the way I lived. So now he was determined to let me feel the real charm of Warsaw. The spring that year was enchanting, bursting out all of a sudden after a very severe winter. Leaves of the most delicate green adorned the trees, the lovely park Lazienki exuded the perfume of lilacs and jasmine, the Saxon Garden was filled with happily shouting children and young couples in tender embrace. Cafés and restaurants set up terraces in the street where crowds of people sipped their drinks, engaged in exciting discussions. In the Aleja Ujazdowska, Warsaw's proudest avenue, lines of light, open carriages with their coachmen and second men in liveries, driven by racy horses, showed to their best advantage the city's elite.

Thanks to Frederic, I soon took part in this intoxicating life. Every day brought something new; interesting luncheon parties at home, or in some other house, or in a good restaurant, always in honor of some great personality in art, science, or politics. The afternoons were given to music; we would play for hours symphonies on two pianos, or I would accompany the mistress of the house. Sometimes Basia joined her mother in a duet, and Frederic, who had a fine voice, would sing his own songs. Evenings were spent in the theater. As we still lived before the era of radio, television, and cinema, the theater and the circus were the only means of entertainment. I simply adored the Warsaw theaters, and the Wielki, the great Opera, was of the highest order, where the best singers of the time— Battistini, la Bellincioni, Anselmi, Caruso, the brothers de Reszke, la Sembrich, the Polish sopranos Korolewicz, Kruszelnicka—all gave unforgettable performances. The Teatr Rozmaitosci was devoted to classical dramas and comedies. Unfortunately, the Russian authorities had banned the fine plays by Mickiewicz, Slowacki, and the contemporaries Wyspiański and Zeromski because they contained too much revolutionary and patriotic stuff, but it was still a joy to see some comedies by Fredro, "the Polish Molière," played to perfection by actors unmatched anywhere.

The most successful Viennese operettas were produced with more verve and with better singers than in Vienna itself. The French farce was certainly not of the highest intellectual order, but the gusto, the perfect ensemble of the actors, the beauty, the purely Polish temperament, and the actresses' touch of risqué that never descended to vulgarity transformed these flimsy and flippant plays into little masterpieces!

Lucyna Messal was the ideal diva of the operetta—a beautiful woman and a great voice. She made me cry when she sang the famous love valse in *The Chocolate Soldier*, but, at the same time, I couldn't take my eyes off her fascinating beauty. Her sex appeal was just there, quite naturally; she didn't have to project it like a Brigitte Bardot, or Marilyn Monroe. And she was not the only one; I remember the soubrettes Bogorska and Kawecka, both lovely creatures who sang and danced ravishingly. And I must not forget to mention the men. In the operetta there was Redo, a fine tenor with good looks, and my favorite, Morozowicz, a comedian of genius. Trapszo, Winkler, and Gasiński were the stars of the farce.

I suppose my non-Polish readers will wonder at this orgy of so many theaters and actors of the past, but I feel the need to express my gratitude to them for their unique performances which enriched my young years and remain engraved in my memory and my heart.

17

After the shows, as before, we had those delightful little supper parties, often attended by some of the stars of the opera or theater. Smoked siga, a Russian delicacy, served with a sauce tartare accompanied by the excellent Polish wodka used to stimulate the reunions. Sometimes we finished by making music—Mozart's *Don Juan* or Moniuszko's *Halka* sung by some of the guests, Frederic or myself at the piano. Our hostess, pani Magdalena,* always insisted on having me as her partner, insisting that there was "a perfect musical understanding between us." The master of the house was usually absent from these late receptions, having supper with his mistress in some *cabinet particulier* of a restaurant. On a few occasions, however, when he did come home and retired early, something shocking would invariably happen: at a very late hour, when we were at the height of our musical or intellectual enjoyment, the door of the salon would open and the old man, clad in a nightshirt, his ghastly face distorted with rage, would yell at the top of his hoarse voice: "Get out, get out, get out!!" and then slam the door so violently that the crystals of the chandelier tinkled for a good five minutes. When this scene occurred the first time I was speechless with terror, but, to my great astonishment, I saw that everyone else in the room took it with perfect composure, almost indifference. I soon found out that they all were used to these outbursts which were almost considered as part of the program. Pani Magdalena actually laughed the whole thing off. "My husband is so nervous," she would say, "the poor man works so hard," and we continued to enjoy ourselves.

One afternoon Frederic burst into the room and shouted: "Arthur, imagine our luck! I just found out that Paul Kochanski is in town, that he is staying with the Styczyńskis. They have invited us both for supper tonight!"

I became quite excited. Frederic had told me so many details about this fabulous young violinist, Paul Kochanski, a Jewish boy my own age from Odessa, whose talent had been discovered by Emil Mlynarski, then a violin professor there. Mlynarski had brought the little prodigy to Warsaw, taken full charge of him, treated him like a son, and given him a solid Polish education. The boy played so well that at the age of thirteen he was

* "Pani" is the Polish form of address for a married woman; "pan" is equivalent to "Mr.," and "panna" is used for "Miss."

appointed by Mlynarski as the first concertmaster of the newly created Philharmonic Orchestra, but only for one year, after which he sent him to the renowed Conservatory of Brussels, where Kochanski studied for a few years. Mlynarski himself and some Polish patrons provided the funds for his studies in Belgium. Now Kochanski was back in Warsaw, after having graduated with honors from the Conservatory.

This short sketch of his life reminds me in so many ways of my own; both of us were practically uprooted from our own families and thrown into the hazardous artistic world a little too soon for our good.

Naturally, I was terribly eager to meet him at last. Frederic and I arrived at eleven at night at the Styczyńskis, a Polish family who helped Paul in his career, and we were received by three young sons of the family, all university students. We had to wait for Kochanski. When he joined us, he announced, before even greeting anybody, that Madame Styczyńska had a headache and excused herself for not joining us and that she had asked him to represent her as the host at supper.

Kochanski was slim and short and had thin, slightly bowed legs, but I felt right away a tremendous core of vitality in him. He had one of the most fascinating and attractive heads I had ever seen—his face square and strong, his chin pointed, and his nose delicately shaped and faintly curved. But his eyes were his most striking feature—coal black, formed like oblique almonds, with a velvety deep expression which could be very moving, especially while he was playing. A black, wavy, unruly shock of hair covered his head.

"Let me look at you. I have heard so much about you!" he greeted me at last in Polish with a distinct but charming Russian accent. We studied each other for a few seconds. Then, without losing a moment, he said: "Come on, let us play the C minor Sonata of Beethoven."

I sat down at the piano and propped the music up on the desk; he tuned his violin and we began to play. And we played as if we had always played together. When he suggested an expression, I took it up at once; when I shaped a phrase, he continued it in the same vein. In short, from a musical point of view, we were made for each other.

When we finished, nobody uttered a word. Paul left the room and shouted: "Supper is ready!" And the gay, loud, tasty meal lasted two hours.

Then suddenly, like a child, Paul declared: "I am tired, I shall go to bed, but don't go yet—come to my room; we can go on talking while I lie in bed." Before he undressed he took one of his photos out of a drawer and gave it to me. On it he had written this inscription: "To my best friend Arthur Rubinstein in memory of [the date]—Paul Kochanski."

I was astounded to read it—he must have written it in a moment of prophetic inspiration. We did indeed become the best, the closest friends. Our friendship fortified, embellished, and ennobled our lives.

Basia used to disappear for whole afternoons, and her "friend" was often a guest at supper, but my ill-fated love was beginning to cool off. Frederic was a great help by introducing me to some beautiful actresses and taking me to receptions where I met some lovely ladies of the best society who impressed me by their regal manners—outwardly they might be reserved and forbidding, but their eyes betrayed a burning passion. And they were difficult to resist.

At that stage, I must confess, I was ready to let myself go; all I ever had on my mind was to get in touch with this or that lady—and I wanted them all; piano practice was neglected completely. To top things I began to be suspicious about Frederic's strange behavior; I never saw him attracted by or interested in any woman. Back in Berlin, he had told me at length of his romantic affair with a servant, a peasant girl, whom he intended to marry but dreaded his father's opposing such a match. Her photo was on his desk; I even remember her name—Helenka Bartosinska— yet he never mentioned her in Warsaw and I never saw her there.

One night late, back in our rooms after a good party, some wodka, and much music, he came out with the truth; it was a painful story, but it solved the puzzle. He confessed that he was afflicted by a chronic physical deficiency which resulted in his inability to make love to a woman. Now I began to understand his strange habit of trying to arouse my interest several times in ladies who were obviously attracted to him. The technique he used was subtle:

"Arthur, did you notice the way the lovely Mrs. X looked at you when you played the other night?"

"No," I would reply. "I was too busy playing."

"Well," he insisted, "she seems to be terribly attracted to you."

"Nonsense," I said, "it's you she is in love with—everybody can see that!"

"Don't be a fool—she is only pretending; she simply tries to draw your attention. Make just a small gesture and you will see for yourself!"

This sort of talk never failed. Right away I would assault the lady with amorous declarations, and in a few instances, where I found a passionate temperament, the battle was won. Yet I never derived full satisfaction from these short-lived victories; a boy, at seventeen, often ends up playing the thankless role of a "Chérubino." At least that was my impression. But I was soon to learn that I was wrong! The first hint came again from Frederic: "Arthur, tonight, when you accompanied my mother, she sang as though she were in a trance—I think she is in love with you."

I laughed. "You are ridiculous, Frederic. I bet one of these days you will tell me that your father is also in love with me!"

But he remained serious. "I know my mother well, and I can assure you that I haven't seen her in such a state since that love affair I was telling you about in Berlin."

I tried to laugh it off again, but I did so half-heartedly. His insinuations really impressed me very much. For some time I myself had been noticing a change in Madame Magdalena. Her naturally cheerful disposition had turned nervous and restless, resulting in frequent scenes with her despotic husband; an especially disagreeable one occurred one day at lunch, when Mr. Harman called the cook, a friendly old man, into the dining room and insulted him, using foul language, for some imagined flaw in the preparation of the meal. Similar scenes had taken place before, but this time the usually composed Madame Magdalena couldn't bear it; she burst into tears, accusing her husband of cruelty and injustice. Enraged, he started to shout at her but broke into a violent coughing spell. And then something horrible happened; his denture jerked out of his mouth and landed on the floor! We all remained speechless; nobody dared to pick up the disagreeable object, so the poor old man had to do it himself. Madame's state bordered on hysteria, and it took us a long time to calm her.

At tea time, more often than not, she would start angry quarrels with her daughters, for no plausible reason at all. At the same time she concentrated her interest exclusively on me, showing an exaggerated concern for my personal comfort, making inquiries every day about my laundry and such. Singing with me at the piano was her greatest bliss, and it seemed she never had enough of it.

It was fate, it had to happen. One night, after a touching song by Schumann, "Ich grolle nicht," overcome by emotion, she took me into her arms and we kissed passionately. Nothing was said. I just left the room.

I was so upset that I couldn't close my eyes all night. Many contradictory thoughts tormented me. I tried to analyze the new situation: to begin with, there was no denying the fact that she was a very attractive woman, and I was extremely vulnerable to feminine charms. But there were other factors involved. I was aware, for instance, that I was still in need of a kind of maternal protection, as my experience with Henny had taught me. Another, rather ugly, thought came to my mind: the circumstances made me assume a dominating position in the household, and this gave me something of a moral revenge against Basia, who had acted so superior by merely being three years older than I; but now, the enormous gap between our ages did not prevent her mother from falling in love with me.

But it was too late to make any decisions; I was irrevocably caught, and there was no way of backing out. I had nowhere else to go, and, last but not least, I was too weak to resist the temptation!

And so began a long period of my life which was attractive and exciting but which, for the same reason, contained a grave danger not only for my artistic future but also for my moral integrity. It would certainly have been the right moment for my parents to have stepped in, forced me to come home, and then made a real effort to find the means to send me to some Leschetitzky in Vienna, or to Busoni himself. But nothing of the sort happened; my whole family seemed to accept my present situation, just as my sisters had, and none of them was aware that it was really the time when I was in desperate need of further disciplined studies.

18

Frederic appeared to be delighted with the new turn things were taking; he looked as though he had expected the latest developments, and I felt he was giving us secretly his blessing. By now familiar with his clever methods, I suspected that he had masterminded the whole affair. His mother seemed pleased to have found in him a complacent confidant, but I was shocked and ashamed, particularly when, after a late supper party, with the last guest gone, only the three of us remained in the salon, he would say: "Arthur, why don't you stay with my mother? She still wants to make some music. I shall go to my room and try to finish my song, but I'll fetch you in an hour."

In order to reach our rooms, Frederic and I had to go downstairs, cross the courtyard, and go up another staircase. He had the only key to his apartment. His offer to fetch me was, of course, a simple pretext to save appearances.

Spending the last days in Warsaw this way, in addition to the extensive social life, was exhausting! Among my new friends, I should mention a Mr. Konstanty Skarzyński, who was married to an ex-soprano of

Joseph Joachim

Professor Barth

Arthur at 13
at the time of
his debut in
Berlin

Frau Professor Engelmann in
größter Verehrung von

Arthur Rubinstein

1 April 1900.

Frau Anna Fröhlich

BERLIN
W. Lützow-Strasse 73.
FERNSPRECHER AMT 6. 1846

SEEBAD AHLBECK, SEESTRASSE.

Die Platten bleiben für Nachbestellungen aufbewahrt.

Sunday afternoon in Berlin

Arthur's parents, Isaak and Felicja,
1912 Lodz - the year of their Golden Wedding
anniversary

the Opera and showed a great interest in me. I didn't pay much attention
to him, but he proved to be of great importance to me in the near future.

When we were ready to go to Zakopane, Frederic and I left ahead
of the others because he was determined to show me Kraków, the ancient
capital of Poland, a halfway stop to the mountain resort. We arrived early
one morning and right away, after breakfast, set out for a tour of the town.
And it was a great experience! The city, largely untouched by time, had a
medieval air with its old fortifications and walls. Wawel, the royal castle,
which had been built on a hill with a view of the city and the Vistula River,
is a majestic structure of vast proportions in the purest Renaissance style, and
the adjoining cathedral contains the graves of many Polish kings. In recent
years the Poles have buried their great sons in an adjacent chapel, honoring indiscriminately war heroes, artists, musicians, and scientists alike.

The next evening we reached Zakopane. Zakopane! The name spells
magic to me. What a wealth of emotions it brings back to me, with its
moments of artistic ecstasy and moral depressions, of daydreams becoming
realities—and of momentous decisions!

Yes, this place was the theater of an unexpected, new turn in my life,
a plunge into the unknown. Zakopane is a village in a valley surrounded by
the Tatra Mountains, which are shared to the south with Hungary, to
the west with Czechoslovakia; both countries, like Galicia, were then parts
of Austria-Hungary. The area was a summer resort, until the energetic Dr.
Chalubinski discovered that its pure air was beneficial to tuberculosis and
other lung diseases, and it became an important health resort during the
winter. Another physician, Dr. Dluski, whose wife was the sister of the
radium discoverer, Marie Sklodowska Curie, built a fine sanatorium on a
hill overlooking the village.

Frederic's family rented a large villa on the outskirts, in a rather
isolated spot, along the road to the highest peak, the majestic Giewont,
which dominated the whole area. By the time we finally arrived, we
found Madame Magdalena, Basia, and the servants all installed in full
possession of the house; everything had been unpacked and put away. On
the ground floor there was a living room with a grand piano, a dining
room, a covered veranda, the kitchen and servants' rooms, and, on the
other side of the entrance hall, two smaller rooms for Basia and her sister,
who was to arrive the next morning. Frederic's apartment, on the left side
of the upper floor, consisted of two charming rooms; there was a fine
Bechstein piano sent from Kraków for his personal use. My room was at
the right of the staircase, separated only by a short corridor and a bathroom from the big apartment of Madame Magdalena. I was very annoyed
by the disposition of the rooms, particularly when I realized that I had

Mr. Harman's room. He was taking a cure in Bad Gastein, accompanied by his lovely ballerina, but planned to join us at the end of the season.

The whole thing was a nightmare for me. Basia, well aware of the situation, put up a front of polite indifference, and the servants, especially Madame Magdalena's private maid, Pauline, behaved as if it were the most natural thing in the world.

The next morning Basia's sister arrived with her one-year-old baby and a nurse, but without her husband. Pola was a lovely creature. There was a certain likeness between the two sisters, but one great difference was in Pola's warmth and softness, as against Basia's touch of masculine hardness.

Life in this secluded villa became complicated from the start. There was a constant tension in the air; with no friends, no acquaintances around, we were left so entirely to ourselves that we were much too aware of one another. Our nerves were permanently on edge. After a few days I noticed that Pola began to ostracize me; she would hardly speak in my presence and appeared only at meals. The two sisters were inseparable, staying mostly in their rooms, or taking long walks, and while Basia's attitude toward me did not change, she had to be superficially pleasant. The feelings between mother and daughters became embittered by frequent quarrels, often deteriorating into scenes with shouting, crying, and doors slamming.

Madame Magdalena took this situation quite in stride, blaming Pola's behavior on her new pregnancy. "She behaved the same way when she was expecting her first child," she said. "And don't think she holds anything against you." But I was not convinced.

I began to feel acutely uncomfortable by Mrs. Harman's constant attentions, and her complete disregard for the rest of the household. Frederic tried hard to be natural, but did not quite succeed; he was so busy composing a cycle of songs that he often late at night would want me for advice; sometimes, not finding me in my room, he would simply knock at his mother's apartment.

Finally, I had had enough of it. I was becoming so morbidly depressed that I decided to start to work seriously on my piano. But in the mornings I liked to take long walks. The countryside was enchanting—with the river Dunajec roaring down from the heights, its pure and transparent water jumping over rocks and stones, making the silvery forms of trout and other fish flash in the sun. Dark, tall pine forests surrounded the village in harmonious slopes. The shapes of the mountains suggested fairy tales; mysterious and aloof, they looked forbidding to outsiders, but not to their own native sons, the Tatra mountaineers, a singular, original race who, quite unlike other Poles, lived in close contact with the mountains.

Lean and tall, their faces like eagles, with high cheekbones and curved noses, mostly clean-shaven, they looked like ideal models for painters and sculptors.

Poland was proud of these people who were brave and loyal to their country all through its history and who formed a sort of aristocracy of their own. My frequent encounters with them, combined with the noble atmosphere of the place, had a wonderful effect on me, stimulating me to work. I regained my natural good humor, which, in turn, affected the whole household, and now at meals, lively conversation and smiling faces appeared again, and our life together became more tolerable.

My piano work had to start at night, any concentration on music being out of the question during daytime. Late breakfasts, my hikes, long luncheons, teas, and dinners left hardly any time. And so, since the salon with the piano was completely isolated from the rest of the house, I began to work when everybody had retired, almost at midnight, and would continue until three or four in the morning. There is no doubt that these nights at the piano were the most profitable of my whole life. Being more and more conscious of my small and dated repertoire, I threw myself with a voracious passion into learning all the music which Professor Barth had kept away from me all those years in Berlin. The B flat Concerto of Brahms; Beethoven's C minor and G major concertos, his "Appassionata"; both of Chopin's grand sonatas, two ballades, three scherzos, several preludes, six études, the F minor *Fantasie*, the *Barcarolle*, and the great F sharp and A flat polonaises; Schumann's *Carnaval* and *Symphonic Études*; Liszt's *Mephisto Valse* . . . all these standard pieces I took up in those two months, late at night, at Zakopane. And this was possible because of my special gift for grasping the meaning and the structure of a piece of music rapidly and my remarkable memory; I could play anything after a few readings, though, of course, neglecting many details, especially when they were due to technical problems. It all sounded fine to the innocent listener; only the initiated, my fellow pianists, would discover what was missing. As for myself, I was too eager to accumulate as much repertoire as possible to worry about flaws; helped by the generous use of pedals and my innate virtuosity, I was able to get away with murder, figuratively and musically.

19

One night, startled by a suspicious noise in the garden, I looked cautiously through a tiny opening of the window curtain and saw the strange, tall figure of a man wearing a long black cape with a hood over his head, standing right in front of the villa. I must admit shamefully that he scared me to death. The poetic legends about the cruel heroes of the Tatras turned suddenly to a prosaic reality, threatening to upset my peaceful work at night. I went quickly to my room and watched from my window the man disappearing in the dark. My account of the incident the next morning met with incredulous faces.

"It must have been your imagination," Basia said. "There haven't been any robbers around here since Tetmajer" (the famous Polish poet and novelist who wrote about the Tatra legends).

Everyone else dismissed my story, too, but that night I saw the same human shape again, standing right outside the salon, and this time it remained even longer. It was still there when I went to bed. This was too much for me. So the next evening, when I saw the man approaching the window of the music room cautiously (Frederic and the servants were standing by in case of danger), I opened the door to the garden, and, my heart beating with terror, I shouted, "What are you doing out there, what do you want, who are you?"

A frightened voice answered politely: "I love music and come to listen to your playing. But if it disturbs you, I will go away and won't annoy you any more."

We all started laughing happily, including the stranger, and Frederic asked him to come in for tea and meet the family. The threatening, ghost-like figure turned out to be a young medical student, Bronislaw Gromadzki, an amateur violinist who went to school in Elisavetgrad, in the Ukraine, as he told us, with a young Polish composer whom he called a genius, and whose name was Karol Szymanowski. "I have copied some of his preludes and études," he said, "and a violin sonata he has written for me. May I show them to you?"

Having had quite a few disappointments with so-called geniuses, I nodded patronizingly and said: "I am working now, as you yourself have heard, on some very serious works, but come tomorrow and let us see some of your friend's little pieces."

Gromadzki returned the next afternoon with a pile of manuscripts which Frederic and I took to the piano without even looking at. We were convinced we would find the naïve scribblings of a schoolboy. It is difficult to describe our amazement after playing only a few bars of a prelude. This music had been written by a master! We read feverishly all the manuscripts, becoming more and more enthusiastic and excited, as we knew we were discovering a great Polish composer! His style owed much to Chopin, his form had something of Scriabin, but there was already the stamp of a powerful, original personality to be felt in the line of his melody and in his daring and original modulations.

We overwhelmed Gromadzki with quesions about Karol Szymanowski: Where was he born? Where did he study music? Where does he live? Where is he now? The poor fellow had a hard time satisfying our curiosity, but felt happy, having proved his point so brilliantly. "Karol was born on his father's estate in the Ukraine, where most landowners were Polish aristocrats," he told us. "He went to school in Elisavetgrad, a Russian city in the neighborhood, where we were schoolmates and became friends, and he studied music there with his uncle by marriage, Professor Neuhaus, an excellent teacher. Later," he continued, "he was sent to the Warsaw Conservatory, where he finished winning a gold medal for composition after having studied with the well-known composer Noskowski."

"But where is he now, where is he now?" I shouted.

Gromadzki answered sadly. "He lost his father a few months ago. It was a terrible shock to him. His family, worried about his despondency, persuaded him to go to Bayreuth for the Wagner Festival, where he is at present. He wrote me about the deep impression the *Meistersinger* and *Tristan and Isolde* had made on him."

We were interested in his story and felt that a powerful personality had entered our lives. What impressed me most was Frederic's reaction. There was not a trace of jealousy visible in him, and there was ample reason for him to be jealous; he could not help but notice how my musical interest was shifting toward this new man, and he honestly shared my enthusiasm.

That night I wrote a long letter to Szymanowski at the address which his friend had given me. I told him what a deep impression his music had made on me, how it had refreshed me musically after a long discouragement, how much akin it was to my own musical instinct, and that I was burning to meet him, to exchange ideas with him. It was one of the most important, most urgent letters I had ever written.

In the meantime we became acquainted with some vacationists, mostly from Warsaw or Lodz, who had heard me or about me and were inquisitive about my plans for the future. Annoyed by their questions, and in order to placate them, I adopted for an answer the line: "I am going to

Paris"—a pure invention; I might just as well have answered: "I am leaving for Timbuktu!" But imagine my astonishment when Madame Magdalena, one morning, showed me a letter from Mr. Konstanty Skarzyński, the man who had liked my playing so much in Warsaw. He wrote from Paris: "I have news of great interest for the young Rubinstein. An impresario, Mr. Gabriel Astruc, has established a Société Musicale for the purpose of presenting new music and musicians to Paris audiences in the grand manner. He has just signed his first contract with the Polish harpsichord player Wanda Landowska. I have a feeling he would like to engage young Rubinstein, so why not persuade this young man to come to Chaville and stay with us for a fortnight or so. I am sure to be able to find an opportunity to introduce him to Mr. Astruc and to some important musicians in Paris."

I was thunderstruck at how my light-hearted declaration had become a reality—it seemed a miracle. The whole household was impressed by the news. I began making plans without losing a second; I was too excited to think of anything else. The burning question was how to find the money! I hated the idea of getting it from Frederic, who would have to ask his mother to give it to him. The only thing to do was to give a concert, hoping that it would be well attended; it was a risk, but there was no alternative, so I rented the theater in the Hotel Morskie Oko, the only sizable hall in Zakopane. The concert was to take place in two weeks, and I was brazen enough to compose a program made up entirely of first performances—that is, nothing but pieces I was still working at. And I was lucky once more. The hall was almost sold out. The summer colony of Zakopane proved to be music-loving, and curious about my progress.

20

Karol Szymanowski wired a brief answer to my letter announcing that he was arriving on a certain day, at a certain hour, in Zakopane, and hoped I would still be there.

Frederic and I went to the station where Gromadzki joined us, and we awaited the arrival of the train with great excitement. Then there he was: a tall, slender young man. He looked older than his twenty-one years, dressed all in black, still in mourning, wearing a bowler hat and gloves—appearing more like a diplomat than a musician. But his beautiful, large, gray-blue eyes had a sad, intelligent, and most sensitive expression. He walked toward us with a slight limp, greeted his friend cordially but without effusion, and accepted our warm welcome with a polite but aloof smile. He was to stay with Gromadzki, who took him to their lodgings; but later, both came to the villa for lunch. Szymanowski did not seem to be at ease during the meal, getting visibly annoyed by the efforts of Pola and Basia to charm him, and the curiosity that Madame Magdalena showed, combined with her jealousy on Frederic's behalf. Szymanowski gave us an account of the Bayreuth Festival but in a detached way, remaining noncommittal. After lunch, under the pretext of having to attend to details of my concert, I left with our guests for the hotel Morskie Oko, where we sat down for a coffee and cognac. And here, at last, the composer opened up. He told me that my letter made him want to come to Zakopane, that he had heard me at a concert in Warsaw, that he was anxious to show me his latest works, that he wanted me to be their interpreter. His voice was soft and persuasive; there was warmth in his eyes under the thick eyebrows. In that instant, to my joy, he revealed his human side! It was a happy afternoon, and I accepted his invitation to spend the evening with them.

"Shall I ask Frederic to join us?" I asked him.

"No, I'd rather not," he answered haltingly, "if you can manage it, of course. I had the impression that he and I had little in common," he added, "both personally and musically."

I had felt it from the first moment at the station. It was going to make things a little difficult for me. But I found some excuse for joining them alone that evening; I said they were going to take me to a friend of Szymanowski's, a young poet, writer, and painter we had met at the Morskie Oko, who wanted to make a drawing of me and whose name was Stanislaw Witkiewicz. Of course, there was no question of any drawing; we simply sat, drank, and talked. From the start, he, too, fascinated me, and I knew immediately that he and Karol and Gromadzki were indeed company after my own heart! I became suddenly acutely aware of the hothouse atmosphere at the villa with its intellectual overtones, and more often than not, with its artificial gaiety, hiding so many dark and unhealthy passions.

In the company of these three young men I felt a wave of fresh air—the presence of youth and true vitality. We soon became inseparable. They came to the villa quite often, sometimes staying on for a meal, but after a polite general conversation, the four of us would gather around the piano and start a lively exchange of views about this or that composer, each one trying to prove his point. I had a great time showing off my memory by playing Wagner, Brahms, Scriabin, and operas and sym-phonies, to the great delight of Szymanowski. On these occasions Frederic somehow didn't belong. His often witty, but too sharp and malicious, re-marks about various composers and interpreters fell on deaf ears; he couldn't adjust himself to the climate of our conversation. And so, little by little, he became a rare guest at our gatherings. His new passion was a young sculptor, a genuine Tatra mountaineer, a very handsome and tal-ented boy. Frederic saw the change in me, but in spite of his personal jealousy, he showed a subtle understanding for my need of a normal and healthy artistic life. His mother, too, tried hard to conceal her impatience with my frequent absences, but she was intelligent enough not to interfere. At night, my work was steadily improving, and soon I was ready for my concert and for Paris. Life appeared in brighter colors.

21

The concert at the Morskie Oko was a success. I played a lot of my freshly acquired repertoire, which I had not yet properly digested, but I put so much fire and enthusiasm into my performance that the lack of finish was not too noticeable. In any case, I had now the money for Paris and I decided to leave as soon as possible.

It was going to be a long journey; overnight to Kraków, a change of trains for Berlin, and from there another night to Paris. Szymanowski, who was going home to his family's estate in the Ukraine, decided to ac-company me as far as Kraków. And so, a few days after my concert, we were driven to the station by Madame Magdalena and Frederic. The farewell was quite cheerful. They were expecting me back in Warsaw in a short time, having little faith in my Paris host's ability to foster my career.

Karol and I found an empty compartment in the train which made it possible for us to lie down for the night. But the minute the train moved, something strange happened: I suddenly burst into tears. An uncontrol-lable crying spell took hold of me, and I did not stop for hours. It was a release of all the worries I had stored up: the break with Barth, which affected me deeply, the anxiety about my unfinished studies, and, mainly, and bitterly, the dangerous Venusberg magic of Frederic's family, to which I had succumbed like another Tannhäuser!

I shall never forget Karol's sweet solicitude for me that night; without saying a word, he put his coat under my head and covered me clumsily but tenderly with some newspapers. "They will keep you warm," he said. Our lifelong friendship was born on that night, and we parted with a big, brotherly hug the next morning.

I reached Berlin late that afternoon. It was raining and gray, which made the city look gloomy. Having two hours between trains, I hailed a cab and asked to be driven slowly past the houses of Henny, of Barth, of Frederic's *pension de famille*, feeling like a criminal haunted by the places of his crimes.

I left Berlin late in the evening with a sigh of relief and in breathless anticipation of Paris and things to come. In the middle of the night, on a stop in Alsace, some young Frenchmen entered my compartment and fascinated me by the way they spoke so easily and charmingly their own language, which I was hearing spoken with the proper accent for the first time.

At 9 a.m. the train stopped at the Gare de l'Est, a dark, smelly, and dirty place. To get to Chaville I had to drive to another station, the Gare St.-Lazare, which looked even less appealing, and then I had to board a smoky and nasty little suburban train for my final destination. Passing mainly through tunnels, I couldn't see anything of the city and arrived finally, a little discouraged, at the tiny depot of Chaville. Count Skarzyński was expecting me. "Welcome to Paris," he said cheerfully. "You are going to see the most beautiful city in the world," and helping me with my bag, he settled me in his elegant landau, and we drove up to his villa.

The house he called a villa was of modest proportions, with a tiny garden in front of it, situated on the main street of the small suburb and surrounded by many similar houses. I was shown to a small, dark room, with a forbidding, old-fashioned washstand, and after a quick and difficult ablution and a change of clothes, I went down to the dining room, where Madame Skarzyńska expected us for breakfast. She impressed me, almost frightened me, by her appearance. Her face showed some remains of beauty, but she projected such a huge bust and stomach, all in one straight line, squeezed mercilessly by a powerful corset, that it looked as though she would burst with a crash at any moment! An opera singer in her youth, she was quite charming and lively, and I soon realized that she was the one who noticed my talent in Warsaw and became interested in me.

"After lunch," she said, "my husband will show you Paris, and to-morrow he will take you to Monsieur Astruc."

And so, early that afternoon, Count Skarzyński and I drove into the heart of Paris. When we reached the Place de la Concorde, he stopped the carriage and took me to the obelisk in the center of this unique square from where you see the four most beautiful perspectives in the world: to the right, the Madeleine, the church where Chopin's funeral took place; to the left, the Chambre des Députés, both built in a pure Greek style; before me, the majestic Champs-Élysées, at the end of which the Arc de Triomphe, bathed in a pink and red sunset, soars into the air; and behind me, the charming, terraced Tuileries Garden leading to the large and venerable buildings of the Louvre.

I was so overwhelmed by the beauty of it all that my voice broke . . . I couldn't utter a word, but I made silently, there and then, a sacred vow never to live anywhere in the world but in this divine city!

Count Skarzyński's carriage, driven by one horse, took us slowly up the Champs-Élysées, which was lined in those times by elegant *hôtels particuliers* and harmonious rows of houses. Strictly a residential quarter, there were no restaurants, shops, or theaters. I was much impressed by the twelve proud avenues shooting out in all directions from the Place de l'Étoile, and could never forget my first sight of the Avenue du Bois de Boulogne with its huge chestnut trees covered with leaves in all shades of green on this glorious late summer afternoon.

22

Monsieur Gabriel Astruc was a descendant of an old Jewish family of Spanish Sephardim, and the son of the Great Rabbi of Belgium. Filled with a passion for the arts and the theater, but without any special qualifications for either, he decided to become an impresario. After a short period with the music publishing firm of Enoch & Sons, he had married "the boss's daughter" and founded, with the financial backing of a friend, the Turkish banker Count Isaac Camondo, the Société Musicale, a kind of agency for the promotion of the performing arts, including theatrical productions.

The house where Monsieur Astruc established the seat of his Société was the Pavillon de Hanovre, the remaining wing of the palace built by the Duke of Richelieu at the corner of the Boulevard des Italiens and the rue Louis le Grand. A large reception room in the form of a rotunda with three wide windows provided a panorama of the whole length of the boulevard, a view which Pissarro loved to paint.

We had scarcely had time to enjoy the sight when Gabriel Astruc appeared at the door of his private office to greet us. He was a man in his forties whose heavy build and premature baldness made him look older than his age. His large black eyes bulged out of a pale face, and he had a long, thin, well-curved nose, and a coal-black, well-trimmed beard and mustache.

Losing no time on preliminaries, or on inquiries about my education or my studies, he just clasped my hand and shouted at the astonished Skarzyński, "Can you bring the young man tomorrow afternoon to the piano house of Pleyel? I shall get some fine musicians to hear him play, and after the audition we can make our plans accordingly!" We agreed, of course, and left in hopeful spirits.

One block down from the Pavillon de Hanovre was the Place de l'Opéra, with the famous Café de la Paix at the corner of the Boulevard des Capucines. With some difficulty we found a small table on the large terrace and ordered some tea, but I couldn't take my eyes off the unique, fascinating life around me. This was 1904; the boulevards were still the heart of Paris. The big theaters, the best restaurants and cafés, were concentrated on these historical blocks.

The sidewalks were crowded. I was intrigued by some of the fast-walking, vivacious Parisiennes who would raise slightly one side of their floor-length skirts with three fingertips; their faces were covered by *voilettes*, and they wore large, ornate picture hats on top of their hair. Probably they were on their way to some romantic rendezvous. Young couples would stroll by in close embrace; *flaneurs*, the Paris version of our "city slickers," were looking for adventure; nobody seemed to be in a hurry. Buses, carriages, cabs, driven by horses, were dashing up and down the street; trees were beginning to shed their golden leaves. The air, filled with the aroma of perfume mixed with the strong scent of horses, was brought to one's nostrils by a mild autumnal breeze.

This was my first encounter with the Parisian street scene, and its fascination has prevailed to this day as I write these lines.

The next day we left Chaville early and lunched in Paris at the old Brasserie Universalle on the Avenue de l'Opéra, where they served twenty different kinds of hors d'oeuvres at a low price. Skarzyński tried hard to get me into the right mood for the afternoon; he knew how nervous I was and what the audition meant to me. I had nothing else in sight for my immediate future.

The house of the Pleyel pianos was still at the Boulevard Rochechouart. While waiting for Monsieur Astruc and the dreaded "fine" musicians, we were shown the hall where Chopin used to give his rare concerts, and his piano stood on the platform. "Play a few bars on it," Monsieur Lyon, the current owner of the factory, proposed. "You will see what a beautiful tone it still has." He was right, and I was in awe as I put my hands on this sacred keyboard. We were interrupted by a man announcing: "The gentlemen are expecting you in the salon."

Monsieur Astruc received us with an encouraging smile and introduced us to the other gentlemen. There were only three: Paul Dukas (the composer of *L'Apprenti sorcier*), Jacques Thibaud, the famous violinist, and Maurice Ravel, at that time still little known. To my relief, there was no professional pianist present.

Thibaud remembered our lunch in Berlin and was pleased to see me again. The other two behaved like a jury in court; they were silent waiting for my performance. Thibaud's presence, however, restored my self-confidence. I reminded him of his magnificent performance of the Bruch Concerto in Berlin, went to the piano, and played it for him; then I switched to the Mendelssohn Violin Concerto and showed him the parts which he had played so movingly.

This unexpected gambit changed the cool indifference of the others into a lively interest. They felt now I was a musician and not merely a seventeen-year-old striving pianist. I did play, later on, a Bach toccata, a movement of a Beethoven sonata, and some Chopin—not too well—but I had won them over. They were unanimous in their praise of my talent, saw a great future for me, and advised Monsieur Astruc in strong terms to take me in hand. This was all he needed and hoped for; he offered me a contract on the spot.

In the cab which took us back to the Pavillon de Hanovre, the three of us, Astruc, Skarzyński, and I, commented on various phases of the audition. When we settled down finally in Monsieur Astruc's office we began serious discussion about the contract. I, for one, was craving for just one thing: a guarantee of monthly payments as advance on my future earnings. This would mean security—what I envied most in Frederic's life in Berlin. Astruc was willing to grant it. He offered me five hundred francs a month ($100 in those days) for five years. The other clauses in the contract were rather hard. He wanted 60 percent on concerts at his own risk, and 40 percent on engagements from other sources. But I paid little attention to such exorbitant terms; for me there were these five hundred francs which shone like five hundred stars in heaven!

And so I consented gladly to everything he submitted. He kissed me on both cheeks and said: "Well, mon petit, all you have to do now is to return to Poland and get the signatures to the contract from both your parents. The contract must be legalized by a notary and the French consul in Warsaw." And he added: "Come back with those papers in a hurry; we must plan our campaign as soon as possible." I shuddered at the idea. My parents had not heard from me since my break with Barth. I had kept them in complete ignorance of my whereabouts, and now I was in their power; they held the decision about my future!

My joy fell to the floor like a stone. What made it even worse, I had to keep my countenance in front of Monsieur Astruc and Skarzyński. They knew nothing of my family affairs, and if they knew, God knows what they might decide.

I wanted to remain in Paris for the rest of the day. "I would like to stroll about the city by myself and perhaps see a play at the Comédie Française—I shall take the last train to Chaville, don't worry about me," I said to Count Skarzyński. He found it natural that I wanted to enjoy this happy day, while I simply felt an urgent need to be alone in order to decide what to do.

I roamed the streets for quite a while, pondering all the time: should I submit to a very probable negative stand of my parents, or drop the whole thing?

After a long walk, weighing the pro and contra, my decision was made; I would go to fight it out in Lodz! And so, full of hope and courage, I had some food in a café and went to the Comédie Française, where I watched, from the gallery, *Les Affaires sont les Affaires*, by Octave Mirbeau, marvelously played by de Féraudy. The play, about a ruthless businessman, calmed my nerves completely; I realized there were worse dilemmas than mine. And I returned to the villa in a hopeful mood.

23

Madame Magdalena and the rest of her family were back in Warsaw. They had moved to another apartment on the fashionable Aleja Ujazdowska. In my letter from Paris I had given her the news about the contract and announced my arrival in Warsaw in a few days. Her answer came promptly by telegram with an invitation on behalf of her husband and herself to stay at their house.

After another week at the Skarzyńskis', who went out of their way to be agreeable and hospitable—the Count was bursting with pride over the success of his protégé—I decided to accept the invitation of the Harmans. I needed their advice on the matter of obtaining the ominous signatures.

The train took thirty-six hours from Paris to Warsaw: two sleepless nights and one day in an overcrowded second-class compartment. I arrived in a state of complete exhaustion, but the sight of Frederic waiting for me at the station brought me to life again. He received me with the warmth of our early days. Zakopane was forgotten; his friendship seemed as fresh as ever. On our way home, he besieged me with questions about my impressions of Paris, which made me feel ashamed of my behavior toward him in Zakopane. At the new home, the whole family gave me a great reception. Papa said pompously: "You won the first battle of your career; the great future is now yours!"

Madame Magdalena embraced me, and even Basia showed some bit of emotion. When I told them of the difficulties I had to face in Lodz they exclaimed indignantly: "Your parents have forfeited the right to interfere with your plans. This is a unique opportunity, and you must not give it up." And Frederic's father added: "If you need my help you can count on me."

The apartment, in a brand-new house, built by a Russian caviar merchant, consisted of the whole ground floor. The house was out of harmony with the other buildings in the elegant *aleja*. The Harmans had larger reception rooms, a more convenient disposition of the rest; it looked rich but cold. They put me up in a real guest room this time. I was separated from the other bedrooms, which, under the circumstances, I found convenient. Certain arrangements in the old apartment had left me with some unpleasant memories.

I wrote my parents, announcing my arrival. The distance by train from Warsaw to Lodz is at least two hours, and it seemed endless. My parents and other members of my family had gathered at the station, and they received me with the usual overexcited shouting, questioning, and fussing, so naturally I felt at home right away.

Later on, when I found myself alone with my father and mother, something unbearable happened: my father burst into tears, crying like a child. I had never seen him in such a state, and it made me feel like a criminal. And I try in vain to forget it.

When he calmed down he was impressed by Astruc's proposition and was willing, to my astonishment, to comply with the legal requirements to make the contract valid. My mother, when it came to the actual signing, showed a sudden reluctance when she was told that the document would give me the legal rights of an adult. However, my father persuaded her that they had no right to block me in my career.

I returned to Warsaw with the papers in my bag but feeling a little guilt at how easily my victory had been obtained.

Back in Warsaw, a few surprises awaited me. Basia's parents had decided to send her to Paris to study with the famous Polish tenor Jean de Reszke, and her father was to take here there. Madame Magdalena also announced, with a smile, that she was going to join her daughter in Paris a few weeks later. Bad, bad news for me!

But other news upset me much more. My uncle Paul Heyman came to Warsaw, called on Mr. Harman at his office, and asked him to help my father by appointing him as his business representative in Lodz, or something of that sort. When Mr. Harman informed me about it, promising to do what he could, I felt ready to kill my uncle for his abominable indiscretion! As I learned later on, the whole thing turned out to be even worse. Mr. Harman, on his next visit to Lodz, approached one of his local business associates on the matter, a man who was related to my mother and who had snubbed my family ever since the bankruptcy. My father, who knew nothing of the whole affair, thought I was the instigator; he refused to have anything to do with it, and I had a hard time convincing him of my innocence. The poor man was deeply hurt.

24

I took the train for Paris in the company of Basia and her father. This time, as I arrived, the dirty, malodorous, and gloomy Gare du Nord looked to me like a royal palace; my newly won independence and the five years of monthly payments made me drunk with pride.

After a sleepless night in a dreary hotel, I was out in the street early, went to the Café de la Paix for a hearty breakfast, and reached the Pavillon de Hanovre, where, armed with the properly signed and legalized documents, I was taken immediately to Monsieur Astruc's office.

"Ah, vous voici de retour, jeune homme," he said, smiling brightly. "I have great ideas for you. I think you will be pleased."

I listened to the details of his plans with mixed feelings. He wanted to introduce me to the Paris public with a great gala, orchestra and all.

In order to finance it, he had approached M. Étienne Gaveau, the French piano manufacturer, an ambitious and resourceful man who was using modern publicity methods to push his product and to leave the old established firms of Erard and Pleyel in the shadow. The prospect of having to play on an unfamiliar piano was disquieting to me. I was so used to the German Bechsteins with their beautiful tone and easy action. However, Monsieur Astruc had already made arrangements for me to choose a Gaveau for my concerts, so it was too late to change anything, and besides, I was informed that it was almost impossible to find a piano of a foreign make in France.

"My pianos have the same quality as the Bechsteins," said Monsieur Gaveau, after I had tried two or three of them. "The Erards have a fine action, but they sound tinny; they have not been improved for a hundred years. But the Pleyels do have a lovely tone—only they are too weak for modern concert halls."

Monsieur Gaveau's opinion of these two pianos was right, but he was a little optimistic about his own product. I tried meekly to voice my criticisms of certain defects in his pianos: their cold tone, their weak treble, and other minor things; but I knew that the deal for the gala had been concluded by the two gentlemen and there was nothing I could do about it.

The date of the concert was set for a day in December. Astruc engaged the Lamoureux Orchestra, conducted by Camille Chevillard, the son-in-law of Charles Lamoureux, the deceased founder, to accompany me in two concertos of my choice, with some solo pieces in between. And, to lend some variety to the concert, he asked a young soprano to sing three songs by Debussy, whose opera *Pelléas et Mélisande* was at that time the subject of a violent fight between his followers and his adversaries. The soprano's name was Mary Garden. She was young and beautiful, had just created the role of Mélisande, was much admired for her beauty and her voice, but sharply criticized for her strong English accent.

Monsieur Astruc had another plan up his sleeve. The Countess Greffulhe (the model for Proust's Duchess of Guermantes) had formed an association called Les Grandes Auditions de France, consisting of the upper crust of the French aristocracy. The members were supposed to give their blessings to some special event of their choice, theatrical or musical, by occupying the best boxes *en grande toilette*, the ladies *décolletées,* the men in tails, white gloves, with the inevitable silk top hats.

Thanks to Monsieur Astruc's excellent connections, the Countess agreed to receive me at the château where she resided during the autumn; she wanted to look me over—to see if I deserved her patronage.

After an hour by train I reached a small station where her carriage waited to drive me to the Château du Bois Boudran. A lackey in livery took me upstairs to a cozy room with a big, blazing fireplace. I sat there a long time before being asked to come down to a large music room, where I found the Countess engaged in conversation with a very tall and handsome young man; some time passed before they noticed my presence. Then she turned around and greeted me in a haughty manner, without a smile, introduced me to her companion, Don Roffredo Caetani, and asked me right away to play something. Her Pleyel was in bad shape and out of tune, but I somehow managed to rattle off the A flat Polonaise of Chopin. When I finished, she said, "Bravo," without conviction, but her friend was pleased. He said he was studying music in Florence and was working on an opera, and revealed himself as a passionate Wagnerian, which was enough for me to go back to the piano and play the whole Overture to the *Meistersinger* for him. And, again, my nonpianistic approach to music won the day. Don Roffredo spoke so warmly of my performance that the Countess did not hesitate; then and there she promised the presence of the Grandes Auditions de France for my debut.

Countess Greffulhe was a striking person; she looked like the pictures and busts of Queen Marie Antoinette. I was told that she tried to live up to that resemblance, giving herself the airs of a queen, and, in a way, Paris society accepted her as such.

The Countess dismissed me, smiling graciously this time. "You will have dinner served in your room, and when you are ready my carriage will take you back to the station," she said in her imperious way. It was hard to believe there had been a French Revolution and that France was a republic!

25

With the help of Monsieur Astruc I found a room in a *pension de famille*, 42, rue Cardinet, a few houses away from his own apartment. The pension was a little, two-story-high *hôtel particulier* transformed into a boardinghouse by its owner, Mr. Cordovinus, who at the same time was the manager and the concierge of the establishment. His wife (one of the ugliest old women I have ever seen) was the cook for the whole house. They lived in the *loge du concierge*, where his function was to open the front door and watch the people come in and out.

The price for the room and pension, consisting of breakfast, lunch, and dinner, was seven francs a day, then $1.40. Very cheap indeed, and the food was the same. We were fed mainly on salad and hash.

The other guests were all Scandinavians, two young sisters from Finland who had come to Paris for singing lessons, but had no talent, a Swedish lady, an operatic soprano with a nice voice, and two students, also from the north.

My room on the second floor was spacious and sunny, and I had a piano sent by Monsieur Gaveau. But no bathroom: in those days there was hardly a bathroom to be found in France; elegant Parisians used portable rubber tubs for a bath, a difficult and inconvenient operation.

The day I moved in Monsieur Astruc invited me to dinner at his house, where I met his wife and his five- or six-year-old daughter, an only child, whom he worshiped. Lucienne, the little girl, with the most beautiful big black eyes, picked me right away as her "fiancé," a position I held for several years.

"I need your program," said her father. "I have to start the publicity for your concert, and I have to have it!"

How I hated this request! All through my life I have had to suffer agonies when my impresarios demanded a program far ahead of time! Once the thing was delivered, there was no way out of it. As a rule, the concertgoer does not care what the artist is going to perform, as long as he is famous and a favorite. But God help him if he tries to change anything in his program at the last minute; the public immediately becomes suspicious and feels cheated!

Well, on that evening it was not too difficult to satisfy Monsieur Astruc; my repertoire was still extremely limited, and so I was going to begin the concert with Chopin's F minor Concerto, then a piece by Brahms, and two études by Chopin . . . Intermission . . . three ariettes oubliées by Debussy, sung by Mary Garden, and the G minor Concerto by Saint-Saëns at the end.

"Saint-Saëns!" exclaimed my host. "But that is wonderful. I will arrange right away a rendezvous for you with the master. I want him to come to the concert!" And so, one of the following mornings, I was invited to visit the great composer. He lived alone on the ground floor of an old house, and received me, to my astonishment, quite cordially. I had heard he was famous for his rudeness. The room was a real "music room"—scores everywhere, big piles on his Erard, the tables loaded with books and music sheets; the death mask of Beethoven hung on a wall, and photos of known and unknown people were scattered all over the place.

Monsieur Saint-Saëns was a small, fat man, baldish, with a short, round, gray beard; two large warts were unsymmetrically posed at either side of his nose. He looked like a French bank official.

"I am glad to hear that you are going to play my concerto," he said. "I conducted its first performance for your namesake, Anton Rubinstein. He learned it in a week." Then he added: "I cannot come to your concert. I don't go out at night, but I shall try to be at the rehearsal."

When I told him I was a Pole, he suddenly rushed to the piano, shouting, "This is my favorite composition of Chopin," and played the E major Scherzo, a little too quickly for my taste, but technically perfect. Later, when I was taking leave, he accompanied me to the door and helped me with my coat; his manners certainly belied his bad reputation.

The rotunda at the Société Musicale was a daily rendezvous of the artistic world of Paris, where a medley of musicians, opera singers, dancers, writers, journalists, would flock in and out, form small groups, start endless discussions about this and that, accompanied by wild gesticulations and uproarious laughter. It was fun watching them, but what they really came for was to attract Monsieur Astruc's attention. Ravel was a frequent visitor; he would try out some pieces for four hands with me, among them Debussy's beautiful Quartet, which was a revelation to me. It was my first acquaintance with his music. Paul Dukas brought me his Sonata and his Variations on a Theme of Rameau, both interesting, but a little labored and unpianistic.

The group of composers was sometimes joined by a fat little man with a round face, black beard, and upcurled, abundant mustachios. He was a Spaniard, a jovial fellow, whose eyes had a charming, smiling twinkle. We loved his stories, which made us scream with laughter. I did not know his name. A few years later, Dukas presented me with a copy of *Iberia*, a Spanish composition whose author, he said, had died recently.

"You remember how we used to enjoy his company?" he asked.

It was Isaac Albéniz, the man to whom I owe my great popularity in Spain and in all Spanish-speaking countries. It was my privilege to introduce his *Iberia*, his major piano work, to his own country and to the rest of the world.

Basia, who was placed by her father in a boardinghouse for young girls, had an audition with Jean de Reszke and was accepted by him as a pupil. Before returning to Warsaw, Mr. Harman left orders that his daughter was not to go out at night with anybody but me! I hadn't yet had a chance to use this privilege when Basia's mother announced by wire her imminent arrival. And there she was, at the Gare du Nord, with her faithful maid Pauline and masses of luggage. Basia and I were on hand to help with everything. She took a suite at the Hotel d'Iena, one of the old quiet places, "to be near my daughter," she said.

After lunch, pretending headaches and exhaustion, she sent Basia home. But she insisted I should stay with her, and she kept me there for the rest of the day.

Overnight I felt caught into the old, dreaded routine; Paris became Warsaw.

My concert was only two weeks away, and here I was, constantly being asked by Madame Magdalena to accompany her to shops, doctors, dentists, chores I hated. On the other hand, I cannot deny that I enjoyed the food in the fine restaurants and, most of all, the theaters of my old passion. But it did embarrass me to be her eternal guest. I, of course, couldn't possibly afford this luxurious way of living on my so proud five hundred francs.

All this was detrimental to my work, and too soon the fatal day arrived. The rehearsal was set for ten in the morning at the Nouveau-Théâtre (now the Théâtre de Paris).

Monsieur Camille Chevillard received me in his room and, without losing time, asked for my tempi. He looked as I imagined a private detective should look: the heavyset body, square shoulders, square head, and square cropped hair, a mustache in the form of a brush, and small, scrutinizing eyes. I felt a little afraid of him. The members of the orchestra were already waiting for us on the platform. At the first look at them, I got a slight shock! Most of them sat in their overcoats and wore their hats; the double bass players looked particularly ridiculous in their bowler hats. The thing upset me, however, because I thought it was their way of showing a lack of respect for a young boy who dared to hire them for a gala. But it turned out to be a wrong guess; they were simply afraid of catching cold in the unheated theater.

Chevillard conducted like a military drillmaster. He had the orchestra well in hand, they obeyed his beat, but he had little use for expression or nuance. The Chopin Concerto was his victim; he couldn't understand the meaning of a rubato, and the unearthly beauty of the Larghetto escaped him altogether.

I was beginning to feel very unhappy when the word was whispered: "Saint-Saëns is here!" And there he sat in a box, ignoring our bows, completely aloof. We settled down to rehearse his Concerto, and I started the initial cadenza, my heart beating wildly with fear. But now Monsieur Chevillard was in his element! He dashed me through the whole piece at a terrific tempo, and the finale sounded like fireworks! We went to greet the maestro, who lisped shortly: "Th'était très bien," got up, and left without shaking our hands. At that moment, Messieurs Astruc and Robert Brussel, his secretary, appeared on the scene. Seeing me looking pale and dismayed, Astruc exclaimed cheerfully: "Mon petit, I don't like your looks. I am going to take you to a good restaurant for lunch—it will bring the color back to your cheeks!"

The restaurant was Paillard's, a famous place just across the street from the Pavillon de Hanovre. Astruc ordered a lobster for me, and made the sommelier put a bottle of champagne on ice, telling me, "This wine will do you good." And he was right. After the first glass of the sparkling nectar I felt better, after the second one I began to smile, and after the third glass I even started to giggle! In this happy mood I went back to rue Cardinet and up to my room, where I dashed to the piano to repeat a passage from Chopin. And at this point occurred one of the most tragic moments of my life! My fingers, which felt like noodles, simply did not respond. It was the champagne, of course. I was in despair, with only five hours to go until concert time. I had never been in such a predicament, and I didn't know what to do. In agony, I alerted the whole household. All the Scandinavians rushed up to my room, the Finnish sisters made me lie down, the Swedish singer put cold towels on my head, the men slapped my face, and massaged my hands, and Mr. Cordovinus brought some strong coffee. Finally, after two hours of this strenuous care, my fingers began to act again! Well, I must solemnly state that after this experience, I have never taken a drop of alcohol on the day of a concert for the rest of my life.

The Nouveau-Théâtre was completely filled; Monsieur Astruc had seen to that by sending free tickets to many prominent people and music students. Mary Garden attracted many of the Debussy addicts, and, last but not least, the Grandes Auditions de France appeared in all its glamour, lending its luster to the gala!

One can well imagine the feelings of the young boy I was, who had played so little in public, who was practically unprepared and inexperienced, and who was facing one of the most sophisticated and spoiled audiences in the world, brought to a pitch of anticipation. I was simply terrified.

A friendly applause greeted my appearance on the platform, and the orchestra rose to its feet. This made me feel so much better that I was now in the mood to do my best. But the Chopin Concerto turned out to be a bad performance, by both the orchestra and myself. My usually good and full piano tone was lost on the unfamiliar and weak Gaveau concert grand, the delicate filigree of the Larghetto was hardly audible, and in the third movement I actually stumbled once or twice. We received a polite applause; we didn't deserve better. Then came my solo pieces. The Brahms Intermezzo, which I played quite well, was received with icy indifference. At that point I became desperate; I had prepared two Chopin études, the A flat, Opus 25, No. 1, and the No. 2, both beautiful but not very effective, so for this last one I substituted on the spur of the moment the grand Étude in A minor, Opus 25, No. 11, which was far from being ready for a performance. I banged out the heroic theme in the left hand with all my might, and smeared up, with the help of the pedal, the difficult passage work in the treble, and finished the piece in a brilliant flash! This provoked an ovation, even some "Bravo" shouts from the gallery. I learned then, on the spot, that a loud, smashing performance, even the worst from a musical standpoint, will always get an enthusiastic reception by the uninitiated, unmusical part of the audience, and I exploited this knowledge, I admit it with shame, in many concerts to come.

Mary Garden, who sang beautifully, had a great success with the pro-Debussy listeners, but less with the rest of the audience. The Saint-Saëns, the final piece of the program, which the orchestra played brilliantly, went very well, but I was again cruelly handicapped by the defects of the piano; there was no spark in the elegant scherzo, and I could not produce enough power in the last movement. Anyhow, the public liked it, and made me play a Chopin valse for an encore. That was the end of the concert, which all in all was (I have to use this ugly definition) *un demi-succès*. What a horrible word!

People were nice afterward in the artists' room; they covered me with compliments, but to me they smelled sometimes like condolences.

I was going to join Madame Magdalena and Basia at Prunier's for supper, when Astruc stopped me.

"Mon cher, you must make the ladies wait. I need you now for an appointment at the *Figaro*."

I was annoyed because I was in no mood to talk to newspaper men, especially at such a late hour, but Monsieur Astruc insisted, and so we drove up to the rue Drouot, where we were shown into a waiting room. A tall, blond young man was pacing the place nervously. Astruc greeted him with, "Bon soir, mon cher, how did it go?"

"Quite well," he answered. "Nine curtain calls."

Astruc introduced us: "Monsieur Henri Bernstein, who has just had the premiere of his play *Le Bercail* at the Gymnase."

"I suppose we are here for the same purpose?" he asked the play-wright with a smile.

"I guess so," the latter replied, noncommittally.

At that point a gentleman entered the room. "Who is first?" he asked, looking at us expectantly.

"I have been here for half an hour," said Bernstein impatiently, and followed him to another room. A few minutes later, another man, a Monsieur Charles Joly, invited us to his office.

"Tell Monsieur Joly what you want him to write about your concert; it is late and his deadline is one a.m.!"

I blushed violently, thinking it was a joke. But they were both serious.

"This is how we do it in Paris," said Monsieur Astruc. "Bernstein, too, is dictating his own critique of his play."

Well, there was nothing else to do but take part in this immoral be-havior of the Parisian press, so I began to stutter out, shamefaced, the few good moments of my performance.

"No, that will never do," shouted Astruc. "Monsieur Joly will write the article by himself; all he needs is your program."

Later, at Prunier's, I found the two ladies waiting in a gloomy mood. They had given up hopes of seeing me at all. It was almost closing time, so we were served in a hurry, and the food was not very good. Madame Magdalena gave me a fine gold watch, my first, "in memory of the great date of your debut in Paris," she said. I was touched by it, but at the same time I was sadly reminded of Frederic's debut in Berlin.

Next morning, I read, to my amazement, a most flattering account of the concert on the front page of the *Figaro*, with a colorful description of the audience, a snobbish reference to the Auditions de France, and a prediction of a fabulous career for me.

The rest of the press was divided about my concert. The daily papers, which had hardly any space for musical matters, stated in a few lines that I had talent, and predicted a fine future. The few weekly or monthly publications devoted to music took it up more seriously. One critic, I forget his name, wrote quite a harsh review. "He is far from ready," he wrote, "to be introduced in such a pretentious way to the Paris public." In his opinion, I was a cold-blooded, immature virtuoso who dared to perform a Chopin étude without having learned it properly. He expressed doubts as to my artistic development but conceded that I was endowed with the gift to excite audiences with my temperament and my technique (!). I shared his opinion on many points, but I found him unjust in denying me a serious talent for music. Monsieur Astruc seemed unconcerned by all that; he looked even pleased and decided to present me the next month in three recitals at the Salle des Agriculteurs, a hall much used for concerts.

"There you will show them what you can do," was his comment. For myself, it meant hard work ahead. And I wanted to work, I wanted to work with all my heart, if it were only to prove to my new friends that I was in some way worthy of their faith in me.

Adversities have always had a salutary effect on me. But I had to face a big stumbling block to all my good intentions as a result of the presence in Paris of Madame Harman. How exasperating it was to find so little understanding for my problems in such a normally intelligent person! She continued to oblige me to spend whole days with her, and when I tried to get out of it, explaining that I had to work, she would force her way into my own modest quarters.

Monsieur Astruc was the only one who could see me whenever he needed me. Needless to say, I loved going out with him; it was fun seeing new faces, and it helped to improve my French.

"Vous êtes un parisien maintenant," he liked to say.

One night after a good dinner at his house, his guests—among them Dukas, Pierre Lalo, the critic of *Le Temps*, Gabriel Pierné, and my old friend Chevillard—asked me to play excerpts from the opera *Die Feuersnot* by Richard Strauss, which I had been raving about during the meal. This was the sort of thing I liked to do, so I gave them long stretches of it, sang the parts, explained the libretto, and pointed out the different instruments. I finally worked them up into such a state of excitement that the incident later reached the attention of Albert Carré, the director of the Opéra-Comique, who decided to put this opera on for the opening of the next season.

Later on, that same evening, Mr. Lalo asked me: "Quels sont vos auteurs préférés?" I gave him some names and mentioned, with special warmth, Brahms. Everybody burst out into laughter.

"Oh, comme il est drôle, il aime la musique de ce sinistre emmerdeur."

I was indignant, I would have liked to hit him, but soon, to my disgust, I found out that all Latin countries bore the same prejudice toward this master; no wonder that, at my concert, his piece had met its fate.

One morning there was a nice surprise: Maître Saint-Saëns sent me his photograph with the inscription, "Pour A. R., avec l'admiration pour son grand talent. C. S.-S." The old man was really unpredictable.

Astruc took me to a lunch given by his friend Count Camondo, who lived at 3, rue Gluck, just opposite the Grand Opéra. His apartment had a suite of eight salon-sized front rooms where he hung his wonderful collection of Impressionists, the finest Renoirs, Degases, Manets, Monets, imaginable.

The luncheon party was amusing; we were only six. Besides the host,

Astruc, and myself, we had the famous boulevardier with us, the writer Henri Gauthier-Villars, who published his books under the name of "Willy" and wrote music reviews for the *Écho de Paris*, signing himself "L'Ouvreuse." He had brought two young ladies with him, who looked like twins, both wearing the same clothes, the only difference being that one had a blue ribbon to hold her short hair, the other a pink one. The first one was Willy's wife, introduced to us as "Colette"; it was still decades before she became the great Colette of French literature. The other one was the actress Polaire, much in vogue in those times. The two of them had almost the same oblong brown eyes, and unusually thin, broad mouths, and they spoke with the drawl of the *titi*, the Paris cockney, spicing their conversation with a lot of argot. I noticed when Mr. Gauthier-Villars came into the room he had a flat-rimmed top hat and carried a strange-looking cane, which he deposited on a chair; he liked to be easily recognized, so one never saw him without these two props. His beard and mustache were modeled after Napoleon III, and his piggish eyes sparkled with malice. He and his two ladies were quite notorious in Paris; people even followed them in the street.

We laughed uproariously all through the lunch as Willy, in his high-pitched voice, tore to pieces every known and unknown personality, and the ladies participated in their own style of making fun of people.

On our way home, Astruc informed me with satisfaction that "L'Ouvreuse" promised to write about me—like the *Figaro*. O tempora, o mores!

26

The programs for the three concerts became a nightmare. I hadn't even begun to think of them. Mr. Brussel suggested I play the Variations of Dukas in one of them; "it would please the critics," he said. I liked his work, but it was a big problem to learn the piece in such a short time, and what made it worse, I dreaded the presence of the composer.

It was not easy to tell pani Magdalena that henceforth I could spend only the evenings with her, but she finally gave in and left me free to do my work.

To make a good program for three recitals was always a hard task, and this time an almost impossible one. I began to patch together all the better pieces from all the work I had done at night—but never really finished—in Zakopane and some remnants from Berlin, and after hours of agonies of indecision, I scribbled some titles on paper which looked like a decent program. I even had the impudence to put the Dukas composition down without the slightest notion of whether I could master it.

And again, thank God, my gift for musical camouflage rescued me. I learned the three programs all right, my memory serving me well, and in the lyrical pieces I always had some good moments, but when it came to difficult passages, I would slip over them with bravura, using a sustained pedal to cover up the missing notes. And the whole mess produced the desired effect, thanks to my brio and temperament.

Most of my concerts went quite well; a French audience of 1904 behaved very differently from one nowadays. In those days, nice passages, in the middle of a piece, would be interrupted by "bravos," or comments like "c'est charmant!" or "quel artiste!" Movements of a sonata would be stopped by applause, and we would have to rise and bow. I must confess that, instead of being disturbed, I was rather encouraged by all this (even now, in private houses, friends often voice their approval in the same manner).

My programs included two Beethoven sonatas: the *Waldstein* and the D major (Pastorale), *Papillons* and *Carnaval* by Schumann, all the Chopin I could muster, two études, a rhapsody, and the *Mephisto Valse* by Liszt, some dated Mendelssohn, a few samples of Scriabin and Szymanowski, and the ominous Dukas, which didn't fare too well. I was too scared of the author. But he was very nice about it and remained my friend.

That night, however, the success was genuine; this time the smaller size of the hall and the more modest publicity turned my critics' attention to the fact that I was a real musician and, if as yet immature, a real pianist.

Willy, "L'Ouvreuse," wrote a lengthy account of the concerts. His article was full of exaggerated praise (he was paid for that), dotted with witty and malicious remarks, devoid of any serious approach to musical matters, but he was always read with avidity by the musically ignorant Parisian or, to use a better term, by the musically indifferent Parisian.

Yes, I am sorry to say, music was much neglected in France, a negligence bordering on stagnation. There were, of course, some good reasons for it, such as the lack of adequate concert halls. The century-old Salle Erard and Salle Pleyel were "salons" rather than halls, with a capacity of three or four hundred; the more recent Salle des Agriculteurs did not hold many more. As a result, concerts given there were treated like private affairs; the general public showed little interest or ignored them altogether.

To be just, there existed a sort of concert life in Paris, a very special one. Every Sunday afternoon, at the same hour, three major orchestras, the Société des Concerts, the Colonne, and the Lamoureux, would play symphonic music—on Sundays only, because on weekdays their members had other musical chores to attend to and, moreover, the theaters where the Colonne and the Lamoureux used to play were unavailable (they had their own daily shows).

The venerable Société des Concerts du Conservatoire, which gave its concerts in the small hall of the Conservatory, was the most coveted by its followers. Because its subscriptions had continued from father to son for a century, it was impossible for an outsider to get in, unless one of the subscribers died childless.

Parisian bourgeois families were well satisfied with these Sunday concerts; they attended them with the conviction that they were doing the right thing. The only audience that showed any real response to music was the gallery, but they were more inclined to demonstrate their disapproval than their enthusiasm. The famous scandals of the first nights of *Tannhäuser*, *Pelléas*, and the *Sacre du printemps* prove my point.

After the intense concert life in Berlin, I felt frustrated by this atmosphere. Even the Grand Opéra, the pride of the city, did not measure up to its looks; the singers were mediocre, the orchestra and the chorus quite poor. However, to be just, I must mention one exception. Monsieur Astruc gave me a ticket for the Opéra-Comique to hear *Manon* of Massenet, and I don't know if it was due to the state of my nerves or some other reason, but this light, sensuous, typically French music simply overwhelmed me. I was so moved that I nearly cried. The tenor Clément and Marguerite Carré were perfect in the main roles, and no other performance, even with Caruso, could compare with this one.

Pani Magdalena returned to Warsaw. She had become restless at the end, seeing so little of me during the two weeks of my concerts. Basia, too, would pay her only short visits, wanting to live her own life, she said, and her singing lessons didn't leave her much time.

I was relieved at Madame Harman's departure, of course, but at the same time, it made me realize something disagreeable, namely, the fact that my five hundred francs, which had seemed so precious, did not get me very far in Paris. After paying my pension, laundry, and other extras, nothing much of the money remained. And I did like my daily visits to the Café de la Paix, which I felt was the center of the world and where I always enjoyed a delicious *mousse au chocolat* while reading papers from Paris, Berlin, and Warsaw, to be found at the kiosk just in front of the terrace.

While pani Magdalena was in Paris, I had had no such temptations. I had been entirely in her hands, with no occasion to spend money. Now, my financial situation was precarious. I badly needed some new clothes, especially a warm overcoat. The air had turned chilly, and I had nothing but my summer things. I had left all my other belongings (there was not much anyway) in Berlin, having told Professor Barth proudly that he could give them away. But I had regretted deeply having to leave behind all my books, which I had collected with so much love.

My concerts had not produced the effect we were counting on; no engagements were forthcoming, and people seemed to ignore my success. "Pourquoi ne jouez-vous pas à Paris?" I was asked sometimes. What was I to explain? The Sunday orchestras took only soloists who could pay for the privilege, or famous artists who would fill the hall.

So, fatally, from that moment on, and for many years to come, I was to live the excruciating life of someone constantly short of money, constantly in debt!

Still, the charm of Paris kept me from becoming misanthropic, and I enjoyed it to the fullest with the modest means at my disposal.

One evening, at a dinner given by a Mr. and Mrs. Dettelbach, a rich Alsatian couple who loved music, I met a young man in the late twenties, already bald, with piercing round blue eyes and a full but pinched mouth.

"C'est un violoncelliste génial," I was told. It turned out to be Pablo Casals. After the meal, the two of us engaged in a lively conversation about music, during which he revealed himself, to my joy, as a lover of Brahms.

"Do you love the D minor Piano Concerto?" I asked him in French.

"I have never heard it; please, play some of it for me."

Nothing could have pleased me more. I played the whole work with passion, the orchestra parts and all. Casals was ecstatic. After a little while, we left the place together and, out in the street, decided to go to a café rather than home. "We must talk some more," said the cellist, and so, by three a.m., happy at having shared our views about many subjects, sipping soft drinks, our acquaintance had grown into friendship.

A week or so after this memorable night, Mr. Cordovinus came up to my room with a visiting card. "This gentleman is waiting for you downstairs," he said, giving me a card that bore the name of the man who had written the devastating critique of the gala. What can he want of me? I wondered, and thought he must be trying to get money, like the *Figaro* and "L'Ouvreuse."

In the parlor, an elderly man in a dark suit, stiff collar, and black tie, with a pince-nez hanging loosely on his nose, rose to his feet and addressed me: "I came to see you, jeune homme, on behalf of Pablo Casals. This great artist, whom I hold in high esteem, has read my review of your first appearance with great indignation. He told me: 'If you really think so well of me, I may assure you that Rubinstein is my equal if not my superior.' I must admit, his words impressed me so much that I decided I should know you better."

It gave me a great satisfaction to be vindicated in such a noble way. The result was predictable: from that day on, the man (I have forgotten his name) was my staunch supporter.

The lack of concert engagements and, consequently, the lack of money made my life miserable. I didn't know how to cope with it. Late one afternoon when, in despair, I was trying to get an advance on my monthly payments from the cashier of the Société Musicale, Monsieur Astruc caught me and was about to forbid it. But seeing me so sad and depressed, he changed his mind, let me have the money, and said in his cheerful and paternal way: "Mon petit, ce soir je vous emmène diner chez une jolie femme!" I didn't protest, so, one hour later, he came to fetch me at my pension and we walked a few blocks to a house on the rue Alfred de Vigny, one of those lanes that surround the Parc Monceau. In the elevator, I asked who the pretty lady was. "Oh," the answer was, "she is an opera singer who used to sing in music halls. Her name is Cavalieri." My heart began to beat faster. "It isn't by any chance the famous Lina Cavalieri?" "Yes, that's who she is," he said.

I could hardly believe my ears. In my early years in Berlin, I used to collect, passionately, colored postcards of Lina Cavalieri, the most beautiful woman in the world, as she was called; she was my "pinup girl." In my daydreams I would have given my life for one kiss from her, and here, on this sad day, I was going to meet her, to have dinner with her . . . it was really too good to be true!

Six or eight people were sipping apéritifs in the salon. And there she was! More beautiful than in the postcards. She rushed up to Astruc and kissed him on both cheeks and then, seeing me, asked in her mellow voice, with a strong Italian accent, "Et qui est ce petit là?" After being duly introduced as a great future star, she also kissed me, saying, "Je suis trai, trai conntánnte de vous connáître."

I was in heaven. And then we went to dinner. She sat between Astruc and the Russian Prince Bariatinsky, her *amant en titre*, as I learned later. The others were Constant Say, a very good-looking young man, heir to a sugar fortune and her *amant de coeur*, another man, her accompanist, and two ladies, one elderly one, probably her secretary, the other one a young, blond actress. I was seated between the two women, with the hostess opposite. The dinner was splendid, with champagne served throughout, and so, when we reached the dessert, the conversation became louder and gayer; we laughed about any silly thing that was said, and we never stopped drinking.

All through dinner I couldn't take my eyes off Lina; from her soft dark eyes with their long lashes, the small, straight nose with rosy nostrils, her mouth in the form of a bow, to the long neck, the classical chin, and the beauty of her skin—everything was perfect, and I gazed at her in ecstasy. The young actress who sat on my right was a rather ordinary-looking blonde with an upturned nose, a prominent bust, and a figure which one would call, now, "sexy." She became a little drunk, and leaned more and more toward me. I began to be excited by her. And then a strange thing happened. The divine Cavalieri turned before my eyes into a most beautiful museum statue, while this woman on my right became more and more desirable; she was made of flesh and blood.

Back in the salon, Lina made me play some arias from operas and some songs she liked; she kissed me again, but the evening finished in an unexpected way. I escorted the blond lady home. But Lina remained a friend for years to come.

Thanks to my "boss" I was invited by a rich lawyer, Maître Nuñés, to a Christmas Eve *reveillon*, in his beautiful house on the Place de l'Étoile. To the French, this is an occasion for a gastronomic orgy. We had fresh foie gras with an exquisite salad, truffles *en serviette*, the famous *canard au sang*, and crepes suzette for dessert, the whole accompanied by the finest vintages. My palate, which had already cultivated a taste for such fare, was now spoiled forever.

As a matter of fact, this period was typical of my life for many years, consisting as it did of the discrepancy between the daily struggle for survival and the frequent escapes into these most refined luxuries.

27

"You have a concert in Nice," Astruc said one afternoon. "I shall be there, and then I am going to take you to Monte Carlo."

My heart leaped with joy; at last a real engagement in sight, and on the Côte d'Azur, to boot. I worked up a very effective program, and we left a few days later for the famous Riviera. The blue Mediterranean, the palm trees, the Promenade des Anglais enchanted me . . . a true fairyland.

The concert itself was a great disillusion, however, because I had to play in the Salon Rumpelmayer, a well-known tearoom. The place held no more than a hundred people, but my audience was composed of only sixty, mostly tired-looking old ladies. It was a dreary affair, early in the afternoon; and my fee was too small even to mention.

We left that same evening for Monte Carlo. In the year 1905 this name held magic. It was the only place in the world where one could play roulette. Famous authors had made it legendary, writing about its frequent suicides, spectacular losses and gains at the tables; newspapers reported celebrated cases of larceny and spread gossip about famous people involved in them; in short, it was a place of universal interest—the Mecca of all the gamblers in the world.

Prince Albert of Monaco was, thanks to roulette, one of the richest sovereigns of Europe. He endowed the small, overornamented theater in the casino with a first-class Opera, with an excellent orchestra, ballet, and chorus; fine singers and great conductors could be heard and seen there. The guiding spirit of it was a Rumanian Jew, Raoul Gunsbourg, a colorful person whom Gabriel Astruc knew intimately. They both had a passion for big productions, for big ideas. Thanks to Mr. Gunsbourg, we had comfortable rooms at the Hotel de Paris and tickets for the world premiere of *Chérubin*, the new opera by Massenet, with Cavalieri and Rousseliere in the main roles. All this was very exciting, but the greatest thrill came when Gunsbourg helped me to penetrate the gambling rooms. The access to these *salles de jeu* being strictly prohibited for minors, he had to sign that I was twenty-one. Astruc gave me two gold pieces which represented forty francs—louis d'or or napoleons, they called them —telling me to try my luck at roulette. "You might make a fortune," he laughed. I walked up timidly to one of those dangerous tables and put one louis d'or on black. And black came out. The croupier put another louis d'or on mine, and I was just going to take both off when he called out "Rien ne va plus." My heart stopped. The ball turned a few times and fell again on black. I now had four pieces. I became reckless; I put all of them on red this time. And luck was with me. In less than half an hour of this hazardous exercise, my pockets were full of louis d'or; in those days one did not use chips.

In the happy mood of a winner, I tried to find Monsieur Astruc to boast about my success when Madame Colette accosted me: "I bet you won, jeune homme. I can see triumph in your eyes." Instead of an answer I clanged the gold pieces in my pocket. "Oh," she said, "this is the first time you gamble, this is your great day, you cannot lose. All you have to do is to put one louis on black or red. If you lose, you put up two, if you lose again, you put up four, then eight, and so forth. But if your color comes up, you still win, and it must come up sometime."

Her system seemed to me as simple as the C major scale, and I went back to a table to follow her scheme. In the beginning it went well, but suddenly I caught a run of eight or nine red against me, and in no time I was completely ruined. I could never forget this disaster, and to this day I hold a grudge against Madame Colette, in spite of my great admiration for her work.

The world premiere of *Chérubin* was a great gala. The Prince of Monaco was present and had Maître Massenet in his box. Opera directors, critics, and conductors from many capitals arrived for the great event. All the men were in tails and wore their medals; the ladies wore the latest gowns, sparkling with jewels. It was a brilliant sight.

Unfortunately, the opera itself proved to be a failure. My beautiful Cavalieri was far from being a prima donna; her voice lacked the right kind of training, and she had an unhappy tendency to sing out of tune. And the music did not help much. It missed the inspiration of *Manon* and *Werther*. Nevertheless, it was warmly applauded, and Massenet had to take many bows. The stage was turned into a garden of flowers for Lina, and everybody tried to pretend that it was a great success. We were happy when it was over and joined Mr. Gunsbourg at a supper given in honor of Massenet and other celebrities. When champagne was served, our host rose to address the composer, but spoke mostly of himself, forgetting his prime purpose. I had never known a man capable of such self-praise.

The next morning Mr. Gunsbourg saw us off at the station to take the train back to Paris.

"Je vais m'occuper de ce petit-là," he said. "Il a l'air d'avoir du talent!"

My boss laughed, incredulously. Later on, in our compartment, Astruc regaled me with many amusing stories about him.

"Raoul is one of the greatest liars I have known," he began, "and he thinks he is Napoleon redivivus. You have seen him walking—his right hand squeezed between two open buttons of his waistcoat, à la Bonaparte. He likes to boast that he had saved singlehanded the battle of Sevastopol. And he thinks, poor man, that he is a great composer. But, with all that, he really is a genius in his own field. He made this Opera, out of nothing, into one of the best in Europe, and last week he introduced to Monte Carlo the greatest Russian basso, Feodor Chaliapin, a sensation. I am bringing him to Paris next month."

Back at rue Cardinet, M. Cordovinus, opening the door, whispered: "A lady is waiting for you in the living room." And I found there, to my surprise, my oldest sister, Jadwiga Landau. At first I asked, in alarm, whether she had run away from her husband and three children, but no. She smiled. "I came to visit you and to see Paris." Now I guessed . . . the family obviously assumed that my career was made, and she wanted to be a part of it.

"My room is next to yours," she said happily. "We will have great fun together—you must show me the city!"

And so, for a few days, we did the sights of Paris: the Louvre, the Invalides, the Bois de Boulogne, the boulevards, and all. Finally at the Café de la Paix, I made her even taste my *mousse au chocolat*. She had enough money, fortunately, so I explained my penury by my great expenses for clothes and big losses in Monte Carlo. But I kept her away from my new friends and acquaintances. Many bad experiences of the past had taught me a lesson.

One Sunday, I was invited to lunch at the Dettelbachs'. It was strictly a family affair, *dans l'intimité*, as they like to say. After the meal, my host went to the races, the two little children were taken by their governess to the Bois, and I remained alone with the lady of the house. She was still young and rather attractive. One night, at the Opéra, sitting behind her in a dark box, on a sudden impulse I had kissed her on her bare back, and since then she had begun to treat me in a flirtatious way. And that afternoon, being alone in the house, I felt that she expected me to improve on my gratuitous gesture at the Opéra. But I was not in the mood; my stiff white collar was so tight that it made me feel uncomfortable. Mrs. Dettelbach, being a woman of experience, sensed it was the wrong moment for tender exchanges, so she proposed instead to take me to some friends, who were offering a quartet ensemble playing Beethoven. We entered a large salon while the performers were in the midst of an adagio, and we remained standing near the door. My neck hurt me dreadfully; the pain became so acute I couldn't bear it any longer. I whispered a few words to my escort and left in a hurry—I simply had to take off that damned collar! Besides, I had a rendezvous with Basia that evening for the concert of a Polish pianist, August Radwan, who lived in Paris and was giving his annual recital, attended by the *tout Paris*, of which he was the *enfant gâté*.

Up in my room, I started to change my clothes, but instead, led by some unconscious instinct, I undressed and went to bed. And suddenly I felt very ill. After a violent attack of vomiting I lay down again and fell into a daze. My sister, as she told me later, found me in that state, delirious and with a high fever. In panic, she telephoned Monsieur Astruc, who was also quite alarmed and sent for his doctor without delay. The diagnosis was scarlet fever, a bad case, considering my age. The fever and delirium lasted for two days and two nights, and the crisis was not over until the third day. I had a trained nurse, but my sister never left my bedside.

A strange telegram from Warsaw startled us; it had been sent on the first day of my illness. I quote: "Last night at spiritistic séance you called for help stop wire how your health is love Frederic."

My convalescence was long and slow, and I owe a debt of gratitude to both of the Cordovinuses for allowing me to stay in their house. I had a dangerously contagious case and the doctor had wanted to send me to a hospital; but my hosts were ready to take the risk. I was, of course, completely segregated from the rest of the pension. My sister and my nurse were the only faces I saw for three weeks. Poor Jadzia was really out of luck. She had come to Paris to have the time of her life, to bathe in my glory, to meet famous people and take in all the attractions of the metropolis. Instead, she was chained to a sickbed, doing all sorts of nasty chores, getting hardly any sleep, and scarcely ever going out. A complicated character, this sister of mine: pretty, in the heavy Oriental way, she had had a superficial education, including those piano lessons, French, and some dancing, as befitted a young girl in the Jewish bourgeoisie of Lodz. After her marriage to a successful businessman, and the birth of three children, she suddenly developed a craving for culture and for the better things of life. This yearning of hers turned into an almost pathological ambition, and here is where I come in. She became so obsessed with the vision of a glamorous, artistic life at my side that she would leave her husband and children to themselves and would try to penetrate my private existence. But I must pay her a high tribute for her sisterly heart, the tender care she showed me during the illness.

One day, feeling a little stronger, I asked her and the nurse to push the bed toward the keyboard of the piano, and when I tried to play something with my pale, trembling hands, she burst into tears and cried disconsolately for a long while. I was deeply moved.

She went back home after my recovery without, thank God, catching the virus. Her husband, however, claimed later on that after she returned, she infected all three children with my scarlet fever.

28

My finances had reached their lowest ebb. I owed money to the doctor, to the pharmacy, and I was, naturally, one month overdue at the pension. To make things worse, I developed abscesses in both ears; it was a disagreeable aftermath of my disease. The most painful incisions, which had to be performed without anesthetic, turned me into a nervous wreck.

To be just, there were some pleasant moments to report, too. Madame Dettelbach, who for some reason felt guilty about my illness, sent, all through my convalescence, lovely fruit and flowers, and Monsieur Astruc showed nothing but concern and understanding like a true friend. He asked me often to dine at his home, selecting carefully the right food for me. "Eat more of it, mon petit," he would say. "You need new strength." And, filling my glass with a fine Bordeaux, "Drink that, there is fresh blood for you."

Basia left her pension and, with two girls, who were also studying with de Reszke, rented a charming apartment on the Avenue Victor Hugo.

"My lover is in Paris," she told me, "so I have to be free."

One evening, after dinner, she invited me to join her and some friends for coffee. The two roommates were English, both charming; the younger one was barely sixteen and wore her long hair loosely tied with a ribbon. Her name was Maggie Teyte, the Maggie Teyte who was to become, of course, the great Mélisande at the Opéra-Comique and the finest interpreter of Debussy's songs. The other girl was Olga Lynn, in later years the most popular singing teacher in London and the toast of the aristocratic set.

Basia's guests, besides me, were two Polish gentlemen: the first, her ominous lover, the painter from Warsaw, the other one, a very tall, strongly built man in his early thirties, by the name of Joseph Jaroszynski. He fascinated me. The minute I entered the room, he shouted with the loudest voice I have ever heard, wildly gesticulating, endangering everything within his reach: "Please, play something, please! I hear you are such a fine pianist!"

And he led me, almost by force, to the small piano the girls rented. I played Chopin, Scriabin, Szymanowski, and what not. The girls sang opera arias to my accompaniment, while Mr. Jaroszynski, shouting like mad, would jump to his feet and perform gymnastic exercises as if in a trance. Such demonstrations of enthusiasm were new to me. Basia's Don Juan did not move from his chair, smoking cigarette after cigarette, watching us with an ironical smile.

After two hours of this infernal noise, our improvised concert was stopped by some angry knocking on the wall, coming from the infuriated neighbors next door. Finally, Jaroszynski and I departed, leaving the painter behind. "He is constantly after me," my new friend complained. "He wants to paint my portrait and I don't like his painting." We went to a café, where, still in the same vein, he spoke and sang so loudly that people nearest to our table sought a more distant one.

The following day he took me to lunch in a good restaurant, and there, in a calmer mood, he told me of his life. He was a native of Podolia, the richest province of the Ukraine, a large part of which belonged to old Polish families, who still held the land from the time when this whole country was a part of Poland, before it had been taken over by Russia.

Jaroszynski was one of four brothers who became heirs to some extensive estates and big sugar refineries. When he was young he wanted to make a career as a pianist; music was his obsession, but his parents would have nothing of it.

"And so I had to study law at the Kiev University." He mused for a moment. "But, instead," he continued, "I spent all my time at the Opera, at concerts, or at my piano."

After the death of his father, he abandoned his studies and went back to the country, where he showed a gift for agriculture, bought more land, and developed it, applying the latest methods. He was a confirmed bachelor.

"All the girls I know are unmusical," he said, "and I like to travel and hear all the music I can."

We became good friends, and again, thanks to him, I enjoyed the rich life of Paris, the fine food, the theaters, the concerts, while, at the same time, my debts were growing and I had not even enough money for a tip.

One morning Jaroszynski declared that he had to leave for the Ukraine. "I have some urgent business to attend to, but I shall return to Paris after a week or so," he said, and then he added, on a sudden impulse: "Why don't you come with me? A change would be good for you."

At these words, a brilliant idea came to my mind: Why not take advantage of this offer and give one or two concerts in Lodz, where the glamour of my Parisian debut had made a big impression and where I could count now on a full house? I wired immediately my brother Staś, the only one I could rely on for this sort of thing, and asked him to announce one concert and, if the sale of tickets seemed promising, a second one. An enthusiastic reply came two days later: "Enormous interest stop have announced two recitals."

The reason for my trip, I told "my boss," was that I needed a short rest with my family, and I did not mention anything about the concerts. It may seem unethical, even a little dishonest, but I felt very strongly that concerts in my home town did not belong in the same category as those of which he kept 40 percent for himself. I needed money too desperately. Joseph approved of my Machiavellian plans, and we left for Poland by the Nord-Express; it was the first time that I had traveled in comfort. I was to leave the train in Lodz at seven in the morning, and he was to continue on to his destination.

This time, my arrival in Lodz was the scene of a riotous farce. The night before, when I had been ready to retire, I asked the sleeping-car attendant to wake me up at six a.m., but he answered so rudely that I had to push him out of my compartment. After this incident it took me a long time to calm down. Finally, I fell fast asleep.

It was still dark when the train stopped, but I paid little attention to it; a stop always startled me, but only for a moment. So this time, again, I dozed on for a while. Suddenly, I heard voices outside, shouting in Polish: "Pan Rubinstein, where is pan Rubinstein, have you seen pan Rubinstein?"

I jumped up from my bed, completely naked, ran to lift the window blind, and was amazed to see my brother Staś, my sister Hela, and two aunts running up and down the platform, looking for me. It was Lodz, all right! When they saw me standing there, with nothing on, they tried, with pantomimic gestures, to make me understand that I must dress and get out in a hurry. I was grabbing my clothes when, brusquely, the train moved on. They shrieked, I shrieked, but there was nothing I could do. I would arrive in Warsaw in two hours and wait there for the next train back to Lodz. So after a little while, in a quieter mood, I decided to dress properly and have some breakfast in the dining car with Joseph. I took out my shaving things, lathered my face carefully, and was about to shave when, suddenly, the train stopped again. Thinking something had gone wrong, I looked out the window and what did I see, to my horror? This unfortunate brother of mine, and my sister, and the aunts running up to my car in breathless excitement, and, seeing me open-mouthed, with a bewildered expression on my soap-covered face, they gave another shriek and . . . the train ran off again. It had stopped for a minute at a new station on the other side of the city, and they had tried desperately to catch me there. When I told Jaroszynski the whole story later at breakfast, he laughed tears, but insisted on beating up the sleeping-car man. I had a hard time stopping him.

But, in the end, all went well; I was on time for the concert and played to a full house. Afterward, there was the usual "small, strictly family" supper for twenty, with pike, *à la juive*, and other delicacies I liked so much.

The second concert, too, was almost sold out, which improved my financial outlook. However, in other respects, things did not look at all satisfactory. The political situation was creating great unrest in Poland and a still greater one in Russia. The Russo-Japanese conflict, provoked by a minor incident involving Port Arthur and treated disdainfully by the Russian military command as a "punitive expedition," had developed into a full-fledged war, with a disastrous result for the Russian Empire. After the Japanese victories on land and the total annihilation of the Russian fleet by Admiral Togo, the Russian bear lost much of his prestige, and Japan became the first Asiatic world power.

At first, people did not take the affair seriously; they were amused by stories about the behavior of the officers on the trans-Siberian trains which transported them to the war—their orgies, the cases of vodka they consumed, the women they had with them became the main topic of conversation. But as the war progressed, the reports of constant defeats and heavy casualties changed all that. There were signs of dissatisfaction and uneasiness which soon deteriorated into angry demonstrations. It was clear that the nation was becoming more and more enraged at the way the Tsar was conducting the war; the people blamed the government—him and his government alone—for the shameful developments.

Finally, in protest, a young Russian priest, Father Gapon, led two thousand citizens of St. Petersburg to the Winter Palace, the seat of the Tsar, in order to submit a petition asking that a constitution be granted to the people. The procession advanced peacefully up to the big square in front of the palace. When it reached the gate, the palace guards opened fire from both sides of the building, and five hundred demonstrators were killed; many more were wounded. The shooting had been ordered by an uncle of the Tsar; the sovereign himself lived with his family in Tsarskoe Selo.

This tragic incident was the spark which set off the revolution of 1905. In retaliation for the massacre in St. Petersburg, another uncle of the Tsar, the Grand Duke Serge, was shot in Moscow. Infuriated mobs attacked police stations and public buildings, intellectuals issued proclamations, students demonstrated in the streets, even the monarchist aristocracy leaned to the side of the people, but the revolution could not win the army or the police, and the all-powerful synod of the Russian church remained loyal to the throne. And so the uprising was quelled by the Tsarist forces. Thousands paid for it with their lives, thousands were deported to Siberia, and the Okhrana, the dreaded secret police, became the real power in Russia. But Nicholas II learned to fear his people. And, as usual, we in Poland ended up as the prime victims.

29

Before returning to Paris, I spent two days in Warsaw waiting for Jaroszynski. Pani Magdalena and Frederic were delighted to see me in good shape again, and invited me to join them later in the summer, the end of July, in Switzerland. They were planning to stay in a hotel high above Montreux, overlooking Lake Leman. I accepted the invitation enthusiastically—it settled my fears about how to spend the summer!

Joseph and I returned to Paris on a lovely spring day, the first day of May, feted in France traditionally as the feast of the lilies of the valley. You saw them everywhere, vendors offered them in the street, and their subtle aroma permeated the whole city. And the city knew how to respond; everything was fresh and gay, the chestnut trees were in full bloom, the pert Parisiennes animated the streets and avenues with their chic and charm, and the pale, blue-gray sky seemed to smile on all of this. Enchanted and happy to be a part of it, we decided to celebrate such a day.

We began with a fine luncheon at the reopened Pavillon Royal, in the Bois de Boulogne, and after a good rest, we went to see at the Palais Royal theater a typical French farce entitled *Chopin*, one of the funniest I have ever seen. One scene in particular delighted me: a retired general was meeting his young mistress every week in a *maison de rendezvous*, but in order to achieve climax in his amorous pursuit, he needed to have a pianist in the next room playing a valse of Chopin. One day, the poor old pianist was taken ill, and he sent as a substitute a young man who, instead of playing Chopin, gave a fiery performance of a valse of Strauss. Catastrophe! The general, red in the face, in his underclothes, burst into the room and shrieked at the pianist: "Nom de Dieu, nom de Dieu, what sort of a music is this?" Neither of them had been able to do a thing! Joseph made the theater shake with his laughter, and I felt proud of Chopin's suggestive powers!

We finished the night at the famous Maxim's—a very different restaurant then from what it is now. Then it was open only at night, and the clientele consisted of the *demimonde* and the men who supported them—the older ones as *amants serieux*, the young ones as lovers. But Maxim's was taboo for the *femmes du monde*. One danced until dawn to the music of a Hungarian gypsy band, and the cuisine and the wine cellar were perfect.

Reigning sovereigns, incognito, Russian grand dukes, theatrical celebrities, and the cream of the "half-world" filled the place night after night. For those who wanted privacy, small rooms (*chambres separées*) were available on the first floor, with discreet back staircases leading up to them. But it was a world of the rich, inaccessible to the impecunious. This was not my first time at Maxim's, but before I had always sat in front, on the terrace, where you could have a ham sandwich for one franc and coffee for fifty centimes, with the right to peep in on what was going on inside. So now I enjoyed it to the fullest; we invited a lovely English redhead to our table, and danced with her.

I remember this day well, because I felt so happy and carefree! And the next day was even better. Monsieur Astruc left a note in the morning which read: "I must see you right away, it is urgent." So I went to the Pavillon de Hanovre with a little guilt complex about the concerts in Lodz and ready to hand over the 40 percent. But a smiling boss received me with an unusual warmth and shouted happily: "Mon petit, they want you for an American tour."

I stood still, open-mouthed, incredulous. "It must be a mistake," I said at last. "I have no contact with anybody in that country, and, frankly, I don't believe my concerts in Paris can justify such an offer."

He laughed. "You will meet the American gentleman this afternoon in my office, and you will find out for yourself."

The American arrived on time, and told me, in broken French, hard to understand, that he had been trying to find my whereabouts for some time and that he was happy to have succeeded at last.

"But what gave you the idea of wanting to bring me to America?" I asked, still suspicious.

"I act only as an agent for the piano firm of Knabe, of Baltimore. Mr. William Knabe heard wonders about you from the most influential critic of Boston, who heard you at Paderewski's house in Switzerland, and ever since, we have been trying to get in touch with you."

Yes, of course I remembered the American guest at Paderewski's villa on that famous evening! Certain events in life can provide a great moral lift, and this one came at the right moment. I left the two men to work on the contract, and out in the street, I ran to the Café de la Paix and had two whole *mousses au chocolat*.

Everybody was impressed by the news, especially my boss and his staff; it had raised my stature, and I was looked on now as a potential moneymaker. A young artist by the name of Sacha Guitry was commissioned to draw my caricature for the press. His father, the famous actor Lucien, had expelled him from home and refused to support him, so the poor fellow had to make his living as a caricaturist.

"My father was infuriated that I wanted to go on the stage. 'There is no room for two Guitrys in the theater,' he said. But I shall not give up." And he didn't, thank God, for the glory of the French art of acting and playwrighting. His excellent caricature of me was unfortunately lost during the war.

The contract for America was signed, and its main points were: forty concerts that would last three months, with traveling expenses paid by the management, living expenses by me. The money was much less than I had expected—four thousand dollars in all, minus the famous 40 percent, of course.

"Ne vous en faites pas, mon petit," my boss consoled me. "This tour will pave the way to a grand career." And, to soften my disappointment, he produced a ticket. "This is for tonight's gala at the Automobile Club. Chaliapin is having his debut, and you will sit in one of the boxes of the Grandes Auditions de France." He knew me well, Monsieur Astruc. My face brightened at once. The Russian basso was a legend in Paris. The French newspapers and magazines had been writing for years about his fabulous success in opera, his unique voice, his resounding love affairs, and there were numerous stories about his modest, peasant origin, his close friendship with the great writer Maksim Gorki, and, the most attractive item for the feminine readers, his exceptionally good looks. It was no wonder that both Astruc and Gunsbourg, in anticipation of his official debut at the Grand Opéra, had decided to present him first at this gala for charity, presided over by the all-important Countess Greffulhe.

And I shall never forget that evening. Chaliapin was to sing the two big arias of Mephisto from the *Faust* of Gounod, but he chose for this occasion his costume for the opera *Mefistofele* by Boito. And what a costume! When the curtain went up, the magnificent body of a naked man came out on the stage. Muscular as Hercules, he was the image of the perfect male. The perplexed audience broke into loud oh's of horror or admiration. And then he began to sing the famous Serenade with a voice of a unique quality; powerful and caressing, soft as a baritone's and flexible as a tenor's, it sounded as natural as a speaking voice. And he was a great actor, too. Gounod's Mephisto tends to be, at times, a character out of a light comedy, but when Chaliapin played him, he personified the very idea of evil as conceived by Goethe.

When he finished, the whole audience stood up as one and shouted "Bravo" in wild excitement. After insistent cries for an encore and more than twenty bows, the Russian giant repeated the aria. I had never seen a greater enthusiasm, and, naturally, I was one of the loudest shouters. That night Chaliapin was crowned the idol of Paris.

After the show Astruc and Gunsbourg took me backstage to meet the great man. He was still in his "costume," and I had to laugh. The impression of nakedness which had caused such a sensation was created simply by a pair of close-fitting, flesh-colored tights covering his whole body, on which he himself had painted the Herculean muscles; he was an amateur sculptor, proud of his knowledge of anatomy. My congratulations, pronounced in my best Russian, provoked an outburst of joy. "Ah, at last, at last I can talk to someone," he said. "I am condemned to be with these two ignoramuses who don't speak my language."

The two ignoramuses laughed. "We must take this boy with us for supper."

In the private room, on the first floor of the Café de Paris, we were served caviar and vodka and, later, champagne. Gunsbourg brought two lovely dancers from the Monte Carlo Ballet, and Chaliapin drank one vodka after another, with each girl in turn on his lap. A tired upright piano stood in a corner of the room, and before long, a little high, I was playing excerpts from *Faust*, *Carmen*, and *Eugene Onegin*, and whatever came to my head, and Chaliapin sang with me at the top of his voice. That night marked the beginning of our lifelong friendship. "Artoosha"—he chose this Russian nickname for me—"Artoosha, you must come with me to Orange in a month. We will have fun together, and you must be my interpreter." Hooray! First Orange, then Switzerland—what a great summer!

In the meantime, Jaroszynski and I continued to probe the culinary art of the French, and their theater. We went to see Lucien Guitry in Bernstein's *Le Voleur*, Madame Réjane in *Madame Sans-Gêne*, and the great Sarah Bernhardt in *L'Aiglon* of Rostand. It was painful, I must confess, to see the great lady play the role of a young boy, and to find her famous golden voice so tarnished and feeble. But Lucien Guitry was my hero. In my humble opinion he was the greatest actor of the French theater; he filled the stage like no one else with his powerful personality. Many actors tried to imitate him, but in vain. Only Raimu, in later years, could come close to him. And Réjane, this bundle of nerves and sensitivity, this charm personified, who was able with her less-than-pretty face to convince you she was a beauty.

Owing partly to my intensive life of pleasure and partly to the presence of her lover, I had been seeing less of Basia for some time. The greater my surprise when one afternoon she came to see me in the company of the painter.

"We need your help," she said at once. "We must have two hundred francs immediately, and I have no money left."

I had only one louis in my pocket myself, so the only thing to do was to ask Monsieur Astruc's cashier for an advance. The three of us went by bus to the Boulevard des Italiens. Basia and her friend waited in the street while I had a hard time obtaining the money from the reluctant employee. Basia thanked me with a hug and kiss. But her lover lit a cigarette and looked away. How the situation has changed since last year, I thought with no little satisfaction.

"Have you seen Chaliapin lately?" asked Joseph one day; he knew I had heard and met the singer.

"Yes," I answered, "and I am going to see him tomorrow."

"Ah, ah," my friend shouted, "you must introduce me to him. As a student, in Kiev, he was my idol. I used to stand whole nights in front of the box office to get tickets for his performances."

Moved by his enthusiasm, I promised to arrange it. And, next day, I told Feodor, with much exaggeration, the touching story of the "poor Polish student in Kiev who went hungry in order to hear you sing and who is dying to meet you and express his admiration." Chaliapin, who, as a rule, didn't like visitors, was visibly much taken by my story.

"Bring him to tea," he said. "I like students."

When the great day arrived, Joseph and I rang the bell to Feodor's apartment at the Grand Hotel. He opened the door himself and shook Joseph's hand with special warmth.

"You don't look like a student," he said to him.

Jaroszynski was confused but didn't answer. A table was set for tea, in the Russian manner—with vodka, smoked herring, sardines, and cold meats. After a few vodkas, the great singer announced solemnly: "I have received a letter from my friend Gorki and his latest short story in manuscript. It is beautiful; I must read it to you," and he left the room to fetch the letter. Joseph hadn't said a word until then. He was overcome with emotion, heightened by the heat and the vodkas. Chaliapin settled down to his reading, a fat little bundle of pages in his hand. And soon, the powerful voice rang through the room with the words of Gorki about the steppes, the forests, the rivers of Mother Russia, about hunger, illness, and poverty, in long, drawn-out sentences. We listened in awe for a long while, and suddenly, I saw to my horror that Joseph was fighting desperately to stay awake. He tried, in vain, to keep his eyes open, then, completely losing control, his head dropped down to his chest, and soon a loud snore was heard. At this, Feodor jumped up from his seat, murder in his eyes.

"Poshol von, poshol von" (get out), he screamed. "You son of a bitch, may I never see you again."

I dragged my poor friend, still in a daze and with tears in his eyes, to his hotel, where he remained, disconsolate, for a whole day. A few days later he left for his Podolia and as I saw him off at the Gare du Nord, suddenly, in a generous gesture, he pulled out two new bills of a thousand francs each. Handing them to me, he said, "You will need them, I know, but don't spend them all at once."

Confirmed spendthrift that I was, I paid no attention to Joseph's good advice. Feeling rich, I ordered four suits of a somewhat pretentious elegance (a dark gray one even had silk lapels), a sensational Panama hat, and a pair of black and white shoes to complete the outfit. The tailor received a small down payment; the rest was on credit.

When the things were ready, I went to the Pavillon de Hanovre to remind Monsieur Astruc of Chaliapin's offer to have me as his guest in Orange. "He had to leave yesterday for his rehearsals," my boss answered, "but he made me promise to take you with me and deposit you safely at his villa."

We left a Paris with half of its inhabitants gone. The Grand Prix, the climax of the horse-racing season, marked the beginning of a general exodus when the wealthy retired to their châteaux or invaded the beach resorts and their casinos; others, after overeating and drinking all through the year, went to offset the lethal results with a severe three-week dieting cure in Vichy or another spa. Those who couldn't afford either and who were forced to remain in Paris had their window shutters carefully closed for the whole summer, as official evidence of their absence.

30

Beautifully situated in the heart of Provence, not far from Avignon of the Popes and from Arles, made famous by Gauguin and Van Gogh, lies Orange, which takes much pride in its perfectly preserved ancient Roman theater, a contrast to the arenas of the neighboring towns. A huge wall, built of large stone blocks, projects at its base a solid platform representing the stage, facing a vast amphitheater, the whole an impressive setting for the annual festival of opera and drama. *Mefistofele* of Boito and *Les Troyens* by Berlioz were the musical events, while the Comédie Française, with *Oedipus* by Sophocles and *Le Cid* by Corneille, represented the drama. The attendance at this popular festival was such that many had to seek lodgings in nearby cities. I was lucky to have a comfortable room in

Feodor's charming villa, only one block away from the amphitheater, and free tickets for all the performances.

"Monsieur Chaliapin est au théâtre, et il vous y attend," said a young and pretty maid, letting me into the house. Anxious not to miss too much of the rehearsal, I left my bag in her care and ran to the place, where, instead of a "naked" Mephistopheles, I saw the stage occupied by ancient Greeks in the act of deploring the unfortunate Oedipus's fate with heart-breaking pathos. Feodor, in street clothes, sat on a stone bench and screamed in ecstasy: "Artoosha, what a genius, this Mounet-Sully! I want to learn from him, he is the greatest actor in the world." And he squeezed my hand at every pathetic outcry of the poor, incestuous king. Mounet-Sully was acknowledged as the greatest tragedian of his time; he was the supreme master of the old school of exaggerated declamation, modulating every word, emoting all the time. I, for one, was unreceptive to this kind of acting, and, to my shame, it sometimes made me burst into uncontrollable giggles.

We started off that morning on the wrong foot, Feodor and I; he gave me a lecture on my incompetence in matters theatrical, and I begged him with fervor not to imitate the old actor. But soon we were in full harmony again, when our eyes fell on a beautiful young *pensionnaire* of the Comédie. It didn't take more than a minute for the irrepressible Fedja to take hold of her arm and whisper into her ear. "Artoosha," he called, after a lengthy colloquium with the girl, "wait for me at the Café du Théâtre. I shall fetch you for lunch." After making me wait a long hour, he came at last and apologized with a smug little grin. "Ah, I asked her to come to my room with me, but, chort pobieri [the devil take it], she had that nasty monthly impediment and so, ah, ah, I had to take her mother instead!" he said, laughing uproariously. "And she wasn't bad, not bad at all!"

This incident was the start of the most riotous ten days of my life. Chaliapin exceeded all normal bounds; any female of sensual promise fell victim to his brutal frankness and, more often than not, gladly. But still he gave a memorable performance of Mephistopheles. When he appeared out of a niche in the center of the wall, in a dim, bluish light, naked to the eye in his painted muscles, and sang the long Prologue in his own inimitable way, the audience went wild with enthusiasm, just as they had in Paris. We celebrated his triumph in the traditional way. Another man, a friend of the singer, who was staying in our villa, possessed a special knack for finding attractive women at the right moment and thus became eminently useful. That night he managed to bring with him four charming creatures of the theatrical world. The hero of the evening, strengthened by a half-dozen vodkas, wanted all four of them for himself, but settled finally on two; the leftovers were for us. This small orgy set the pattern for our daily program, and, I must confess, it was utterly delightful.

The *Troyens* of Berlioz impressed me deeply; it was the first operatic work of this strange genius I had heard. I call him strange because, in my opinion, the sublime in his music alternates often with the banal. Inspired by Beethoven and his own super-romantic temperament, he conceived forms of colossal dimensions, using excessive orchestral and choral apparatus. Chopin said of him, "He makes too much noise." But I learned to love him more and more with time. *Oedipe Roi* turned out to be a great experience. My prejudice against the declamatory vanished in the face of the perfect unity of style, to be found only in productions by the venerable Comédie Française. Mounet-Sully's real emotion and his powerful, almost musical conception of the Sophoclean tragedy provoked no laughter but brought tears to my eyes. Feodor was right, and I made my amends to him.

The time had come to leave for Switzerland, where my friends were expecting me. "We can travel together to Lyon and spend the night there." my boss advised. "Your train leaves early in the morning and mine takes me later to Aix-les-Bains, where I go for my cure."

I accepted, of course. After a gay luncheon with some musicians and critics, I went back to the villa to pack my things and to take leave. Fedja embraced and kissed me, saying, "Come to Russia, Artoosha—there I can give you a really good time."

A really good time? I thought, almost scared. And what was wrong with this one?

The pretty maid, another of the singer's victims, brought my bag down.

We found good company in the train, Astruc and I, and spent a few hours in lively and interesting conversation. A bad surprise, however, was awaiting us in Lyon, where we arrived at midnight. There was no room to be found in any hotel of the city. "Ne vous en faites pas, mon petit," said the ever-resourceful impresario. "I know of a good place where we can go to bed, and, eventually, sleep," he added, with a grin. His "good" place turned out to be the finest bordello in town, where my boss seemed to be at home. "Wake us up at eight tomorrow morning with a nice breakfast," he said to the madam, and left me in the care of a tall, full-bodied brunette, choosing for himself a skinny blonde. On this night I was initiated into this underworld of love.

The next morning we separated at the station, and I took the train for Montreux. Lac Leman lay quietly in the sun, the mountains looking down on it from their majestic height, and the whole countryside wore the full dress of summer. It was very hot when I arrived at my destination.

After a quick snack at the station buffet I proceeded to the Grand Palace de Caux from nearby Territet by a funiculaire which, after a half-hour's steep ride, reached the hotel. Frederic greeted me at the landing with his usual warmth and charm and led the way to the hall, where his mother and Basia received me with a hearty welcome. It is strange to say, but in spite of the abnormality of our relationships, I felt as if I had come back to my family.

The Caux Palace was a five-story building of vast proportions, perched on a protruding cliff above the lake. A balustrade, on the edge of a precipice and following its outline, offered a perfect panorama of the entire lake and its guardians, the snow-covered Alps. A truly majestic view!

Inside the building, the discreet elegance and the meticulous order so typical of Swiss hotels exuded a pleasant feeling of comfort. A wide, carpeted marble staircase led from the entrance hall to the first-floor lobby, a large place with tall bay windows. Here, the hotel guests would get together, play cards, sip their coffee, or just gossip. The adjoining dining room, in white and gold, had an open balcony where, on clear days, one could eat and enjoy the sun. The food was excellent.

My friends occupied an apartment of three connecting rooms on the second floor; mine was at the end of a long corridor. Frederic, the lucky man, had a grand piano rented from Lausanne. He was deeply engrossed in the composition of a concerto which kept him for long hours at the instrument and left me with hardly a chance to prepare something new for America, as I had intended to. The sad result of it was that I spent weeks without touching a piano, but truthfully I was not too unhappy about it.

Life in the Caux Palace resembled closely the kind of life I was to know later on transatlantic luxury steamers. Here, as there, we were closed in, shut off from the world. The only available outlet was to climb and descend the mountain, both difficult undertakings. The ride down and up by funiculaire meant a whole day lost. So, our daily walks along the balustrade seemed as monotonous as the ones on the promenade decks of ships. No wonder, isolated as we were, that we fell into the bad habit of watching with a malicious eye everything and everybody around, making loud remarks in our own Polish, which made us feel safe from being overheard. I have often observed on my travels, whether on boats, by air, or on trains, that we are inclined to use a sharp eye on our fellow passengers, to hate this one, or like that one, for no other reason than that we are herded together.

Our behavior in Caux confirmed my theory; we felt a pang of irritation every time a German family entered the dining room just because the man looked like a butcher, the wife was too tall and too thin, and the children too blond and too freckled. But we watched with tender sympathy a pale, fragile-looking lady from Argentina with her two daughters in their teens and a good-looking young man, evidently her lover. A loud group of Italians aroused our deep-felt wrath, while an Englishman became the main target of our curiosity. He was, in his own way, perfect. Impeccably dressed, he changed his clothes three or four times a day, always the right outfit for the occasion, and at night his dinner jacket, pleated shirt, patent pumps, and silk socks were the last word in elegance. He ate alone, and his well-shaven ruddy face, with a monocle in one eye, giving him that look of social superiority so charac-teristic of the English, was awesomely admired. We were also favorably intrigued by three haughty Russian ladies, one of them a Baltic Baroness. I thought she was beautiful, but pani Magdalena hated her, which was natural.

After a few days of this cold-war atmosphere, we began, shyly at first, to get acquainted with some of the guests of the hotel, and after knowing them better, we had to admit, with shame, how superficial our appraisals of them had been. The Germans, for instance, revealed them-selves as passionate music lovers; I caught them one day standing at Frederic's door and listening intently to his playing. This, naturally, brought us together. Our quarrels about Brahms versus Bruckner were enjoyable hours to remember.

Señora Amelia Luro, the Argentine, was ill with tuberculosis, the disease which gives its victims, sometimes, before they die, a radiance of transcendental beauty, as was her case. She would sing, accompanied by her guitar, some lovely popular songs of her country, with a mezza voce of a sweet and warm timbre so touching that it moved me to tears. I still recollect some of these songs. Her young man was a painter from Cambo, in the French Basque province where they all lived, and a life-long friend of the family, not her lover as we had been so convinced. Needless to say, we all fell in love with Amelia and our groups became inseparable.

When the three haughty ladies from St. Petersburg learned that we spoke Russian they dropped their snobbish airs and begged us to be allowed to join our company. And so, after meals, our coffee table in the lobby became the center of things. Animated conversations on serious subjects such as art, philosophy, religion, or politics, or simply gossip, good stories well told, witty repartées or funny imitations greeted with bursts of laughter, filled our afternoons and evenings with undiminished joy.

The mornings were spent in Frederic's room, where he would show

me the progress of his concerto. He was having difficulties with it, having
adopted, owing to my influence, a Brahmsian style not well suited to
his nature. From time to time he did let me play the piano.

Our glamorous Englishman was still attracting our attention; his
studied nonchalance, his perfect table manners, which could have served as
an example for generations, were indeed subjects for admiration. We were
also impressed by his personal valet, a prototype of Wodehouse's Jeeves,
who would appear daily in the lobby after lunch and dinner carrying a
large silver box for cigars, choosing the right one and cutting and lighting it for his master with the hand of an expert.

It is difficult to describe my astonishment when, one morning, I
surprised my Englishman and Frederic walking in the corridor, engaged
in a lively conversation. My friend called me.

"Arthur, this is Mr. John Watson, and you'll be interested to hear
that he knew, intimately, Oscar Wilde. Isn't that fascinating?"

Aha! I said it almost aloud! The image of the exalted son of proud
Albion fell crashing to the floor . . . and Mr. Watson dropped his monocle
and started to tell us, with a growing volubility, stories about his friend
Wilde.

"I can show you a book by him where he mentions me," he said, "and
I wanted to meet you." He turned to Frederic. "I overheard you the
other day when you spoke of Oscar with such an enthusiasm!"

The relationship between these two became quite obvious to me,
but I was delighted to note that Watson had a twinkle in his eye and a
real sense of humor. From that day on, he became one of us. He kept
his mask on for the general public but opened up completely with the
Harman family and me. One night, late, when we were quite alone in
Frederic's room, he felt an urge to tell us the truth about his life.

He spoke French with a charming accent. "My 'trade,'" he began,
"is cheating at cards!" We laughed, taking it for a joke. "No, no, don't
laugh," he continued, "I am in earnest. I know you won't give me away,
so I can tell you my story." And he told us the true story of a professional cardsharp. "I have two partners; one is a German Baron, the other
an Englishman with a good name, but we pretend not to know each
other. We meet at the right hotels, in the right season, and try to get
some exact information about the financial situation of the people who
interest us, and then we establish our working plan. Of course, as you
saw for yourselves, we *must* impress the hotel guests; it makes it easier
to approach our would-be victims; their snobbery makes them often forget their losses." He smiled: "The actual method of cheating I cannot
reveal to you. That I must keep secret."

We sat still, half amused, half appalled by this candid admission of a criminal offense! But he told it in such a casual and ironic manner that we began to doubt if the story was true; it sounded too absurd! At the same time, we felt flattered by his confidence in us. And so, whether or not he was a swindler, we liked our fake English lord.

Oscar Wilde, whose works and colorful life were much discussed in those days, was often the topic of our conversations. On one occasion, when we were discussing his plays, I gave a vivid description, acting it all out, of *Salomé*, the drama he had written for Sarah Bernhardt, which I had seen at a private showing in Berlin, produced in German by Max Reinhardt.

I must have been at my best that day; my imitations of the gestures and voices of the actors and my dramatic account of the feverish progress of some scenes impressed my small audience to such a degree that Mr. Watson, forgetting his usual calm composure, cried ecstatically: "Why don't we perform it here?" We looked at him as if he had proposed to jump the balustrade. "Don't make those silly faces," he persisted, unperturbed. "It is perfectly feasible. We have a stage here, and we must all take part. In life, you are pretty good actors," he added, smiling maliciously. He was right; on the ground floor of the hotel we had a ballroom with a small stage used for dancing on Saturdays; it was closed on weekdays.

The whole thing seemed crazy, but just because it was crazy, we liked it.

In planning this exotic venture, we forgot the most important question: which language to use! The play was written in French for Sarah Bernhardt, who never played it, so it was first published in its English version. Being the instigator of the whole affair, I insisted on German. "I remember the Berlin performance in every detail," I said, "and I can stage it exactly as I saw it," I added proudly, and I won my point.

Of course, this left out lovely Amelia Luro and her suite; they had no notion of the language, and the Baroness and her friends had refused from the beginning to take any part in the venture. Watson spoke a little German, but his English accent was so unbearable that we had to discard him. So, finally, after all the eliminations and considerations, we came to the conclusion that the principal roles must go to our Polish quartet.

A Lausanne bookshop had three German copies of the play. I read it to the cast, and the distribution of the parts was quickly decided. Pani Magdalena was Herodias, I was to play Herod, Basia was, of course, to be Salomé, and Frederic chose Narraboth, a short and minor role. The problem arose as to who would play Jokanaan (John the Baptist). Watson found a candidate, a young boy he had met in Territet, who gave his name as Germain d'Esparbès. I still doubt it was his real name; I presume he borrowed it from a French poet who was quite well known then. The young man was about twenty, tall, extremely handsome, and Watson's penchant for him was obvious. I must add, the boy was intelligent and showed a marked enthusiasm for the role. And so, we had no choice but to accept him. We wrote out our respective lines and started right away rehearsing. After a few days of ardent work, the thing began to take shape, and, to our great satisfaction, it showed promise of a real, almost professional job.

The whole hotel, from the management to the last guest, jocularly skeptical at first, became more and more interested in the affair. The director, a Swiss with a passion for the theater, suggested we should charge admission and distribute the proceeds among the employees of the hotel. If we agreed, he would help us secure a set for the stage, lend us some German-speaking waiters for the short appearance of the Jews and Nazarenes in the play, and some stage hands and the musicians for Salomé's dance of the seven veils. His proposition was so attractive that we did not hesitate. We decided to put on the show in a fortnight; the director announced it in the Montreux and Lausanne papers and got busy with his part of the production. I remembered an old Jewish tune, wrote it down for Frederic, who arranged it for the six hotel musicians, and that was to be Salomé's dance. Basia tried a few steps for the seven veils and did very well—she had the right temperament for the part. Even the German-speaking waiters were delighted to participate in the play, and learned their lines and gestures under my direction. The whole thing was staged by me, as I had seen it in Berlin.

Frederic and I decided to start the show with a performance of *L'Apprenti sorcier* of Dukas arranged for four hands, which we played brilliantly; it would put our audience into a receptive mood.

The great evening finally arrived. To our amazement, a lot of people arrived from Lausanne, Montreux, Territet, Clarens, and other places in the neighborhood, and the hall was packed! The Dukas received an ovation, and the play was a real success. While doing my role of Herod, I had the strange sensation that I was acting out my own life story, and Herod's impassioned wooing of Salomé brought back for that evening my old love for Basia and at the same time a pang of hatred for Herodias —Magdalena—her mother; it was a curious coincidence, a quite disquieting one.

After the show, all of us and the crew were offered a gay supper by the very happy hotel director. A nice couple who had come from Lausanne to see the play praised our performance but were especially impressed by the piano duet. The man introduced himself as a Colonel Clayton, an Englishman and personal aide-de-camp of the Duke of Connaught, King Edward VII's brother. His wife was French, a Baroness de Fouquières, a very charming lady. They invited me to come to London for a few days, stay with them, and play at a great reception they were giving in honor of the Duke and his daughter, Princess Patricia. I was to receive a fee and traveling expenses. The offer was extremely attractive, a fine opportunity to see London and meet "high society," so I accepted gladly, agreeing to spend a week in November at their house there.

Our lively and adventurous summer in Caux came to an end. We left for Paris via Geneva, where we stayed for two days, and although I liked the city very much, I was not as overwhelmed by it as Paderewski had promised. From Paris, Frederic and his mother took the train for Poland. Basia remained in town, and I returned to my quarters at rue Cardinet and began to prepare the programs for my American tour.

The weather before my trip to London was rainy and depressing, but I managed to see one or two good plays and hear some concerts. I recall also a rather disagreeable incident during that time. The Russian composer Scriabin, whose piano pieces I knew well, arrived in Paris for a concert of his own compositions. Monsieur Astruc was charged to organize it in a grand manner. Nikisch was to conduct the *Poème d'extase*, another symphonic work, and a piano concerto with the composer as soloist. "This young man is one of your greatest admirers," said Astruc, introducing me to the Russian master, who spoke little French and was therefore delighted to find an interpreter and admirer in France, where he was still unknown. "Come and have a cup of tea with me," he said amiably, and we went to the nearby Café de la Paix and ordered some tea and cakes. Scriabin was short and slender, with wavy dark blond hair, a carefully trimmed pointed beard not unlike Nikisch's, and cold brown eyes which seemed to ignore everything around him.

"Who is your favorite composer?" he asked with the condescending smile of the great master who knows the answer. When I answered without hesitation, "Brahms," he banged his fist on the table. "What, what?" he screamed. "How can you like this terrible composer and me at the same time? When I was your age I was a Chopinist, later I became a Wagnerite, but now I can only be a Scriabinist!" And, quite enraged, he took his hat and ran out of the café, leaving me stunned by this scene and with the bill to pay.

Later at his concert I had a little revenge for his outburst. The *Poème d'extase* was received with boos and shouts of disgust by the audience. I saw Dukas, Bruneau, and Fauré climbing up on their seats and whistling into their latchkeys with gusto. But I, on the contrary, admit that I was impressed by the work, and some parts of it pleased me immensely. A few years later, in Moscow, the conductor Koussevitzky took me for a visit to Scriabin, whose compositions I was then playing at my concerts. This time he received me very politely, offered me some tea again, and treated me to an hour-long detailed description of his latest work, called *Mystère*, designed to be played in a specially built temple! He was a bit strange, Scriabin, but I still have a great admiration for his music.

31

I left for London with a great feeling of insecurity. In the continental countries I had known until then, people were in awe of the English, of their way of living, their language, their habits, their clothes, their table manners.

Queen Victoria, with her sixty-four-year reign over one-fifth of our planet, had attempted to impose strict rules of behavior on her subjects. Her heir, King Edward VII, who had been known only as the Prince of Wales, had the reputation of a *bon vivant*, a lover of women and of wine and gambling, in spite of the strong admonitions of his mother. I happened to arrive in London just at the beginning of the Edwardian era, so it was fascinating to watch its influence on English society.

The journey to London was most uncomfortable (it couldn't have been worse!). We had to sit in a smoky compartment for three hours until Calais, then cross the Channel on a small steamer, where we were crammed on a deck which smelled of the stale remains of seasickness, refurbished from time to time by new victims of the high waves. After one hour of this ordeal, landing in Dover completely exhausted, we had to stand in long queues for the examination of documents and to go through customs. Another hour and a half in an express train which shook us from our seats brought us finally to London. But my excitement at being in London for the first time made me instantly forget all these discomforts.

I followed the instructions in Mrs. Clayton's letter and took a two-wheeled carriage, called a hansom, with the driver sitting behind and above me. A little depressed by the dim, foggy streets, I rode to 78

Portland Place. There my hosts received me in a boudoir; Colonel Clayton was dressed up in tails, and his wife wore a rich evening gown.

"We have been invited to dine at Lord Morley's, and you are too. So change your clothes right away; we will leave soon and send the carriage back for you."

A severe-looking old butler in tails and black tie showed me the way to my room. Without a word he went to the bathroom and started my bath. While I was busy undressing, he emptied my bag and left the room, taking my evening clothes to press them. I was just beginning to enjoy the warm comfort of the bath when the man reappeared, in a state of alarm. "I can't find your top hat, sir . . . I looked for it everywhere, sir . . . can you tell me where you have left it?"

I became panic-stricken. I just did not possess any top hat, and he made me feel suddenly that a man without a top hat had no right to live! Fortunately I had the presence of mind to explain: "This is terrible. My man in Paris must have forgotten to pack it. I really don't know what to do. I can't very well go to a dinner without a top hat."

The butler said: "I'd better give you one of the Colonel's hats for tonight. I hope it will fit you." Well, it did not fit me at all; my head is very large, and I can never find ready-made hats of my size. However, I took Colonel Clayton's hat and kept it in my hand, pretending it was too hot to put it on.

It was a small dinner at Lord Morley's. We were not more than ten, but everything was very formal. We had to enter the dining room in pairs, offering our arms to the ladies. Once we were seated, the conversation was rather subdued, great attention being given to the food, which was not very tasty but was served with absolute perfection.

While we were having dessert, the host rose and said solemnly, holding his glass of champagne: "Ladies and gentlemen, I give you the King." We all got up and sipped our wine in silence. After dinner, Lady Morley led the ladies back to the drawing room, and the men remained at the dinner table, where coffee and port were served. And now, with the help of a few glasses, the conversation became loud and lively, some good jokes provoked explosions of laughter, and our host had a hard time, after a long half-hour, making us join the ladies. I felt terribly out of place at that party; nobody seemed to know that I was a musician —I had been invited only as the house guest of the Claytons. Nevertheless, I enjoyed my acquaintance with what seemed the typical London society of that time.

My hosts were most hospitable. They made me visit the National Gallery and the British Museum, which pleased me immensely, and more so because both are easily accessible; you can see their masterpieces right away, like the famous Elgin marbles taken from the Parthenon, or the Venus of Velázquez, the only nude he ever painted, at the Gallery, whereas my visits to the Louvre used to exhaust me, what with the vastness of the rooms, the climbing of steep stairs, the bad lighting, and the difficult disposition of its masterworks; one had to walk miles to see the Venus de Milo and the Mona Lisa on the same visit.

The great party at the Claytons took place two days later. The whole house had been turned upside down, large pieces of furniture removed, others brought in, and the main drawing room was transformed into a concert hall, with beautiful flower arrangements adorning every corner. We lunched in town so as not to disturb the preparations for dinner.

"Let us have some lobsters at Scott's," said Colonel Clayton. Scott's was the name of a famous restaurant on Piccadilly Circus, the only place where you could find fresh lobsters with claws larger than tails.

That evening, all dressed up, the three of us waited for the dinner guests in the lower drawing room, where drinks were set up. At eight sharp, punctual to the minute, the distinguished gathering assembled. The Duke of Connaught, accompanied by his son, Prince Arthur, and his daughter, Princess Patricia, were the last to arrive, by protocol, I suppose. To my great satisfaction, there was less formality in the proceedings than at Lord Morley's. The Claytons introduced me to everybody, making nice remarks about my talent, and I heard, in response, some intelligent comments on musical matters. When the butler announced that dinner was served, the Duke offered his arm to Mrs. Clayton, and Colonel Clayton escorted the Princess, but the rest of us went in without ceremony. I was seated on the other side of the Princess, both an honor and a pleasure, because she was charming and beautiful, a tall brunette with a perfectly shaped head and black, intelligent eyes. She treated me like a grownup, was interested in my impressions of London, inquired about life in Paris, and at the end of the dinner we were on friendly terms. The other guests, I found out later, belonged to the intelligentsia of high society; they were interested in the arts and literature, and were seen frequently at concerts and serious plays.

After the excellent dinner (our hostess was French!), toasts were dispensed with and the men remained for drinks and coffee for only a short time, then we went up to the big room for the concert. New guests kept arriving, and soon both rooms on the first floor were filled with people.

I have forgotten the program I played, but I do remember the last two pieces: "Isolde's Love Death" from Wagner's *Tristan*, arranged by Liszt, and the famous "Ride of the Valkyries" in my own arrangement.

Both were big successes, as Wagner was much in vogue at that time. The Duke and his daughter were particularly pleased; they knew this music well, and the rest of my audience behaved as warmly as a similar audience in Poland had.

A lavishly laid-out buffet supper was served after the music, and the last guests left late at night.

"Vous avez été splendide," exclaimed my charming French hostess, kissing me, and her husband shook my hands with obvious satisfaction. I should mention that all through that visit I talked French, my English still being poor, but it actually turned to my advantage because I held the upper hand in my conversations with the English.

The last four days were spent most agreeably. The Claytons took me by train for a weekend in the country with Lord Burnham, the owner of the *Daily Telegraph*, the important daily newspaper. He was a stocky, strong man in his sixties, completely bald, with a big, round nose and very red cheeks, probably from living outdoors so much. We were received by him and his large family with loud greetings. And I had thought the English were cold and reserved! When I expressed my astonishment to Mrs. Clayton, she laughed. "My dear," she said, "Lord Burnham is a Jew. We have quite a few Jews in England who, when they succeed in their respective careers, receive titles and honors. Queen Victoria gave her favorite prime minister, Benjamin Disraeli, the title of Earl of Beaconsfield." My racial pride was much gratified by this information. The weekend was gay and lively. After dinner I played first some serious music, and later I made the young people dance. We also improvised some games and stayed up until long after midnight.

The next morning we returned to town for my last day in London. My hosts gave me a warm farewell and then took me to Victoria Station. Mrs. Clayton gave me a pair of beautiful cuff links made of white enamel on gold, with a small diamond in the center, surrounded by tiny rubies on one side and emeralds on the other. I was delighted with my visit, but a little disappointed at not having met any English musicians. The world of the Claytons was strictly aristocratic.

I reached Paris, this time less tired by the intricacies of the journey, and in the proud mood of one on intimate terms with English royalty, aristocracy, and plutocracy! On my way home I was struck by the contrast of the short, fat, bearded aspect of Frenchmen. . . .

Cheered by the welcome my friends at the pension gave me and by the fine chocolate ice cream for dessert, I decided to go out on a spree. "If you want to have a good time, go to the Folies-Bergère," said one of the Scandinavian students. "It's the best show in town." I believed him and, alas, followed his advice. The place was sold out; there was standing room only, which I took eagerly.

The Folies-Bergère with its revue, *à grand spectacle*, as they called it, was in 1905 at the peak of its fame. A tourist with a little ambition felt dishonored if he missed seeing it. But I must confess *"le grand spectacle"* disappointed me. The main attraction consisted of a dozen or so half-naked girls descending a staircase in a slow procession; some of them exhibited bare bosoms, but they had to stand still like statues, so, after a while, one stopped looking at them. The other girls, adorned with strange headgears supposed to illustrate topics currently in the news, wore inscriptions like: "I am the Panama Canal," or "I am the Senate," or "I am the Slaughterhouse"; they paraded without rhythm or grace, keeping a stereotyped grin on their faces. To make things worse, a *compère* and a *commère*—the French kind of M.C.'s—were constantly around to explain the nonsensical procedures in song, talk, and gestures. As a much needed relief there were some first-class vaudeville numbers.

I, for one, was more fascinated by what was going on in the hall than on the stage. The standing room was quite different from what I expected it to be; it was called *le promenoir*, and it was actually used for promenading. But the place seemed to be reserved for men, many of whom wore evening clothes and silk hats, and for prostitutes in search of clients. The *promenoir* was connected with a large foyer, a sort of entrance hall, where, during intermission, you could see an Oriental belly dancer, buy obscene postcards or funny gadgets, and sip refreshments at small tables. A long bar where drinks were served by pretty girls was the place where the prostitutes and the promenaders made their arrangements. There is a beautiful picture by Renoir, *Le Bar des Folies-Bergère*, showing a scene of this kind.

I was watching it all with the ardent curiosity of my eighteen years when a woman, a gorgeous blonde, stopped me. "Tu viens, mon chéri?" she whispered. "I live close by, we can spend a moment together, you won't regret it . . . I'll give you much pleasure." Her talk and her voice excited me so that I couldn't resist. Without further words, she took my arm and led me out of the theater across the street to a small hotel. A moment later we were shown into a room with an adjoining alcove which was occupied by a huge bed. A waiter brought a bucket with ice and two bottles of champagne, which he uncorked at the same time. He was followed by a tall woman with black hair, who was introduced to me by my blonde as "my best friend," and the two of them started to pour out the wine into three big glasses. We finished the two bottles in less than half an hour. By that time I was in a state of complete surrender.

They made me take my clothes off, put me on the bed, and began working on me in the most expert and rapid way. I felt as though I were in a clinic, subjected to a ticklish and tantalizing operation performed by two vicious nurses. When their job was finished they prepared to leave and asked for their money; at the same time the waiter brought the bill for the room and the champagne. All in all, it amounted to over two hundred francs. And I felt rich, poor fool that I was, with eighty francs in my possession. I was terrified, learning they might arrest me or beat me up. But, suddenly, I remembered the precious cuff links, still in my pocket.

"I would like to talk to the manager," I said to the waiter. After a while a fat man came up, a stern expression on his face. "What can I do for you?" he asked. "I forgot to take more money with me," I said, trying to be casual. "These ladies brought me here a little by surprise," I said with a sickly smile. "But fortunately I still have these cuff links which I bought this morning in London. Give me a hundred and fifty francs and you can keep them until tomorrow; I shall come to redeem them in the morning."

The man was impressed by my manner and by the beauty of the stones. "All right, here is the money, but don't fail to show up tomorrow," he said. I sighed with relief. After paying the hotel and the women —not without a struggle, they wanted *all* my money—I swore never to get into such a mess again! It took me three weeks, on the day before leaving for America, to get the money to recover the cuff links. The fat man smiled cynically: "Monsieur, as you did not come the next morning, I sold them at a loss!"

32

A few days before New Year's I embarked on *La Touraine*, a French transatlantic ship. Monsieur Astruc gave me a bag outfitted with toilet articles and such, as well as some extra money for tips on the boat, which were important, he said. At the Gare St.-Lazare, he wished me success and gave me instructions on how to behave in case of danger, and how to fight seasickness. His talk did not cheer me up; I was scared of my first experience at sea, and when we reached Le Havre on a gloomy and foggy night my spirits fell very low.

La Touraine, compared to modern luxurious liners, looked like a modest riverboat. The entrance lobby served for all purposes—-as a salon, with a Pleyel grand in a corner, as a lounge for the passengers to get together in at tea time and after dinner, and also as a reading and writing room. In the center, there was a large staircase, leading to the cabin decks and to the dining room.

My cabin was quite Spartan: two cots, one above the other, occupied half of it; no bathroom, of course—such a thing was unheard of in France in those times—only a small basin where a trickle of cold water came out when one pushed a button and held on to it. I was gratified, but not consoled, to learn that there were no better cabins on the boat except two on the upper deck. And I had another satisfaction—I had my cabin all to myself. Fortunately, I was asleep before we sailed out into the open sea, so I missed the first contact with it. The next morning I decided to stay in bed until lunch. Shaving and dressing in the tiny room was a major problem because one had to ring for hot water and it took time to get it. However, I managed to go down to the dining room, a not very engaging place; it was smelly and not too clean. I was one of the few passengers who had made it, and felt proud to be a good sailor. But that didn't last. The ship began to dance in the most alarming way, the terrifying noise of the waves battering it from all sides. We ran to our cabins and went to bed. This marked only the beginning of one of the worst crossings in years; we were ten days at sea before we reached New York.

After two long, sleepless nights during which I was often seasick, I couldn't stand the stale air of the cabin any more. After dressing summarily, I struggled up to the lounge and tried to go out for a walk on the promenade deck, but found all the doors locked. It was dangerous to go out, I was told. So, instead, I decided to try to play the piano. The hardest thing, I found, was to stick to the seat, but the playing went quite well. After a while I made a brilliant discovery: when playing a piece which had a strong rhythm I would breathe with that very rhythm and not with the heavy, irregular up-and-down movements of the ship, which make one so promptly seasick. As further experiments confirmed my theory, I decided not to leave the lounge, so as to have the piano within reach in case of emergency. A kind steward agreed to bring me food; he liked music. To my amused surprise, some of the passengers, looking like hospital patients after an operation, started to ascend and settled themselves in low chairs to listen to the music. They declared that even listening to it made them feel better.

On New Year's Eve most of the passengers made a big effort to
dress and come down to dinner. The captain invited me to his table with
some "notables." Four or five of them were important French businessmen. The only lady present was an American, and we were later joined
by a pale young Frenchman, Count Armand de Gontaut-Biron.

The menu de luxe for the occasion was lost on us, our stomachs re-
belling at the fresh foie gras and the duck à l'orange. I could barely
swallow the consommé and some fruit, but later, in the lounge, where
the presence of the piano restored me, I did indulge in some champagne
to toast the New Year and my debut in America. By general request,
I gave a real concert, during which a comic incident occurred. At one
moment, a sudden jerk of the boat made me lose my balance and I fell to
the floor, although I was not hurt. When I scrambled to my feet again,
the captain gave orders to two sailors to attach my legs with leather
straps to the stool, which was secured by hooks to the floor; so was
the piano. I continued my concert without further incident, and enjoyed
the fact of being "chained to my art."

"Bravo, bravo," shouted Count Gontaut-Biron, when I had finished,
his cheers being the loudest of all present.

"Will you join me for another glass of champagne?" he invited me
in the most gracious manner. "I adore music above all, and you play
after my heart."

He was a young man of medium height, about twenty-five years
old, with light blond hair parted in the middle. A thick mustache à la
gauloise covered a thin, curvy mouth, his nose had a fine longish shape,
and the very blue eyes and small ears lent to these fine features an air of
great distinction. He was the image of the French aristocrat of the
eighteenth century.

That night, on the rolling boat, we became friends. We invited the
lonely American lady to join us, drank a whole bottle of champagne,
and stayed into the early hours of the morning. The lady, an attractive,
middle-aged woman, was the widow of a wealthy man from Los Angeles.
She raved about that small city, of which we had never heard, claiming
it was a paradise and had the friendliest people and the finest flowers
and fruit in the world. And yet, she said angrily, Americans ignore it,
flocking instead to that vicious, Godforsaken, wide-open city of San
Francisco, which should be razed to the ground. To both of us, it all
sounded like fiction, and everything she talked about seemed far away
and unrealistic. Anyhow, she invited me warmly to visit her and make
music with her—she said she played the harp!

From that night on, the three of us spent all our time together.
When after five days the high waves subsided a little, we moved around

with more freedom and our appetite for real food returned. One evening, the businessmen from the captain's dinner invited us to join them in a game of poker. I was usually rather good at card games, but I didn't know this one.

"There is nothing difficult about it," said Gontaut, who was eager to play. "You will learn in a few minutes." As a matter of fact, poker is easy to understand, but it takes time and talent to play it well. Still, the game fascinated me. In spite of the very low stakes we were playing for, I was a loser every night. I hadn't learned to conceal my joy when I held a big hand, with the result that they stopped betting against me, while I was an easy prey to their bluffs and better hands.

"Arthur, put on your poker face!" Armand tried to teach me, but it was too late, I had lost all the money I had with me, including the sum Astruc had given me for tips, and I was out of the game. Fortunately, we were due to arrive in New York the next morning.

My steward promised to wake me up in time to see the Statue of Liberty, France's gift to America, but I was up and dressed hours before; it was too exciting to land in the New World! When we passed the statue I was impressed by its colossal height and, poor Polish Jew under the hard Russian rule that I was, I was moved by its symbol of liberty.

Before we were allowed to touch the quay, a small boat brought a doctor and the immigration officials on board, and at the same time a swarm of newspaper reporters invaded our ship, trying to interview many passengers about our delay; they had had reports of the difficulties of the crossing, of some damage to the boat, and of the hardships we had endured. Finally, when all this was over, we could land. As I put my feet to the ground, a tall man came up to me and introduced himself as a Mr. Ulrich, the manager of my tour on behalf of the Knabe firm.

"Dear Mr. Ulrich," I said with an embarrassed smile, "please help me out. I have lost all my money at poker and need some change for tipping the various services on board; ten dollars will do."

"Well, well, young man," he laughed, handing out the money, "I hope you play the piano with more success than poker."

I ran back to the boat, finished my business in a hurry, and returned to Mr. Ulrich. This time he was accompanied by a few photographers and newspapermen who subjected me to rapid questions which I had some difficulty understanding.

"Who were the poker players? How does it feel to be chained to a piano? You were the hero on board, weren't you? You are the son of Anton Rubinstein? Do you break strings at every concert? Aren't you a pupil of Paderewski?"

They didn't wait for my answers. Finally, Armand came to my

rescue, and I introduced him to my new manager. The reporters became excited: "Are you a *real* Count? Have you come to America to
marry an heiress? Do you sometimes wear a crown?" and other questions of that kind. Gontaut had experience; he got rid of them quickly.

"Where are you going to stay, Arthur?" he asked me, but Mr. Ulrich answered: "I've reserved a nice room with a piano at the Netherland
hotel." Armand laughed scornfully: "This is impossible—you can't stay
at such a place. The only hotel for you in this city is the Waldorf-Astoria." "But it is very expensive," said Ulrich. "All really good things
are expensive," replied Armand, philosophically. And so I decided on the
Waldorf-Astoria. A "four-wheeler," as they called it, driven by a horse,
took Ulrich and me to the huge, red-colored building on Fifth Avenue
and Thirty-fourth Street. After my distaste for the slummy and shabby
streets of the neighborhood on our way from the dock, I was doubly
impressed by the dimensions of this hotel. Mr. Ulrich smiled: "Wait until
you see the Flatiron Building; it is the tallest *apartment house* in the world
—twenty-one stories high."

We walked up to the reception desk and asked for a room and
bath. The room had to be large enough to accommodate a piano.

"To have a piano in a bedroom is against the rules of the house,"
said the receptionist, "but we can give you a small suite, where you
could use your instrument. The charge is twenty-one dollars per day."
Ulrich was ready to leave. "This is an exorbitant price," he whispered.
"You can have a nice room at the Netherland for only four dollars a
day!"

"No," I answered, "I like it here. I will take the suite, never mind
the price!" There was finality in my voice. He gave up, and
after I had signed the register, we were taken up to my rooms. And what
comfortable rooms they were! A charming sitting room with a couch and
easy chairs, a writing table, a small bar in a corner, and some books on a
shelf. The bedroom was so cozy I could have stayed there for weeks
without leaving it. Each room had a telephone. But what enchanted me
most was the bathroom, the first bathroom I had ever had all to myself.
It was perfect, with ten snow-white towels hanging on neat little racks,
and a bathtub with fragrant soap and a bottle of bath crystals for my
use, and there was even a tap for ice water. Mr. Ulrich laughed at my
ecstasy: "In the United States every hotel has private bathrooms," he
said. I was ashamed to admit that Europe was so far behind in matters
of hygiene. After washing up, we went down for tea and talked about
my tour.

My debut was set for two days later, as a soloist with the Philadelphia Orchestra at Carnegie Hall. They selected for it the G minor

Concerto of Saint-Saëns, my old war horse, and the same concert was to be repeated in Baltimore, Philadelphia, and Washington. The other orchestral engagements were booked for Chicago, Minneapolis, and Cincinnati, and the rest of the tour would be only recitals.

Well, this looked like a real grand concert tour, my first one; and my heart beat with hope and excitement. Back in my room the telephone was ringing and it was Armand de Gontaut inviting me to dine with him in the Grill Room of the hotel. At dinner he told me everything about his own life, and his story fascinated me. His was the aristocratic world of leisure which I thought had disappeared after the French Revolution, a society in which the young men still did not take up a profession other than the military, and their main occupations were riding, dancing, fencing, and *faire la noce*, the French definition of the gay night life. Armand had lost his mother at an early age, and after his military service he shared with his older brother Louis an apartment in Paris where they lived exactly the life he had described. "My brother married a few months ago," he continued, "and I was bored living alone, so I took a job in secret. I work now as an agent for the French automobile firm of Panhard-Levassor, and this is my second trip to America for them. But make no mistake about it—I am not a regular salesman. They have here another man for that. My work is simply to praise their automobiles discreetly at parties in the houses of wealthy New York society to which I have an easy access, thanks to my name." He laughed. "And they all think that I am hunting for a millionairess!" His frankness charmed me; I had been frank with him, too, so this exchange sealed our friendship, and we decided to spend as much time as possible in each other's company.

Next morning, awakening late, I wanted to order my breakfast but couldn't find the button to ring for service. I searched in vain in the corridor for a waiter or a maid, and a kind neighbor, who saw my distress, gave me the needed information.

"You can get service only by telephone," he said. "Call 'room service' for food, 'valet' for your clothes and laundry, and the 'operator' for anything else."

This sounded efficient, but in my case it became a major handicap; I was used to a personal contact with servants to whom you could explain what you wanted by words or by gestures, whereas by telephone it was difficult to make myself clear and to understand the American way of speaking English.

I had another bad surprise that morning; my shoes, which I put out the night before for cleaning, as one does in Europe, were left there

without being touched. You had to send them down to the barbershop
and wait for hours to get them back. But these were minor flaws in the
American hotel system.

My breakfast, a very tasty one, was served after a hard struggle with
the telephone. The "newsstand," too, answered my call for the morning
papers. I was curious to see if they had mentioned anything about me.
And bang! there it was. A large photo of me at the dock, and big headlines, on the front page of one paper: "Rubinstein, the young Polish
pianist, acclaimed as a hero by passengers of *La Touraine*," followed by a
story of my being chained (*sic*) to the piano, playing a whole night to
calm the panic-stricken passengers of the battered and damaged French
liner. Another paper, also on the front page, published to my amazement
a completely untrue account of our innocent poker game: "Young pianist
victim of cardsharps! French gamblers took all his money at marathon
poker game." These were more or less the words which I remember, and
I was really shocked by the sensationalism of the American press. Armand
called me up; he was alarmed, too, having been one of the players. I
promised to ask Mr. Ulrich to protest.

That morning there was another shock in store for me—my encounter with the Knabe pianos. Three concert grands were placed on
the stage of Carnegie Hall for my choice, and all three proved to be
unsatisfactory; their tone was muffled, the action was hard, and the bass
was weak. As unhappy as I was, I had to pretend that I was pleased. There
was nothing else to do, so I picked the one which had a little better tone
and implored the tuner to ease up the action and to make it more brilliant.
It had to be ready for the rehearsal and the concert, the very next day.

I returned to the hotel a little depressed, but found a Knabe practice
piano in my room which sounded better than the concert grand, so I put
my hope in the hands of the tuner!

Armand had come up to fetch me for lunch when the telephone rang.
"Three gentlemen want to see you," announced the operator, and when I
asked who they were, he answered: "You met them on the boat and they
insist on seeing you." I was scared, and wanted to refuse to see them, but
Armand said, "Let them come up. I shall take care of them." Our French
poker players, murder in their eyes, came into the room.

"Vous êtes un joli coco!" the youngest of them shouted. "You made
us look publicly like crooks, and all I won was ten miserable francs and
my friends won not much more! We are going to sue you for slander!"

I was terrified. I didn't know what to say, but Armand again rescued
me.

"Messieurs, don't forget that I, too, am a victim of this slander, but
I happened to be present when my young friend asked his manager for

money because he had lost it at poker. The manager thought it was a good story for the press, but he forgot to ask us how high the stakes were, and that caused all the trouble. The papers will publish an apology tomorrow, so don't worry, sit down and have a drink." The men calmed down immediately, and we all enjoyed our apéritifs.

After lunch I practiced my concerto the whole afternoon; the Knabe pianos left me with a sense of insecurity which I tried to overcome. Toward evening, a strange visitor interrupted my work. He was my first cousin, Adolf Neumark, and I remembered him well from my childhood in Lodz. He had been expelled from the Russian school, so his father decided to send him out into the New World to make his own way in life. We had never heard of him since, so here in New York, far away from home, I received him with affection. He was impressed by the newspaper reports, felt sorry that I lost so much money to "these dangerous cardsharps," and we laughed a lot when I told him the truth.

A funny incident occurred. When I asked him to go down with me to the Grill Room for dinner, he answered rather nervously, "Can't we go somewhere else?" "No," I said, "I don't want to go out tonight because of my rehearsal and concert tomorrow, and, besides, I like the food here." "But I cannot go there with you," he insisted. "Why? Do you owe them money?" "No," and he blushed. "But you see, I was employed there as a waiter quite recently." This was something new to me—my first notion of the real democracy! I was happy! In my heart I had never considered anybody's condition or occupation as lower than my own, and I have never treated anybody condescendingly, not even a talentless pianist. I took my cousin Neumark's arm and we went down proudly to the Grill Room, where his ex-colleagues served him without any sign of astonishment. My first day in New York ended in a nice way.

33

Anxious to see what the tuner had done to my piano, I arrived at Carnegie Hall half an hour before rehearsal time, but I found many of the orchestra's musicians already on the stage enjoying the familiar cacophony of tuning and trying out their respective instruments. At ten sharp, the conductor, Mr. Fritz Scheel, appeared and, without losing a second, began to rehearse the overture of Weber which was to precede my concerto.

Scheel was the typical German musician, well trained, solid, but cold. The orchestra played splendidly—it would have been a dream, I thought, to hear it under a Nikisch! When my turn came, Mr. Scheel asked me right away, "Are you related to the 'great' Rubinstein?" I had heard this question often before, but it irritated me this time more than ever. The piano sounded better, to my great relief; the tuner had kept his promise, so I played my long solo introduction to the concerto better than I had feared I would; after a few minutes I had the orchestra on my side. The rehearsal went very well. Mr. Scheel was efficient and indifferent, though my dynamic tempo in the last movement did stir up some reaction in him. I returned to the hotel in good spirits and spent the rest of the day in anticipation. In the evening, well ahead of time, Mr. Ulrich came to take me to the concert.

"The hall is well filled," he said with satisfaction, "and William Knabe and his brother Ernest and their wives have arrived from Baltimore and invite you for supper after the concert." I had sat barely twenty minutes in the artists' room—the overture was short—when they called me to go up on the stage. The well-lit hall, filled with people, looked twice as big as in the morning. My appearance was greeted with a warm applause. As I made my bows I became aware of a gift which served me well through my entire concert career: the bigger the hall, the larger the audience, the more confidence and self-control I felt, and I had none of the paralyzing stage fright which afflicts so many of the best concert performers. And so I attacked my concerto with a tremendous impact. The public applauded each movement, and at the end of the brilliant finale I received a roaring ovation. I brought the conductor out, twice, to acknowledge the applause, and shook hands with the concertmaster, but the public would not give up and shouted "Bravo," and "More, more," called me back three or four times, and finally forced me to give an encore. I played the A flat Polonaise of Chopin with pride. The ovation doubled, and I had to add another piece before they calmed down. An anticlimax awaited me in the artists' room. "How dare you give encores!" Fritz Scheel screamed at me, foaming with rage. "You ruined my concert—I won't let you play again with my orchestra;" And he left the room, slamming the door behind him.

I was speechless. I hadn't known that encores were taboo at symphony concerts; in Europe they were generally accepted. Scheel's threat was a great blow; it killed the joy of my success. Suddenly the door opened, and a real crowd entered the room. Mr. Ulrich, beaming, shook my hand as if it were a pump, slapped me on the back, and shouted, "Great, you were great, you made it!" Then he introduced me to the two members of the Knabe family, who were very nice, and their wives; the two men gave me a hug, their wives kissed me. William, the elder brother, said cheerfully, "Take your time. After you have had a rest, we will take you to a good supper." At that moment Armand appeared, followed by some friends whom he introduced to me. I, in turn, introduced him to the Knabes. His title, as usual, produced a magic effect. They babbled, "Will you do us the honor and join us at supper, Count?" "Count, this is a real pleasure." It was as if they were trying to learn how to pronounce "Count," they used it so often. Armand, courteous as ever, kissed the hands of the ladies and accepted the invitation. He was determined anyway to spend the evening with me.

When I told Mr. Knabe and Mr. Ulrich about Mr. Scheel's outburst, they were indignant. "He is obliged to continue the concerts with you," said Mr. Knabe. "We paid for it." Vastly relieved, I started to sign cheerfully some autographs for the waiting crowd, while my party waited patiently. Finally we were able to leave. Three hansoms, the English-styled two-wheeled cabs, took us to Delmonico's, one of the two most fashionable supper places in New York then (the other one was Sherry's). The place was packed, but the Knabes had a table reserved. Both brothers were in their early thirties, tall and rather good-looking; their wives were young and pretty. And the four of them were gay! My success was toasted at every drink, but "the Count" remained the center of their attention. They invited him to come to their home town of Baltimore, where I had my next concert, and Armand promised to come. I was well pleased with my debut in America. The critics, next morning, expressed divided opinions about my performance; two reviews were enthusiastic, one augured a great future for me, another one praised my technique and brilliance but thought less of my musicianship, and one critic, a Mr. Krehbiel, did not like me at all. But the balance was in my favor.

And so, after a hearty breakfast, I decided to make a grand tour of the city. Frankly speaking, New York was an ugly town in those days. This long and narrow island, squeezed between two large rivers, was cut vertically by avenues and horizontally by streets which to my surprise bore numbers instead of names. The geometrical design was said to be practical, but for me it was monotonous. The majestic skyscrapers had not yet been built, and the only attraction the famous Flatiron Building had was that it had the shape of one. The best thoroughfares were Broadway and Fifth Avenue. The first one was the vital center of New York, a replica of the boulevards of Paris, and the latter had a certain "grand air," thanks to the many palatial structures of the rich, especially where it faced Central Park. The houses of the Vanderbilts, Morgans, Fricks, Astors, and others had some real architectural beauty. The side streets of the "distinguished" part of the city had been patterned after some London centers with the small, neat, and narrow private houses in even rows. The rest of the city had an air of negligence and poverty; the streets were dirty and smelly, filled with crowds of ill-dressed, sad-faced people who seemed to be constantly in a hurry. What I disliked most, from an aesthetic point of view, were the "ladders" which hung from balcony to balcony in front of most houses. Later, on one of my frequent returns to New York, I was shown some nicer aspects of the city, like Wall Street and its surroundings, the quaint old streets which had names, exotic Chinatown, and Riverside Drive.

Returning that evening from my exhausting sightseeing tour, I found messages and a letter from the Knabes inviting me, and "the Count," to their box at the Metropolitan Opera that night. Caruso was to be singing in Aïda. This was really exciting! I telephoned Armand to tell him the great news, but he knew it already and recommended that I dress in a hurry, put on tails, white tie, and silk hat; he would wait for me in the lobby.

The famous opera house looked from the outside like anything but a theater; you could walk by without noticing it. Inside, it was quite impressive, all in red and gold, which gave it a grand air. We sat in a first tier box on the famous "Diamond Horseshoe," a name describing its shape and the jewels worn by the boxholders.

I already loved Aïda, but I loved it much better after hearing Caruso. He had the most phenomenal tenor voice I have ever heard. It was very powerful and soft at the same time. Perfect breath control and beautiful phrasing showed he was a musician and not just a tenor, though; when he sang a tender aria, the sheer timbre of his voice brought tears to my eyes. Only Battistini's baritone and Chaliapin's basso and, later, Emmy Destinn's soprano had the same effect on me.

During intermission I was taken backstage to meet Caruso and Mr. Conried, the director of the Opera. The singer was from Naples, exuberant and cordial.

"Ah, bravo, bravo, I heard of your great success," he said, embracing me (probably he hadn't heard a thing about me, but I was flattered). In later years, thank God, I heard him often, and, a few times, we performed at the same concerts. Heinrich Conried, a German, received me in his office ceremoniously; he felt important and was pompous.

"Have you heard any good singers in Europe lately?" he asked me, pleased by my enthusiasm for Caruso.

"I know only one," I answered, "and he is a genius; the Russian basso

Feodor Chaliapin." The opera director laughed, a little derisively. "Mein junger Freund," he said in German, "I know he is good, but no basso can ever have a success in New York after Edouard de Reszke!" I didn't insist, and it did take years for Feodor to conquer America.

The Knabes, Armand, and I left by train for Baltimore early the next morning. I did a silly thing before leaving. I kept my expensive rooms for the three days I was absent, just because I was too lazy to pack and hated to see the piano removed. This lightheadedness was a vice which caused me no end of trouble.

Traveling south of New York was a complicated affair in 1906. You had to drive by horsecab to Twenty-third Street, and from there a ferry-boat took you slowly across the river to Jersey City, where a train waited to take you to Philadelphia, Baltimore, and Washington, and farther south. We settled in a Pullman car, a novelty for me; Europe did not have them yet. I liked the comfortable swivel chairs and the Negro attendant who brushed my shoes, coat, and hat.

The three concerts in the three above-mentioned cities where I played for three consecutive days went well, more or less as in New York, except that I gave no encores, of course. My relationship with Mr. Scheel became normal, if not friendly. The Knabe brothers gave a big party in their home town, to have their friends meet "the Count," and seemed pleased with my success. I continued my tour in company of the excellent tuner, George Hochman, who became a helpful and gay companion.

On my return to New York for my first recital, I found a letter from the Marquis Melchior de Polignac, a good friend of Armand's. He was the owner of the well-known champagne firm Pommery & Greno and had come to New York on business. This letter was very amusing. As a pretext for a simple invitation for lunch, he composed a long epistle in a poetic form, in which he mentioned Venus, Lucullus, and the Muses as inspirers of the party. The inclusion of these legendary personages meant in my prosaic translation simply that the food was going to be of the highest quality, that he would like me to play something, and that we would enjoy the company of some ladies of light morals. Armand, when I showed him the letter, agreed with me. "Polignac," he informed me, "is a passionate music lover, a gourmet, and an inveterate chaser of women."

The luncheon was given at the St. Regis hotel, in a private suite, and the guests were, besides Gontaut and me, three ladies, all three very attractive, and not too young, exactly as I expected. One of them, tall and blond, had a generous bust and a round, curved seat. She was my choice right away. The Marquis was a wonderful host, and the menu surpassed my highest expectations. We were served caviar in its original box and *canard au sang*. The salad, cheese, and dessert were chosen with care, and we drank the best-vintage Pommery during the whole meal. A culinary feast of this kind cannot fail to produce the desired effect. The wine untied our tongues, we talked loudly, all at the same time, laughed at the slightest provocation, and flirted with the ladies.

As for myself, I had my hand, whenever it was possible, on the thigh of the one to my right and tried to find out what kind of legs she had (the long skirts covered them in those days). The lady responded to my advances without false modesty. Coffee was served in the next room, where a table was laid out for a poker game. I remained for a moment with Dorothy—that was her first name—in the dining room and whispered excitedly, "When and where can I see you? You please me and I want you!" She smiled sweetly. "Here is my address. Come next Thursday at five o'clock," and kissed me furtively. Inventing some pretext, I excused myself from the game. My finances didn't allow me to play poker for the time being—particularly since the cost of the hotel had begun to weigh on me. To make things worse, Armand liked to bring some of his wealthy friends to my room, and I used to offer them drinks and play for them, too. The picture of the young, penniless pianist that I was, entertaining without remuneration millionaires like the Belmonts, Goulds, and Astors, amused me very much.

On the Thursday of my rendezvous, a few minutes before five, I drove to Dorothy's house, on Thirty-ninth Street, east. (I still remember her address.) My heart was beating with excitement. When I rang the bell, a butler opened the door, took my hat and coat, and asked me to go up to the first floor. I ran up, in hopes of finding Dorothy in a negligee lying on a couch or, better still, on a bed. So, imagine my open-mouthed stupor when I entered a room full of people and recognized among them some well-known ladies of the best New York society. It took me quite a while to compose myself and to be able to kiss the hand of the hostess in a natural way. She made the rounds of her guests with me, introducing me with style. Humiliated by the lesson she gave me, I made an effort at polite conversation, had a cup of tea, and was preparing to leave when she stopped me at the door. "You are not going to leave, are you? You must stay for dinner!" she decided, without waiting for an answer. In my bitter mood, I was anticipating a long, boring affair. Yet another surprise was in store for me . . . the guests began to trickle slowly out of the house, and I was the only one who stayed. Venus and Lucullus made their reappearance! We had a delightful dinner downstairs, Dorothy and I.

After we had had coffee and liqueurs in the salon, she dismissed the servants for the night, and when everything quieted down, we went up to her bedroom. Our "liaison" was short-lived. I was too seldom in New

York, but it remained in my memory as one of the highlights of my stay. I liked her best when, in the moments of ecstasy, her wide-open light blue eyes would start to squint. Mythology ascribes the same characteristic to Venus.

34

So far, things had gone smoothly and agreeably; the first week in and around New York had seemed promising, both artistically and personally. Now, I was facing the real start of my American tour, a tour de force in a way, as my contract called for forty concerts in less than three months, which meant one concert every second day. My manager, Mr. Ulrich, had some bad news for me: my two New York recitals were to take place in the afternoon in a theater that belonged to the Shubert brothers. A musical comedy was playing there with a famous comedian, Eddie Foy, as the star. Ulrich admitted that I would be the first artist ever to play under such conditions.

"Why make a scapegoat out of me?" I asked. Ulrich answered by giving me a lecture on the musical life in America.

"The main musical interest of this country," he said, "is concentrated in New York and especially in the Metropolitan Opera with its expensive singers and conductors. The other cities, with the exception of Boston, follow New York in all artistic matters. Publicity is the dominating factor in our concert life, and it creates, unfortunately, sensationalism rather than real love for music. As in your own case, pianists are brought to this country by the piano manufacturers only to help to promote their instruments. That explains our arrangement with the Shubert theaters. You see, it is very expensive to run concerts in our cities. The Shubert brothers have theaters all over the country and have agreed, on a percentage basis, to let you 'play their circuit,' as they call it, and to assume all the publicity for the tour."

Needless to say, I became depressed by this picture of music in America, and by the prospect of my "circuit." Ulrich noticed it and tried to console me: "Don't be sad," he said, "things are not as bad as they look. We have engagements for you with some fine orchestras in Chicago, Cincinnati, and Minneapolis and a recital in Boston in a real hall."

My first recital in New York at the Shubert Theater set the pattern for all the others to follow. At noon, while trying out my piano, I was surrounded by half-dressed chorus girls who formed a strange background for the Bach Toccata I was rehearsing; unaccustomed to classical music, they kept interrupting me with requests for popular tunes. Some of them were quite lovely, which added to my distraction.

Just as I feared, this theater was not fit for piano recitals, and my listeners were not musical. They applauded at wrong moments and were bored by long pieces; what they loved best were my short and effective encores. This time the critics were more severe. My loyal followers still praised my talent but found fault with this and that, imputing it to "my visible nervousness." Mr. Krehbiel condemned my performance mercilessly, betraying his obvious prejudice; he was to be for years my implacable enemy.

We took the train for Chicago, Hochman and I. It was the first time I had seen an American sleeping car—a novel experience. The chairs were transformed into beds, two chairs making a booth, a lower and an upper berth, as they called them. At the opposite ends of the car were the washrooms for men and women. I had an upper berth, and it was the most uncomfortable place to sleep in. Fully dressed, you were able to get into it only with the help of a ladder, and once settled, with a heavy darkgreen curtain drawn, you had to undress in a bowed sitting position; it was a truly acrobatic exploit. If, still half asleep, you happened to raise your head, you would receive a hard knock from the ceiling. Both sexes used the same car, so watching the ladies climbing up the ladders into their berths lent a certain piquancy to the scene.

As we arrived in Chicago just in time for my rehearsal, Hochman dropped me at Orchestra Hall and took our luggage to the hotel. "Hurry up, everybody is on the stage waiting for you," a house employee shouted, showing me the way. Without losing a second, just dropping my coat and hat on the floor, I struck the first octave of the Saint-Saëns Concerto, and we played the whole piece through in less than a half an hour, with no repeat, no stop. Mr. Frederick Stock, the young conductor, jumped down from the stand and kissed me, and the orchestra shouted "Bravo," a rare tribute at a rehearsal. What impressed them most was the sight of my undaunted energy after the exhausting journey. Nothing is more encouraging for me than the approval of my fellow musicians; my spirits rose.

Chicago had the reputation of being a windy city, and on this day it was bitterly cold. The snow-covered, slippery streets made walking a hazard, and the sharp, icy wind threatened to blow my head off. I had to give up the idea of exploring the city on foot, and I must confess, to my regret, that throughout my tour I had hardly a chance to see anything;

we were moving too rapidly from one city to the next, so, except for some special incidents, all I remember are the stations, hotels, and the halls where I played.

That night in Chicago, however, I wouldn't give up. I decided to enjoy my free evening and happy mood. "Let us take a cab and go to a burlesque theater," Hochman proposed. "You might like it, it is typically American." And I loved it. The burlesque shows were, in the old days, very different from what they are today. They offered a combination of vaudeville, comedy, and operetta with the emphasis on short sketches played by comedians who were often vulgar but always irresistibly funny. Ever since that night I have never missed a "burlesque" if I could help it; my favorites were the comedians Weber and Fields—their antics and their marvelous American slang made me fall off my chair with laughter.

The Chicago I knew in 1906 had another, very original attraction to offer. The whole block of South Michigan Avenue, the so-called red light district, was wide open to visitors. What made the place peculiar was the fact that each of the bordellos featured a different race. You had the choice of the houses with only Negro, Japanese, or Chinese girls, or of the more expensive ones with various European imports. It must have been a source of learning for students of ethnology, but Hochman and I became quickly tired of it. At every entrance door, a fat Negress would invite us inside a room where an old man played tunes on an upright piano. A moment later two or three girls, half-asleep and half-dressed, would come down and stare at us, waiting for the drinks we were supposed to order. We would visit these places as one visits a museum; we looked around without touching the objects on display.

All in all, I am grateful to Chicago. A young Swiss American, Rudolf Ganz, who was successful in America, had warm words of praise for me, and has befriended me ever since. My concert with the Theodore Thomas Orchestra under Frederick Stock was a big and solid success with both the public and the press. The "windy city" remains my faithful friend even as I write these lines.

Despite the strain and the rush of the tour, I enjoyed it more and more. The Shubert theaters in some cities had no shows at the time, so I had the exclusive use of them, and in contrast to New York, they were more open to concerts and the audiences more appreciative of music.

Some amusing, and some less amusing, incidents broke now and then the monotony of the tour. At a concert in Columbus, Ohio, I had just begun to play the first movement of a Beethoven sonata when the nail of my thumb, twisted between two white keys, ripped open. A gush of blood covered the whole keyboard, but I continued to play, ignoring the pain, completely involved in my work. Only when I had finished the movement did the pain become so acute that I had to leave the stage to have the finger bandaged. When I returned to continue the sonata on the freshly cleaned keyboard, my listeners burst into applause. They had been in doubt, when they saw the blood, whether I would be able to finish the concert. The papers, next morning, gave more space to my "Spartan feat" than to my performance.

Another incident, this time a comic one, occurred in St. Louis, the most "western" city of my tour. The morning after my concert I was having my breakfast in bed when I heard a knock on my door. Thinking it was a servant, I shouted "Come in," and in came a strange-looking man in a light-gray checked suit. He was unshaven and had some long black side whiskers, and he wore a dirty brown bowler hat which he didn't take off. He looked the perfect villain in a melodrama. Without explaining his presence, he sat down on my bed and started to talk rapidly and excitedly in the worst Middle West nasal jargon. Instead of listening to what he was saying, my attention was focused on the golden watch and the money I had left on a table which was out of my reach.

The man became impatient, seeing the blank expression on my face, and began to gesticulate in a strange manner, putting one hand, then the other, then both hands into his mouth. I was in a panic; I was sure he must be insane! I was too scared to call for help or to use the telephone. Suddenly, the man jumped to his feet as if ready to leave, pulled out of his pocket a long sheet of paper, and threw it at me. I picked it up and looked at it; it was a program for a vaudeville show. He pointed to a number on it—and, ha!—the whole thing became clear. The man's stunt was to imitate musical instruments, particularly the violin, the cello, and the trumpet. His trick was to "play" using only his mouth and hands. But he needed a pianist, and had read about me, so he decided to team up with me for a vaudeville circuit! When I tried timidly to explain that this was impossible, he became furious, shouted, and with his eyes popping looked at me threateningly. Helpless in my bed, scared to death, and still concerned about my things on the table, I nodded, finally, my acceptance and promised to sign a contract the next morning. Oh, what a sigh I let out when I heard the door close behind him. I picked up the telephone, called George Hochman, and asked him to come to my room. When I told him my story, he became scared, too, and so we decided to leave the city right away, by the earliest train.

To describe my tour in detail, city by city, and concert by concert, would be a difficult and thankless task. As it went along, it became a routine, interrupted now and then by an exceptionally good or bad performance. Sometimes, I did have the chance to meet interesting people.

On the way back to New York for my second recital, George talked, as he always did, of nothing else but San Francisco; he had a real passion for that city.

"What a shame we are not going there," he said. "It is the most beautiful city in the world and the gayest one at the same time. It is the only place left in the old Wild West with the saloons, gambling, women, shows, and everything you can think of. It is made for you."

Such tales made my mouth water, so one can imagine my joy when I returned to New York and Mr. Ulrich announced that I had been engaged for two concerts in that fabulous city, at the end of my tour.

It was another New York I found this time. My friend Armand de Gontaut had left for Paris. Without him I felt a little abandoned despite the fact that the "upper four hundred," as one called the rich, continued to extend invitations to me.

My second recital at the Shubert went better than the first one, but the critics did not come this time (they used to review only debuts). The papers were full, however, of the Josef Hofmann affair. A married lady of a distinguished family of South Carolina had eloped with the famous pianist, taking her children with her, and they had left for an unknown destination. The outraged husband swore to bring them back. This scandal became, naturally, a great topic of conversation.

Continuing my tour, I remember with pleasure my concert in Boston at Jordan Hall. It was bitterly cold, but I had an almost full house, and it felt more like Europe than anywhere else in America. I missed Miss Drew, my Berlin friend whom I had hoped to see again in her home town.

My concerts were coming to an end. Besides the prearranged calendar, I had some flattering return engagements in important cities like Baltimore, Washington, Providence, Cincinnati, a proof that my tour was a success. Unfortunately, the opinion of the whole country took its cue from New York, so, as a result, Mr. Krehbiel's adverse criticism did me a lot of harm. Apropos, I must denounce here some perverse ways of American publicity: in his harsh review of my first concert, Mr. Krehbiel wrote something like: "He missed the meaning of the piece, despite *the phenomenal dexterity of his fingers.*" Mr. Ulrich promptly took these last words out of their context and used them throughout my tour in all my advertisements!

There was a letter from Baltimore which was a heavy blow for poor George and a great disappointment for me. The Knabes wrote that the trip to San Francisco was abandoned and that I had a return engagement in Chicago instead. The reason for this change was easy to guess; it was much cheaper to send us to the "windy city" than to the distant metropolis in California.

The Chicago concert was my last. I was on my best mettle that day, and the audience gave me a warm farewell. I was delightfully surprised later when my old friend Miss Drew showed up during the intermission. Her husband, she told me, was the minister of a church in the suburbs, and they had lived there since their marriage. The next day, I had lunch at their modest, charming home, and I gave them a colorful but careful account of my life in Berlin after they had left.

That evening, when George Hochman and I were going to a burlesque show, the hotel clerk stopped us at the door with the news that San Francisco had had a terrible earthquake and that the whole city was on fire. He handed us the special issue of a paper which had the full description of the catastrophe. It had happened at night, the city was taken by surprise, and the population fled for safety into open spaces; there were countless dead and wounded, blocks of collapsing houses, and many other dreadful details. We were horrified. "We would have been right there," George cried, "and your first concert was set for yesterday." He was wringing his hands in amazement. "And I, like a damn fool, was cursing the Knabes for not letting us go there, and now," he cried, "they have saved our lives!" I, for my part, was deeply moved by our miraculous escape.

My money situation had become alarming. The money I received by contract was completely gone. The Waldorf-Astoria, the small parties in my room, and the expensive days in Armand's company had ruined me. My extravagance was in a way explainable, however. It was the first time in my life that I had had a rather large sum in my possession, and I hadn't learned yet how to use it. Money as such had no other meaning for me than to be spent. In short, I was totally devoid of a sense of economy—a failure that has proved fatal for most of my life.

I wrote and wired Monsieur Astruc for help, as he was holding a small part of my money as provided per contract. William Knabe, very generously, made Ulrich pay my last bill at the Waldorf. And so, one day, at the end of April, I was all packed and ready for my return to Paris. My ship was again the old *Touraine*, of dreadful memories. I was deadly afraid of it, but George assured me that sea travel in April couldn't be better. Mr. Knabe, Mr. Ulrich, and George Hochman came to the pier to see me off, and later, in my cabin, I found lovely flowers, a basket of fruit, and a bottle of champagne sent by some of my new friends. Also a charming note and a box of fine handkerchiefs from Dorothy.

When an interviewer asked me about my impressions of America, I gave him the usual banal answers: "great country, in full progress, fine hotels, good orchestras, etc.," but I had to think about what my impressions really were, for a long while.

The greatest part of the America which I had seen in 1906 was ugly. With the exception of a few large cities, the country presented a drab picture. Most towns had been planned and developed in a hurry; all built after the same pattern. Restful squares with their benches and trees and fountains or parks were practically unknown . . . the open countryside which I was able to observe from my Pullman car windows looked desolate and unattractive. I was appalled by the sight of the long stretches of uncultivated land, by the uninviting forests, and by the heaps of dirt and waste on the outskirts of little towns lying near the railway tracks. My American friends sang the praises of Niagara Falls, the Rocky Mountains, the Grand Canyon, and Florida. I was disappointed in not having seen them, but still they were the work of nature and not of men. On the other hand, I was fascinated by the people in America. The quite recent mass immigration of a mixed variety of Europeans had succeeded in creating a harmonious whole, despite their disparity. Their dynamic will to succeed in their new surroundings was exciting to watch. America was called the land of opportunity, and rightly so. And how I loved their witty and sharp, pointed slang! It was refreshing to hear after the traditional, polite, and repetitious use of their language by the English.

Speaking of my own personal contact with the people, my impressions were mixed; concert audiences, in general, were still living under the regime of the crude, big-drum publicity used by the old Barnum system. To quote: Jenny Lind's title as "The Swedish Nightingale" made her more popular than her singing; Paderewski's lion's face with the golden hair and his personal train became a symbol—people would wait a whole night near the railway tracks to see his train pass but wouldn't make the slightest effort to hear him play. In my own case, the name of the "great" Anton Rubinstein had still a magic touch. Often, when asked if I was his son and I answered in the negative, people refused to believe me.

To my astonishment, I hadn't met any American musicians on my tour, except the charming Rudolf Ganz and the few conductors I had played with. My fellow pianists seemed to boycott me and my concerts. I tried in vain to find an explanation for it, but later, on the boat, I learned the reason.

I seemed to be characterized as "a great talent, a fine temperament, the promise of a brilliant career, but still immature . . . he has much to learn." I must admit that this was also my own opinion.

35

The first day at lunch, in the dining room, I discovered two famous pianists, Raoul Pugno, the Frenchman, and Joseph Lhévinne, a young Russian who had made a sensational debut in New York. Later on, in the lounge, both of them came over most graciously and talked to me, inviting me to take my meals with them at their table. This was the beginning of one of the most delightful crossings of my life. Mr. Pugno was in his fifties, very fat and stocky, but the picture of the debonair Frenchman. Joseph Lhévinne, about thirty, had a clean-shaven, sensitive Semitic face with a sad expression in his somewhat bulging eyes, and wore a curly, artistically arranged wig to cover his premature baldness. When he spoke or laughed, his high-pitched voice sounded like a child's. And there was something of a child in his nature. I loved and admired Joseph Lhévinne both as a man and as an artist.

On the second morning of our crossing, I decided to walk on the promenade deck to fight off any possible discomfort, and I discovered a man in a cape and beret doing the same thing. We were walking in opposite directions when he stopped me, suddenly. "Aren't you the pianist Rubinstein?" he asked. "Yes," I answered, continuing to walk (I had the sea on my mind). But he wouldn't let me go. "What do you think of Pugno?" he asked. "Fine," I said. "And of Lhévinne?" "Wonderful," I said. "And of Paderewski?" "Magnificent, colossal, great," I said unhappily, not feeling too well. "And how about Josef Hofmann?" the man insisted. This was too much. I was about to be seasick, and I lost my temper. "Hofmann!" I burst out. "Hofmann must be a madman to run away with an ugly old woman and all those children!" The man said quietly, "How right you are. You see, I am the husband of that lady." Imagine the expression on my face!

George Eustis, the unfortunate husband, was a distinguished gentleman; he and a friend of his, Robert Chanler, became members of our group on board. I am happy to add that the sea was threatening only that morning, and our crossing turned out to be smooth.

At dinner one night, I complained to my senior colleagues about the boycott I felt I was a victim of, and they both laughed. "It happens to all of us," said Mr. Pugno. "The American piano makers hire us for their publicity, and since each of us plays a different piano they keep us isolated.

The best proof is that I played the Baldwin, Lhévinne the Steinway, you the Knabe, and in spite of the fact that we all toured the same country at the same time, only now do we meet!" And Lhévinne added, "There is such a competition among them that they consider us like boxing champions who have to fight it out for them," and he had a fit of laughter.

At nights we played poker for very small stakes, but very noisily. Bob Chanler, a well-known painter, a member of the rich Astor family, and a great eccentric, was the leader of the riotous games. He was the man, incidentally, who later married Lina Cavalieri by way of an advertisement in a paper. In many ways, he reminded me of Jaroszynski—the same huge frame, the bellowing voice, the irrepressibility. Chanler liked practical jokes; he loved to collect leftover bits of sausage, fish, or smelly cheese and stuff them into shoes which were put out for cleaning at night. Once, at poker, when Lhévinne showed an unexpected full hand, Chanler hit him, jokingly, on the head and upset his wig.

As was the custom, the purser had to organize a benefit concert for the orphans of sailors on the eve of our arrival. This time, he was embarrassed by the abundance of pianists. Which one to choose? So we decided to help him out, and arranged an original and amusing program. Each one of us, in turn, had to play a valse and then accompany two singers of the Metropolitan Opera who were also on board—the baritone Gilibert and his wife, a soprano.

Preceded by the traditional captain's dinner, the concert began with Mr. Pugno's elegant performance of the Valse by Saint-Saëns, followed by an aria from *Faust* by Mr. Gilibert. As the next, by seniority, Lhévinne played the difficult paraphrase of the "Blue Danube" by Schulz-Evler in a dazzling way and gave, as an encore, the Nocturne for the left hand alone by Scriabin. Lhévinne's left hand was fabulous; it was the envy of all the pianists.

After Micaela's Aria from *Carmen*, sung by Madame Gilibert, I banged out the *Mephisto Valse* by Liszt. Finally, the Giliberts sang a duet from an operetta by Messager, which I accompanied, and that finished the program.

Everyone was delighted with this concert, the poor orphans received a substantial sum of money, and the captain treated us to a lavish "souper." *La Touraine*, this time, did her best to make me forget the nightmare of my first crossing.

The landing at Le Havre was full of frenzy with passengers rushing up and down, and back and forth, worried about their luggage, and greeting their relatives and friends. All this agitation around me gave me a fit of sadness. I had loved those eight carefree days spent in the company of such talented, lively, and intelligent people.

My return to Paris was a big question mark. With no concerts in view, with little money left, and still in debt to Mr. Cordovinus and the tailor, I saw my immediate future in the blackest of black colors!

36

"Did you get a contract for next season?" asked Monsieur Astruc when I entered his office.

"No," I said. "They have engaged Busoni." And I tried to explain how difficult it was for the Knabes to use the same pianist two years in succession to promote their pianos.

"You see," I continued, "my tour was only an experiment, so now they need an artist of international fame."

He was disappointed and gloomy—and so was I!

My reappearance at Mr. Cordovinus's pension was not reassuring. The poor man lived under the illusion that an artist made a fortune overnight in America, so, seeing me as impecunious as ever, he lost both his illusion and the hope of getting the money for my three-month-old bill soon. But he had a good heart, Mr. Cordovinus.

"Try to pay me in small installments," he suggested. I understood; he was willing to let me stay in his pension for the time being.

Depressed and discouraged, I spent my first week in Paris without seeing anybody. One morning, however, I decided to find out if Armand de Gontaut was in town. He answered the telephone himself.

"Quelle bonne surprise, mon cher," he said. "I have been trying to find you for several days, but nobody knew your whereabouts." Dear Armand, he was the only one who had no illusions about America and the result of my tour, and who was certainly well aware of my actual situation.

"If you have nothing better to do," he continued, "have lunch with me at a small bar called Fouquet's at the Champs-Élysées." A true friend's voice is the best balm, I discovered.

Fouquet's, now the popular Fouquet at the corner of the Avenue George V, was then a tiny, oblong room with an important bar and four or six small tables where you could be served lunch or dinner. The bar, for the apéritif, was the meeting place of the young aristocratic and plutocratic set, the *jeunesse dorée*, whose life was centered on horse racing, sports, and the opposite sex. Armand was an active member of this group but had in addition his cultivated mind and his love for music.

"Where do you live?" was his first question, after we sat down to eat. When I described the pension, he exclaimed, "It sounds like an abominable place! I have a better plan for you. Come and stay with me. My brother's room in the flat which we shared became free after he married, and is yours. You will find a decent Pleyel in my living room where you can work undisturbed."

I knew his offer was too generous to accept, but I hadn't the moral strength to refuse. My fortunes were at their lowest, and here was my salvation.

"Merci, merci, mon cher," I said, quite moved. "I accept with all my heart, but I hope I shall not be a nuisance. At least, you must let me pay for my food and my laundry."

"Nonsense," he answered. "In the morning my butler prepares a light breakfast and I lunch and dine out. The washing is done by a woman who comes twice a week. So you have nothing to worry about."

Happy as a lark, I managed somehow to scrape up enough money to pay one month of my debt to Cordovinus with the promise to pay the rest in the near future. My bags couldn't take all the books and music I had accumulated, so I had to leave many of them behind. That same day, in the late afternoon, I moved to Armand's lovely apartment at the Avenue Kléber. His brother's room, which I inherited, looked like a paradise to me. It had a wide, soft comfortable bed, a gay light wallpaper, Louis XV furniture, and—oh, joy—running water. An elegant salon and a small dining room separated my room from my friend's, and the corridor led to a vast bathroom, the kitchen, and the servants' quarters. Ferdinand, the valet-butler, immediately took charge of my bags, emptied them in no time, and disappeared with things to clean, press, or wash.

From that day on, my life entered a new phase, not the right one for my artistic and moral development, but a most exhilarating and fascinating one for a boy of nineteen. Looking back on it, I can only say I learned the meaning of dissipated living.

Armand de Gontaut-Biron was a favorite of the *jeunesse dorée*. He introduced me to his friends in the most flattering terms: I was the greatest musician, the most intelligent fellow, a great polyglot; "et il raconte des histoires à mourir de rire." Such an introduction could not fail; they adopted me right away as their steady, somewhat exotic companion. By some strange association of thoughts, I saw here a certain analogy with my Berlin *Lesekränzchen*.

The days started late. I would have my breakfast of coffee, croissants, and honey in bed, reading *Le Gaulois,* the most reactionary and royalist morning paper, founded and edited by a converted Jew, Mr. Arthur Meyer, who was married to a French Duchess. Such an absurd paradox! Only a few years had passed since the tragedy of the Dreyfus case, which broke up families and divided the country into opposite camps. Armand subscribed only to *Le Gaulois* and a sports paper.

At noon, in my robe, I had barely the time to play a few passages on the Pleyel when it was time to dress and go out for lunch. The young men would assemble at the bar at Fouquet's for an apéritif and make plans for the day. We lunched usually right there, unless we preferred a real restaurant, just for a change. Afternoons they would spend at the races, when there were any, or gambling in some club, or having private poker parties; this was the only time of the day when I could be alone to practice or read. At sunset a new reunion at a bar established the pro-gram for the rest of the evening and especially for the night. We had a weakness for music halls, the French café concerts, on the lower Champs-Élysées, mostly open-air places like the Ambassades, and the Alcazar d'été. We loved to acclaim the popular singers of the day: Mayol, the irrepres-sible homosexual; Dranem, the pathetic clown; Fragson, who sang senti-mental songs; and, of course, Yvette Guilbert, the famous red-haired, black-gloved diseuse. After the show, supper, usually at Maxim's, where the best corner table was kept for us. More often than not, we finished the night at Montmartre, at some special cabaret *en vogue.* We would drink only champagne throughout the night. I seldom saw my bed before four in the morning!

How could I afford to lead this kind of life with the little money I had? Well, as astonishing as it may sound, I was never allowed to pay for anything in company of Armand and his friends. My status as the "youngest by ten years," the foreigner, the artist, disqualified me from any part of the bills. So, as a matter of fact, I was able to keep more of the five hundred francs paid out by Monsieur Astruc than when I stayed at the pension Cordovinus.

During the two months of this *dolce vita* I saw little of the outside world. Frederic and his mother had answered my two letters from Amer-ica and were now the only ones who knew my change of address. Basia had left for Warsaw, and my absence from the concert stage cut me off from any contact with the musical world. My longing for the theater and for concerts was drowned in the turmoil of my night life.

All in all, it was a deplorable state of things, but it had some good sides, too. Armand and a few of his closer friends, the Count de Ganay, the Marquis de Polignac of New York memory, Count Recopé, Georges

Brocheton, a half-Spaniard, and a fat, tall, charming Baron Grandmaison liked to hear me play. Soon, thanks to their propaganda, I began to receive invitations to luncheons and dinners by members of their families. Armand himself started a whole campaign on my behalf. He began with his own family. One day he announced that his father and his sister expected me for lunch. Count Antoine de Gontaut-Biron, a distinguished gentleman of around sixty, received me very warmly. "I am grateful to you for the good influence your music and your ideals have on my son. I hope it will take him away from the empty life he is leading."

Ha, I said to myself. In reality it is the other way around.

Another family we visited often were the Leishmans, the in-laws of Armand's brother Louis. Mr. Leishman was a wealthy American who became later the ambassador in Rome.

Thanks to these connections and without, at first, realizing it, I was accepted by the proudest branch of the *grand monde*. The faubourg St.-Germain was the current habitat of the old regal aristocracy in contrast to the imperial one created by Napoleon. The families of the faubourg used to shut their doors to foreigners, unless they showed true blue blood, and they disdained marriages with aliens. They lived in their own world.

In those years, in all the European capitals, the aristocrats were still the dominating patrons of the arts, and followed the old tradition of offering to their guests private concerts in their own palaces. Because of the propaganda of Armand and his friends, I was engaged for several of these *soirées musicales;* Monsieur Astruc made the financial arrangements and obtained, to his great delight, a thousand francs for each appearance.

I remember particularly well the first one given by the Count and Countess de Ganay. A hundred guests, *en grande toilette,* filled the cream and gold salon and sat on dainty gilded chairs, ready for the music. As at a public concert, I came out from a side door, bowed in response to the polite applause, and began to play the printed program. My elegant audience broke immediately into lively conversations, interrupting them from time to time by a "Bravo," usually after a loud passage. At the end of the program, when the last chord had been struck, the doors opened to a vast dining room where a buffet was served. In no time, the table with the food and wine was besieged by the guests, who behaved as if my concert had given them an inextinguishable hunger and thirst.

The other soirées were quite similar, save the one at Count Jean de Castellane's, where I had the honor of having Gabriel Fauré in the audience and, as I was told later, Marcel Proust, who was still unknown; Anne de Noailles, the famous poetess, was also present.

.   .   .

At the Café de la Paix, one afternoon, I was accosted by a tall, bearded old gentleman. "I am Count Jan Zamoyski," he said in Polish. "I heard you play in Warsaw—come and sit with me." I had heard of him; he was the famous patron of music who gave Bronislaw Hubermann a priceless Stradivarius. We talked about Chopin.

"Princess Marcelina Czartoryska, the favorite pupil of Chopin, was my aunt," he informed me. "She taught me how to play his mazurkas." And, to prove it, he began to sing some of them in a creaky and asthmatic voice. Pleased by my respectful attention, he invited me to a dinner at his niece's—"a small family affair." That next day was the Sunday of the Grand Prix de Paris at Longchamp, and, besides, Armand and I had accepted a dinner invitation that evening at the Marquise de Laborde's. I explained it to the Count.

"Come, then, after dinner," he insisted. "I would like my niece to hear you play!"

I agreed to come at ten, and before we parted he gave me an address near the Étoile.

The Grand Prix was run without me. I stayed home. Horse racing was not to my taste, disliking as I did the excited, pushing crowds, the long wait between the races; and since I couldn't afford to bet, I was indifferent as to which horse was going to win. Instead, happy to be alone, I worked at the Pleyel for the first time in weeks. When Armand returned, we changed into tails, and, silk hats on our heads, we drove in a rented cab to the Île St.-Louis. At eight sharp we rang the door to the apartment of Madame de Laborde. The Marquise and her two daughters received us in a very elegant Louis XV salon. We were the only guests. The mistress of the house was a stately matron with impeccable manners, slightly haughty, but with much charm. The daughters were beautiful, both still in their teens; Lili, the elder, a striking brunette, was desperately in love, so Armand told me, with his brother, Louis de Gontaut. The younger one, Françoise, was a tall, ravishing blonde. It was difficult, in France of the 1900's, to mingle with young daughters of the old families. They were always brought up in convents, and later on they were seen in public only at some *bal blanc* during the Carnaval season. So, naturally, I enjoyed this rare opportunity. The Marquise took my arm to enter the dining room, but once we were seated at the round table, formality stopped, and we had a very refined French dinner. The young ladies' conversation was full of wit and charm. I told some stories which made the Marquise fall into fits of laughter, and Armand looked the happiest of us all.

After we had had coffee in the salon, the hostess retired to an adjoining room, leaving the doors wide open, and left the four of us in the salon. Now we had a really good time. Lili, happy to be with the brother of her beloved, held us spellbound by her charm and vivacity. Françoise led me to the piano, and I poured out all my repertoire of Viennese valses while she sat close to me on the piano bench. Armand and Lili began to dance, when, suddenly, I looked at my watch. It was ten thirty! And I had promised to be at ten at Count Zamoyski's niece's. "What shall I do?" I asked Armand in panic. "Hurry, my cab will take you there—the party is certainly still going on," he said.

I thanked both girls for a lovely time and dashed out of the house. It took me half an hour to get there. I looked up; the lights were still on. "Thank heaven," I sighed, but the moment I rang the doorbell the lights went out; the door opened, however, on a dark staircase. A voice called from the top, "Who is it?" I answered meekly, "Rubinstein . . . Count Zamoyski asked me to come, but I see it is too late." The staircase and a part of the house were suddenly alight, and I saw at the top of the stairs a gentleman, and a lady, evidently the hosts, still dressed. "Oh," the lady said in Polish, "I am *so* sorry. My uncle is not well and could not dine with us, and the other guests are gone, but please come up and have a glass of champagne."

We entered an oval-shaped boudoir, the most exquisite room I had ever seen; the wall had panels hung with a light blue silk; a love seat, two armchairs, a small round table, all in a delicate Louis XVI style, and, in a corner, a brown Erard piano made up the furniture. Two rosy pictures in round frames, presumably Bouchers, gave the finishing touch to this idyllic evocation of the eighteenth century.

The Count looked like a man in his fifties; he was completely bald, wore a black pointed beard, had an *embonpoint* and very red cheeks. Count Zamoyski's niece, who could not have been more than thirty, was a striking beauty. She was dressed in a black velvet gown which accentuated her pale, alabasterlike *décolleté*. Her small head, poised on a proud neck, was covered by long black hair, arranged in a very feminine fashion, and she had the greenest eyes I ever saw. And what a nervous little nose, and what a sensuous red mouth she had! I was speechless with admiration.

"Have you been at the races?" the Count asked me, and, without waiting for my answer, he continued. "This horse, Spearmint, what a surprise, eh? Nobody believed in him, but I knew he would win! And the jockey, Bartholemew—what a master, eh? I always bet on him." And he continued this monologue while the Countess and I sipped our champagne.

"Would you play something for me?" she whispered in a low, soft voice. "Gladly," I answered, and we went to the piano. Her husband stopped talking and settled himself comfortably on the little sofa, and she pushed one of the armchairs nearer to the piano.

"What will you play?" she asked, putting a vase with dark red roses on the side of the piano stand.

"Something of Chopin," and I began to play the long D flat Nocturne as though in a trance, inspired by her beauty. The Count closed his eyes; when his chin dropped, a barely audible, soft snore announced that he was asleep. When I reached the coda with its pianissimo descending sighs, the Countess, suddenly, leaned forward close to me and, covered by the open stand and the flowers, kissed my mouth with a wild passion. I struck a wrong note, too loudly—the Count woke up, and the charm was broken. We finished our champagne, I kissed her hand several times, with ardor; the Count accompanied me to the door, and I left the house. I never saw either of them again.

My readers might be astonished by this long account of an unimportant event, but I shall always remember the evening which so completely transported me into the romantic days of Chopin and Liszt.

37

"Arthur, I have to leave in two days for New York," said Armand after a lunch at Romaine Brooks's, the latest mistress of Gabriele D'Annunzio. I had enjoyed that luncheon party. Mrs. Brooks was an American, a painter of talent with an original taste for interior decoration. I was much impressed by a large sofa in white satin, covered with black velvet cushions. Her guests, besides the two of us, were two ladies from Chile, a Madame Errazuriz, a woman in her late forties, and still beautiful, known in Paris as "la belle Madame Errazuriz," and her daughter. After lunch, to please Madame, I played excerpts from *Tristan*, and the whole *Après-midi d'un faune* by Debussy. She seemed entranced. I could not guess, on that day, what an important role she would play in my life in later years.

And right after that, in the street, this sudden announcement of Armand's departure! What was to become of me? was my first thought. Seeing the disturbed expression on my face, the charming fellow tried to calm me.

"You can stay in the apartment as long as you wish," he said with an encouraging smile. "I am taking Ferdinand with me, but I shall give orders to the concierge to prepare your breakfast every morning, and fix your room." My eyes thanked him; I couldn't speak.

I saw him off on a hot, sunny day, at the Gare St.-Lazare, and as the train moved off, I cried. A short period of my youth, with a special quality of beauty and happiness, had come to an end.

Things changed right away; I was on my own from now on. Most of the money I earned I had spent senselessly on articles of elegance. Always ready to emulate Armand, I had ordered expensive batiste dress shirts with narrow doubled cuffs, pleated in front and bordered with frills, and of course they had to have monograms. My ankle-long nightshirts were of the same material and make (pajamas were still unknown in Paris). Long black silk stockings and patent leather pumps rounded off this finery. Yes, I had become quite a dandy that spring.

Now I was punished for my extravagance. The concierge, the food, the laundry, the newspapers, the cabs, everything had to be paid for; it took time to get accustomed to the change. As before, my steps led me mechanically to Fouquet's for the apéritif. The usual companions were as hospitable as ever, but I became too shy, in Armand's absence, to accept their invitations. Life became difficult again. The season was over, and the *beau monde* left the torrid city for the summer resorts. Paris was taking a rest; my concierge complained that she had a hard time getting bread for my breakfast, but I had a harder time getting the money to pay for it.

Astruc left orders to give me my monthly stipend piecemeal; he knew of my debts and did not approve of me. And so I went often hungry to bed; after my breakfast, all I could afford for the day was a casual sandwich and coffee at a cheap brasserie, or some fruit bought in the street. Still, I would appear at Fouquet's on time for the apéritif, although I did not have one; I went only to have someone to talk to.

One evening, Georges Brocheton and Henri de Grandmaison, both of the *jeunesse dorée*, invited me to have supper with them at the Café de Paris, and this time I accepted because I was near starvation.

What a wonderful place the Café de Paris was! Forming the corner of the Avenue de l'Opéra and the rue Daunou, it was made up of two long aisles in the shape of a V. The tables of the right aisle were always reserved for the "right" people, while transient tourists and such were relegated to the left side. I admired the art with which this monstrous snobbishness was handled. But the food was divine!

Another thing which made this restaurant popular was its music ensemble which played for dinners and suppers. The leader was a pale, consumptive-looking Dane who drew from his fiddle the schmalziest tunes in the schmalziest way.

When my friends and I, seated at the "right" table, were beginning to eat our steaks, my first meat in a week, a pretty brunette, sitting at a table oposite us, began to sing at the top of her mezzo voice a song by Grieg, "Ich liebe Dich." Mr. Moeller, the Dane, and his band accompanied her discreetly. After she had finished, we all applauded. She responded with a gracious smile when, suddenly, looking at me, she shouted: "Rubinstein, Rubinstein, I have heard him in New York, I want to meet him!"

My companions knew her escort, a German, a Baron von Hochwaechter, so it made things easy. At coffee we all sat at the same table. Our singer's name was Mrs. Olive White, an ex-chorus girl who had married a rich New Yorker. Her husband, detained by business, had sent her, in the company of a girl friend, for her first visit to Europe.

"Boys," she addressed us with a typically American familiarity, "what are we waiting for—let's go to my place for a nightcap!"

My friends declined politely, but I accepted; I couldn't resist the call of a pretty woman. We drove, she, the Baron, and I, to 80, Avenue du Bois de Boulogne, where she had rented a flat with a balcony overlooking the beautiful avenue. Her friend, a plump, pleasant blonde in her thirties, brought us the drinks.

"Ruby, please play something," said Olive. And, despite my fear of neighbors, I played softly some tunes I had heard in America. She sang some of them, and then she began to dance, kicking her legs like a chorus girl. The fun continued late into the night hours. When we were ready to leave, she threw her arms around me. "Ruby," she called, "you must come tomorrow for lunch and stay the whole day. You can practice here if you like. Alec will fetch you in my cab." I promised, and we left, Alec and I. Walking up the avenue, Alec, the Baron, raved about Olive's beauty, charm, and wealth. I couldn't make out if he was her lover or just a devoted friend, but I did guess that he was not rich.

And again I was off on a mad merry-go-round for three full weeks of dinners, of suppers at the Bois de Boulogne, the Café de Paris, the cabarets at Montmartre, Olive singing "Ich liebe Dich," and always the four of us, with Alec paying for everything out of Olive's purse. From what I observed, the Baron was seriously in love, and in hopes she might divorce, and marry him, while she led him on to believe it. She was a frivolous and sweet little thing, Olive; petite, black eyes, black hair, with too much makeup and the wrong rouge on her lips, but good-hearted and irrepressibly gay. And she loved music. She treated Alec and me frequently to a hot kiss, without giving it much meaning. Her girl friend was always laughing, always willing to be patted, to have her big breasts cupped or her fat bottom smacked.

By Jove, we had a jolly good time! Only once was this riot interrupted by a disagreeable experience I had, all through Olive's fault.

Prince Bariatinsky, the *amant serieux* of Lina Cavalieri, invited me on behalf of his mother-in-law to a formal dinner at her villa in Neuilly. I knew he was married to the daughter of the Princess Yourievskaya, the morganatic wife of the late Tsar Alexander II. It was evident that he intended to make me play, but it was an important affair, so I accepted.

On the afternoon of this party, Olive, who had developed a growth on her finger, or on her toe—I don't remember which—had to have it removed by a surgeon.

"Ruby, Ruby," she cried, "I won't let him do it unless you play during my operation!"

I'll be brief. The surgeon was late, I played impatiently, Olive cried in pain, I ran to change in a frenetic hurry and, ugh, I arrived at the villa forty minutes late!

When I entered the grand salon, the old Princess rose from her chair and, without even a glance at me, offered her arm to a stout gentleman and led her twenty guests into the dining room in a slow procession, as at a royal court. Nobody paid any attention to me; only Bariatinsky, in passing, hissed: "You have gone too far, my friend."

Feeling like a culprit, shyly I found my way to my seat between two ladies to whom I was not even introduced. I tried to explain my predicament to them, but they seemed incredulous. From time to time the Princess would give me a resentful glance, destroying my appetite; I felt so miserable.

After dinner, when we went back into the salon, I begged Prince Bariatinsky to ask his mother-in-law if she would allow me to play for her guests. The answer was in the affirmative. I never played with a greater desire to please my audience. It took me a long time, but after a smashing performance of the Grande Polonaise, they clapped and shouted, and the Princess, with the severe look still in her eyes, said in a deep, almost masculine voice: "You are an angel!"

Soon after that evening Olive received a telegram from her husband ordering her to come home immediately. He had reserved passage for her and her friend on a boat sailing from Cherbourg in two days.

"He must have heard some horrible gossip about us," she complained, "and I wanted so much to take you to Trouville for a week." But there was nothing she could do; she had to leave. We decided that the last night before her departure we must have a glorious finale. We all dressed up and started out with a gala dinner at the Café de Paris, where Olive sang her Grieg song with a quiver in her voice, then we proceeded to a small place on the rue Pigalle to drink another bottle and finally came back to Olive's flat for the last loving cup. From that moment on, strange things began to happen. Shirley, Olive's companion, declared suddenly that she was not going to return yet to America. At that, the Baron, quite a little drunk, jumped to his feet and shouted: "Let us all drive right away to Cherbourg and spend the last day with Olive!" Recently we had been driving around in a rented automobile which was still waiting to take Alec and me to our respective homes. When we objected strenuously that we were wearing the wrong clothes for such an expedition, he screamed hysterically: "The least we can do to show our love and respect for Olive is to see her off in style!"

None of us was sober, and so, infected by his enthusiasm, we agreed, without further thought.

I shall never forget that horrible trip at night, and in the open car! The wind, the dust on the old roads, the stops for a flat tire or for other reasons, the bad coffee in a roadside inn—it was a nightmare that lasted fourteen hours. We arrived finally in Cherbourg exhausted and dirty, only three hours before sailing time. At the hotel, where we went to wash up and eat something, Baron Hochwaechter called me to another room and handed me an envelope.

"Take these two thousand francs," he said. "I know you are hard up. You can pay me back whenever it is convenient to you."

I blushed; I knew well it was Olive's delicate way of letting me have that money. I thanked him, however.

We accompanied Olive to her cabin. Shirley was busy retrieving her bags, as all their luggage had been sent by train. Suddenly, when the signal called for us to leave, Alec, in a voice high-pitched from emotion, declared: "I stay on the boat! I can't let her go alone!"

"How can you?" I cried, in consternation. "Just like that, without a ticket, without your things, in your evening clothes?"

"I can find all I need on the boat," he answered, "and there is Shirley's cabin." Olive was amazed but flattered.

"Alec, you are crazy," was all she had to say.

"What will become of Shirley and me?" I asked him. "How shall we get back to Paris?"

"The car will take you home. All you have to do is to pay for the gasoline. The chauffeur and the car are taken care of. Leave Shirley at 80, Avenue du Bois."

It was late. We had barely the time to kiss Olive and rush down the gangplank!

The return trip was another sort of a nightmare, but this time only for me. Our plump Shirley was romantic—a tendency which now surfaced. She found in her Baedeker some odd cathedrals to visit, and some off-the-road places for good food. From time to time, she would stop the car to pick some field flowers, or to admire the quaint headgears of the

Bretonnes. And we were still wearing our evening clothes! Fortunately, Shirley made no demands on my time; she was leaving the next morning for Switzerland. But the worst was to come. At my final stop, at Avenue Kléber, the chauffeur, whom I was making ready to dismiss with a good tip, pulled out a lengthy-looking bill.

"Monsieur," he said, "the Baron owes me some money for arrears in gasoline, and he paid for the car only up to our excursion to Cherbourg. And driving at night costs double." The whole bill was for seven hundred and some francs. And I had felt so rich in possession of the two thousand, with visions of my debts paid up! Anyway, I paid the chauffeur, but my tip was smaller than intended.

As for the Baron Hochwaechter, he came to London in 1920, just after the First World War, to claim the money I owed him, he said, and I gave it to him at the prewar rate.

38

Frederic wrote from somewhere in Poland: "My family has left for a cure in Marienbad. I am staying here in the country near Warsaw with friends of mine, the Barylskis. They have four sons, charming boys who are gay and intelligent. Their parents have heard you play and would love to have you with us. Do come! You can ride horses, work if you feel like it, read, or rest. The food is simple and healthy; fresh milk and fruit, and vegetables from the garden. I am sure it would do you a lot of good."

It sounded attractive, although I felt a little nervous about the boys in connection with Frederic. In the meantime, I still followed my lazy routine, getting up late, playing some études, and later, Fouquet's, the summer theater at the Champs-Élysées, and Maxim's at night. I had become thin and pale, with hollow cheeks and rings under my eyes.

Paul Dukas saw me one afternoon, sitting on the terrace of the Café Weber, having coffee and brioches; it was actually my breakfast. "What are you doing in Paris? I thought you had left long ago," he said.

"Oh," I bragged, "I am having the time of my life! Parties every night, you know, then Maxim's, and, oh, the beautiful, beautiful girls! How can I leave a town like this?"

He smiled indulgently. "Come to my place, if you have nothing better to do. I want to show you something."

I followed him to his flat on rue Washington; he lived on the fourth floor and there was no elevator.

"Excuse me for a moment, I have to do something in the kitchen. Look at these photos—they will please you." He took out of a drawer a carton, handed it to me, and left the room. Expecting to see some nice snapshots of his travels, I opened it casually; it contained a large collection of pornographic pictures in color. My eyes filled suddenly with tears. I was hurt and ashamed. This man, whom I respect and admire and who was my friend, is now disappointed in me, I felt, and his gesture with these lewd pictures was his answer to my stupid talk!

The door opened, and Monsieur Dukas came in with a large tray and put it on a table.

"Come and have a bite with me," he said kindly, and seeing my distress, he added softly, "I didn't mean to offend you. But tell me about yourself."

We sat down to a meal of cold meat, cheese, bread, and tea, and I poured my heart out to him.

"My musical career is finished," I cried in an emotional outburst. "I am nothing but an empty-headed *noceur*."

"Nonsense, mon ami, at your age nothing is lost, but you ought to do something about your health. My earnest advice is: go to the country for a good rest and recover your strength; your mood for work will come back by itself."

I suddenly remembered Frederic's letter, and thought, How amazing, his proposition fits exactly the master's advice. I decided to leave for Warsaw as soon as possible. Dukas was delighted to hear it.

"Before you leave, I shall show you bits of my opera, *Ariane et Barbe-Bleue*. I am working on it just now. Come tomorrow morning—we can play some of it four hands."

I thanked him for everything from the bottom of my heart. He had brought me back to my senses. I ran to a post office to wire Frederic my decision. Back at Avenue Kléber, I found a letter from Armand announcing his return in a week. It contained a very amusing description of the scandal caused by the arrival of Olive and the Baron on the same boat. He wrote: "Mr. White, the husband, became incensed by the insinuations, and snapshots, which were published by some gossip papers. When he heard that Olive and Alec were together on the ship, he took a friend with him to the dock, and when Hochwaechter emerged, the two of them beat him up very severely. Olive screamed for help, and they all landed in a police station. The newspapers printed lusty accounts of the whole affair. Hochwaechter is in poor condition, he sails for Europe by the next boat."

The last days in Paris were spent with Dukas, playing the lovely *Ariane et Barbe-Bleue*. I paid a last visit to Fouquet's to say goodbye to my friends and packed my few belongings. I also left a long letter for Armand on his table.

The long journey to Warsaw tired me more than ever before; I was completely run down. Frederic was at the station and cheered me by his affectionate welcome. He had a cab waiting to take us across the river to the St. Petersburg railway station. There we boarded a train which deposited us in an hour at a depot where two good-looking boys expected us.

"This is Kazio and this is Zygmunt," said Frederic, introducing them. "They are both very musical."

A spacious carriage drove us to the estate, about two miles away. We stopped in front of a vast house which had no architectural proportions, the whole built on the ground floor, where long wings had been added later, probably for the steadily growing family. The owner, Mr. Barylski, belonged to the Polish upper middle class. His important position in a Russian insurance company made him rich and influential.

In his early fifties, but already gray-haired, he was an intellectual interested in everything, particularly in music. Madame Barylska was not much younger but kept still a youthful appearance; dignified, relaxed, energetic, and full of vitality, she took part in everything around her. She was all I felt a Polish matron should be.

The boys, one more handsome than the other, were still on vacation and enjoying it to the fullest. They adored riding, fishing, playing tennis, and all the outdoor sports, but in the evening they would read good books, play chess, or have long political discussions, mainly on the subject of Poland.

The estate was really a large farm, with horses and cattle, and the house with its flower and vegetable garden was called, in Polish, the *dwor* —the manor.

The regime of the household was ideal. I would ride with the boys after breakfast, then spend an hour or two at the piano while they played tennis. Lunch on the terrace would consist of clabber, hot potatoes, cold meat, and wild strawberries or raspberries with cream. In the afternoon Frederic was busy with his composition, and the rest of us loved more than anything to go picking mushrooms in a nearby forest. Tired but happy after the long walk, we had the traditional Polish "tea," all kinds of baked goods, iced lemonade, jam, honey, cheese, sausage, and fruit; it was the most popular meal of the day. Evenings we ate little, but I drank my two large glasses of milk. With such a diet it didn't take me long to put on weight, and to recover my strength.

Sometimes, if we felt like it, Frederic or I would play Chopin, but it was never forced on us. Madame Barylska liked to draw me into a game of piquet, or we would spend the evening peeling and eating fresh nuts. My suspicion about Frederic and the boys proved to be groundless; all four sons were perfectly normal and healthy in every way.

The summer was over, and it was time for us to return to town. Our farewell was most affectionate. Madame Barylska made the sign of the cross over us and kissed our foreheads. The family made us promise to visit them in Warsaw. I was quite moved, my heart filled with gratitude for what they had done for my morale and my health.

39

Autumn was my favorite season. I loved the fresh breeze shaking the golden leaves off the trees, and the faster moving clouds, the shorter days, and the freer circulation of the blood. Warsaw was filling up again. It was good to see the men return to their work with renewed energy, still brown from the sun, still exhilarated by the long rest. And the women, lovelier than ever, brought excitement simply by their presence.

Frederic's family had returned from abroad. Pani Magdalena welcomed me in her own demonstrative way, yet I felt a subtle aloofness in her which might have been developed by our long separation. Her husband, on the other hand, was exuberantly cordial. My American tour had much impressed him. His impression, as I soon discovered, was shared by the whole country! Several Polish newspapers had published some favorable reports about my "successes" in France and America, thanks to which I became now "the famous Polish pianist." As a result the advantages didn't take long to materialize. Emil Mlynarski, the director and chief conductor of the Filharmonja, engaged me on the spot at a good fee for three concerts as a guest artist. A new concert manager from Lodz came forth with a proposition for two recitals in my own town. I started to work on my programs with fresh enthusiasm.

Joseph Jaroszynski arrived in Warsaw and was planning to stay for my concerts. He had never met the Harmans, and I was loath to bring him to their house; they just were not fit for each other. So, instead, it was Joseph who introduced me to his own friends, a childless couple, Mr. and Mrs. Rzewuski. They had a charming apartment with a fine Steinway and were passionate music lovers. Stanislav Rzewuski had lost a leg in a duel, was often ailing, and lived on drugs. His only daily occupation was playing bridge for very high stakes at the best club in town. He confided to me: "I play ten percent better than anybody, and that provides me with a yearly income of about thirty thousand rubles."

His wife, a former beauty, was still attractive, and full of vitality. She had been born in the same Ukraine where Balzac's Madame Hanska and Liszt's Princess Wittgenstein came from. Both Rzewuskis worshiped Wagner, and never missed their annual pilgrimage to Bayreuth for the festivals. She liked to identify herself with Brünnhilde. I soon became *l'habitué de la maison*, playing for them *Walküre* and the *Götterdämmerung* for hours. The Rzewuskis, in turn, introduced me to the most important people in Warsaw. The result of it was that I began to be lionized by the uncrowned queen of the city, the Marchioness Wielopolska, and by the rich Epsteins, close relations of the Rothschilds of Paris. My concerts were a real success. Mr. Mlynarski was not only a great conductor but proved to be a great teacher as well. He gave me invaluable hints about the interpretation of the concertos I played with him. The Harmans were quite proud of me, and pani Magdalena gave a big supper after my first concert at which I was even honored by the presence of her husband. My sister Jadzia came from Lodz for the events and brought alarming news of our brother Ignacy. He was back from his exile in Siberia and had become involved again in revolutionary activities. This time, if caught, the sentence would be very severe; he might be condemned to death.

"He must go abroad right away," she said, "and the best thing for him to do would be to go to Paris, where he wants to study violin. We will somehow manage to send him a monthly allowance, and he will have the advantage of being near you."

She took two hundred rubles from me for his ticket and for his initial expenses, and she also made me try to find a way to get him out of the country. "With your connections it should be easy," she said. I was lucky; by some obscure machinations I obtained a document which allowed him to pass the ominous Russian frontier. In those happy days, no passports were required anywhere but in Russia and Turkey! Anyway, Ignacy reached Paris safely. But Jadzia dealt me another blow; she asked me to pay the bill for some dresses she had bought, and it amounted to three hundred rubles.

"I am afraid to show this bill to my husband," she explained. "It infuriates him when I spend too much." So I was out of pocket for five hundred rubles, and it was more than my fee for one concert. Still, I couldn't blame her entirely. The general opinion had it that I had made a lot of money in America, and my new elegant outfit did not help to change this impression. I tried in vain to convince my sister that the last months of high living in Paris had swallowed up a great amount. No wonder that I was received in Lodz this time not as the prodigal son but as the conqueror of America. Consequently, I felt morally obliged to make a gift of half my earnings to my parents. The outlook for a return to Paris with a substantial sum of money was not too good; I was left with just enough for a month or two.

Back in Warsaw, the arrival of Karol Szymanowski cheered me up; it was a happy renewal of our friendship. He brought some recently published compositions with him, among them the *Variations*, Opus 3, dedicated to me. I started to work on them right away, and on his études and preludes as well. Karol's friend Gregor Fitelberg, a composer and conductor, joined us sometimes. Only a few years older than Szymanowski, he put on grand, superior airs. He was a broad-shouldered, strong man, though only of middle height, and he had thick, wavy black hair, a round, shaven face, and behind his eyeglasses a stern expression. One could call him handsome, in a way; he resembled the photos of the young Anton Rubinstein. Instinctively, I did not like him. However, thanks to his efforts and energy, young Polish composers were able to see their works published and performed.

A Prince Ladislas Lubomirski, a member of one of the oldest families in Poland and a wealthy landowner, had a genuine passion for music, not often to be found among Polish aristocrats. Fitelberg, his protégé for years, suggested to him that he emulate the famous Russian "Five" by creating something similar in our country. The Prince liked the idea and founded, with a large sum of money, an association of young Polish composers, over which he presided. The first members were Fitelberg, Szymanowski, Ludomir Rózycki (my old offender), and Apolinary Szeluta. After my last concert, at which I had played as an encore an étude of Szymanowski, the Prince came backstage to express his appreciation, and I thanked him, in turn, for his great contribution to music.

Life at the Harmans followed its old routine. The master carried on his affair with his ballerina, Madame continued her tea and supper parties with her usual cronies, and Frederic worked on the orchestration of his concerto. He planned to take his compositions to Paris and try his luck in the French capital. Basia was out most of the afternoons, probably spending them with her lover, who was back in Warsaw. The other daughter, Pola, would come daily at tea time for a visit to her mother. She had changed since Zakopane and treated me now in a civil way. My close relationship with Madame Magdalena was cooling off, as I have mentioned before. It was partly that the disposition of the apartment made things more difficult, but mainly because she disliked the fact that I was moving now in circles other than her own. Feeling often at odds with my delicate position in their house, I offered to move to a hotel, but the entire family insisted on my staying on.

And then, out of the blue sky, the most incredible, unexpected thing happened. At sunset one day, Pola and I were still sitting and talking at the tea table, all by ourselves, after the others had left the room, when suddenly, compulsively, we became silent. My heart began to beat faster. I searched her eyes questioningly, intently; she did not withdraw hers. Then we both knew; we were in love, deeply and passionately in love. I reached for her hand, she took mine, our fingers entwined, and we sat like that, blissfully, without uttering a word. Someone was coming; we started as though waking up from a dream. Pola stayed for dinner, but all through the meal we did not dare to speak to each other. Her mother thought we had quarreled. I reassured her about that, and she asked me to take Pola home.

"I don't like to let her walk alone at this late hour. And she lives only five blocks from here."

It was a gift from heaven. We walked hand in hand; we were too shy to speak. Only at her house door, before she could ring the bell, I took her into my arms, held her closely, and we kissed—it was a long, long, passionate, thirsty kiss. She whispered, in tears, "Tomorrow morning at eleven, at the *cukiernia*." The door opened, and she entered the house. I returned in a daze.

Frederic was still up, waiting for me. I told him what had happened, unable to withhold it from him.

"I saw it coming," he said calmly. "You were bound to complete the cycle; it was inevitable."

He was right—it was fatal, inexorable. Ever since I had met him and his family I lived under their magic spell, and I was not able to free myself—near them or away from them. And now I saw myself irrevocably caught in their dragnet.

Next morning, at the *cukiernia*, or café, I found her sipping tea at a table in a corner. She looked terribly agitated. "We can't be seen here together," she said quickly, with her eyes fixed on the entrance door. "Some people I know come here. We must leave at once, and separately. I shall find a better place where we can meet." At that, she squeezed my hand and ran out.

She was right, of course. There was no legitimate reason for us to be seen together anywhere but at her parents' house. After endless but impractical ideas, Pola one day proposed a rendezvous at the apartment of a young girl who was in love with Frederic and evidently glad to be of service to his sister. I jumped at the idea; I would go anywhere to be with Pola for one second alone. Sophie Kohn, our savior, was the daughter of a well-known lawyer. She was a lively, charming, well-proportioned, elegant young girl. Unfortunately, a long, formless, reddish nose with its tip almost reaching her mouth marred her otherwise pleasant face. She received us (we came separately, of course) in her bedroom, furnished with a virginal-looking bed (it had white curtains with ruffles), facing a huge Bechstein concert grand. A small sofa, two easy chairs, and a low table filled a corner. For weeks, this room was the shelter for our love. Sophie, always very discreet, would leave us alone, under pretext of having things to attend to. But in spite of that, all we dared was to sit still, hold hands, and repeat the same old words which sound so divinely new when you are in love! We were, naturally, shy in this unfamiliar place and, moreover, bewildered by the sudden dramatic turn our lives had taken.

Frederic had left for Paris and wrote that he had found some pleasant quarters in the apartment of an elderly English lady, and that she had a room available for me whenever I decided to come. His parents and Basia were leaving for Germany to spend Christmas with some relatives and, of course, I felt I should leave, too, but I wasn't ready to face the separation so soon. Szymanowski and Fitelberg helped me out; they pretended they needed me for a vast musical project. Thanks to them I could stay another fortnight.

"You can remain in the apartment," pani Magdalena said. "The servants are there, and Pola can come from time to time to see if everything is in order."

Those two marvelous weeks passed like one day. Pola came often to the house, where, at last, I could hold her sometimes in my arms, always afraid, however, that someone might surprise us. At every meeting we swore each other eternal love, and she promised to write, but begged me not to answer. "It is too dangerous," she said.

Just before Christmas, she was giving a dinner for two brothers of her husband and their wives. She insisted I should come, too. "It looks strange that I have never invited you, especially now, when you live alone in my parents' house."

It was the wrong thing to do. I felt out of place. The three men behaved in an unfriendly way, they were barely polite, and the ladies snubbed me with a typical anti-Semitic overtone. Pola became nervous and unnatural. The minute we got up from the table, I begged to be excused and left. My presence had spoiled the party, but I couldn't make out why. Unless they knew or had heard something about us, or about me?

At Sophie's the next morning, Pola explained that they had simply resented me as an alien element at a family reunion. I was not quite re-assured.

Our farewell took place two days later at Sophie's again. Pola cried, and I was disconsolate; after she was gone, Sophie kept me for an hour, brought some coffee, and tried to soothe me. Finally, she forced me to go to the piano and play my heart out. That helped! And I can state right now that once again my music had the power to console and calm.

40

Twenty-five, rue Lauriston was my new address in Paris, and my landlady, Mrs. Cowl, was an Englishwoman in her sixties, petite and alert, always neat in her English dresses invariably made of printed materials. She tinted her dark hair an off-color yellow, and she had an odd assortment of chains of amber, crystal, and metal hanging from her neck, and some similar noisy bracelets on her wrists which made her presence known by their clank. Mrs. Cowl was the kindest creature, not very educated, but eager to learn. She lost her heart to Fred and, to please him, received me, too, with open arms. We were her only tenants, and as both of us had to have pianos in our rooms we were separated from each other by the living and dining room.

My first step on my return to Paris in 1907 was to see Astruc. Our relations, of late, had not been too good, and for plausible reasons. He was obviously disappointed by the poor progress of my career, and even more by my dissipated life of the summer before. But the moment I entered his office his good smile reassured me; he was still on my side; he had not given up on me.

"Alors, jeune homme," he said, giving me a friendly tap, "what shall we do next? All I have for you is a concert at the Société Philharmonique, and then we will see." This concert was a recital at the small Salle des Agriculteurs, and the grand name of Société Philharmonique stood for a modest number of subscribers to a short series of concerts of chamber music or recitals.

"But I have a good idea for you," continued Monsieur Astruc. "We are organizing a colossal benefit matinée; all the celebrities in town are lending their services. Francis Planté, the great French pianist, who is eighty-six years old, is coming especially from Tarbes, where he lives, to play a tarantella by Gottschalk with the band of the Garde Republicaine and a solo piece. As he is listed at the end of the program, which will last at least three hours, you could play one or two short pieces at the beginning. It would be excellent for you to have your name on such a bill."

His idea didn't please me, but I felt it wasn't the right moment to refuse anything, so I said yes, and gave him "Two pieces by Chopin" for my program.

"Don't be late," he recommended. "It begins at three and you will be the third or fourth on the list."

The list was formidable: Sarah Bernhardt was going to play a whole act of *Adrienne Lecouvreur*, Lucien Guitry a scene of his latest success; Mounet-Sully, Coquelin *aîné*, Le Bargy, de Féraudy, monologues and recitations; Félia Litvinne, the great soprano, and Lucienne Breval, Vallandri, and the tenor Alvarez of the Opéra were going to sing, and last, but not least, the great Francis Planté was to make his first appearance in Paris after ten years of absence.

No wonder that I felt rather proud to see my name on posters among such glorious company.

I was on time at the Théâtre Sarah Bernhardt. The house was sold out—and at high prices. Parisians loved this kind of show, feeling they were getting their money's worth. When I arrived backstage it was full of confusion and disorder. Men and women, in costumes or informal clothes, were running in all directions, talking and gesticulating. When I tried, in vain, to get hold of a printed program, a man caught my arm and pushed me toward the stage.

"Thank God you are here," he said excitedly. "Vallandri failed us, so *you* are on now!" I found myself suddenly in front of the public. I bowed, and recovered my senses only when I was seated at the piano. The nocturne and the étude of Chopin were practically drowned by the loud conversation of the audience, which infuriated me, so, in answer to a tepid, polite applause, I responded by playing my sure-shot war horse, the Polonaise in A flat. This time they were bound to listen, and I took three bows. Pleased with myself, I was about to go into the theater to watch the rest of the program when the *régisseur*, the man who had pushed me on the stage, stopped me again.

"Bravo, bravo," he said, tapping my shoulder, "it will give you pleasure to know that Maître Planté wants to meet you! Come with me."

We knocked at the great pianist's door. It was quite a sight: Planté was a little man, bald, with a pink wrinkleless face, and a short round gray beard. He had his shoes off, and sat, all dressed up, with his feet in white stockings on a small electric heater. As soon as he glanced at me he shouted: "Ah, ah, comme il est gentil, ce petit! Oh, I can see he has a great talent. Isn't he charming?" he addressed the *régisseur* as if I weren't there.

"I am *so* sorry that I couldn't hear you, but I know you had a great success," he went on, "and what did you play, mon jeune ami?"

I told him. When I mentioned the Polonaise, he looked at me suddenly in a stunned fury, overturned the heater, stood up, and shrieked: "He stole my piece, this rascal, he stole my piece! I am leaving! It is the only piece I practiced, and he has stolen it!"

I ran out, terrified, retreated into the theater, behind the boxes, and watched, with other standees, the proceedings. It took two long hours before the great master appeared on the stage to a thunderous applause, and also, to my great relief, as if to belie his age, he played the Tarantella with a perfect control of his fingers and with the élan of a young man. After the well-deserved ovation had subsided, he raised his hand and addressed the public: "My young colleague has given you a fine performance of the piece which he, inadvertently, took away from me. I have not prepared anything else to play," and he left, smiling graciously.

Unexpectedly, this concert, in spite of the dramatic interlude, had good results for me. Coquelin *aîné*, the great actor, who was impressed by my success, invited me to play at a gala concert which he was arranging for the benefit of the home for old actors. As Caruso and Geraldine Farrar had promised to take part in it, he politely advertised the *three* of us as the great foreign stars, to Astruc's and my own delight. This concert took place in the hideous hall of the old Trocadero, which had, however, three thousand seats. After the immense success of the opera arias sung by Caruso and Farrar, I had the good idea to play as my last piece the "Liebestod" from *Tristan and Isolde* in the Liszt transcription; it brought the house down. Saint-Saëns, who was present, complimented me very warmly. "It sounds better on the piano than for the voice," he commented. I played that piece often at my future concerts.

With those two successful appearances to my credit, I caught the attention again of the *grand monde*, and three engagements followed in succession for the "unmusical" *soirées musicales*. One of them, however, was exceptional. The Countess de Béarn, an authentic music lover, asked the famous soprano Félia Litvinne to sing at her party the poetic cycle of songs *Dichterliebe* by Schumann, and the singer expressed the wish to have me for her accompanist. I still remember this evening as one of my most moving musical experiences. Félia and I became good friends after that, and I went often to her house.

My brother Ignacy was now studying music at the Schola Cantorum. In my opinion, it was a loss of time: he had no real gift for the violin, and the whole idea stemmed from his desire to emulate me. He seemed to have forgotten all about the social revolution. I saw little of him; we never had much in common.

My old pals at Fouquet's told me that Armand de Gontaut had left again for New York, insinuating that this time he was really out to catch an heiress.

To make up for his absence, they were nicer than ever toward me. The young Recopé, one of Armand's friends, transmitted an invitation to me for lunch by a Count Nicholas Potocki.

"A real Potocki of Poland and a very rich gentleman," he added. "He does not speak Polish, but he is devoted to his old country and to his compatriots. When I told him you were a Pole, he asked me to invite you."

The site today of the Chambre de Commerce on the Avenue Friedland was then the palace of the Count. He lived all alone in this huge building, which had a spacious garden, a garage, and a stable attached to it.

Entering the vast *salon de fête*, we were greeted by a rather tall gentleman in his late forties, with a bald head, a light blond mustache, and the kindest blue eyes in a round, well-shaped face. Being lame, he walked up to us with the help of a cane.

"I wish I could greet you in Polish," he said, "but I never had the chance to learn it. I was born in Siberia, where my parents were sent into exile after the revolution of 1863, and when they died, I came to live in Paris."

The salon began to fill up slowly with men of all kinds and callings, young and old. Some looked very formal, others seemed at home, but most of them came in as though they were entering a restaurant. Recopé explained the matter. Count Potocki kept a so-called open table, a remnant of a grand old Polish tradition—which meant he would offer standing invitations to lunch to a number of persons whom he wanted to see or would like to meet. They were welcome whenever they were free. The table was set daily for twenty-four persons. On that particular day I remember two ambassadors, a Russian general, a few Poles, the then famous portrait painter Bonnat, the not less famous caricaturist Sem, the actor Le Bargy, and some members of the government. There were about sixteen at the table; the other seats were empty. The food was excellent, and the conversation was on a high intellectual level.

I became a frequent guest at the Avenue Friedland. From that very first day, both the Count and I felt a great liking for each other; he won my heart because of a loneliness I sensed in him, linked with the love I felt he had for Poland, and I seemed to stimulate him with my vitality and my interest in everything. And he did adore music. Quite often, after lunch, I played for him when the other guests were gone.

My life in Paris at that time was filled with the richest artistic experiences, which provided a new, invaluable impetus for work. Pola's sweet, tender letters and Fred's intelligent support kept my spirits constantly high.

Monsieur Astruc had important plans for the season. Influenced in no small measure by my persistent effort to persuade him, he decided to bring to Paris *Salomé*, the new opera of Richard Strauss, with the original cast. There was a great political risk involved, as it would be the first time since the Franco-German war that the German language would be heard in public. The scabrous text of Oscar Wilde's play was another concern of his; Salomé's sordid love for John the Baptist and her long scene kissing his severed head on a plate might provoke in Catholic France great indignation. Undeterred, however, by these considerations, Astruc, with his usual *savoir-faire*, again obtained the support of the Countess Greffulhe with her Grandes Auditions de France, and, even more important, the promise of the President of the Republic, Monsieur Armand Fallières, to be present the opening night.

Six performances at the Châtelet were announced, with Strauss himself as the conductor. Emmy Destinn, the star, was, in my opinion, the greatest dramatic soprano of the time. I had even had a crush on her in the old days in Berlin, where she was known for her love affairs with several young music students.

All afire over this production, I took an active part in it, rehearsing with various groups and some of the soloists. Destinn herself asked me to run through the last scene with her, the most difficult and intricate part of the opera. Without realizing it, I soon knew the whole score by heart.

The six gala evenings, all sold out at a hundred francs a seat, were a boon to Astruc. Strauss and his wife, who behaved rudely at first, were now pleased. Earlier at a rehearsal, Mrs. Strauss, a mediocre liedersinger, had shouted in her Bavarian German from the balcony to her husband, who was in the orchestra pit, "Ach, wie schrecklich! This dirty theater! Ach, and this foul orchestra! I told you the French were no good," and more of the sort.

On the first night, before the beginning, the Countess Greffulhe called me to her box.

"Do you know Madame Destinn personally?" she asked me. When I said I did, she continued: "Please beseech her in my behalf to kiss the head of John the Baptist as lightly as possible; the best thing would be if she could manage not to kiss it at all!"

I left the box, amused by her apprehension; this kiss was the climax of the whole opera!

There was another amusing incident. Sacha Guitry liked to take me sometimes, just for fun, to a super-elegant *maison de passe*, a house where you could enjoy the services of beautiful call girls at very high rates. The madam of this establishment was the widow of a governmental official who took great pride in her important and rich clients. She had a penchant for Sacha and his sparkling wit. Our visits were purely platonic; neither of us could afford to enjoy the charms of her protégées. She liked to show them off, however.

"Viens ici, petite," she would call a statuesque brunette. "Show your lovely derrière to these gentlemen," and, pleased with our appreciation of the fine exhibit, she would let us admire, for an encore, a pair of hard, pointed breasts belonging to a beautiful blonde.

One afternoon, during the *Salomé* performances, I met Guitry on the street.

"Allons faire une petite visite à la vieille!" said Sacha, and I went with him. The madam offered us sherry and biscuits, I told some funny stories about Strauss and *Salomé*, and she gratified us with an ampler view of the brunette's anatomy.

Two days later, at the Pavillon de Hanovre, I was given a letter; it was from the madam and she had written, more or less, the following: "A very important client of mine is a collector of autographs. He craves to own one of Maître Strauss. Could you possibly help me in this matter? I don't dare to offer you money for this service, but I have a better proposition for you. Vous pouvez coucher gratuitement avec la belle brune."

When I showed this letter to Strauss, Astruc, and other members of the cast, it provoked a riot; they couldn't stop laughing. The poor woman, of course, never got an answer from me.

When Sacha and I, a few weeks later, strolled over again for a visit to the *maison*, I was prepared to parry any reproach for my not answering by denying that I had ever received the letter. When we entered the small salon, she embraced me. "You angel," she screamed, "I don't know how to thank you for the beautiful autograph! My client was delighted!" I must have made a silly face; I was stupefied. Strauss's old bearded Berlin stage manager, while reading the famous letter, took a good look at the address and exchanged the letter in which Strauss thanked him for his "precious contribution to the success of the opera" for a couple of hours with the gorgeous brunette!

After the last evening at the Châtelet, Emmy Destinn invited me for supper in her suite at the Hotel Regina, where she stayed with her sister. They changed into their dressing gowns, and the three of us sat down to a snack of cold meat and champagne. I expressed my admiration of her art to the great singer and cited some particularly impressive moments in her *Aïda*, *Carmen*, and, now *Salomé*.

"The way you sing is a great lesson for me," I said. "You taught me how to use judiciously the rubato, that much misunderstood definition of the free expression of a melody. I try to translate your perfect breathing control into my own phrasing, and I feel certain that Chopin had exactly that on his mind when he required rubato in his works."

Emmy Destinn listened to my long talk with frowning attention, but suddenly she picked up her glass of champagne and smashed it to bits against the fireplace.

"All right, all right," she screamed, in a rage. "I know I am a good singer, but I am also a woman!"

I was aghast. Her sister stood up calmly and left the room, and here I was, with Pola in my heart and on my mind, expected to prove that I was a man, too! She was a strange woman, Emmy Destinn. And she really frightened me when I saw the threatening head of a serpent on her thigh. She had a bright-colored tattoo of a boa encircling her leg from the ankle to the upper thigh; it took me some time to get over my shock. I am afraid I was not at my best that night, but she seemed not to mind; later she became quite mellow and maternal.

Well, anyway, she had to leave the next day for London to take her important part in the great season of the Covent Garden Opera. And here is another unaccountable trait of this great artist—for weeks she sent me letters in the form of poems in verse in a fine calligraphic handwriting on a special de luxe paper. Like a romantic teenager, indeed.

Meanwhile, my stunt of being able to play the whole score of *Salomé* from memory proved to have solid earning power. After its phenomenal success, the opera remained for quite a while a topic of in-

terest among the musical elite of Paris. Many amateurs wishing to become better acquainted with the intricacies of this modern work would
ask me to play it "professionally" for them privately. This proposition
delighted me by its novel form of earning money. Five hundred francs
was the uniform price I established for such a performance, but, as well,
I was not a little flattered by the great impression my memory made on
my listeners. The atmosphere at these gatherings was vastly different
from the one at the regular *soirées de musique*. Here, only a half a dozen
or so of the latest Strauss devotees made up my whole audience, and they
listened to the music while reading scrupulously the score and the words.

Monsieur Astruc had yet another surprise up his sleeve for the spring
season: a grand festival of Russian music for four nights at the Théâtre
de l'Opéra. The program was truly sensational. Arthur Nikisch was the
general musical director of the concerts, but a few composers conducted
their own works, among them Rimsky-Korsakov, Glazunov, Rachmaninoff, and Scriabin. Chaliapin—and this was his real Parisian debut—sang
long excerpts from *Boris Godunov* by Moussorgsky, and *Prince Igor*
by Borodin. Symphonies and large scenes from different operas were
performed under Arthur Nikisch.

The plan for this ambitious undertaking was conceived by a Russian
nobleman, Sergei Diaghilev, and became a reality thanks to Gabriel
Astruc. The young Russian had the patronage of the Grand Duke
Vladimir and, especially, of his wife, the Grand Duchess Maria Pavlovna,
but most of the money required by the huge apparatus of the festival
had to be found by the ingenious Astruc. Fortunately, he was up to the
task, and the contracts could be signed.

Needless to say, Frederic and I were among the most assiduous and
passionate listeners at the festival and happy to witness the immense
impact some of the music had on the usually so critical and skeptical
public of Paris. Chaliapin scored a major triumph with Galitzky's song
from *Prince Igor* and the long scene of Boris Godunov, but this time he
had to share it with Moussorgsky and Borodin, whose music made a
deep impression. Rachmaninoff brought the house down with a beautiful
performance of his Second Concerto, which was heard for the first time
outside Russia. In the artists' room after the first concert, Chaliapin embraced and kissed me.

"Artoosha, what a wonderful surprise! Come and join us for supper
at the Café de Paris."

As I entered the restaurant I expected to find him in the company of
some fresh feminine conquests, but, to my astonishment, I saw at his
table two distinguished and elegant ladies.

"This is my wife Masha and this is her sister," he introduced me in a formal way. It was amusing to see him so different from the Don Juan he had been the year before in Orange.

The festival of Russian music brought with it unforeseen consequences; it opened the way to the creation of the fabulous seasons of Diaghilev's Ballets Russes. I shall try to give a short résumé of the string of developments which culminated in this unique artistic explosion.

The revelation, thanks to Chaliapin, of the beauty and novelty of the excerpts of *Boris Godunov* and *Prince Igor* aroused a clamor in the Paris press for the complete performances of these operas. Both Astruc and Diaghilev responded and went to work at once. With Astruc's assurance of large financial support, Diaghilev left for Russia to assemble the artistic forces he needed for such a venture. And this was the occasion when he revealed a genius for finding just the right elements for his productions. Instead of using the usual old-fashioned stage sets, he commissioned some modern painters, whom he had supported financially for a long time, to produce new ideas. He found a brilliant young dancer, Fokine, who longed to create something new for the dances in *Prince Igor*. And, of course, Diaghilev chose the best singers, with Chaliapin as the star, and his ballet dancers were all hand-picked from the Operas of Petersburg and Warsaw. Such an ensemble could not fail; the Opera that season was the sensation of the year. But what excited Paris most were the dances in *Prince Igor*. One had never seen anything like it before: the music, the daring colors of the décor, the explosive sensuality of the dances—it was overpowering, and quickly became the talk of Paris.

"What about a full season of your kind of ballet for the next spring in Paris?" Astruc asked Diaghilev.

Even before this question was uttered, the Russian had all sorts of fantastic plans in mind. As a result, Paris was given the most brilliant theatrical event of the century. Nothing seen before or after surpassed the success of the ballet *Schéhérazade*, for which Diaghilev used the symphonic poem of Rimsky-Korsakov, the dazzling green and blue decoration and fantastic Oriental costumes by Bakst, the debut of Nijinsky as the amorous slave and the beautiful Karsavina as the adulteress in the harem. The two of them danced again in *Le Spectre de la Rose* with music by Weber, and Nijinsky was sensational when he leaped through the window so lightly that he seemed to jump into the sky.

But the outstanding revelation of that season was Anna Pavlova, who was immediately acclaimed as the greatest classical dancer of the time. She inspired poets to write odes to her wherever she appeared. On stage she was a sylphid, a fairy, while Karsavina danced like a full-blooded, sexy woman. From that unforgettable season on, the whole world was waiting impatiently for the next visit of the Ballets Russes. Astruc was the master of its organization, Diaghilev the genius of its artistic production. It was Diaghilev who, after hearing a short piece for orchestra by a young pupil of Rimsky-Korsakov's, commissioned him to write the first original score for a ballet. The young man was Igor Stravinsky, and the ballet was *The Firebird*. It was a triumph. The following seasons, up until the World War, brought his *Petrouchka* and the famous scandal of *Le Sacre du printemps*, the great success of *Daphnis et Chloé* by Ravel, *Jeux* by Debussy, and many others, major and minor successes. The greatest painters of our time provided the decorations and costumes, among them Picasso, Matisse, Braque, Rouault, Chagall, Derain, Dufy, and Marie Laurencin. Diaghilev revolutionized the whole artistic world and not only the fine arts; fashions, interior decoration, color schemes for materials were deeply influenced by his productions. Yes, one can safely call the years before the First World War the epoch of the Ballets Russes. After Diaghilev's death many ballet companies were started, and thanks to the great American impresario Sol Hurok, the ballet reached its golden age.

41

One morning Frederic came into my room and made me read a letter from Basia. I could see from his face that it meant bad news for me. Basia, in her terse style, simply asked her brother to make me return Pola's letters to her at once! No further comment. Deeply hurt, I gave the treasured letters to Frederic without uttering a word. But, at that moment, life lost its charm for me. Finally, after several sleepless nights, I came to the conclusion that this abrupt break must have been forced on Pola, and I lived for the day when I could see her again to find out the truth.

Meanwhile, a pleasant surprise took my mind off this nightmare. Because of my stunt of playing *Salomé* by heart, I received an interesting engagement in London. A rich American lady, Mrs. Potter Palmer, had rented for the season the town palace of the Dukes of Sutherland so that she could entertain London society. When she heard that the opera

Salomé had been banned in England for its religious implications, and that King Edward VII had expressed curiosity to hear it, she decided to arrange a performance for him. As no room was big enough to accommodate an orchestra, she hit upon the idea of having me perform it on the piano; she had heard me doing it at one of the soirées in Paris.

The regal fee of a hundred guineas, the chance of seeing Emmy Destinn again (she was the star of the Covent Garden Opera season), and the honor of playing for the King of England made this engagement most attractive. I arrived in London with great expectations. At our first meeting, Mrs. Potter Palmer expressed anxiety about the length of the opera.

"Could you play just a few excerpts from it?" she asked.

"Yes," I answered, "though I am afraid they would be too fragmentary. But," I added, "I could play the 'Dance of the Seven Veils' alone and if you would engage Emmy Destinn to sing the great last scene of *Salomé* accompanied by me, it should make a perfect program."

"Hurrah, hurrah," she cried, "that is a brilliant idea! I am going to arrange it right away!" And she dashed out of the room to put her secretary to work on it. To my disappointment, however, through some sudden impulse of patriotism, she engaged the American soprano Olive Fremstad for the final scene.

Emmy Destinn received me joyously and kept me for dinner, but she seemed slightly piqued about my collaboration with Fremstad. Still, she invited me to hear Caruso and herself at Covent Garden in *Aïda*.

The concert and the reception took place at three in the afternoon. There were not more than thirty guests, and the King was the last to arrive. Four of the ladies present were pointed out to me as sometime mistresses of His Majesty. He had good taste, I must admit—all four of them were beautiful. Mrs. Potter Palmer had had a small platform built at one end of the room, with a fine Bechstein grand rented especially for me. The King settled down in front, quite close to the platform, and the others sat around him.

My performance of the "Dance of the Seven Veils" was well received; at least, they listened to this modern music in silence; the English have better concert manners than the French. Olive Fremstad was a wonderful soprano; she sang the difficult long lament of Salomé with perfect intonation and in a grand style (but I missed the intense, heartbreaking quality of Destinn's voice). She had a well-deserved success, making me share it most graciously, and we had to bow several times to the applause.

When I termed her success "well deserved," I may add that she deserved it even more, but for a quite extraneous reason: all the while she was singing, the King puffed at a big cigar and blew the smoke right into her face; it was something short of a miracle that she was able to overcome such a handicap.

After the concert tea was served, Madame Fremstad and I were introduced to His Majesty. What struck me most in him was the elegance and art with which he covered his *embonpoint*. His fame as the best-dressed man in the world was well deserved. That day, he wore a long, dark single-breasted frock coat with large silk lapels. (This formal dress is replaced now by the cutaway.) Instead of the usual front buttons, two sapphires at each end of a small golden chain were inserted into the corresponding buttonholes, allowing the coat to fall in a graceful line.

The King had a sonorous low voice and spoke with a slight German accent. He had some warm words of praise for Madame Fremstad and then turned to me for a discussion about the merits of Strauss's opera.

"I did not notice anything shocking in what I heard, and I cannot understand why our censors objected to it," he said. Obviously, he expected to be a little scandalized and was secretly disappointed.

That same evening I saw *Aïda* with Destinn and Caruso, an unforgettable event in my life. At that performance Emmy received greater ovations than her partner, but I attribute it to the fact that Verdi endowed the role of Aïda with more beautiful music than that of Radames.

I stayed a few days more in London, spending every day at the charming house at Tavistock Square which Destinn and her sister had rented for the season. We made much music, enjoyed the cuisine, or went to the Opera to hear great singing. I remember with pleasure our short love affair; it was romantic, but neither of us was intensely involved.

My return to Paris brought me back to reality. The *grande saison* with its parties, balls, races, concerts, and theaters was coming to an end, and I had no plans for the summer.

Frederic had signed a contract for a tour in America as an accompanist of a concert singer. Without him I lost my contact with the dear Barylskis, and I did not feel like going to Warsaw or Lodz. The Whites (Olive) had left for Deauville, and Armand de Gontaut was still in New York. And yet, Fortune smiled on me once more. The Baronne Gustave de Rothschild invited me to play at a soirée which marked the end of the *saison* and was considered the most important social function of the year. When I went to the palatial house at the Avenue Marigny to discuss the program, the Baroness, an elderly lady, showed the vitality of a person half her age.

"I want you to play a short program alone," she said, "and after an intermission you will accompany Miss Destinn [this time] in two arias from *Carmen* and in the last scene of *Salomé*. Your fee is a thousand francs."

She spoke with a tone of finality. With the same authority she directed her secretary, her butler, her gardener, her carpenter, and the other help in the disposition of the podium, the piano, the chairs, the arrangement of the flowers, and all the minute details for the evening; she acted like a general.

And the party turned out to be the most brilliant *soirée musicale* in which I had the privilege to take part. The *tout Paris* was there. The old aristocracy, only a few years after the ghastly Dreyfus affair, the Académie Française, the University, artists, writers, musicians, were all well represented. The white and gold paneled grand salon with its priceless paintings, the harmoniously placed flowers, and the elegance of the audience made a dazzling sight.

The concert was a triumph for Destinn and quite a success for myself. When the applause subsided, we were invited to join the guests at a mile-long buffet laden with an endless variety of food. Cold langouste and fish with their mayonnaise and green sauces, cold duck and chicken, hot dishes of curry, especially prepared ice creams, pyramids of cherries and strawberries, and delicious pastries filled the table. Champagne was the only wine served.

I brought Emmy to her hotel at a very late hour, but she did not let me stay; she had to return to London early in the morning.

There is a sentimental sequel to my so vivid memory of this particular night. At the end of World War I it so happened that I, and later my wife, too, became close friends of Robert and Nelly de Rothschild, the heirs of the indomitable Baroness Gustave. And when we returned to Paris after World War II, this friendship became even closer with the next generation of this great family and continues to this very day.

42

"Why have you been absent from my luncheons for such a long time?" asked Count Potocki, when I appeared again at his "open house." I gave him a full account of my visit to London and made him laugh with my imitations of the King of England and other celebrities. When I mentioned the Rothschild party, Count Potocki exclaimed: "Let us have a musical party right here!" He fixed the date and sent out the invitations that same day. My concert in his palace was very different from the others. The guests were chosen among the cream of the *demimonde* mixed with a trickle of famous actresses; I remember the presence of Bartet, Cecile Sorel, and Eve Lavalliere. The men, all very wealthy, some of them high government officials or members of the Jockey Club, were mostly the lovers of the ladies of the *demimonde*. The others were the Count's daily table companions. An assembly of that sort, not the kind to be seen at concerts, has obviously little understanding of classical music. So, while I played some Chopin, the general conversation went on and became louder and louder. But when I finished, they stood up and applauded heartily! The high point of the evening came when supper was served at small tables. The host gave us a fine sample of the Polish hospitality. At my table sat an Italian beauty named Mariella who was intelligent and had a complete lack of inhibition. And she came to the party unescorted.

"I loved your concert," she said, "but my God is Puccini." And, later, warmed up by the champagne, she told me all about herself.

"J'ai un ami serieux," she said, "the banker Oppenheimer from Cologne. I call him l'O. de Cologne, ha, ha; he has set me up in a charming apartment, comes to visit me every month for a few days, but the rest of the time I am free. Tomorrow I am having some charming friends for dinner. Will you come?"

I accepted with pleasure. Her guests were two young women from her milieu and the banker Édouard Weisweiller, a good musician and an amateur pianist. Mariella liked to entertain in her cozy flat; she had prepared the spaghetti herself, the wine was of a good vintage, and she had a way of telling funny stories with her low-voiced Italian accent. In appreciation, I played all the Puccini I could think of and was rewarded with hugs and kisses.

On the way home, Weisweiller asked if I could give him some piano lessons. I quickly accepted his offer, thinking that he seemed somewhat gifted, and I anticipated a large fee. As usual the money I had just melted in my hands, and my debts were growing again from day to day. I owed money to the tailor, to Cordovinus, to dear Mrs. Cowl for a whole month, and my allowance from Astruc was heavily overdrawn. It was a *cauchemar*.

One morning Mr. Biernacki, Count Potocki's Polish secretary, brought me a present from the Count, a pair of cuff links made of four cabochon sapphires set in platinum, along with a letter, inviting me to spend the weekend at his country place near Rambouillet; he would take me down in his motorcar. This was pleasant news, but his gift disappointed me. I had hoped to receive a nice sum of money for my playing, and I was

Donnerstag, den 12. Februar 1903

Abends 7¹/₂ Uhr

IM BEETHOVEN-SAAL

Klavier-Abend

von

Arthur Rubinstein

PROGRAMM.

1. Sonate E-moll op. 90 . . . . *L. v. Beethoven*
   Mit Lebhaftigkeit und durchaus mit Empfindung und Ausdruck. —
   Nicht zu geschwind und sehr singbar vorzutragen.

2. Capriccio H-moll, op. 76 No. 2 . . . . . . }
   Intermezzo B-moll, op. 117 No. 2 . . . . . } *Joh. Brahms*
   Variationen über ein Thema von Paganini, op. 35 }
       Heft II . . . . }

3. Davidsbündlertänze op. 6 . . . . *R. Schumann*
   Lebhaft — Innig — Etwas hahnbüchen — Ungeduldig — Sehr rasch und
   in sich hinein — Mit äusserst starker Empfindung — Frisch — Hierauf
   schloss Florestan und es zuckte ihm schmerzlich um die Lippen —
   Balladenmässig — Einfach — Mit Humor — Wild und lustig — Zart
   und singend — Frisch — Mit gutem Humor — Wie aus der Ferne —
   Ganz zum Ueberfluss meinte Eusebius noch Folgendes: dabei sprach aber
   viel Seligkeit aus seinen Augen.

4. Mazurka G-dur op. 50 No. 1 . . . . }
   Mazurka F-moll op 63 No. 2 . . . . } *Fr. Chopin*
   Nocturne G-dur op. 37 No. 2 . . . . }
   Rhapsodie hongroise No. 12 . . . . *Fr. Liszt*

LA VIE DE PARIS

Arthur Rubinstein

— Un pianiste qui se nomme Rubinstein ! C'est impossible ! Qu'il change de nom tout de suite !

C'est par cette vive riposte que me répondit une personne, très affinée d'ailleurs et aussi très avisée, à qui j'annonçai récemment l'arrivée à Paris du jeune virtuose porteur de ce nom redoutable.

— Voulez-vous l'entendre ? rétorquai-je à mon tour.

— Très volontiers !

Rendez-vous fut pris aussitôt, et quelques jours plus tard, durant deux grandes heures sous l'inspiration de sa propre fantaisie, ou obéissant au désir inattendu des personnes présentes qui voulaient éprouver sa technique sa mémoire, et surtout ses facultés d'interprétation, le jeune Rubinstein remplit ses auditeurs d'admiration et d'étonnement : admiration pour la sûreté et la majestueuse simplicité de son art d'où semble exclue toute difficulté d'exécution et où l'esprit des maîtres se réfléchit comme en un miroir ; étonnement pour sa culture vraiment prodigieuse, puis

qu'elle lui permet de jouer indistinctement, de mémoire et toujours avec l'expression qui convient, non seulement tous les maîtres de la littérature du piano classique et moderne, mais les symphonies d'Haydn, de Mozart, de Beethoven, de Schumann et de Brahms, les poèmes symphoniques de Richard Strauss et les drames lyriques de Wagner.

Les rares privilégiés qui eurent l'occasion d'entendre le jeune Rubinstein reçurent la même impression de surprise. Edouard Colonne, Camille Chevillard, Paul Dukas, Ernest Van Dyck, Gaston Salvayre, quelques autres encore, tous furent émerveillés par l'étendue de son savoir musical autant que par la maîtrise de son exécution.

— Ce qui me frappe chez cet artiste, disait après l'avoir écouté M. Pierre Lalo, le très distingué critique du Temps, c'est que, malgré sa grande jeunesse, il sait, rompu à toutes les difficultés de la technique, se placer au-dessus des détails de l'œuvre interprétée pour en donner une exécution synthétique. Il voit et il joue large. Il ne se perd pas dans les détails où d'autres se complaisent, car les difficultés d'exécution sont chez lui résolues d'elles-mêmes. Cette sérénité lui permet de se donner tout entier à l'interprétation des maîtres, et voilà pourquoi il se classe d'emblée parmi les plus grands. »

Tel est le jeune artiste — il n'a pas dix-huit ans — que Paris entendra pour la première fois le lundi soir 19 décembre, au Nouveau-Théâtre, avec le concours de Mlle Mary Garden, de l'Opéra-Comique, et de l'orchestre Lamoureux, sous la direction de M. Chevillard.

De taille moyenne, svelte et naturellement élégant, le cheveu abondant et typique, d'une allure fière où vient adoucir une timidité charmante, Rubinstein porte sur son jeune visage le masque expressif des passions dont il est l'interprète. Ses yeux, qu'une lueur fugitive d'inquiétude sillonne parfois, accusent l'émotion que traduisent ses doigts.

Né en 1887 à Lodz, grande ville manufacturière de la Pologne russe, il est l'enfant de cette patrie de Chopin, terre de prédilection, riche de poésie, féconde en musiciens de génie, où toute vie semble devoir se traduire par un geste d'art. Comme tant d'autres, il eût pu faire profession d'enfant prodige, car la nature l'avait doté des dons les plus rares qui se manifestèrent dès sa plus tendre enfance. Mais sans doute la Providence lui réservait une destinée plus haute, puisqu'elle mit sur sa route un homme qui lui traça, en l'aplanissant, la route qu'il devait suivre ; cet homme occupe depuis un demi-siècle la plus haute situation qu'un artiste puisse envier : il a nom Joachim.

Joachim avait entendu Rubinstein tout enfant ; il le fit venir à Berlin, lui choisit un maître renommé — le professeur Heinrich Barth, — assura son existence, surveilla ses études, fit tant et si bien qu'à l'âge de douze ans son jeune protégé donnait un grand concert avec orchestre, à la salle Beethoven, devant une assistance extraordinaire, aux premiers rangs de laquelle, à côté du vénérable Joachim et du professeur Barth, se pressaient Max Bruch, Humperdinck, Gernsheim et toutes les notabilités du monde musical. Nous ne suivrons pas Rubinstein dans ses nombreux concerts à Hambourg, à Dresde où, âgé seulement de quatorze ans, il produit une sensation inoubliable dans un concerto de Mozart, à Varsovie où il provoque l'enthousiasme du public de la Philharmonie.

Mais je veux conter une anecdote :

S. A. I. la grande-duchesse de Mecklembourg, désirant entendre Rubinstein, l'invite un jour au palais ducal de Schwerin. Elle l'écoute une heure, deux heures, tout l'après-midi ; Son Altesse en oublie même d'aller à l'Opéra. La soirée passée, Rubinstein est encore invité quelques jours plus tard, à la fête de la grande-duchesse, où, seul artiste engagé, il joua trois concertos avec orchestre devant un parterre royal.

N'est-ce pas le plus bel exemple à citer de cette sorte de fascination qu'Arthur Rubinstein exerce sur tous ceux qui l'entendent ? Je puis ajouter que lors d'une entrevue récente, Rubinstein impressionna très vivement le plus spirituel des critiques musicaux, j'ai nommé Henry Gauthier-Villars :

— Son art d'interprète est tel, disait ce dernier après avoir entendu le jeune artiste jouer plusieurs pièces de Brahms, qu'il arrive à colorer et à rendre sympathique une musique que, pour ma part, je trouve d'une riche aridité et à laquelle les concerts français n'ont pas encore fait la même place qu'à celle de Beethoven et des autres grands maîtres. »

... Et voilà pourquoi Arthur Rubinstein ne changera pas de nom !

Charles Joly.

Cl. Paul Berger

ARTHUR RUBINSTEIN

C'est un jeune, très jeune virtuose. La presse n'avait pas encore propagé son nom. Tout au plus sait-on de lui qu'il débuta sous l'égide de Joachim. Cependant, des artistes éclairés le tenaient pour un des interprètes les plus extraordinaires de Chopin, de Brahms et de Schumann. Il vient de se révéler au monde musical parisien dans un concert donné au Nouveau-Théâtre. Et l'opinion qu'avaient de lui des initiés s'est élargie au public, qui lui fera bientôt une renommée universelle.

ARTHUR RUBINSTEIN MAKES
HIS AMERICAN DEBUT

POLISH PIANIST'S WONDERFUL TECHNIQUE
DAZZLES CARNEGIE HALL AUDIENCE

Plays a Saint-Saens Concerto with Marvellous Digital Skill and Great Intelligence, Sweeping Audience Off Its Feet and Creating a Furore.

Those hands!—dozens of them—those fingers!—scores, hundreds, seemingly—galloping up and down the keyboard of the concert grand—dashing from clef to treble, from sharp to flat, from end to end—rushing, bounding, swirling—tirelessly, wondrously, with stupendous digital dexterity—then a crash—discordant, with the intonation of a miniature peal of thunder— a slim figure rises from the chair at the piano, bows once, thrice, five times to the audience—bows to the orchestra, to its leader!

Arthur Rubinstein, the Polish pianist, has made his American debut.

It happened at Carnegie Hall on January 8, the Philadelphia Orchestra, with Fritz Scheel conducting, furnishing the instrumental music. The concert stamped Rubinstein as one of the world's greatest pianists —not in the overworked, abused sense of the word "great," but in its real meaning —great because of his stupendous technique, because of his indisputable talent, because of what he has accomplished in spite of the limitations of youth. This is the opinion of one, endorsed by the great audience which acclaimed Rubinstein and forced him to play three encores—it is to some extent the opinion of the erudite New York critics—one of whom slept throughout the greater portion of the boy's recital and another of whom confessed to a lady beside him, and in hearing of the writer, that he it was who really wrote the critiques of the man who slept.

Rubinstein is very young, very boyish—very immature, so far as the great sorrows which make the great artists are concerned. Let the next five years or less bring him some genuine heartache, such as befalls the majority of us—let some American girl twist his heartstrings around her dainty little finger and then break the alleged seat of affection, and—Arthur Rubinstein will be the greatest of all pianists. He has the genius, the physical ability, the tremendous nerve force necessary—let him gain a quota of blighted affections and all will be well with him.

Personally, he is a charming youth—slender, graceful—the gentleman. He has a well-poised head, crowned with dark brown hair, not too much, yet enough to set off his face to advantage. His hands are long, shapely and evidently tremendously powerful. He plays without undue exertion—performs the most marvelous digital contortions with the utmost ease— has none of the mannerisms usually associated with the great in all lines of endeavor—he is, as yet, an unspoiled boy.

This was proved by the delighted manner in which he received the applause of the audience and in the avidity with which he responded with three encores. There was nothing stagey about it—just happiness that the American public liked his playing well enough to demand more of it. It was also proven by the incidental happening that when he first sat down to play he found the chair too low, and was forced to place the scores of Brahms' Second Symphony and Schumann's "Liebesfruehling" on the chair that his seat might be high enough.

He played Saint-Saens' concerto in G minor and rendered it with dash and verve, with wonderful intonation and most intelligent shading. The tone which this slim youth manages to produce is really astonishing and shows that he possesses considerable muscular force to produce the technique which amazed his audience. For an encore he played Liszt's "The Mephisto Waltz" in "The Episodes from Lenau's Faust."

The Philadelphia Orchestra was at its best when playing the beautifully blended "Liebesfruehling," the lights and shades of the overture being exquisitely intoned.

The Brahms symphony and especially the fourth movement, allegretto grazioso quasi andantino, was played very well indeed. Max Schillings' symphonic prologue to Sophocles' "Oedipus Rex" closed the evening's entertainment.

Press comments:

New York "Herald": "Brilliancy from the outset marked his treatment of it and won him a real ovation from the house. His touch proved remarkably crisp and firm, his fingers wonderfully fleet, his pedaling judicious and his notions of phrasing generally excellent."

New York "Times": "He has a crisp and brilliant touch, remarkable facility and fleetness of technique—though this is not altogether flawless—and much strength of finger and arm. He knows how to make all these things count for the utmost; and his performance of the concerto was imposing. His delivery of the preluding of the opening movement, with its suggestion of Bach, was emphatic. There was grace in the scherzo, and the tarantelle of the last movement, which he took at a great speed, was brilliant."

New York "Tribune": "In Mr. Rubinstein's performance there was an exhibition of amazing digital skill. His fingers flew with lightning speed over the keyboard and bounded with marvellous elasticity from the keys to the scherzo."

New York "Press": "A few bars only were needed to show that here was a boy of unusual gifts. His confident attack; his round, full tone; the massive, yet delicate beauty of his touch stamped him at once as a born virtuoso. The impression grew stronger as he played on. In spite of many an objectionable feature in his performance, the impression remained that Rubinstein had all the essentials that go to the making of a great pianist. He has magnetism in plenty; he has temperament to an excess; he has musical grasp and remarkable technical capacity."

YOUNG RUBINSTEIN AN ARTIST OF PROMISE

A very slender youth, dressed in the most fashionable evening clothes, with a leonine head topped by waves of light brown hair; this is the interesting outward personality of Arthur Rubinstein the Polish pianist, with the revered name, who played in the Light Guard armory Wednesday evening. The social and musical element of Detroit, which usually attends concerts, was conspicuous by its absence, and the audience was one of strange faces and stranger clothes as concert gatherings go. A man in dress clothes was not to be seen aside from the manager at the door, and the very correctly garbed young artist on the platform. That a musically apprecia-

tive and brilliant
greet Rubinstein is
the young player i
and played an att
a manner to arrest
interest.

Rubinstein playe
in this country in 1
a month ago, and
quent appearances
Boston he was cri
judgment and by
less forceful young
escaped with "pre
have been allowed
notice by kind ind
whole Rubinstein o
rather than rebuffe
erican reception. a
he—a youth of 19,
lustrious name—sh
critical controversy
pliment and an ach
ing Wednesday ni
sive proof that the
add another great
honor—a second
knows? The youn

EIN W WIEDNIU

cja. z Wiednia pióra
Warszawski" 24.XI.)
m.in. takie oto re-

instein porywa. Jego
estionuje. Poddaję się
siły, jej szlachetnej
rowi jej wyrazu, któ-
owiadać najsubtelniej-
i stany uczuciowe.
ucha się zawsze z za-
nem. To jest talent z
ent torujący sobie sam
tym talent wyrosły
podłożem nam wszyst-
tóry trafia do naszych
ej, że czuje się w nim
ską i nawskroś polski
stęp jego zwolenników
każdym występem.
a Musikvereinu była
orzód wyprzedana".

jer Warszawski
24, 1912

RUBINSTEIN IN VIE

Correspondence from Vi
(*Kurjer Warszawski*, 24 No
along with other news these
". . . I am carried away b
His playing fascinates me. I
charm of his strength, his nob
the seduction of his expressi
how to portray the most sub
emotional states. One alwa
Rubinstein breathlessly. It is
talent that forges its own
grown out of and linked v
that are so close to us all,
reaches to our hearts, espe
one feels in him the Slavic s
Polish sentiment. The numb
mirers grows here with his
ance. The enormous Musikv
sold out a week before the co

told that sapphires did not fetch a good price when sold because they are too easy to simulate.

The Count called his place a shooting box, but what I found was a great villa, big enough to accommodate a dozen guests. I was the only one this time. The master of the house lived there with his mistress, a Madame Mathilde d'Avignon, all through the summer and the September shooting season; his grounds bordered on the estate of the summer residence of the presidents of France. I was given a beautiful room in white and pink, with an adjoining boudoir with flowers and fruit on the tables and some good books on the shelves. It was a pleasure to enter the bathroom. From my window I had the view of a graceful lawn and lovely flowers.

Biernacki told me about the Count's passion for horses. "Being lame, he cannot ride anymore," he said, "but he is very active as the president of the Éperon, a club which organizes the yearly Concours hippique in Paris."

On Sunday morning, Count Potocki took me in a cabriolet to his stables, holding with assurance and elegance the reins of his four-in-hand. He showed me with pride a few fine thoroughbreds and led me to a manège especially equipped for learning to ride. We sat in a box, like one in a theater, which he used to direct the proceedings; he noticed with satisfaction my interest in horses.

"You must come here this summer—I shall teach you how to ride like a gentleman," he said.

"I would love to learn," I answered politely, but I almost jumped with joy. I was so grateful to find a place to spend this wretched summer!

Mathilde d'Avignon (one of those adopted names) was a woman in her forties with an indifferent face and a good figure. She tried hard to look distinguished by copying the gestures and manners of her actress friends, to no avail. And she was deaf, poor woman.

Back in Paris, I began my work with Mr. Weisweiller. He played quite well, for a banker, and wanted to improve, but his technique gave him trouble and he had not much time for practice. My fee was a louis d'or per lesson, not enough, I thought, but Mariella had warned me. "He is stingy," she had said with the knowledge of experience. I made it up, however, by giving him an hour daily.

Frederic anounced one morning, "I am leaving tomorrow for Brittany because my singer needs me for rehearsing," and seeing me look rather distressed, he continued: "You won't miss me, Arthur; anyhow, for quite some time now, we have hardly seen each other. I think, to be frank, that neither my presence nor my absence would make any difference to you."

It was a harsh statement, but he was right. In the beginning I did try to make him meet my friends, but he refused, declaring, "Ce n'est pas mon monde." On the other hand, he was worried about the life I was leading, neglecting serious work for playing in "salons." As to Pola, he was completely noncommittal.

Nevertheless, we parted as the friends we really were. Mrs. Cowl, who worshiped him and felt lonely after his departure, decided to close her apartment and go to England for the summer. This put me into a difficult situation. I owed her a large sum of money which I was in no position to pay. But she was kind and generous. When I offered her the small amount I could afford as an advance on my debt, she refused to accept it.

"You will repay me whenever you can, my dear, so keep the little money you have; you will need it for the long summer ahead of you."

I embraced the noble creature with deep gratitude.

A hotel at the Avenue Carnot was anything but inviting, its only attraction being its low rates. The room I took situated on the highest floor was so small that no piano, even an upright one, could possibly be placed there. It was almost unendurable for me to live without an instrument. However, the fatalist that I was, and am, I accepted this as a punishment for my neglect of the piano at the rue Lauriston.

I remember these last weeks of July mainly as a sordid fight for survival; my funds were quite insufficient for both food and room. And so I became shamefully dependent on invitations from friends for meals. Dinners at Mariella's and, especially, the two splendid ones offered us by the accommodating O. de Cologne at Voisin's allowed me to go without food until the next day, and the splendid luncheons at the Avenue Friedland used to appease my appetite for the rest of the day. Overdrawn with Astruc, my only source of income was my lessons with Weisweiller, who reduced them to three a week; it was too hot, he said.

To my great relief, Count Potocki reminded me, as if I needed to be reminded, of my promise to spend the summer at his "shooting box" in Rambouillet.

"Come on the first of August and stay as long as you wish. I have ordered a good piano to be sent especially for you."

This great lift to my sinking spirits restored immediately my natural zest for living, and also, alas, my carelessness in handling money. So one night I went through an experience not easily forgotten. After indulging at Maxim's in a caviar sandwich and coffee, I returned late to my hotel and asked the night porter for the key to my room.

"I can't give you the key unless you pay your bill," the man said.

"This is absurd," I answered. "I am only a few days overdue. I shall pay my bill tomorrow."

"I have strict orders not to deliver the key if I don't get the money right now," the man said.

I became exasperated. "I have no money in my pocket, and it's impossible to raise it in the middle of the night, don't you understand? I assure you, I shall pay tomorrow, but now you must let me get into my room!"

He did not answer, just picked up a newspaper. I banged my fist on the desk. I was out of my mind with rage. "You have no right to do that, I shall call the police," I screamed, but he merely shrugged his shoulders. This was too much for me. I ran out into the street to think of something, but nothing came to my mind. Finally, I sat down on one of the benches on the Place de l'Étoile and fell asleep from exhaustion. The early dawn woke me up. I began to pace the nearby Avenue Wagram waiting for a café to open, and when it did, I settled down to three or four coffees with croissants to warm me up and began to consider seriously what to do. At nine o'clock, I decided to telephone Mr. Weisweiller and ask him to help me out. I would pay him back with lessons. The man whom Mariella called stingy appeared in less than a half-hour at the café, went with me to the hotel, and demanded to see the manager. The manager turned out to be a tall, thin-lipped lady who asked me coldly, "Did you bring the money?"

At that, my friend picked up the bill, read it carefully, and threw the right amount on the desk. And then he gave it to her: "You treat hotel guests in a barbaric way, Madame," he shouted. "This young man is a great artist and you might have damaged his health forever out there in the cold." (It was actually hot.) "I really should sue you!"

She didn't say a word.

"Go and pack up your things." He turned to me. "I am going to take you away from this horrible place."

When my things were brought down, he hailed a cab, but before we left, he snapped at the woman: "You can tip your employees yourself—you trained them to become just as wicked as you are."

He gave an address to the *cocher* and, during the ride, told me his immediate plans for me. His proposition had an amusing, unmistakably Parisian touch.

"J'ai loué un petit pied-à-terre pour une charmante petite amie et je l'ai mise dans ses meubles," he said, "mais elle a fichu le camp avec un autre type," he added, smiling sadly, "and now that she has run out on me and as I am stuck with the lease for a whole year you can move in right now if you like it. There are no strings attached, and I am going to give you an advance on our future lessons. You must have some money to live on." And he pushed into my hands a bill of five hundred francs. A wonderful fellow, this Weisweiller! Another appearance of my by now familiar *deus ex machina*.

The little flat was, by a strange coincidence, on the rue Cardinet, at the other end from the Pension Cordovinus. It consisted of a living room, a bedroom, a *cabinet de toilette*, and a small kitchenette. Darkness reigned as in a cellar; the ground floor on a narrow street did not allow the sun to come near it. And what furniture! The *petit salon* contained a square table and four chairs made of a cheap wood and another table instead of a buffet. But the bedroom was the worst; the bed must have been on sale in a bordello; its head was made of wickerwork painted in gold, and the rest was in pink—sheets, cover, and walls. A large bidet was the main object in the *cabinet*, besides the washstand and a tiny tabouret.

I suddenly realized why the girl, if she was really nice, couldn't stand living there. Still, I decided to stay for the time being: hotels scared me, and I needed a roof over my head. Mr. Weisweiller arranged with the concierge to serve my breakfast in the morning, and offered to put in a piano, but I did not let him. I was about to leave anyway for the country. As a matter of fact I stayed only three days more. On the eve of my departure we dined together at a brasserie. I couldn't resist saying to him: "How on earth is it possible that some people say you are avaricious? After what you have done for me, I will make them eat their words!"

He laughed it off. "I know where this gossip comes from," he said, and then, more seriously, he continued, "These lovely creatures of our *demimonde* have an insatiable appetite for money, jewels, furs, and all the other luxuries, and I know many married men whom they have completely ruined. I am still a bachelor, but I refuse to spend my money in such an idiotic way, or live like my friend Oppenheimer from Cologne. But if I can be useful in matters of art, and especially of music, which I adore, I even forget the meaning of money!" Here was a man who had his heart in the right place!

43

The Potocki villa was paradise after my last week in Paris. The summer, now at the climax, deployed all of its magic. Flowers of all kinds, shades, and sizes occupied every free space of the garden and reached beyond into the park. Under my window, jasmine filled the room with its strange and sweet aroma. The heavy, leaf-laden branches of two huge oaks moved in the wind with a quiet, majestic rhythm.

I was given again the little suite I liked so much, but the rest of the house was not empty this time. Two distinguished gentlemen, close friends of the Count, arrived to spend the summer; the Russian Count Strogonoff, a man of about sixty, whose careful walk made him look much older than he was. The other guest, a cousin of our host, was one of the most interesting and intelligent persons I have ever met. Stanislav Rembielinski, a descendant of a noble Polish family, was a man in his early fifties. Tall and slender, he had a pale, narrow, sensitive face with round, penetrating black eyes and bushy eyebrows, a thin, aquiline nose, thick hair, and a long, square black beard with a fine mustache.

The Pleyel concert grand stood in the hall, a very large room in the English style. It had a big, open fireplace, two long tables laden with magazines and newspapers, and a few comfortable sofas and armchairs. On the walls hung colored engravings of hunting scenes. It was the most attractive place in the house; little chance, I thought, of being able to practice without someone present.

After dinner, back in the hall, Count Potocki asked me to try out the piano; I had tried it before, but now I felt like playing. And I was delighted to discover that all three gentlemen were deeply affected by music! My fears about playing in the hall disappeared, and from then on the place belonged to me. The Count took me to a corner of the room.

"Jeune homme," he said, "tomorrow morning we are going to start seriously on our work. Be ready at eight o'clock. My butler will bring you a pair of jodhpurs which I hope will fit you. I have also some leggings for you at the manège."

When he spoke of serious work, he certainly meant it. Next morning, punctually at eight, his four-in-hand trotted us to the manège. On this very first day, comfortably seated in his box, he began to teach me in earnest the art of horsemanship.

"Bring in the mare," he ordered a stable boy. "She is the safest for a start; and no saddle!"

Proud, in my perfectly fitting riding breeches and leather leggings, I mounted the horse, helped by the boy.

"Go slowly, relax, let her walk, and hold your reins with one hand," the voice from the box commanded. This slow exercise lasted the whole hour of my lesson. The next day I was allowed to trot, but for only ten minutes. The Count shouted: "Keep your feet inward, sit erect, and let your body take the rhythm of the trot." I tried, but it was hard to hop on a bare horse back. When I reached the stage of being allowed to gallop my teacher became quite excited.

"Sit still, hold on to her with your knees, and don't pull on your reins," he screamed, observing my progress through binoculars. From time to time he would make me stop close to his box and fish out of his pocket a carrot or a piece of sugar for the sweat-covered mare. Jumping over the fence without a saddle was a torture. His admonitions, "Lean slightly forward, try to be light on her, follow gracefully her movements when she jumps," were of little help. I was thrown off the horse several times, quite ungracefully. Fortunately, the floor of the manège was covered by a corklike substance which did not hurt. He permitted me to mount a saddled horse only after a month of such strenuous preparation.

Life at the villa was interesting and amusing. At meals, Mr. Rembielinski held us spellbound by his intelligence, his art of telling a story, and his wit. He spoke to his cousin with an almost imperceptible touch of condescension, and treated poor Madame d'Avignon with a devastating irony.

"Arthur, venez faire une petite promenade," he would call to me often at sunset. These long walks in the park are among the best memories of my youth. Our conversation ran from religion to philosophy, from music to architecture, from politics to economics—his knowledge seemed to have no limits, and, what I liked best, his talk was full of vitality and humor. I grew very fond of this man, and he too, I felt, befriended me in a delicate, undemonstrative way.

Mr. Biernacki told me strange and romantic stories about Stanislav Rembielinski's past: "He was the greatest Don Juan of his time," he said, "and in his youth he traveled all over the world. The Khedive of Egypt was so impressed by him that he offered him the post of supervisor of finance and general director of museums and archaeological research. They say, also, that he wanted him to marry his daughter, if Rembielinski would become a Moslem. But he refused all of it."

"How could he refuse such an offer?" I asked, intrigued. "He told me himself that he was poor, that he had a modest flat in Paris, and that he comes to Rambouillet mainly for reasons of economy."

"If you can keep a secret, I shall tell you something else about him," the gossiping Pole answered, and after I promised, he continued his story.

"Money had no attraction for him; the fortune he inherited was spent on travel and women. You probably know that our Count Potocki was married to a very beautiful Italian Princess; you saw her portrait by Bonnat in the Count's library. Well, she left him after only a few years and guess with whom? With Rembielinski! She was madly in love with him."

"But how it is possible?" I exclaimed. "They are the best of friends."

"That is the beauty of it," he smiled. "The lovers separated after a year or so; she became too possessive and he was too independent. So, after some time had passed and things calmed down, Rembielinski came back to his heartbroken cousin and told him at length how the Countess forced him to elope with her, what a domineering and ruthless woman she was, and how he suffered, causing his dear cousin such a distress," and he added, with a sardonic grin, "and now you see how they are. This whole affair brought them closer together—both feel they are the victims of the same woman!" And he laughed.

Even if it were only half-true, it was a good story.

Monsieur Astruc called one day to ask if I would arrange a meeting with Count Potocki. It was a matter of importance, he said. Knowing his persuasive ways when he needed support for his projects, it seemed clear to me that he intended to use Potocki's friendly disposition toward me to ask him for financial help in my career. Despite my aversion for this sort of thing, I thought it reasonable to comply, considering realistically the poor outlook of my future. The Count agreed right away to this meeting: "If he is as remarkable a man as you say, I shall be pleased to hear what he wants to consult me about, but I would not be astonished if it were something concerning you."

Count Potocki received him in the room he was using as his office, and the two men settled down for a long talk. I was waiting hopefully in the hall. When Astruc finally came out, looking happy and excited, he embraced me and shook my hands, but when I saw him to the car his only comment was: "Quel grand seigneur!"

Later that day Count Nicholas said with a confidential smile: "You were right about this man—he impressed me very much—and I hope you will be pleased with the result of our conversation."

So I still didn't know what this result was, and I didn't dare to ask, but I decided to go to Paris and find out. When I learned the truth, my disappointment was as great as my surprise.

Ever since I had met Gabriel Astruc, he had been obsessed with the idea of creating a modern theater on a grandiose scale. Disgusted with the shabby look of the Châtelet and having no access to the Opéra, he decided to endow Paris with the most beautiful building for the theatrical arts. The main hall was to be the home of grand opera and ballet with a device for turning it into a concert hall. Another, a middle-sized theater for drama and comedy, and a smaller one for experimental productions would complete his scheme. He assured himself of the services of the best architects, of the sculptor Bourdelle for the embellishment of the façade, of painters like Vuillard and others for decorating the lobbies and ceilings.

Of course, a project of such magnitude would cost an enormous sum of money. In order to find it, Astruc, like Diaghilev before him, tried to obtain financial support mainly from international personalities. He created an Association des Amis de la France to make it look more official. The members were rich foreigners who lived in Paris and whom he knew how to flatter by telling them: "Vous êtes si Parisiens!" This brings me back to my story. Count Potocki was so impressed by his enthusiasm that he vouched a hundred thousand francs for the theater, insinuating that he did it out of friendship for me! As to myself, I was left completely out. But ever since, when I see the beautiful Théâtre des Champs-Élysées, I always think that a little piece of it owes its existence to me.

August passed like a dream in the idyllic atmosphere of the villa, and I still remember well some special incidents. One was pathetic. It was late when I returned from Paris, discouraged by the news of the deal which excluded me so completely. As I entered the hall I found that everybody had retired for the night, so instead of going to my room, I opened the lid of the piano and sat down to play the Sonata with the Funeral March of Chopin. (The hall was at an inaudible distance from the bedrooms.) Reaching the trio of the march, I was startled by a loud sob coming from somewhere near the fireplace. There I found poor Count Strogonoff, sitting in a tall armchair with its back to the room, crying disconsolately. "It is over, it is over," he said between sobs. "This march told me it is over." I took him to his room, helped him to go to bed, and left him still crying. He died in Paris only a few weeks after that night. I have been superstitious ever since, and refused to play the Funeral March in a private house.

Another incident was amusing. Mr. Fallières, then President of France, offered a gala banquet at his official summer residence, followed by fireworks in honor of the King of Cambodia. Count Nicholas and his guests were invited, but not to the banquet, only to watch the fireworks. Our host was visibly piqued. The others refused to go, but I yearned to see it all. So as not to disappoint me, this fine gentleman promised to take me to the fete. We wore tails, white ties, white gloves, and top hats (they found one for me), and a magnificent landau driven by two perfectly matched black horses took us to the château. In the entrance hall, servants wanted to take our hats, but the Count said to me, sharply, "Don't take your hat off!" And so, hatted, we entered the grand salon, and from there the wide terrace, where the President and his exotic guest of honor, surrounded by high dignitaries and other important personalities, were waiting to watch the fireworks. "Act as I act," whispered the Count, while we walked up to the President. Mr. Fallières, tall and heavy, looked like a good-natured peasant. His wavy gray hair and gray beard, his carelessly worn clothes, made him look untidy. Very politely, he stood up to greet us. Count Nicholas ceremoniously took his hat off, and so did I, but he put it on again almost immediately, as one does in the street, and I copied him. We performed the same maneuver for the King of Cambodia, but for other persons who came up to pay their respects, he just touched his hat with one finger, in the English way, and I, of course, did the same.

"You must teach these 'bourgeois' manners," he said later when we were alone. "One doesn't invite a gentleman for after dinner!" Now I understood what the game with the hats was all about.

Nevertheless, we enjoyed the brilliant fireworks and had the surprise and good fortune of seeing a short performance of the beautiful dances by the women of the King of Cambodia's harem. The harmony of the slow, dignified movements of head, torso, and limbs was a pure enchantment to watch. The famous sculptor Rodin was so entranced by their dances that he accompanied them on their journey back to Cambodia to draw his famous sketches.

September brought great changes into the life at the villa. With the opening of the shooting season, the house was restored to its original purpose. The Count and Biernacki were busy with lists of invitations, a delicate affair in view of the rivalry between the château and the villa for the best shots. My riding lessons came to an end, and Rembielinski returned to Paris for a week. The hall suddenly resembled a hotel lobby with people rushing in and out, and my poor piano was available only at late hours. In addition, a little incident of a disagreeable kind annoyed me greatly. A young girl, not more than twenty, a godchild of Count Nicholas and a protégée of Madame d'Avignon, came to stay for a few weeks. Blond and blue-eyed, with the pretty name of Emmanuela and a good figure, she was quite attractive. What I liked in her best, however, was her passion for music; she begged to be allowed to listen whenever I played, and I have seldom seen anybody so enraptured. No wonder that one night, seeing her in tears when I finished my beloved *Barcarolle* of Chopin, I gave her a hard, long kiss, to which she responded. The sudden crash of a fallen chair broke the spell. From behind the chair emerged Biernacki, white with fury.

"You ought to be ashamed of yourself! This is an outrage! To attack a young girl!" he shouted at me in Polish, while Emmanuela ran out of the room.

"How dare you shout at me?" I answered. "And what you saw is none of your business."

"Aha, well, well, is that what you think?" He spoke now with a fiendish smile. "But I shall *make* it my business to tell her godfather and Madame Mathilde about it!"

"Do as you like," I said, and left. He did make his report about my "attack" to both of them, painting it in the most sinister colors. The Count laughed when I told him the *real* story, and Madame d'Avignon even gave me an approving twinkle. Emmanuela herself explained everything to me.

"He has pursued me with his love for two years; he even proposed to me," she said indignantly. "At his age—imagine, he is over fifty, you know." After a pause, she added, "And he hopes my godfather will settle a big dowry for me. I simply can't stand him and I refuse all his advances."

Poor Emmanuela was aflush with anger and spite. Biernacki turned into a veritable Iago, vowed revenge on me, and never left the poor girl out of his sight.

Meanwhile, the great hunting went on. Guests, all good shots, were coming and going: the tableau laid out in front of the house was made up of hundreds of massacred partridges, pheasants, wild ducks, and hares; at meals we were served nothing but delicate game prepared every fancy way: it was a constant feast. When the bulk of the season was over, the Count promptly switched from shooting to fishing, another hobby of his.

"Do you like to fish, Arthur?" he asked.

"I love it," I answered, "and I am ashamed to admit that as much as I feel an aversion for shooting beautiful birds I am cruel enough to hook any fish in cold blood."

He laughed at my sally, and we decided to open our private fishing season. Like everything else, it was meticulously organized. Two men carried fish lines, tackle, nets, buckets, and comfortable field chairs to the nearby river (I think it was the Eure) and searched for the most advantageous sites. It was the most luxurious fishing bout of my life!

But I had to pay a heavy price for it; one day, while taking my fish off the hook, the tip of my right forefinger got caught by it; I felt a sharp pain, but paid no attention. I was completely absorbed by the sport. Well, that night, I was awakened by a painful throb in my finger. I couldn't close my eyes, for fear that something had happened to my hand. I rang for the valet, early in the morning, and sent him to the Count for some medicaments. Alarmed by my request, Count Potocki himself rushed into my room, carrying an assortment of bottles and salves. After washing my finger in sterilized water, he poured iodine on the sore spot, put a soothing salve around it, and bandaged the finger in an expert fashion. A hospital nurse couldn't have been more skillful in treating an injury. To be able to endure the pain, I had to hold my hand rigidly upright for hours. When the Count took off the bandage next morning, he declared it was a *panaris*, a dangerous inflammation of the finger just under the nail. He decided that I should leave for Paris right away to see a specialist. An hour later I was on my way in his car, and he advised the doctor by telephone of my arrival. After one look at the injured spot, the doctor confirmed the Count's diagnosis.

"If you don't want your finger to lose the articulation of a joint, you will have to submit to a very painful operation," he said. "In order to allow your blood to flow freely again, I must remove every trace of the infectious matter."

"Please, please, doctor," I begged, panic-stricken, "you must save my finger, my life depends on it. I promise I can stand any pain if it will help!"

Well, thank heavens, he cured my finger of that ghastly *panaris* and restored the free movement of the joint. But I still shiver when I think of the torture he made me endure! Without using any anesthetics he pierced the very spot of the infection with a small silver stiletto and began to dig around inside the tip of my finger for a good minute or two, while I squirmed on my chair and shrieked at the top of my voice. The pain was indescribable!

"This is the only way to get all the pus out," the doctor said when I came to after a short spell of faintness.

He tortured me three more times before the ordeal was over. Since he never asked me for his fee, I suppose he sent the bill to the Count.

Paris made me feel dismal after the glorious days in Rambouillet. The indecent, gloomy flat at rue Cardinet had a demoralizing effect on me. I used it only for the night.

To be out in the street did not bring much relief either; the stench of the horses, the strong odors of the city intensified by the oppressive heat, was even more apparent the last days of summer. But what completely undermined my morale was the fact that I had no money. And with both Astruc and Weisweiller out of town I couldn't think of anybody to turn to for help. The small sum which I obtained at the Mont de Piété (the municipal pawnshop) for a suit and a coat was good for a week with one frugal meal a day. And what a frustrating experience, this first visit to a pawnshop! When I arrived there, by Metro, the Mont de Piété was closed for the day, and I had to walk back, ashamed of being seen on the street with the two heavy garments on my arm. A cup of coffee and a roll was all I could afford to eat that day. I had to go through the same agony next morning, but this time I found the sordid place open!

One touching incident will give a picture of my plight at that time. Ever since I had come to Paris I would buy my newspapers at the kiosk in front of the terrace of the Café de la Paix. I was on good terms with the saleswoman; we liked to laugh about things. Well, on that memorable late afternoon, with just one cup of coffee and a brioche as all the food I had had for the day, I walked up to the kiosk to read the headlines of the papers with no intention of buying one.

"Hello, young man, don't you want your paper?" she asked.

"No, thank you, not today," I answered. She examined me with sharp eyes—I must have had the hungry look.

"Take it anyhow." She forced it on me and pressed at the same time a five-franc piece into my hand.

"Prenez ces cent sous et allez manger quelquechose, jeune homme, vous me les rendrez quand cela vous conviendra."

I blushed and accepted—she had done it in such a motherly way.

When my few francs melted to nothing, I decided to go to the Pavillon de Hanovre and try to get some money from the cashier, who was often tolerant about my monetary irregularities.

"Ah," he exclaimed, "I am glad you came. There is a letter for you and I didn't know your address."

The letter was from Warsaw—an invitation to take part, with two other performers, in a great gala concert for charity. The fee was to be four hundred rubles. The program they had chosen for me was the Chopin Concerto in F minor. Paul Kochanski was to play the Tchaikovski Concerto, and the other artist was Basia!

While I read the letter my heart began to beat faster. This is what I had been waiting for. Now I would find out what had happened to Pola: whether she still loved me, or whether she did not want to see me again. I was sure to see her at the concert—she couldn't miss Basia's debut.

But soon I returned to reality: the date of the concert was a week hence; I still had time to make it, but the question was where to find the money for the train. And for other expenses before the concert? The friendly cashier was willing to lend me twenty francs out of his own pocket. "It's all I can do," he said. I took, gratefully, the louis d'or and left. Out in the street, my mind was made up, and a hard decision it was. Count Potocki! It was Count Potocki whom I would ask for the money! Biernacki, in the early days of our acquaintance, had told me that the Count hated to be solicited for loans. On the other hand, I remembered how easily Astruc obtained his large contribution to the theatrical project. In my own case, I knew that the Polish nobleman took it for granted that I was well taken care of and that my career was in full swing. He did not know, fortunately, that I had sold his sapphire cuff links a long time ago. And so, with a heavy heart, I called the villa at Rambouillet and asked the butler to announce me to his master.

"Mon cher comte," I said, trying to sound cheeerful, "I am leaving in a few days for Poland and I would like to come to say goodbye, if I won't disturb you, and to show you, also, how my finger has healed thanks to you!"

I heard a delighted chuckle on the phone. "Parfait, parfait," he answered. "Tomorrow is Saturday. Come for dinner and stay over Sunday. We might even try some little brushing up at the manège, eh?"

Half of my louis d'or was gone when I arrived at the villa, just in time for dinner. Count Potocki came out to the hall to greet me, carefully examined the perfect functioning of my finger joints, and expressed his pleasure and pride about it. Then he led me to the dining room, where we found Madame d'Avignon, Emmanuela, Rembielinski, who had been back for a week, a lawyer I didn't know, and the ever-somber Biernacki. The dinner was excellent, but I felt no appetite in spite of my chronic hunger. I was too preoccupied with the choice I had to make: Shall I ask him tonight or tomorrow morning, when he will be in a happy mood on the terrace? It was a lovely, mild evening, the air was perfumed, the birds twittered around us, a cricket gave us a concert.

"Come for a walk, Arthur," Rembielinski said suddenly. "Nicholas won't mind." The Count hated to walk because of his lameness. When we reached the park and were out of hearing distance, my companion stopped.

"How much do you need?" he asked me, brusquely.

"What do you mean?" I said, taken aback.

"Don't pretend, Arthur," he continued softly. "I observed you all through dinner; it was written on your face. You need money and you intend to ask Nicholas to give it to you. Don't do it, my dear, don't do it; he might lose his affection for you and will certainly lose his confidence in you. If the amount you require is within my means, I shall be glad to help you out."

"No, no," I almost cried. "I can't let you do it. It is a big sum—I need three hundred francs. It is nothing for a rich man like the Count, and you told me yourself that you are living on a small allowance!"

Rembielinski smiled. "Let us sit down . . . and listen to me," he said, approaching a bench, and when we were seated, he continued, assuming the role of a mentor.

"Take my advice! I have learned much about human relations through long experience. I give it to you in a nutshell: if you are in trouble, go for help and understanding to a person who is also in trouble! If you lose a dear one, if you are afflicted by an incurable disease, or even by a vulgar toothache, you will find real sympathy and understanding only in people with similar pains and miseries. Your best friends, in such cases, usually perform the ritual gestures, they send condolences, they visit you at hospitals with flowers, they recommend to you the best dentists, but their hearts are not involved—they live in another world, in a world where people haven't lost anybody, aren't ill, and have no toothache!"

He paused for a moment, then continued: "Nicholas has a kind heart. He wouldn't hesitate to give any amount of money to a friend from the Jockey Club who incurred gambling debts; he knows the implications, he respects debts of honor. But in your case, he would be at a loss to understand why you, with your talent, your good manners, a young man received by the *grand monde*, chose to come to him for a small sum instead of taking it simply from your bank or from Mr. Astruc, or from your family!"

He laughed. "And now, mon cher Arthur, forgive my little digression on human behavior and ethics, and let me tell you that the three hundred francs are not going to ruin me. I shall return with you to Paris tomorrow night, and on Monday morning you will have the money."

He tapped me on my shoulder and brushed away my vain attempts to thank him with a charming gesture, raising both hands, as if in defense.

After a good night's sleep I was brilliant at the manège the next morning, and the Count was highly gratified. "Now you can mount almost any horse," he said, with a teacher's satisfaction.

How happy I was not to have had to ask him for money.

In the evening, as we were leaving, he and the others—except for the sinister Biernacki—bade me a warm farewell.

Early on Monday I rang the bell of Rembielinski's flat at the quai Voltaire; he lived in two bright, spacious rooms with walls covered by books from floor to ceiling. Pan Stanislav received me with a cheerful smile. "This is my domain. I am happy here to be all alone with my books!" He showed me some precious old editions, some flattering inscriptions by famous contemporary writers, and finally handed me the money.

"You must be on your way, and I am detaining you," he said, seeing me to the door. "Bonne chance, cher Arthur." We embraced. It was the last time I saw him; he died of consumption some time later in Switzerland.

44

Warsaw looked different to me this time. I took a room in a modest hotel and felt a bit like an exile, banned from my usual home. During these years I had not written a word to anyone except the few love letters and some urgent, unavoidable messages. My aversion for writing was almost a disease.

No wonder that I had lost contact with Frederic and his family. And I had no way of knowing what they thought about me after the story with Pola's letters. I had to wait until the concert, when I hoped Basia's behavior would give me a clue to the mystery.

Meanwhile, I was delighted to see Szymanowski again and to discover that he, Paul Kochanski, and Fitelberg, the conductor, were staying at the same hotel as I. The Victoria just across the street from Philharmonic Hall was convenient for all of us.

The charity concert was sold out. An elegant audience filled the hall, and young ladies of the committee were selling programs. My number was the first, Basia's last. She wasn't supposed to arrive before intermission, and that gave me the chance to play my Chopin quite decently. Great applause and an encore. Paul Kochanski played the Tchaikovski superbly; nobody could touch him in this work. And then the intermission. Basia appeared in the artists' room alone, visibly nervous; she greeted everybody politely, trying to avoid me. When I insisted on being noticed, she gave me a cold nod and shook hands without a smile. I asked her about her family.

"My parents and Frederic are in the hall. Pola did not come," she answered, cutting off any further questions. After intermission it was her turn to sing some Mahler and Strauss with orchestra; Fitelberg was conducting. I joined the audience to hear her sing and, furious as I was, wished her bad luck for her debut. She sang her first song very well, with a fresh voice, good intonation, and the right expression. But while the orchestra played a short prelude to her second number she caught my eye at one moment and forgot her entrance. Fitelberg stopped the orchestra, and they had to start from the beginning, this time without a hitch; but I was well pleased with my private little mesmerism.

When the concert was over, the artists' room was invaded by a crowd of friends led by Frederic and his parents, who came to embrace Basia for her brilliant debut. Then they turned to me with enthusiastic praise for my performance, and Madame Magdalena invited Szymanowski, Paul, and me for supper. My friends declined, pretending other engagements, but I accepted, of course. To my regret, there, too, was no sign of Pola, and nobody even mentioned her name. The party, as usual, was wonderful: food, wine, gaiety, with talk galore. Frederic gave us a very amusing account of his American tour, which broke up after one month; the season was wrong and they played to poor houses, but he himself was lionized wherever he went. He brought back some nice, new American tunes which he played and sang for us with his particular charm. When it was my turn to tell them about my life in Paris, I described in vivid colors the Rothschild party, the reception given by the President of France, the shooting season at Rambouillet, the dinners given by Count Potocki with all the details of the menus. I gave even a not bad imitation of King Edward, but I took good care not to reveal anything of the reverse side of the coin. Having duly impressed the master of the house, he invited me to stay with them again, as before. I refused politely, saying that I had work to do with Szymanowski and Kochanski, and had to keep close to the Philharmonic Hall. But I promised to come as often as time would permit. At the door pani Magdalena gave me an enticing glance to which I responded with a grateful smile. I left, disgusted with myself.

One morning Sophie Kohn telephoned. "I have important news for you," she said, after some cordial greetings. "Pola is coming for a short visit this noon; I thought you might want to see her."

"Oh, thanks, thanks," I shouted, dropping the telephone and running to my room to get ready.

It was a strange meeting. Pola, dressed in dark blue, looking lovelier than ever, stood up politely and greeted me like a casual acquaintance. "How are you?" "Very well, thank you." "Was it hot in Paris?" "No, it was quite bearable." "We had a mild summer." "And how are your children?" "Very well, thank you." When Sophie got up to leave the room, Pola said, alarmed, "I must go, it is late, I must go," and left in a hurry. Zosia, the pet name for Sophie, smiled consolingly. "Don't worry, she will come again, I am sure of it; you must give her time to find out where she stands," and she insisted I stay for lunch.

The hospitality at the Kohns' had a quite unique character; their dining room was busy all hours of the day. Zuzia, their middle-aged governess, housekeeper, and friend, was ready to serve, on the spur of the moment, breakfast, lunch, dinner, or supper to members of the household or to unexpected guests. Such hospitality was too alluring to resist, and there was also the attraction of the fine Bechstein in Zosia's bedroom. So, from that day on, I became a frequent visitor of the dining room as well as of the piano.

Pola did come back, pretending to be surprised to see me, and always in a rush. She was never quite herself; when I tried to touch her, she went into a panic. And every time we met at Zosia's she continued to play the same comedy. I questioned Frederic, but he gave me evasive answers. The rest of the family never mentioned her, as if she did not exist! It was a mystery to me.

Meanwhile, my concert career began to progress. Two recitals in Warsaw had good financial results; other Polish cities made good offers, and a bold impresario from Lodz actually engaged me for a thousand rubles! My visit to the city of my birth was, as always, an occasion to celebrate. The whole family showed up at the concert, and later at supper. I gave half my fee to my father toward the expense of this banquet.

A great surprise was in store for me; my brother-in-law Maurycy Landau (of Dresden fame), who made a fortune in wool, traveled often to Russia on business. On his last visit to St. Petersburg he talked about me to Aleksandr Glazunov, the composer and director of that city's famous

Conservatory, which was founded by Anton Rubinstein. Glazunov, Maurycy told me, showed interest and expressed his willingness to present me in a concert to the students and professors at the institute.

"The date he proposed is a week from today," Maurycy said, without waiting for my response to this project. "I will take you myself to St. Petersburg."

"But how is it possible?" I asked, puzzled. "As far as I know, Jews are not allowed to live in the big cities of Russia, only in the peripheries."

"You can stay there for twenty-four hours, and that is all you need," he answered, with resignation. "I, as a first-class merchant, as they call it, have the permission to stay as long as I want, but I have to pay a special tax for it. The only Jews who have the right to live in any town in Russia are those who graduate from universities and conservatories."

I felt a rush of loathing for these infamous discriminations, but the thought of having a chance to play for my colleagues in the hall built by Anton Rubinstein was irresistible. I thanked my brother-in-law for his initiative, and I decided to go.

We arrived in St. Petersburg early in the morning. A fat *izvozchik* —a Russian coachman—drove us to the Hotel d'Europe, the best in town, Maurycy said. At the desk a man took my passport and said, "You shall have it back tomorrow morning before you leave." After washing up and eating breakfast we went to the Conservatory, where Mr. Glazunov received us in a most gracious way. He led us straight to the hall. "This is the place where we admired Anton Grigorievitch and his great art!" he said. I was impressed by a picture which hung on a wall; it represented Rubinstein playing in that very hall to a worshiping audience. "You want to practice, I suppose," said the composer. "The concert is at three o'clock, so you have a good hour to try out the piano, to eat something, and change your clothes." They left, and I started to play. The piano was of a Russian make, a Becker, if I remember well, not much to my liking, but just adequate. While repeating a difficult passage, I was interrupted by a young violinist I had known in Berlin.

"Well, well, I see you are getting along," he said. "Glazunov does not do these favors often," and he added, with a nasty chuckle: "The school thinks that Rubinstein is not your real name, that you took it to impress him . . . ha, ha."

I had to make a great effort to control my nerves and "not to give in." At lunch I couldn't swallow a thing, but by the time of the concert I was completely self-possessed. The hall was packed; all the students, male and female, seemed to be there. Mr. Glazunov, my brother-in-law, and the professors of the Conservatory sat in the first row, and even the stage was filled to the brim with young people. When I walked up to the piano, I was a little afraid of some hostile demonstrations, but, instead, I was received with loud applause. My first piece of the one-hour-long program, one of the slower preludes and fugues of Bach, had an unexpected success. They shouted "Bravo, bravo," and clapped for a long time. The sonata which followed brought wild enthusiasm from the house, and at the end of the concert, pandemonium broke loose; the whole audience stood up, shouting, stamping their feet, applauding. The boys and girls on the stage surrounded me—some girls kissed me, the boys tried to lift me from the floor—and my encores were played amid screams of delight. When I finally succeeded in retreating to the artists' room I was overwhelmed with emotion. I never dreamed of a triumph like this!

Glazunov and Maurycy came in. My brother-in-law was overcome. "I must wire home about it right away!" he cried. Mr. Glazunov kissed me on both cheeks, mumbled some compliments about my playing, but when Maurycy shook his hands, exclaiming, "What a success, what a triumph!" the composer said quietly, "They are always very polite in St. Petersburg." I cooled down in an instant. This was a good lesson for the future: Always find out first how the public behaves at concerts of other artists!

I returned to Warsaw the next morning, without having seen anything of the Russian capital. With my finances improved of late, I decided to change the Victoria for the Hotel Bristol, one of the two best hotels in town. Karol Szymanowski left for the country to finish the orchestration of his new symphonic work, but Paul remained in town and was my daily companion. Our friendship grew from day to day. We discovered many affinities in each other, and a great resemblance in our lives and careers. I admired immensely his talent, and he had a great respect for mine. Besides, he had a divine sense of humor, and we had another trait in common: he was a fine mimic. We loved to play billiards, and we would meet every day at four p.m. punctually at Lourse's, a popular tearoom. We were both mediocre players, but we put so much zest and animation into the game that a friendly group of kibitzers gathered around our table, betting on the winner and prodding us with encouraging or disparaging remarks. Apropos, these meetings remind me of an amusing incident. One night, an important music critic insisted on taking me to his club for a poker game. We sat down at a table with three not very engaging gentlemen. I was the winner for the first four or five hours, and then I wanted to leave. But they wouldn't hear of it, and in fact were rather discourteous about it. So the game went on without stop until four p.m. the next day! And by then, of course, I was a loser! When I found myself out on the sunny street I nearly collapsed from fatigue, but decided to hold out until the normal time for a good night's sleep. But I suddenly remembered that Paul was waiting for me at Lourse's. I was received with mocking boos by our supporters, but the betting was on the minute we started to play. Paul was in great form that day; mine was unmentionable. At one point, he made an unusually long series of hits, while I was standing still, leaning on my cue. When my turn came to play, I was still standing in the same position, but I was fast asleep! And no booing or shaking could wake me up. I had to be helped into a cab and into bed.

Paul and I decided to give a concert with three violin and piano sonatas; we were by then equally popular in Warsaw, and hoped to draw a good audience. Emil Mlynarski, who was a sort of adoptive father to Paul, made us perform our program for him. His remarks about balance between our instruments, phrasing, tempi, have remained forever in my mind: "Play freely, but try to mold your phrasing; don't play for effect—the music ought to be allowed to speak for itself—and remember that a slow movement gains by being played a little faster and a presto by being played a little slower and . . . rehearse, rehearse, and rehearse!"

But this was a problem; we had no place for rehearsals. Having no piano at the Bristol, I was satisfied using Zosia's Bechstein daily for an hour or two. The only solution was to introduce Paul to the Kohn family. I took him there after our billiard game, late one afternoon. The minute we entered the room, Mrs. Kohn shouted: "Zuzia, dinner!" And ten minutes later we were served a complete meal. The entire family adopted Paul in no time, and Zosia's father, a well-known lawyer, whose affairs took him all over Europe, was so fascinated by Paul's personality that he never left his side. When we retired to our music in Zosia's bedroom we found it a paradise to work in.

The concert was a solid success; the critics noticed our perfect ensemble and style, especially in Beethoven's *Kreutzer* Sonata. After this concert we were much in demand, and were often invited by the Rzewuskis, the Epsteins, and by Paul's friends the Styczyńskis.

I remember an amusing incident that took place about this time. A young, handsome Persian Prince came to Warsaw as an exile and stayed at the Bristol, where he took a suite on my floor. All of Warsaw society showered invitations on him, and the press loved to print stories about his social life and his great wealth. Another resident of our floor was a high-grade prostitute, a voluptuous blonde.

One night, as I was going up to my room, she stopped me.

"You must help me," she said in a pleading voice. "I am dying to meet the Persian Prince. I noticed you talking to him and I know you can arrange it. Please, please!"

I laughed. "My dear woman, I am not a pimp, and I don't intend to help you. But why don't you try to catch him when he returns from his party? I wish you luck!"

I entered my room and went to bed. Two or three hours later, a terrifying shriek made me jump up and run to the door. What I saw was a startling scene. The blond beauty, stark naked, was dashing out of the Prince's apartment, yelling at the top of her voice: "Help, help, he wants to kill me!" By then most of the hotel guests were out in the corridor; a few caught up with the hysterical woman and dragged her into her room, where she kept on sobbing, "He tried to kill me."

Since I had met the Prince socially, I ventured to enter his apartment through the still-open door. I found him standing there in his dressing gown, perfectly composed. He offered me a seat and explained in his best French what had happened.

"I came home late and was just opening the door when this girl appeared from nowhere, said something in Polish which I did not understand, then kissed me and followed me into my apartment. I found her attractive, I must admit. I had not the strength of character to throw her out." He paused, then said a little haltingly. "She undressed completely, settled comfortably on this couch, and made a sign for me to join her." He continued in a confidential way: "I must touch upon a delicate subject. We Moslems are not allowed to have intercourse with women who keep their pubic hair. I tried to explain it to her, but she couldn't understand what it meant. So I went to the bathroom to fetch my razor, and came back to shave off her offensive tuft. When the girl saw me lifting my arm with the razor in my hand, she gave that shriek, and you know the rest."

My visits to the Harmans' became less and less frequent, not because of negligence on my part or a change in our relations. There were two reasons—one was that neither Paul nor Karol had any desire to be drawn into their circle, and the other was that pani Magdalena still believed that we could continue our long-since-faded love affair. Nevertheless I attended with pleasure their after-theater suppers, and helped Frederic with the cadenza to his concerto. Only once did I find myself face to face with Pola at the door of their house, but she passed me, without stopping.

Early one morning a bellboy knocked at my door and brought me a letter. It was important and personal, he said. I opened it with care. Its text was, I remember it well, the following: "I advise you strongly to leave the city at once. If you persist in staying, I shall give you a good thrashing wherever I see you!" It was signed by Pola's husband.

Everything became suddenly clear. He must have caught her writing to me, forced her to recover her letters, and probably obtained her promise never to see me again. In all probability, he had been suspicious about our meetings at Zosia's, and that prompted him to send me this rude letter.

His vulgar threat called for a strong reaction. But I was completely inexperienced in matters of that kind; nobody had ever threatened me before. I could think of no one better to consult than Stanislav Rzewuski, the incontestable arbiter in questions of honor. When I called, he received me instantly, and read with frowning attention the insulting note.

"This is a provocation for a duel," was his verdict, when he finished studying its content. "You must react to it without delay. Someone you can trust ought to go immediately to Mr. K. [Pola's husband] and speak to him in the following manner: 'My friend Mr. R. sent me to exact a written apology for your insulting letter. If you do not accede to his request, he challenges you to a duel. The seconds of both parties can meet tomorrow to discuss the details.'" Mr. Rzewuski smiled; he was in his element. "This will teach him," he said. "I shall wait for you to hear what he has to say."

I chose Fitelberg for this disagreeable errand, and he did me the favor without difficulty. He returned in less than an hour to make his report.

"It was fascinating," he said. "When he heard I came in your behalf, he was convinced, I saw it on his face, that I brought him your promise never to annoy Pola again if he lets you stay in Warsaw without harm, but I have never seen anybody as stupefied as this man when I announced to him that you were challenging him to a duel! For a moment he was speechless; when he recovered from his shock, he said he would appoint his seconds in the afternoon."

I thanked Fitelberg for the correct performance of his mission and ran to Rzewuski to report its result. Pan Stanislav was delighted. "It worked perfectly," he said, "and I shall be glad to be your second, of course, but we must find the other one." After we reviewed a few not quite desirable candidates for this role, our choice fell on Jaroszynski.

"He is in Kiev," I objected. "Never mind," Rzewuski answered, "I shall wire him myself and I feel sure he will come."

He was right. Joseph arrived next morning, a little bewildered at first, but he was soon coached for his assignment. The two gentlemen rented a room at the Bristol for the meetings with their counterparts. The high social standing of my seconds impressed Mr. K. beyond words. The best he could find were his half-brother and a trainer of race horses. For two days the four of them discussed the place, the hour, and the arms. Our opponents proposed the traditional épée, but pan Rzewuski insisted on pistols with two shots exchanged from a fair distance. He made a point of the fact that I had the right of choice, being the offended party.

On the eve of the duel, Mr. Rzewuski gave me precious instructions.

"Do not aim at him," he said. "Your hand might shake at that moment, but raise your arm, and when the signal is given, bring it down with your finger on the trigger and shoot. If you do as I advise, you can't miss him." I repeated this exercise a few times for his satisfaction. His lesson terrified me, and I was determined to miss, not to kill the poor man. Seeing me distressed, both Rzewuski and Jaroszynski tried to convince me that they would obtain an apology signed by my adversary before the shooting. Full preparations for the duel, they said, were routine procedure in questions of honor. Despite their assurance, all that night I had such dreadful visions of death and blood that I couldn't sleep.

On that cold and cloudy morning, at seven o'clock, pan Stanislav, Joseph, a doctor, and I drove in a covered coach to a carefully selected place beyond the Lazienki park. The other party was already there. We bowed ceremoniously to each other, and our seconds began to count out the preestablished distance between the duelists. The seconds examined carefully the pistols and handed K. and me the corresponding ones. The doctor busied himself at assorting his stuff for first aid. I was shaking; my hands were sweating and ice cold. When we were placed at our posts, the pistols in our hands, waiting for the signal to shoot, a customary procedure required the seconds to give a last chance to the offender to retract his letter and the threats contained therein. To everybody's relief Mr. K. gave his assent, and our duel was stopped. A protocol was worked out on the spot, endorsed by the four gentlemen, and signed by Mr. K. It read, approximately: "I hereby take back every word of the letter I wrote and sent [the date] to Mr. A. R. I acted solely in defense of a certain person" (sic).

We returned to town, and I felt like one condemned to death whose life was spared. Warsaw was not the town to pass up this tidbit of gossip. Fantastic stories ran from mouth to mouth; people invented all sorts of incredible reasons which supposedly led up to the duel. But, luckily, the name of Pola was never mentioned; we simply had never been seen together. Anyway, my new status as the young man who knows how to defend his honor enhanced considerably my social standing. The one most thrilled by the outcome was Mr. Harman. He knew the true story, of course, like the rest of the family, and never expected that I would behave as I did.

Frederic's father wasn't on good terms with his son-in-law; he blamed him for his ineptitude for work and resented his inability to support his wife and children, so he was secretly delighted with the lesson I had given K. The result of it all was that I became a hero in his opinion, and that Pola was again admitted to the family circle with my presence as though nothing had happened. Frederic and Basia were noncommittal, as usual, but pani Magdalena called me to her room for a hard talk.

"What was going on between you and Pola?" she asked angrily.

"Nothing at all, I assure you. Last year we became good friends after we learned to know each other better," I answered very quietly.

"Tell me the truth, Arthur, you must tell me the truth," she insisted. "I heard that she was writing to you and that you were meeting her at some secret place."

"This is sheer nonsense," I answered. "She did send me a few nice letters, and why shouldn't she? And as to the 'secret place,' it was simply her friend Zosia Kohn's apartment where Paul Kochanski and I were rehearsing our concert." And I added, disdainfully, "K. was foolish enough to have listened to some silly gossip."

She seemed to believe me; at least, she recovered her composure. But, all of a sudden, she asked me, almost in a whisper: "Are you in love with her?"

There was a short silence; I was taken aback for a moment.

"Yes and no," I answered cautiously. "I did fall in love with her last fall, but the same thing had happened once before with Basia, as you well know. It is a curious phenomenon that all the ladies of this house have an erotic effect on me!" I tried to make it sound funny, but she was not amused. "As a matter of fact," I said, "the whole thing is quite dead and buried. I am incapable of loving without reciprocity, and you can see by yourself that Pola treats me with an utmost indifference." This time, I think, I calmed her suspicions.

The last two months in Warsaw of this year 1907 were a constant merry-go-round of musical, social, and some less commendable activities. Mornings I used to play at Zosia's house, alone or with Paul, and we often stayed for lunch. One day I had the bad idea of introducing Jaroszynski to the Kohns, and to their famous dining table, whereupon he too picked up the habit of coming to Zuzia for meals at any odd hour of the day. The four p.m. billiard contests became a daily exercise which we never missed. The parties offered by lovely Varsoviennes filled agreeably the ends of afternoons. And from time to time the Rzewuskis invited Joseph and me to one of their Lucullian dinners, which were inevitably followed by long sessions of Wagner operas accompanied vociferously by Joseph. Theaters remained my greatest attraction, concerts only when a major musical event took place. But I never missed the irresistible supper parties at pani Magdalena's. Pola came seldom to her mother's house and stayed away from Zosia. After the duel affair her position became somewhat ambiguous. In spite of all the odds against us, my instinct told me that the same secret current of our love was still alive.

Four successful concerts in Kalisz, Piotrków, Częstochowa, and Lublin brought a much needed respite to the turmoil of my life in Warsaw, and provided me with a nice sum of money.

On my return to the capital, Frederic tried again his old trick of using me to substitute for him in his relations with women. Or was it in his plan to take my mind off his sister? I shall never know. This time his choice was a tall, statuesque, gorgeous creature with a spectacularly curvaceous figure. He arranged a little supper for the three of us, after which she invited us for a nightcap to her suite at the Bristol; she was the mistress of an old Polish Count who kept her living in luxury at the hotel. She was quite a character, this Genia Chmielnik! Her favorite gesture was to raise her skirt, revealing her strong, round thighs, slap them with both hands, and exclaim: "I am the real whore! So what of it!?" And her behavior did not belie her claim. When it was time for us to leave, she said to Frederic: "My dear, I always wanted to sleep with you, but I know you have no use for me, so I will try out this young boy," meaning me. At the door, ready to go, Frederic said to me, "I leave you in good hands," the way a mother entrusts her child to school for the first time.

"Go to the bathroom and take a hot bath," said Genia imperatively, "and when you are quite dry, come to my bedroom." I didn't dare to disobey her. I did exactly what she told me to do and found her lying on her bed without clothes, waiting for me. She kept me there for the whole night, and when we rose in the morning for breakfast I felt like a graduate from a college of the art of making love.

The consequences of this new adventure were quite exciting but more often than not frankly disagreeable. Genia acquired a dreadful habit of calling me at my friends', where she was sure to find me, whether at some social function or making music at Zosia's. She always gave her full name and pretended that I had asked her to call. My strong objections to her behavior only made things worse. One afternoon, when I was having tea with Frederic's mother, Pola, and Basia, she rang up again. The maid was instructed to declare that Mr. R. had left. Genia's impudent answer was: "You lie; go and look for him in Madame's bedroom!" I don't need to describe the fury of Madame Magdalena. However, I was not unhappy to find a touch of jealousy in Pola's reaction.

Another concert with Paul in the Philharmonic Hall and a very well attended one in Lodz closed my concert season in Poland. And I could not find a plausible reason for extending my overlong stay in Warsaw. The colorful and often boasting descriptions of my social successes in the French capital had created the general impression that I was on the road to a brilliant career in Paris.

When are you leaving? When is your next concert in France? Are the Rothschilds giving another party? were now frequent questions I found difficult to answer. My friends were more discreet, but I became well aware of their misgivings about my long absence from Paris. I suddenly felt I had no choice: I had to leave.

After a riotous New Year's Eve party with my friends I announced my departure for the first week of January. I was given a great send-off with gifts of books, candies, and my favorite *torciks* from Wedel. "What a lucky devil, this Arthur, who lives in Paris! I would give anything to be able to go with him!" was the kind of remark I overheard at the station. Paris was, and is, every Pole's Mecca.

The rather ironic truth of the whole thing was that I had no intention at all of going back to Paris. I had decided, instead, to stop in Berlin!

45

Why did I choose Berlin, of all places? I have tried in vain to find a logical answer to this question. My departure from Warsaw, which was in a way morally forced on me, left me in a complete vacuum. One thing I knew for certain: It was impossible for me to return to Paris. Monsieur Astruc had no plans, no concert engagements to offer me. He was frankly disappointed in me and discouraged by my *manque de serieux*, as he called it, and by my nonchalance toward my career. My Polish successes never reached him or the Parisian press. On the other hand, the idea of staying in Weisweiller's disgusting little flat and making a living on his lessons presented a very poor alternative, not to speak of the nightmare of my still unpaid debts. As to hopes for more of the *soirées musicales* which had been so profitable the spring before, I was well aware that my *Salomé* performances had become dated and that the moment had come to prove myself in some major public appearance.

Only when I arrived in Berlin at the old, familiar Friedrichstrasse station, on that cold and windy morning, did I realize that my decision to stay in this city was nothing but a cowardly compromise. The rest of the money I had earned in Poland could last two or three months, depending on my way of living. I rented at a monthly rate a nice room with a bathroom at the Hotel Bellevue, a not very expensive but quite distinguished residence at the central Potsdamer Platz. Mr. Metzger, the owner and director of the hotel, loved music, and did not object to my having a piano in my room. The house of Bechstein, the famous piano makers, sent me a baby grand without charge.

I was determined to remain incognito and to try to avoid meeting or visiting any of the old friends whom I had left so abruptly in 1904, especially the ones I liked best. *Why* I felt that way is difficult to explain. If I remember well, I went through a crisis, a sort of an inferiority complex, made up of a mixture of shyness and ambition. My career seemed to have reached a dead point, and I had no valid reason to offer for my presence in Berlin.

The only person I wanted to see was Emmy Destinn. She would not be interested in asking why I was in Berlin; she would simply take it for granted. I called her up and was touched hearing the familiar warm timbre of her voice: "How lovely to know you're in town! Come right away to dinner—I want you to meet a friend of mine, and tomorrow you must see me in *Carmen*. It is a gala at the Opera, and Emperor Wilhelm will be present. I shall have a ticket for you."

The prospect of seeing and hearing her again was the best medicine for my melancholic state of mind. When I entered her living room, she threw her arms around me, kissed me on both cheeks, and introduced me to her other guest.

"Arthur, this is my fiancé," she declared. "He is a dancer, a member of our Opera ballet"—and then, without transition—"Doesn't he look like Napoleon?" she asked, with a proud look in her face. Yes, indeed, he did look like Napoleon, as we see him in pictures; the same thickset body, the shape of the head, the short neck, the chin, the nose, even his hairdo. But the completely un-Napoleonic expression in his eyes betrayed a man of little intelligence and vitality. Emmy took my arm and led me solemnly to the next room, where I saw, to my amazement, a whole museum of Bonapartiana. The furniture was made up entirely of authentic pieces in the Empire style; there were arms, costumes, documents signed by the Emperor, and other memorabilia set in beautiful order.

"Napoleon is my idol," she said. "I have worshiped him since I was a child." The little man smiled benignly; he accepted the homage as befitting the great man. I had a dreadful vision of the two of them making love and Emmy reaching the climax, singing at the top of her gorgeous voice, "Vive l'Empereur, vive la France!"

The next night I had the chance to observe at close range a live Emperor, the notorious Kaiser Wilhelm II. It was a spectacular affair, this gala, or rather this command performance, as they called it. The entire audience was there by invitation; no tickets were on sale. It was obligatory to wear evening clothes, white tie, uniforms, medals. The army, that privileged class of Imperial Germany, was predominantly represented. The Kaiser, accompanied by the Empress and two sons, occupied his box close to the stage. I have never heard *Carmen* sung better than on that evening. Destinn surpassed herself. Nobody in the crowded theater dared to applaud without the signal given by the Emperor, who, unmusical as he was, paid little attention to the proceedings on the stage and orchestra. Yes—at one moment he did burst into loud laughter, when Zuniga, José's superior officer, twirling his mustache and smacking his lips, set his eyes on Carmen and said, "Don-ner-wet-ter!!"

On the way home, Emmy was quite upset by the Kaiser's behavior. "Imagine how he treated me," she complained. "When I was brought to the Imperial box for the usual congratulations, he took me aside and asked me with a vulgar twinkle of his eyes: 'How is little Farrar* doing?' as if he were questioning a madam about a girl of her bordello!" I mention this incident because it shows yet another facet of this man whose ambition and envy led to the disastrous world wars and the misery of our present times.

Besides Emmy Destinn, I visited also my Aunt and Uncle Meyer, who lived far enough from my old friends and had never communicated with them. I liked to go to museums, bookshops, and cafés. Theaters attracted me as before, and I tried not to miss a good concert in spite of my fear of meeting people I wanted to avoid.

At this point in my life, I wanted simply escape; I seemed to be waiting for something to happen, to wake me from a kind of torpor. My daily routine was simple; I practiced and played a little after breakfast, took all my meals at the excellent hotel restaurant, then strolled aimlessly along the street. If there was nothing new at the theater, I would go early to bed with a book and read late into the night.

One day this quiet *train de vie* was interrupted by the arrival of my sister Jadzia. Aunt Salomea Meyer had written her about my presence in Berlin, adding that I had no immediate plans for the future. Nothing could have pleased Jadzia more, so she grabbed yet another occasion to be with me, believing that I was leading the life of an *homme du monde*, basking in wealth and glory: she wanted to share it with me, at least for a few weeks. My family was still convinced that after the American tour my success was assured.

And this time, alas, things looked even worse. I had nothing to show; my career had come to a stop.

* Geraldine Farrar, the American soprano, whose name gossip linked with the Crown Prince.

Having no earthly reason for avoiding her, I decided to at least be a good companion. At first the financial side was no problem; my sister was staying with the Meyers and had enough money to spend on the theaters, concerts, nightclubs, and other attractions she liked to go to with me. I invented some plausible reasons for my long stay in Berlin and made it clear that my means were very limited for the time being. When these problems were settled, we started a merry-go-round of shows, shops, and museums. Jadzia paid for the tickets, but, unfortunately, she took a liking to the food at the restaurant of my hotel, and so I became, involuntarily, her frequent host at meals. Besides, I took care of transportation and tips. My sister proved to be indefatigable at this kind of a life.

Such artificial euphoria as this could not last. One day, my sister announced that her funds were dwindling and that she would have to return home. The state of my own reserves had become quite alarming; my hotel bills were overdue, and I had only a small sum left. The only person who could understand and appreciate the intricacies of my life was Joseph Jaroszynski. He knew all the facts about Pola, about Paris and all the rest of it. I wrote him a long letter about my present situation and begged him to send me five thousand marks, a rather large sum of money (the equivalent of $1,250), which would enable me to return to Paris and possibly give a concert there on my own. Without his help, I wrote, it was the end; I was standing on the edge of an abyss. I dropped this letter into the mailbox with a strong heartbeat, feeling my immediate future was in his hand.

"You know what I did?" said Jadzia on the eve of her departure. "I pawned a bracelet and a brooch which I never wear, so I am sure that Maurycy will not notice it. Here are three hundred marks for you, I know you are hard up, but please keep these pawn tickets, and redeem them when you have the money."

Jadzia's departure left a void. I felt suddenly very lonely. Her vitality and her devotion to me had a soothing effect on my frequent attacks of depression. I didn't want to see anybody, not even Emmy Destinn or the Meyers. My mind was concentrated on one thing—Jaroszynski's answer. Still, I did go to a few concerts, but only when I could get free tickets.

One day, I met in the street Ossip Gabrilówitsch, who, besides being a fine pianist, was a lovable human being. He took me almost by force to visit Joseph Lhévinne, who was married and living in Berlin. His wife, Rosina, herself a brilliant pianist, is still, in the year 1972, one of the great piano teachers.

The Lhévinnes were pleased to see us and kept us for dinner, after which the four of us plunged happily into a riot of music making! Lhévinne and Gabrilówitsch played a concerto on two pianos, then Gabrilówitsch and I performed some Schubert for four hands, then the Lhévinne couple played delightfully a suite by Rachmaninoff, and we didn't stop until two in the morning. That night, forgetting my worries, I managed to take a good breath of life.

Two days later I went to hear Gabrilówitsch in a recital at the Beethoven Saal and was enchanted by his Schumann and Chopin, played with perfection and tenderness. After the concert I went to the artists' room to thank him for his beautiful performance. The place was filled with other enthusiasts, among them quite a few pianists. Ossip Gabrilówitsch was liked and admired by his colleagues.

"Ah, Rubinstein," he exclaimed, "how nice of you to have come. You must join us for supper—we are all going to the Austern-Keller!" I accepted his invitation with pleasure. And so we flocked to the restaurant, where a large table for at least twenty persons had been set in a private room. I was seated next to Yolanda Mero, a young Hungarian pianist who had just made her successful debut. As she looked at the menu, a startled expression came over her face.

"Everything is so expensive here," she said. "I hardly dare to order." I smiled. "Don't give it a thought. I am sure Gabrilówitsch can well afford it."

"But you are wrong," she replied. "Tonight everyone has to pay for himself."

This gave me a shock, and I had to act quickly, so I said to Yolanda Mero, "Please tell them that I had to make an urgent call. I shall be right back." I ran down the stairs, picked up a telephone, pretended to speak to someone and then sent a boy with a message to Gabrilówitsch: "Mr. Rubinstein is very sorry, but he had to leave in a hurry to see a sick friend."

Out in the street, all alone, cold and hungry, I felt pretty miserable.

Mr. Metzger, the hotel owner, sent me a stern letter about my unpaid bill. My credit at the restaurant was canceled, he wrote, and no food would be served in my room unless it was paid with cash. And still no news from Joseph. I wrote again, this time a registered letter addressed to his country place near Kiev. I did not mention my plans for Paris; anyway it was too late for it. Now it became simply a question of survival. "You must get me out of this dreadful hotel," I wrote, "and I do need some money for food and for my fare to Warsaw, where I hope to get some engagements. You always believed in my talent and my future, so you have no right to let me down." While writing this letter I felt as if I were drowning and yelling for help.

This time the waiting for his answer was even more agonizing than before. I had to look cheerful and reassure the manager that the money I expected was coming any day.

My daily diet consisted now of no breakfast at all, of a wurstel and dry roll at Aschinger's Automat, which cost ten pfennigs (2½ cents), and the same menu for dinner. And the rest of the day? A vague fumbling for some right notes on the piano, a listless wandering along the streets, and a chronic state of despair.

But just at that time, a curious phenomenon occurred: every night, the moment I fell asleep, the most fantastic, extravagant dreams invaded my unconscious mind, and in all of them I played the role of a powerful and happy personality. I was recurrently a famous composer, I conducted my new symphony, which was received with endless ovations, or I played my own piano concerto, a most original work. All the beautiful women were at my feet. In other dreams, I fought victorious battles for Poland, I would be saving Jews from persecution, or I was fabulously rich, the benefactor of humanity. My awakening brought the usual painful, tragic contrast, another disagreeable letter from the manager under the door, the hopelessness of the situation, and my empty pocket.

In my distress I decided to accept my dreams as reality and my days as mere nightmares. I tried to sleep as long as I could.

Two more weeks went by without news, and I gave up all hopes. I had reached the bottom. The idea of death by suicide was not novel to me, it had been on my mind before, but from that moment on, I couldn't think of anything else—it became an obsession. There was nothing left for me, life had driven me into an inextricable position. I wanted to die; I was ready for it. But even a decision as final as that had its problems. How to carry it out? I had no arms, no poison in my possession, and the idea of jumping out the window was revolting—I might have to go on living with broken arms and legs. The only thing to do was to die by strangulation, to hang myself. Well, on that sad afternoon, left so utterly alone, not even able to think of anyone to write to, I prepared for the finish.

I took out the belt from my old worn-out robe and fastened it with a knot. My bathroom had a clothes hook which was placed high enough to hold me. I pulled up a chair, secured the belt on the hook, and put it around my neck. As I pushed the chair away with my foot the belt tore apart and I fell on the floor with a crash.

If I saw today such a scene on television, I would roar with laughter, but in my role as the living hero of this tragicomedy, my first reaction was a severe nervous shock; I cried bitterly, disconsolately, for a long time, lying where I had fallen, with no strength left. Then, half-consciously, I staggered to the piano and cried myself out in music. Music, my beloved music, the dear companion of all my emotions, who can stir us to fight, who can inflame in us love and passion, and who can soothe our pains and bring peace to our hearts—you are the one who, on that ignominious day, brought me back to life.

When one stops crying, the suffering subsides, the same as when laughter dies, the fun is gone. And so, nature claiming its own, I began to feel hungry. "This time I shall have two sausages," I decided.

Out in the street, however, a sudden impulse made me stop. Something strange came over me, call it a revelation or a vision.

I looked at everything around me with new eyes, as if I had never seen any of it before. The street, the trees, the houses, dogs chasing each other, and the men and women, all looked different, and the noise of the great city—I was fascinated by it all. Life seems beautiful and worth living, even in prison or in a hospital, as long as you look at it that way.

This revelation is easy to explain: in attempting suicide I was completely dismissing the world I was going to leave behind, so no wonder that after my "suicide manqué" I felt as if I had been reborn. My "rebirth" brought yet another surprise: it created a revolution in my whole psychic system. I suddenly started to think. The life I had been leading consisted of a series of events for which I had no responsibility; I acted entirely by instinct, following blindly the road drawn out for me by circumstances; I never tried to analyze anything.

Well, on that night, right there in the street, on my way to Aschinger's for my dinner de luxe, my brain was full of philosophical thoughts, and it resulted in a new conception of life and a new criterion of values, all for my private use. The eternal, unsolved question—What gave birth to the universe? What is the reason for its existence?—would involve a long dissertation. Let me say only that in this chaos of thoughts I discovered the secret of happiness and I still cherish it: Love life for better or for worse, without conditions.

46

When I got back from Aschinger's, that very same night, I wrote the truth about my situation in a letter to my brother Stanislav, and begged him to try to gather, somehow from somewhere, a thousand marks to save me. Staś, as we called him, had a heart of gold; he kept my secret from our parents and obtained from Maurycy, Jadzia's husband, the bulk of the sum; he himself couldn't contribute more than three hundred. I received the money by telegram, paid the hotel half my due, which they accepted reluctantly as part of a payment to be made later, and left happily for Warsaw, with a feeling of the greatest relief in my life. I had yet to find an explanation acceptable to my friends for my unexpected return. The need to justify was rooted in my inveterate vanity and pride, and a certain lack of humility. I simply couldn't bear to be seen in a state of weakness or inferiority; the façade of success had to be kept intact, even when my affairs were at their lowest—which is a rather unpleasant trait of my character, I admit.

And this time again I hit upon a perfect alibi: my coming of age at twenty-one. I became due for military service, and it was imperative to find ways to avoid it.

Upon arrival, the first person I met at the Hotel Victoria was Paul Kochanski. We were happy to see each other again and went up to my room for a chat. When I told him why I was in Warsaw, he clapped his hands and exclaimed: "This is great! We are in the same hole—I am twenty-one, too." And he already had some plans for our defense campaign.

"I shall introduce you to Colonel Stremoukhov. He has a passion for music and can help us a lot. And we have plenty of time," he added. "As far as I know, we will be called only in November."

"Good news," I said, and changing the subject, I asked: "Where is Jaroszynski? What is he doing?"

"He has been in Warsaw all this time," Paul said, "but he just left for Kiev and is supposed to come back in a few days. But wait," he continued, "I must tell you a wonderful story about him. As you know, my family left Russia and settled in Leipzig, where my two brothers study music and where my sisters found work. I helped them to get there, and now I have to support my parents. Well, this spring, when the concert season was over, I was completely broke—I had barely enough for my own expenses, and I had to find the money for their rent. I asked Joseph to lend me some money until autumn, and you know what he did? He simply *gave* me four thousand rubles! Enough for my parents and to see me through the whole year. Isn't it fantastic?"

It is easy to imagine the effect this "wonderful story" had on me, and the mixed feelings it awakened. In a way, I was glad for Paul, I wished him well with all my heart, but I couldn't help seeing in Joseph's élan of generosity a sort of treachery toward me. I was well aware that he was entranced by Paul's playing and by his irresistible charm, but at the same time I used to think of Joseph as my close and devoted friend, and there was never anything which had come between us, so I was at a complete loss to understand his indifferent and cruel behavior. Unless it was a case of the popular French saying: "Les absents ont tort."

"My congratulations, Paul," I said, "you certainly are a lucky devil, but now I am going to tell you my own wonderful story, and you must swear to keep it secret." He did. During my long account of the Berlin nightmare, he listened with mixed feelings. When I finished, he was quite pale.

"How could he do such a thing!" he shouted indignantly. "I feel as if I had stolen that money from you!"

"Don't get too upset," I said. "There is a chance, a slight one, that he hadn't received my letters, or, perhaps, he did have some secret reason for acting that way."

"In any case, let us wait until his return—then we shall know."

My fear of seeing astonished faces and hearing indiscreet questions proved to be greatly exaggerated. Everybody seemed to accept my reappearance in Warsaw with nothing but pleasure. Szymanowski and Fitelberg were living at the Victoria, and we celebrated our reunion at the Bacchus restaurant with herring and wodka.

The "Kohn establishment," with Zosia, Zuzia, the Bechstein, and all, reopened its wide doors to me. Frederic showed me with pride the finished score of his concerto; pani Magdalena, unchanged, kept me for dinner. Pola remained invisible. This whole tableau restored my confidence.

But what really evoked my state of euphoria, that feeling of joy which swept over me, was again the magic of the Warsaw spring, the intoxicating air, when everything looks fresh and festive, when you feel wings, walking the streets.

One morning Paul received a telephone call from Jaroszynski; he was calling from the Bristol, had just arrived, and suggested meeting for lunch. Paul announced that I was back in town and that he was lunching with me. Expecting to hear a voice of bad conscience, he was surprised when Joseph reacted to the news of my return joyously. Needless to say, Paul and I were completely stupefied.

When we entered the restaurant, Joseph got up from his seat, embraced me, and shouted: "Arthur, I am so happy you are here and safe. I began to feel worried about you. But I was sure you would get out of this silly mess!"

I asked, timidly, "Did you receive two letters from me?"

"Of course," he laughed. "They were both very sad, but, knowing you, I imagined you were having a jolly good time in Berlin."

Suddenly I understood; the whole thing began to make sense. I remembered the fable I had read as a child about the boy who cried "wolf" too often.

It was a perfect analogy. I had written Joseph before for money in more urgent and pathetic terms than the occasions actually warranted, and he had generously responded without delay. My last fatal appeal for help must have left him with doubts about the seriousness of my situation, which explained his indifference. He had just given a large sum of money to Paul, so, in his heart, he had done his best for art and artists.

All these suppositions ran through my head; true or not, they helped me to recover my equanimity, and I was able to lunch and talk in his company as naturally as before.

Paul told him later the story of my Berlin disaster with all the details. The tale of my suicide manqué was too much for him, and he came to my room almost in tears. We talked and talked for hours; he frankly admitted that I hadn't convinced him with the colorful picture of my misery. "I thought," he said, "that you wanted that money simply to satisfy your passion for pleasures. Life in Berlin is very exciting, I believe."

It turned out to be exactly as I thought. The *affaire* was closed: I held no grudge against him.

We resumed more or less the life we had been leading before. Much music and frequent meals at the Kohns', billiards with Paul, and the usual social activities. A novelty was my acquaintance through Paul with Colonel Stremoukhov, a fanatical music lover. He would invite us for dinner, but after offering us a quickly served cold snack instead of a real meal, he would listen without budging to six or seven sonatas for piano and violin. As a person, he was a shattering bore, but he was very useful to us in connection with the military service.

Jaroszynski had to return to Zarudzie, his country place, and offered to take me with him. "It will do you good to stay a few days in the country," he said.

I was willing. I did need a rest. We left by train the next night and arrived the following morning in Kiev, where his horses were waiting to take us to Zarudzie. The Ukraine has the richest, most fertile soil in Russia, and Joseph's estate was in the center of it. He felt a real passion for land and bought up every piece of it, whenever there was one for sale. Already he was known as one of the largest landowners of the region. His many estates and farms, sugar factories, and other products yielded a very large income. Zarudzie was his main seat. The place looked very simple; the house had been built with no regard for form, but it was spacious and comfortable. A large veranda overlooked a horizon of endless steppes. The interior decoration was without interest: large bedrooms, bathrooms without bathtubs, bad plumbing. The dining room had cheap furniture. In the living room I found to my joy a fine Bechstein grand, but the rest of the place was quite primitive. A strange fellow, this Joseph; I began to know him better and better.

We spent a week in complete leisure. I slept without dreams, played most of the day to his usual shouts of delight, and we had simple, uncomplicated meals, but everything served was fresh and off the land. Back in Kiev, where we had to wait several hours for our train, Joseph took me to his town house, the big family home, where he occupied the second floor. Here, in the rooms he had used as a student, everything I saw was in good taste.

"I shall be gone for an hour," said Joseph, "and when I come back, I will take you to the Continental hotel for lunch."

"Can't I come with you?" I asked.

"No, you better wait here. I have some business to attend to."

He returned in less than an hour, out of breath, all flushed and a little embarrassed.

"I have a surprise for you, Arthur!" He pulled out of his pocket a large and fat envelope and put it into my hands. The envelope contained forty bills of a hundred rubles, four thousand rubles in all. For a surprise, it was really a big surprise!

"I went to my bank to settle some transactions," he said. "While I was handling the money I thought of the injustice I had done to you. So here is my debt. I only hope that you can still go back to Paris and pick up your career."

"Thank you, thank you, Józio, you are the most generous friend in the world," I exclaimed, kissing him on both cheeks. "Paris is out for me at the present—the concert season is over. A summer spent in France would ruin me. Besides, you know, in the autumn, Paul and I have to work something out about our military service."

Exhilarated as I was by his gift and feeling all this money in my pocket, I suddenly fell into my most exuberant and frivolous mood.

"Józio," I shouted, "I have a great, a magnificent idea. You suspected me of using your money for nothing but pleasure—well, let us do just that, but this time together, you, Paul, and I. Let us make a grand tour of the capitals, Berlin, Paris, and London, and enjoy every minute of it. What the devil is money made for but for living? And this I call real life—all the rest is nothing but mere preparation for it. It is true that Berlin can be exciting, Paris, when you have money, is all yours, and in London the great season is only beginning. I know it all sounds crazy, but it could be divine. What do you say?"

Joseph listened with a perplexed, bewildered expression on his face;

my vitality and my enthusiasm had always had a hypnotic effect on him.

"It sounds wonderful," he said, after a pause, and then, trying to find an argument against it, he added shyly: "I intended to take a cure in Karlsbad in August."

"Why not?" I answered quickly. "We can come with you and have a good time without the cure."

I won. It began with a smile, then, suddenly, he felt in his element; he jumped up, did some of his famous gymnastics, laughed uproariously, and shouted: "You devil, you—you could get away with murder!"

After his excitement subsided, he asked: "Are you sure Paul will like the idea?"

When we got back to Warsaw I found that to persuade Paul to join us on the "unique tour of the grand capitals of Europe exclusively for pleasure" was the easiest thing in the world. Even before I could finish the outline of the project, he interrupted me with enthusiastic signs of approval. "I shall take my violin to Hill in London—it needs some repairs —and in Paris I may find a good bow by Tourte," he said with a greedy grin.

We lunched with Joseph in a happy state of anticipation and fixed the date of our departure.

Another long sonata session at the music-devouring Russian colonel's, a delicious dinner at the Rzewuskis', my farewell evening with pani Magdalena, Basia, and Frederic, and a whole day of music and food at the Kohns' finished nicely our stay in my dear city on the Vistula. We left Warsaw with light hearts.

47

Berlin in 1908 was a Berlin I had known only from hearsay. When I was there as a teenager, I had simply lived the same kind of life as other boys in town: I was one of them. My recent unhappy stay had been nothing but a long inferno: I had been indifferent to the city as such, I was an exile, I lost the contact; even the "distractions" in the company of my sister had no stimulating effect on me.

On that lovely spring day, however, the three of us arrived as con-

querors. In my proud role as a guide and interpreter, I was in charge of
all the arrangements.

We stayed at the Kaiserhof, one of the best and most expensive hotels
in town. "When I was a boy, I wanted to see the interior of this place,"
I said. "I always looked at the façade with envy." Our windows had the
full view of the distinguished and "exclusive" (I hate this word) Wilhelm-
strasse, where most of the ministries and foreign embassies had their seat.
Right across the street was the site of Hitler's future underground shelter,
where he found his ignoble nemesis.

My first move was to run to the pawnshop and redeem Jadzia's
jewels. I felt much relieved when I had placed them safely at the bottom
of my bag. On my return, after a good rest, we sat out on a classical
Baedeker tour. Our first stop was the Kaiser Friedrich Museum, the gallery of paintings which contained, among others, a unique collection of
Dürers, Cranachs, Holbeins, and some of the finest Rembrandts. At the
sight of my favorite Rembrandt, *The Soldier with the Golden Helmet*,
Joseph put up such a show of shouting and gesticulating that the other
visitors were scared away.

The next thing on our program was the Zeughaus, the showcase
where the Prussians displayed, among other items, the arms and trophies
won in their war with France in 1870, and the Schloss, the residence of
the Imperial family. Before being allowed to enter the apartments of state
we had to put on some soft felt slippers which made us glide on the shiny
parquets as though we were on a skating rink. Our flock meekly followed
the uniformed guide, whose monotonous singsong and impersonal delivery
of the thousand-times-repeated descriptions put our attention to a severe
test. Back in the fresh air, rid of the gliding slippers and the palace, we
let out a sigh of relief.

"If you intend to show us more places of this kind, I am taking the
first train to Paris," said Paul. Joseph said nothing: he was just groaning.

After a fine meal and a short walk on Unter den Linden we returned
to our hotel. In the hall a woman's voice called Paul's and my name. It
turned out to be a friend of ours from Warsaw, the wife of a banker.
Small and somewhat corpulent, but agile in spite of her age—she must
have been well over fifty—she was attractive with her slightly faded
vestige of beauty.

"What are you doing in Berlin?" she asked.

"We are on our way to Paris," I answered cautiously, "and this is
our friend Joseph Jaroszynski."

"Please, dine with me tonight, all three of you. I promise you a good
dinner—the restaurant of our hotel is still the best. After dinner let us go
to the Wintergarten, and I shall take a box."

Her liveliness was so infectious we accepted. And the dinner, at which she ordered schnapps, caviar, and other delicacies, was perfect. A bottle of a French champagne brut helped to heighten our spirits. Paul was brilliant. He told some of his best Jewish stories—she was a Jewess—in his inimitable way and made us roar with laughter. My own imitations of some persons we all knew contributed to the fun. We left for the Wintergarten, singing in the street.

The show was exciting. Acrobats, jugglers, magicians, comedians, tightrope walkers filled the program. On our way home, grateful for the splendid entertainment she had offered us, we decided to reciprocate.

"Chère Madame, will you join us tomorrow evening for dinner at the same place, the same hour, the same table?"

She was visibly touched. "How sweet of you, boys, to spend so much time in the company of an old lady."

"You shouldn't say such a thing," we protested with false indignation. "Your charm, your gaiety, make you younger than you are!"

After our thanks and wishes for a good night, we retired to our respective rooms.

I slept until noon, my companions even longer. Well rested, giving up breakfast, we just had a light luncheon. After coffee, I arranged the menu for our dinner with the maître d'hôtel and asked the porter to reserve a good table for the show at the literary cabaret which I had seen before with Jadzia. The rest of the afternoon we spent shopping on Unter den Linden.

The dinner that evening was my responsibility, a great occasion for showing the taste which I acquired in Paris for the *haute cuisine française*. We had caviar again, with vodka instead of schnapps, a consommé double followed by a *canard à l'orange*, especially recommended by the chef, and a *soufflé au chocolat* to finish. I chose the wines with great care.

The cabaret was packed, but our porter secured for us one of the best tables in the place. We ordered champagne. The lights went out, the show began. In the overcrowded room we were forced to sit too close to each other—we could hardly move our arms or legs. In this position, suddenly, I felt the touch of a soft warm hand on my thigh followed by a light squeeze. Our lady friend did not stop at that. By and by, the squeeze developed into a series of provocative motions under the table. Her fat short leg found mine and clung to it all through an amusing sketch. Even the brilliant Jewish comedian Fritz Grunbaum, whose jokes provoked shrieks of laughter, did not interrupt her sensuous movements. By then, thoroughly aroused, I began to respond. Our exciting activity continued until the end of the show. After the last curtain call, during the noise at the exit doors, she whispered close to my ear: "Come to my room later on, third floor, room 39."

Back in the lobby of our hotel, the effusions of thanks, kisses, and good-night wishes continued for quite a while. Finally, we took the elevator to our different floors. At last alone, I waited until all the noises died down, then, cautiously, I slipped out of my room, climbed the stairs to the third floor, and entered her half-opened door. She was already in her nightgown and sat on a couch, waiting. The unusual amount of champagne I had absorbed and her art of arousing potential sensualities produced its combined effect. We made love right away, without losing time. She began to moan and talk incessantly, using a quaint vocabulary: "You are doing fine, you work beautifully, oh, you are working so well, oh, this is fine work!" This blabber went on in a crescendo.

When I got up, ready to leave, she kissed me and said, "Thank you, my dear, thank you—and don't worry about consequences. I promise you have nothing to fear."

Poor woman, that was pathetic.

Next morning, I woke up with a hangover. I had my breakfast in bed and was trying to go to sleep again when someone knocked on my door. It was Paul.

"What is the matter with you, are you ill?" he asked.

"No, I am just exhausted from last night," I said.

"Is that all?" he asked again, inquisitively.

"What do you mean by that?" I asked, a little alarmed.

He gave me a long look with his coal-black velvet eyes. Suddenly, with a diabolical grin, he started: "Oh, you are doing fine, oh, how you work beautifully, oh, what fine work," and he went on and on. It was her voice and her accent, to perfection!

For a moment I sat up, open-mouthed. Then, looking at each other, we both burst into uncontrollable Homeric laughter.

"Paul, you rascal, when did it happen to you?" I asked, when we were able to speak.

"After the Wintergarten show," he replied. "Don't you remember? I was the one that night who sat next to her."

Our passionate friend returned that night to Warsaw. We saw her off with flowers. Paul left to spend a day in Leipzig with his parents and returned next morning.

The last days in Berlin were spent mainly in pursuit of our individual interests, but we did meet for lunch at Dressel's. Joseph was visiting agricultural exhibitions and tried to explain to us with his usual passion the use of modern tractors. Paul practiced the whole morning in his room. I followed his example at Bechstein's storehouse, happy to put my hands on a piano again. Our afternoons were more diversified; Joseph's dynamic constitution compelled him to take long siestas after our copious meals. Paul indulged in shopping; he had a mania for collecting gadgets of all kinds, especially those made in Germany. My own preference was visiting bookshops and music stores in search of new publications. One morning, in a spell of courage, I called up some of my old benefactors and friends. Most of them had left for the summer, but Mr. Martin Levy, still in town, received me with his usual kindness. I gave him a highly colored account of my successes in Paris, America, and Poland, and I noticed with pleasure that he was impressed.

A few more shows, one of them *The Dollar Princess*, the brilliant operetta by Leo Fall, and another one, an amusing comedy by Arthur Schnitzler, put an end to our glorious Berlin adventure. My companions called it a great success. As for myself, it was something more: it was a private retaliation for the agonies I had endured in that city.

48

We arrived in Paris one gray morning. The Gare du Nord looked more shabby, more dirty than ever (the first glimpse of this beautiful city is so often discouraging). Tired and hungry, we lost much time getting through customs and finding a cab. But, finally, when our horse trotted us down to the Avenue des Champs-Élysées, the sky cleared and the Ville Lumière smiled on us again.

Joseph took us to the Champs-Élysées Palace, where he had stayed before—a new hotel on the avenue of the same name, close to the Place de l'Étoile. The pretentious air of the place, the showy hall in white and gold, and the bright uniforms of the porters were quite a contrast to the small, uncomfortable rooms we had and the poor service; we had to wait hours for the valet or the maid to answer our call. With sighs of resignation, we managed, however, to empty our bags, hang up our suits, take hot baths, and put on some fresh clothes. Then, all spick and span, we went out to lunch at the Pavillon Royal, in the Bois de Boulogne, a restaurant which Józio and I remembered with affection because we had gone there quite often in the early days of our friendship.

That same afternoon, while Joseph and Paul took a walk around, I tried to phone my friends, such as Count Potocki, Mr. Rembielinski, and Armand de Gontaut. I wanted to apologize for my silence, to tell them how grateful I was for all they had done for me. But one by one the reply at the other end of the line was that Monsieur was out of town, was on vacation, was taking his cure, or had left for America. I dropped the wretched phone in a fit of frustration; I had wanted so very much to make up with these fine men who had been so good to me. That evening when they returned, Paul and Joseph seemed equally depressed to have found the Café de la Paix swarming with foreigners and hardly a word of French spoken. Even an evening at Maxim's, where the same old guard were still on hand, did not improve our spirits, and the next day when Paul found his violinmaker's atelier closed, it was the last straw. After a thorough exploration of the Louvre and the Invalides and a memorable evening at the Comédie Française, we left for London the next day.

Journeying there by train, boat, and train again can be one of the most complicated and uncomfortable ways of traveling, often made worse by the heavy seas of the Channel. Yet we arrived in the evening at the Victoria Station in a state of anticipation rather than exhaustion. On the train, we had had lengthy discussions about our financial arrangements. Joseph very generously had paid the large bill of the Kaiserhof, except *our* dinner in honor of the lady from Warsaw. Paul and I, by turns, were responsible for all the other expenses. In Paris we automatically did the same. For London, however, we decided to do the reverse—assume the hotel bills and let Joseph pay for restaurant meals. Smaller outlays for cabs, tickets, tips, and such we left to our discretion; we hated to be too meticulous.

Infected by the universal snobbery of those times for England and everything English, we chose to stay at the Carlton, the place for the "right people." But there was nothing available there, and we had to settle for rooms at the Victoria, which the kind reception clerk at the Carlton found for us.

The old Victoria hotel was the prototype of most of the provincial hotels in England. Our rooms were less than pleasant. The one which Paul and I shared had two extra-long beds made for the tall English, a washstand, a toilet table with a standing mirror, two chairs, and an old-fashioned armoire with squeaky doors. Joseph's room was smaller but had the same furnishings. Neither had a bathroom. Having decided not to lose our good humor, we didn't bother about unpacking or changing our clothes; we just left the hotel in a hurry and returned on foot to the Carlton.

We were lucky in finding a table at the Carlton Grill, famous for its French cuisine. Here, ha, ha, we felt like the "right people" again. After a good, long dinner, we managed to see at least the last part of the variety show at the Empire Music Hall. We were so delighted with what we saw that we swore to return the next night for the part we had missed. Variety shows and big revues were typical of the English stage then.

A cab took us back to our hotel. We dreaded a little the return to our uninviting quarters, but we woke to a glorious morning. London is known for its bad climate, but when you hit upon one of those perfect summer days, it becomes the most beautiful city in the world. We were pleasantly surprised to find that the hotel did serve us a very good breakfast in our rooms.

Ready and out in the street, Paul asked me to accompany him to Hill's, the best-known dealer in old violins. Joseph preferred to visit the National Gallery, where we promised to join him. We strolled down to the Old Bond Street, enjoying the sun and the mild air. At Hill's I witnessed an emotional scene. Here, Paul was in his element. When he had explained the matter of the repairs on his violin and had left his instrument in good hands, he began to inspect with a greedy passion the priceless Stradivari and Guarneri del Jesu with the sign of the cross carved inside. He handled and stroked them tenderly, he tried out their feel under his chin, and he played and played and made them sound heavenly. I was very touched by this scene. If I were a millionaire, I would buy all of them for him, I wished in my heart.

Before joining Joseph, we couldn't resist giving in to our secret vices, Paul's for gadgets and traveling bags, and mine for clothes and new ties. He rushed to Asprey's, his favorite shop, and I went to order a full dress suit at a renowned tailor's, who promised to have it ready in a week. We both arrived late at the Gallery and found Joseph in a distant room, sitting on a bench, exhausted and angry.

"What kept you so long—what were you doing all this time?" And then, addressing Paul, "Did you play your whole repertoire at Hill's?" he shouted.

"We were walking up and down on Bond Street and the Burlington Arcade, window shopping," we lied, covering our bad conscience with a smile. We didn't want him to know how we were spending his money. The luncheon at Scott's on Piccadilly Circus, which specialized in lobsters with claws larger than an entire *demoiselle de Cherbourg* of Paris (the delicate lady lobsters from Brittany), calmed his temper.

We had a delightful time in the English capital. Visits to the British Museum, the Tower of London, the Wallace Collection, and an excursion to Windsor occupied our mornings. In between I had to rush surreptitiously to the tailor's for my fitting. We took most of our meals at the Carlton or Savoy Grill and some more at Scott's.

Apropos of restaurants, I recall an amusing incident. Paul and I, quite unintentionally, had in London a financial advantage over Joseph. Our hotel was obviously cheaper than the luxurious Carlton, while the restaurants where we usually ate were even more expensive than in Paris or Berlin. Now, Joseph, with all his generosity, had a streak of stinginess, so characteristic of the rich, which he, with his unrestrained frankness, could not hide. On frequent occasions during our meals, he would let out one of his special, sonorous sighs, complaining: "Ay, ay, ay! Always hungry, always lobsters? Always steaks? Always champagne?" while enjoying these delicacies himself with an irrepressible appetite. We were vexed enough to feel we should teach him a little lesson. One night, preparing to go to the Covent Garden Opera to hear Caruso in *Pagliacci*, we took time changing into our evening dress for the great occasion.

"Hurry up, hurry up," Joseph shouted from his room. "It is getting late for dinner."

"We don't feel like dining tonight," we answered. "We ate too much at lunch." A long sigh was his answer; he could not afford to insist. We drove to the theater on empty stomachs.

At the Opera, after *Cavalleria Rusticana*, which preceded *Pagliacci*, we remained in our seats during the entire intermission. The theater offered an impressive sight. The boxes were occupied by the flower of the English aristocracy. The ladies, beautifully dressed, showed off their sparkling jewels and tiaras.

Caruso in *Pagliacci* was unsurpassed; his great aria, "Ridi Pagliaccio," moved us to tears. At the end of the opera, the audience gave him a standing ovation. When we were out in the street, looking for a hansom, Joseph suggested something about supper.

"No, Józio dear," I replied with a Machiavellian cruelty, "Paul and I are tired and sleepy, but why don't you go by yourself?"

Poor Joseph was caught in a trap; to have supper by himself would amount to a frank admission that he was the one who was always hungry, always ready to eat, while we had plainly shown our indifference to food. And so, meekly, he returned with us to the hotel. It goes without saying, of course, that we were both starving to death, but decided to play the game to the bitter end. We went to bed, but couldn't sleep, partly through hunger, but mainly because of the loud groans and moans coming from the other room. At seven in the morning we heard Joseph ring for breakfast. We did the same and invited him to join us for the heavenly meal. While gulping down voluptuously our eggs and bacon, croissants and toast, with jams and marmalades, and sipping coffee, we confessed to our dear friend our fiendish meanness, and he showed what a really wonderful fellow he was. Instead of bearing a grudge for what we did, he began to insist henceforth at our meals on our having lobsters, caviar, and what not.

We were enjoying our stay in London more and more when Joseph announced that it was time for him to leave for Karlsbad, where he had his hotel reserved for a certain date.

"Do you really intend to come with me?" he asked. We were both taken by surprise; my suit wouldn't be ready for a day or two, and, as a matter of fact, I had ordered another one which they promised to deliver at the same time. Paul's violin saved me from my embarrassment. I answered: "Of course we intend to go to Karlsbad, but we cannot leave right away. Hill's has still some work to do on Paul's fiddle, but it won't take more than two days. I shall stay with Paul, and we will join you there."

Joseph left the next morning. We saw him off at the Victoria Station, and from there, behaving like two naughty boys who got rid of their governess, we took a bus for the White City at Shepherd's Bush, a real madhouse of an amusement park. Here we let off all our boyish steam. We took in everything: the scenic railways, the Prussian mountains, the water chutes, the labyrinths, the shooting galleries, and other devilish devices. We loved every bit of it. When we returned, dead tired, we still had the energy to go to hear Kreisler at the Queen's Hall.

Two days later we were ready to leave: both suits and the violin were in our possession. While packing, I saw Paul fishing out from under his bed two brand-new leather bags. "These last a hundred years," he said with pride. I knew better; he would buy some new ones in no time.

The journey to Karlsbad was long and tedious. We arrived the next day at sunset. At the Pupp, the hotel where Joseph was staying, there was a note for us, saying that all the hotels in town were full, but that he had found a room for both of us in a private house, close by. We went there on foot, accompanied by a porter with our luggage. The life in front of the hotel was quite exhilarating. Under a sky inflamed by the last rays of the sun, crowds of old and young people in gay summer attire were walking up and down the esplanade, listening to a band which played Viennese waltzes. We promptly spotted among the promenaders some remarkably attractive women. Anxious to join this animated throng, we hastened to settle down in our new lodgings—which turned out to be a drab attic room in a house run by a fat Czech woman who left us to take care of ourselves. By the time we had settled in we were famished.

"Let us go quickly to the Pupp," said Paul. "We can dine there on the terrace and watch the people." It was an excellent idea, I thought. But when we arrived at the esplanade, the whole place was empty. It looked dead, as if it were infested by a pestilence which had chased the inhabitants out of town. Not a soul to be seen, the band had disappeared, the streets were dark. The hotel was closed for the night, the tables of the terrace were overturned. We stood there, stupefied, speechless for a while. Only hunger brought us back to our senses.

"There must be a place where we can eat," I said. "It isn't late, it's only eight thirty." We wandered around, hoping to find a café or a tavern still open. Finally, in a narrow street we passed what looked like a shop, but in the show window, a bottle of wine and two apples caught my eye, and we managed to get a small bite.

After a long night's rest, we got up at nine, dressed, and went to have our breakfast at Pupp's. Joseph came down from his room to sit with us.

"I have my breakfast at seven, after my first glass at the hot spring," he said.

When we told him the story of our arrival, he laughed. Then he gave us a lecture on Karlsbad. The life of this little town was centered entirely on its mineral springs. Thousands of people, year after year, would come in the hopes of restoring their damaged livers and stomachs by drinking the precious waters.

"But we have to submit to a very hard discipline," he continued. "The cure begins at six in the morning with a glass of water at the hot spring, followed by showers, massages, and a hot bath. At seven we have our breakfast, then to bed for a rest. Another glass before lunch at noon, with a special diet, of course. Long walks in the afternoon, the part I hate most, and the last glass before dinner at six. After dinner we are allowed to enjoy the music on the Alte Wiese, and that is where you came in," he said, smiling. He added, "So no wonder that everybody retires at eight and is fast asleep at nine."

"Such a program is not for us," Paul said. "Arthur, we must organize our own life in this restrictive place, and right away." We left Joseph to his liver-curing chores and started out on a thorough exploration of the town. The head porter of the hotel, duly tipped, gave us some precious information. Following his instructions, we found after a short walk a small square with a fountain in the center, surrounded by flower beds. Two café-restaurants with large terraces lent an air of gaiety to the charming place. A waiter told us that the cafés served meals until two o'clock in the morning. This was good news, indeed.

We adopted the square as our headquarters for the whole stay in Karlsbad. My own problem, an urgent one, was to find a piano. I hadn't touched one since we left Berlin, and I was becoming quite alarmed about the state of my fingers. To my great relief, this problem, too, was solved on the same afternoon. We had a Kursaal in town; every health resort apparently has to have one. "Ours" had a large hall for dances, theatrical entertainments, or concerts. And right there stood a concert piano which was still in good condition.

The administrator of the building, to whom I went to ask permission to use it for an hour or so, was a music lover.

"You can play here the whole day, undisturbed," he said. "The Kursaal is always empty anyhow—the people are too busy with their cures. But I hope you will allow me to listen to you sometimes." I thanked him; I liked the man.

From that day on, Paul and I arranged our "anticurist" life to our entire satisfaction. In the morning, at seven, we would take turns going down to buy some of those delicious Viennese croissants and rolls and then would come back to sleep. We had learned our lesson when we found nothing but hard, dry toast at our own breakfast time, at nine or ten. The rest of the mornings we spent practicing on our instruments, Paul in his room, I at the Kursaal. One day on the esplanade called Die Alte Wiese a very young girl, a striking blond beauty, addressed me in a haughty, authoritative manner.

"I am Piedita Iturbe, a pupil of Leschetitzky's. I hear that you are a talented pianist," and she continued her promenade. Years later, in Madrid, I saw her again. She was married to a Prince Hohenlohe. We became friends, which we still are.

In one of the restaurants on the square, where we used to take our meals, we met a few attractive young people, also "anticurists" who had come to Karlsbad with their parents. At night, when the rest of the town was safely settled in the arms of Morpheus, we would get together at our lively meeting place to play some billiards or to talk on the terrace, sipping cool drinks.

We saw Joseph only at intervals between his daily "glasses," but the cure became more congenial for him, and, in a way, for us by the arrival of many of our friends and acquaintances from Poland, the Rzewuskis among others.

One nice day, our good old Joseph became exasperated by his monotonous routine. He dropped the whole thing and joined our revolutionary anticure camp. Our new friends were at first a little startled by him but learned soon to appreciate his colorful personality.

One afternoon at Pupp's, where I sat with a group of Poles, Joseph appeared all flushed, waving an envelope in his hand.

"Guess what I have?" he shouted at me, and, not waiting for an answer, he announced triumphantly: "A ticket for *Parsifal* for tomorrow at Bayreuth!"

I was thunderstruck. It had always been my dream to be at a Wagner Festival in Bayreuth and especially to see *Parsifal*, which at that time could be seen only at this Wagnerian Mecca.

"Is this ticket for me?" I asked, my heart beating with excitement.

"No," he answered, "a bank had only this one ticket for sale and I had to pay for it one hundred and twenty-five kronen!" (about $25, five times the original price). "You might find something for the next performance."

"And you have the courage to go all by yourself and leave me here eating my heart out?" I cried. "You know very well that everything has been sold out since January. You're just trying to give me false hopes, but I will go with you anyway and see what can be done, and if I fail, you will have to share with me your miserable ticket!" I became quite hysterical.

For once Joseph was immovable. "You can come with me if you like," he declared tersely, "but forget about taking my ticket."

The distance between Karlsbad and Bayreuth was more than two hours by train. We arrived at noon. The friendly Bavarian town, Wagner's shrine, had a festive air. Flags and banners hung from the windows. Crowds, mostly ticket holders for the festival, were walking up and down the main street in search of souvenirs. We went to a small hotel, where Joseph found a room for me, against all odds. I rushed down to inquire at the hotel desk about possible ways of obtaining an entrance to the Festspielhaus. The clerk was more than pessimistic.

"There is only one chance," he said. "You could wait in front of the box office for a ticket which might be returned." I did not hesitate. Equipped with two ham sandwiches, I ran to the place he had indicated, where about five men stood already in line for the same purpose. It was one o'clock, and *Parsifal* started at four. The three hours of waiting was one of the greater tests of my life. Finally, as the ominous hour approached when people began to enter the hall, the box office opened its windows. The five men ahead of me were sent away, one by one, empty-handed. When it came to my own turn, I was so distressed that I had not the strength to open my mouth—I just made a pathetic questioning gesture. The man in control opened his arms widely and shrugged his shoulders, indicating that he could not help me.

By that time the entire audience was inside the theater, and the entrance doors were closed. In Bayreuth, even the King of Bavaria wouldn't be allowed to enter the theater when a performance has begun.

I was walking away, frustrated, with my head down, when a policeman who had watched me for some time and noticed my despair addressed me: "Young man, you seem quite upset. Can I be of any help?"

I grumbled something about the ticket.

"I thought so. Have you twenty marks to spare?" he asked. I nodded in the affirmative.

"Then I have one for you, a very good one," he said. "We have arrested a fellow who stole one and tried to sell it at an exorbitant price.

The ticket is now at the police station, and you can buy it for the original price."

I couldn't believe my ears. I shook his hand so hard I almost broke it. We went together to the police station, which was around the corner. In less than ten minutes I was in possession of the precious bit of paper. I ran back to the entrance door of the theater. The man in charge of it had a forbidding look. I didn't say a word. I just opened imploring eyes on him. He must have noticed my distress, too, as the policeman had, because, after a short while, looking at me sharply, he muttered: "Can you swear that you will remain seated on the first step nearest to this door without moving until the end of the act?" I swore—I would have sworn to anything. He opened the door just enough to let me slip in. I was fortunate enough to have missed only the great orchestral introduction to *Parsifal*. The first act, from the start, made an overwhelming impression on me. Ever since Berlin, I had been a fervent follower of Wagner, thanks to the wonderful performances I had seen of *Tristan and Isolde*, the *Meistersinger*, and the whole tetralogy.

In Bayreuth, on that day, something strange happened to me. I was caught by a mysterious spell. I cried part of the time. Now, after all those years, it is easy to explain: I had found the whole town entirely concentrated on Wagner and his musical drama. His devotees gathered at his shrine year after year, walking up to the Festspielhaus in procession like pilgrims in search of their salvation. Seated in the dark auditorium, the music seemed to come straight from heaven. The careful choice of the singers, the gorgeous sound of the orchestras, the many months of preparation, and the great conductor, Karl Muck, in charge of the whole production, made up the rest. The result was irresistible. I can well understand how at my young age I was so swayed by the magic of Wagner's genius. It was like a disease. I have since called it my "Wagneritis."

During intermission we were served dinner set up in the park adjoining the theater. When Joseph saw me, he had the guilty look of someone who had let me down. One can imagine the change of his expression when I told him my little story. He gave out a loud shout and started some of his gymnastics. When we settled down at a table, we were bubbling over with enthusiasm in wild excitement. A fanfare called us back to the theater. After the unforgettable evening, exhausted from our emotions, we went to sleep without a word.

Early in the morning, before returning to Karlsbad, Joseph went to town hunting for tickets for the next performance of *Parsifal*. This time he found no fewer than three good seats.

"We must make Paul come with us," he said.

Back at our health resort we couldn't stop talking about our experiences. It was quite contagious. Everybody dreamed of going to Bayreuth. Even Paul, who took his Wagner rather coldly, became more interested. The news of our euphoria reached Marienbad, our neighboring spa, where Madame Magdalena, in company of Basia, was taking her cure. Both ladies came to Karlsbad for a visit. I had tea with them at Pupp's. The conversation, naturally, centered on Bayreuth and *Parsifal*.

"Mother has a ticket," said Basia. "She bought it from a gentleman who suddenly decided not to interrupt his cure. But what about me?" she added, putting on her charm.

"There is nothing, absolutely nothing you can do," I answered, unmoved.

"But *you* have a ticket, haven't you?" she insisted.

I was loath to part with my seat. "Come with us to Bayreuth and I will do what I can," I said. At worst, I thought, I shall have to sacrifice one act for her.

The day we arrived in Bayreuth, Paul persuaded us to look around, and we had lunch at a charming rathskeller served by Bavarian "dirndls" and enjoyed the food and the atmosphere so much that we forgot to look at the time. At three o'clock I felt a pang of conscience toward Basia. I hadn't tried anything about a ticket for her, and I hated to lose a whole act because of her. All I could do so late was to return to the box office on a faint chance, but with the reassuring thought, this time, of having a ticket in my pocket. About twelve men and women were standing ahead of me when I took up my position. I waited impassively, without the slightest hope, when a respectable-looking man moved toward me, brought his face close to my ear, and whispered: "Ask at the control desk for the ticket of Otto Schulz," and he walked away. I was abashed. I didn't know what to make of it. It might be a trap, I thought, remembering the stolen ticket of my previous visit. Still, it was too tempting an offer. I decided to follow the man's instructions.

The scene of the week before repeated itself: the same slow progress of the people ahead of me who heard the same fatal answer, "There are no returned tickets for today." I became frightened, I was ready to run away, but it was too late—I had already reached the desk where three men in dark clothes sat like judges in court. I stuttered softly: "T-t-ticket for O-t-t-o Sch-sch-ulz," whereupon one of the men handed me an envelope without saying a word. I asked tremulously, "How much?" "No charge," came the answer. I walked away, absolutely stupefied. The envelope contained a ticket for a seat in the privileged box next to Cosima Wagner.

I gave my own seat to the overjoyed Basia, and kept the other one for myself, so as not to involve her in case of some trouble.

The theater became calm, the lights went out, and the first majestic notes of the introduction resounded from the orchestra pit. Again, this powerful music filled me with an indescribable emotion. I shall never forget the beauty of Karl Muck's conducting this work. The first act was sung even better than the time before, but my attention was hampered by the mystery of the ticket and the strange man. Also, a disturbance was caused by a comical incident in the audience. A lady who sat in one of the back rows wore an enormous picture hat topped by ostrich feathers, blocking the view of the people who sat behind her. In protest, they whispered, "Hut ab" (hat off), then hissed louder, "Hut ab," then almost shouted, "Hut ab, hut ab." The lady tried to ignore them at first, although she was well aware of what they wanted her to do. Soon it became obvious that she would rather die than take her hat off. Suddenly she couldn't stand it any longer. With a face distorted by rage, crying hysterically, "Tas de chameaux, tas de chameaux," she ran out of the theater. Basia explained to me later that this wretched French woman was wearing a complicated coiffure and her hair was attached to the hat, making it impossible to take it off without ruining the whole thing.

During the long intermission, instead of joining the others at dinner, I walked around the grounds in search of the mystery man. I was delighted to find him standing near the box office, in conversation with the comptroller who had given me the envelope. Obviously, there was nothing to fear from him. When I approached, he called, "Young man, how did you like the performance? You are a musician, aren't you?"

"Yes, I am. I don't know whom to thank for the wonderful seat," I said, "but I am anxious to know what happened to Mr. Otto Schulz." Both laughed.

"Don't worry about it," said my man, "there is no Otto Schulz. We always hold at the box office one or two tickets for a last-minute emergency or for a guest or a friend of Frau Cosima Wagner. We simply couldn't bear to see once more the same distressed face you had last week."

I blushed with shame for having inspired pity, but I did feel grateful for their discreet and sensitive response. And they were pleased to learn that they had done it for a musician with a passion for Wagner. I felt uneasy about telling the true story of the ticket to my friends. They might laugh at me, I feared. And they did.

"You and your faces," Paul giggled. "The devil in hell would let you go free if you turned a face on him." We all returned to Karlsbad in high spirits. Back in our attic room, Paul and I had our nightly conversation. We spoke about *Parsifal*.

"I am completely shattered by this genius, Wagner," he said, and by a strange association of thoughts, he added, "You and I will never amount to anything—we are too lazy, we are not good enough." His pessimism was contagious.

"I absolutely agree with you," I answered.

One morning Paul and I were rehearsing a violin and piano sonata at the Kursaal when the administrator, who was listening, interrupted us: "What a shame you can't give a concert in my hall!"

"Why?" I asked. "Is it prohibited in this town?"

"No, of course not," he answered. "We had one last year and it was a disaster. We couldn't gather more than twenty people. The cure guests retire too early in the evening, and the townspeople will not spend their money on expensive concert tickets."

"Let me think about it—I might have an idea," I said. I suddenly felt an urge to give a concert. I hadn't played for ages before a public. I called Joseph and Paul for a conference, and Paul quickly devised a clever plan: to charge twenty-five kronen (about $5) a ticket for the five front rows.

"Most of our friends and their acquaintances are very rich," he said. "They are sure to come, and they can't afford to take cheaper seats. The rest of the hall we can give away at a minimal price. That might attract some people from town, just out of sheer curiosity."

We adopted his idea right away, and so did the administrator, who offered his hall without charge. The expenses for publicity were covered by the Kursaal's yearly contract with the local paper and the billboards in the street. We were responsible only for the printing of programs, but we had the right to charge for them. It was easy for us to make up a good program: a Beethoven violin and piano sonata by Paul and myself, and four groups of solo pieces played in turn by each of us. Joseph agreed with pride to play the accompaniments for Paul; he had done it often and did it very well.

Our concert took place at seven p.m., and it was an all-around success. Paul was right. The first five rows were sold out in one morning. The next six or seven rows were almost empty. But the rest of the hall, sold at a nominal price, was packed with a noisy and enthusiastic crowd. We earned the net amount of more than three thousand kronen, a big sum for those times. The administrator thanked us exuberantly.

"You saved the honor of our Kursaal," he said with pathos. "Now we can face a better future."

The time had come for us to leave the quaint health resort. Most of our friends had finished their cures and returned home. Jaroszynski, who had stayed longer than he intended to, was called back to attend to his many business obligations. He promised to join us later in Warsaw. Paul was going to visit his family in Leipzig before returning to Poland. And myself? As the incurable Wagner addict I had become, I decided to go to Munich for the opening of the Wagner Festival at the Prinzregenten (a theater especially built for performances of Wagner's musical dramas) to hear the great Felix Mottl conduct the *Ring of the Nibelung* and, on top of it, *Tristan and Isolde*.

49

Munich, the capital of the kingdom of Bavaria, was very different in 1908 from the city that we came to know later as the cradle of Hitler's rise to power and as the scene of the shameful Munich Pact.

My first impression of the city was most gratifying. At the station I found a friendly, talkative cab driver who took me to the Hotel Vier Jahreszeiten. On the way, he gave me practical hints for my stay which proved to be very useful. Thanks to him, I found the tickets for the various performances without being overcharged, and an inexpensive *Keller* where the food was simple but excellent. With my inexhaustible passion for sight-seeing I did the official tour of the city in one single day. I paid a long visit to the Pinakothek, and saw three fine churches and the inside of the lovely baroque Residenz theater, where they played the operas of Mozart. However, my imagination was filled with the romantic past of the city so closely linked with Wagner: the handsome, youthful King Ludwig II, whose passion for the master had brought his country to the verge of ruin and revolution; the Spanish dancer Lola Montez, who was mistress of King Ludwig I and who later ran away with Liszt; the most pathetic case had been the marital drama of Hans von Bülow. This fine musician and Wagner fanatic had the courage to conduct the world premiere of *Tristan and Isolde* in Munich. While he devoted himself to this difficult work, rehearsing month after month, his wife, Cosima, the daughter of Liszt, eloped with Wagner to Luzern. The *affaire* had stirred up a great scandal. The press covered poor Bülow with ridicule, while the happy couple was violently attacked.

But all this was ancient history to the Munich I came to visit. In 1908, the whole city basked in the glory of the composer of *Tristan*. The costly Prinzregenten theater had been built to compete with Bayreuth, and was superior in many ways—better acoustics, more comfortable seats, and a noble architecture.

Rheingold was a revelation to me. I had seen it before, but I had never realized what it could sound like. Everything was perfect and Felix Mottl supreme.

During the days that followed I became so involved that I could not think of anything but Wagner. Instead of practicing I played the scores of *Siegfried, Tristan*, whatever I could lay my hands on. By chance the first night I had run into two singers who had collaborated with me on the *Salomé* performance in Paris, and touched by my fervor, they arranged for me to visit the festival workshop. I had the privilege of hearing two full rehearsals by Mottl of *Tristan*, an unforgettable experience. The two singers, both Bavarians, were indefatigable in showing me all the attractions of their city. After the magnificent performances of the *Ring* and of *Tristan and Isolde*, we used to exchange impressions late into the night, eating sausages and drinking the dark Löwenbräu, the only beer I liked. I reciprocated by inviting them after to lunch at my hotel.

On one free evening—they were busy that night—I wanted to see something of the more elegant life of the city. My hotel man recommended a restaurant to me, supposedly the best in town, where Munich "society" used to dine. "A Hungarian gypsy band is playing there during dinner time," he said. I put on my best clothes and went to the place, looking forward to some dishes more refined than the thick soups, the *Knödels*, and the sausages that I had been eating daily. The restaurant lived up to my expectation. The waiters wore tails and white ties, the guests were distinguished, and the food looked promising. The gypsies, dressed in red coats with gold trimmings, sat on a platform and played some Hungarian tunes.

When the maître d'hôtel showed me to a small table in front of the band, the pianist suddenly stopped playing, got up, and left precipitately through a side door. The members of the band looked baffled. One of them went to find out what had happened. When he returned he came to talk to me.

"Our comrade refuses to come back and play as long as you are in the restaurant," he said.

The blood rushed to my face. An anti-Semite, I thought.

"This is preposterous," I replied, angrily. "Nobody has the right to make me leave this place."

"But you are mistaken, mein Herr," the man said. "He is simply afraid of you."

I was puzzled. Who on earth could be afraid of me, and why?

"Let me talk to your pianist," I said. "I must find out what it is all about."

He led me to a small room where the musicians changed their clothes. As the pianist jumped up from his chair, I looked at him intently.

"Fritz, Fritz Müller," I called. It was *the* Fritz Müller, my friend and rival of our old Berlin days, the promising composer, Joachim's protégé.

"Why, for heaven's sake, are you afraid of me?" I asked.

"I am not afraid, I am ashamed," he answered, and began to cry. I could not bear it—I was about to cry, too.

"If my presence here embarrasses you, I shall leave right away, but you must promise to come to see me tomorrow morning at my hotel." He promised, and I returned to my *Keller* for ham and cabbage with *Knödels*.

Fritz arrived early, and we had breakfast. In his street clothes he looked the same as I had known him; he had not even grown much. I asked no questions about his playing in a gypsy band. I took it for granted that he needed money to be able to compose without starving.

"Have you composed a lot lately, Fritz?" I asked.

"No," he answered. "I was left without money in Berlin, so I ran away to Hamburg, where I accepted a job playing in a café. They liked me there, and it opened my way to this new career. I began to love playing light music, and now here in Munich I have a good job with this band and am earning good money."

I became quite upset. "But, Fritz," I insisted, "you cannot abandon your great talent, give up a fine career as a concert pianist, as a composer?"

"Serious music does not attract me any more," he said. "I am sick and tired of it. My hysterical behavior of last night was simply due to the fact that you are the only person in the world who could make me feel ashamed of my costume and of the stuff I am playing."

I offered to help him, to take him with me to Warsaw, but it was useless. All I could do was to wish him luck with his new career.

The performance of *Tristan and Isolde* was the last of the festival, and my last day in Munich. The orchestra and Mottl were superb, so much so that it put the singers into a shadow. I even forgot their names, and it was not until many years later when I saw the Danish tenor Melchior and the Norwegian soprano Flagstad that I heard the best Tristan and Isolde of my life.

I left the next day for Warsaw. My "Wagneritis" had reached its limit.

The old, smelly, shabby, but homelike Victoria hotel became a refuge for musicians. Gregor Fitelberg, Karol Szymanowski, and Paul

Kochanski were still living there, and the latest addition was Paul's younger brother, Eli, a brilliant cellist. My return was greeted with hurrahs. Without delay, I was informed about the revolutionary changes which had taken place in the structure of the Filharmonja Orchestra. In the last year or two, since Emil Mlynarski had given up his post as its director and conductor, there had been a great decline in public attendance. The quality of the orchestra had deteriorated under second-rate guest conductors and carelessly chosen programs. The whole institution was on the brink of bankruptcy.

The generosity of a great Maecenas, in the person of Prince Ladislas Lubomirski, saved the situation. He pledged to finance the orchestra through the eight months of the concert season and to underwrite a probable deficit. However, he made two stipulations: that his protégé, Gregor Fitelberg, be appointed as the general director and conductor of the Orchestra and that it be called, instead of Filharmonja Orchestra, the "Orchestra of Prince Ladislas Lubomirski." The Committee accepted both the offer and the conditions. Such was the state of things when I arrived.

Fitelberg was, without doubt, a good musician and a talented conductor, but a ruthless character. Nothing was sacred to him; he would walk over dead bodies to reach his goal. Professionally, he was a fine exponent of Richard Strauss, Gustav Mahler, and Max Reger. His close friendship with Szymanowski, on whom he exercised a great influence, both musically and personally, was based on his genuine faith in Karol's genius, as well as on full awareness of the advantage of being accepted as the only authorized interpreter of the Polish composer. Szymanowski's delicate, sensitive nature, full of complexes, was an easy mark for this man's forceful personality.

Before I had finished washing and unpacking, Fitelberg knocked on my door.

"Arthur," he started with a beguiling smile, "I have good news for you. I have chosen you and Paul for my opening concert as my soloists. You can play your Saint-Saëns, and Paul his Tchaikovski."

"Thank you, Ficio," I said, "this will indeed be a wonderful beginning of the season. I am glad to play the Saint-Saëns Concerto, too—it is my old war horse."

He laughed and was ready to leave.

"Wait a minute," I said. "You did not mention my fee."

He looked at me disapprovingly.

"I did not expect such a question from you, Arthur," he said. "To take money for playing with our orchestra would be a gross ingratitude toward Prince Ladislas. Paul accepted without even mentioning such a thing."

I had no choice but to agree, although it disturbed me very much. I have always had a strong conviction that all professional work should be remunerated, unless it is offered to a charity. Paul had the same opinion. I was somewhat pacified by an engagement for three concerts in the provinces. The fees were small, but at least I was to be paid.

Frederic telephoned that his mother had invited me for dinner. I accepted with my heart beating with excitement. I was still under their spell. I would never be free of it, I thought.

To my astonishment and my delight, Pola was there. As soon as I saw her, I could barely conceal my emotion. My love had never died. I had known it all along—through all the events of the last months, it was always there simmering in me—but now, in an instant, it was aflame.

The dinner was, as usual, animated. There were two amusing guests at the table, and the story of my Bayreuth adventure was quite a success. After dinner, as we moved to the salon, Pola held me back at the door for a split second and whispered nervously, "Tomorrow at eleven at the central post office."

I was there a quarter of an hour ahead of time. The post office was always crowded with people going in and out, and I was afraid I would miss her. Suddenly I felt a hand touching mine. It was Pola—she had arrived before me! We went to a corner and sat across from each other at a desk where one writes telegrams.

"I love you," I said.

"I love you," she said. We could not speak for a while. She had tears in her eyes. "Arthur," she murmured, "I can't live like this any more. I want to be with you. Can you arrange for me to come to your room without being seen?"

I swore I would make it possible. She smiled through her tears. "Tomorrow, same place, same hour. You will tell me how it can be done," she said, squeezed my hand, and rushed away.

Back at the hotel I tried to solve this difficult problem. She couldn't possibly use the front entrance. We had no elevator. The staircase was the greatest risk of all. Only one solution was left, a rather difficult one. The hotel had a large side door used by horse-drawn vehicles to enter the courtyard and discharge their merchandise. It might have been used also as a service entrance. However, there was a serious inconvenience. The door was always locked, and one had to ring for the watchman to open it. I had to get in touch with this watchman: in other words, I had to bribe him. And that is exactly what I did.

We were both on time at the post office that morning. I gave her my instructions in a whisper: "All you have to do, my love, is to push gently the large door and slip in; it will be open from four to five—you don't need to ring. Inside, there is a staircase which is used for service but only in the morning and at night. On the first floor, you will find my room across the corridor."

She blushed and said softly, "I shall be there at four. I can hardly wait."

That day is engraved on my memory. It was the beginning of our beautiful love story. Twice, three times a week I would wait in my room, my ears trained to the soft squeak of the side door. An instant later my Pola was in my arms. We made love and we talked and talked and we made love again. It was heaven.

The opening concert of the "Orchestra of Prince Ladislas Lubomirski" under Fitelberg was a triumph for everybody concerned; it might have been called a gala. To begin with, the house was packed. The Polish aristocracy, rarely seen at concerts, came en masse. The new title of the orchestra was an attraction for them. The rest of the audience, the real music lovers, were delighted to hear two soloists instead of one, not to mention their natural curiosity about the new conductor. Praise was unanimous, both from the public and from the press. The season had started most auspiciously. Prince Lubomirski seemed to be particularly pleased with my playing. He had a long talk with me, mainly about Wagner. He, too, suffered from an attack of "Wagneritis." Emulating the poor King Ludwig II of Bavaria, he obliged Fitelberg to conduct some parts of *Parsifal* in the morning when he sat alone in the empty hall.

Spurred by my love, I began an intense musical life. Paul and his brother Eli and I developed into a fine trio. We played all the available scores of Beethoven, Schubert, Schumann, Brahms, and were soon ready to appear in concerts. Zosia Kohn's room was our favorite place for rehearsals, which would last sometimes until well past midnight and were followed by Zuzia's suppers. The smaller towns offered me the opportunity to develop my repertoire, which I needed for my frequent appearances in Warsaw. During that season I gave twenty-one or twenty-three concerts in Warsaw alone, and I still hold the all-time record for the greatest number of concerts given in the same town in one single year.

One morning my brother-in-law Maurycy Landau burst into my room with an angry expression on his face. Without even taking his hat off, he shouted at me from the doorway: "My wife should be proud of her young brother, eh? What a scandalous thing to make her pawn her jewels for you! And for what? For spending money in nightclubs and loafing for months in Berlin! Your sister was nice enough to try to keep it from me, but I found out anyhow. You better give me now those pawn tickets. I only hope you did not lose them, or throw them away."

I was hurt and furious. This man had a good heart, and he could be very generous, but all that was ruined by his innate coarseness. Without answering, I opened my traveling bag, took out the precious jewels, and handed them to him.

"I wanted to give them back to Jadzia personally," I said, "but you deprived me of this little satisfaction. Now I want you to leave. I have work to do." Finding nothing to say, he put the jewels into his pocket and left.

There is a beautiful sequel to this story. After his charming visit, my brother-in-law went to a bar for a snack and wodka, and when he returned to his hotel, he found his pocket was empty—the jewels were gone. I must confess with shame that I thought it served him right.

Fitelberg invited me to play three more times at his subscription concerts, using the same sly approach as for the first one. He simply never paid his soloists. I profited, however, by gaining more experience in playing with orchestra and by trying out new, unfamiliar concertos.

Paul and I had to begin to think seriously about the military service which would be threatening us any day. Colonel Stremoukhov promised to help us, but we had to pay him in advance with endless performances of sonatas. A Jewish doctor who was a member of the medical commission of the army obtained a year's deferment for us, and thanks to our boring colonel we did not have to appear before the recruiting board. However, we were not allowed to leave the country; our passports were invalidated. The doctor received, of course, a rather large sum of money for his services.

Just about that time, I was offered a concert in Kraków and another in Lwów, the two most important Polish cities after Warsaw and Lodz. I was anxious to accept, but, paradoxically, both cities were Austrian, which meant that I couldn't get there without a passport. My dilemma was solved, however, by the above-mentioned doctor.

"Go at noon to the Café Bristol. There you will see near the first window a little man who is completely bald and who wears a red tie. He will help you."

I did what he told me to and recognized the man from his description.

"Sit down and have a cup of coffee," the man said, "and listen carefully. You can't take the regular night train to Kraków—I have no connections there. Take, instead, the day train to Częstochowa. When you arrive in the evening, a police inspector will be at the station and will drive you to a hotel. Invite him to have supper with you in your room and give him plenty of wodka. Early in the morning he will take you personally across the frontier into Germany, where you will find an express train for Kraków. All told, you will arrive only three hours later than the regular train from Warsaw."

It sounded strange, but I had no choice. The man charged me twenty-five rubles; he had to share the fee, probably, with the doctor.

The plan worked out as scheduled. A high police officer in uniform was expecting me at the station and escorted me across the street to a hotel. He accepted my invitation quite naturally, entered my room, and called a waiter. We ordered smoked herring, onion, and a bottle of wodka, and an unbelievable drinking orgy ensued. My policeman swallowed a quart and a half of wodka; I nursed three cups for hours. For food, he ate nothing but the herring and a lot of onion. I had an omelet and coffee, to keep awake. The orgy lasted until six a.m. He sang gypsy romances and called me Artoor, and I had to call him by his pet name, Vassia. An amazing detail—he was not drunk. Finally he looked at his watch and said, "Artoor, it is time to go."

We went down. I paid the bill, and we left for the German frontier. We passed the passport control without being stopped, and I was in Germany. By then I was dead tired. It was difficult to sleep in the train during the daytime with passengers getting on and off at every station. After five hours I arrived finally in Kraków. I decided to go to bed right away and rest until it was time to dress for the concert.

In the cab, on the way to the Grand Hotel, I noticed that posters announcing my concerts had strange red stripes pasted across them, which intrigued me. I stopped the cab to see what was written on them. To my horror, I read "Rubinstein's concert postponed because of difficulties at the Russian frontier." I drove straight to my manager's office to find out what had happened. He could not believe his eyes when he saw me.

"How the devil did you get here? I was told you were arrested at the frontier!"

"Who invented such a story?" I asked indignantly.

"Your friend Szymanowski," he said.

"What? What? Karol Szymanowski? He wouldn't do such a silly thing!"

When we calmed down, the story was explained. It was another Szymanowski, Alexander by name, and no relation of the composer. He was a fanatic admirer of mine, who followed me around all the time and had become quite a nuisance. It was he who had taken the regular night train from Warsaw to be present at my first concert in Kraków. Knowing about my problems with passports, naturally he became panic-stricken when he realized that I had not arrived. His next move was to inform the manager about my arrest. In his opinion, there couldn't be any other reason for my absence at the station.

The concert, that night, was definitely canceled, but fortunately the hall was free for the next night. However, my appearance in Lwów had to be postponed until spring. The one advantage in the delay was that I could have a good night's rest. Nevertheless, my nerves were on edge before the concert. The Kraków public was known for being difficult to please. Besides, another detail worried me: it was to be my first performance of Karol Szymanowski's *Variations on a Polish Theme*, for which I felt a great responsibility. I was determined to do my best for his work.

The concert began with a Beethoven sonata which I played stiffly and tensely, owing to my nerves. The response of the audience was cold; there was very little applause. When it came to the *Variations*, something happened to me. Call it inspiration or the will to conquer—whatever the reason, I had never played this work with more élan and passion than I did that night. The success was instantaneous. The public shouted "Bravo" and made me bow half a dozen times. When I retired to the artists' room, the door opened and in came Alexander Szymanowski. Haggard and shaking, he threw himself on a sofa and had a fit, crying spasmodically as though he couldn't stop. The poor fellow had gone through agonies for having caused the whole trouble. My great success had provoked his hysterical feeling of guilt mixed with joy. We had to call a doctor to calm him.

This memorable concert was the start of my popularity in this "foreign" part of Poland, and it never let up. I returned to Warsaw armed with a pass signed by the mayor of Kraków, bearing another man's name. I discovered at that time the existence of a vast organization in the three divided parts of Poland which provided false documents for those who needed them to pass the Russian frontier.

In Warsaw, life ran smoothly all through the season. Our concerts remained attractive, because of their diversity. We appeared with orchestra, in trios, in duos, and gave, of course, some solo recitals, too. Besides, I was much in demand in Lodz and in many smaller cities. They paid little, but it would have been enough for my needs if I had ever learned to economize.

Our hotel was bursting with activity, what with the five of us musicians all living there. Day and night, the telephone would ring for one of us, and there was only one receiver for the whole place, in a small booth, near the reception desk. On our free evenings, we would go out together, or separately, to concerts, theaters, dinner parties, cabarets. I never went to bed before two or three o'clock.

One evening, at about ten o'clock, utterly exhausted, I decided to go to bed early and get at last a decent night's rest. Entering the hotel, whom did I see but my friend Paul, who stopped me at the door and addressed me sternly in the following way: "Arthur, if we don't give up this kind of life we may land in a hospital with nervous breakdowns. We must stop it from now on. I am set on that, and I urge you to do the same. Now, since it isn't late, we can play a little game of piquet until eleven o'clock."

I followed him to his room, pleased to have found Paul's mood not unlike my own, and we began to play piquet with relish and for small stakes. But our will to win was insatiable; we both pretended to be past masters at this intricate old game. Paul won the first round.

"Let's double the stakes," I said tersely. He agreed, and again he won. I couldn't bear that: we played for double or nothing. This time I beat him. Now it was Paul's turn to exact a *revanche*. By then it was midnight, but I couldn't refuse—it wouldn't be fair. We went on playing. Paul was totting up on a sheet of paper what we were winning or losing; neither of us would put a stop to the game, and so we played on and on and on, ignoring the time until, at seven in the morning, the sun burst into the room and a ravenous hunger for breakfast brought us back to our senses.

Paul had lost the staggering sum of one thousand, three hundred rubles ($650), on credit, of course, and on a paper which we tore up into little bits. Neither of us would have ever considered paying our debt—we barely had the money for breakfast. But we wouldn't have dared mention our famous determination to change our ways.

50

An urgent telephone call woke me up one morning. It was Pola's maid.

"Madame is in great danger! The Master and Madame's mother are threatening to kill her, they are beating her, she is screaming for help. . . ."

I dropped the phone, ran up to my room, dressed in a hurry, and dashed out for a cab. When I reached Pola's apartment, the maid opened the door.

"They are gone," she said. "They have taken the children away. Madame is in her bedroom."

I found my sweet, lovely Pola moaning on her bed. She showed me the bruises all over her body. Her head was swollen. "They have stolen my babies," she cried desperately. "They want to shut me up in a madhouse! You must save me, Arthur, you must!"

I had to act without delay. "You have to get out of the country by the next train," I said. "My sisters Jadzia and Hela are in Bad Reinerz—it is a resort in German Poland, right across the frontier. I shall wire and ask them to take care of you for a while. Get dressed, have the maid pack your things, and I shall fetch you in an hour."

I kissed her tenderly and rushed to send an urgent telegram to Jadzia and to tell the whole story to Zosia and beg her to help me with Pola's departure.

After thinking it over, she herself offered to take Pola to the station. My ever-ready-to-help Alexander Szymanowski would follow them in another cab with the luggage so as to make the whole operation look inconspicuous. I myself was to wait for Pola in the train. Our plan was carried out up to the last detail. Pola had her passport, her ticket, and some money; everything was in order. The train started moving. We sat silently, looking at each other disconsolately until we had to part at the last station before the frontier.

After a sad, long kiss, I had to leave the train. Standing there alone on the platform, I was heartbroken. True, my sisters had phoned and asked me not to worry; they were going to take good care of her, and I was sure of it—they were both such kind-hearted women. But I felt an acute moral responsibility because I had induced Pola to take such a fateful and dangerous step without any hopeful plans for the near future. On my journey back to the capital my nerves cracked. I had to run to the washroom, where I vomited and cried for a good half-hour.

After my return to Warsaw I made a great effort to regain my composure, and decided to go to the concert to hear *Also Sprach Zarathustra* by Richard Strauss, conducted by Fitelberg. But I did not expect to derive any emotion or consolation from this music; I simply knew that it was important to be seen in public that evening. Karol and Paul had seats in a box, so I joined them, and everything seemed normal, nobody showing any signs of being aware of what had happened. After the concert, at the cloakroom, I noticed Mr. and Mrs. Harman standing near the exit door. When he saw me, he raised his cane and shouted coarse insults at me. Infuriated by his gesture, I walked up to him, tore the cane out of his hand, broke it into two pieces, threw them at his feet without saying a word, and left the hall, while Karol and Paul watched in utter amazement. When I gave them the full account of the events of the day, they became seriously concerned.

"This is a fearful mess," Paul said. "It will be hard for you to get out of it. Have you any intention of making her get a divorce and marrying her?"

"Certainly not," I answered. "It goes without saying. First of all, she is a Catholic, so she cannot get a divorce, and, second, I could not support a wife at this stage of my career, and, I must frankly admit, it is not in my nature to marry a woman who is older than I and who has children by somebody else."

"Then you don't really love her?" said Karol, slightly shocked.

"How can you say such a thing?" I cried indignantly. "I love her more than ever, I adore her! She has a noble heart, she is lovely, intelligent, and musical. Her love saved me from that diabolical charm which her family exercised on me—their irresistible attraction which brought me to the verge of moral turpitude. All I care for, at the moment, is Pola's safety; as for the rest, we will see!"

Paul was not wrong about the "fearful mess." It started the next day. Suddenly everybody in Warsaw seemed to know everything about me, and my adventures with the family. Sarcastic rhymes about mother, daughter, brother, sister appeared in the gossip columns. In some papers I was treated as a gigolo who was after the rich girl's money, and the father was a frequent target for ridicule.

Public opinion was divided. My friends, my concert followers, stood up for me, sometimes too aggressively for my taste, but I noticed, also, signs of disapproval, of harsh criticism among the so-called respectable set.

Of course, Pola's disappearance was the main topic of speculation, with many people pretending to know where she was, but the secret was well kept, and my presence in Warsaw remained a puzzle.

What hurt me most in those difficult days was Frederic's reaction. I didn't pay much attention to what the other members of the family had to say. The father, in his blind rage, pretended that I was trying to extort money from him; the mother called me a human demon. Basia was in Berlin, preparing her opera debut, but Frederic? I had confided in him about Pola and me, and he had given us his brotherly blessing. Now, of course, his father threatened to withdraw his allowance if he were ever to speak to me again, and I was well aware that he lacked the courage to disobey, but he could have sent me a message or tried to meet me in secret, if only out of concern about his sister. I saw him only once again, years later, after the First World War. It was after one of my concerts in Warsaw. He burst into the artists' room with the enthusiasm I knew so well, and, without warning, he asked me to leave with him for a talk.

I would have gladly complied, but I was unavoidably committed to attend a supper in my honor. Three years later, sitting on the terrace of a café in Pernambuco, Brazil, I read in a local newspaper that Frederic had died of a heart attack while conducting the *Meistersinger* overture at the Philharmonic Hall in Warsaw.

It gave me a great shock; I couldn't think of anything else for days. Poor Frederic had a glorious death—in a moment of musical ecstasy. I learned later that it was when he reached the climax of the overture, which he always loved, that his heart collapsed. His mother heard the concert with its tragic end over the radio.

51

A letter from Pola, full of praise for my sisters, who had found a nice room for her and were kind and not inquisitive. The rest of the letter was pathetic—all about the children, our love, the terrible morning in Warsaw, the whole situation. She had communicated with Basia, and her sister had advised her strongly to come to Berlin; she would try to arrange a meeting for Pola with her father. What was my opinion: should she see him? My answer was: "Yes, by all means." I hoped, against odds, that he might help her to get her children back and see our love in a better light. After all, the blind, vindictive rage of her mother was nothing but a wild outburst of jealousy, a feeling her husband couldn't possibly share.

Pola left for Berlin. I was waiting in suspense for the outcome of this all-important meeting. A few days later, she sent me a full report: he spoke to her quietly, almost kindly, promising to help her recover her children and to provide her with a monthly allowance. But there was a condition: she had to enter a sanatorium for a much-needed rest which would calm her nerves and give her a clearer point of view of the whole situation. The sanatorium was on the outskirts of Berlin, where she was to stay for a whole month, and she had to promise not to communicate with anybody, especially with me. "This way, my child, you may come back to your senses," he had said to her, as a final touch.

This letter upset me instead of giving me hope. I am of a suspicious nature, I admit. The fatherly approach he had adopted did not fit his personality, and I was afraid that he was trying to trick her. But it was too late to warn her—she had accepted his conditions and was on her way to the sanatorium.

My instinct proved to be right. That same week I received an envelope from Germany with my name and address in a strange handwriting. Inside, I found a short note from Pola saying in substance: Wait for me in a cab next Friday at eleven p.m. near the gate of the sanatorium (and the address).

There was no time to lose. Paul lent me three hundred rubles for any emergency. I got a valid passport from my man at the Café Bristol, and took the train to Berlin the same night, where I found an unobtrusive hotel in a quiet street and registered as husband and wife. "My wife arrives this evening," I told the room clerk. At ten p.m. I picked a cab with a good horse and we drove to the sanatorium; it was a twenty-minute drive. The street was pitch dark. We stopped a short distance from the place and waited. At about eleven fifteen I heard a short squeak of the gate, and saw Pola with one bag in each hand rush toward the cab. She jumped in and fell into my arms. On the way back to the hotel she could hardly speak; she clung to me, crying and laughing. I held her tight and kissed her eyes and mouth and hands; it was heaven to be together again. And then she told me what had happened.

"Darling, this sanatorium is nothing but a clinic for mental cases, a real madhouse. Father took me there and talked to a nice, smiling doctor who assured me that I would be very happy there and get a good rest. When my father left and I was shown to my room, I noticed iron bars on my window. Later on, in the corridor, I saw the ominous, pale faces of some inmates, and I suddenly knew what kind of place it was. Fortunately, as my case was considered a very mild one, they allowed me to walk unaccompanied in the garden. The man who guards the gate had a kind expression on his face. I felt by instinct that he wanted to help me. It was he who sent you my note and prepared my flight with much danger for both of us. He even refused to take my money!"

We entered the Schmidt hotel as man and wife, and it was our first night spent together. Our love made us forget all our worries.

Back in Warsaw, Pola drove straight to a modest but comfortable *pension de famille*, where she found a nice room, and I returned to the good old Victoria.

The news of Pola's escape from the "sanatorium" gave Mr. Harman quite a shock. He had been very pleased with himself for having so neatly disposed of her for the time being.

So this was the definite break. From then on she had no access to her home or to her children, but at least she did have a small monthly

allowance because her grandfather had left in his will a sum of money
for his grandchildren.

The conditions of my life in Warsaw had considerably changed.
Gone were the carefree days, the late nights in restaurants and cabarets,
the telephone calls at the Victoria. Gossip and slander had their field day.
The scandal, far from being subdued, became "the *affaire*." Echoes
reached me about Mr. Harman's insinuations that my elopement with his
daughter was a simple case of blackmail. This was too much for me. I
composed a document in which I swore on my honor that I would *never*
touch one cent of Pola's or her family's money. A Catholic canon whom
I had met at the Harmans' and who liked me countersigned my declaration and promised to deliver it personally to Mr. Harman. From then on,
the ugly insinuations stopped.

Fortunately, I still had some concerts on hand, but the season was
nearly over and I began to feel with a shudder the black clouds of a
long summer hanging over me again. But what made me unhappy was
the fact that our love had been degraded and besmirched by this horrible
scandal.

The sweet privacy, the intimacy, the secrecy of our meetings was
no more. It became impossible for me to visit Pola in her room for more
than a few minutes; she, on the other hand, hated to come to my hotel
again, and so we could be together only at Zosia's, or meet furtively in
some out-of-the-way café, bar, or tearoom.

For a necessary contrast, there must be always a "comic relief," so
dear to the makers of movies, and I might just as well tell my little story
about a fellow called Kapnik.

At the beginning of the concert season, at the Philharmonic Hall, a
meek young man stopped me in the lobby during the intermission. He
was short, had colorless, blondish hair, washed-out features, and a pair of
big, sad eyes.

"Colonel Stremoukhov sent me to you for advice," he addressed me,
almost in a whisper.

"You are a pianist?" I asked.

"No, I am a singer," he replied.

"Ha, ha," I laughed, "you speak to the wrong man. I don't know
anything about singing."

"But the Colonel assured me that you are the only one who can advise me," he insisted.

I knew that I could not afford not to comply with the Colonel's
wishes. "All right," I said, "come tomorrow morning at ten to my hotel
and bring some music."

Next day, I had forgotten about him and was still asleep when he knocked on the door. I jumped out of bed, put on a dressing gown, and let him in.

Without saying a word, I grabbed the sheet of music he held in his hand, went to my piano, put the song on the desk, and waited for him to begin to sing. He remained silent.

"What are you waiting for?" I said. "I will accompany you. Come on, sing!"

"I don't sing yet, I don't know any songs, but I have a fine voice," he said.

"Then why the devil did you bring this music?"

"You told me to do so."

"This is crazy." I became angry. "I am not an expert in voices, but, well, give me a sample."

He let out a long, loud note, without vibration; it sounded like a trombone. That did it. I went to my desk and wrote a short note. "Here is a letter of introduction to the great basso Edouard de Reszke, who lives in Warsaw. He can tell you if you have a voice or not." And without taking any further notice of him, I took off my dressing gown and went back to bed. He opened the door and stopped.

"I suffer terribly from my stomach," he said, looking at me with his teary, light-gray eyes. "There is only one medicine which can cure it, but it costs five rubles and I am very poor. Can you help me?"

I had, all in all, thirty rubles, but I gave him the five he asked for, not out of pity for his ailment, not at all. I simply wanted to get rid of him and, at the same time, please the Colonel. I didn't know then what a fateful gesture it was. I fell into a deadly trap. This man was a leech, a vampire, a demon incarnate—he never left off. He always knew when I had some money coming, and he was right there beside me with his damned teary eyes. When I tried to hide from him, he would sit on a bench in the square for four, six, eight hours, watching the hotel entrance and catching me every time. This went on for two or three years. I became the laughingstock of my friends. Paul would jeer at me: "Why don't you marry him?" or, "Why don't you call the police?" It was of no avail. I had no power to resist him, and I continued to dish my money out to him. He never became a singer, de Reszke didn't even take the trouble to answer my note, and as to the Colonel, I found out that he had never sent him to me.

There is a funny epilogue to this story: years later, in St. Petersburg (now Leningrad), I was giving a concert in the great Hall of the Nobility which was right across the street from my hotel. When I reached the artists' entrance (it was ten degrees below zero) I was stopped by a young man who asked me for a ticket.

"I have no tickets, and it's cold—let me pass," I said angrily. "But you are a great friend of my brother," he said. "Who is your brother?" "Kapnik," he answered.

I gave a shriek of horror, ran inside, and slammed the door behind me. My heart was beating as if I had been attacked by a serpent.

I tell this lengthy episode as a warning to my readers. There are quite a few men of Kapnik's type running around freely. The Jews have a name for them: they call them schnorrers. Well, I must concede to my Kapnik the title King of Schnorrers.

52

Pauline Narbut was the widow of a retired Russian general, by thirty years her senior, who left her his fortune and a big farm with a spacious house. A tall blonde of about forty, with an attractive figure, high cheekbones, and light blue eyes, she was endowed with an unusual vitality and intelligence. This Polish Jewess of mysterious origin (she never revealed her maiden name or the place where she came from) became the life of the intellectual and artistic set in Warsaw. My feeble attempt at describing her personality is the expression of a deep gratitude toward this fine woman. I owe her one of the happiest periods of my youth. A passionate supporter of my case against the Harmans, she invited Pola and me to spend a few weeks with her in the country. A gift from heaven! It meant not only a substantial relief from financial worries, but the promise of a blissful lovers' honeymoon.

Pani Paulina was the ideal hostess; one never felt the weight of her presence. We could be late for lunch or dinner, be gone for a whole day without explanation, I could play the piano the whole night—she didn't mind, didn't interfere.

Our room was large and sunny, with windows overlooking the garden. The rustic, comfortable furniture, the whitewashed walls, the shelves with books of quality, the daily fresh flowers, made us want to stay inside all the time.

Our hostess had two other guests besides us, the poet and playwright Tadeusz Miciński and the fabulous, legendary Franc Fiszer. Miciński, a mystic, wrote dramas and poetry of the highest intellectual level. The Polish literary circles held him in high esteem, but his difficult style made him not quite accessible to the masses. Looking back on his work, I find in him a certain affinity with the French poet Paul Claudel.

The other one, Fiszer, was one of the most colorful personalities I have ever known. Tall, very fat, grayish blond, with a noble beard and mustache like a hidalgo painted by Velázquez, he had small, sparkling, mischievous eyes, a strong, straight nose, and long ears. He was over fifty when we met, but he struck me as being ageless. A Falstaff in appearance, with the wit and intelligence of a Voltaire. Judging him by the way he lived, one might describe him as a pre-Sartre existentialist.

Pola and I loved the company of these men. Our discussions and quarrels, our shouting and laughing, would keep us at the table for hours. Fiszer's stentorian, declamatory voice invariably predominated: nobody could outtalk him.

It takes a great writer to draw a true portrait of as picturesque a personality as his. All I can do is to give a few sketchy snapshots of his character.

Franc was the descendant of a hero of the Polish revolution; he owned a piece of land near Warsaw, but the country bored him. His vast knowledge and love of literature and the arts drove him irresistibly to Warsaw, where he joined a group of young, brilliant writers and poets. Every night, a large corner table was reserved for them in a popular café.

Fiszer was an inveterate spendthrift—he treated his young friends to caviar and champagne, took them to expensive places for dinner, and dished out his money freely to anybody for the asking. The group had admitted a single outsider, a shy, middle-aged bachelor bank clerk with a passionate love for poetry. Late one night Fiszer asked this man: "Have you by any chance a sofa in your apartment on which I could sleep? It is too late to drive to the country, and I have not a cent left."

"Yes, of course, you are welcome," said the man. From that night on, Fiszer stayed with him. He had had to sell his estate to pay off his debts and was now happy to be free of the "dirty mammon." His host was just too proud to have him, and Franc was supported, provided with ready pocket money, wined, dined by everybody who came into contact with him. This modern Diogenes was a philosopher after my own heart. He never put on paper or published his brilliant thoughts because, as he explained, every day brought new ideas, and changed his outlook on life.

One morning at breakfast, Franc asked: "Arthur, have you read Spengler?"

"No," I said indifferently.

"Oh, but you must, you must read him right away, I shall give you his latest articles—he is a great genius, the best brain of our epoch," he exclaimed enthusiastically.

Pola and I read and studied this Spengler with great concentration and discussed him. I found in his work some very original ideas, some striking points, but his theories didn't convince me, or Pola.

When I returned the pieces to Fiszer and commented rather shyly: "It is very absorbing work, Franc, with lots of new ideas," he threw the articles on the table with a disdainful gesture.

"Spengler is a raving idiot—one should burn this nonsense! Go back to Nietzsche, Arthur, he was also mad, but he, at least, was a poet!"

I must confess that ever since my old Altmann days I have read every philosopher within reach. I admired Kant's logic. I enjoyed Nietzsche's lofty, exalted mind, and Bergson's serenity and clear-cut sentences; Schopenhauer's pessimistic utterances about women disquieted me; but none of them ever seriously influenced me in any way. I was determined to look at life with my own eyes and to have the courage to face it.

The summer of 1909 at Pauline's was an unforgettable idyll. My heart swelled at the sight of the soft rhythm of the wheat in the wind, of the weeping willows overhanging the pond. Our love bloomed in this pure, Polish atmosphere.

In September, however, I became restless about plans for my concerts. I had had no time to prepare anything. It was imperative for me to return to Warsaw. Pola decided to remain in the country for the time being.

The city was still slumbering in the *dolce far niente* of the summer. Most of my friends were abroad. Paul was staying with the Mlynarskis in Slgovo, their estate in Lithuania; Karol had returned to his family in the Ukraine. Only Fitelberg remained in town—but no—I forget, Kapnik was there, too.

Mr. Dropiowski, a resourceful impresario, engaged me for a concert in Kraków and found a good date and a special occasion for my belated debut in Lwów. Other dates, including Warsaw, were confirmed, but the season was still far off, and I had not enough money to hold out so long. The problem of food became alarming. The young director and owner of the Victoria, a great music lover, was very considerate about my growing hotel bill. Whenever I received my fees, I paid off some of my debt, but I couldn't afford to give up my room for the summer out of fear of being stranded in the street. His kindness, however, made me feel uncomfortable about taking my meals on credit.

And so my pearl tie pin and my gold watch found their way to the pawnshop. On one occasion, Kapnik, trying to extract another contribution, induced me to go with him to the Jewish ghetto and sell one of my best suits.

But, glory be to God, as the Irish say, a new *deus ex machina* in the person of the Prince Ladislas Lubomirski appeared out of nowhere at just the right moment. I noticed in the newspaper that he was about to arrive in Warsaw for a conference with his brother Stanislav, the banker, and my unfailing instinct told me that it was of utmost importance for me to see him. I entered the restaurant of the Hotel d'Europe at lunch time with the air of one who is expected by friends, when a loud voice called: "Panie Arturze, what are you doing in Warsaw?"

It was the Prince sitting at a table with his brother and another man. I greeted him, pretending great surprise.

"I am waiting for the opening of the Philharmonic concerts," I said.

"But you should be heard in the great cities, in Berlin, Vienna, Rome, Paris. To stay in Warsaw is not good enough for your great talent."

"I would love to be able to follow your advice, Prince, but it is impossible for me," I said, and gave him an idea of what it would cost to give concerts in these cities when one is not well known.

"Unless you want to become my manager, Prince?" I added, playfully.

"And why not?" he answered quite seriously. "I shall deposit ten thousand rubles [$5,000] in my brother's bank. You can draw on this sum to cover the expenses of these concerts," and without losing time, he put this agreement on paper, signed it, and handed it to the third man at the table, a Mr. Gintovt, the director of the Lubomirski bank.

"Here is to your success," they toasted me with the last sip of wine, and without listening to my thanks, they got up and left.

I was in heaven. This was the great moment of my life! Nothing more to worry about! How overjoyed Pola will be! Yet, as strange as it seems, in some corner of my subconscious I had known this would happen. Ever since the first time the Prince heard me play I felt a secret "antenna" between us.

When I told Fitelberg what the Prince had done for me, he looked green with envy. "Why would he do such a thing? Why waste money on such a useless project?" he muttered.

When Karol heard the good news, he wired: "Congratulations. Come to stay with us for a week or two if you can."

I accepted his invitation with pleasure. Mr. Gintovt gave me two hundred rubles toward initial expenses, and I left the same day for Tymoszovka, where I arrived the next morning. Karol's elder brother Felix and his youngest sister Sophie waited for me with a *britchka* at

Kamenka, a station miles away from their place. We drove through end-less, fertile steppes—Russia's larder—to the Szymanowski place, a vast but unpretentious house, where Karol's family received me very warmly. His mother was a tall, distinguished lady with light-blue eyes, a noble, arched nose, and beautiful hands. Nula, her oldest daughter, was a nervous, un-happy person, and Felix, the oldest son, was the head of the family, in charge of the estate. The Szymanowskis were typical examples of the old Polish landed nobility; highly cultured, they represented the finest heritage of the country, in contrast to the aristocracy who preferred to live abroad and impress Paris, Vienna, and Rome with their importance and wealth.

Karol and I shared a small guest house. After breakfast we liked to play four hands on his upright piano, mainly Beethoven quartets, and he also showed me parts of his new sonata, which enchanted me. Often the youngest sister, Zioka, a tomboy but also a gifted poet, would saddle two fine horses and ride with me over the fields. Luncheons and dinners were amusing what with the large family, which included an aunt and cousin, making ten or more at the table.

I spent a delightful ten days in Tymoszovka and was deeply moved by Karol's devotion to his family, the love and care which he maintained toward them until his death.

I returned to Warsaw enriched by a lovely experience.

A day after my return I had a nasty surprise. Mr. Gintovt informed me in a polite letter that for the time being he was not entitled to let me take any money out of the fund. Soon enough I found out who was be-hind it. Fitelberg, during my absence, had started a series of intrigues against me. Iago couldn't have invented anything more fiendish.

He had told the Prince that he felt it his duty to warn him that I was too young and too inexperienced to be entrusted with the money he put up for me; that he, Fitelberg, would be willing to help me with the arrangement of a concert in Berlin and might even agree to conduct the orchestra for me. What a horrible hypocrite! His offer to conduct was nothing more than an attempt on his part to use my concert to promote his own career.

And the Prince believed him, seeing it simply as a friend's concern about me (he told me so later in Kraków). So there was nothing else for me to do but "faire bonne mine à mauvais jeu."

The concert season was ready to start, but the orchestra had under-gone some great changes. Prince Lubomirski had relinquished his role as the sole responsible patron because the experiment proved too expensive even for him. The members of the orchestra, after many meetings, de-cided to continue as an autonomous body. They created their own

administration and hired a manager who had the power to engage conductors and soloists, and who had to build up the programs for the season.
I was happy about this change, because now they began to pay us real
fees; Fitelberg's exploitations became a thing of the past.

My concerts started auspiciously. I gave quite a few in Warsaw, one
with orchestra, one solo, a sonata evening with Paul, and two big charity
concerts, which helped to create a better image of me since "the *affaire*."

When I played in other towns, Pola came with me; it was our only
chance to be together. I took her even to Lodz, where she met my
parents, who treated her after my concert to one of the famous Rubinstein suppers, with pike, noodles, and all. I was happy to notice that Pola
enjoyed the warm atmosphere of my large family, so different from her
own.

With my credit blocked at the bank, the money situation became
alarming again, largely through my own fault, of course. The minute I
received my fee, I had to pay some old debts and some advance payment
on my hotel bill; and I would buy some clothes or a new tie, or a present
and flowers for Pola. In my great moments of extravagance I liked to
treat her to a grand dinner de luxe served in a private room of a fine
restaurant: caviar, wodka, crayfish on rice, good wine—nothing was too
expensive! Not to mention Kapnik.

After our sonata concert, Paul and I were invited to a supper by a
Jewish banker and his wife. We went without changing our clothes, each
with his fee (three hundred rubles) in his pocket. The fine food, a few
wodkas, and a third guest who told amusing stories put us into a happy
mood. After supper, at the host's suggestion, we settled down to play
poker for high stakes, an ill-fated, disastrous idea. Both the banker and
our amusing table companion turned out to be champion poker players.
At four in the morning Paul and I were left without a cent; they had
ruined us. Out in the cold night, we discovered that we had not enough
change for a cab.

So, still in our concert clothes and in our low patent leather shoes,
we—poor fellows that we were—had to wade through the high snow all
the long distance to our hotel. Not a proud memory, this!

53

The concert in Berlin took place at the end of the year. My forebodings were entirely confirmed; in fact I had been too optimistic. Fitelberg had rented the Philharmonie, the largest hall in town, and engaged the great Berlin Philharmonic orchestra at a high price.

He insisted on my playing the G major Beethoven and the B flat Brahms concertos, dismissing my preference for the Chopin or Saint-Saëns. He refused to conduct anything he had not chosen. I guessed right away why he was so adamant. Both the Beethoven and the Brahms are predominantly symphonic, orchestral works, giving the pianist little chance to shine as a virtuoso and provoke enthusiastic demonstrations, a thing which all conductors dread.

Our concert included the Fourth Symphony of Mahler, a novelty in those days, which Fitelberg advertised as the main attraction of the program. This ambitious work required a soloist, a first-class soprano. The cost of the whole thing amounted to almost half of the fund, with little hope for great returns at the box office. And this was not all; worse followed. My rehearsal was scheduled for the morning of the concert from ten to one. When I arrived at the hall, and I was on time, Fitelberg rehearsed the Mahler without stop until intermission at eleven thirty.

I sat down at the piano, waiting. The orchestra was seated again, I was ready to play, when he suddenly decided to continue the Mahler. This was too much. I shouted with rage: "What is the matter with you? What about my concertos? We have hardly time to play them through, and you call that a rehearsal?"

He turned to me with a smile. "Don't get excited. The symphony is the most important work on the program, and your concertos we have played before. This orchestra knows them by heart."

I was ready to kill him.

"Du verfluchtes Schwein!" I screamed in German, right in front of the orchestra.

He pretended to ignore me, turned to the players, and said, "Beethoven." He raised the baton—we began to play. It was a strange rehearsal. We didn't speak to each other. When I needed a change of tempo or expression, I spoke directly to one or another member of the orchestra.

This Berlin concert has remained in my memory as one of the

greatest tests of my nerves and my endurance. The knowledge that I had to perform this heavenly music accompanied by a man I loathed kept me in a state bordering on hysteria. I would have canceled the concert if I hadn't been the true professional musician I was. And somehow, considering the circumstances, the concert went quite well. The opening of the Beethoven put me into a trance, I closed my eyes playing it, I put my heart into my performance. It was in this very hall that I had heard it for the first time, played divinely by Eugen D'Albert.

The Philharmonie was half empty, and most of those who were there had free tickets. Free ticket holders are usually severe critics; people show enthusiasm only when they have to pay. On that evening, however, they were quite receptive. I was called out three times alone. I ignored Fitelberg, but I made a great point of shaking hands with the concertmaster and the solo cellist in the Brahms. After the concert I had secret hopes of seeing some of my oldtime friends, but nobody showed up. As I found out later, Fitelberg had given orders not to let anybody backstage.

But Professor Barth had been present. I received a letter from him which the Philharmonic manager forwarded to Warsaw. He addressed me as "Dear Mister Rubinstein." I lost this letter in the First World War, but I remember what he wrote. He loved the beginning and the second movement of the Beethoven but found the rest "muddy." He was impressed by my "power" and my "rhythmical energy" in the Brahms, but "you should pay more attention to details and use less pedal." I was touched by the great moral effort it must have cost him to write to me, and decided to visit him on my return to Berlin. The critics found more to praise than to blame. All in all, it was not a *great* success, but an "honorable" one.

After an enjoyable Christmas Eve at Pauline Narbut's, with Pola, Fiszer, and some of her other friends, and a boisterous all-night affair on New Year's Eve with Paul, Jaroszynski, two brothers Moszkowski (I shall tell more about them), and their fiancées, I was set to prepare for Kraków and Lwów. Mr. Dropiowski assured me that both cities were excited by my coming. Lwów interested me particularly.

The year 1910 was the centenary of Chopin's birth. Lwów was planning to open the celebrations with a gala Chopin recital at the Opera. Two pianists were to share the program, Ignaz Friedman, the noted Polish virtuoso, and myself. He was in charge of the first part, including the *Funeral March* Sonata, and I had the second part with the B minor Sonata. In the middle of the program we were to join forces for the performance of the Rondo for two pianos. A very original combination, though it looked to me a little like a competition. To my surprise, the concert in Kraków was almost sold out, a rare occurrence in this city. It was such a triumph from beginning to end that the people wouldn't leave and I had to play four encores. And with what a satisfaction I heard of the presence of Prince Ladislas Lubomirski in the audience, especially on as brilliant an occasion as that! He came backstage, beaming with pride, and genuinely moved by my performance.

"Bravo, bravissimo, panie Arturze," he exclaimed, "how lucky I am to be in Kraków at this time. Come to lunch tomorrow—I have many things to discuss with you."

I couldn't have dreamed of anything better.

The Prince lived with his family in Rajcza, his large estate in Galicia, but he spent most of his time in Vienna, where he ran horses during the racing season. The Lubomirski family was in Kraków for the carnival, which explained his presence at my concert.

The luncheon took place in his vast apartment in the center of the town. The Princess, a well-born Viennese, a tall, soft-hearted lady, introduced me to her four children, two boys and two girls, all four still in their teens. A charming, simple, and gay quartet. All through the meal, the Prince, addressing me, assumed with relish the grand air of an impresario.

"How was Berlin? Which cities come next? When are you playing in Vienna?"

I answered evasively without committing myself. I waited for the right moment to speak.

"By the way," he continued, "Countess Betka Potocka telephoned me: she wants you to play at her palace in Lwów on the eve of your concert. I promised to answer her this afternoon."

"Please decide for me, Prince. I will do as you wish," I said, addressing him in the third person (so, the exact translation would sound: "If the Prince will kindly decide for me, I will do as the Prince wishes").

After lunch, he took me to his study, picked up the telephone, and, having obtained the communication with Lwów, he got the Countess on the wire. I remember well his replies in this conversation.

"Hello, Betka. . . . Yes, he is here, and he accepts the invitation to dine and to play for your guests. . . . No, he doesn't care for presents, he wants money. . . . His fee for private concerts is three thousand kronen [$600]. What? Too much? You can afford ten times that sum! . . . No, no, no! He can dine, but he will not play," and he slammed the phone down with rage. "That rich woman! She owns the finest castle in Europe, has fifty servants in livery, she lives like a queen in Vienna and Rome, but she is too stingy to pay a decent fee to an artist! But I did give her a lesson, eh?" He laughed, pleased with himself. This was the right moment for me. I told him the whole Fitelberg story in a calm, diplomatic way. No vain accusations, a simple statement of facts.

The Prince listened quietly, showing neither concern nor surprise. "I always knew he was a great egoist, a man who will stop at nothing to get what he wants. But this time, I did believe his intentions were sincere."

It was then that the Prince related to me verbatim Fitelberg's Iago talk in Warsaw.

"Well," he concluded, "I shall stop him from interfering with you and take up your affairs myself. First thing, I want you to make your debut in Vienna in the grand way, with orchestra and a Viennese conductor. Do you know how to go about it?"

This was easy. My manager, Dropiowski, was offering me his services for concerts abroad, especially Vienna, where he had good connections. Prince Ladislas charged him with the arrangements, guaranteeing the expenses, and Dropiowski was lucky in obtaining the best hall in Vienna, the Musikvereinssaal, and the fine Tonkünstler Orchestra with their conductor, Oskar Nedbal, for a date in February. The Prince was satisfied. "I shall be there," he said.

On the eve of my departure for Lwów, the Lubomirskis gave a small dinner party for me. We were ten or twelve at the table. One of the guests was an extremely good-looking young man, the "tall, dark, handsome" type, *par excellence*. This Count Alexander Skrzynski, a Pole from Galicia, was an attaché of the Austrian Embassy at the Vatican in Rome. Very rich, (he owned oil in the Bucovina), intelligent, and musical, he was one of the most popular bachelors in Europe. (Princess Lubomirski gave me all these details.)

After an excellent dinner, I opened the lid of the piano and played some excerpts from Wagner operas to my hosts' delight, and some pieces of Chopin to everybody's satisfaction. Count Skrzynski was particularly impressed. He spoke with a soft, melodious voice, pronouncing his *r*'s in a special, charming way: "This was ma-h-velous! You a-h a g-h-eat a-h-tist. You must come to Uh-ome—the Uh-oman public will ado-h-e you."

The Prince jumped at this last sentence.

"Panie Aleksandrze, if you guarantee Rubinstein five thousand lire [$1,000] he will come to Rome," he said, playing with joy his new role as my manager.

"I shall be delighted to do that," answered the Count, "but I am su-he-e he will ea-h-n much mo-h-e."

"Never mind that," said the Prince. "All we want is your guarantee."

"I pledge it," replied the poor soul, completely ignorant of the concert business. "The best time would be Ma-h-ch. On my uh-e-turn to Uh-ome I shall make the necessa-h-y app-h-oaches. I shall wi-h-e you the uh-sults."

The Prince was proud of his bargain. I was a little ashamed.

54

A little man with a sad expression on his face caught my arm when I descended from the train at the Lwów terminal. "My name is Türk, I am in charge of your concert," he explained, and he added, without a smile: "We are sold out for tomorrow!"

He drove me to the Hotel George, where the porter gave me a letter containing a printed invitation for dinner at the Palaïs Potocki. So Countess Betka did invite me after all? Or was it simply to teach Prince Lubomirski a lesson for his rudeness? I decided to accept and find out. And the evening deserves a description.

Countess Betka and her husband, Count Roman Potocki, received their guests in the great ballroom. We were sixty at dinner, and a hundred more arrived later. The Countess, all smiles, complimented me on my success in Kraków and added graciously: "The whole town is going to your concert tomorrow, and we are all looking forward to it." She never mentioned Prince Ladislas or their little dialogue over the telephone.

We dined at small tables. I was seated between two ravishing young ladies; one was a Princess Radziwill, a niece of the hostess, the other a Countess Tarnowska, Alexander Skrzynski's sister. Both fascinated me with their Polish charm, and I had a wonderful time. They flattered me by their attentions, laughing at my stories, and we had fun. I still wonder, when I think of it, if they were sincere, or if all this was a comedy, a well-planned scheme to make me play after all. When we joined the other guests in the ballroom, my two sweet table companions attacked me right away: "Please, please, play something for us, only for us, we are dying to hear you," said the young Princess Radziwill. "And I beg you, don't tell my aunt about it— she would be very angry with me."

How can you resist a pair of sirens with so much charm?

Countess Betka acknowledged my offer to play with a gracious nod. She clapped her hands and, when silence was established, announced:

"Pan Rubinstein is kind enough to play for us. Please take your seats around the piano."

I played three or four short pieces and was duly applauded and kissed by my young seductresses. The hosts uttered a few words of appreciation. "Can you come to our large preconcert dinner party tomorrow at eight?" asked the Countess. "As you play after intermission, there is plenty of time." I answered politely that I never eat before a concert. I left the palace with a little feeling of guilt toward Prince Lubomirski.

Ignaz Friedman was a Kraków-born pianist, by ten years my senior. He belonged to the famous Leschetitzky school of brilliant and elegant virtuosi who were much in vogue in those days. A gay, witty, convivial companion, a good colleague, he was also a formidable hand at poker. Bound to be compared to this well-established favorite of Lwów, I was a little afraid of being completely overshadowed by him.

As it turned out, fate and some unexpected circumstances changed the whole picture of this dreaded evening. Friedman and I had lunch together, and later in the afternoon, all dressed, we went to the Opera house to rehearse the two-piano Rondo. The concert was to begin at eight thirty, so we had ample time for a sip of coffee and a good rest in our respective artists' rooms. When Friedman was ready to go out on the stage, Mr. Türk appeared with a worried expression on his chronically sad face.

"I am afraid we have to wait a few minutes," he said. "The papers must have announced the wrong hour, I suppose, because the house is sold out but it is still half empty." And we waited five, ten, fifteen minutes before the people began to trickle into the theater, but they did not nearly fill the house. When the public became restless and started stamping their feet, Friedman decided to start the concert. I did not hear his program, I was too nervous for that, but I heard the great applause after the *Funeral March* Sonata. This was the cue for my entrance for the last piece before intermission, the Rondo for two pianos. We played this piece (not one of Chopin's best) with gusto, and it was well received.

After the long pause there was a startling surprise. When I reappeared on stage, I noticed the theater looked entirely different. It was packed to the brim. And this new audience looked like one you see rather at gala openings at the Opera than at concerts. Loges were filled with the flower of the Lwów *beau monde*, with the Potockis and their guests presiding in the center.

When the lights were dimmed and complete silence fell on the house, I felt that special secret current between the public and me, the current which inspires me when I play. My success, on that night, was one of the most important ones of my career. From then on, until the First World War, Lwów was the *only* city where I could count on a sold-out house.

I felt indirectly responsible for the unpardonable behavior of the public toward Friedman, but I could guess the reason for their discourtesy. Friedman was the well-known pianist, a frequent visitor in Lwów, and I, on this occasion, was announced as the great, promising newcomer. The papers mentioned Prince Lubomirski, the success in Kraków, the gossip from Warsaw, and the Potocki party. No wonder that the people wanted to see and hear me, and in order to have time to dress, to finish quietly their dinner and their smoke, they decided to go to the Opera only for the second half of the program. I must add that Friedman behaved very elegantly when he dismissed the whole thing with an indulgent smile.

Countess Betka never sent me a word of thanks, or mentioned money or presents. I had similar experiences later, in America. Mrs. W. K. Vanderbilt (Birdie, by her pet name), who invited me often to her house, asked me at one of her great parties to play "professionally" (*she* used this term), but she never paid. A relative of hers, Mrs. Cornelius Vanderbilt (Gracie), did the same thing, only more crudely. She asked me about my fee, and I directed her to my manager. Again, I played, but she neither got in touch with him nor sent me money. Women, I have observed, are more tight-fisted than men, especially when they haven't earned their money themselves.

To return to my story, I stopped in Kraków on my return to Warsaw, in order to make final arrangements for my impending concert in Vienna. My program was ambitious: Beethoven's Fourth, Brahms's Second, and the G minor Saint-Saëns!

"The most important thing," I told Dropiowski, "is that I must have a fine Bechstein for the concert. It is the only piano I can play."

Back in Warsaw, I was bragging about my adventures in Kraków and Lwów, and Pola became excited. "I must go with you to Vienna—I don't care whether the Prince is shocked or not to see us together."

It was wonderful to have her with me.

We arrived in the capital of the Austro-Hungarian empire early on a Saturday morning. I remember it, because my concert and the second rehearsal were on a Sunday, the next day (the first rehearsal was Saturday afternoon).

The morning was glorious, cold and windy, but with the sun piercing through the blue-gray sky. The air was invigorating. Mr. Kugel, the manager of the Musikvereinssaal, Mr. Dropiowski's correspondent, was waiting for us in the hall of our hotel. A nice, polite, suave man whom you couldn't identify the next time you saw him, he gave me a full account of his preparations for the concert, a story larded with self-praise.

"I have made miracles in getting for you a fine audience," he said.

"A Sunday is a bad day for concerts, even for the critics, but *my* publicity will force them to come. Your second rehearsal is at nine tomorrow morning, but you will have the assistant conductor; Mr. Nedbal is guest-conducting abroad." Seeing me disappointed at that news, he quickly added: "Don't worry, *I* saw to it that everything will be all right." After he left, I took Pola for a sightseeing tour of the city.

Vienna in those days was still the Vienna of Haydn, Mozart, Beethoven, and Schubert and, more recently, of Brahms and Bruckner. The valses of Johann Strauss were still in the air, and his successors, Lehár and Fall, were the toasts of the town. The old Emperor Francis Joseph remained the absolute ruler of a vast Empire, and the idol of his citizens. The city was swarming with Czechs, Poles, Hungarians, Croatians, Italians; the great families of Bohemia (now Czechoslovakia), Hungary, and Poland had magnificent palaces, some of them showpieces of the capital.

We took a fiacre to drive around the town. Our coachman, chic in his short, fur-lined coat, his bowler hat, and a carnation in his lapel, charmed us with his soft Viennese accent and his eagerness to show and explain the most interesting sights.

We bought some flowers and drove to the cemetery to pay our homage to the great ones in music. A guide took us to the famous corner, and there we stood, in awe, holding our breath, surrounded by the graves of Haydn and Beethoven, Schubert and Brahms, even Hugo Wolf and Johann Strauss. Mozart's grave was there, too, but only as a symbol—the wicked Viennese had let him be buried in a common grave. Pola and I couldn't utter a word, we were so overcome by the emotion of gratitude and love for these immortal geniuses.

On our way back to the hotel I vowed to give my best, not to let them down at my concert.

At the hall, that afternoon, the young conductor (I forget his name) met me at my dressing room, led me to the stage, and introduced me with a few kind words to the already assembled orchestra. I thanked him and told the musicians what an honor it was to perform with them in the very hall where Brahms had played and conducted. They gave me a warm welcome, tapping the back of their instruments with their bows. When I opened the lid of the piano, I saw, to my dismay, that it was a Bösendorfer, made in Vienna, and not the Bechstein I expected to find. When I protested, the manager assured me that his efforts to obtain one had been in vain. I was very annoyed: "This is absurd! The Bechsteins have always provided me with their pianos. I shall see to that after the rehearsal." For the moment there was nothing else to do but to play the Viennese instrument. And it turned out to be quite good.

The rehearsal went well; the orchestra played with obvious pleasure, and the conductor proved to be a very fine accompanist. We finished in less than three hours.

The minute it was over, I hurried to the Bechstein store to get there before closing time. Fortunately, it was still open. Two clerks were busying themselves in the shop, and I asked to see the director. After a while, a tall, heavily built man came in, looking the typical Prussian: the hard, round face with the characteristic scar acquired in one of those student duels, a barbaric German custom.

"What can I do for you?" he asked, visibly impatient; it was late. I explained to him, in a few words, my problem. "I haven't received any instructions from Berlin about it," he said coldly. "Do *you* have a letter for me from Mr. Bechstein?"

"No, I never needed one," I answered, slightly irritated. "The Bechsteins and their agents were always delighted to be of service to me."

"It might be so," he said, "but here we need formal instructions from Berlin."

I became furious: "Berlin will hear from me about this," I replied sharply. "Your attitude is outrageous. It is in your own interest to have your pianos used at a concert of that importance and at the great Musikvereinssaal. And, to tell you the truth, I am not displeased to have to play the Bösendorfer—it is a fine instrument."

I left, banging the door behind me.

Pola waited at the hotel to be taken to dinner. She laughed at my encounter with the nasty Prussian. "You certainly let him have it," she said, "but is this piano really satisfactory?" I assured her that it was very good.

"Was there a message from Prince Lubomirski?" I asked her.

"No, nothing yet."

I was secretly a little restless. The Prince had promised me in Kraków to come to this concert, and I hadn't heard from him since. The porter of the Hotel Sacher, when I called, gave me the equivocal answer: "The Prince is out"; it could mean out of the hotel or out of town. I did not call again. I hate to importune people. The rehearsal on Sunday morning was very satisfactory, and the piano sounded very good.

A little contretemps occurred just before the concert. When I arrived at the stage door at seven forty (concerts in Vienna begin at eight) to have the time to warm my hands, brush up, adjust my tie, and comb my hair, the manager, in a panic, grabbed my arm, took my hat and coat, and pushed me onto the stage, shouting: "Hurry up, hurry up, you are late, the public has been waiting for ten minutes!" Concerts on Sundays started half an hour earlier, but nobody had taken the trouble to inform me about it.

The public gave me a lukewarm reception, and the musicians of the orchestra glanced at me, implying that I must have been having fun with a woman and forgotten all about the concert.

All this stopped at the majestic opening of the Beethoven G major Concerto. This hall and its great memories and my emotion at the cemetery inspired me for this performance. The conductor and the orchestra were in complete accord with me. At the end there was a spontaneous applause, the real one. After a short interval, we attacked the Brahms. Here I was in my element. Ever since the first time I had heard it I considered it as "my" concerto. That evening I felt as if Brahms were in the audience. I played it for him alone. We received an ovation. I bowed many times with the conductor, the concertmaster, and the first cellist, who played beautifully his great solo.

During intermission, behind the stage I noticed a very old gentleman in a short fur coat, with a muffler around his neck and his hat on. Slightly bowed, he walked up to me slowly and introduced himself.

"My name is Ludwig Bösendorfer. I am eighty-six years old, and I do not go out at night any more, but I had to see and hear the young Rubinstein who refused to play my piano while the great Anton Rubinstein preferred my instruments to all the others."

I blushed with shame for having hurt this fine old gentleman's feelings, especially since it was his piano that had helped me so much to my success. When I tried to explain he interrupted me with a light tap on my shoulder.

"Don't take it to heart so much, young man," he said, "I know very well what was behind it all, and I am glad that you found your way to my pianos. Come to see me tomorrow at noon at the piano store; I have some ideas which might interest you."

I thanked him and he walked slowly out into the street.

The Saint-Saëns did its duty. A huge ovation with shouting and an encore. Pola came back with tears in her eyes. It was a great evening for us. There was only one dissonant note—the absence of Prince Lubomirski. And no message, no sign of any sort. Was it Fitelberg again? Or had *I* done something wrong? Pola insisted that her presence in Vienna was the cause of it, but I felt sure he wouldn't mind that—it was not like him. Pola decided, however, to return the next day to Warsaw because she felt she was in my way.

55

Mr. Ludwig Bösendorfer received me in a private office of the large piano store on the Herrengasse.

"Sit down close to me, I don't hear as well as I used to," he said. "You see, the factory does not belong to me any more—I sold it to my friend Hutterstrasser, a younger man and a good businessman. But I still own my concert hall, the Bösendorfer Saal. Can you stay another week in Vienna?"

"Yes, I believe I can," I said.

"Well, then, young man, I intend to introduce you to the Viennese public in the proper way. My hall is taken for the whole season, but I can put off a singer until next autumn and give his date to *you* for a recital next Friday. I want it to be a special affair; I shall send out my personal invitations to all the people who count in Viennese artistic circles and to all the musicians, of course. Do you like the idea?"

I was so moved by the old man's gentle ways that I could only nod in response.

He smiled. "You see, my boy, I do it simply because you made my piano sound so beautiful."

I dashed back to the hotel to tell Pola. The desk clerk had a telephone message for me: "Prince Lubomirski invites Mr. Rubinstein for supper tonight at the Hotel Sacher. At ten and informal."

I was relieved at last; no intrigues by Fitelberg, but his absence was still a puzzle. Pola left late that afternoon. I hated to let her go, but I felt that she was right.

At the old Sacher, the most fashionable hotel in Vienna, I was taken to a private dining room where I found the Prince and two guests sitting at a table laid out for supper.

"Panie Arturze, I am glad to see you again," he said in a jovial tone, with a hint of uneasiness. He introduced me to his companions, a fat, red-faced man—"He has the best race horses in Austria"—and to a very pretty young woman—"This is Rosy." Then he rang for the headwaiter.

"You can serve now supper—and put the champagne on ice." Suddenly he burst into laughter. "You won't believe it, panie Arturze, I have had the tickets to your concert for two weeks in my pocket and I forgot, like a fool, that it was yesterday, ha, ha!"

I didn't laugh or smile.

"Your absence made me very sad," I said. "My concert last night was a tribute to you for all you have done for me."

He became at once serious. "I know, I know, I am very sorry myself —and I was so much looking forward to it. But now, tell me how it went." My account of the concert and of the Bösendorfer project enchanted him.

"I told you Vienna is the place for you!"

In the meantime the waiter was serving caviar and the champagne. The Prince raised his glass: "Here is to your success in the world! Rosy, kiss him!"

Rosy did.

My short stay in Vienna was spent agreeably. The mornings were devoted to practicing my program for the impending concert; the Bösendorfer piano store put a special room at my disposal. A light lunch at the Opernkeller, consisting mostly of the famous *Wiener Würstel* with mustard and a cold potato salad, would be followed by coffee and cake at one of the old cafés, where they show you the *very* table on which Schubert "wrote some of his songs." In the afternoons I visited the great Imperial art gallery or one of the many magnificent private collections, the Liechtenstein, the Harrach, or the Czernin. And then it was time for the theater. I was lucky enough to see the great comic actor Max Pallenberg, an operetta by Lehár, and one or two excellent plays. After the show, every night, Prince Ladislas expected me in the now familiar room at the Sacher. Rosy was always present and, sometimes, one or another of his racing friends; on the walls of the room hung many engravings of crack race horses and hunting scenes.

The Prince couldn't do enough for me now. His suppers were culinary orgies; we always had caviar and champagne followed by some Viennese specialties and the inevitable Sacher torte. The famous Frau Sacher, who ran her hotel and the restaurant with an iron hand, came often to inquire if everything was all right.

"I have arranged a concert for you in Berlin," said the Prince one night at supper. "This time you will play alone at the Beethoven Saal. I want you to show the Berlin public what you can do!"

He actually got in touch with the Hermann Wolff bureau all by himself and was happy to have succeeded in giving me another chance after my painful experience with Fitelberg.

One or two days later he called me at the piano store. "Come at once to the Sacher. I received a telegram from Skrzynski."

In less than ten minutes, I was at the hotel.

The Prince, dressed in a bathrobe, received me in his bedroom. "Tell me what you think," he said, giving me the telegram to read. I still remember the approximate wording of the wire: "Concert organizations refuse to engage Rubinstein pretending he is unknown in Italy stop if he still intends to come to Rome let me know date of his arrival, I shall of course keep my promise, greetings, S."

A little abashed, I said: "I am not astonished; I expected as much the moment the whole idea came up in Kraków. Naturally, there is no question of my going to Rome."

"Nonsense," cried the Prince. "You must go, I insist on it. You can very well give a concert in Rome without anybody's help. And don't worry about Skrzynski—he is rich and he will be very pleased to have you. I shall order your ticket for next week and wire him the time of your arrival."

And without waiting for my consent, he dismissed me. "I must dress now. Don't be late for supper."

I left in a state of uneasiness, but at the same time, I was excited at the prospect of seeing Rome.

My recital at the Bösendorfer Saal turned out to be a gala. The elite of the city responded en masse to Mr. Bösendorfer's invitation, and many well-known musicians were present. Professor Leschetitzky came with his Polish wife, his fifth; the world-famous pianist Moriz Rosenthal, the not-less-famous Emil Sauer, the violinist Arnold Rosé of the quartet of his name, Franz Schalk, the main conductor of the Vienna Opera, and the most important critics sat in the front rows. The Polish colony, including two ministers of state, was well represented. Prince Ladislas brought Princess Maria Lubomirska and her daughters, relatives of his.

As one can well imagine, I was terribly nervous facing an audience as intimidating as that. The ideal acoustics of the hall, however, and the really wonderful piano gave me courage. The presence of so many musicians managed to stimulate me. Only Professor Leschetitzky annoyed me all through the concert by fixing a huge pair of binoculars on my fingers! To sum up: I played quite well, and I was much and heartily applauded; my encores brought out some shouting—the kind of demonstration that was seldom heard by an invited public. Many people came backstage to compliment me, among them Rosenthal, famous for his wit and malicious tongue. To my surprise, he said nothing but some kind, encouraging words.

I missed the dear, old Mr. Bösendorfer at the concert, but it was too late for him, and he sent me a warm message.

Prince Ladislas gave a supper party for me. He had the Princess Maria and her daughters and some other distinguished guests. Rosy was not invited.

I had gained a foothold on Vienna; the critics were full of praise, and people began to take notice. And most important: two managers made me offers for the next season. At our farewell supper the Prince gave me a first-class round-trip ticket to Rome with a private sleeping compartment.

I wrote a long letter to Pola with all the sensational news and begged her to come to Berlin for my recital at the end of March. It was a long separation, and I missed her very much.

56

To be alone in a sleeping compartment of a "train de luxe" for the first time was a voluptuous experience. I felt too comfortable, too happy; I could not close my eyes. It was probably due to my excitement about Rome. The long journey was a continuous joy, our stops in Venice, Bologna, Florence making my heart beat quicker; the very names of these cities sounded like music to me.

Before we reached Rome I became restless. How would Count Skrzynski receive me? Would he try to get rid of me by paying the money and sending me right back? (I had never been happy about the whole thing; I still felt that the Prince had taken advantage of the innocence of the Count and that I, unwillingly, had become a partner of this dubious transaction.)

When the train came to a stop I tried to hearten myself for any eventuality. When I descended to the platform, my eyes caught sight of Count Skrzynski, all smiles, expecting me.

I shall not bore my readers by continuing to reproduce the way he pronounced his *r*'s but give him a chance (in this book) to enunciate them normally.

"How wonderful that you decided to come in spite of these fools who don't know who you are," he said, taking my arm. "I put you up at the Excelsior; the Grand Hotel, where I live, is filled for the whole season." On the way to the hotel, he told me his plans.

"I have arranged a concert for you at the ballroom of the Grand Hotel day after tomorrow. Don't be afraid—it is a fine place, they use it often for lectures and concerts. You will play for the most select audience. I have invited the *tout* Rome. Before your recital I shall have twenty people for dinner, among them four ambassadors and their wives. What do you think of it?"

"I think it is wonderful of you to do all this," I said, but without conviction. The whole idea reminded me of the Bösendorfer introduction, minus the presence of musicians. When I questioned him about it, he said: "Music, in Rome, means opera; that is why I could not find anybody capable of arranging a public concert for you. However, there is one man, Count San Martino, the president of the Academy of Santa Cecilia, who has organized a good symphony orchestra and built a splendid hall on top of the mausoleum of the Roman Emperor Augustus. He was the one I approached, and he answered that he had no date for you and that in any case he wouldn't engage a completely unknown artist. But he will know you after he has heard you tomorrow. I invited him to both the dinner and the concert."

We arrived at the hotel. In the lobby, at the reception desk, he recommended me to the room clerk, invited me for dinner, and left.

In my lovely room with bath, after unpacking, I grabbed my Baedeker for Italy and studied carefully the sights marked with four stars, which were the first I wanted to visit in the Eternal City. I went about it as meticulously as a German pedant. This first day was devoted to the ruins of the old Roman Empire. A cab took me to the Forum Romanum, and my passion for history came to life again. I explored everything, not leaving a stone unnoticed, and I was proud of being able to decipher some Latin inscriptions. The arch of triumph erected in honor of Titus for his victory over the Hebrews and for the destruction of the Second Temple gave me a pang of sorrow. After a quick bite in a trattoria I continued my pilgrimage into the past glory of Rome. In the huge, awe-inspiring Colosseum I could visualize the cruel fights of the gladiators and the early Christians thrown to the lions. The Temple of Vesta, the Via Appia Antica, the catacombs with the graves of the martyrs, brought back to me my lessons with Altmann; I suddenly missed him.

I was so caught in the spell that I almost forgot the dinner. After a rapid wash and a change of clothes, I was on time at the Grand Hotel. When I called up his apartment, Count Skrzynski came down and took me at once to the dining room.

During our long dinner à deux he showed me the list of his guests for the concert, a staggering mass of titles, from dukes down to barons, the most "never-seen-at-a-concert" crowd imaginable. But he gave me also an outline of the state of things in Italy, politically, socially, and artistically. It was a brilliant résumé by a remarkably intelligent man.*

* He became, after the First World War, the foreign minister of free Poland.

His preparations for his reception and the concert were made with a professional efficiency.

"The acoustics are perfect," he said, showing me the hall, "and here is the address of Madame Bretschneider, the local Bechstein agent. She will take care of your piano and be at your service."

My morale was considerably strengthened while I walked back to my hotel on the Via Veneto. It will amuse my readers to learn that the now so famous Via Veneto, the rendezvous of the *dolce vita* and the cinema world, lined with crowded café terraces stretching from the Excelsior to the gate of the Pincio, was in those days a quiet, distinguished street, with its center focused on the Palazzo Margherita, the residence of the Queen Mother.

Early next morning I went to the address on Via Condotti to see the Bechstein representative about the piano. A charming old lady, Mrs. Bretschneider, showed me the instrument, which was in good condition, and promised to send me the best tuner in town. What a contrast with the Prussian in Vienna!

A sip of coffee at the four-or-five-centuries-old Café Greco, where Byron and Shelley, Chateaubriand and Stendhal, Mickiewicz and Slowacki had their table, and I dashed off to the Vatican.

But I cannot omit the deep emotion I felt when I saw for the *first time* the frescoes on the ceiling in the Sistine Chapel, Michelangelo's masterpiece. Lying on the floor for a long time, I contemplated in silent wonder the overwhelming conception and execution of this monumental work. The admirable paintings by Botticelli, Ghirlandajo, and others which hang on the walls of the same chapel were overshadowed by Michelangelo's genius, but the frescoes and stanzas by Raphael, this Mozart among painters, enchanted me by their simplicity and tender expressions.

Later in the afternoon, in the Museo delle Terme, I saw a great collection of sculptures. The monotonous line of busts of Roman emperors began to bore me, when I noticed in a niche a beautiful statue of a Venus callipygous that had been recently found in Cyrenaica. Her rump was of so great a perfection that I could not refrain from stroking gently her marble buttocks as if she were alive.

In the evening, after dinner, I went to see a variety show at the Salone Margherita. Pasquariello, a popular singer of Neapolitan songs, was the great attraction. The place was full, but I was struck by the way a good many of the men behaved. All through the opening numbers they sat with their hats on, reading huge evening papers and paying no attention to the proceedings on the stage. But the minute Pasquariello appeared, the hats were taken off, the papers folded, and these same people became suddenly transformed into the most noisy, enthusiastic audience I ever saw. And I was one of the noisiest. Pasquariello enchanted me with his warm voice and his lovely songs. I still remember two of them, and sometimes, when I am alone, I play them with nostalgia.

57

The concert, better called the party, was a triumph for Count Skrzynski. His *savoir-faire* made it into the kind of event one talks about for a long time. The dinner, I was told, was superb. I missed it because, as usual, I did not dine before playing.

Later, when his guests began to enter the ballroom, one heard nothing but ah's and oh's of admiration for what he had done to this banal place. The disposition of the flowers and the way he placed the red and gold chairs turned the big room into an elegant salon. My listeners were sitting not in straight rows as at a concert but around me in informal groups. I had never played under better conditions.

The greatest names of Italy were present. The Princes Colonna, Doria, Aldobrandini, Boncompagni, Rospigliosi, among many others, represented Rome. From Venice came the beautiful Countess Annina Morosini and the lovely sisters Princess Potenziani and Countess Arrivabene. The Duke and Duchess of Trabia were the most distinguished Sicilians.

In Italy even more than elsewhere titled society was still the predominant factor in the life of an artist.

I played without stop for more than an hour. The Bach Toccata was timidly applauded, the real success came with Chopin, and the last piece, Liszt's paraphrase of the "Liebestod" from *Tristan and Isolde*, was acclaimed. Skrzynski introduced me to many people who complimented me, and I received several invitations. Count San Martino expressed the wish to have me as a soloist in one of the symphony concerts at the Augusteo.

"He did find out who you are, didn't he?" said Skrzynski with a twinkle in his eye, when I told him. "Tomorrow I shall remind him of his offer and not let him get out of it."

The great evening had another, a more immediate consequence. The Marchesa Rudini, a wealthy and beautiful young woman, invited me to give a concert at her housewarming party. She had rented a wing of the great Palazzo Barberini, which contained a big, empty chapel, ideal for a concert, she thought. Skrzynski, whom she consulted about my fee, promptly demanded two thousand lire ($400 in 1910), and she agreed to it gladly.

Overnight I became quite popular in Rome. The few days before the Rudini reception became a mass of social activities: a luncheon here, a dinner there, a tea in between was my daily program. I don't know how I managed to continue my sightseeing and to put in some work at Mrs. Bretschneider's.

Count Skrzynski was pleased to have obtained a date for my debut at the Augusteo during the winter season.

"These miserly people," he said. "They refuse to pay more than six hundred lire, which is barely enough for your traveling expenses. Still, I advise you to accept, because of its importance. Ah, what a shame that Luisa is not in Rome."

"Who is Luisa?" I asked.

"The Marchioness Casati," he replied. "She is the most interesting and charming woman in town. I only hope that she will be back soon."

An invitation from the American Embassy proved that the ambassador was the same Mr. Leishman whom I had known in Paris. Both he and his wife received me like an old friend. Countess Gontaut-Biron, their daughter, gave me news of Armand, whom I hadn't seen for a long time. Mrs. Leishman asked me to consider the embassy my home.

The Rudini housewarming was a magnificent affair, the *clou* of the season. A gallery of five or six regal rooms with fine frescoes covering the walls and ceilings led to the chapel, which was transformed into a concert hall with a podium and rows of seats. Some beautiful tapestries were its only adornment.

A brilliant assembly entered the chapel in a slow procession and took their seats. Never in my life have I seen a more elegant crowd. The Skrzynski guests, again present, were outnumbered three times.

I played a whole recital program, announcing the pieces one by one. And this audience "de luxe" listened attentively and responded with their heart. They showed their inborn love for music, these Italians— I became happily aware of it.

They gave me an ovation after my Beethoven sonata, and the Schumann, Chopin, and Liszt which followed provoked salvos of applause and a growing enthusiasm.

After the concert, a buffet supper was served in three rooms. Dora

Rudini, the pale-faced, dark-haired, beautiful hostess, was radiant. She introduced me to many interesting personalities, among them Maestro Sgambati, the famous pianist and composer who was befriended by Liszt and Wagner, and to Modest Tchaikovski, brother of the Russian composer. Both men fascinated me, and they, in turn, seemed to like me. We stayed until late in the night, Tchaikovski talking about Russian music and his brother, and Sgambati telling some amusing stories about Liszt and Wagner. Altogether it was a memorable and significant date in my life.

58

The morning mail brought me my feé from the Rudinis. The minute I had the money, I decided to go to Naples; my Baedeker was burning in my hand. "See Naples and die!" goes the saying. My paraphrase was: "Die if you don't see Naples." When I told Skrzynski at lunch about it, he laughed.

"Why hurry to see everything at once? You will have plenty of time in the future to visit Italy calmly."

I flushed with impatience. "I do not believe in postponing anything in life. If you feel an urge for something and if there is a chance of getting it, don't wait, grab it. These moments of luck are unique gifts from heaven, and they never return at your will!"

He had an indulgent smile for the raving young artist.

"Anyway, don't stay too long in Naples, and let me know when you return. My dear friend Luisa Casati will soon be returning to town, and I want you to meet her."

I left that night. It took only six hours to get to Naples by train, but I didn't want to waste a precious day on traveling. I arrived at seven in the morning. Here, my French and my English, sufficient for Rome, were of no use, and I had a hard time understanding the Neapolitan dialect. My gesticulations and facial expressions had to speak for me. I directed my cab, driven by a tired horse, to an inexpensive hotel (one star in my book). Fortunately, the window of my room gave me the full view of the beautiful bay, with the impressive Vesuvius on the left. I went down for breakfast to await nine o'clock, the hour when they opened the Museo Nazionale, which contained the finest collection of bronze statues and busts found in the ruins of Pompeii and Herculaneum. When the time came, I picked a cab with a stronger horse, and said to the driver: "Museo Nazionale, Museo Nazionale," while gesticulating: Go ahead, go ahead. The driver smiled and nodded. "Si, signore," and the horse trotted off quite cheerfully. This driver must have taken a liking to me because he insisted on explaining the sights and monuments we were passing, especially those I was not interested in. "Garibaldi, Garibaldi," he would scream, or "Grande Magazzino," showing a department store.

In a narrow street he stopped suddenly, pointed excitedly at a house, and made me step down. Expecting to find that somebody of importance (to him!) was born or had died there, I followed him into the doorway. At the bottom of a staircase stood a little girl, not more than ten, smiling at me. "Bella ragazza, bella ragazza," chanted the driver, rolling his eyes in ecstasy. At that, a fat woman appeared from nowhere, pushed the child toward me, and kept repeating, "Mia figlia, mia figlia." Seeing my indifference, she unbuttoned the girl's blouse, exposing her round little breasts, and forced my hand to touch them. They were hard as stones. And all that at nine in the morning! Dear Naples! In 1910 it was the most attractively immoral city.

I ran back to the street and shouted angrily at the driver, "Museo Nazionale," and he complied with regret.

The bronzes from Pompeii and Herculaneum seemed to me supreme works of art. The mastery of these ancient sculptors was unsurpassed. While admiring the beauty of the statue of Caesar (?) on a horse, I was struck by the notion that modern sculpture, in comparison with music and painting, had progressed so little since these ancient times.

The first floor of the Museo contained the collection of paintings and tapestries, many rooms of them, but I saw only *one* picture, *The Danaë* by Titian; all the others faded in my memory. If I owned only this one picture, my life would be enriched a hundredfold.

The rest of the day was devoted to a visit to Pompeii, where I plunged with gusto into the glorious past and felt for a few hours a noble patrician of that time. The many pornographic and obscene relics shown in Herculaneum and Pompeii tend to prove that the Naples I had seen then had inherited some of its ancestral customs. In the evening, this great city seemed to be a huge bordello. Pimps would stop you at every corner, cabdrivers offered to take you to sensational whorehouses, and in many windows you would see young women waving at you with the inviting gesture "come right up." I escaped these dangerous traps unscathed thanks to the fatherly warning printed by my friend Mr. Baedeker. He advised me instead to climb the Vesuvius and not to leave Naples without seeing the Isle of Capri. I confidently submitted to his better judgment.

In the morning a bus took me to the Torre del Greco, the village from where one ascends the volcano. At first glance, the ascension on foot looked forbidding. I was just about to give it up when a man came up with an attractive offer; he would provide me with a saddlehorse and take me to the edge of the crater. The price seemed not too high, so I agreed. At the start, being a good rider, I enjoyed sitting on a horse again in spite of the slow progress. My mount was placid and I had to encourage it by tapping it lightly with my Paderewski cane which I had brought with me. After a while, however, the man began to annoy me when, instead of walking ahead or leading the horse by the bridle, he would hang on to its tail, making the poor animal drag him up the steep path. When I tried to stop him, he answered angrily, indicating by gestures that he would comply only if I let him have another horse for himself. Reluctantly, I gave in. He ran back to the village, kept me waiting half an hour, and returned astride a . . . mule. "Same price," he said mockingly.

When we were halfway to the summit he pointed to a cabin and made me dismount; he did the same. "Lacrimae Christi," he said solemnly. I expected to find a sacred chapel as we entered the place. It was a tavern with a bar. The barman, or whatever he was, spoke French, and explained that Lacrimae Christi was the name of the regional wine and that it was the custom to drink it on the way to the volcano. My man nodded approvingly. The barman opened a bottle and filled three tall glasses for the three of us. The wine was sweet and heavy. When I offered to pay, he said: "He will pay for you." My guide finished the bottle, and we continued our ascent. There was another cabin en route— and another bottle of Lacrimae Christi.

Finally we were near the top; only a short, steep stretch remained to be climbed on foot. As I took my first step I realized that the soil was nothing but a pile of soft ashes. My legs were buried up to my knees. I tried hard to advance, but to no avail. The fellow had a way with the ashes, for he was soon standing above me, holding out a rope to pull me up. "Twenty lire," he said, keeping the rope out of my reach. I was boiling with rage. "No, never," I cried, suffering the tortures of Sisyphus. In the end, completely exhausted, I gave in and grabbed the damned rope.

"You will pay for it, you fiend," I muttered, but my threat was lost on him; he laughed. Now I advanced cautiously to the very edge of the crater and looked down into it. Suddenly, it gave off a thunderous noise,

big stones erupted from the depth of the volcano, huge flames threatened
to engulf me, and I felt a tremor of the soil under my feet. I shrieked,
the Paderewski cane slipped from my hand and fell into the flames, and
I slid down the ashes in terror. The horse and mule were waiting peacefully, obviously used to it all. My torturer, perfectly composed, made
me understand that the Vesuvius is *always* active, that there was nothing
to be scared about.

We rode back in silence. In Torre del Greco he invited me to enter
his office and pay my bill. His office was a den where five or six men,
looking like a band of cutthroats out of a Western movie, drank wine
at a table. They were the good friends of my guide and had no love
for me, I felt. When the fiend presented me the bill, I was horrified at the
amount. He had multiplied every item and charged me for four (!)
bottles of the sickening Tears of Christ. When I raised my voice with
indignation, his friends seemed not to approve of that. "I better pay at
once," I said to myself, and did so in a hurry.

Back at my hotel I looked scornfully at my Baedeker. But I couldn't
let him down on Capri. My Hotel del Vesuvio (was it an omen?) had an
agency for economic tours, among them a one-day excursion to Capri.
The price included the boat round trip, a luncheon in a hotel restaurant
at the port of Capri, a visit to the famous Blue Grotto, a tour of the
city, and the ruins of the villa of the Emperor Tiberius. The schedule
was: departure at nine a.m., return at seven p.m. Great things to be seen;
I had heard wonders about this paradise island.

The boat, medium-sized, resembled the ones which sail between
Dover and Calais. The morning was sunny and bright, the sea calm, the
air fresh but not cold. I joined a flock of happy tourists on the upper
deck.

A tall man in a yachtsman's dress and cap, who stood aloof from
the rest of us, addressed me suddenly in English: "Is this your first visit
to Capri?" I nodded.

"You look like an artist. Are you one?" When I answered that I was
a musician, he said, "How interesting. I guessed it right away."

He looked not more than forty-five, and though a little forward
and voluble for an Englishman, he was obviously a gentleman.

"I live in England," he said. "I write books, but I spend two months
every year in Capri, to get away from the foul climate at home. Tell me
about yourself."

I gave him a good account of my (in)glorious ascension of the
Vesuvius. "These wicked Neapolitans," he laughed. "One has to beware
of them—they are a dangerous lot."

Our conversation turned to literature, my favorite subject. He showed a vast knowledge of French and Russian authors, and I, on my part, expressed my admiration for Dickens and Oscar Wilde, and so we went on talking animatedly.

When we reached the port, he whispered: "Don't visit the Blue Grotto with this crowd—they will spoil it for you. I would like to take you there in a canoe which can enter the cave—they will see it only from the outside."

I accepted gratefully. It was noon. A guide was collecting the tourists.

"The best thing for us is to lunch while they are gone, and leave when they come back," said my new friend. His impressive authority and knowledge of the island made me trust him implicitly.

The visit to the grotto was a pure delight. Our canoe, handled by an expert oarsman, penetrated the cave by a narrow opening and circled gently the sapphire blue water. After our return, my voluntary guide took a cab and made me admire the poetic streets, squares, and fountains of this lovely town.

In a café, where we had some ice cream, I noticed Maksim Gorki, the great Russian writer, sitting at a table, engrossed in a book while sipping tea with lemon from a tall glass. My indiscreet, wide-eyed curiosity did not disturb him in the least. I did not have the courage to approach him.

It was getting late—a quarter of six—and I was getting ready to return to the port when my cicerone stopped me: "You cannot leave without having seen Anacapri by sunset and watch Naples and Ischia shining like diamonds. The drive alone is worth your visit. Besides, there is plenty of time for your boat."

I had to agree, and so we drove in an open cab onto the road which was cut out of the rocks high up above the sea. It was truly magnificent.

We were driving quietly and comfortably along when, suddenly, I became aware that the man was pressing his heavy body against me. I tried to move away, but he pressed closer and closer. He acted exactly as one might behave with a woman.

Terribly embarrassed and frightened, I said that I didn't feel well and would like to return right away. He understood, stopped annoying me, and told the driver to take us to the port.

Night was falling, and we made slow progress. When we got there, a most disagreeable surprise awaited me—my boat had left! Everything became clear. He had made me miss the boat on purpose.

"Don't get upset," he said. "You have a boat at nine in the morning. The hotel is completely full, but you can spend the night in my apartment. I have two rooms. Let us wash up and have dinner—I am terribly hungry." And, seeing my distress, he added, "Cheer up, you will be in Naples tomorrow before noon." I said nothing, but I was afraid.

A short flight of stairs led to his apartment. He showed me into a large room and opened the door to a smaller one.

"This is your room," he said with an engaging smile. I was panic-stricken. There was no other door but the one to his room! And it had no key! But I kept quiet. We washed our hands and went down to dinner. I could not figure out whether he was the gentleman he seemed to be who took me for a homosexual and saw his mistake, or a sex maniac who might attack me and threaten me with a knife.

I decided to flee. Pretending a violent headache in the middle of our meal, I went up to my room. He remained, polite and unruffled, continuing to eat. Upstairs, I organized my flight. First of all, I barricaded the door with a heavy chest of drawers topped by two chairs and whatever else I could find in the room. Then I examined the window, my only means of escape. It was not too high to jump—the room was on a low first floor—still it was a risk. But there was a balcony at the end of the corridor. I could reach it with my right arm and pull myself onto it. With some skill I could make it. I lay down, without taking my clothes off. There was no question of sleep. After an hour, I saw the knob of the door moving up and down. Then, a short knock and push. When he felt the resistance, he must have understood that it was hopeless to insist without creating a scandal. I didn't dare to move or to sleep. It was one of the longest nights of my life.

At five in the morning I heard noises coming from the port. I tiptoed to the window, where I saw two large boats prepared to sail, giving forth short blasts as signals. There was no time to lose. I crawled out of the window as far as I could, holding on to it with one hand while I tried to reach the balustrade of the balcony with the other. When I succeeded in getting a tight grip on it, I found a narrow foothold on the wall, and by a brisk suspension in the air I grabbed the balustrade. In a few seconds I was inside the balcony; I opened the door to the corridor and ran down to the lobby. I woke up the sleeping night porter and asked him where these ships were bound for. "Napoli, Napoli," he answered. Hurrah!

The captain of one of the fishing boats took me on as a passenger for a few lire, and four hours later I was in Naples.

At the Hotel del Vesuvio I found out that a train for Rome was leaving in an hour. I took that train, but I didn't care to look again in my Baedeker; I was afraid that I might find I had missed some other four-star attraction.

59

When I got back to Rome, I changed from the Hotel Excelsior to the Bertolini Splendid on the Corso Umberto 1°. It was much cheaper, and the Corso was the liveliest street in town. When I phoned and announced my return and my new address to Count Skrzynski, he was pleased.

"You are back just in time," he said. "Luisa is in town and expects me for tea. You must come with me. I told her a lot about you, and she wants to meet you."

We drove to a large, modern villa where a butler opened the front door. "La Signora Marchesa si trova in la sua camera," he said, and showed us in. From the way Skrzynski had talked about her I was prepared to find a blonde or dark beauty endowed with an irresistible charm, but when we entered her drawing room I could scarcely suppress an exclamation: the lady sitting on a couch was the same ghost who had once scared me so terribly by emerging from the other side of my desk in the dark writing room of the Vier Jahreszeiten hotel in Munich. The same mauve hair, the uncanny painted eyes, the long yellow teeth!

Luisa Casati had a good memory, and she said, smiling, "Don't be frightened. I remember your scream in Munich, and I promise not to harm you."

She said it so nicely that I felt immediately charmed by her. I told Skrzynski about her ghostlike appearance in the dark room and my panic. He joined us in a good laugh. She had a personality one doesn't forget (I don't mean to be sarcastic) and a remarkable intelligence.

That afternoon we became good friends, and we remained so for many years. Would I play for her, she asked, if she gave a party for me? Skrzynski whispered something to her, and she answered, of course, how could he doubt it?

Later, in the street, Skrzynski told me, "You have another fee in the bag!" He was learning quickly; he had the stuff of a good impresario.

Right after the Casati party, I was due to leave for Berlin, where Pola was going to join me. I had only five days left in Italy, and a more conscientious pianist would have spent them practicing for the forthcoming concert; not me. The program for Berlin was a difficult one, but I had played it quite often and was reluctant to overprepare it. And so, led by my inborn lightheartedness, I decided to explore more of Italy.

I took a morning train to Florence and occupied a seat at the window of a first-class compartment. Opposite me sat a distinguished elderly French gentleman who had heard me at the Rudini party. He introduced himself, said a few words of praise, and drew me into a friendly conversation. A middle-aged couple from Poland entered the compartment and took the two seats at the door. At the last moment, a breathless, red-faced German and his wife settled in the remaining center seats.

The train was running smoothly when an amusing quid pro quo took place. The Frenchman and I started a hot argument about art. To make my point, I threw my arms up in the air and shouted: "Mais, monsieur, Michel-Ange est le plus grand de tous." The Polish lady looked at me disapprovingly.

"Patrz jak ten smarkacz sobie pozwala z tym starszym Panem,"* she said to her husband. And she kept on: "These French boys have no education—they lose all sense of respect. If my boy dared to behave this way, I would spank him to teach him a lesson!" And then, "He looks so nasty, God knows who his parents are!"

I was enjoying this and remained completely impassive. But things became still funnier. While playing in Rome, I had hurt a finger and I was still nursing it with a small bottle of alcohol. The German's wife watched it and asked me in German: "Was haben Sie? Tut der Finger sehr weh?"

I told her in German what it was. She said, "My husband is a chemist. He can help you." The man got a box out of his bag, examined my finger, and put some stuff on it. I thanked them in my polite German. From the moment the Germans spoke to me my Polish lady got very excited.

"I knew it, I knew it," she said with a sardonic laugh. "To jest ordynarne szwabisko!" (meaning "He is just a vulgar Swabe"—an insulting term for a German). "How could I have taken him for a French boy—only a German could be so arrogant."

I enjoyed it more and more. I bided my time. I knew from their talk that these Poles were from Kraków. The Frenchman and I kept up our conversation, and from time to time I spoke German with my neighbors. Shortly before our arrival in Florence, I produced a box of fine chocolates and offered some to my co-travelers. The Frenchman took one, so did the Germans, but when I held them out politely to the Poles, the woman refused with a disdainful gesture.

"They looked delicious, but I wouldn't touch anything coming from this brat," she said in Polish to her husband.

* Polish, in free translation: "Look how this cheeky brat dares to speak to this old gentleman."

When the train came to a stop and we made ready to leave, I addressed her in my best Polish: "How are things in Kraków, Madame?"

She looked at me with a distraught grimace, and let out a long "Aooh." Her husband gave her a murderous look and led her quickly away. I told the Frenchman the story, and we laughed tears.

Florence enchanted me. Before visiting scrupulously the four-star wonders, I strolled for hours along the streets, the Lungarno, the Piazza della Signoria, the Ponte Vecchio, and took a long breath of the charm of this romantic city.

I loved the tender Botticellis at the Uffizi, the refined Donatellos at the Bargello, the delicate terra-cotta enamels by della Robbia. The elegant *Perseus* by Benvenuto Cellini touched me, as I remembered his passionate account of the progress of this statue in the story of his life. Fra Angelico's frescoes left me cold, however. I have never been able to appreciate the art of the primitives, and I find Giotto the only one among them who makes me realize his grandeur. But of all my impressions of the great day, the gigantic *David* of Michelangelo stands out in my memory.

Filled with gratitude for the privilege of seeing all these incomparable treasures, and for the revelations of this gem of a city, I continued my route to Venice.

Sitting quietly in the corner of my compartment (incognito this time), I tried to brush up on my history of the city of the doges. The long paragraph in Mr. Baedeker did not satisfy me. Now it was up to me to teach him a thing or two. I noticed with glee that my own knowledge went much deeper than his.

To me, Venice felt like home. I loved this city as one loves a woman. I had studied her history with passion; I knew all there is to know about her. Her great painters were my favorites. Old chronicles, novels, and news about her were subjects of constant interest to me, even the lengthy memoirs of Casanova.

When the train moved slowly into the terminal, I hurried down to the Grand Canal and jumped into a gondola. "Al albergo Luna," I commanded the gondolier. By then, my Italian had somewhat improved. Right from the start I had to argue with him about the route to take. He intended to make the usual shortcut through the narrow canals, whereas I was set on entering my dream city by the only tolerable course—by the majestic Grand Canal, with no regard for time. A few additional lire persuaded my reluctant oarsman, and the gondola advanced swiftly down the famous waterway.

"Ecco il ponte del Rialto!" I greeted the well-known bridge, taking my hat off. All through our passage I called out excitedly the names of the palazzos, as if I were meeting old friends. "Il Vendramin, dov'è morto Wagner," I shouted. "La bella Ca' d'Oro! il palazzo Mocenigo! palazzo Papadopoli! il Desdemona! il Dario!" and so on, until we reached the hotel. It took me a minute to register and leave my bag, and I rushed to the Piazza—the Piazza San Marco, that finest of all squares and places. I was so moved to find it looking exactly like the old paintings I had seen, measuring up to my most exalted vision of it, that I walked right up to the terrace of the Café Florian, took a chair at the table, and admired the golden aureole on the cupolas of the St. Mark Cathedral, shimmering in the glorious sunset.

I lived a *moment of eternity*—an expression I use only for those rare moments when time loses its importance. Whether they last an hour, a day, or a year—nothing can improve or diminish their perfect form of beauty.

For two full days I walked, strolled, and ran along the narrow streets and bridges of this paradise for those who like to walk (I hate the word "pedestrian"). Sometimes when I lost my way, a passer-by I questioned would invariably answer: "Sempre diritto, passa il ponte e dopo demanda!"—Go straight ahead, pass the bridge, and then ask! And I would follow this advice, only to be completely lost. However, somehow I always found my way back to the Piazza.

Too soon it was time to return to Rome for the Casati party and to think of the Berlin concert. I had written Pola a long letter about Venice and how I missed her in this city of love, again begging her to join me in Berlin.

Leaving Venice was leaving a dear friend. There is nowhere in the world where I play with more joy and feel more at home.

Back in Rome there was no time to lose. I spent a few intense hours practicing at Madame Bretschneider's; the few days without a piano had left their mark.

Luisa Casati's party was in some ways more interesting than the previous ones. Aside from a scattering of illustrious names, she gathered the real intellectuals, the real music lovers, the ones who are part of a concert public. And so I played as if it were a dress rehearsal for my concert in Berlin. Skrzynski asked me for lunch at the Grand Hotel on the day of my departure and gave me the two thousand lire for the concert and the remaining thousand of his guarantee. He also presented me with a lovely silver cigarette case with my initials in gold.

"I have written Prince Lubomirski about your success in Rome, and bragged a little about myself; I think he had it coming to him for being so offhanded with me. By the way," he continued, "it's a pity that you must leave; the season is still in full swing, and I feel sure you could have played some more *dans le monde*."

He bade me a warm farewell, and I thanked him from my heart.

A night train brought me to Berlin the morning of the concert. At the hotel, Pola, who had arrived an hour before, was waiting for me in our room. We held each other tightly for a long while and kissed. It had been a long time since we had been together in Vienna, and we had so much to tell each other that she finally had to remind me that I had a concert. We had a rapid breakfast, and she sent me away to see the hall and the piano.

"I shall call up Professor Barth and ask if he can receive you this afternoon. You promised to visit him, you remember?" She was an angel and she was wise.

The new manager of the Hermann Wolff office, Mr. Fernow, a powerfully built giant of a man with a short beard and a neck bulging with two fat rolls, was waiting for me in the hall. "We are having trouble with your concert," he said sternly. "The proprietor of the Hotel Bellevue has a claim against you for an unpaid bill. He threatens to seal off the box office receipts. What will you do about it?"

My heart stopped beating, but I smiled. "It is nothing. I shall settle it right away," I said cheerfully. "Let me have six good tickets for tonight. He and his family are great music lovers."

It took me less than half an hour to try out the piano and to set my stool right. On the way to the Bellevue I fell into a nervous depression. Again that nightmare?

Mr. Metzger received me in his office. He was set on getting his due; the announcement of my concert at the Beethoven Saal made him think I was swimming in money. I had a hard time explaining that the concert was guaranteed by Prince Lubomirski and that any box office receipts were simply deductible from the deficit. Metzger called up Fernow to get confirmation of what I said and finally accepted a small sum on account and the six tickets. When I returned to Pola for lunch I felt twenty years older.

Professor Barth was expecting me early in the afternoon. It was a very difficult visit. Frankly, I was terrified to face him again. He had moved to another apartment, which helped, because I would have hated to see him in the same surroundings. A maid showed me to a small living room, where he was sitting in his swivel chair.

"Wie geht es Ihnen, Herr Rubinstein?" he said politely, as if I were a new acquaintance. I stammered a few unintelligible words. "I shall come and hear you tonight," he said. "What are you going to play?"

"The Beethoven Opus 53," I began, and he nodded approvingly. "The *Symphonic Études* by Schumann," I continued, and he nodded again. "A ballade and two études by Chopin"—another nod—"and, to finish, two pieces by Debussy," I concluded. At this, suddenly, he banged both fists on a table. "Diese Schweinerei! Wie können Sie so eine Schweinerei spielen!" he shouted, and went on about my playing "this piggish music." Here was my old Barth back again. I tried to tell him that he might finish by liking these particular pieces, but he wouldn't listen to me; it was like old times. When I took leave, he mellowed a little and wished me good luck.

Poor Pola was quite upset, as I looked pale and tired.

"Will you be able to play at all after such a strain?"

I tried to reassure her, but I myself was apprehensive. We drove up to the hall as to a funeral. When Mr. Fernow told me that it was time to begin, I was in a panic. But from the moment I took my first bow my self-confidence was back. The presence of many friendly faces in the audience helped a lot. Mr. Metzger with his family sat in the first row. It was pleasant to show him that I could play, too, not simply be his debtor. Anyway, I played much better than I had the last time with Fitelberg, and the success was genuine and deserved. Even the Debussy pieces were applauded, to my special satisfaction. Frau Emma Engelmann and her son Hans came backstage to see me, as did Professor Max Friedländer and his wife and a few other old friends. Warm and kind as ever, they treated me as if I had never left. Pola was duly introduced as "an old friend from Warsaw on her way to Paris."

Out in the street, near the stage entrance, I saw Henny waiting for me. She was a little shy seeing me with Pola, but she took my hand and said something nice about my playing, mentioned that I had grown (!), and rushed away. She had come, I suppose, to the concert in secret. Professor Barth did not write that time, but I learned later from a pupil of his that he was impressed and had mentioned: "Der Kerl hat doch ein wenig gearbeitet"—The fellow must have worked a little.

I took Pola to Dressel's for supper, where we celebrated our reunion and the good concert. She talked about her hope to recover her children.

"We must be more careful than ever, darling," she said. "The less we are seen together in Warsaw the better."

I hated to let her go back so soon, and I proposed an idea I had been nursing. "What about going with me to Rome?" I said. I explained that there were prospects for more private concerts, that I could still make money there, and we could enjoy being together in that divine city. She was worried again about whether she would be in the way, but I reassured her. Berlin had nothing to offer us but bad memories.

In the morning, at breakfast, we read the papers. Most of them praised me for my talent; all of them liked best my Chopin and Debussy. One critic found my Beethoven sonata not "deep" enough, a term profusely used by the Germans but which I cannot understand. If he meant "with deep feeling" it would make sense, but that couldn't apply to me, because in spite of all my technical faults and other defects, the "deep feeling" was the real essence of my talent.

Mr. Metzger sent me a letter with thanks and congratulations. I hoped to find in the envelope an acquittance of my debt, but in vain; an elegant gesture was something unknown to this German innkeeper.

Nevertheless, I did live up to my motto: "Nie dam sie." I shall not surrender!

60

In Rome, at the Bertolini Splendid, I took two rooms this time and Pola registered in her own name. Even though she had to remain "incognito," none of these little inconveniences lessened the delight of our being together.

The first thing I had to do was to call up Count Skrzynski, but we found that he had left for Vienna. Very disappointing news. I had counted on his gift for obtaining engagements for private concerts. And there, unexpectedly, I was on my own. All I could do was to leave my visiting card (it was the custom then) at the palazzos of some of the important people I had met.

In answer, Luisa Casati and Dora Rudini asked me for lunch, which I had to accept, hating to leave Pola to lunch alone, but I refused Countess Arrivabene's invitation to a ball. The Leishmans were kind enough to invite both of us to tea; I introduced Pola as an old friend from home. Meanwhile, no engagements materialized. I still had some money, but it was dwindling away—a fact that I, improvident as ever, ignored.

We lived a happy week, Pola and I. We admired all the treasures of Rome hand in hand, open-mouthed like a couple of children; we enjoyed the Italian food; we threw, superstitiously, some coins into the Fontana di Trevi, to guarantee our return to Rome; we went to hear Pasquariello, who made Pola cry. What we loved best was to stroll the streets, have a coffee at the Café Greco, and look at shop windows. In the Piazza di Spagna I bought her a dress which I noticed she had looked at twice.

That same evening, after dinner, I had to tell her. "Darling, I am afraid you have to go back to Warsaw. I have not much money left, and there is hardly any hope of another engagement. The season is almost over."

Pola listened in silence, but then she became upset. "But, Arthur," she said reproachfully, "why didn't you tell me in Berlin? I was ready to leave then—"

I interrupted her. "No, my darling," I said, "I wouldn't have given up one single hour of our beautiful week even if I have to go to prison for it. Every minute we live is unique and irretrievable, while money can be earned, won, inherited, found, or even stolen!" She nodded sadly with resignation, but she was anxious about me.

"Don't worry, dear," I said. "I wrote Mr. Türk to announce a concert in Lwów, where I am sure to fill the house." I saw her off the next evening with a sigh of relief. I couldn't bear to make her a victim of my improvidence.

Being used to money troubles, I prepared to face them all by myself. In my letter to Mr. Türk I asked him to send me a few hundred lire as an advance on the box office receipt. Türk answered by wire: "Concert now inadvisable better wait till winter stop Paderewski just played twice at much raised prices emptying people's pockets."

It was discouraging news, but I still had to get out of Rome, and even a half-filled hall could help me. I wired back: "Announce concert urgently right away I guarantee expenses stop please send date and money."

I lived in expectation. My daily diet consisted of spaghetti, fruit, and coffee.

Mrs. Leishman wrote me a letter inviting me for dinner, and she mentioned: "It will be of interest to you to know that Mr. John Pierpont Morgan, the great banker, is going to be our guest of honor. We hope you will be kind enough to play for us after dinner."

I knew, of course, that I would have to play, and not for money—they were dear friends of mine—but why should meeting Mr. Morgan be of interest to me? I mused. Certainly he is not going to tell me, "Arthur, I like your playing—here are a million lire, go and have fun!" So, I kept on ruminating, I, the penniless pianist, will give all I have by playing for him, while he, one of the richest men in the world, will get it for nothing.

I went to the dinner with an angry prejudice against this potentate. It was a small party, and we were all waiting for the guest of honor, who was late. When he entered the room, I received a shock. He was rather tall, gray-haired, heavy-built, and could have been quite inconspicuous if it had not been for his nose. You couldn't call it a nose; it was a huge, blue, brown, and mauve tubercle, which showed pus in some places. I felt, suddenly, acutely sorry for the man; it must have been an agony for him to meet people. He excused himself very politely for being late, and we entered the dining room, where he sat at the head of the table between Mrs. Leishman and another lady. Twice, during dinner, he was called to the telephone; he expected some important news from London.

Later, when we had coffee and I was introduced to him, he asked, "Have you played in America?" and "How did you like it?"—but I, playing the naïve, inquisitive boy, asked him, "Is it true, Mr. Morgan, that you could keep a fleet of your own and attack any country? And that you could live comfortably a thousand years without having to work? I just read all these things in the morning paper." He frowned. "You shouldn't read such nonsense. I am a hard-working man." He proved it, because he rose to take his leave after I played my second piece. "Poor Mr. Morgan is at his desk at seven every morning," said the ambassador, explaining his early departure.

Back at the hotel, warm in bed, I thought how much happier the penniless pianist was than the multimillionaire, who had to get up at seven a.m. in order to take care of and keep clean a huge mountain of gold which he believed to be his own, but which he couldn't take with him to his grave.

Türk wired a date and sent five hundred lire. Once more I was safe.

The journey to Lwów was a very, very long one, second class and no sleeper. Besides, I was traveling under a strain—what if the concert were a financial disaster? How careless of me to have given my promise to cover the expenses! Dirty and utterly exhausted after two almost sleepless nights, I arrived in Lwów prepared for the worst. There on the platform stood Mr. Türk with an expression on his face as if he were at the funeral of his whole family killed in an accident. My heart dropped to the floor. We shook hands. "Is it as bad as all that?" I asked timidly. "Not *one* ticket sold?" He answered, shaking his head sadly, "*Sold out.*" "What?" I screamed. "You are joking, aren't you?" "No," he said, "it was sold out in two days, and, if you agree, I shall announce a second concert." I was ready to strangle the man.

"Why the devil are you looking so sad?" I shouted at him. "You scared the life out of me!"

He seemed astonished. "How can I look happy if I have nothing left to sell?"

Quite a character, this pan Türk. Anyway, I gave two sold-out concerts with crowds shouting for more. God bless Lwów and its faithful public.

My journey back to Warsaw was rather eventful. The visa on the fake passport which I had used on my way to Kraków had lost its validity. So, for my return, pan Türk provided me with an Austrian pass signed by the mayor of a vague village, a not too safe document. But I had no choice, and took the risk. At midnight, at the frontier, the Russian gendarme took my paper and disappeared with it. While I was waiting, the other passengers were allowed to continue their journey. After a long hour, the gendarme came back, led me to the first-class waiting room, and locked me in. I was arrested! My brain was working fast: Colonel Stremoukhov—he might help—when a policeman came in with some tea and crackers. He left without a word and locked me in again. Exhausted, I was dozing intermittently in an easy chair when two gendarmes woke me up at six in the morning, handed me back my paper, and declared sternly that the document was insufficient (!) and that they were going to put me on a train back to Austria. Ough! Once again on free soil, I took a train to the German-Russian border and had the impudence to present there to the Russians the same discreditable scrap of paper. And, this time, I passed the frontier without trouble. I arrived in Warsaw in a shaky but happy condition.

61

At the Victoria, I had a joyous, happy reunion with Karol and Paul. My appearance had taken them by surprise, and we spent the evening and half the night together. I treated them to a dinner at the Europejski, the best restaurant in town, where I told them my odyssey with all the details. They enjoyed most the Vesuvius and Capri episodes, which proves my theory that disagreeable incidents and dangerous adventures later become the funniest stories. Pola, whom I called up immediately, was overjoyed to hear that Lwów had saved me. We fixed a rendezvous for the next morning.

The Warsaw spring lavished on us its incomparable charm. We couldn't resist it, and my Pola resumed her visits to my room, cautiously, but using this time the main entrance to the hotel.

Thanks to Paul, I made some wonderful new friends—the Moszkowski family. The father, a stock broker, was the cousin of the composer Moritz Moszkowski. He was a debonair and witty old gentleman, not unlike his famous relative. The mother was a remarkable woman, in her middle fifties, with the vitality of a young girl. A keen reader of the best literature in

three languages, she was a perfect wife and mother. The three sons, whom
Paul had known since childhood, were slightly older than we—one an
engineer, one an architect—but the whole family was passionately devoted
to music; they never missed a concert, and Paul and I were their favorites.
I soon became as privileged a guest of this stimulating household as he was.
Now and then we would play some of the music we were rehearsing for
a joint concert, which we had decided to give in Warsaw and Lodz, in
order to see the effect on the musical ears of the Moszkowski family and
to hear their comments.

One night Antek, the eldest son, brought a Russian newspaper and
pushed it at me. "Read this story," he said. "It might interest you." It was
a detailed account of the forthcoming Anton Rubinstein competition for
pianists and composers to be held in St. Petersburg during the summer
(I forget the exact date). Aleksandr Glazunov was going to be the president of the jury. The age limit was twenty-five years (I was twenty-
three). There were single prizes of two thousand rubles ($1,000) each for
the pianist and the composer.

My great namesake did things very nobly; he made me feel proud to
bear his name. It was he who had created this first international competition without regard for race, creed, or color. In order to ensure impartiality
he ordered the competitions to run every fifth year alternatively in St.
Petersburg, Berlin, Vienna, and Paris, and in each of these cities under the
presidency of the actual director of their state conservatories.

"Well, well, what do you think of it, Arthur?" asked Antek.

"I think it is a great thing for young talented pianists," I answered.

"But you don't get my point," he insisted. "I want you to go to St.
Petersburg and win the prize."

I smiled. "It is good to hear that you have so much faith in me, and I
would like nothing better, but I am not prepared for it. You know very
well that I was never able to learn a piece up to the last finish—there is
always a bit of improvisation left. Also, the program which the competitors
have to perform is very difficult; it would take me months to learn it."

Antek was not convinced by my arguments. Paul began to take his
side. "You underrate your talent, Arthur."

"Talent alone does not win prizes," I said. "They demand more than
that." They gave up. The discussion was over, but inwardly I was disturbed. Frankly, I envied the young pianists who were able to work eight
hours a day and know their pieces to perfection. I tried to forget about the
competition. The concerts with Paul were wonderful. In the Franck and
the Brahms sonatas we inspired each other, and the public felt it.

The Siren, Warsaw's emblem, was at work again. I fell under her
spell with more reason than ever before. Pola's love, tenderness, and charm

filled me with a new vitality and power. Her courage had liberated me forever from the sordid *envoûtement* of her family. And so, thanks to her, I could enjoy fully the enchanting Warsaw atmosphere including everything, friends, theaters, streets, cafés, people with their spark of humor! My ego, too, was flattered by the fact that Warsaw and Lodz had heard echos about my success abroad.

My happy love affair with the Warsaw Siren came one morning to an abrupt end.

The press brought out an article which made my blood boil. It concerned the Rubinstein Prize. Glazunov and the jury had signed a petition to the Tsar asking for a relaxation of the law which prohibited Russian Jews from remaining in the capital for more than twenty-four hours, and for the permission to allow the Jewish contenders to stay for the duration of the competition.

The Tsar did not answer, but Stolypin, the premier, did. His refusal was rude and categorical.

This insolent, outrageous injustice was more than I could bear. Besides being personally humiliated as a Jew, I resented the insult to the memory of my great namesake, who would never have tolerated discriminations of that sort. I was burning to take my revenge.

Paul and Antek had read the article.

"Antek, I am going to Petersburg to compete!" I said grimly. "If they try to stop me, I shall make an international issue of it, a real scandal!"

Paul said, "I hope you know that it starts two weeks from now—how will you manage to learn the repertoire?"

"I don't care about the music," I answered. "I am going simply in protest to Stolypin!"

Antek said calmly, "Arthur, I am going to get all the music of the program. Come tomorrow morning to our house and read it through. Then you will see what you can make of it."

To that I agreed. Next morning, Madame Moszkowska, smiling, treated me to a second copious breakfast of coffee, eggs, cakes, and jam. "And now, boys, go to the piano," she said cheerfully.

First I read the Rubinstein Concerto in D Minor, a piece every contender had to play. It sounded difficult at concerts, but it proved easier than I thought. The rest of the program for the competition consisted of a full recital: a four-voiced fugue by Bach; one of the last sonatas by Beethoven; one of the important pieces by Schumann; one of the ballades, a nocturne, and a mazurka by Chopin; and one of four specified études by Liszt.

All this did not look too bad. I had studied with Barth the Sonata, Opus 90, by Beethoven; one of the easier ones, it had only two movements. For Schumann I had the choice of *Papillons* or the *Carnaval*, Opus 9. The

Chopin pieces were familiar to me, but I had no étude by Liszt, nor a four-voiced fugue, in my repertoire. Still, and I knew it only too well, *none* of these pieces was really ready for a competition. I was always able to give them a fine, musically sound outline, but I neglected detail and technical finish, a vice which lasted for many years.

Antek and the rest of his family were optimistic.

"You could learn it in no time if you really decided to work."

"That is just my trouble. I love to *play* music the whole day long, but I get tired practicing after an hour."

"Look here, Arthur," Antek said, "just to amuse yourself, and us, learn the first movement of the Concerto before luncheon."

I could never resist a challenge. "All right, I shall try." Antek left the room and locked me in, the rascal.

At about two o'clock I knew two movements by heart, and was starting on the third.

"Lunch is ready," shouted pani Moszkowska.

After an invigorating and gay meal, we resumed the same procedure.

Antek's clever scheme proved successful. He knew how to prod my ambition and my sporting spirit. I actually enjoyed being locked in and forced to work with the proud satisfaction of beating his challenge. And so, after ten days of this regime, I felt sure I could at least make a decent showing at the competition.

It was Antek who arranged all the formalities, like sending itemized details of my birth, my musical education, and so on. Zosia's cousin, a journalist who lived in St. Petersburg, offered to share his room during my stay.

Pola, who tried at first to dissuade me from this risky adventure, was impressed by my firm resolution and gave me all the moral support. I left with my friends' blessings.

62

Stefan Grostern, Zosia's cousin, had a friendly, boyish face with blond curly hair, and the blinking eyes of the shortsighted. On the way from the station to his home he gave me some precious information.

"I know your situation," he said, "and I think you have nothing to worry about. A good friend of mine right here in Petersburg, a Jewish lawyer, is interested in your case. If there is any trouble he will represent you without charge. He was so incensed by Stolypin that he was ready to start an action against the government—which, of course, would be of no avail—but he is sure that you will win."

In his room, before I settled down, Grostern asked me for my document.

"I have to deliver it to the janitor," he explained. "He is responsible to the police."

"What shall I do if the police order me tomorrow to leave immediately?" I asked.

"You must declare that you have the right to compete. This they will investigate. If the answer is negative, the lawyer will step in."

A little, but not entirely, reassured, I gave him my old passport. After a long sleep and breakfast, I left for the Conservatory to register and to see Mr. Glazunov. All the contestants were there; we were not more than twenty. With four of them I was well acquainted; they and a few others were quite well-known concert pianists. Mr. Glazunov received me in the director's office. He was visibly disturbed.

"You shouldn't have come," he said. "I am afraid they won't let you stay."

"If that happens," I said emphatically, "I shall create an international scandal. Besides, a local lawyer is ready to take up my case."

"What worries me," he answered, "is the fact that you are the only one involved in this predicament. The other Russian Jews have graduated from Russian conservatories and became *svobodnyia houdojniki* [free artists], and the Jews from abroad have foreign passports."

"Whatever happens, sir, please allow me to compete," I said beseechingly. He agreed; he had no right to refuse.

Downstairs, in the assembly hall, I joined the others for signing applications and drawing numbers for the order in which we were going to perform. I drew number twelve. Later on, we gathered informally around a buffet, where we became better acquainted with one another. Soon, loud talk and gossip in many languages filled the air. A Russian pointed out a young man who wore glasses.

"Alfred Hoehn, a German," he said to me. "He will win the prize."

"How can you be so sure about it? Is he a genius?"

"He has a letter from the Grand Duke of Hesse for his sister, the Empress Alexandra of Russia," he said, "and I am sure that our jury will be notified about it."

Pure gossip, I thought. Still, I was interested in knowing this German pianist better. After a few minutes of conversation it was clear that we had much in common, Hoehn and I. His ideas about music and the piano were not unlike mine; and we both loved Brahms.

The competitors having their choice of piano, my first concern was to find the Bechstein representative. I found him in the person of André Diederichs, himself a piano manufacturer, the nicest man imaginable. He made me try out the instrument he had prepared for the competition, a splendid Bechstein, and listened intensely to my playing.

"You have the stuff of a winner," he exclaimed. "I bet that you and my piano will be the champions!"

His encouraging words were followed by an invitation to luncheon. At the restaurant, learning that my coming was a protest against Stolypin and that there might be trouble with the police, he showed his indignation so vehemently that I had to calm him down. I found in him a precious and faithful friend. He took me back to Grostern's quarters, sharing my anxiety about the police. Grostern, who had been on the alert the whole day, told us that there was no investigation as yet. I decided to follow quietly the course of events.

The competition started the next morning at ten.

Number one was Swiss pianist Edwin Fischer, who performed the first and second movements of the Rubinstein Concerto (the committee had discarded the third). The jury, presided over by Glazunov, sat in the two front rows. They were twelve, all professors of the various Russian Imperial conservatories. The most important among them was the great pianist Annette Essipova (the third wife of Leschetitzky). The attendance was poor, owing to the early hour. Fischer, who became famous in later years, commented bitterly: "The first performer at any competition is a victim," he said. "They all wait for the next ones in order to be able to compare." He played, accordingly, with a certain indifference.

The Rubinstein Concerto, classical in form, contains some nice melodic material. It strives for grandeur but results in grandiloquence. A good performance of this work demands sweep and passion. The performers this first day were well equipped with technique and power but lacked these two elements.

That evening, Diederichs, who had inquired, told me that there was no sign of the police. "I think they have forgotten you," he said in a jocular mood. We went out for a cheerful supper.

On the afternoon of the next day it was my turn to play the Concerto. Some five pianists had played in the morning, but the general atmosphere of the contest was still colorless, and the public not responsive. I had no lunch, only two cups of coffee at the buffet. My nerves were on edge— it was the first time in my life that I would be taking part in a competition.

À Mr. Gabriel Astruc en
témoignage de ma plus grande reconnaissance
et sympathie.
Arthur Rubinstein

62 rue Caumartin, Paris

2. 05. Paris.

*Arthur during his first tour
in United States, 1906*

Kochanej pannie Zofji w dowód przyjaźni
Artur Rubinstein

Warszawa 25. 6. 09.

left to right

Arthur, Mrs. William Knabe, Mr. Knabe, and their
daughter in the Bois de Boulogne Paris, 1906

Arthur in Paris wearing his
first pearl stick-pin given
by George Brocheton 1909

Arthur in Warsaw 1910
with Antek Moszkowski.

From left to right
Arthur Juliusz Wolfsohn Leo Sirota

left to right
Fitelberg, Szymanowski, and Arthur

left to right
Karol Szymanowski, Paul Kochanski, G. Fitelberg

And I had refused to rehearse with the orchestra, thinking that an unprepared performance would sound spontaneous!

They called me; my fingers were icicles. I bowed graciously and sat down ready to faint. But with the first chords of the Concerto I was transformed into another person, I was in a trance. I played as if driven by an unknown power. My performance must have been electrifying, because people started shouting before I had finished the cadenza. With the last note, thunderous applause broke out. The public clapped, yelled, and stamped their feet. *The jury stood up and applauded.* I was afraid that the second movement, a charming romanza, might calm them down, but their enthusiasm did not subside. During the intermission all members of the jury came to the artists' room to congratulate me. Glazunov said: "I thought I was hearing Anton Grigorievitch [Rubinstein]." Madame Essipova kissed me. I was in heaven.

Diederichs took Grostern and me for dinner to Cubat, the best French restaurant in town. We celebrated until late hours. I began to forget the police and Stolypin.

The morning papers brought glowing accounts of my playing, and all mentioned how the jury had honored me.

The rest of the pianists did not do more justice to the Concerto than the previous ones. Hoehn played it meticulously, but without spark. The composers—there were five of them—presented their works for a whole day before the piano solo recitals were to begin. We had two free days to practice on the piano of our choice, and we would listen to each other with great interest and not a trace of envy. All of my colleagues were accomplished pianists, and many among them made fine careers. Two Russians, Pyshnov and Borovsky, were pupils of Madame Essipova, and had hopes of winning. I continued to discover musical affinities with Alfred Hoehn, a scholarly and modest young man; Emil Frey, from Switzerland, competed both as a pianist and as a composer, which impressed us all.

On the third day, Edwin Fischer was again the first to play. This time the hall was packed. The public, the press, and the whole of Russia became passionately involved. At that phase of the competition, practically every one of us had his partisans, but, frankly, I had the most. If I had been a race horse, my odds would have been about 10 to 1.

After Fischer, I heard Sirota, Pyshnov, and an Englishman. They depressed me—they played too well. All four had the kind of technical polish which I never possessed. And they never missed a note, the devils. It is better for me not to listen to the others, I decided, lest I run away from the competition, police or no police. As a matter of fact, I am afflicted with an inferiority complex with regard to my playing; any youngster who performs properly a Scarlatti sonata makes me feel that he is a better pianist than I. Of course, I want my reader to know that as a musician in its true sense, I have no complexes.

Finally, a day later, in the afternoon, someone called: "Number twelve!" I felt as if I were going to the scaffold. The house was full to the brim. After having heard eleven pianists, the public had reached the stage of a feverish expectation. Even the members of the jury looked nervous. It would take a good psychoanalyst to decipher my own state of mind.

Curiously enough, the atmosphere of tension and excitement is favorable to a good performance.

My first piece, the Bach Prelude and Fugue, sounded well on the Bechstein; it had clarity and dignity. The public applauded warmly, and the jury gave me many approving nods. The Beethoven Sonata which followed worried me a great deal by its shortness and its ineffective, inconclusive ending. The first movement is magnificent and moving, but the last has a too-much-repeated, beautiful theme which dies out at the end. Professor Barth told me that Anton Rubinstein touched people to tears with this movement. With that in my mind, I played this Sonata with all my heart, giving a new and stronger meaning to every repetition of the lovely melody. At the conclusion, the public, disconcerted at first, gave me a fanatical applause, so typical of partisans; it wasn't really meant for me but against the others. Still, I began to feel as though I had won the battle.

The *Papillons* of Schumann were a genuine success and the Chopin pieces a triumph. The Mazurka made Madame Essipova wipe her tears. I smashed the Liszt Étude with a number of false notes but with an irresistible élan.

The response a few days before had been mild in comparison with what took place after my recital. The Russians can be the most savagely enthusiastic audiences in the world. They proved it on that day. Screaming and shouting, they tried to mob me. I had a hard time getting to the artists' room, and the jury could make it only one by one; some of them arrived slightly disheveled. Glazunov said some touching things. Madame Essipova thanked me for the Chopin, "which I shall never forget," she said.

The jury returned to their seats and resumed their duties. A Frenchman played well but indifferently.

The morning papers printed long articles about me. All, without exception, called me "the winner." One "liberal" daily, much read by Jews, went too far. The headlines said: "Golos naroda, golos bojyi" ("The voice of the people is God's voice!"); "It takes a Rubinstein to win the Rubinstein." The Warsaw press reprinted this exaggerated outcry. Pola, the Moszkowski family, and Paul sent me enthusiastic telegrams.

On the last day of the competition I spent the whole day listening to the five or six remaining pianists; among them were Borovsky, Hoehn, Isserlis (a Russian), and Emil Frey. Borovsky was a good pianist and a solid musician, but he lacked personality; everything he played was too deliberate and therefore uninspired. But his many friends from the Conservatory were warmly responsive to his playing.

For Hoehn's recital there was great anticipation. The story of the letter to the Tsarina was circulating among the audience, the sort of thing which led to rumors about Hoehn's being a natural son of the Grand Duke of Hesse. In reality Hoehn was a serious, unassuming young man. He chose for his Bach a slow and long fugue which requires much nuance and a variety of tone which he did not have, and so, in spite of his musically excellent performance, it sounded monotonous. His second piece was the greatest of all the Beethoven sonatas, the so-called *Hammerklavier*, Opus 106. He played this great work magnificently, as a mature master. This music was in him—it sounded as spontaneous as if he had just composed it. I was deeply impressed by the noble conception of the first movement and moved by the simply and beautifully played Adagio. The final, difficult fugue was splendid; the whole sonata was a masterly performance. After the sonata, Hoehn received a well-deserved ovation. The rest of his program was less interesting; he was not romantic enough for Schumann, nor did he have the right feeling for Chopin. And virtuoso pieces, such as a Liszt étude, were decidedly not in his vein.

Isserlis sounded dull after a personality of Hoehn's caliber, but Frey was quite marvelous. He had impressed the jury with his trio and was considered as the only candidate for the composition prize, but one had never expected him to be the fine pianist he revealed himself to be. His *Hammerklavier* Sonata was technically more perfect than Hoehn's, if not as moving, but the whole program he played was a sheer delight. This Swiss musician appeared to be my most dangerous rival; the public cheered him enthusiastically, and the jury looked puzzled!

The contest was over. Nobody moved. We all thought that the announcement of the prize winner would be made right away. Instead, Glazunov decided to postpone it until the next day, at two in the afternoon. It was cruel to make us spend twenty-four hours in such agony. My friend André Diederichs had a small party for me in his apartment; he had intended it as a celebration of my victory—a little prematurely, as it turned out. Anyway, the dinner was excellent, his guests were my faithful supporters, and André himself, who swore by me, seemed to have been very active on my behalf. He told me that Alexander Siloti, one of Liszt's last pupils, wanted me to be the soloist at two of his fashionable symphony concerts in St. Petersburg.

"I did not promise him anything yet," André said. "I hope to get something more substantial for you. But I didn't discourage him, either."

We sat, drank, and talked for half of the night. I had to wake up poor, hard-working Stefan Grostern at three in the morning, and I slept until noon. André came to fetch me at one for a quick *zakouska*, a Russian substantial hors d'oeuvre, and we went to the packed concert hall of the Conservatory. My entrance provoked a loud demonstration of enthusiasm which warmed my heart. It was two o'clock. We waited patiently for a whole hour, but nothing happened. Many of us went to the adjoining buffet for a cup of coffee. An attendant promised to call us when we were wanted. Another hour passed, there was no more coffee to be had, and still no news. Tired from sheer nervousness, we went back to the hall. It was after three full hours that Glazunov and the jury appeared on the stage. They were received in dead silence. Glazunov, pale and sweating, came to the fore and announced with a tremulous voice: "The prize for composition, two thousand rubles, conceded by unanimous vote to Mr. Emil Frey."

Ovation. Frey went up on the stage and received the congratulations of the jury, and a long applause from the public.

Glazunov continued: "The prize for pianists, two thousand rubles, conceded by unanimous vote to Alfred Hoehn."

There was a moment of stupor, soon followed by booing interspersed with bravos and clapping. Glazunov tried to stop the noise by raising his hands, implying that he had some more to say, but in vain. It took some time before he obtained silence. Speaking much louder, almost shouting, he announced: "A special first prize, a document of praise, unanimously conceded to Arthur Rubinstein," and, without interruption, "A special second prize, a document of praise, conceded to Alexander Borovsky," and he invited us—Hoehn, Borovsky, and me—to mount the platform and receive the compliments of the jury. The whole maneuver, so cleverly done, disconcerted the people. They finally understood that I shared the first prize with Hoehn but that he alone received the money. They did not approve the solution, but it calmed them down. André remained the only militant dissenter, shouting, "Shame! Shame!" As to myself, I went through a mixture of emotions and analytic thoughts. It would be pointless to deny that the general acclaim had made me sure of winning and that the verdict was a bitter disappointment. In my heart of hearts, however, I must confess that after hearing Hoehn's performance of the *Hammerklavier* Sonata, a work so much more important than my short

E Minor one, and, on top of it, after the fine recital of Frey, I became less confident of actually deserving the prize.

André Diederichs and I had one of the gloomiest dinners of my life. The Russian language is one of the richest in invective, and my friend showed his thorough command of it through the meal. He claimed, among other things, that the Tsarina had given the order and that the "swine" had obeyed!

I did not like such accusations.

"André," I said, "you seem to forget that Hoehn is a fine pianist and doesn't need anybody's influence. He won by merit."

He wouldn't listen to me; partisans are blind and deaf to arguments.

"Enough of this talk, André," I said, a little impatiently. "Your spite makes you unjust, and I am too tired."

He gave in and drove me to my quarters. Stefan Grostern was waiting for me.

"Guess who was here to see you?" he asked, and not waiting for my answer, he continued: "The police. A policeman brought back your passport with the order for you to leave in twenty-four hours, and he added, without a twinkle in his eye, 'Jews who have no exemptions must strictly obey this order.' When he left, I laughed."

I joined him, with loud guffaws. This "comic-relief" ending of my drama-filled day was just perfect.

"I shall leave tomorrow night for Warsaw," I said, "and, dear Stefan, I am glad to deliver you from the tiresome roommate I was!"

He protested, of course, but looked rather relieved. Early the next morning André entered the room with a bang.

"Arthur," he shouted, "you have won the competition in spite of all! You must leave tonight for Kharkov!"

The open-mouthed, puzzled expression of my face made him laugh. He came out with the whole story.

"Last night Serge Koussevitzky called me up from Kharkov. He wanted to know the result of the competition. My story of the injustice done to you angered him very much. He decided on the spur of the moment to compensate you for it. And here is what he proposes: an engagement for a concert tour in Russia, including two appearances at his symphony concerts in Moscow and Petersburg and, as an equivalent of the Rubinstein Prize, two thousand rubles as an advance on the tour."

No words could express my joy. I thought I was dreaming.

"That is not all," André continued. "Koussevitzky invites you to Diergatchi, his country place near Kharkov. He wants to meet you and discuss the details of his proposition."

I told him about the police. He laughed.

"So, these bastards remembered you suddenly, eh? Well, there is no time to lose, you must leave tonight for Kharkov. I shall announce your arrival to Koussevitzky and ask him to send a carriage for you."

I embraced him. I embraced Stefan, too. I could have embraced the whole world!

Koussevitzky was already well known in Europe as the best double-bass player of his time, an authentic virtuoso of this awkward instrument. Nikisch and other great conductors used to engage him as soloist at their concerts. He began his career as a first double-bass player in the Moscow Opera orchestra. A very wealthy and intelligent lady fell in love with the tall, good-looking young man who played so beautifully his instrument. Their love resulted in marriage. The young bride's wedding present was a full-fledged symphony orchestra of his name. After studying for a time with Nikisch, Koussevitzky opened a great season of concerts in Petersburg and Moscow. At the same time he set up a concert bureau in Moscow with representatives all over Russia; Diederichs was his agent in Petersburg. This was the situation in 1910, and Koussevitzky was the man who stood up for me so nobly. Everybody knows that he became later one of the great conductors and for twenty-five years the beloved music director of the glorious Boston Symphony Orchestra.

63

Diergatchi was a suburb of Kharkov; it took me less than half an hour to reach it by the horse carriage. Serge Koussevitzky and his wife received me most graciously in their simple but spacious villa. During dinner we talked about the Rubinstein competition, and I gave a full account of my role in it from the beginning in Warsaw until the surprise ending. What they liked best was my decision to fight Stolypin's decree and my secret victory.

"Aha, they didn't dare to touch you, eh?" he said, delightedly.

After I had had a restful night and a delicious breakfast, he took me to his study and told me about my concert tour.

"I want you to play the Rubinstein Concerto with me," he said. "It will be sensational. I heard wonders about your performance."

I frankly would have preferred to play a concerto of a greater importance, but I had to agree.

"My bureau will organize recitals for you in Moscow and Petersburg, Kiev and Odessa, and possibly in Kharkov."

"I promised André I would play the *Hammerklavier* Sonata at my recitals—I want to start working on it right away," I said.

"It is all right for the two capitals, but I wouldn't advise you to play it in the provinces."

When we were called to lunch, he reached into his pocket.

"Here is your ticket for Warsaw," he said. "Your train leaves at nine, so we will dine early. Oh, I must not forget." He opened a drawer of his desk, took out an envelope, and handed it to me.

"This is your Rubinstein Prize," he said, "but you will have to play for it again," he added, smilingly.

In the afternoon I opened the piano, a nice Blüthner, to try it. As they were both anxious to hear me, I played a whole concert program. Madame Koussevitzky, who impressed me as being very reserved and tight-lipped, showed a warm understanding for music and became much friendlier toward me. Her husband listened attentively and reacted not unlike Diederichs.

"You have the stuff for a great career," he said. "If you persevere in your work, there cannot be any doubt about it."

He drove with me to the station and kissed me goodbye on both cheeks. The journey took a night and half a day.

In Warsaw, my friends received me with congratulations mixed with indignation and rage. They accused the Russians of treachery. The most virulent among them was Antek Moszkowski.

"The members of the jury ought to be shot on sight," he declared with a ferocious grimace. The Koussevitzky sequence, however, changed their mood. I noticed with pleasure how the whole country had taken my side during the contest and that my popularity had grown considerably.

I found Pola looking pale and not feeling too well. She had had an invitation to go with friends to Zakopane, and I encouraged her to accept it in spite of this new separation. She dissuaded me from trying to join her there. The poor thing lived with the hope of getting back her children, and was still afraid to be seen in my company in too conspicuous places. Karol Szymanowski was planning to spend the rest of the summer in Tymoszovka and persuaded me to join him. We left a few days later. Before leaving, however, I was proud of being able to pay my debt to Mr. Shaniavsky of the Victoria hotel. And, it goes without saying, Kapnik received enough money to buy pills for a whole family.

Karol's mother and the rest of the family seemed to be happy to see me again. It was the same curriculum as before: mornings making music with Karol, then riding, then practicing alone or reading Karol's sonata and the new symphony; evenings playing cards or word games, going early to bed. I stayed more than four weeks, and it did me a lot of good.

Back in Warsaw at the Victoria, refreshed and revitalized, I began to work on the formidable *Hammerklavier* Sonata. The concert season was slow in starting, so I had some free time to dispose of. Pola came back a little later, feeling much better. We resumed our clandestine meetings; our love was unchanged.

A letter from Rome confirmed my engagement for a symphony concert at the Augusteo. The date was set for a late Sunday afternoon in January 1911, five days before my debut in Moscow. Count San Martino asked me to play two concertos of my choice and two or three solo pieces of Chopin in between. A big order, this, and, to boot, for a fee insufficient for the expenses. Anyway, I was proud and happy to appear in public in my beloved Rome!

The brighter outlook ahead encouraged me to enlarge my repertoire. This time I didn't need to be locked up. I liked to work on the new pieces. My social life, too, had taken a turn for the better. Thanks to the Petersburg success, I regained my previous popularity; "the *affaire*" was forgotten. As to concerts, I became fastidious and refused a number of poorly paid appearances in the provinces, and agreed to play only once in Warsaw and once in Lodz. In view of Rome and Russia I ordered some new clothes.

And so I spent a very rewarding autumn basking in my love and my work, and enjoying my friends' company.

In the middle of December I received a telegram from Koussevitzky: "On way to Berlin change trains in Warsaw please meet me at the station and bring programs of recitals." He added the date and the hour.

The train was on time. We drove to the other station, where we had a nice talk at the restaurant, drinking tea. He liked my programs, suggested some small changes, and left after half an hour.

My concert in Lodz had a dramatic interlude. The hall was well attended, my family sat expectantly in the first rows, and I was playing quite well when, suddenly, during the intermission, an uncle, looking pale and scared, came into the dressing room.

"The police are here. A policeman inquired about your military service. I begged him not to interrupt the concert and promised to arrange everything tomorrow morning. I had to give him your address, and he accepted a few rubles."

I finished the concert by a superhuman effort at self-control. Back at home the whole family was in a panic. The only way to deal with the situation was to bribe the policeman, which was risky, but in those days one had no alternative way of coping with the Russians. And it worked—for the price of five hundred rubles. The policeman promised to drop the inquiry. My first concern in Warsaw was to see the man who took care of my draft deferment for another year.

"You have nothing to worry about," he said. "I have the paper for this year, but I need seven hundred and fifty rubles to get one for the next year." My prize money began to dwindle, but the worst was to come. My poor Pola had to undergo an operation. It was urgent, she said, and she needed the money for it. There were a few days of terrible anxiety, but the operation went well, and Pola was recovering her health. Christmas with its traditional obligation of giving presents and the expensive celebration of the New Year finished by ruining me completely.

As the day approached for my departure for Rome and right after it for Moscow, I was penniless—I had no money left for my ticket or for my traveling expenses. I asked Paul, Antek, and his brother to lend me the necessary amount, but their pockets were just as empty as mine. I did obtain a decent passport, a French one, from Paul's friend Jean Styczyński, who happened to have been born in France. All I would need to do with it, Jean said, would be to get a new French visa for my return to Russia. "When you are in Vienna you can send a hotel boy to the consulate saying that a friend asked you to do it for him."

On the eve of the day on which it was imperative for me to leave, I became desperate and enraged. "It is too absurd to lose opportunities like Rome and Russia just for this stupid ticket money," I mumbled to myself, "and to have nobody able to help!"

Suddenly I remembered André Diederichs. The devoted friend! The representative of the Koussevitzky bureau! He could send me the money right away and get it back after my concert in Petersburg! I sent him a night telegram beseeching him to send immediately by telegraph five hundred rubles as advance on the Petersburg concert.

The earliest I could expect the money was by noon, but I couldn't close my eyes during the whole night. It was useless to try to sleep, to play, to read, or to eat. All I could do was to wait, to wait, to wait! Nothing by noon, nothing at one, nothing at two—I had given up when I heard a knock on my door. I opened it and there stood a postman—to me, an angel from heaven.

"Are you Arthur Rubinstein?" he asked in Russian. "Yes, I am," I said. "Do you expect money by telegraph?" he continued. "Yes, yes, I do, I do!" I shouted.

"From Moscow? A thousand rubles?" he asked.

For a split second I didn't answer, I was so taken by surprise. But in less than a second I calculated: André didn't have the money on hand, so he telephoned the bureau in Moscow which had made the elegant gesture of sending me twice the amount I had asked for.

"Yes, of course, yes!" I said.

He gave me the telegram and the postal check on the Bank of Commerce in Warsaw. I dressed in a hurry. The banks were closing at four. From that moment on, everything ran on schedule. With the money in my hands I felt again like a millionaire. I bought a return ticket (second class) to Rome, I invited Pola to a dinner de luxe in a private room of the Bristol, and later, at the Victoria, I offered a farewell bite with plenty of wodka to Paul and the Moszkowski brothers, and left at midnight for Vienna, where I arrived at noon of the next day. Straight from the station I drove to the Hotel Imperial for lunch; I knew the Austrian capital inside out. I said to the head porter, giving him my passport: "Please send a hotel man to the consulate of France and have this document visaed for Russia. My friend Mr. Styczyński is in the country and asked me to have it done."

I fortified my request with a few gulden. The man promised, and I went in for lunch. While I was having coffee, my emissary came back.

"I am sorry, sir," he said, returning the passport to me. "They refused to give the visa. They say that this gentleman did not do his military service in France."

My coffee stuck in my throat. This was a severe blow. There was absolutely no time for me on my return from Rome to struggle for a pass in Kraków or Lwów. I had to go straight to Moscow with a half-day stop in Warsaw. For the moment I could do nothing but wait gloomily in a café for the train to Rome.

The director of the Bertolini Splendid hotel in the Eternal City received me with an even brighter smile than on my previous visit; a poster hung in the hall, announcing my concert at the Augusteo, with my name in big letters. Count San Martino sent me a welcoming letter giving all the details about the concert, that I was to have three rehearsals, the conductor was Mr. Molinari, and the piano a Bechstein.

To my great regret I learned that Count Skrzynski was in Poland, and my thoughts turned to the only person who could help me with the passport—Modest Tchaikovski. I took my courage in both hands and telephoned him. He answered himself in the most friendly manner and accepted my shy invitation for lunch. To be correct, I sent a bellboy to deposit my visiting cards at the Leishmans', Rudinis', and Casatis', and, of course, at the home of Count San Martino.

Modest Tchaikovski arrived on time and kissed me on both cheeks in the Russian tradition. I took him to a nice restaurant where I used to lunch with Pola.

"I look forward to your concert," he said. "What are you going to play?"

"The Beethoven Concerto No. 4, the *Barcarolle*, a nocturne and the Polonaise, Opus 53, by Chopin, and, to finish, the G minor Saint-Saëns Concerto."

"A formidable program. Can I come to a rehearsal?" he asked.

"Of course, I shall be honored to have you."

Meanwhile, I was tortured at having to tell him my trouble with the passport. Should I tell him the truth? How would he react? His interest in my concert reassured me somehow. I told him honestly the facts, and this noble gentleman understood my predicament perfectly.

"I know the Russian consul very well," he said. "I shall try to explain the matter to him in a way he can understand. He might help you out."

He stopped my thanks with a large gesture, and smiled. "You can thank me when you get the paper. But now I shall go to the consulate. Wait for me at your hotel; I shall bring you the verdict."

I returned to the hotel with a much lighter heart. A windfall in the form of a letter from the Marchesa Rudini cheered me up. "Dear Rubinstein," she wrote, "can you come and dine with me tomorrow night at nine if you are free? And I hope you will play for me afterwards (professionally, of course). Yours, etc."

These two thousand lire were very welcome, considering the mean fee for the concert.

Tchaikovski arrived an hour later with a sad expression on his face, saying, "He refused, the nasty fellow, and, as if this were not enough, he told me in a severe tone that he will not denounce you as a special favor to me."

So that was that. A hopeless situation. Tchaikovski was desolate.

"Please don't despair," he said. "I must, I will find a way to help you out. I shall see you tonight at the rehearsal, and meanwhile I shall think of something." His sympathy touched me deeply, which was in itself a consolation.

The rehearsal in the magnificent Augusteo went very well. The conductor, Bernardino Molinari, was an expert accompanist, and the orchestra was with me from the start. Count San Martino, who heard only the Beethoven, expressed his satisfaction.

Tchaikovski declared that I was born to play with orchestra. "I hope to hear you play my brother's concerto one day." I promised to learn it. Then he went on: "Are you free on Saturday afternoon?" he asked. It was the day before the concert, and my last rehearsal was to be that Saturday, so I said yes.

"You see, we have here a small Russian club. It was formed by members of the Russian nobility who live here. Next Saturday, at four, we are invited to hear a lecture by Prince Serge Volkonsky, the intendant of the Imperial theaters in Petersburg. The Russian ambassador and his whole staff will be there. I want you to go with me as my guest. Something might turn up. . . ."

"And the consul?" I asked.

"He isn't a member and isn't invited."

I was skeptical, but I would have accepted any suggestion from Modest Tchaikovski. The Friday morning rehearsal was very long. Molinari worked out every detail and repeated many passages, especially in the Beethoven. He tired me out, but it was worthwhile.

I rested in the afternoon in order to be fresh for the concert at the Rudinis'. Dressed in my tails, white tie, black overcoat, and wearing my top hat, I drove to the Palazzo Barberini, and arrived at nine sharp. A butler opened the door, took my hat and coat, and said that the Marchesa would be ready in a few minutes. I thought that I had mistaken the hour and was too early. He showed me the way through a long gallery of salons leading to a small boudoir, where a young man, dressed in a dinner jacket, was reading a book. I bowed, and he bowed politely but continued to read. I took a seat and waited, as if I were at a dentist's.

After a while we started talking in French. He was an Argentine, and spoke with a strong accent: "I am here for pleasure," he said. "Life in Buenos Aires is dull, and Rome and Paris are the only cities where one can find some amusement."

Here was a young man who knew what he wanted. He was handsome, too, with his Spanish-type black hair with sideburns, and strong eyebrows. Our small talk was interrupted by the entrance of the Marchesa, beautiful as ever, dressed in a house gown.

"Oh, dear Rubinstein, I am so happy to see you again," she said, holding out both hands to me. "You don't mind, I hope, dining informally *en trois* with my dear friend." (She introduced us, but I forget his name.)

Aha, I thought, the party will take place very late, probably around midnight!

We entered the dining room, rather a sort of breakfast room, and were served a dinner, a grand dinner with desserts, wines, and all. I hardly ate at all, and refused the wine, thinking of the party and my playing. However, I began to feel a little uncomfortable. Dora Rudini had not uttered a word about the concert, nor when, where, and how it was going to be. When I inquired politely about the Marchese, she answered with a smile: "Oh, you did not know. We are separated."

The conversation at dinner was of no interest. They talked of sports, racing, and gossip. The young man mentioned parties, dances, and the merit and character of the tango, and I told some stories about Russia and Poland. When coffee was served, she ordered the butler to take it to the music room. We went to one of the larger salons, where Dora and the Argentine sat down on a sofa, with me in an armchair facing them, and the coffee table between us. There we sat in silence, sipping our coffee, when Dora said, with her endearing charm: "Caro Arturo, play for us, please. I would love to hear again the *Barcarolle* of Chopin, which I loved so much at my party." Only now did I understand. *This* was the *party!*

The piano was behind me. I hadn't noticed it because it was covered by all sorts of objects—flowers, photos, and books. "I hope you will like my piano. I bought it only recently," she said. All three of us cleaned the instrument of its encumbrances, and I sat down to try it. It was a good Blüthner, and it was in tune. Dora and her friend went back to the sofa, and I started the *Barcarolle*. As they sat behind me, I was supposed not to see them. But the glossy lid of the piano shines like a mirror. So, while I was playing, I saw Dora, apparently excited by the music, kiss her beau passionately, clinging to him, while he, evidently less musical, seemed to respond to her caresses, but without élan. My own position was most embarrassing. I did not quite know what to make of it. The situation reminded me of the French farce *Chopin*. Should I have felt offended for being treated as a paid *exciteur* or be proud that my music was capable of inspiring love? Anyway, I continued to play, and played with pleasure. Music makes me forget everything else. But I want to reassure the reader: my "public" didn't go *too far*.

I left about midnight. Dora Rudini, recovering her cool, charming poise, kissed me good night, the Argentine shook hands with the dignity of a Spanish hidalgo, and in the entrance hall the butler helped me into my coat and gave me my hat and an envelope. I returned to the Splendid richer by two thousand lire.

64

The last rehearsal on Saturday morning was excellent. I learned to appreciate the slow, careful preparation for a concert with three rehearsals after the hurried single ones which I had had to endure so often.

Tchaikovski, who was enraptured by our performance, invited me for lunch.

"I want to give you some additional information about the Russian club," he said. "There is a little detail which will interest you. After his last concert in Rome, Anton Rubinstein left his piano as a gift to the club. If it so happens that the lecture isn't too long, there might be an opportunity for you to give them a little concert on the 'Rubinstein Piano.' With the ambassador present, something might come out of it. Not a bad idea, eh?" He laughed, pleased with himself.

The Russian club was a sober-looking gray building in a quiet street. The entrance hall led straight into a large music room. An elegant audience of not more than a hundred occupied a few rows of comfortable seats. A high desk was set up on one side of the podium; the piano stood in the center. Tchaikovski and I took two seats in the rear.

Prince Serge Volkonsky approached the desk, threw down a fat pile of written sheets of paper, took a long draft of water, lit a small table reflector, and began his lecture. The subject was the history of the theater and the art of acting. His delivery was halting, and his voice was monotonous, with a touch of haughtiness and pedantry. The effect was soporific, and after an hour I saw many heads lowered in discreet slumber. When the lecture was over, a tired applause rewarded the lecturer, and the members of the audience rose to their feet. As a much needed outlet, they burst into loud, animated conversations. While coffee was served, Tchaikovski took me to the place where the ambassador greeted his friends. Prince Dolgorouky, the Russian ambassador, was the very prototype of the old-fashioned elderly aristocrat, tall and slender, with his well-shaped eagle nose, short mustache *en brosse*, and a very large monocle in one of his light-blue, deep-set eyes. He wore a dark morning coat, striped gray trousers, a white waistcoat, a hard white collar, and a tie-plastron held together by a black pearl pin.

Modest Tchaikovski introduced me to this elegant gentleman: "Excellency, this is a very talented young pianist, and his name is Rubinstein."

"Ah, ah, ah, how interesting, and the same name? And also a pianist, ah, ah."

"If it is not inconvenient for Your Excellency and if the other members of the club agree, the young Rubinstein would love to play some Russian music on this, for him, sacred piano of the never to be forgotten Anton Grigorievitch."

Tchaikovski uttered these words unctuously, in spite of having been, like his brother, rather antagonistic toward Anton Rubinstein.

"Ah, ah, mais c'est charmant! Of course we want to hear the young man."

The piano was an old Russian-made Becker, but it was in tune. I played all the possible Russian music I knew. Two preludes and an étude by Scriabin, a famous prelude by Rachmaninoff, and something by Medtner.

After the deadly dull lecture, the music had a most vivifying effect on these people. My success reminded me of Petersburg, and of the fact that no public in the world reacts to music like the Russians.

The ambassador, in his enthusiasm, dropped his monocle.

"Ah, ah, bravo, bravo, how beautiful, how exquisite, how charming!"

I poked a finger in Tchaikovski's back.

"Excellency," he started (it was the right moment), "this poor young man had a terrible thing happen to him; he lost his passport. Tomorrow he plays at the Augusteo, and Monday, early in the morning, he must leave directly for Moscow, where his concert tour begins with a great concert with orchestra."

"How sad, ah, how sad!" the Prince said with deep sympathy, and then, smiling again: "The consul will help him out right away, I am sure of it, ah, ah?"

"The consulate is closed until Monday morning, and the consul himself is absent," my advocate lied shamelessly.

"Ah, oh, oh, there must be a way—they are waiting for him in Moscow, he must get there!"

Honestly concerned, the ambassador called a young attaché of the embassy. The two whispered together for some time, the Prince interrupting from time to time the other man's whispers with short exclamations like: "Why not?" "Pour un seul passage!" "Ah, ah, never mind." After his short consultation, the ambassador turned toward me and said in the most gracious way: "Young Rubinstein, ah, ah, I am coming to your concert tomorrow, and I will bring you a nice present, ha, ha, ah, ah!"

This kind of graciousness is the endearing side of the true aristocrat. We left the club, Tchaikovski and I, in a hopeful mood.

"He will bring you a little note signed by him, and it will be good enough for the frontier, so you needn't worry any more," Tchaikovski said.

My debut in Rome was a great event for me, and it remains an unforgettable one. It was the beginning of a love affair between the Italian public and myself which has lasted until this late day of my life.

The concert started with the Beethoven Concerto which went very well but lacked the ultimate inspiration. Both Molinari and I were distracted by noises, latecomers, and a parterre filled with the not-too-musical *grand monde*. Fortunately, the balcony was packed with music students and music lovers. My next number was a solo, three Chopin pieces. The first one, the *Barcarolle*, was always a great favorite of mine which never fails to inspire me for the rest of my program. And it did not let me down on that occasion. As I played the last notes, the audience was with me, making me bow three or four times before I could play the Nocturne. From that moment on, my success grew until it reached an explosion of enthusiasm after the A flat Polonaise. The balcony shouted and yelled: "Bravo, bis, bis, bravo." I left the stage at intermission time, but the public did not stop yelling "Bis." I had to bow five or six times to a growing demand for an encore, which I reserve for the end of the concert. Suddenly, behind the stage, appeared a breathless Maestro Sgambati, who screamed at me: "Presto, presto, play something. They are getting furious—they might do something to you!" He scared me. I rushed to the piano and played an étude of Chopin which appeased the dynamic temper of the Italian public.

Prince Dolgorouky, escorted by Modest Tchaikovski, entered my dressing room. The ambassador, very impressed by my success, kissed me on both cheeks.

"Ah, ah, you bad boy, you made me cry, ah!" He gave me a large envelope.

"And here is my present, my dear." He called the same young attaché who stood in the corridor. "Take from the young man the data which he needs and put it all into the document. I have signed it already."

As I started to utter some words of thanks, he stopped me with a large gesture of his hand.

"Ah, ah, no thanks, no thanks, it is nothing. When you have passed the frontier, just tear up the paper and get another passport; all this is nothing, ha, ha, but you made me cry, ah, ah!" And he left. The attaché took a large paper out of the envelope and asked me where I was born and how old I was.

"This is a diplomatic passport," he said casually, "and I must fill it out."

After a second of hesitation, I answered calmly: "Born in Warsaw in

1889," quickly making myself younger than the draft age. He wrote it in and handed me the document. On a large stiff sheet of paper the text, written in Russian (and also in French), read: "Number 1—In the name of His Imperial Majesty Nicholas II, Tsar of all Russias, we beg to give aid and protection to our subject Arthur Rubinstein," and the date. It was signed by Prince Dolgorouky himself. An unbelievable thing! Even Tchaikovski was slightly abashed.

"I didn't expect him to do a thing like that."

The Saint-Saëns Concerto went as if it were a tornado. Molinari and I had to bow endlessly, and I had to play two more encores. Many new friends came to compliment us, and Maestro Sgambati said with a smile: "I saved your life—you might have been killed by one of your enthusiasts."

Count San Martino offered me a date for the next season, and I took leave of Modest Ilyitch with my heart overflowing with gratitude. I have never forgotten the generous understanding by this great gentleman of a delicate and controversial case, considering that he was a Russian patriot and I, at heart, a subversive Russian subject.

My return journey to Poland was long and tedious. The miraculous document, however, burned in my pocket. "It is too good to be true," goes the saying: Does it apply to my passport? Will they arrest me for carrying illegally such a document? Tormenting thoughts of this kind occupied my mind until we reached the Russian frontier. With my heart beating fast and with my hand trembling I delivered the ominous sheet. The gendarme opened it, read it carefully, folded it, and gave it back to me with a military salute and a click of his heels. He took me out to the buffet, invited me to sit down, and ordered tea and *zakouska* to be served to me immediately. To admit that I was impressed would be an understatement. All I can say is that I gained considerable respect for my diplomatic passport and decided not to tear it up.

When I got back to Warsaw the greatest puzzle awaited me. I found at the Victoria hotel a telegram from André Diederichs: "Have just returned from two-week vacation in Finland and find your urgent telegram stop if you still need the money wire and I send it immediately affectionately André."

An incredible mystery! I couldn't make heads or tails of it. How the devil could I receive money from Moscow when Diederichs did not receive my request for it? Pola and Zosia, Paul, and the Moszkowskis were overwhelmed by both my impressive passport and this latest mystery. Anyway, I had to leave for Moscow. They all saw me off and wished me luck. Pola was disconsolate; this one was going to be a long separation.

I arrived in the old capital of Russia on a bitterly cold morning. On the train, looking out the window, I saw nothing but snow-covered plains, a desolate land, and poor peasant huts. Even the cities we passed looked sad and cold.

Mr. Avierino, the director of the Koussevitzky bureau, and an excellent viola player whom I had known in Warsaw, was at the station. On our way to the Hotel Metropole he explained to me the riddle of the money: a fantastic comedy of errors, a most impossible, improbable *deus ex machina*.

"Do you remember having seen Koussevitzky in Warsaw when he was on his way to Berlin?" he asked.

"Yes, of course."

"Well, here is the story. A few days after you two met, I received from him a telegram at the bureau which said: 'Send by express telegram thousand rubles Rubinstein saw in Warsaw everything in order Koussevitzky.' He left out the word 'stop' between 'rubles' and 'Rubinstein.' You see? And I was the damn fool who read the wire carelessly, and sent the money to you instead of to him! When I read his wire more attentively it was too late!" And I had got it on the very day!

The disagreeable sequel to the affair was that I had to reimburse the thousand rubles to Avierino. I gave him five hundred on account, which almost emptied my pockets, and the rest was to come from the future concerts in Russia.

Koussevitzky introduced me in the most charming terms to his orchestra. As we rehearsed the Rubinstein Concerto, I found to my great regret that he was not as good an accompanist as I thought. After the rehearsal he took me to lunch at his house, where his wife received me very graciously.

The concert at the great Hall of the Nobility took place on the next day, in the evening. The house was full. The Concerto had a great success, especially the first movement, but I felt that a Beethoven, Chopin, or Saint-Saëns would have introduced me much better. At the Rubinstein competition there was a sentimental element present which was missing at a public concert in as musical a city as Moscow.

The critics liked my performance but reserved their final appraisal for my recital.

Our program was repeated two days later in St. Petersburg, at the beautiful Dvorjanskoye Sobraniye—the Hall of Nobility. Here I received a heartwarming welcome from my fans even before I played. The performance itself had more or less the same reception as in Moscow. The Rubinstein Concerto is definitely not attuned to my musical sensibility: it lacks inspiration; it is simply a vehicle for a good interpreter. Still, my performance gave it its due, and my success was quite legitimate.

André Diederichs was pleased; so was Koussevitzky. The three of us had supper after the concert, at which the talk was mainly about the story of the thousand rubles.

My two recitals in both capitals were by far more interesting. The inclusion of the *Hammerklavier* Sonata was much commented on. All the critics made too obvious comparisons between my conception of this work and Hoehn's. Some of them found mine too romantic, others thought Hoehn's less exciting. The truth is that we were both right.

"How is it possible?" asked André Diederichs, my unconditional partisan.

"I can prove it," I answered. "André, if you ask ten famous artists to paint you, your face will be *different* on each picture, but the painters will assure you that they *interpreted* your face exactly as they see you."

"All right, I agree," said André, "but where is the link with music?"

"It is obvious," I said. "You see, André, each creative work becomes a part of the universe, just like a flower, or a human being. Consequently, a sonata sounds *different* to each gifted interpreter. This is the real mission of our particular talents. Nietzsche, in his book *The Birth of Tragedy*, calls music Dionysian, and all the other arts Apollonian, explaining that they *interpret* nature, or their visions and ideas, while music is an independent metaphysical force of creation. I like his metaphor. And, in my own immodest way, I consider the great creators of music as the Dionysians and us, their interpreters, as the Apollonians."

I smiled, a little ashamed of my pretentious lecture.

André seemed impressed, but he still insisted that my conception of the Sonata was the right one.

"I can see your point, André," I said, "and it is interesting, because the most important thing for us is to be able to *persuade* our public, and we try hard to achieve it."

Back in Moscow, the Sonata had a much greater success; they had not heard Hoehn!

My recitals in both cities went very well, the public showing a warm appreciation, at some moments even enthusiasm, but my success was not what I would call sensational. There was a reason for it. For once, my name rather hurt me than helped me. Josef Hofmann, in those times, held a pianistic monopoly in Russia. Having been a pupil of Anton Rubinstein, this legendary idol of the country, he was generally accepted as the rightful successor of the great man, a fact which made me appear as a false pretender to the sacred name.

Nevertheless, my success was established and my return assured. I stayed in Moscow for more than a week.

My first impression of this ancient capital of Russia was disconcerting. Instead of the brilliant, London-like metropolis that I expected to see, I found a city which looked as if it were an amalgamation of small townships and villages, built around a medieval fortress and castle, the Kreml (Kremlin), protected by an inaccessible wall. The modern, beautifully planned St. Petersburg and the shapeless, somewhat Asiatic Moscow seemed to belong to two distinct countries. Yet, the exterior ugliness of the latter was compensated by the intense inner life and the character of its inhabitants. The town belonged to the merchants. One saw many of them in the traditional garb of the muzhiks, their trousers tucked into high boots, shirts with colored hems, the collars buttoned on the side. Their heavy coats were lined with cheap, smelly furs. Most of them had long beards and wore their hair parted in the middle. Even the rich among them did not disdain this attire, but their long fur coats were made of sable, astrakhan, or seal. At the same time, some of them had an acute sense for beauty. The merchants Morosoff and Shtchoukine bought up whole exhibitions of French Impressionists at a time when Frenchmen were still slow in their appreciation of these masters. A museum built by these two men contained one of the finest collections of Cézanne, Renoir, Monet, Manet, Degas, Pissarro, Gauguin, Van Gogh, and already some paintings by Picasso and Matisse.

Moscow was proud of its Bolshoi Opera, where Chaliapin and the tenor Sobinov were the great stars. The Imperial Conservatory which was created by Nicholas Rubinstein with Tchaikovski as its professor of composition continued their great tradition.

My unbounded admiration, however, went to the Moscow Art Theater of Stanislavski and Nemirovitch-Dantchenko. They had created it in honor of Chekhov, who wrote for the opening *The Seagull*, which became the emblem of their theater. I saw there several plays, among them *The Cherry Orchard*, an unforgettable evening. There were no stars; every actor or actress had to play big or small roles as befitted his or her individual personality.

Thinking back on those days, I remember an amusing sample of the culinary habits in this fascinating city. A friend of Koussevitzky invited me to lunch with him at one of the best restaurants. We arrived there at one o'clock and went straight to the buffet bar, where about thirty delicious hot and cold hors d'oeuvres were lined up, surrounding several tiers of trays with small vodka glasses that looked inviting to the thirsty Moscovites. After having enjoyed these tidbits for a long while, we took a table in the dining room.

"What do you recommend?" my host asked the headwaiter.

"We have a fine choice of fish," he said, and showed us a large tank, from which we selected a big, lively one.

"It will be ready in an hour," he said.

"Let us play a game of billiards while we are waiting," said my companion. We played for more than an hour.

"Your fish is ready," announced the waiter. We returned to our table and ate it with delight. The same procedure took place with the next course, the meat. We chose a chunk of raw beef to be cooked, and went back to the billiard table for another hour. The preparation of an elaborate dessert allowed us to play two long games of piquet. We washed down the whole meal with a fine French Burgundy. This luncheon lasted until nine in the evening and must have cost a fortune.

My tour took me to Kharkov and Rostov on the Don River. I had been engaged in both cities by the Imperial Russian Society of Music. Both cities received me with a genuine enthusiasm. There is nothing to be said about either of them. The hotels were primitive and uncomfortable, and the people in the streets and in the concert hall looked drab and unrefined. My next and last stop was Kiev, which I remembered from my previous visit. This concert was arranged by the Moscow bureau of Koussevitzky and managed by a Pole, Mr. Idzikowski, the owner of a large book and music shop. I arrived in this capital of the Ukraine on the morning of the concert. It was a bitterly cold day. After a hot bath and breakfast I went to see Mr. Idzikowski, an elderly little man with an intelligent face, who received me in his private office.

"We are so glad to have you play in Kiev," he said, "but it is a pity that you don't have anything of Szymanowski on the program. We have here quite a large Polish population and they showed great interest in our young composer."

"How wonderful!" I exclaimed. "Kiev seems to know more about Szymanowski than Warsaw. Please, put the *Variations* of Szymanowski on the program instead of the Schumann."

He smiled. "I am afraid you will have a poor house tonight. You see, the public doesn't know you, but I feel sure that the change of the program will help a little. I have heard you in Warsaw, and I predict a great success."

He took me to the hall, which belonged to the Kiev Merchants Club. Situated in the city park, it had fine proportions and perfect acoustics and looked very engaging. The piano, a good Bechstein, was in tune. I worked on it for an hour or so, had a light lunch, and took a long rest. To play Karol's *Variations* for an understanding public was a pleasure I was looking forward to.

In the evening, at concert time, I found the hall practically empty. Besides some young people in the standing room, there was a scattering of no more than fifty people in the hall. I felt pretty depressed but even more determined to play my best. In contrast to many of my colleagues who act "offended" facing a small audience, I always considered the few people present as the selected representatives of a full house. And so I played my Beethoven Sonata which opened the program with care and love. My small gathering proved to be a musical elite, who showed full understanding for the music I was playing. After the Sonata, the door opened and eight or nine persons, dressed in evening clothes, came in and occupied seats in the front row. They looked a little shy about being late, but I smiled, putting them at ease.

The next piece was the Szymanowski. I loved this work and played it with all my heart. It was received with respect but without warmth. Only the newcomers applauded enthusiastically, and during intermission one of them came to the artists' room and introduced himself as a Count Pruszynski, a Pole. He spoke French better than Polish and excused himself and his companions for having missed the beginning of the concert.

"Concerts in Kiev start too early," he said, "il faut bien dîner, n'est-ce pas? We came to hear you, but especially the music by Szymanowski. Dmitry Lvovitch Davydov and his wife are his neighbors and great friends, and ils m'ont chargé de vous inviter à souper avec nous après le concert."

I gladly accepted; his friends intrigued me—they looked attractive and interesting.

The end of the program was a great success. My young public left the standing room, came to the front of the podium, and shouted for more and more. They calmed down only after my fourth encore.

Count Pruszynski was indignant.

"What bad manners they have! To force you to play and to stand in front of us as if the place belonged to them."

I laughed. "Don't blame them too much, Count, I happen to like this kind of manners at my concerts."

He took me to the restaurant of the Grand Hotel, where we found his companions waiting for us. A surprise was in store for me: Dmitry Davydov was the nephew of the composer Tchaikovski and, consequently, of my friend Modest Tchaikovski to whom I owed so much. His wife Nathalie proved to be one of those rare human beings one cannot forget—a person who emanated a luminosity, a nobility of heart and intelligence, which captivated me immediately. Their friends were interesting and lively, and the supper at the Grand Hotel was the beginning of a friendship which I cherish in my memory. Moreover, all of them banded together and insisted that I could not leave Kiev without giving the people another chance to hear me. When I asked pessimistically how did they know whether anyone would come this time, I was told: "Dmitry Davydov is the president of the Ukranian nobility, and Goudim-Levkovitch, his brother-in-law, is the son-in-law of General Trepov, the governor of the Ukraine. The two of them are able to fill ten halls in Kiev."

That stopped my arguments. I promised to see Idzikowski about a second concert. The poor man received me with a sad face.

"The Koussevitzky bureau lost a little money yesterday," he said. "I hope you will have better luck next year."

When I told him my plans and the names of my sponsors, he clapped his hands and in Polish used the expression for good luck: "Pan się w czepku urodził!" (You were born with a bonnet).

He announced the concert for the end of the week, and I had five days to prepare my program. The Davydovs adopted me the whole time I was in Kiev; I spent my days in their house, practiced on their piano, and had my meals with them. They gave a great reception at which they introduced me to Kiev society. On the day of the concert every seat was taken. It was a brilliant evening, with the governor in his uniform, bedecked with medals, sitting in the first row, surrounded by his aides-de-camp and their wives and all the prominent people of the city. I played much Chopin, which had an enormous success. As I learned from himself, later, Vladimir Horowitz, then a little boy, was brought to hear me. Dmitry Lvovitch and his wife gave a great party at the Grand Hotel.

Idzikowski was exultant.

"We must announce another concert right away," he exclaimed. "A whole Chopin recital."

Altogether I gave four concerts in Kiev. The last two were just as successful as the second one. The capital of the Ukraine was my only real Russian conquest. When I settled my accounts with Idzikowski, expecting to receive a large amount, he gave me an accounting of less than a thousand rubles.

"Is that all I have earned for three sold-out concerts?" I asked.

"I am the representative of the Koussevitzky office," he replied, "and they sent me a whole bill against you. I had to deduct the deficit of the first concert and the five hundred rubles you received in Warsaw. And, besides, the expenses for the four Kiev concerts were very heavy."

I had to believe him and take the money against my better judgment, but I promised myself for the future to watch the box office with more attention.

The Davydovs insisted I should spend the summer or a part of it at their country place, Verbovka, and I promised, of course; we liked each other better every day.

Count Pruszynski was an excellent guide. He showed me the city, which was not beautiful but very interesting. There was a huge underground monastery called the Lavra where the monks kept billions of rubles in gold, and when some of the Tsars were in need of money they had to beg these monks for it. The city was built on a hill overlooking the majestic river Dnieper. The Sobor of St. Michael was a magnificent piece of architecture, with an interior rich in stained-glass windows, golden and jeweled objects, and fine mosaics.

One morning, Count Pruszynski, gay and relaxed, invited me to accompany him to a Russian *banya*, or steambath. "The Russian Banya is the best institution in Kiev," he said in a mocking tone. "C'est tout simplement merveilleux." Being curious, I accepted, in spite of my dislike of sweat.

A nice building on the main street harbored the Russian Bath. We entered a large hall laid out in marble where a tall, athletic man, wearing a white apron, led us to a smaller room and asked if we wished a sweat or another kind of bath, a shower or a massage.

Count Pruszynski said in his broken Russian: "Krassivoyou jenshtchinou dlia nievo e maltchika dlia menia" (a pretty woman for him and a boy for me).

Aha! Suddenly I understood his predilection for these places, and his "choice" was no surprise to me: I had been informed about his homosexual habits. What shocked me was his rather high-handed method. However, I was curious to see the young woman he asked to have provided for me. He himself was assigned to another room, and I was left, waiting. After a while, a tall, heavily built woman entered the darkened room. At a close look I saw to my horror that she was in the last months of pregnancy! When I recovered from my shock I told her in a kind way that it would be better for me to resist the temptation and for her to give up violent exercises for the time being. She smiled gratefully when I gave her a few rubles for the lost time.

Pruszynski, when I told him my misadventure, became red with anger.

"Ces bandits, ces voleurs," he cursed. "They will never see me again. Do you want to try another *banya*?"

"No, thank you," I said.

My last evening in Kiev was a small party at the Davydovs', where I played until late in the night.

"We expect you in Verbovka!" they shouted at my departure.

65

In Warsaw, on the morning of my arrival, Pola was at the station. A telegram from Kiev announcing my return was the only news she had had from me since Moscow. It had been entirely my fault. My inveterate hatred for writing letters developed into a vicious practice of postponing ad infinitum my most urgent correspondence. No wonder I found her reproaching me bitterly for my lack of heart but still happy to find me the same as when I left. Anyway, she knew all about me: Joseph Jaroszynski had given her a full account of my success in Kiev.

My usual program began right away. Concerts in the provinces, one or two in Warsaw, one with orchestra, and a recital with Paul.

Karol and Joseph were in town, the former delighted by my friendship with Mrs. Davydov, whom he loved, and the latter proud of my success in "his" city.

The Warsaw spring was, as usual, irresistible, and I took advantage of every minute of it. I made the round of the theaters, of charming dinner parties, of gay suppers with my friends, and we had, of course, long sessions of music with Paul and his brother.

One afternoon, while playing billiards at Lourse's, Paul said, in his casual way: "Don't laugh, Arthur, I have a good surprise for you—I am going to get married."

I looked at him incredulously.

"And whom, please, are you going to marry?"

"Our Zosia, of course," he said. "It is official."

I could hardly believe my ears. In all those years I had never noticed in him the slightest sign of love, or even of a simple attraction, for her. He never changed his manner of treating her as a good and useful pal. As for Zosia, I was quite sure that she was not in love with Paul, and with good reason, for she had confided to me her passionate love for Kazio, the oldest of the four Barylski brothers.

"Paul," I said cautiously, "think it over carefully; in my opinion you are making a big mistake."

"Don't be so pessimistic," he replied. "Zosia declared that she feels proud to become my wife, and her whole family is happy about it. Her father made me a present of a wonderful Stradivarius violin he bought in Russia."

The thought crossed my mind that this gift might have been the determining factor in Paul's decision. I kept silent, but remained categorically opposed to this union. And I refused to attend Paul's wedding. He swallowed the humiliation and came, on *his wedding day*, as usual, to join our billiard game.

My passion for life was never greater than on that spring. I was a happy man! And I dare say that I still am the happiest person I have ever met. A statement as pretentious as that sort needs explaining. My conception of happiness was born on that sad day in Berlin soon after my attempt at suicide. It had been a sudden revelation, and ever since that time I had learned to love life *unconditionally*.

Most people, in my opinion, have an unrealistic approach toward happiness because they invariably use the fatal conjunction "if" as a condition. You hear them say: I would be happy *if* I were rich, or *if* this girl loved me, or *if* I had talent, or, their most popular "if": *if* I had good health. They often attain their goal, but they discover soon some new "ifs."

We are born into an unfathomable, unaccountable, illogical, absurd, and dangerous world with the unanswered question: Who or what created it and for what ends was it created? As for myself, I love life for better or for worse, unconditionally, because in my eyes it is the only modus vivendi.

I remember the charming story of the emperor who was advised by his astrologer to wear a shirt belonging to a happy man. After a long search for such a man, a peasant was found who declared himself to be perfectly happy, but . . . he had no shirt.

Far from me to pretend that I have an exceptional constitution and fortitude, or that I am able to "smile in the face of adversity." On the contrary, I am as much a prey to nervous depressions, to outbursts of anger or impatience, as anybody else, with the only difference being that my subconscious accepts them as a necessary *contrast* to the state of euphoria.

Life can deprive us of freedom, of health, of fortune, of friends, of family, of success, but cannot take away from us our thoughts or our imagination, and there is always love, music, art, flowers, and books. And the passionate *interest* in everything.

It may sound paradoxical that my conscious love of life was really born in Berlin on that unhappiest day of my life.

Antek and Wacek Moszkowski invited me to visit a great friend of their family, Dr. Goldflam, who wanted to meet me. He was a man of an exceptional quality: a noted doctor of medicine, rich by inheritance, who practiced without remuneration and preferred to care for the under-privileged.

We went one evening after dinner to his apartment in a fine old house which belonged to him. The doctor opened the door himself and greeted me very cordially, and I noticed immediately that his dark eyes and his face bore the marks of wisdom and kindness.

"Ah, I have the pleasure of meeting you at last! I have heard you so often, and Antek has told me so much about you!"

I felt at ease, right away. He was a tall, alert man in his fifties, grayish, who looked younger than his age. In his spacious library, where he served us coffee and cakes, he showed me his fine collection of small bronzes, including a lovely Rodin.

"These bronzes are my passion," he said. "They are the companions in my solitude. I am a bachelor, you know. I have never had the time for marriage—my patients keep me too busy."

His vast library and the quality of the books bore testimony to the fact that Dr. Goldflam was a well-read man. Conversation with him was extremely interesting. We touched on every imaginable subject, delighted to find some points for discussion. He seemed to be omniscient; his arguments were those of a professional.

Antek, at one moment, opened up the question of anti-Semitism in general, and in Poland in particular, a frequent subject of conversation among Jews. My point of view was that anti-Semitism, in many ways, was justifiable.

"When I see these rich Jews and their wives behaving in public the way they do, showing off their wealth, their jewels, their furs, pushing themselves forward wherever they go, I can understand the indignation of the Gentiles."

Goldflam answered softly: "You seem to forget that the Jews you mention represent only a small minority. Your criticism cannot apply to the whole Jewish race."

It may be that my years spent among soft-spoken Protestants and distinguished Catholics had a bearing on my judgment.

"All right, doctor, all right," I argued hotly, "but what have we on the other hand? The ghettos? These masses of meek little men with their beards and side curls, afraid of everything and everybody? Why don't they use their born gifts and intelligence for something better than buying and selling old clothes? It infuriates me when anti-Semitic Poles slander us, calling us Jews usurers and thieves. I know that we have, fortunately, a highly cultured elite, too, and I would like to vote for you, doctor, as its president, but it is too small—it is unable to offset the bad effect of the rest."

The doctor became sad and serious. After a pause, he said in a low voice: "I am sorry to hear your pessimistic opinion of our race. There is much true observation in what you said, but have you ever tried to think about the causes of all these phenomena which you criticize so harshly?"

I had to admit that I was only aware of the results.

"Then you must promise to read with attention a few books I am going to send you. After reading them, bring them back, and we will continue our discussion."

"I love good books more than anything, doctor, and I promise to read them and take good care of them."

On the way home I regretted having been so outspoken to a man whom I had learned to respect and admire.

The doctor sent me four volumes of *The History of the Jews* by Heinrich Graetz, in German. I spent a whole week or more, mostly in bed, reading them. The origin of our race and the biblical era presented nothing new to me: I was quite well informed on that subject, the principal feasts of the Jews were always reminders of the main historical incidents, and, besides, I remembered the essence of my Berlin lessons in religion. However, when I read the description of the terrible war against the Romans under the Emperor Titus, the heroic defense of the Jews, the destruction of the Second Temple, and the beginning of the Diaspora, my interest grew from chapter to chapter, and developed into a feverish impatience to know more. I hated to put the book down.

When I finally finished the four volumes, a great change in my outlook on the Jewish question had taken place: I was acutely conscious of being proud to be a Jew. And I shall never be grateful enough to Dr. Goldflam for opening my eyes to the real, fundamental character of the Jews.

Living in exile for two thousand years, they kept heroically their racial and religious identity. Ostracism, persecutions, inquisitions, tortures, killings, expulsions—nothing could break their stubborn resistance and their faith in their destiny.

I took the books back to Dr. Goldflam, who was busy with his patients, but he invited me to dine with him that same evening. This time our conversation was a happy exchange of ideas and observations. He said: "The characteristic thing about the anti-Semites throughout the world is that they gladly tolerate the kind of Jews you criticized the other day; they even like them. They are impressed by the wealthy Jew: money has an immense power. The scions of the finest and most noble Christian families often marry the daughters of rich Jews. They do not mind even the so-called usurers, the bankers who lend them money; they need them. As to the others, the ghetto Jews, well, they are considered an inferior human race; the anti-Semites like to treat them kindly and protectively, as they treat servants or slaves."

"So, when we look at it closely," I said, "their real hatred is concentrated on the Jews who possess the highest standards of ethics, intelligence, and talents, on those who, whenever allowed to compete, become prominent in all possible fields like science, art, or economy. They hate them for their refusal to be absorbed by the nations where they live, for their devotion to their families, for their sobriety, for their charity. To the true anti-Semite, all these characteristic traits are simply unacceptable."

Dr. Goldflam smiled. "Doctor," I asked, "don't you think that at the bottom of it there is a lot of envy?"

"Yes, of course," he answered. "Envy is a poisonous state of mind which can lead to crime, not only to slander and injustice."

I must confess that I am grateful for being still alive in this year of 1972, when I am writing this book, and to have seen the miraculous rebirth of the State of Israel. My father, as long as I remember, talked and dreamed of the return of our people to Jerusalem. I feel somehow, in my heart, that I represent him at this glorious moment.

The Jews, back in their old country after two thousand years of the Diaspora, are showing to the world of what mettle they are made. They turned a desert into a beautiful, fertile land in less than a quarter of a century. They developed industries, scientific centers, and the fine arts. They speak Hebrew soberly, without the singsong of the jargon, and have proved their indomitable courage and their consummate military art in fighting successfully a foe a thousand times more numerous. Yes, the meek Jews of the ghettos became formidable fighters!

66

Pola became more and more depressed by being separated from her children, and she dreaded being seen with me in town. So we started meeting again at Zosia's, and we spent a rather melancholic week at Pauline Narbut's.

As the summer of 1911 progressed, I decided to accept the reiterated invitation from the Davydovs. They used the same railway station as the Szymanowskis, so the journey was familiar to me. Verbovka, their estate, was about ten versts from Karol's Kamenka, but their place was quite different from the old Polish Tymoszovka. It had the appearance of a suburban villa, a white façade, elegant and spacious but devoid of character. The garden could have been a small city park. The interior was in the English style with furniture that was quite modern for those times. The rooms were not large, but they were comfortable and made one feel at home.

I received a most cordial welcome from the family, including their three young sons, who seemed to be delighted to see me again.

"You are going to stay in the room and sleep in the bed that my uncle Peter Ilyitch Tchaikovski used when he spent his summers here," Dmitry Lvovitch said. "There he composed some of his finest works."

One can easily imagine how impressed I was. At night, sometimes, the famous composer haunted my dreams, but always in a pleasant manner.

All in all, my life at Verbovka was delightful. Nobody expected me to do things, leaving me discreetly alone, and even meals were not served at set hours.

Karol arrived one day accompanied by his cousin, Harry Neuhaus, a very talented young pianist and composer, the son of a German piano professor married to Mrs. Szymanowski's cousin. Karol had finished his Sonata, and he brought the manuscript for me to read. It was a very complicated and difficult work, but a masterpiece, full of new ideas and an irresistible élan and passion. We were all moved, and I was yearning to learn it right away. He left the manuscript with me, and I started right away working on it. I had sensed that Karol was deeply attached to Natalya Michailovna (Mrs. Davydov's first name followed by her father's name)—perhaps even in love with her. And Natalya Michailovna never left the room while I worked on this great sonata of his.

One night, the Davydovs took me to a ball in their neighborhood, given by a Russian Princess Yashvil. The whole atmosphere, the decorations, the guests, reminded me of the ball in Tchaikovski's *Eugene Onegin;* the only thing missing was the music of the opera, but the dances were the same—a polonaise and a real Polish *mazur*. It was enchanting, and we didn't get home until six in the morning. The days were too short for us, what with the long conversations with the enchanting lady of the house and much music. I played all I could remember of Tchaikovski, but the mornings were devoted to Karol's Sonata, which I began to know by heart. One afternoon Madame Nathalie and I visited the Szymanowskis and a funny incident occurred. The old aunt—the one who always stayed with them—had just received the new novel by the most popular Polish writer of the time, Stefan Zeromski. The novel, *Popióly* (*The Ashes*), was in two volumes. The aunt had just finished the first volume and was kind enough to lend it to me. Back at Verbovka, I started reading it and finished it at seven in the morning. The book described Poland during Napoleon's days, and it was fascinating. I could not live without having the second volume, so I begged the Davydov boys to have a horse saddled for me, galloped back to Tymoszovka, threw myself at the feet of the aunt, and implored her to let me have the precious second volume! The saintly woman gave it to me, and I galloped back happily with the treasure in my possession. A second sleepless night followed, and I read to the end. Later, this novel became the inspiration for a sequence in Karol's Second Symphony.

My stay at Verbovka had come to an end. I was sad to leave, and I had to promise to return the next summer.

Back in Warsaw, I found that Pola, who had not left the city, had nothing but bad news to report. Her family had ostracized her completely, and cut off all communication.

"Why not force their door and create a scandal?" I suggested. "After all, a mother has always the right to see her small children." But she would not listen to me—she was too frightened after what they had done to her. The poor thing had a very hard time, and I was of no help to her. My only hope was to be able to travel with her abroad, but for the time being, my only concerts were in Poland and Russia, where I could not take her with me. She was afraid of Poland, and my Russian fees were too small for traveling expenses for two persons. Our only consolation was our love.

The Warsaw concert season started brilliantly. Eugène Ysaye, the great Belgian violinist, and Raoul Pugno, the French pianist, gave two sonata recitals at the Philharmonic Hall, a memorable event. Fitelberg, Szymanowski, Paul, and I, spent much time in their company. After every concert we had supper together and stayed up late, telling stories and eating and drinking a lot. Ysaye took a liking to Paul and me.

"Come tomorrow afternoon to our hotel room, where we have a piano, and play a sonata for us," he told me. We agreed eagerly, of course, but we were scared to death to play for these giants. Anyway, we rehearsed in the morning the *Kreutzer* and a Brahms sonata and went bravely to this audition. The two masters listened attentively to our performance. When we finished, Pugno, quite spontaneously, kissed Paul on both cheeks and exclaimed, "On ne joue pas mieux que cela," and Ysaye rushed to embrace me and screamed, "Je n'ai jamais entendu la *Kreutzer* jouée comme cela—vous êtes un poète." We were amused by this little show of disloyalty toward each other by these two great artists.

Another famous visitor to Warsaw was Chaliapin.

The circumstances of his arrival were characteristically unusual. A wealthy caviar merchant from Astrakhan, who worshiped our basso, engaged him for a big sum of money to make a short concert tour in Russia and Warsaw, just so he could travel in his company. They arrived four strong, Zhizhin the merchant, Chaliapin, Koenneman, his accompanist, and Avierino, my old friend from the thousand rubles fame, who contributed to the program with some pieces for viola.

The concert was a huge success. Feodor Chaliapin, who had a very limited recital repertoire, found a clever stratagem for covering up this weak point. Instead of having a printed program, he would distribute small booklets containing about five hundred songs, all numbered; so all he did was to announce to his audiences a number for his next song, which they had to look up. I, for one, always guessed his number; it would either invariably be "The Two Grenadiers" by Schumann, "The Flea" by Moussorgsky, two songs by Anton Rubinstein, and two or three more. That was all. But the innocent public was amazed by the immense repertoire of the clever fellow.

After the concert, the caviar merchant arranged a supper party in a private room at the Bristol. His other guests were two lovely ballerinas from the Opera, and a Russian singer, a friend of Feodor's. The supper soon developed into a veritable orgy, as we all drank quantities of wodka. The girls were kept busy by Fedja's enthusiasm for their shapely figures, I played all sorts of things on a dreadful piano, and Zhizhin, the caviar man, started hugging and kissing me, shouting tearfully: "Artousha, you must swear that you will come to Astrakhan for a concert. I shall make you famous in Astrakhan, and I will give you a *real* supper—this here is only a joke!" How to resist such arguments? I swore, of course, that I would come (and I kept my word!). It took me a few days to recover from this night.

One day Karol asked me to play his Sonata for some friends of his in the house of a very music-loving old lady, a Madame Spiess, the widow of a wealthy manufacturer of chemicals. She gathered a small group of admirers of Szymanowski (her son, Stefan, was Karol's close and helpful friend), including Fitelberg, who was going to show some excerpts of Karol's Second Symphony.

The Sonata made a deep impression, especially on Mrs. Spiess. "This is a master work," she cried. "It ought to be made known to the whole world."

After Fitelberg and Karol had played four hands some parts of the first movement of the Symphony and the whole beautiful second movement, the old lady was in tears.

Portrait of Arthur by Kramsztyk
done in 1914 in Paris

The picture was thrown out to the
garbage by Nazis who occupied and
robbed our house of all its contents
during World War II. Thanks to the
concierge of the square it was saved
and returned to us after the war

Arthur in Prague in 1914

Arthur, 3rd from right, at a banquet given by the Friends of the Philharmonic of Valencia after the concert

ciembre
1916

À la Sociedad Filarmónica de
Bilbao, recuerdo, de

"These two works are of the same source of inspiration—they complete each other," she said, deeply moved.

At that, Fitelberg's opportunistic mind quickly picked up the opening her remark offered.

"Madame," he exclaimed, "how wonderfully you guessed the close relation between the Sonata and the Symphony! If I had a fortune I would not hesitate to give concerts of only these two works in Berlin, Vienna, and Leipzig. I am sure that Arthur agrees with me," he added, turning to me for support.

"It certainly is a brilliant idea," I said, "but a very expensive one."

Mrs. Spiess looked puzzled for a moment, then, with a sudden air of determination, she said: "If Ficio promises to conduct the Symphony and if Arthur will play the Sonata, I am ready to finance the whole project."

Fitelberg and I, for once in accord, played to perfection our speechless amazement at that wholly "unexpected" and "never-dreamt-of" offer. Whereupon, joined by Karol, we poured out an avalanche of thanks to the generous and enthusiastic old lady. Ficio, as was to be expected, took over all the arrangements and, of course, the handling of the money in connection with these Szymanowski concerts.

As to myself, I felt proud to reveal to the world Karol's masterpiece. At the same time I couldn't help being worried about this new collaboration with Fitelberg after my earlier bad experiences.

We planned these concerts for January or February in 1912, which gave me enough time to give a few concerts in Poland and five or six in Russia, including the promised one in Astrakhan.

Pola came to Kraków. She hid carefully in the hotel, but she did go to the concert, pretending to be "casually" in town. In addition to Kraków and Lwów, I played in other cities in Austrian Poland, feeling wonderfully safe with my miracle passport.

In Russia, I played in Moscow, Kharkov, Rostov, and Saratov in the small halls of the Imperial Russian Music Society, for absurdly low fees. A primitive train with no electricity, only candlelight, took twenty-four hours to deposit me in Astrakhan. It was a weird journey all along the Volga and down to its delta. Yellow-faced Tartars, Kalmucks, and other Mongols filled the cars, and in the smelly diner, their faces, illuminated by the flickering candles, made an eerie effect. Fortunately, there was an end to the nightmare when I arrived in the caviar city.

Mr. Zhizhin, my sponsor, greeted me with cries of delight and hugs and drove me to the only decent hotel in town. On the way he reassured me about my concert.

"I filled the hall with my friends," he said, "and they promised to applaud as if you were Chaliapin himself." Being in a good mood, I began to enjoy the novelty of the whole adventure.

The concert was a riot. His friends (my audience) kept their promise and applauded with a vengeance at every stop in my performance, even in the middle of a piece.

After the concert, Zhizhin invited me for a supper.

"I have a little surprise for you," he said. I could tell from the expression on his face that the surprise was a formidable one. And I was not disappointed. He took me to a large room at the hotel where I was staying. There, a huge table was set for about thirty people, and it was laden with an enormous hollow block of ice, completely filled with unsalted, fresh caviar. It was the most delicious caviar I had ever tasted. Before I knew it I had gulped down two or three vodkas.

A Tartar chorus appeared from nowhere and sang a cappella the so-called Military Polonaise in A Major of Chopin. All through the performance the guests stood at attention, thinking that it was the Polish anthem. After that we settled down for supper.

My host introduced me to his mistress, who sat between us, a beautiful, tall brunette with an astonishing white skin, big eyes with long eyelashes, but a dull face. She wore a magnificent Persian costume and was covered with diamonds.

The caviar we ate with large soup spoons, washing it down with vodka. The supper was endless: fish, Caucasian shashliks flambés with rice, followed by an array of sweets, Turkish halvah, *rahat loukhoum*, and cakes; ice cream; fruits of all kinds, dates and nuts filling large silver containers. It must have been four or five in the morning when I saw that everybody was drunk but myself, but I had to pay for this advantage with a violent attack of nausea. A friendly soul led me to the men's room, where I vomited the whole supper.

A little later, recovered and refreshed, I returned to the party, which continued full blast.

There was a show in progress. Turkish or Persian belly dancers were exercising their bare abdomens in quick jerks and slow rotating movements. From time to time, they would turn around and, for variety's sake, exercise their behinds in the same manner, to the great enjoyment of the spectators. I was absorbed by the show, when my host suddenly shouted at his paramour: "Don't sit there like a mummy! Get up and give our guest some pleasure!"

The poor young woman, who had been stolidly eating and drinking without uttering a word, rose to her feet and settled herself comfortably on my lap, putting her arm around my neck. This unexpected gesture made me feel rather unhappy, and I was afraid that the man, now completely drunk, might suddenly recover his senses and, seeing me in this position, would try to cut my throat. My qualms, however, were soon allayed by my host's assurance that the whole thing was nothing but a demonstration of the traditional Oriental hospitality.

As much as I would have liked to have the girl in my room, his offer, made so publicly, was not appealing to me. And so, I reacted to the girl's caresses as if I were a virgin.

The early morning brought new life to the party. A regal breakfast was served, beginning with a new display of caviar accompanied by the unavoidable vodka, followed by eggs, cold meats, sausages, cheeses, and finally by some hot coffee with a vast variety of rolls, breads and cakes, honey and jams. All this lasted until noon, when I had barely the time to pack and catch my train. Zhizhin and his girl had the strength to take me to the station and give me a tearful farewell with hugs and kisses.

"That was one real, authentic orgy!" I sighed, sitting at last in my compartment, completely exhausted.

67

The first Szymanowski concerts took place in Berlin, a few days after the New Year, 1912. Fitelberg had again chosen the great hall of the Philharmonie and the Philharmonic Orchestra. But this time, thank God, I was on my own. The program consisted of the Symphony No. 2, a long intermission, and the Sonata No. 2.

In a way, it represented two separate concerts. Karol insisted that the Sonata be played last, saying that "it made the right musical balance." The concert was a great event for us. Fitelberg obtained fine results in his two full-time rehearsals, making the orchestra conscious of the importance and beauty of the Symphony. As for the Sonata, I chose the finest piano available at Bechstein's and worked on it feverishly.

Natalya Michailovna Davydov arrived from Kiev for the concert, and Karol's cousin, Harry Neuhaus, was in Berlin at that time to study with Professor Barth (!).

The concert turned out to be a genuine success. Of course, the large audience—mostly "paper" (admitted by free passes)—was nevertheless composed of well-known musicians, among them Busoni, and of genuine music lovers. The newspapers sent their leading critics, and there was the tense atmosphere of expectation that is always felt at musical events of real significance.

Both works were received with great respect, although the opinion about them was divided. They admired Fitelberg for his masterly conducting, while I was praised for my fine conception, my memory, and my temperament.

Madame Nathalie offered the four of us (Harry joined us) a supper at Dressel's, where we toasted each other, our tongues loosened by the excellent champagne. We left the restaurant very late, and as we said good night Karol asked Harry to lunch with us the next day at one.

We slept until noon, had no breakfast, and waited for Harry to appear for lunch. We waited for an hour and finally decided to begin to eat, but Karol was concerned about his cousin.

"It is not like him to miss an appointment. And it is difficult to reach him because he has no telephone." After a quick bite, Karol and I drove to his boardinghouse and found the landlady worried.

"He behaved strangely," she said. "He didn't touch his bed and left early in a hurry. There is a letter on the table for a Mr. Szymanowski."

Karol opened the letter with trembling hands and became ashen after reading it; he couldn't utter a word, just passed it to me.

I remember clearly what the letter said but not the exact words. Harry wrote that the concert had made it clear to him that he would never be a composer or a pianist, that because he could not go on living convinced that he was a failure, he had decided to leave for Florence, which he loved, and to die there.

"There is no time to lose, Karol," I said. "You must leave immediately for Florence and stop him from doing something irreparable."

"Yes," Karol muttered. "He is subject to terrible depressions, but please come with me, Arthur—I simply can't face it alone." We rushed to our hotel, inquired about trains, and left that same evening for Florence, where we arrived in the early afternoon of the next day. Karol went straight from the station to a bar in Via Tornabuoni to wait while I ran to the next police station and inquired if they had heard something about a young man of Harry's description. After a few telephone calls, they told me that a young Russian by the name of Nicolsky had cut his wrist in the bathroom of a hotel, but, panic-stricken, he had called for help and was now safe and recovering in a hospital. My instinct told me that this Nicolsky must be Harry. Back at the bar I found Karol sipping, gloomily, a drink. I dragged him out, and we drove to the hospital, where all our apprehensions were confirmed. There we found poor Harry in bed, his face white, his eyes half-closed, and his bandaged arm in a sling.

Our appearance gave him a start. He tried to say something, but Karol stopped him with a big, brotherly hug, and the whole nightmare dissolved in the happy tears of the three of us.

Fortunately, the doctor pronounced him able to travel, so we packed him into a sleeping car back to Berlin. Karol and I spent the whole night keeping watch over him in turn.

Harry's wrist took a long time to heal. However, after the First World War, he remained in Russia, where he made a great career. He became the director and professor of the famous Moscow Conservatory and gave some remarkable concerts. A few of the finest Russian pianists enjoyed his guidance and were inspired by his universal culture and his intense knowledge and understanding of music.

A curious phenomenon of my stay in Berlin was the fact that none of my old friends or acquaintances had shown up or communicated with me, as if the concert had taken place in another city. After my return from Florence it was too late to visit anyone. We had to leave for Leipzig. Our concert in this Saxon city of music fame proved less gratifying than the one in Berlin. The fine Gewandhaus, the concert hall made famous by Felix Mendelssohn, being unobtainable, we had to content ourselves with a large, circular, unpopular place with bad acoustics. The orchestra, an improvised body composed of heterogeneous elements, was not adequate to the strong demands of the Symphony. As to the audience, it certainly was not representative of the Leipzig musical elite.

The orchestra, with a few exceptions, remained indifferent to the music, but the public applauded warmly both Ficio and myself. When we requested Karol to take a bow, the applause became barely polite. The critics found much to praise, with some reservations about the density of the orchestration. As to the Sonata, they liked its dynamic progress and originality, and generally it received more favorable reviews.

By a curious coincidence Paul and Zosia were in Leipzig on a visit to Paul's family. Their presence at our concert was a wonderful surprise. I dined the next evening at Paul's parents' apartment, where I met his whole family.

Right away I liked his mother, who had the same black velvet eyes and some of the vitality of her son. His father was less interesting; he struck me as a typical Russian Orthodox Jew except that he was uncommunicative and taciturn. The two sisters were lively and hospitable, though not attractive, but a younger brother, a pianist who had just graduated from the Conservatory, displeased me by his manners and lack of sincerity. There was another guest, a charming and pretty young English girl violinist, Sylvia Sparrow, who had studied with Paul in Brussels. She became very soon a dear, lifelong friend.

Zosia was visibly ill at ease in this company. These simple people were not "refined" enough for her, but she tried hard to cover up by smiling engagingly at everybody, by overpraising the food, and by offering her help to the mother. Thanks to Paul's warm introduction, I was received with open arms.

Our caravan left for Vienna a few days later, where we established ourselves at the Hotel Kranz, a friendly and distinguished place. The owner, Mr. Kranz, loved music and expressed his pleasure in having us.

I was looking forward to the concert in this city after my promising debut. The newspapers took an interest in it, treated it as an event, and published stories about us. Fitelberg managed to get the fine Musikvereinssaal and the Tonkünstler Orchestra with three rehearsals. As for the Sonata, I did not hesitate this time. I chose a Bösendorfer. The organizer told us with pride that there was a great demand for tickets. Prince Lubomirski was in town and gave a splendid dinner at Sacher's.

This concert in Vienna was a complete triumph. We were cheered by the public, and Karol had to bow several times. The press was unanimous in praising both works, calling them "great masterpieces which enrich our musical heritage." And Leopold Godowsky, who became the head of the Meisterclasse at the Vienna Conservatory, came to compliment us and invite us to his home.

Our concert turned out to be one of the musical events of the season. As a result, Szymanowski was offered a long-term contract by the very important music publishing house, the Universal Edition, a great step toward the general recognition of his music. A few days later, Karol showed us the signed contract with deep satisfaction, which we shared with him with all our hearts.

Shortly after, Prince Lubomirski, at a luncheon at Sacher's, announced with pride that, thanks to his recommendation, Fitelberg had been offered the post of a conductor at the famous Vienna Opera, with the title of a Kaiserlicher und Königlicher Hofkapellmeister, the Imperial and Royal Court Conductor. This sensational news was a big surprise only for me. The others had known about it but had kept it secret until it became official. We toasted Ficio and the Prince with many glasses of wine.

Even I received a small share of the wide interest shown our trio. Godowsky proposed to me to take over the preparatory piano class for his Meisterschule at the Imperial and Royal Conservatory with the title of a K. und K. Professor! A tempting and flattering proposition indeed, but something I was completely unprepared to accept at that period of my life. I had learned to love my freedom, in spite of the many hardships I had endured in order to preserve it. Subconsciously I always lived in a state of expectation of the unforeseen, of a miracle, of the sudden change.

The three of us, Ficio, Karol, and I, enjoyed our Viennese success. We were lionized by many influential people, and the local musicians showered invitations upon us for concerts, theaters, and parties. A young critic by the name of Hans Effenberger, a good-looking man with dark, dreamy eyes and a black beard, used to follow us around like a dog. He said he was an illegitimate son of a Polish nobleman and a Polish countess, that his real name was Śliwiński. Found abandoned on the steps of a church, he had been adopted by a childless Austrian couple, the Effenbergers, who lived in Prague. He had graduated from the Prague university, and became a critic of music and literature, and was one of the librarians at the Imperial Hofburg.

It was a lovely, romantic story which we accepted with a dose of skepticism, but we liked him for his suave charm and his enthusiasm for Karol's music.

The Godowsky household became our second home. The great master loved to play his recent compositions for us in his inimitable way, handling their hair-raising difficulties with nonchalance. His wife, a lively brunette, treated us like close family, and so did their four children, two boys and two girls, all still teenagers. The younger daughter, Dagmar, was quite beautiful. At thirteen, she looked like a Persian miniature, reminding me very much of Mania Szer of Lodz. Her heavy black braids, almond-shaped eyes, pretty nose, and full, red, arched mouth made her look older than her age. Both Karol and I became sensuously aware of her presence; and she was coquettish and provocative toward us. She liked to tell about her "*friendship*" with Franz Lehár, the famous composer of operettas, and with Josef Hofmann, the great pianist, whom she called "Uncle Franz and Uncle Josef." She was quite a girl, this Dagmar.

One morning I read in the paper that Pablo Casals was about to make his debut in Vienna in a few days, which was thrilling news for me. His name was already known, and there was a filled Musikvereinssaal to greet him. To our astonishment, he chose for his performance with orchestra a concerto by a Swiss composer, Emanuel Moore, who was known only as the creator of a piano with a double keyboard. The concerto proved to be insignificant, but Casals played it with his inimitable tone and such a deep concentration that it was impossible to resist him. And when the time came for encores, Vienna was completely conquered. Later, in the artists' room, where we all went to congratulate him, he introduced me to his English manager, who had come with him for this important event. Mr. Montague Chester was the head of Vert's Concert Agency, an old London firm, Casals told me.

"He wants us both to have lunch with him tomorrow," Casals explained. "He has something interesting to propose to you."

I accepted, of course, and we lunched at the Bristol.

"I know all about your success in Vienna," Chester started, "and Casals has spoken well of you. He has suggested that I arrange some concerts for you in London during the big season, this May and June. What do you think?"

"Do you mean you want to engage me for a fee?" I asked, hopefully.

"No," he replied. "My firm acts only as an agent, but I am willing to manage your concerts for a small percentage of the gross receipts. I propose that you give three recitals in the Bechstein Hall, and as I feel sure of your success, you will get some well-paid engagements right away."

I smiled sadly. "Mr. Chester, I haven't the money to give concerts I know will be a sure loss, and I know how expensive they are."

"How could you afford your first concerts in Vienna and Berlin?"

"I had a sponsor," I said, "who believed in my talent."

"Oh," Chester exclaimed, "let me talk to him—he might do it again for London."

Casals interrupted our conversation.

"I am giving a concert in London at Queen's Hall at the very beginning of the season. If you are willing to play sonatas with me, it might be a useful introduction for your recitals."

Chester clapped his hands. "Pablo, you are a wizard—you are offering Rubinstein his success on a platter." Then, turning to me: "As you must know, Casals will pack the house, and you will be heard by all London. Now, give me the name and address of your sponsor, because I am sure he will guarantee your recitals." He became quite excited. "I shall telephone him right away and ask him to receive me."

A few hours later the Prince called me.

"Is this Englishman who came to see me a reliable person?" he asked.

"Yes, he is the manager of the famous cellist Pablo Casals."

"Then tell him that I agree to his proposition."

He dropped the phone without listening to my thanks. Chester and Casals were so pleased with the news that we made our plans for London right away, and I agreed to play a Brahms and a Grieg sonata with Casals for my debut. I also promised to send three different programs for the recitals.

Karol wanted his sister Stanislava, a very fine singer, to appear in a recital of his songs and asked me to play the accompaniments for her and a few of his solo pieces. It was not the best thing for the progress of my career, but I agreed out of friendship for him and my admiration for his work. The concert took place two weeks later in the hall of a club. Stasia sang very well, I played Karol's *Variations*, and some études and preludes. We had a small but appreciative audience.

In the meantime my life in Vienna continued in the same lively fashion. A Mr. von Oberleithner, the owner of a large department store who had a passion for composing operas, often invited me to lunch or dinner at that time. His latest opera, *Aphrodite*, had just had its premiere at the great Vienna Opera House with the young, beautiful, and brilliant Maria Jeritza in the title role. Jeritza sang beautifully, but the music was devoid of real talent and originality, and frankly I was slightly shocked that the Vienna Opera had put it on.

After the premiere, Mr. von Oberleithner gave a splendid supper party in a private room at the Sacher for the singers, the conductor, and a few Vienna notables. There was a good piano in the room. The minute we got up from the table, I was asked to play, and I complied with pleasure; it was the right kind of an audience.

Fitelberg, Karol, and I used to take our meals at the hotel. Ficio held the strings of the purse and paid the hotel expenses, so I did not give much thought to money. Still, I had to spend quite a lot on my own in drugstores, at haberdashers, on mail, barbers, tips, and transportation, and once again I began to reach the end of my resources. One morning, I decided to ask Fitelberg for a small amount of pocket money. When I couldn't find him or Karol in their apartment I went down to the front office to inquire if they had left a message for me. The room clerk answered that the two gentlemen had left the night before for Venice.

I was speechless. The heartless beasts! They had abandoned me to my fate! Of course, it was Fitelberg's doing. Karol was only an irresponsible child completely dominated by him—but Fitelberg! He had done it again.

That night, fortunately, I had dinner with the Prince, who wanted to learn the details about London.

Well, I could not resist; I told him the story about Venice. The Prince knew that I had given up a few important engagements for this Szymanowski tour, on which I played without any fee, and that it was a sacrifice from the point of view of my career. So, when he heard what Fitelberg had done to me, he shouted, "He is a scoundrel! I shall break his engagement at the Opera! I shall tell them what sort of man he is."

I had a hard time calming him, and I begged him not to do anything of the sort, saying that it would create too big a scandal and involve all of us. Prince Ladislas promised, began to smile again, and finally, when I was taking leave, gave me a bill of a thousand kronen and said: "I don't want to see you as a victim of this scoundrel."

A few days later, the two "scoundrels" came back from Venice, and Fitelberg simply said to me by way of explanation, "We became suddenly so tired of Vienna that we decided to take a rest."

I didn't reply; as a matter of fact I stopped talking to him. But I did have a few words to say to Karol. Instead of apologizing, he attacked me suddenly on the subject of Dagmar Godowsky. I saw hatred and jealousy in his eyes.

"You became very irritating, constantly making eyes at her, trying to impress her, and you did it only to annoy me. If you ever as much as look at her again you can count me out as your friend."

I was boiling with rage.

"All right," I shouted, "from now on I shall really start to flirt with her!" and I left, slamming the door behind me.

The next time we dined at the Godowskys', I invited Dagmar to visit the Fine Arts Museum with me. She readily accepted, and her parents weren't against it. From that day on, Karol and I ceased speaking to each other for a whole year, when Dagmar herself brought us together again. The whole thing was a bitter experience for me.

Four

ENGLAND
& THE FIRST
WORLD WAR

68

As the time to leave for London grew nearer, I became more and more excited about my English season; my imagination ran away with me. This is the place where I shall start my great career, I daydreamed.

With such imaginary prospects in mind, naturally I wanted Pola to share them with me. I knew, of course, that my money couldn't last for more than two or three weeks for both of us, but I had faith in Chester's promise to get me well-paid engagements, and I expected Casals to pay me for my collaboration. I wrote Pola a long letter explaining all this and begging her to join me in Paris on our way to London. She wired back how happy she was and that she would meet me at the Gare du Nord.

I was overjoyed. Simply as a precaution I decided to ask the very rich Mr. von Oberleithner to lend me a thousand kronen, hoping that he was going to give it to me as the fee he never paid for my playing at his party one time. When I called, he offered to come to see me at my hotel. He arrived all smiles, shook both hands, and seemed to expect an invitation to a concert or some other pleasant proposition. At my request for money his face changed into that of a stern bank cashier, but he felt somehow obliged to comply.

"All I can give you is eight hundred," he said. "I am short of cash at the moment."

I took his eight hundred, and he asked me to sign a receipt. As a result I left Vienna in better financial condition and full of anticipation for London.

Pola arrived in Paris at the Gare du Nord looking fresh, lovely, and happy. We spent that day and the night in the Ville Lumière, having a glorious time—one of those perfect days of happiness which I like to call "moments of eternity." The next morning we took the boat train to London. It was the same long, smoky journey to Calais, the smelly channel boat, and, finally, at Dover, the pleasant compartment with the English tea so richly served. We arrived at Victoria Station unannounced. I didn't want Chester to find out right away that I was not traveling alone.

An Englishman in Vienna had recommended that I take a flat at a place on Hanover Square, even promising to make a reservation for me. We drove up to the place and found a pleasant-looking building with a uniformed doorman in the entrance hall, which had a nice marble floor. A very polite manager showed us a small flat consisting of a cozy living room and a large bedroom for two with a little hall and a bathroom between them. What we liked best was the comfortable, solid English furniture and the clean look of the place.

Afraid that such a place was beyond my means, I was already preparing an elegant retreat when the man mentioned it was five pounds a week ($25!). "You can also have all the meals served in your rooms. We have no open restaurant, but a fine cuisine and not an expensive one."

Ah, these were the golden days of living in great comfort for so little money. I almost kissed the manager. All I had to do was to sign my name; Pola's was not required. When the man left, we hopped and danced around the rooms.

My first visit in the morning was to Bechstein's. They had a factory in London and a large store near their concert hall which was in great demand for solo recitals (and still is). The local head of the firm received me very kindly. Chester had been in touch with him about my coming concerts, and the man assured me of his full collaboration. What a contrast with his friend in Vienna! He himself offered to send a small piano to my flat and invited me to visit his store and to choose a concert piano.

The Vert's Agency was near enough so that I walked the two or three blocks and found Mr. Chester in his office, pleased to see me. "I like my artists to arrive well ahead of their public appearance. It gives them a chance to get familiar with the hall, the piano, and, eventually, to meet the press. Casals is on tour in the provinces and will arrive two days before the concert to have two rehearsals with you. The Queen's Hall is sold out for your sonata recital."

He offered to take me for lunch, but I refused; Pola was waiting for me.

The four days before Casal's return were spent enjoying the city. We visited the National Gallery twice. Pola was awed by the marvels of the British Museum. We saw a well-played comedy by Pinero, with Mrs. Patrick Campbell, and a brilliant variety show. Our flat was such a constant delight that we had almost all our meals at home. The breakfast and the afternoon tea were perfect, the lunch and dinner indifferent but wholesome.

Casals came to the flat for our first rehearsal. From a musical point of view, it was a very interesting experience. In the Brahms E minor Sonata we disagreed several times in our conceptions of the work. Brahms, it is true, was to a certain degree influenced by Schubert and Schumann, and his music is full of exuberance, but there is always the restraining hand of the classicist in him, and this is the way I understand his music.

Casals played the first movement with his inimitable singing tone and his passionate warmth, but he added a certain pathos to it which I thought unnecessary, although I did not dare to criticize—his playing was simply too beautiful. His phrasing in the Trio of the second movement, however, was too sweetly romantic for my taste. We disagreed on the rubatos he wanted me to make and, finally, we both compromised. The Grieg Sonata went smoothly from beginning to end, and Casals shouted "Bravo, bravo," when we finished. I was proud to play with this great master.

The concert at Queen's Hall was a matinée at three o'clock in the afternoon—the English music lovers' favorite hour for concerts.

I was nervous about it and not a little afraid of being considered as a mere accompanist of the great soloist. But I had nothing to fear; Casals came up to the platform holding my hand, and we bowed to the applause as equals.

The Brahms made a deep impression on the public; we had to come back four or five times. The next number on the program was a Bach sonata for cello solo, an acknowledged master performance by the great cellist. After intermission we played the Grieg, and as I expected, this work seemed to appeal the most to the audience. We received a great ovation with shouts of approval, and finally we had to repeat the last movement. Casals embraced me in the artists' room.

I invited him to dinner at the flat in secret from Chester, because I wanted him to meet Pola (she was not present at our rehearsals). When we were alone, I explained to him the situation, which he took quite naturally. At dinner he was visibly charmed by Pola, who was at her best, still flushed with joy over our success.

The severe London critics had nothing but praise for the concert and treated me on the same level with their well-established idol. I remember one critic writing: "Their playing together was the most perfect chemical mixture." I didn't question what he meant by that, but simply took it as something favorable for me. Anyhow, Mr. Chester considered me already as "the coming man."

My first recital at the Bechstein Hall took place a week later. Chester told me with a self-satisfied grin: "I *gathered* a nice audience for you," a well-known remark that meant that it was mostly "paper." I was prepared for it. The English were known for being slow to accept young newcomers. They loved veterans like Joachim, Paderewski, Melba, de Pachmann, worshiping without discrimination such favorites who could do no wrong.

The Bechstein Hall was well suited to intimate recitals. It held nine hundred people, and I had about six hundred of them in the place. My program was of a kind which I call "introductory." A fantasia and fugue of Bach, a Beethoven sonata, the *Symphonic Études* of Schumann, a small bouquet of Chopin pieces, and a Liszt rhapsody. I was in good form and felt the audience with me from the start; the success grew with every piece. The Liszt drew shouts for encores, and I played three. Tired but happy, I returned to the artists' room, where Pola choked me with kisses and hugs. Later on, people poured in to congratulate me, among them, Destinn and Jacques Thibaud.

"I hear that you had a wonderful recital with Pablo," Jacques said. "Why not play two concerts with me right here in this hall?" I didn't know what to answer, but Chester jumped at the idea.

"You must agree to it," he shouted. "This is sensational. You will have given six concerts in less than six weeks!"

"We will make it strictly two sonata recitals without any solos," Jacques added. I was thrilled; six sonatas with Thibaud!

Then Destinn appeared, bringing a pale-looking man with her, probably her new lover. "Didn't I tell you that he is wonderful?" she said to him. He looked unconvinced.

An old couple also came in and introduced themselves as Mr. and Mrs. John Bergheim.

"We had a letter from our friend, Mr. von Sachs, from Vienna. He wrote us to be sure to hear and meet you." (Mr. von Sachs was a wealthy, retired businessman who adored music, and he liked to give small tea parties for young promising male artists, but the atmosphere at his parties was too homosexual for me and I always felt I did not belong.) The old gentleman went on excitedly: "But he didn't do justice to you—you are much better than he said."

Mr. and Mrs. Bergheim invited me for dinner with an insistence that could not be refused. I hated to be invited without Pola, but, on the other hand, I had not the courage to introduce her as a "lady friend" who travels with me. So, when I tried to find an excuse, Pola whispered in Polish: "Do accept, please—they are so anxious to have you and they look so warm-hearted." So I accepted, and Mr. Bergheim fixed a date right away, gave me his address, and said he would send a car for me.

The press, next morning, had very favorable reviews about the concert. Two or three found me too exuberant and hoped that I would calm down; others, on the other hand, praised me highly for the same exuberance, but all of them conceded that I was a "born" pianist and predicted a great future. What struck me was the uniform style of the London critics. They never voiced their personal impressions or their preferences or dislikes with arguments for their opinions. They simply brought in their verdicts, like judges at a court, with an incontestable finality. I am afraid that their style, in all these years, has not changed.

69

The Bergheims lived in the northern suburb of Hampstead. At the angle of a short street called Belsize Park, a drive-in courtyard led to their house, a large but unpretentious three-story building which stood by itself.

Two maids opened the door and took my coat and hat. One of them preceded me into the living room on the first floor, opened the doors, and announced loudly: "Mr. Arthur Rubinstein." There were several guests. Mr. Bergheim received me enthusiastically and introduced me—to my annoyance—as the "young genius." A short man in his seventies, he had sharp gray eyes, which were bloodshot, constantly bulging with excitement, and a well-shaped but unmistakably Jewish nose. Mrs. Clara Bergheim, not much younger and no taller than her husband, was slim and neat, her gray hair dressed à la Queen Mary. She was wearing thick-lensed glasses and had a tendency to blush so violently that even her nose turned red.

Their guests were interesting: among them were Sir Edmund Davis, one of the well-known Jewish millionaires to have made their fortune in South Africa; Ralph Peto, a young very good-looking gentleman, and his wife, a tall, lovely brunette, a niece of the Duchess of Rutland and a cousin of Lady Marjory and Lady Diana Manners, two famous English beauties; Sir George Henschel, a noted concert singer and the first conductor of the Boston Symphony Orchestra, and his daughter Helen, a promising soprano.

Dinner was served downstairs in a large dining room. The table was adorned with exquisite orchids in different shapes and colors, and the food was in the best English style, not much to my taste. At the end of dinner, the host produced a few bunches of huge black grapes.

"From my own hothouse," he said proudly.

When the ladies had left the room, we were served port, and Mr. Bergheim opened a door leading to the garden and showed us a long row of greenhouses.

"Here is where I raise my orchids and grow my fruits," he said, and gave us a long lecture on the merits of hothouses.

Englishmen, after dinner, like to be left to themselves to talk and drink. So it was a while before Mrs. Bergheim opened the door and invited us to join the ladies. When we went up to the living room, Mr. Bergheim took me aside and begged me to play. "We have a fine, well-tuned Bechstein," he said, "and our guests are devoted to music." He did not need to ask me—I was ready to play anyway. In my short conversation with Sir George Henschel, I had found him to be an oldtime Wagnerite, so I began with the "Liebestod" from *Tristan*, followed by my own concert arrangement of the "Walkürenritt," two of my sure-fire hits. And the impact was overwhelming. I can't remember when my playing pleased a small group of people more. It was touching the way Sir George hugged me, and Mrs. Peto kissed me. Everyone there became my devoted fans for many years. When we were ready to leave, Mr. Bergheim asked me to stay a little longer. He took me to his den, which looked like an office.

"I wanted to tell you a little about myself," he started. "It might interest you." He went on to describe how he had been born in Jerusalem (Palestine was still under Turkish rule). "My father was a businessman, but I became interested in oil and came to London to look for opportunities. A Canadian, a Mr. McGarvey, joined me as a partner. Soon we bought some concessions for oil in Galicia, Poland. We established a company there with two Poles, a Count Skrzynski and a Mr. Bernstein, whose son became a French playwright. And so I made my fortune in Poland."

"Did this Count Skrzynski have a son?" I asked.

"Yes, he had a son by the name of Alexander, and two lovely daughters."

"Ha, ha," I laughed. "Now it is my turn to tell you about Alexander and about Henri Bernstein." My tale amused him very much.

"I suppose you want to leave now. It is getting late. My car will take you home. And please accept a small fee for your magnificent performance." He opened a desk and gave me twenty-five pounds. I gladly accepted the money, knowing it would be a help. So far Mr. Chester had never mentioned anything about engagements, receipts, or money.

As I left, this charming old couple made me promise to come again to lunch *en famille*.

When I got home, I found Pola reading in bed, waiting for me. She wanted to hear all about the party, and as I finished my story, she said with satisfaction: "I knew that it was important for you to go," and she added, with her little air of a Pythia: "They are going to play an important role in your life."

The morning papers had wonderful news. Diaghilev's Russian Ballet was coming for a short season to the Covent Garden, opening with *Schéhérazade, Le Spectre de la Rose*, both with Karsavina and Nijinsky, and the dances of *Prince Igor*. A divine surprise for both of us; we had never seen the Ballets Russes. With Chester's help, we obtained two good stalls, paying for them, of course.

And it was a fantastic evening. Pola and I sat in ecstasy, holding hands through the whole performance. The ballet was still so fresh that the decorations of Bakst and Roerich were immaculate. Nijinsky's grace was breathtaking, and so were his leaps, and as to Karsavina—I simply fell in love with her. Pola was not at all jealous, because she felt the same way. We left the theater, emotionally exhausted.

At my second recital I had fewer people than at the first. "But most of them paid for their tickets," said Chester with a grin. This time I played some first performances: the Fifth Sonata of Scriabin, two pieces by Medtner, and an étude and two preludes by Szymanowski. The critics judged the new compositions more or less favorably, but they could not resist offering the composers some suggestions for improvement. The public received them with much applause but felt more at home when I attacked the A flat Polonaise of Chopin, followed by favorite encores.

Later in the artists' room Pauline Narbut appeared, our good friend from Warsaw. She was in London for business, she said, and was *dying* to see the Ballets Russes. Pola was delighted to find a companion for shopping and sightseeing. She did get a little lonely sometimes, the poor thing, as I became more and more involved in my career, practicing for the concerts, accepting invitations without her, and so on. That evening we took Pauline to dinner at the Carlton Grill, my favorite restaurant.

Alas, I had to continue to go alone to dinner parties, as I had no plausible alibis. Lady Davis invited me to a big supper for twenty guests, all great names in banking and industry. A French painter, Edmund Dulac, who was *en vogue* for his book illustrations, was there, too. The Bergheims were not invited. I played at that party, hoping for a substantial fee, but all I received were a thousand thanks and a hundred praises.

My last recital was quite well attended by both a paying public and "paper." At that concert my audience began to look familiar. I was able to recognize quite a few persons who had come to all the recitals. My program included the Sonata of Chopin with the Funeral March, which impressed them. The Bergheims were in tears when they came to congratulate me. My last number was the Liszt transcription of the "Liebestod," which never failed with any public.

After my three recitals I was anxious to know how much money was coming to me, so I went to see Mr. Chester at his office. When I asked, he looked genuinely astonished. "I don't understand what you are talking about," he said. "I am preparing all the accounts for Prince Lubomirski. He still has a deficit to pay for, which amounts to less than two hundred pounds, but there is certainly nothing for you."

What a naïve fool I was! In my uncommercial mind I had taken it for granted that the Prince assumed the responsibility for the expenses of the concerts and that all the box office receipts were for my own benefit. After all, I gave all these concerts without a fixed fee, but I had to provide for my traveling, board, and food; in short, I had to live. It seemed to me the London venture had been a pipe dream.

"Frankly, Mr. Chester, you rather misled me in Vienna with your colorful picture of well-paid engagements if I were to prove successful," I said bitterly. "Well, you must admit that I am not a failure; both your public and your press approve of me, but in spite of all that you have nothing to show as yet."

"Don't blame me," he answered meekly. "I am doing my best, but it is a little too late in the season. Everything was booked before you came. However, I have two good concerts for you for next spring." And suddenly, changing the subject, he said, "A young American singer and his wife, a very interesting couple, have been at all your concerts and are raving about you. May I take you to their house tomorrow for tea? They begged me to ask you to come."

I accepted, but only to be agreeable; my talk had hurt him, I felt.

Pola, at lunch, tried to dispel my discouragement. "I've been reading the cards for you," she smiled, "and they say that you shall overcome obstacles. You shall always be the winner."

And there was a letter from Mrs. Bergheim with a new invitation for dinner. There was no question of refusing; I was sure to earn some money again.

The next day when I met Paul Draper, the American singer, and his wife, Muriel, I knew they were people after my own heart; it took us less than five minutes to understand each other to perfection. Paul was a tall and slim young man in his late twenties. His well-shaped head, a narrow, clean-shaven face with regular features, gave him an air of distinction, and he moved and wore his clothes with an impeccable elegance. What particularly attracted me to him was his almost touching devotion to music. His wife was made of a completely different mettle. Her age did not matter; she might as easily have been forty as twenty, but she was actually only a little younger than her husband.

She had a fine, graceful figure, a pale, silky complexion, and remarkably beautiful hands. But her face was disquieting: her narrow, long head, topped by hair that she kept closely under a net, her high cheekbones, her short, slightly flat nose, and exuberantly large mouth with thick red lips made her look like a white Negress. Many people considered her ugly, others beautiful. In spite of her aggressive personality and exceptional intelligence, she had a great feminine charm.

When Chester left, Draper sang in a thin, raspy tenor voice but with great musical feeling some songs of Schubert, whom he worshiped. With such people I felt no hesitation in telling them about Pola, and they invited both of us for dinner that very evening. Pola liked Paul Draper very much, but Muriel's ironic smile, strong opinions, and loud laughter disturbed her a little.

In the meantime, the Bergheims developed a passion for my company. Hardly a day passed without an invitation or a message. Whenever I played, I received the usual check of twenty-five pounds. Once, at a party, Mr. Bergheim asked me to play the Funeral March of Chopin. I refused, giving as an excuse that the March was a part of the Sonata which was too long for the occasion, but, in reality, I had been superstitious about playing it ever since the sad evening with Count Strogonoff at Rambouillet. Mr. Bergheim kept insisting, and I hated to tell him about my vow never to play it for friends in private. Finally, I gave in, and again after my performance this dear man was in tears too.

Here I must relate a curious incident. One day the Bergheims invited me for lunch, saying they wanted me to meet a very interesting Polish lady. "We became good friends on a cruise to the Canaries, and I feel sure that you will like her," Mr. Bergheim told me.

When the maid opened for me the door to the drawing room, I was stupefied! There were two ladies sitting on a sofa: one was Pauline Narbut, the other . . . Pola! A scene out of a comedy.

Pauline, with her quick wit, took hold of the situation. "Arthur," she shouted, "what a lovely surprise to find you here. We talked with Pola a lot about you—she was so lucky to hear you at all your concerts." Pola smiled a little shyly. All through lunch we continued our comedy. As I had guessed and as Pola confirmed later at home, Pauline instigated the whole thing in order to embarrass me, because she disapproved of my cowardice in not introducing Pola to the Bergheims, as my love. I was angry with her at that time, but now, when I think about it, I feel that she was right.

The concerts with Thibaud were a sheer joy. We were musically in complete harmony and enjoyed our rehearsals almost more than the concerts. Jacques brought with him the pretty and charming Sylvia Sparrow, his and Paul's ex-pupil, whom I had met in Leipzig at Paul's parents'. They lunched with us at our flat before we began our work. On one of these afternoons Thibaud wanted to rehearse before we had had our coffee. Sylvia, most obligingly, poured the ambrosial liquid for us. At one moment she put a cup of coffee for me on the side of my music stand just when Thibaud, trying out a difficult passage, touched the cup with his bow, and smack! the coffee inundated the inside of the open piano. All four of us cried out in horror, and I was particularly upset at being responsible for an instrument which did not belong to me. Pola and Sylvia did not lose a second. With the gift women have for this sort of thing they sucked out the liquid buried under the cords with tiny pieces of a sponge. After much strenuous work the harmony board was dry. A great sigh of relief! But this poor Bechstein must have kept the fragrance of coffee for the rest of its existence.

Pola decided to leave for Warsaw with Pauline Narbut and to spend some time in the country with her. Poor Pola, her quest for her children was always on her mind.

During the night before she left we went through a shocking experience. We were sound asleep when at three a.m. the telephone rang, and we woke up with a start. It was Paul Draper calling from our entrance lobby. "I must see you right away," he said in a strange-sounding voice.

"Why . . . what happened?" I asked, quite alarmed.

"I am coming up. I have to talk to you," and he dropped the telephone. We had barely the time to put on our robes before he stood at the door. I let him into the living room, where he sat down and began to talk incoherently in a breathless voice; his bright shining eyes and red cheeks heightened our alarm. It was then that we realized that he was completely drunk. After a while we were able to make out what he was trying to say.

"Arthur, I must have the complete list of the Schubert songs you want me to learn," he mumbled. There was for me nothing else to do but pick up a piece of paper and scribble some names of songs which I could remember. He grabbed it, stood up, and left in a hurry.

We decided to call Muriel. "She must be in agony not knowing where he is," I said, but she answered in a sleepy voice: "Don't worry about him, he is out on one of his drinking bouts which last four or five days. When it is over he comes back to normal." Strangely enough, that calmed me.

After Pola's departure I decided to remain in London for the time being, in hopes of another check or two from Mr. Bergheim or of some belated engagement procured by the wretched Mr. Chester. My remaining funds were dwindling fast. The seven weeks with Pola in London had emptied my pocket, and my rent was a week overdue.

Casals was in town again and asked me to lunch with him at his hotel, the Dieudonné, which had a good restaurant. The old Madame Dieu-donné catered almost exclusively to French artists.

Casals was a surprising man. That morning the papers had a front-page story about the assassination of a Spanish Minister of State by the Catalan anarchist Ferrer, who had shot him point-blank in the Cortes, when the parliament was in session. When I spoke of it with indignation to the great cellist, he said impassively: "Ferrer has simply done his duty. I am myself an anarchist."

During our meal I brought up my disappointment with Chester. "He let me down," I complained. "I played in six concerts without receiving a penny, and he was not able to provide me with a single engagement."

My intention was to remind Casals that he had neglected to give me even a small share of his receipts for the concert at Queen's Hall. When Casals failed to react to my insinuation, I asked him for a loan of ten pounds. After a moment of hesitation, he took me up to his room, where he wrote out a check for that amount and gave it to me. I thanked him a little coldly and left.

As I continued to see more of the Bergheims their friendship for me grew. I was often a guest at their family luncheons, where I met a niece, Nina, and a nephew, Peter—orphans of Bergheim's brother—whom the Bergheims had adopted and who lived with them. On our walks in the garden we talked of many things, and I was impressed to learn that Mr. Bergheim was one of the first contributors to Wagner's Festspielhaus in Bayreuth. He wanted to know everything about me and became impatient when I told him about Chester.

"You must get rid of that man. Next season, I shall take your career in England into my own hands, and you must stay with us." I was deeply touched. I came to love this old man.

Muriel Draper informed me that Paul was at home and well again. One afternoon when we were alone, she told me the sad story that Paul had been a chronic alcoholic ever since his college years, that in reality he hated alcohol, knowing what it did to him and to his voice. "So he fights it for weeks, but if, on some unlucky day, he happens to take one sip of the stuff, nothing and nobody can stop him. He disappears for three or four days and it's difficult to trace him in this big city. Sometimes I have to ask the police to help me to find him. . . ."

What a terrible disease! What made it even more tragic was the un-believable contrast between his sporadic drinking bouts and his periods of sobriety, when Paul was always the most courteous, lovable, enthusiastic, and charming human being. We used to spend happy hours at the piano; he was quite a good pianist himself, and he sang Schubert, Schumann, and

Brahms with just the right feeling. With a better voice he might have been one of the best liedersingers of the time.

Thanks to him I received an unexpected windfall. The Drapers were moving, and Paul asked me to choose a Bechstein concert grand for the large studio in the new house. I was very careful with my choice and found an exceptionally beautiful instrument for him. The next day the Bechstein firm sent me a check for thirty pounds—my commission on the sale!

I left London with blessings and a check for fifty pounds (a bonus?) from Mr. and Mrs. Bergheim and a great farewell from the Drapers. When Chester mentioned the two engagements he had for me for the next season, I asked him to get in touch with Mr. Bergheim, anticipating with pleasure what he was going to hear from the old gentleman.

70

My first stop was Vienna on my way to Russia. I had promised to spend the rest of the summer with the Davydovs in Verbovka, but I had to get a new passport to pass the Russian frontier. The diplomatic one which the ambassador in Rome had given me was, in a way, a dangerous document. It was too spectacular, too important for a young, unassuming pianist. Though I did pass the frontier town Alexandrovo unharmed on the way to Warsaw, Brody, at the frontier leading to Kiev, was notorious for its secret police. The idea of being subjected to a close questioning about a diplomatic passport made me tremble with fear.

The one man who offered to help if ever I needed it was Karol's and my loyal follower, Hans Effenberger; he had mentioned it once while we discussed that subject.

In the morning, after a quick breakfast at a café, I walked to the Hofburg and found my way to the Imperial Library. The man in uniform whom I asked to announce me to Hans Effenberger said that it was not necessary, that he would take me to him right away.

When Hans saw us coming in, he closed precipitately the sloping top of his desk, pushed some books into drawers, and jumped up to greet me.

"What a good surprise," he said, "I hope that you are going to stay some time."

"It depends entirely on you," I answered and told him that I needed his help.

"I am sure Maria can help you out."

"Who is Maria?"

"A charming woman, my mistress."

When I pressed him for details, he told me that she was a married woman, that they were in love, and that he wanted us to lunch with her.

"All that is just splendid," I said, laughing, "but where the devil can she get a passport from?"

"Her husband has one and will certainly let you have it. He is a very nice fellow."

Unlikely as it sounded, I couldn't afford to dismiss any possibility. "Hans," I asked, "why did you close your desk in such a hurry when I entered the room?"

He looked around to be sure that we were alone.

"You see, Arthur," he whispered, "I am preparing a catalog of international pornographic literature. I am getting a good price for this work. But my desk is littered with the hottest and dirtiest stuff I ever read. Not only is it detrimental to my health, as I am constantly sexually aroused, but you can imagine what would happen if this clandestine occupation of mine were discovered. I'd be disgraced—they would kick me out."

I must confess that the juxtaposition of the sacrosanct Court of the Emperor Francis Joseph of Austria and a catalog of the world's pornographic literature had an amusing, ironic touch!

It was time for lunch; Hans closed his desk and drawers with four different keys. We left and drove to a café.

"Maria has a date with me in this café," he informed me. "You can wait for us in the fiacre."

They came out hand in hand, beaming. "This is Maria," Hans said, introducing a short but well-formed brunette with sparkling eyes, a small upturned nose, and an inviting smile. Bursting with vitality, she never stopped talking, and would change her expression every second—in other words, to use a popular term, she was good company. No wonder that the dreamy, quiet, serene Hans fell in love with her. At luncheon, he immediately broached the subject of the passport. Maria clapped her hands with satisfaction.

"You will have in your possession, this very afternoon, the nicest, the jolliest passport you have ever seen. My husband doesn't need it anymore."

I gave her a big kiss and swore my eternal gratitude.

Effenberger brought the coveted document in less than two hours, and we spent a gay evening at Ronacher's Variety Show. I returned to the Kranz hotel for a good night's sleep. At seven in the morning, someone rapped at my door.

I thought the maid must be waking me by mistake, but, when I opened the door, my heart stopped at the sight of Hans with a bandaged head, blood around his nose and mouth, an arm in a sling, and his body sagging.

"For heaven's sake, what happened?" I shouted, making him sit down.

"They have beaten me up," he said with a trembling voice.

"Who?"

"Her husband and her two brothers," and he cried. "They threatened to beat me up again if I try to see her."

All my sympathy was with him, but also I became alarmed about the passport. He reassured me that Maria had told him her husband would never miss it and that we could send it back if we wanted.

I arrived in Verbovka two days later, and the first thing I did was return the document to Hans.

The summer of 1912 in this Ukrainian village was sweet. The peace, the remoteness of the place, and the simple, unobtrusive beauty of the landscape were a boon for my nervous system. The last months in Vienna and London had left their mark on me. The constant agitation, the decisions to make, the many disappointments and responsibilities, the eternal worry about money had undermined my moral resistance. It took me only a few days, in this peaceful haven, to recover my senses.

The Davydovs were an ideal household to get along with. The father and the three sons were lively and amusing and had, thank God, the gift for discretion. They never intruded upon my privacy, never asked me to play unless I invited them. Madame Nathalie was an ideal companion. She sat still in a corner when I played, and at other times we would talk for hours about life, art, literature, and people. She gave me many Russian books to read which I had not known. She painted with talent and had organized a school for the development of popular art among the peasants of the village. One of these country women wore on a chain a gold medal which she had won at an exhibition in London.

My favorite reading spot was a bench surrounded by beds of flowers and a few birch trees. From there I could enjoy the view of the majestic sunsets on the rich, shimmering fields followed by the seemingly endless Ukrainian steppe. I did not visit the Szymanowski family that time, my silly feud with Karol being still too fresh in my mind; besides, I had heard from Natalya Michailovna that Fitelberg and Karol had taken an apartment in Vienna and were staying there for the summer.

One day I received a letter with the most upsetting news. Mr.

Bergheim had been killed in a motorcar accident, while his wife, who was with him, had suffered only minor contusions. The dear old gentleman. I cried like a child, feeling guilty for having played the ominous March. It was horrible to think of it, but I wrote a long letter to Mrs. Bergheim and a card to the nephew who sent me the dreadful message.

I spent the rest of my stay mostly at the piano, this great comforter. Natalya Michailovna showed much sympathy, since she knew all about Bergheim from my account of our so short-lived friendship.

The Davydovs kept me for a week longer than I intended to stay. "We don't like to see you downhearted," they said. They were right, and I pulled myself together, determined to attack London in Mr. Bergheim's memory—and without Chester.

I returned to Warsaw to find a letter from Mrs. Bergheim at the Victoria hotel. She was staying in Vienna with another niece of her husband, Marjorie, who was married to Fred McGarvey, the son and heir of Mr. Bergheim's partner. In her letter, the old lady gave me a detailed account of the accident, telling in simple terms how her husband had been thrown from the car they were driving and killed instantly.

In a postscript she added a few touching words: "I remember my dear husband's intentions in respect to you, and I intend to follow them up. So, please, my dear boy, accept my invitation to stay in my house when you are in London and let me know if I can be of any use to you in your career."

This postscript went straight to my heart; it was a happy surprise. I had underrated her, I am ashamed to have to admit. Mrs. Bergheim came from Protestant, upper-class English stock with all the Victorian overtones. Since she seemed, in my eyes, to live happily in the shadow of the overpowering personality of her husband, I had not realized how strong a character of her own she possessed.

I answered her with warm words, accepted with thanks her invitation, and promised to visit her in a short time in Vienna, where I was going to give a concert.

Pola, back in town, was shocked by the news of the accident. "I, too, had a premonition on that night when you told me the story of the Funeral March," she said.

My season began with a concert in Lodz, where my parents and the rest of the family were curious to hear my account of the concert season abroad. Of course, they already knew every detail, being the best detectives in the world.

After two or three concerts in Russian Poland, I left for Kraków for my annual appearance. The manager of the hall was pleased to tell me that I was going to have a very good attendance. "Soon we will beat Lwów," he boasted. His secretary, Rudolf Eisenbach, a cousin of the pianist Ignaz Friedman, was actually in charge of the concerts. After the exceptionally good results of my recital, I thanked him for his excellent work. He asked to see me in private; he had a proposition to make. We sat down in a café, and I was ready to listen.

"You know what I think of you," he began shyly, his ears turning red. "You have it in you to make a glorious career, but you need somebody to help you to achieve it."

"I don't agree with you," I interrupted him. "If my concerts continue to show the same kind of results as this one in Kraków, I have nothing to worry about."

"But you are wrong," he replied heatedly. "You are an artist, and it takes a businessman to run things profitably and successfully. You need someone who can exploit opportunities, who gets in touch with concert organizations, and who knows how to talk about money."

He became excited: "And I am the man for you. Here is my plan: I shall be your private manager. I shall arrange your tours in a practical way, send out your publicity to the concert managers, obtain better fees, and run your own concerts in cities where you are apt to fill a house. I would travel with you to see that you are not taken advantage of." He stopped to take a breath.

"My dear fellow," I said, smiling sadly, "your plan is perfect, it sounds wonderful, but from where would I get the money to pay you for all this? I have hardly enough money for my own expenses, and you want to travel with me?"

"No, no, you did not let me finish," he said hastily. "You don't have to pay me anything now. All I want is ten percent of your net earnings when you will be able to afford it, and I shall see to it that you make enough to make it possible. I shall be responsible for my own traveling expenses until the time comes when it will be easy for you to pay me back."

I was astounded. His proposal sounded too good to be true. The vision of a personal manager who would run my affairs without any commitment on my part was irresistible. I would have agreed on the spot if I hadn't been afraid that I had overlooked some detrimental factor in his plan.

"Give it to me in writing," I said. "I shall discuss it with your manager here. I will abide by his opinion, as he has known your work for years."

He agreed. With his paper in hand (I studied it carefully) I presented the case to his boss.

"He's had this idea on his mind for a long time," said Trzciński, the manager. "I know I am losing a good secretary, but my advice is: take him, he will be invaluable for you."

Eisenbach and I made up a contract for three years and signed it. He started on his work without losing time, and results were quick to show. My concerts in Lwów, under his control, yielded more money. Besides, he obtained a few engagements in Galicia for higher fees. Thanks to his efficient correspondence with Russian societies of music, he arranged for me a nice tour including St. Petersburg. For publicity, he had some neat little brochures printed with my picture and excerpts from reviews, and he dispatched them to important music centers.

He kept me busy all through autumn. The concerts in Russia were particularly successful, especially in Kiev, where I was wined and dined by my friends. The Davydovs were in Petersburg at the time of my concert and insisted on taking me to all sorts of parties. We had a luncheon at the Winter Palace (in the absence of the Tsar), given by the general in command of the place.

Eugene Onegin at the Marjinski Opera was lovely. A large reception took place in the sumptuous house of Baroness Üxkull-Gilenband, whom I had met in Kiev. Hundreds of people filled the five or six reception rooms. Tired of being introduced by the hostess to the many princes and counts without finding anybody to talk to but my friends, I tried to find my way to the buffet. Passing a boudoir, I noticed a huge monk sitting on a taboret talking to a group of persons who surrounded him. I was sure it was Theodore, the monk who escaped from his monastery, published pamphlets against the powerful Synod, and became popular in certain Petersburg salons. He looked so repulsive with his dirty hair and beard that I walked away. Later, out in the street, Dmitry Davydov whispered: "The monk was Rasputin. He has a dangerous influence on the Tsarina and the Tsar." I regret now that I did not take a closer look at him.

I spent a few weeks around Christmas and New Year's in Warsaw. Eisenbach joined me there for further plans. My only remaining engagements were for two concerts in Rome. It was important to appear again in Vienna, Berlin, and London after the promising debuts there. But we did not have the money for the heavy expenditures involved. We studied the problem carefully and found out that I could afford to risk two concerts in Vienna. London with Chester was out of the question. We had to find another manager.

We left for Vienna, where Eisenbach began to prepare my recitals at the Musikvereinssaal. A week later I took the train for Rome. The Augusteo was well attended, the public acclaimed me, but the fee was so derisively small that it barely covered my traveling and living expenses. All my "important" friends were out of town, and there was no chance of a nice, profitable little private concert. "During the winter season they go skiing or stay on the Riviera," Count San Martino informed me.

I spent only a few days in Rome, stopped in Venice for less than a week, and returned to Vienna. Eisenbach, who fetched me at the station, sounded a little pessimistic about our concerts.

"For the first recital we have a great annual ball against us," he said, "and on the second night there is a gala premiere at the Opera."

I listened without becoming upset or discouraged. Lifelong observation has taught me that whenever a public is slow in buying tickets the local managers will find some real, indisputable reasons for it: the mayor's birthday, a patriotic celebration, or an epidemic of catarrh. But when the people *really* wanted to hear an artist, not wars or revolutions or general strikes would deter them from coming to the concert.

At the Kranz I received a postcard from Mr. von Sachs inviting me to tea, "to meet Mrs. Bergheim." I telephoned my acceptance and learned from him that our friend was back in Vienna staying with the McGarveys. I found their number in the book and called right away. Mrs. Bergheim was glad to hear my voice. She introduced me over the phone to her niece, who asked me for lunch on the next day.

"Aunt Clara has been telling us so much about you," she said. Fred and Madge McGarvey lived in a large, comfortable apartment on the Arenberg Platz, two houses away from the Godowskys. They were alone when I entered the living room.

"My aunt will be with us in a minute, but we don't need her to get acquainted. We know you very well from her stories about you, and we have been looking forward to meeting you." I was instantly at ease with them, and when Mrs. Bergheim came into the room she found the three of us chatting as if we had known each other for ages. Their aunt seemed to have recovered from her shock; she looked the same as when I had left her. "Arthur, my dear." She kissed and embraced me. "I am so glad to see you," and, lowering her voice, "You remind me so much of him." She was crying, and I was deeply moved.

At table we started an animated conversation about music; both Fred and Madge McGarvey were very musical and felt a passion for the piano. They were thrilled by the news of my concerts in Vienna.

"And what about London?" Mrs. Bergheim asked. "When are you coming? You remember, I hope, your promise to stay with me?"

"I don't think I shall be able to come this year," I said. "I have no concerts in London."

Mrs. Bergheim was puzzled. "I thought it was all arranged," she said. "Johnny told me that he was going to take care of it. What made you change your mind?"

Her curiosity was soon satisfied by my irrepressible loquacity. After my half-hour of talk, she and the McGarveys knew everything worth knowing about me. What fascinated Mrs. Bergheim was my unusual contract with Eisenbach. "I want to meet this secretary of yours, or is he your manager?"

"He is both," I said.

That very afternoon, Eisenbach, in a long interview, outlined to Mrs. Bergheim his plans for my immediate future and obtained from her a credit for up to fifteen hundred pounds and from Fred McGarvey an additional one for five hundred pounds. The money was to be used to promote my concerts in London, Vienna, Berlin, and other important cities. My secretary was to account periodically for his expenditures.

After the success of his visit Rudolf recounted his personal triumph with the air of Napoleon after the battle of Austerlitz. Mrs. Bergheim nobly refused to be thanked. "I only did what Johnny had intended to do." And Fred McGarvey, when I began to express in awkward terms my gratitude, stopped me, putting his hands on my shoulders. "My dear fellow, Poland helped me to my good fortune, and you simply gave me a chance to reciprocate."

Both concerts in Vienna gave me great satisfaction. At the first one I performed the formidable *Hammerklavier* Sonata of Beethoven, this stumbling block for the average pianist. To be able to hold the listener's attention during the long, calm, majestic Adagio was a difficult problem which I seemed to have solved on that evening. The program for the second concert was in a lighter vein. After Bach and Chopin, I played my usual successful stuff. We had a deficit at the first recital, but the expenses for the second one were almost covered.

Godowsky was present at both concerts and had praise for the Sonata. "But you must practice," was his post-comment.

To our great relief, young Dagmar Godowsky managed to bring about a complete reconciliation between Karol and myself. At Demel's famous tearoom, happy to see each other again, we laughed off our absurd, childish feud. From that day on, our friendship remained unscathed until Karol's premature death.

"How are you getting along with Ficio?" I asked. It was a fatal question.

"Don't utter the name of this shameless creature," he exclaimed with a grimace of disgust.

"What has he done to you?" My curiosity was aroused. Karol, with intense indignation, a finger pressed to his nose, said in a viciously hissing voice: "Arthur, just imagine—this beast brought a woman to our flat while I was away, and he had the infernal cheek to sleep with her on my bed, right under the picture of my mother, you understand, Arthur? Under the *picture of my own mother!* I should have killed him for that!"

I couldn't help it—I chuckled.

This incident reminded me of a similar one between Chopin and Liszt, who committed the very same indiscretion. Anyway, I was not displeased to see Karol getting a taste of the "real" Fitelberg.

Eisenbach arranged a recital in Berlin at the old Singakademie, the hall where I had heard Joachim and Hausmann play the Double Concerto of Brahms with the Meininger Hofkapelle under Fritz Steinbach. I felt it an honor to appear in this venerable hall.

A pleasant surprise awaited me. Mrs. Emma Engelmann, in a letter forwarded by our agent, invited me to be her guest during my stay in Berlin. She had lost her husband and was living with her son Hans in an apartment near the Kurfürstendamm. I wired my grateful acceptance.

On the morning of our arrival in the German capital, Hans, now a tall, fattish young man, awaited me with a broad smile and drove me to their new home. Rudolf took a room in a nearby hotel.

I found Mrs. Engelmann almost unchanged; she was the same friendly, agile, round little lady as when I had seen her last. At breakfast we had much to tell each other, mostly about musical matters. It was good to taste the familiar atmosphere again.

The concert went well. The not large attendance was very appreciative. I played with great attention to detail and with technical precision but without the usual aplomb. In Berlin, my natural enthusiasm would often lose its spontaneity, as if I were still under the spell of the old Barthian days. Apropos Barth, the Professor was at the concert, and wrote me a letter full of critical innuendos, yet he had a few words of praise for my Chopin. No trace in his letter of a serious approach to the pure essence of music—there was nothing but some advice for a better handling of technical problems.

Mrs. Engelmann played with me during a whole afternoon: quartets of Beethoven and Schubert arranged for four hands. This was heaven. That afternoon remained in my memory as the highlight of those days in Berlin.

We left for Kraków, Rudolf and I. He had some business of his own to attend to, and I had to give two additional concerts in Galicia. One of them was in Czernowitz, a well-to-do industrial center near the Rumanian frontier. Its inhabitants liked to call their city the Vienna of the East.

An old gentleman whose name I forget met me at the station and introduced himself.

"I am the man who engaged you," he said.

On the way to the hotel, when I questioned him about the piano, he answered somewhat arrogantly: "My dear boy, you can be proud of having the chance to play in Czernowitz. The subscribers to my concerts are the most important people in town—they are more elegant than any public in Vienna."

I was impressed by his boast, although a little unconvinced. The hall was well proportioned and in good taste, the acoustics were perfect, and the piano was a good Bösendorfer. A detail, an odd feature, was not to my liking: one side of the hall had a row of ten doors opening directly onto the street. The feeling of having to play so close to street noises was disturbing. I was used to halls which were well protected from outside sounds.

In the evening, at the concert, the sight of the audience was really impressive. The hall was filled with people dressed up as if they had been invited to a ball by the Emperor, and not to a simple concert. The manager was right, it was the most elegant—but also the most indifferent, bloodless audience I had ever faced. After every piece I played, and I played well, begloved hands trying to produce a sound with two or three polite claps were faintly heard. The sound died before I had a chance to bow. No wonder, therefore, that I planned to finish the recital as quickly as possible. After I played the last chord the public regaled me with three additional claps and made ready to leave. All the exit doors were opened wide and a gush of cold wind blew into the hall. Back in the artists' room, I was reaching for my coat and hat when the noise of a genuine applause struck my ear. I peeped into the hall and saw, to my amazement, the whole public standing up with their coats on, clapping with energy.

Aha, I thought scornfully. They applaud here only when they want encores, not before? Well, I'll teach them. I went up to bow with ice-cold dignity. The applause grew louder. I bowed two or three times more, and finally I couldn't suppress a smile. Now they began to shout "Bravo, bis, bravo, bis," shouts which no artist can resist. Well, I played an encore. When I finished, hell broke loose. They made me play three more encores and I finished by enjoying my success.

All through the concert, the old manager was sitting quietly in the artists' room, apparently satisfied with me and the audience. But, from the moment when the applause started, he became restless. I heard him mumbling angrily: "I must stop that, I can't bear it any longer, I *will* stop that!"

His anger grew with every encore until, in a paroxysm of rage, banging his fists on the table, he shouted: "I shall call the police, I must call the police!"

"What has happened?" I asked solicitously. "Are you in trouble, can I help?"

"No," he said, with a discouraged gesture. "It is useless, nothing would stop you from playing your encores."

This was too much. "What have my encores to do with your rage?" I asked sharply. He calmed down and said, with a quivering voice: "You see, it is the fault of these damned exit doors. They open them at the end of the concerts, and while my public is leaving the hall, hundreds of hoodlums who have been waiting for this moment in cafés and in the streets pour in and applaud noisily to make my artists give them a free concert, and I have no way of stopping them!" He sat down with a heavy sigh. I said a few words of sympathy but I made a vow to play in Czernowitz in the future only for the "hoodlums."

When we returned to Vienna, Mrs. Bergheim had left for London. I saw much of the McGarveys, who were helpful in every way. They invited me to practice on their piano, which was better than the one I had at the hotel.

My repertoire needed expansion. Two major Beethoven sonatas, short pieces by Brahms and Schumann, and the great B minor Sonata of Chopin were added to it in less than two weeks. As before, and as would prove true for many years after, the processes of my means of approach to the music at hand were made up of a peculiar combination: a clear conception of the structure of a composition and complete empathy with the composer's emotional intentions were always within my reach, but because of my lazy habits, I would neglect to pay attention to detail and to a finished and articulate performance of difficult passages that I hated to practice. I used to put the whole weight on the inner message of the music.

Effenberger, completely recovered from his contusions and from his infatuation with Maria, finished his illicit assignment. Back to his normal self, he became a charming companion, making my life richer by his vast knowledge, which embraced anything worth reading, seeing, or hearing. It was he who acquainted me with the first novels of Thomas Mann, with the poetry of Rainer Maria Rilke, and with the music of the young Austrian composers.

Karol showed me sketches of a piano concerto which he intended to write for me, but he used them later for the First Violin Concerto, which he dedicated to Paul Kochanski. I was later compensated by the gift of his beautiful Symphony Concertante for piano and orchestra.

We saw the *Rosenkavalier* with Lotte Lehmann and Elisabeth Schumann, a wonderful ensemble. But the outstanding event of the season was the Double Concerto of Brahms, played by Ysaye and Casals. I had to stand behind a double bass in the orchestra, because there was no seat left in the house, but my discomfort could not spoil for a second my joy and my emotion listening to the unforgettable performance by these two great artists.

71

The London season had just begun. We arrived, Rudolf and I, on a sunny morning, after a long and tiring journey from Vienna. At Victoria Station we found Mrs. Bergheim's chauffeur, who drove us through the crowded city to the remote, peaceful Belsize Park. The old lady welcomed me with her typical straightforward simplicity.

"I hope you will be comfortable, my dear," she said, taking me to a lovely room on the second floor. "Nina and Peter are your neighbors, so you won't feel alone. If you need anything, call Wiggins, my housemaid—she will look after you."

I felt as if I had never lived anywhere else. Wiggins unpacked my trunk, placed everything in order, and took my clothes to be ironed, all with silent efficiency.

Eisenbach was driven by the chauffeur to a place where Mrs. Bergheim had reserved a room for him.

At lunch I met the two other members of the household. Nina Bergheim was a tall, slender young woman in her late twenties. She was shy and amiable and of great help to her aunt in running the house. Unfortunately, her face was so utterly commonplace that I wouldn't be able to recognize her in the street. Her brother Peter was a businessman; he had a responsible post in a large steel company. A Jew, born in Jerusalem like his uncle, he tried to look and behave more English than the English themselves, an attitude which gave him a look of cold aloofness. In later years he even changed his name.

I spent a restful week in the quiet, clocklike routine of the house. In the morning, after breakfast, Mrs. Bergheim liked to invite me to her boudoir to read aloud the letters she had just received in the morning mail—a ritual, I guess, that she must have performed daily with her late husband. As soon as the last letter was read I was free to practice the new repertoire without being disturbed.

Eisenbach reserved two dates for my recitals at Bechstein Hall, the first at the end of May, the second one in June. The manager he had chosen this time was Daniel Meyer, who had many artists on his list and could be trusted. . . . Anyway, he couldn't be worse than old Chester!

Paul Draper sent me a letter asking me to come that night for supper. "Later we shall have some music," he wrote. I telephoned that of course I would.

The Drapers had left their charming house in Kensington and moved to 19 Edith Grove, a short, uninviting street situated amid a poor, dreary neighborhood. Muriel Draper had the magic to know just how to transform the banal, uniform look of Number 19 into a most agreeable place to live. There was an odd structure on the rear of their house; it might have served as a studio, a stable, a workshop, or a cellar, God only knows. Muriel had emptied and cleaned it inside, leaving only the naked brick walls; she broke through a wall to make room for a door and staircase leading down to the place, and then, miraculously, she created out of it a magnificent, spacious, square, noble music room. On one side of the huge fireplace stood the Bechstein concert grand, some music stands, and shelves with music. On the wall opposite was a large, majestic sofa flanked by two long Renaissance tables and an oversized armchair. The mantle over the fireplace was covered by an old Gothic tapestry. Dark wooden beams crossed the ceiling, and huge candles were posted in prominent places. The whole gave the impression of the interior of a Florentine palace. But the most precious aspect of the room was its power to attract great artists to make music.

The night I was about to enter the enchantment of this place, I heard from the entrance door the theme of the second movement of the F major Quartet by Beethoven, the Opus 59, No. 1. Nothing more beautiful has ever been written. Paul Draper showed me the way to the music room, and we sat down on one of the steps so as not to disturb the musicians. Convinced that I had been invited to a *soirée musicale*, called in England an "at home," I was happily surprised to see not more than six or seven persons listening intensely to the accents of proud resignation of this sublime work. When the finale with the Russian tune came to an end, I descended the stairs to greet Muriel Draper and to be introduced to her guests. Three of them were Spaniards: Enrique Arbós,

a violinist and conductor, and Agustin Rubio, a cellist, were both professors at the Royal Academy of Music; the third, Pedro Morales, was
a viola player. The others were: Eugene Goossens, a young violinist and
composer of Belgian descent, who later became a famous conductor; an
anonymous lady; and the great American painter John Sargent, who was,
I discovered, a fervent lover of music.

The London String Quartet, led by the young, brilliant Albert Sammons, was on its way to becoming the best "ensemble" of its kind. The
four players invited me to join them in a quintet. "Yes, yes," Muriel
shouted, "Arthur will play, but first we'll have supper."

We followed her upstairs to a small dining room where a table laden
with cold lobsters, champagne, fresh fruit, cheese, and desserts offered a
pleasant sight. Mixing happily food and conversation, we spent a delightful hour getting better acquainted. Arbós made us laugh tears with his
funny stories. John Sargent exchanged with me memories of Joseph
Joachim, whom he admired and whose portrait he had painted. After
the last drop of coffee, we returned cheerfully to the music room.

We settled down to play the F minor Quintet of Brahms. It meant
for me a first sight-reading, but I knew this particular work from ear,
having played it many times for four hands. I played a little cautiously
at the beginning; the original version was much more difficult than I
thought. Soon, however, I warmed up, and inspired by the sensitive and
powerful cooperation by Sammons and his colleagues, we gave a fine
rendering of this masterpiece, to the warm approval of our listeners.

As is customary among musicians, we entered into long discussions
and comments on every facet of our performance. Our interminable
chatter was stopped by Muriel's imperative voice: "And now, please, the
Schumann!"

We obeyed. The Quintet of Schumann, this jewel of chamber music,
gave me a better opportunity to show my born gift and love for ensemble playing. It was easier to read at sight than the Brahms, and I
plunged into this work with delight and passion. When we finished, a
loud cheer was our reward. By then, I had become drunk with music.
Discarding the quartet players, who needed a rest, my greedy eyes fell
on Goossens and Rubio.

"Please, please, come on, let us play a Schubert trio!" I prompted
them. They resisted at first, but when I dragged them almost by force
toward their respective instruments they gave in and we settled down
to play the great B flat Trio. With trios I felt at home; they were my
domain. I had played them dozens of times with Paul Kochanski and his
brother. Consequently, our playing had the quality of a concert performance. The beauty of the music whetted our appetite for more. We

attacked, without delay, the other grand Schubert, the Trio in E flat, which came off even better than the first. Getting up from our seats, glad, and a little tired, we were ready to call it a day or, more precisely, a night, when Muriel announced with an air immune to objection: "Paul, give us a few songs from the *Winterreise*."

And Paul sang, with me at the piano, almost the whole of Schubert's winter journey cycle with his small, well-trained voice and great intensity of expression. He stopped, but I continued to play my favorite songs by Brahms, Schumann, Hugo Wolf, and others, anything I could think of. After this orgy of music, it was really time to go home.

"Come up for a little snack," called Muriel from upstairs. "You must be hungry." Yes, we were indeed, without being aware of it. The "snack" was a hearty meal of scrambled eggs, cold meat, cheese, and coffee. Chatting, joking, laughing, we finally took leave and dispersed in different directions. From that night on, the music room at 19 Edith Grove became a temple of glorious music making such as the world has not known; it remains in my memory as the supreme musical euphoria of my life.

I woke up at noon the next day. At lunch, Mrs. Bergheim asked: "Was it a dance last night? I heard you come in at five this morning."

I told her what kind of party it was. The old lady was perplexed. "But this is preposterous! How wicked to ask guests to play and to order them about! And two suppers, you said? They must be very rich."

"No, I don't think so," I said, "but I am sure that they will give more of these parties, and I would love to take you to one of them."

Poor Mrs. Bergheim. It took me some time to make her understand what they meant to me. Anyway—to pacify her—I submitted stolidly to her reading of her mail.

May 1913 passed off like a dream. The month included some parties, plays, great concerts and lesser ones; often stimulating, sometimes amusing, they were always interesting, but the nights of music at Edith Grove were inspiring—they were inspiring in the best sense of the word. The company of great musicians dedicated to the purest expression of their art enriched, ennobled, exalted the lives of those present, whether performing or listening.

Our next gathering at the Drapers' occurred on the spur of the moment, quite unexpectedly. We all went to Jacques Thibaud's concert with orchestra at the Queen's Hall. Entranced by his beautiful playing, the Drapers, I, and many musicians went to the Green Room to thank him.

"Let us all go to have supper at Edith Grove," said Muriel in her tone of finality. And, turning to a group of musicians, "Go and fetch your instruments. Jacques and Arthur will want to make some music."

"Mais, avec joie, ma chère," said Thibaud, who had played before in their former house. The Drapers, he, and I took a taxi, and arrived well ahead of the others. The supper was on the table; she had ordered it by phone from the Savoy Grill.

On that night I met Lionel Tertis. "This is my friend, a viola player," said Albert Sammons, introducing an unassuming little man in the middle thirties with the kindest eyes in the world behind his glasses, and a ready smile. A thick, tobacco-blond, oppressive mustache belied the rest of his friendly face.

"Come in and eat," ordered Muriel, clapping her hands, and the hungry lot of us rushed into the dining room and actually devoured the succulent delicacies from the Savoy Grill. When the happy noise around the supper table subsided, Thibaud gave the signal: "Come on, boys, let us play a little quartet!"

Paul set up the stands, and Jacques, Sammons, Tertis, and Rubio settled down to play the one by Debussy.

From the first bars on, I became aware of a new element in their ensemble, a sonority I had never heard before. The sound came to light by the powerful, singing, soulful tone of the viola as played by Lionel Tertis. Here was one of the greatest artists it was my good fortune to know and to hear. Our close, lifelong friendship dates from that night on.

After the Debussy, I played with him, Thibaud, and Rubio the C minor Piano Quartet by Brahms. The sound of his solo in the first movement still rings in my ears. It was a glorious night of music.

My first concert was carefully prepared by Daniel Meyer and, if not full, was quite well attended. I played a few pieces of my new repertoire for the first time and had qualms about them, but the presence and acclaim of my friends and fellow musicians encouraged me throughout the recital.

During intermission, Meyer and Eisenbach brought good news of an invitation from Sir Henry Wood to play with his orchestra in July, a wish come true; I had hoped for this for a long time.

The concert ended with a clamorous success of the Polonaise in A flat of Chopin and the unavoidable encores.

Later, in the crowded artists' room, Muriel Draper sought out with great cunning the right people to take back for supper. This time she had prepared it. A good opportunity for Mrs. Bergheim to find out what a Draper "party" was like, I thought. "May I bring Mrs. Bergheim to your supper?" I asked Mrs. Draper discreetly. "You may, if you must," she answered in her manly, ungracious way. Undeterred by her rebuff, I invited the old lady in her name.

The supper was superb, with lobsters and champagne aplenty. On that night there were some other guests besides Mrs. Bergheim: John Sargent again; John Warner, Paul's roommate at Harvard, a pianist and organist; and three ravishing American girls, sisters, Sarah, Hoyty, and Olga Wiborg. All the musicians present had brought their instruments; it had become the rule of the house.

The music began with the Piano Quintet of Schumann, on which Thibaud and Tertis did wonders, followed by the Franck Sonata played by Jacques and myself. We were all charmed when little red-haired Paul Junior, aged four, appeared in his pajamas to hear the music. After a while his mother took him back to bed. Later on, we had the joy of hearing the String Sextet of Brahms performed by Sammons and Goossens, violins; Tertis and Gertrud Bauer (the pianist Harold Bauer's sister), violas; and Rubio and May Mukle, a newcomer, cellos. A beautiful work beautifully played.

After a short snack we had a charming interlude. The Wiborg sisters asked me to accompany them in the Terzetto of the Daughters of the Rhine from Wagner's *Götterdämmerung*. They sang it delightfully with their young, fresh voices. Paul, excited by their singing, kept me at the piano and sang "Ich grolle nicht" of Schumann, and Schubert's "Erlkönig."

Mrs. Bergheim, imbued with the Victorian tradition of how a "party" should be run, was, at first, shocked by the informality which reigned at Edith Grove. Muriel's brusque, self-assertive ways, her sarcastic remarks and loud laughter, offended her bourgeois background. But soon, after supper, the charm of the place and the beauty of the music, played and heard with an enjoyment hitherto unknown to her, exercised their magic. She fell, in the end, completely under the spell of Edith Grove. On our way home, she never stopped babbling about the many features of the party.

From that night on, my time was divided between Belsize Park and Edith Grove, which was quite a big physical effort: the long waiting for buses or taxis, the seemingly interminable distance between these two points, had a telling effect on my nerves.

A great solace to me was the arrival of Paul Kochanski and Zosia. With the beginning of June, when the London season reached its peak, most performing artists would come to the British capital, as all artistic activities on the Continent were at rest until autumn. Paul Kochanski was immediately recognized by the Drapers as a full-fledged partner in all musical activities at the studio, and both he and Zosia were soon intimates of the Bergheim and Draper households.

My second recital, in spite of being well attended and well received, fell a little short of my expectations. It was simply lost in the avalanche of concerts by the perennial favorites of the English public: Paderewski, Ysaye, Casals, and Kreisler filled Queen's Hall to the brim; Caruso, Melba, and Destinn reigned at Covent Garden. Premieres of plays by Bernard Shaw, James Barrie, and John Galsworthy were the great attractions of the season. And, last but not least, a visit of Diaghilev's Russian Ballet was announced for July.

We were ardent participants in this orgy of performances, Paul, Zosia, and I—sometimes finding good seats, often standing through a whole performance.

Nevertheless, music at Edith Grove went on as before, or, better still, it entered a new era. Musicians who heard about our reunions begged to be allowed to join them, and snobs who couldn't bear to be left out tried to force their way in. Muriel was inflexible on that point; performers were always welcome, even if they had no chance to perform, but she would not tolerate anybody but a few listeners of distinction, mostly men like Sargent, Henry James, or Norman Douglas. When forced to invite some musicians' wives, she prepared for them a cozy corner upstairs where they could chat without disturbing the music. She did get on quite well with Zosia, in spite of their frequent verbal skirmishes.

I remember the night when Rubio brought Casals for the first time to Edith Grove. We were having supper while a quartet of Mozart was played in the studio. Pablo stood still at the front door and asked suddenly: "Who plays the viola?" He discerned Lionel Tertis's tone from that long distance. It was a happy meeting for these two great artists. A curious coincidence: both are born on the same day of the same year, and right now, as I am writing this, they are both alive and well at the ripe age of ninety-six.

Paul Kochanski and I were very fortunate in that year of 1913 to have made so much chamber music with these giants. Rubio worshiped Casals and always called him Pablissimo. He himself was quite a personality. A man in the sixties of a tall, commanding stature with a flowing gray beard and a wavy shock of hair, a strong nose, and blue eyes burning with faith and passion, he could have served as a model for Michelangelo's statue of Moses.

On that night of Pablo's first contact with the music room, I heard for the first time the String Quintet with two cellos by Schubert, played with deep inspiration by Thibaud, Paul, Tertis, Casals, and Rubio. My emotion at hearing it is indescribable. All I can say is that ever since that night my desire is to be escorted, at the hour of my death, by the sound, real or imaginary, of its heavenly Adagio's peace and resignation.

Returning to my career: Mr. Daniel Meyer obtained for me two engagements for "at homes," the first one at Lord and Lady Esher's, the second one in the beautiful house at Belgrave Square of Sir Otto Beit, a South African millionaire. The English "at homes" were more formal than the *soirées musicales* in Paris; they were considered as concerts given in private homes. Some snobbery was involved in the proceedings. It reminds me of a story: An English Duchess requested Paderewski to play after a dinner she was giving for King George and Queen Mary. The great pianist demanded a very large sum of money which was readily granted. A day before the event he received a letter from the Duchess: "Dear Maestro, accept my regrets for my not inviting you to the dinner. As a professional artist, you will be more at ease in a nice room where you can rest before the concert. Yours, etc."

Paderewski answered: "Dear Duchess: thanks for your letter. As you so kindly inform me that I am not obliged to be present at your dinner, I shall be satisfied with half of my fee. Yours, etc."

I know of another charming answer: Pablo de Sarasate, the famous Spanish violinist, freshly arrived in London, received the following note:

"Dearest friend, how lovely to have you back in town! Can you dine with us tomorrow? Yours devotedly, etc. Postscript: Please, do not forget to bring your Stradivarius."

Sarasate replied: "Delighted to see you again. I most certainly accept your invitation to come to dinner tomorrow. Yours affectionately, etc. Postscript: My Stradivarius does not dine."

The beginning of July brought a quick succession of interesting events. Paul Kochanski gave a brilliant recital at Bechstein Hall followed by much more music at the Drapers.

My own first appearance with orchestra as a soloist in Chopin's F minor Concerto was well received by the public but did not please the critics. In their peremptory opinion, Paderewski's conception of this work, which was so much more sentimental and romantic than mine, was the definitive one.

Kreisler, Casals, and Harold Bauer gave a splendid matinée of trios at Queen's Hall. The three great artists, so distinct as to temperament, merged in complete unison.

A young boy aged ten, a pianist, showed great talent in a concerto of Mozart. His name was announced simply as Solomon.

Mrs. Bergheim, by then a converted partisan of the Draper "parties," not without a touch of jealousy, tried to emulate them in her own modest way. The small receptions with music *furnished* by a young, inexperienced trio were not very successful. So she decided, on my suggestion, to give a real English "at home." I offered, of course, to play a whole recital program. The large dining room was emptied of its furniture, and a good concert grand was sent in by Bechstein's. The place was filled with her friends and their own musical friends, with Muriel's chosen coterie and my new acquaintances. It was a brilliant affair.

The old lady was exultant with pride; she enjoyed every minute of it. She kept Zosia, Muriel, and the two Pauls until late hours, talking about the party. Her "at home" gave her a new shot of vitality. The result of it was an almost daily tour of sightseeing. In the morning, after breakfast and the reading of the letters, she would take me to the Kew Gardens or to Hampton Court, to the exhibition at the Royal Academy, or the Chelsea Flower Show, putting me often into a state of collapse, while she remained fresh as a daisy; in addition, she made me inspect every day *all* the hothouses in her garden. Nina and Peter Bergheim took no part in all this.

Late one afternoon, I was in my room reading when Wiggins called: "Mr. Rubinstein—Mrs. Draper is on the phone." Expecting to learn of a project for the evening, I shouted: "Take a message, please." After a short while, Wiggins called again: "Mrs. Draper wants to talk to you." I went downstairs, picked up the phone, and said cheerfully, "Hello, Muriel." A soft, pathetic voice answered: "Arthur, come at once if you can. I need you, I am unhappy, it's Paul." I didn't lose time; a taxi took me to Edith Grove. I found Muriel sitting at her desk in the small room which led to the studio. The Muriel I saw at that moment was a completely different person from the one I knew so well. Dressed in a loose pink tea gown, there sat a soft feminine figure with silky blond hair falling in large waves over her shoulder and part of her face. Big blue eyes looked up at me in distress. My question, "What happened?" she answered with uncontrollable sobs. Then, calming down a little, she spoke.

"Paul disappeared four days ago, and, this time, nobody has seen him anywhere. He is completely lost. I tried desperately to find him, calling up all the bars I knew about. I finally called up the police and they brought him this morning in a state which I cannot describe—I thought he was going to die. He is upstairs in bed now, still only half-conscious. The doctor gave him a sedative." She began to cry again, and added: "Arthur, I can't take it anymore. I am all alone with it—I try to hide it from people. You are one of the few who knows, you have seen him in that state—please help me, Arthur!"

I found nothing to say. There was nothing I could do. There was a long silence. And suddenly I took her in my arms, I kissed her. I spoke to her soothingly and stroked her hair tenderly. I fell in love.

72

The Russian Ballet brought the London season to a glorious end; the whole town lived for two weeks under its spell. For me, personally, there was the revelation of a great composer, Igor Stravinsky. His *Firebird* as danced by Karsavina, Bolm, and the corps de ballet was beautiful to watch, but my attention was completely absorbed by the music. The richness of the orchestration, the rhythmic pulse, the subtlety in the treatment of melody and modulation, and the majestic crescendo of the final hymn absolutely carried me away.

My rapture was even greater when I saw *Petrouchka* for the first time. During the entire performance of this masterpiece, the action on the stage enthralled me as much as the music. Here, the orchestra produced an orgy of the most authentic Russian sound since Moussorgsky. The death of the puppet by Nijinsky with its disconsolate music moved me to tears. We also saw the enchanting *Après-midi d'un faune*, Nijinsky's novel creation, and *Daphnis et Chloé* by Ravel. The last production was *Le Sacre du printemps*. The excited accounts of the scandalous tumult which broke out at the premiere in Paris had created in London a feverish expectation. We sat on pins in the packed Drury Lane theater. The short prelude sounded lovely and promising. But when the curtain went up, the music was difficult to grasp, and with the progress of the ballet, the noise and the monotony of the score and the incomprehensible action on the stage began to exasperate me. When it came to the last hysterical dance of the sacrificed maiden, my nerves could not take it any more. I was defeated and unhappy.

The audience gave a polite applause accompanied by some hissing; the well-bred English public felt respect for the author of *Petrouchka*. It took me weeks of study to understand the greatness of this work. Ten years later, in Paris, young pupils of the Conservatory played this score as if it were a study of Czerny.

Pierre Monteux, the great conductor, held the baton throughout the season. And I saw almost all the performances in the company of the Drapers, the Kochanskis, or Mrs. Bergheim, whom Muriel now called "Aunt Clara" but, behind her back, derisively, "Clarita."

Paul and Zosia left for Poland. So did Eisenbach. I meant to leave with them but changed my plans. I simply couldn't tear myself away from London. Edith Grove became, in time, my second home. I spent whole days with Muriel and Paul: we would lunch at the Savoy Grill or at some Italian restaurant in Soho; I escorted Muriel to dressmakers, or art dealers; we went to theaters and variety shows, or made music at the studio.

I discovered a new side of Paul: he was an inveterate gambler, who would bet on the horses with an uncanny luck. It all came out at lunch one day at the Savoy. Paul suddenly got up and left the restaurant. Seeing me look worried, Muriel reassured me: "This time it is all right, Arthur." He came back after a few minutes, a little flushed, and declared, "I won three thousand pounds." Then he told me his story. He had always felt a passion for horse racing, and would study every day the tips and speculations of the turf specialists. In time, he said, he developed a sort of divination, an instinct, a clairvoyance.

"When this feeling comes over me," he continued, "I run to the phone and make the bet. My bookmaker, the firm of Ladbrokes, with whom I established my credit, takes any bet at the last moment before the race." He added with a smile, "I always bet for big stakes, but I also have to take big risks."

Muriel confirmed the story. "Paul's intuition for the winning horses paid for Edith Grove, the music, the suppers, the good life, and also for his lessons with Zur von Muhlen." She laughed contentedly.

During these last days in London I found a new friend, the well-known writer Norman Douglas. He appeared now and then at Edith Grove for a drink and a chat. Muriel, whom he had known as a young girl, was devoted to him. A supreme master of the English language, he liked to use in conversation a mixture of profanity and ribaldry such as would make a Rabelais blush. With all that, he was a man of a rare intellect, knowledge, and wit, endowed with a tender heart and love for music. In a sentimental mood, he reminded me of my dear Franc Fiszer from Poland. Douglas liked to take me to Soho for a lunch and talk. Honored by the friendship of a so much older and more experienced man, I confided to him my love troubles and, especially, my feeling of guilt toward Pola.

"Hairy Christ, Arthur, this is all bloody nonsense. Follow your instinct, always be yourself! If this Pola lost your love, it is her own fault;

she is not strong enough to hold you." I felt the same way, but I hadn't the courage to admit it.

At Edith Grove, Muriel said casually: "Arthur, Paul and I are leaving for Florence to stay with Mabel Dodge, an old friend of ours. She has a beautiful villa in the hills near the city. She writes: 'Bring any of your friends.' Would you like to join us?"

I accepted without the slightest hesitation, but, secretly, with a pang of remorse. I had promised Pola to come to Zakopane, where she was spending the rest of the summer.

"Aunt Clara" took the news of my departure for Florence with an indulgent smile.

"I am not surprised, my dear," she said. "I rather expected it." She gave us a nice farewell supper, and we left the next day.

The journey was long and tedious. Descending from the train in Florence, we looked like chimney sweeps. The hundred-odd tunnels between Genoa and Florence almost choked us to death.

Two horsecabs took us to the villa, where we refused to be seen by anyone before washing up. Finally, when the gong rang for dinner, I was the last to go down, and I entered a huge room where Muriel introduced me to Mrs. Dodge and her guests.

Villa Curonia was a beautiful place. Reached from Florence by a climbing, sinuous lane, it crowned the hill of Arcetri. The Renaissance palazzo in the center was surrounded by tall cypresses and fragrant flower beds. A vast loggia opened onto the soft neighboring hills and the shimmering-in-the-sun Tuscan landscape.

If Muriel and I had been alone in the villa, it would have been heaven. In reality, it was hell.

Mabel Dodge was a young woman of around thirty with a pleasant face, a slightly too generous figure, and the fixed, absent smile of a Mona Lisa. She spoke in monosyllables, save when addressing her servants, and she answered any query with a short nod. Life at her Villa Curonia was a constant carousel. Our hostess showed a gift for gathering together the most incongruous combination of guests in the world. There was the art and music critic Carl Van Vechten, a genius at arguing; Robin de la Condamine, a charming, stuttering actor whom nobody had seen on a stage; John McMullen, a young, good-looking amateur interior decorator and Muriel's pet friend. John Reed, a journalist and poet, and a militant Communist, was sullen and very aggressive. He was Mabel's choice companion. There were two shrieking Englishwomen whose names I have forgotten, and, as if it weren't enough, a continuous flow of extraneous persons were constantly invading the premises from morning until night. We had Gertrude Stein, engaged in some interminable vocal battles with

Van Vechten, Reed hating everything and everybody, Norman Douglas using with relish his most profane repertoire in swearing, and last but not least, myself, persistently jealous and irritable. Whenever or whatever I played, whether Beethoven or Stravinsky, some of those present would leave the room in protest, hating the one or the other.

Paul Draper, disgusted by it all, decided to return by himself to his lessons in London. Muriel was the only one who kept her unruffled poise amid the general hubbub. I even suspected that she enjoyed it. Her loud voice and shrill laughter got on my nerves, and I hated the way she dressed à la Scheherazade, with turban and all. Besides, I could never see her alone, as our rooms were on different floors. After ten days of this ordeal, we all had had enough of it. Muriel, McMullen, and I decided to go to Venice for a short rest.

As we took our leave, Mabel Dodge gave us another of her enigmatic smiles and a significant nod, and we were on our way.

Venice, dear Venice, thank you for those three days of bliss! In the noble calm of this miracle of a city I rediscovered the Muriel of the day when I had fallen in love with her. Here, at last, she released her golden hair from the confinement of the hated net, learned to speak softly, and regained her feminine charm.

We sat in the Piazza for hours, admiring its beauty in silence, we walked to the Accademia to see the Carpaccios, we enjoyed our grilled scampi at Martini's, and we talked endlessly and happily. John McMullen was an agreeable and amusing companion.

On the last morning, while having breakfast on the terrace of our hotel, Muriel announced with a happy smile: "Darlings, I am leaving today for London to bring the good news to Paul. I am pregnant." I took the shock bravely. Both John and I gave her the customary response: Isn't it wonderful! Good girl! Lucky Muriel, lucky Paul! . . . and the good wishes and hugs and kisses.

In the afternoon, we took her to the station in a gondola, kissed her goodbye on the platform, and saw her settle down comfortably in her compartment. When the train started, I suddenly jumped in, driven by an uncontrollable impulse, shouting to John: "I shall return for the luggage." Muriel was good-humored, and we spent the rest of the day and the night talking, eating, sleeping, and talking, until Paris. I saw her off at the Gare du Nord and remained, depressed, a whole day in the hot, deserted city. On my return to Venice, I thanked John for his help, paid the hotel, and took the train for Vienna, Kraków, and Zakopane.

Pola—I had wired her—expected me at the station and greeted me with her usual sweetness and kindness. I couldn't bear it, and felt I had to tell her the truth. On the way to her place, I confessed to her the whole story. She listened quietly, bending her head, and remained silent for a long while. Then, turning toward me, she said, softly: "I have seen it coming for a long time, Arthur. I really am too old for you, and I gave you nothing but trouble."

"No, no, no," I cried, "it's not true, you don't understand me. I love you more than ever, my darling, and I admire you! I simply couldn't help falling in love with that woman, but I *don't like her!*" Pola did not answer.

Our horse-driven cab stopped in front of a spacious house, built in the Zakopane style which I liked so much. The place was a private home and not a boardinghouse. The owner, pani Zagórska, was a distinguished lady, a cousin of Joseph Conrad. After the death of her husband she had been obliged to take in a few paying guests who were, as a rule, her personal friends. Pola was one of them and obtained a room for me next to hers, where we talked and talked until late and had a lovely night of love.

Madame Zagórska had an unmarried daughter, Aniela, living with her, a very lively and remarkable young woman who was actually the master spirit of the house. Known, moreover, as an excellent translator of Conrad's novels, she was held in high esteem by writers and poets. Thanks to her, the Zagórska home became a favorite meeting place of the Polish literary world. Stefan Zeromski, the popular novelist, Leopold Staff, a fine poet, and my dear old friend Witkacy* were daily paying guests at dinner. We were treated to and took part in the most interesting intellectual discussions I can remember.

From time to time, a tall, lean, somber figure of a man appeared at the dinner table. He had a small head with strong features, bushy eyebrows, a thick mustache, and a cropped haircut. Taciturn and uncommunicative, he would take leave of Aniela and her mother with a polite kiss of the hand, paying no attention to anyone else. Derisive tales about him were current, hinting that he was training hunchbacked and crippled students in military maneuvers. But it turned out that this man was Józef Pilsudski, the future liberator of Poland and the victor in the war against the Russian armies under Trotsky.

The six or seven weeks in Zakopane restored me completely after all the turmoils of the past "Season." Thanks to Aniela's solicitude I was

---

* Pet name for Stanislaw Witkiewicz. At the beginning of the century, his writings were considered literary extravaganzas by an otherwise gifted and attractive personality. In the 1950's, the intelligentsia of Communist Poland found in him the philosophical predecessor of Sartre and Camus. Now the literary world has discovered him.

able to work undisturbed on the piano in the living room which she reserved for me every morning. The rest of the days were filled in a way I liked best: reading, taking long walks with Pola, hunting for mushrooms, and, as my favorite pastime, having endless philosophical discussions with Witkacy at the Café Morskie Oko.

Pola and I lived in perfect harmony, happy in each other's company. *She* was never mentioned, and, anyway, I had not heard from her or communicated with her. Mrs. Bergheim sent some cards from a resort in England but did not mention the Drapers.

Eisenbach came for a few days to consult me about my coming concert tour, which looked promising. He helped me organize a charity concert which I offered to Dr. and Mrs. Dluski for their tuberculosis clinic. The concert took place on the eve of our departure. That night my playing was nostalgic and sentimental, as my memory went back ten years to the day when, in this very place, I had tried out my wings for the flight into a solitary and unknown future.

Zakopane always retained a mysterious and happy significance in my life. Many years later I returned to the same dear place to woo my future bride.

73

With the beginning of the autumn the Zagórska circle disintegrated. Pola left for Warsaw and I went to Kraków, where I remained until my first concert of the season. Eisenbach did things well; I might even say, too well. He made me travel and play all through the autumn and winter, allowing me barely two weeks of rest around Christmas. The tour began in Galicia; my concerts in Kraków and Lwów became annual events, a standing rule. For Lwów I prepared a surprise that involved quite a great risk: I announced four recitals of only Chopin's music—a remarkable feat to venture, but in reality it was a dangerous adventure. My repertoire of Chopin contained merely two programs, not four. Hence, I was obliged to learn haphazardly dozens of pieces, while on tour. It was Eisenbach's idea; he was greedy for the ready money from my faithful city of Lwów. Fortunately, there was no catastrophe; each piece was properly memorized, but far from what these masterworks should sound like.

I remember a little incident in connection with the Chopin recitals. At one of them, a scholarly piano professor, known as a severe critic, came to hear me. Panic-stricken, I sent him a note before the beginning of the concert: "Dear Professor—I beseech you, as a personal favor, not to remain in the hall. Tonight, my physical condition is such that I cannot meet your high standard. If you will kindly agree to have supper with me at George's restaurant after the concert, I shall explain to you my reasons for this unusual request." He left the hall, but he came for supper.

The rest of the Galician tour was long, tiring, and not very profitable. At its conclusion, I paid my first visit to Bucharest, the capital of Rumania. Here I was in my element; the city and the people in the street reminded me of Warsaw. A colorful and musical crowd attended the concert and listened with the kind of genuine attention so necessary to the artist. They liked me and I liked them, especially the lovely, dark-haired, sparkling-eyed Rumanian women. Later on, I was taken to a place where I heard their folk music so beautifully explored and expressed by my friend Georges Enesco. Less languorous than the Hungarian, it is more vivid and exciting.

The next day, at the Royal Palace, I played for the old Queen Elizabeth, who was well known for her sentimental German poetry, published under the name of Carmen Sylva. She and her lady-in-waiting listened distractedly for half an hour to my playing, which was frankly bad. The minute I stopped, the Queen said a few kind words in German and pinned to my lapel a shiny medal which bore the inscription "Bene Merenti," meaning "the well-deserving one"!

I returned to Warsaw with pleasure but stayed only a few days. Eisenbach saw to it that I had no respite; he kept me busy with concerts in Poland until Christmas. I did play in Lodz, where my parents and the whole family were duly impressed by the better turn my career was taking.

Yuletide in the Polish capital had a beauty of its own, which I have always considered a privilege to be a part of. It was a feast of pure, unmitigated good will and serene peace. Pola and I basked in this perfect holiday. But there was nothing comparable to a New Year's Eve spent in Warsaw. Poles possess a born gift for gaiety, for fun, and for a full enjoyment of anything life has to offer. They shout, they sing, they dance, and they drink, but they do it all out of sheer joy, never losing their natural sense of dignity, courtesy, or elegance.

And so, we ushered in the ominous year 1914, making a riotous, boisterous, jolly night of it, my friends and I. Early in January, I was off for my tour in Russia, a quite extensive one. Beginning with Kiev and Odessa, I followed the route toward Rostov on the Don, playing along the way in Poltava, Kremenchug, and Kharkov. After a concert and a short rest in Moscow, with daily visits to the theater of Stanislavski, I continued my tour. My last concerts took place along the Volga in Nizhni Novgorod, Kazan, Samara, and Saratov.*

Quite frankly, I did not derive much pleasure or profit from this lengthy round of concerts. The halls were small, and the audiences were dull. The powerful Imperial Music Society which had engaged me for the whole tour obviously neglected its provincial branches, leaving them in the hands of incompetent organizers. And to make matters worse, my fees were barely sufficient for the travel and hotel expenses.

Glad to be back home—Warsaw meant "home" to me—I prepared for the forthcoming important concerts in Vienna, Rome, Berlin, and London. Pola was uneasy about this last city.

"You will see her again," she said.

"Yes, I suppose so," I answered, "but don't worry, darling. I am completely cured." I could tell from her eyes that she was not reassured, and, I must confess, neither was I.

It was good to learn that Paul and Zosia were coming again to London. After a round of farewells to my friends, I left with Eisenbach for Vienna. A freezing cold and icy wind greeted us on our arrival in the Austrian capital; Moscow felt warm by comparison. Walking in the streets was hazardous, as the ice on the sidewalks made them slippery. Fortunately, on the day of my first concert, the weather changed. Everything went well. The public welcomed me warmly, and my own friends were all present. I had dinner with Prince Ladislas, visited the McGarveys, and lunched with Godowsky and his family. Mrs. Bergheim wrote a long letter with an invitation to stay with her again at Belsize Park. Effenberger brought me a few good books and introduced me to some talented young musicians.

The second concert with the Rosé Quartet was very interesting; the world-famous ensemble had invited me to play piano quintets with them at the Musikvereinssaal. We played the Brahms and the Schumann quintets; both were familiar to me thanks to the nights of music in London. The success of our collaboration was much spoken of, especially as neither the public nor the critics believed that I could be good for chamber music.

* The Soviets replaced the names of these and many other cities by those of some Red leaders but changed them again when the leaders fell into disgrace.

Arnold Rosé proposed that I join his Quartet for a tour in Spain in 1915. Nothing could have pleased me more. Ever since my childhood I had felt a predilection for Spanish tunes and rhythms. In later years, anything Spanish, whether music, art, books, or history, held a special interest for me. And so, in spite of having to appear for the first time in Spain only as an auxiliary and not as a soloist, I gratefully accepted his proposition.

Eisenbach gave me a sad report of our finances. Whatever small income there was, he said, the expenses for the two of us had swallowed up.

We arrived in Rome with empty pockets and little hope for filling them sufficiently for the near future. Count San Martino wanted me to play in his concerts but refused stubbornly to raise my fee; the orchestra cost him too much, he argued. I had a windfall, however, in the form of a well-paid *soirée musicale* given by the Marchesa Casati. At the Augusteo, with Molinari conducting, I played the G major Beethoven Concerto, which did not provoke calls for encores but had a solid success with musicians.

My recital in the hall of the Santa Cecilia had much Liszt and Chopin, which pleased the audience immensely.

From Rome we left directly for Berlin, where Rudolf arranged a recital at Beethoven Hall. As at my previous appearances, I had the *Lampenfieber*—or stage fright. The house was only half full and with much "paper." I made a huge effort to play *all* the notes and as few wrong ones as possible, and as a result, it sounded labored, not inspired.

To my astonishment, the public, including my personal friends and the press, praised this particular concert as my best to date. Luckily, we had no trouble with the deficit. Eisenbach had sent a deposit which covered the loss.

Berlin lived in a state of unrest because of the tense political situation in Europe. German papers printed disquieting stories about Russian troops holding threatening maneuvers close to the Austrian frontier. I did hear in Vienna reports about Ukrainian students in Lwów rioting and clamoring for autonomy, and about an open revolt in Bosnia and Herzegovina against the Austro-Hungarian Empire, but Vienna did not take it very seriously. "We are used to that. We can cope with them," said the easygoing Viennese.

The Germans did not take it so lightly. Living in constant awe of their army and navy, they lost their sense of proportion. And Emperor Wilhelm's persistent verbal attacks against England, France, and Russia kept them in a state of nervous alertness. We left Berlin with a sigh of relief.

74

London was bathed in sunshine. The whole city wore the festive air of the beginning of spring. Londoners, weary of their long winter of cold, dark, foggy days, squatted on the steps around Nelson's column in Trafalgar Square, around the Eros fountain in Piccadilly Circus, and crowded the green lawns of the parks, drinking in the heavenly rays as if they were champagne. Belsize Park took a share of the sun feast. The house looked clean and white, the greenhouses were shining, and the garden showed buds promising a wealth of flowers.

Mrs. Bergheim, dressed in light gray, welcomed me with a motherly warmth. She had guests for dinner to celebrate my return. "I hope that you will find your room in order," she said. "Wiggins has taken care of it. And I had the piano tuned," she added with a smile of satisfaction. During a long, pleasant talk over tea and muffins, I gave her a good account of my travels, of Vienna and Berlin, and she, in turn, told me about her own activities and about people, but she never said a word about the Drapers. It puzzled me very much. Since the sad farewell at the Gare du Nord in Paris, I had not heard from them or about them, and I did not care to ask. After two or three days of acute impatience, I rang up the number of Edith Grove. A maid answered.

"This is Mr. Rubinstein. Will you call, please, Mr. Draper to the telephone?" Moments later, I heard Paul's voice, cool and deliberate: "How do you do?" Startled, I answered in the same tone: "Very well, thank you. And how are you and your family?" But this was more than I could stand. "Paul," I said, "this is bloody nonsense. Something has gone wrong between us. Have lunch with me at Scott's tomorrow. We must talk it over." He answered with his natural voice, "All right, I shall be there."

At Scott's, the next day, he came out with the truth. He had been jealous in Florence, observing my own undisguised jealousy. When Muriel returned and told him that we were in Venice together, he refused to believe that we were not alone there.

I answered: "I admit that I was in love with her like all the other men around her, but now it is all finished. My happy summer with Pola made me forget Florence and the rest. As to Venice, Paul, I swear on the most sacred oath that John McMullen was constantly with us and that I was never alone with her. So forget the whole thing. But the thought of a London without Edith Grove, the studio, the nights of music, is unbearable. I would rather leave town right away."

Paul finished his coffee. We stood up and were ready to leave.

"Arthur," he said, "come and see our new baby."

We found Muriel down in the music room, sitting on the couch in front of a table covered with cups and cakes, pouring tea. "Hello, Arthur," she said, "you lost weight."

"I am glad to see you looking so well, Muriel—*you* must have gained some weight."

A guest, a young woman, sat at the table.

"This is Ruth, my kid sister. She is our house guest," said Paul, introducing me.

"I am happy to meet you at last," she said with a soft, musical voice. "Paul has written me so much about you."

There was no resemblance between sister and brother, but she had some of his warmth and charm. She had a thin, delicately shaped face, dark hair, a sensitive, slightly curved nose, and dark, expressive eyes.

The four of us, sipping tea, started a long conversation about music. At that moment, Nancy, the Irish nurse, appeared with the baby and its older brother, Paul Junior. Muriel stopped our talk and took the baby, which looked like any other baby, into her arms. "His name is Smudge," she announced. (I have never known his real name.)

Ruth and I broke into the classical repertoire for these occasions: "What a lovely baby! It looks exactly like you, Muriel! Yes, but it has Paul's eyes!" etc. The baby began to cry and was taken out of the room by Nancy. Little Paul, a good-looking red-haired boy of four or five, remained and ate some cakes.

Muriel, more self-possessed than ever, her hair kept neatly under the net, told us about the wonders of the coming Diaghilev season.

"We shall have both, opera and ballet. Chaliapin is going to sing *Boris Godunov, Prince Igor,* and *Khovantschina.* And we will see again the *Sacre du printemps* and *Petrouchka.* I bought a box for all the first nights."

"What a marvelous time we are going to have!" I exclaimed. "But who has sponsored all this?"

"Thomas Beecham's father, who made all this money with his pills. He guarantees the whole season, and all he wants is to see Thomas conduct a few ballets and to have the words Beecham Pills, Beecham Pills, Beecham Pills printed in all the programs."

"That is all right," I said. "He intends to promote Russian art and

English laxatives at the same time." But nobody laughed at my sally. Russian art was sacred in those days.

The days passed quickly in London. Before I knew, my first recital was on, Paul* and Zosia were in town, and the great season had started. Muriel had a gorgeous party, with great music and a surprise. The active musicians were, besides Paul and myself, Sammons, Tertis, Sylvia Sparrow, Rubio, and a very tall, excellent cellist, Felix Salmond. The guests included Henry James, John Sargent, Norman Douglas, the three Wiborg girls, who were back in town, and, even Montague Chester, more pompous than ever, who appeared dressed in his tails and wearing white gloves. Our program began with the E flat Trio by Schubert with Paul and Salmond. As there was no problem of sight-reading or technical difficulties— we knew this work well—we played it with all our heart. Then came a lovely Haydn Quartet with Sammons, Sylvia, Tertis, and Rubio, which was followed by the Brahms Quintet, played by Paul, Sammons, Salmond, Tertis, and myself. Our listeners were ecstatic, save Henry James, who didn't seem to like music, but was fond of Muriel, and Chester who, when pleased, produced just a short snort.

After a nice, long supper at which Pierre Monteux appeared with a viola case in his hands, we returned to the studio.

We expected Muriel to suggest loudly, as she always did, which work she would like to hear, but, instead, she began to whisper something in Draper's ear. He answered with another whisper, then both of them whispered intently to Ruth, who at first said, decidedly, "No," but after some more whispers, gave in.

Now Muriel announced very loudly: "My sister-in-law, Ruth Draper, will do a monologue."

There was a moment of a general consternation; here we were ready to play great music, and the Drapers were going to impose upon us some prattle fit for a family celebration at Christmas or for grandpapa's birthday!

Ruth fetched a worn brown shawl, threw it over her head, and tucked it under her chin. Then she explained quietly: "An old Irish immigrant arrives in America to live with her daughter, whom she has not seen for twenty-five years. She expects to find her ashore, waiting, but the daughter does not turn up."

Suddenly, she *was* the old woman searching the crowd with keen eyes in anxious expectation of the happy reunion. She asks people for information, but they do not understand her Irish twang. In time her face

* In order to save the reader from confusing the two Pauls, I shall call, from now on, Draper just Draper and Paul Kochanski just Paul.

and her body seem to shrink; she begins to dread the outcome until, at last, the woman, now a tragic figure, expresses in only a faint murmur her fate of loneliness, dejection, and poverty in a strange land.

Ruth took off her shawl. We all had lumps in our throats. Henry James stuttered: "My dear, you are a genius." Ruth smiled and announced cheerfully, "I will do now an English lady showing off her garden to friends." She gave a smoothing touch to her hair, and became at once the fastidious British aristocrat: "Don't you adore my petunias, my deah? Aren't they simply divine? And here are my sweet little dahlias. . . ." And she went on with this prattle, imitating to perfection the accent, the inflection of voice, of the high-born English.

Enchanted and excited, we shouted our bravos and praises. "Where did you learn all that?" we asked. "Who wrote your stories?" Ruth answered modestly: "Oh, I made them up myself. I always liked to imitate and to caricature people."

Draper and Muriel were proud of their "surprise." It was, indeed, a great revelation.

My recital at Bechstein Hall was a genuine success; the great Fantasia and Fugue in G minor and the *Symphonic Études* of Schumann were much applauded. I was really beginning to make my way in London. Eisenbach was happy to tell me that we had no deficit.

We had music later at Edith Grove. Thibaud, Paul, Tertis, Monteux, Salmond, and May Mukle played beautifully the two sextets of Brahms. Ruth gave us two of her funny sketches. This time Sargent came mainly to study her face; he was making drawings of her in her different roles. I asked Norman Douglas what he thought of her. He answered: "I fuck the bloody old Irish bitch, but I like her comic stuff."

My life reached a frantic tempo, each day bringing something new. London was the most hospitable city in the world. It was the style to be invited for dinner and opera, or theater and supper or concert. I met a great many interesting people on those occasions. One of them, Lady Colefax, wife of Sir Arthur Colefax, K.C., was the greatest lion hunter, a genius in her field, and a very charming woman to boot. Using a technique of her own, she would send a wire to Bernard Shaw: "Please come to tea tomorrow; H. G. Wells is anxious to meet you." And another wire to H. G. Wells: "Bernard Shaw is coming to have tea tomorrow—hopes to see you, can you come?" Both men would appear. She used this trick on politicians, artists, musicians, and anyone who was in the public eye.

Besides my social activities, there were the more important ones, my concerts. The next one was a sonata recital with Paul. On Draper's invitation we would often rehearse at the studio.

One morning Muriel said, "I hear that Casals is in town; let's ask him to come tonight and play the Quintet of Schubert." Draper and Paul volunteered to try to find him. While we were waiting for their return, Muriel called up the other musicians, and they all promised to come. Two hours later, the two Pauls came back to the studio.

"Well," I asked, "did you see him? Is he coming?" They sat down with somber expressions on their faces. "What is the matter? Why don't you answer?" They maintained a stubborn silence. I couldn't stand it any more. "Paul, tell me at once what happened." I spoke in Polish, "I feel it concerns me personally." Paul gave in, reluctantly. "Yes, Casals refuses to come to a house where you are present."

"Wha-a-t?" I uttered in complete consternation. "Why?"

"We don't know—he didn't want to tell us. We insisted, we begged him to give us a reason, but he was adamant."

I sat down. I was deeply hurt by this cruel, unexpected insult. What offended me most was the mystery; it made me look as if I had committed a crime. In all honesty, and exerting my best mental effort, I couldn't remember having done anything to deserve such treatment. I sent him a letter in the following (approximately) terms: "You have insulted me very gravely. I consider your refusal to tell what is at the bottom of it as inadmissible and intolerable. There must be a misunderstanding. My conscience is clear; I always kept a monument in my heart for you and your great art [a terrible phrase, but I *had* written it]. You have no right to keep back the truth. I demand an immediate answer."

His answer came the next day, and I remember every word of it: "Friends who borrow money and do not pay it back cease to be friends." And he signed it.

After reading the note, I had a good laugh. "So that is all there is to it!" Yes, indeed, I did remember the ten pounds he lent me; I had not repaid it because I considered it a token of the fee for my collaboration at his concert. And I still had not the money to repay him; I had to borrow money from Paul. Then, I wrote him: "I learn with great relief that it is nothing but a vulgar question of money. If I remember well, I owe you fifteen pounds, which I enclose with my regrets for the long delay in my repayment."

My letter received no answer. Quite naturally, this affair was widely talked about. Some of the comments must have reached his ears, because, four or five weeks later, he sent me a letter with five pounds in the envelope. The letter read: "Going through my bills and accounts, I find you overpaid me by five pounds, which I herewith restitute."

This was the end of a sad, absurd story. We did make up, years later, Casals and I; it was Rubio who brought us together again. We even played again, once or twice, but the charm was broken. My "monument" shrank to a small lump of admiration for the great cellist, not for the man. We did not look at life with the same eyes.

The fabulous season of Diaghilev's Opera and Ballet began with a gala introducing Chaliapin in *Boris Godunov*. His impersonation of the unhappy and demented Tsar was unsurpassed. On that opening night he sang more gloriously than ever. It was an immense triumph. The Kochanskis and I sat with the Drapers in their great box, completely entranced. After Feodor's twenty or thirty curtain calls, we all went backstage to greet him. Fighting our way through a crowd of enthusiastic Londoners who behaved as if they were Russians, we finally reached his dressing room.

"Artoosha, it is good to see you!" he shouted, kissing me three times in the best Moscow tradition. After the introductions, he promised to come to Edith Grove on his next free night.

I was fortunate enough to have seen all the first nights of the operas and ballets, either with the Drapers or with Mrs. Bergheim, who had seats for many of them. Karol Szymanowski and Joseph Jaroszynski arrived in London, attracted by the glamour of the season. Mrs. Bergheim invited Karol to stay at Belsize Park, knowing the pleasure it gave me. He accepted, of course, but soon regretted it, unaccustomed as he was to such fussiness as that of our hostess. Edith Grove, however, enchanted him. Both he and Joseph, in addition to Chaliapin, soon became habitués of the studio. On that occasion Feodor generously pardoned Joseph's past indiscretion. One night Feodor brought his friend Jeanne Granier, then a famous operetta singer and comedy actress. After supper, Draper sang some new, difficult songs by Szymanowski, accompanied by the author. Too modern, too complicated, they sounded unconvincing to all of us. Alone, Jeanne Granier shouted: "Bravo, bravo, c'est merveilleux!" Chaliapin, who hated insincere compliments, rebuffed her: "Don't pretend, my dear—you didn't understand one single note of the songs."

She replied angrily: "How dare you say that? I have *always* loved his songs. I sang, when I was young, his whole *Amour d'un poète*." Obviously she was referring to the *Dichterliebe* of Schumann; the poor woman thought that in Poland Schumann meant Szy(u)man/owski(!).

To change the subject, Feodor produced the piano score of Moussorgsky's *Khovantschina*, made me play it for him, and sang through the whole opera.

Paul and I had a great artistic success at our concert of sonatas, but a poor attendance. My own second recital suffered a similar fate. The overpowering attraction of the Russian Ballet absorbed the whole interest of London concert lovers. Anyway, I was well satisfied with my success, and Daniel Meyer obtained three important engagements for me for January and February, 1915.

We saw *Petrouchka* again, one night. I sat in the stalls with "Aunt Clara," and Karol, Paul, and Zosia joined Muriel in her box. The ballet had the same tumultuous success as on the first night. After a few curtain calls, a little man appeared to take a bow. A prolonged ovation greeted him; it was Igor Stravinsky in person. I jumped up from my seat, said excitedly: "I must meet him," and rushed out of the theater and backstage. Stravinsky was still on the stage, taking more bows. By now I knew almost everyone in the company so when I saw a familiar bearded electrician nearby I begged him to please introduce me to the master. "All right," he answered in Russian. With the last curtain call, Stravinsky turned around, ready to leave, when the man pointed a finger at me and said, "This is Rubinstein." The composer stopped, waiting for what I had to say.

"I have studied carefully your *Sacre du printemps*," I said shyly, in Russian, "and I am anxious to find out if my conception of this great work is right or wrong. Could you spare a few moments for an exchange of ideas on the subject?"

He had been prepared to dismiss me at once, but he became interested and listened. When I stopped talking, he hesitated for a second: "I am occupied all day tomorrow," he answered in a low, resonant voice, "but if you care to come at nine o'clock in the morning, you will find me at breakfast and we could talk for half an hour. I am staying at the Hotel Cecil on the Strand."

I thanked him and ran back to my seat. The next morning I was up at seven so as not to be late. At nine sharp I knocked at his door. When I entered, he was sitting at a table near the window, finishing his breakfast. He bade me sit down, and without losing time, I began to explain my impressions of the *Sacre*, but not before telling him first my profound admiration for the *Firebird* and *Petrouchka*.

"The first hearing of the *Sacre* disconcerted me beyond words," I said. "My musical instinct revolted against the savage onslaught of your work. But I was loath to follow the trend of the typical conceited contemporary who dismisses a work he cannot grasp with the cheap comments: 'He must be mad,' or, worse, 'He is not sincere!' After a long study of the score I came to the conclusion that your basic idea was to evoke the evolution of sound at the birth of nature rather than to illustrate some tribal rites of the sacrifice of a maiden in order to pacify their gods."

Stravinsky was impressed; he admitted that much of what I said was close to what he meant.

"The *Sacre*," he declared, "was essentially my revolution against the existing musical traditions. I simply tried to infuse new blood to music, to give it new life."

From that point on, we started one of these interminable discussions about every subject at hand: art, literature, language, politics, religion, and love. Suddenly, he stopped in the middle of a phrase: "Here we are talking, and I forgot my appointment! Ah, never mind, they are bores, anyway!" And we continued our talk. It was almost noon when he suggested with a twinkle in his eye: "Let us sneak in on Richard Strauss's new ballet; they are rehearsing it just now. Diaghilev ruined himself on the décor and costumes by Sert; I want to see if it was worth it."

It was only a short walk to Drury Lane. We entered the dark theater and sat down in the last row. Sert's décor was actually a pastiche of the biblical scene of Joseph and Madame Potiphar by Veronese or Tintoretto (I don't remember which of the two).

Strauss himself was conducting that last rehearsal. The music had the characteristic Straussian *Schwung*, the orchestration had his rich, polyphonic texture, but its substance was empty and uninspired.

Stravinsky pinched my arm at some salient moments and criticized the music in unprintable terms. We left the theater without being seen. Out in the street, he said: "It's time for lunch. Do you know of a good place where we could eat?"

I was expected to lunch at Edith Grove with Paul, Zosia, Karol, and Jaroszynski.

"Would you like to join me for a good meal at my friends' house, where you will meet a few interesting people who speak French and Russian?"

The idea pleased him. We were still in time, as Muriel liked to lunch late. The unexpected guest was received with all the honors, of course, and he, in turn, found our group entirely to his taste. The conversation at table was animated beyond measure. We had coffee in the studio. Stravinsky sensed immediately the charm of the place, but at the sight of the concert grand he made some denigrating remarks about the piano as an instrument.

"The piano is an instrument of percussion and nothing else," he said. Karol argued: "I don't agree with you. The greatest composers have written for the piano masterpieces which demand a singing tone."

"They were all wrong," said the Russian composer. "I am sure that a new music will be written treating it in the right way."

Karol, to win his point, became personal: "If you had heard Arthur play your *Firebird* or *Petrouchka* you would have changed your opinion about the piano."

"Is Rubinstein a pianist?" asked the astonished Stravinsky. Everybody laughed, taking it as a joke, but I suddenly realized that I had neglected to tell him.

We stayed at Edith Grove until four in the morning. There was chamber music in the evening, two suppers, plenty of champagne. On my way home by taxi, I dropped Stravinsky at his hotel. We kissed goodbye and decided to call each other by our first names, using the familiar "thou" in French and Russian. We lunched every day together during the week of his stay in London, and in spite of many artistic quarrels and arguments, we remained brotherly friends forever.

On June 28, 1914, the Archduke Francis Ferdinand, heir to the throne of Austria-Hungary, was killed in Sarajevo by a fanatic Serbian patriot. The whole world was aroused by this new tragedy in the house of Hapsburg. There was an outcry of sympathy for the poor, so sorely tried Emperor. King George decreed a week of court mourning.

Our own group was not overly affected by this political crime. Life went on as before; we still had the operas and the ballets at Drury Lane, all the great artists were still in town, our music nights were enriched by fresh repertoire and new performers, and our gay suppers were more gay than ever. Yes, indeed, life in London was intoxicating! And the glorious season had not ended yet.

Draper told me, in confidence, one day: "Arthur, don't tell anybody, but I am ruined. Luck has been against me for a fortnight. I played for higher and higher stakes to recover my losses, but it's all gone. My only hope is the Derby; I put up five thousand pounds on a horse which cannot lose. Do come with me to watch the race, I feel that you will bring me luck."

I promised, and so, on Derby Day, this sacred holiday of the English, Draper, Paul, and I left by taxi for Epsom. It was a hot, sunny day; a throng of more than a million packed every space at the huge racecourse. We pushed our way through the dense crowd, reached the barrier, and clung to its metal rail. The King and Queen arrived in a carriage driven by four horses, and took their seats in the royal box. The great race of the year was ready to start. Twenty-odd horses, one by one, ridden by tiny jockeys garbed in their multicolored accessories, appeared on the racetrack in slow procession. The riders, clinging to their saddles in a squatting posture, paraded their precious mounts before the excited crowd.

Draper, pale with anxiety, pointed to a chestnut colt: "That is Kenymore," and I said "merde" for good luck. The horses were brought into line behind a gate. A sharp signal, the gate went up with a jerk, and the race began. At first, the horses moved for a while as a bunch, closely bound together, but at the first curve they formed a line which, after a while, was lengthened by four or five of them, who detached themselves from the lot and advanced now rapidly.

The crowd broke into a wild, ear-splitting clamor. People yelled hysterically the names of the horses they had bets on. Draper yelled with the others: "Kenymore, Kenymore!" Four horses were now far ahead; Kenymore was not among them. Draper shouted with the voice of a frightened chicken: "Kenymore, Kenymore." Then his voice became weaker and weaker, and finally, when the race was over, I heard him still murmur, "Kenymore." A pathetic, heartbreaking scene. I can never forget the name of the horrible horse; it rings forever in my ears.

We returned to town in an overcrowded bus, standing up most of the time. Draper couldn't open his mouth, he was so completely shattered. Paul, who saw the race, separated from us by the crowd, was well aware of the drama—Draper had told him everything.

At Edith Grove, Muriel, Ruth, and Zosia were having tea while waiting for us.

"Muriel, we are ruined, completely ruined," said Draper in a loud voice, as he entered the studio.

"Sit down, all of you, and have tea," said Muriel, evidently prepared for the bad news.

"But, Muriel," he insisted, "I mean it. We have lost today every penny we had."

"Don't be a bore. We have a dinner at the Savoy Grill tonight, and we still have some credit."

Draper sank into a chair and gave up.

Their financial situation was really desperate. Besides having lost his own money, Draper was in debt with the bookmaker firm of Ladbrokes. To have gambling debts in England was a serious matter. They had long debates and conversations, consultations with experts, talks with creditors. They mortgaged the house and the studio. At last an angel, in the person of Ruth Draper, came to the rescue. Ruth, who was devoted to her brother, offered the bulk of her inherited capital to deliver him from the most urgent debts and to keep him afloat for the time being. Draper was deeply affected by her gesture, but Muriel played the queen who receives a gift from her vassal.

Politics came again to the fore. Austria demanded extraordinary concessions because of the murder of the Archduke, but Serbia refused.

Eisenbach brought one morning the *Neue Freie Presse* of Vienna and cried excitedly: "Read that, read that, it means war!" I read that the Austrian government had served an ultimatum on Serbia the night before and that if the latter persisted in its refusal, Austrian troops would cross the Serbian border.

I dropped the paper: "There is nothing to worry about; this war would be nothing but a penal expedition by a great Empire against a small, rebellious neighbor!" But I changed my mind the next morning. The headlines were all about Russia's threatening Austria with armed intervention in case of an attack on Serbia.

London newspapers printed articles calling it a serious crisis, but the man in the street paid little attention to it and remained unconcerned. The situation, however, worsened from day to day. Kaiser Wilhelm seemed to have been waiting for just such a crisis. He urged the senile Emperor of Austria to attack Serbia without delay, and sent the Russians a note threatening them with war if they interfered in the Austro-Serbian conflict.

The governments of England and France were now genuinely alarmed. The tripartite Entente Cordiale between these two countries and Russia called for each partner to intervene if one of them were at war.

Ordinary people, including ourselves, would not, and could not, believe that a war of such monstrous dimensions could occur in our civilized world. But the news was disquieting.

Paul and Zosia left for Lithuania and took Sylvia Sparrow with them. They were invited to spend the summer with the Emil Mlynarskis on their estate. Karol returned to Tymoszovka and Jaroszynski to Kiev. I was supposed to leave with Paul and Zosia but decided to stay, partly because I like to be where important things are happening and, mainly, because I was still in love.

Paul Draper decided, all of a sudden, to leave for Germany, of all places, right in the middle of the dangerous political crisis. The reason he gave us was vague and unconvincing: he wished to learn German, to hear German songs, or something of the sort. In my opinion, he wanted to escape from the mess he had created and which he was unable to face. Muriel took his departure with perfect calm. We went to the ballet that night, the last of the season.

The Kaiser was now openly threatening France as well as Russia. In one of his bellicose harangues, he swore to his people that he would fight the enemy to the finish. German troops were standing on the alert at the Russian and French borders. The situation deteriorated rapidly. The French and Russian governments answered his threats by ordering the general mobilization of their armies and navies.

Now thoroughly alarmed, Londoners stood by the thousands in front of the posters, reading the fateful words from abroad in silent anxiety. Newspapers printed bulletins every half-hour.

King George and Tsar Nicholas besought the German Emperor, their cousin, with urgency to reconsider his inflexible decision; they were ready to join him at a conference table and work out a satisfactory solution of the conflict. The Kaiser coldly rejected their proposition. In a solemn address to his subjects, he declared that the general mobilization ordered by France and Russia was a hostile provocation to which the only answer was war.

And then came the day when we read the stupefying headlines: "Belgium invaded by the German army."

England, which hoped against all odds that some miracle might stop the fatal outcome at the last minute, was outraged by the brutal assault on this small, peace-loving country. The parliament voted unanimously for the declaration of war; the King signed it. France was already at war; so was Russia.

The tragic catastrophe, which gave birth to so many others, had begun. The long era of the easy, peaceful intercourse between nations, of gracious living, of good taste, of good manners, of prosperity, was gone forever. The world lost its confidence in the future.

75

In the first days of the war, the perplexed Londoner took offense at the Germans chiefly because of their lack of consideration. "Fancy these Germans starting the war on our bank holiday!" But, at the same time, the whole country stood up for their King, ready for any sacrifice.

Mrs. Bergheim, fussier than ever, but, in reality, happy to be active again, saw Peter Bergheim off in uniform as he joined his regiment. Nina, his sister, entered some work in hospitals. London looked like a military camp. Eisenbach had the jitters because as an Austrian subject he was in a dilemma. Staying in England meant that he could be sent to a prison camp; on the other hand, all the roads were closed for him to return to Kraków. I read in the papers that the Austrian embassy staff was to leave for Trieste by sea. "If they take you along, you are safe," I said to my poor frightened secretary. "I have met your ambassador at one of the 'at homes'; he is a nice man, so there is a chance. But it is doubtful that he will want to see me under the present circumstances."

The Ambassador, Count Mensdorff (he had been a close friend of King Edward VII and was the most popular diplomat in London) did receive us immediately and promised to help. That evening I received a telegram from him with instructions for Eisenbach to join the members of the embassy at Southampton on such and such day. A gesture of a *grand-seigneur*, indeed.

Muriel Draper, the American from Boston, became overnight a most zealous English patriot; I could read in her eyes that she disapproved of me for not joining the war. It was of no use explaining to her that in the three divided parts of Poland brothers were forced to fight against brothers, that I would like nothing better than to fight the Germans, but not on the Russian side.

A manifesto by the Grand Duke Nikolai Nikolaievitch, a cousin of the Tsar and commander in chief of the armed forces, proclaimed that Russian Poland was allowed to fight the war under her own flag. At the same time came the news that the thousands of Poles who lived in France were forming a Polish Legion which would fight the enemy in the ranks of the French army.

I decided to leave for Paris without delay and enroll in the Legion of my compatriots. Equipped with the meager amount of money I had left and a small bag containing only the strict necessities, I took the train at Victoria. Mrs. Bergheim and Muriel came to bid me farewell. Dear "Aunt Clara" gave me five pounds in gold. "In case you need some extra food; I don't trust these French," she said in the best English tradition. Muriel saw me off with the pride of having won a new recruit for the war.

I arrived in Paris toward evening and drove straight to the Hotel Scribe on the Boulevard des Capucines, where I took a room for one night. I intended to report to the Russian Embassy the next morning and enlist immediately at the seat of the Polish Legion.

Out in the streets, beflagged as though it were the Fourteenth of July, the city lived in a patriotic turmoil. Troops, led by their bands, marched in regular intervals through the densely crowded boulevards. Throngs of excited Parisians cheered the soldiers, shouting, "Vive la France, vive la Belgique," waving their hats and handkerchiefs; women threw flowers at them, girls rushed to kiss them. Some of the marches played by the bands invariably brought a lump to my throat with their stirring, exalted pathos; the "Sambre et Meuse" and "Le Chant de Départ" produce the same noble stir as the "Marseillaise."

I could not sleep that night. The vision of myself as a soldier carrying a gun, prepared to kill other men, kept me awake with nightmarish thoughts. I felt capable of shooting the Kaiser in cold blood, but the idea of killing innocent young Germans, and among them, possibly, my friends from the *Lesekränzchen*, seemed so flagrantly unjust that it revolted me.

On the terrace of the Café de la Paix, where I ate my breakfast, everybody was reading anxiously the latest war news. "The enemy has reached the French border. The invasion is imminent!" The papers extolled King Albert of Belgium and his brave army for their heroic stand, which gave the French the all-important respite for regrouping their armies.

It was time to go to the Russian Embassy. A taxi deposited me at its entrance on rue de Grenelle, where I found groups of stranded Russian citizens standing in the courtyard waiting to be allowed to enter the premises. I asked an usher in livery to give my visiting card to the military attaché. "Count Ignatieff is in St. Petersburg," the man said, "but Colonel Osnobishin, who replaces him, might see you." He disappeared with my card. The name Osnobishin sounded familiar to me. After a while, a tall, fat Russian officer entered the corridor. He looked at me and then at my card: "Rubinstein?" and, suddenly he laughed, "Artūr Roubinshtain? What on earth are you doing here?" At that instant I recognized him; he was a friend of Colonel Stremoukhov, the great music lover who had protected me and Paul from military service in the old Warsaw days. Sometimes, I remembered, this fat man would listen to our playing with visible pleasure. I told him what brought me to Paris and came to the point.

"The French army requires a document signed by the Russian military attaché legalizing my enrollment in the Polish Legion fighting in France."

Colonel Osnobishin became serious: "His Majesty the Tsar revoked the manifesto of our commander in chief. The Poles fight under the Russian flag, and there is no Polish Legion in France."

A shattering blow! For a moment I did not know what to say or what to do. After a while, already resigned, I said: "There is nothing else for me to do but enlist in the Foreign Legion. Do you think that they will take me?"

"Of course, they will," he answered, "but take my advice: Don't do it. Service in the French Foreign Legion would ruin your hands forever, even if you were lucky enough to come back from the war without being hurt."

I said something, feebly, about my intention to fight.

"Nonsense," the colonel objected, "we have enough men in the field. But it is our duty to preserve men with great talents for the good of mankind. Leave your address, Roubinshtain; I shall try to find for you some war work which will not hurt your precious fingers."

He dismissed me with a cordial handshake. On my way back to the hotel, I thought with relief: How lucky for me that Count Ignatieff is in St. Petersburg! He might have sent me straight to Russia!

While waiting for news from the colonel, I tried to find the whereabouts of my brother Ignacy: I knew that he lived in the district of Montparnasse, but I had lost his address. After asking around, I found the café where I was likely to meet him, the Café de la Rotonde, then very much in vogue as the rendezvous of artists of all nationalities. The large terrace of the place was filled with a miscellaneous, colorful crowd. Most of the men bore the unmistakable look of painters, musicians, or writers. Longish, unkempt hair, beards, and mustaches were everywhere. They were dressed in a picturesque mixture of clothes—a workman's corduroy trousers, well-worn sweaters, open-collared shirts, tired, shiny winter suits with stiff white collars, and an amusing variety of shoes: moccasins alongside patent shoes, brown boots next to sandals or slippers; and, yet, it all harmonized perfectly. One heard every known and unknown language, except French, for all young Frenchmen were mobilized. Most of the women were models and *les petites amies* of the painters. Everybody seemed to know everybody, shouting from table to table.

I loved the place. Noticing a table where three men spoke Polish, I asked one of them if he knew my brother. "Yes, I know him very well," he answered. "He must be out of town; otherwise he would be here." Since nobody knew Ignacy's address, I decided to come to the café often.

A week passed without news from Colonel Osnobishin. I became nervous. My room at the Hotel Scribe was much too expensive, and besides, it was an expenditure I hadn't anticipated. The worst of it was that I did not dare to leave the hotel, as I had given that as my address to the Colonel.

The news from the front was alarming. The German army had taken Sedan and St. Quentin and was moving rapidly toward Paris. General Joffre, the French commander in chief, retreated to more secure positions to put up a stand in defense of the threatened capital. One morning, bulletin boards appeared in the streets. General Gallieni, the military governor of Paris, had signed an appeal to the citizens. He warned them of the imminent danger and entreated them to leave the capital. Only those engaged in war work should stay.

Paris was empty, anyway. The declaration of war turned the annual escape from the city into a veritable exodus.

There were new orders from the police: all public places had to close at nine o'clock, lights had to be dimmed, and other regulations and restrictions were issued from hour to hour.

Early one morning, a strange noise woke me from my sleep. I jumped up from bed and rushed to my balcony to see what was happening. The noise came from the boulevard, where an unending line of taxis was transporting troops to some unknown destination. Terrified by what I saw, my first thought was: The garrison of Paris is fleeing, Joffre has lost the battle, and Gallieni is about to surrender the city.

I dressed in a hurry and rushed to the Russian Embassy for information. At the rue de Grenelle, two French policemen stood on guard in front of the building and did not let me pass.

"I have an appointment with the military attaché," I said sternly.

"He left last night with the whole embassy for Bordeaux," one of them said.

I didn't believe him. "This is impossible," I said. "An embassy has no right to leave, if the government remains in the capital."

"The French government left for Bordeaux yesterday morning," he answered and turned away.

My heart stopped. This was the last straw! I went back to the hotel in despair; I had visions of Germans arresting me as a spy and burning my hands in torture. At the Scribe, I packed my bag, paid my bill, and walked out in search of a cheap room in some modest hotel. Passing along the terrace of the Café de la Paix, I heard shouts and screams coming from the Place de l'Opéra. Newspaper vendors brandished the last bulletin: "Grande bataille sur la Marne. La garnison de Paris, transportée au front par Gallieni, enfonce un flanc de l'ennemi. L'armée de von Kluck en retraite!"

Blood began to flow in my veins again. The crowd shouted, "Gallieni, Gallieni!" I shouted with them.

At the nearby rue du Helder, I found a tiny room for three francs a day at the Hotel du Nil (absurd name, had nothing to do with Egypt), a really modest place, but it looked clean. I unpacked, went down, and took a bus for Montparnasse.

The Café de la Rotonde was overflowing; many patrons were standing with a cup of coffee or a drink in their hands. Everybody was talking at the same time about the battle of the Marne. I found my Poles at the same table and was invited to share half of a chair with one of them. Getting better acquainted, I discovered that my "co-chairman" was a doctor of medicine who loved music, as do most members of his profession. We stayed for hours in that crowded place; from time to time one of us fetched a new bulletin, but the news was the same: the enemy was retreating.

At nine the curfew began; everybody had to leave. The Polish doctor suggested that I accompany him to his hospital, where he served as an intern at night.

"You can have a cup of tea at our messroom," he said in Polish, "and we even have a piano there."

I couldn't resist, not having seen a piano since I left London. The Hôpital Lariboisière was a lugubrious place that night; ambulances would arrive every minute with seriously wounded soldiers from the front, and left, losing no time, to fetch others. In the messroom, my Polish intern introduced me to a few doctors who sat at a long table, sipping tea or coffee. They discussed impassively some difficult cases and could never finish a drink without being called away to perform some new surgery.

For the first time I became acutely conscious of the absurdity, of the real horror, of the war. Young innocent men who were healthy and carefree yesterday were butchered today by other young innocent men. What an intolerable, tragic farce it all was!

Timidly my eyes caught the upright piano in the corner of the room, and I approached it, opened the lid, and struck a few notes. It was abominably out of tune; two or three keys were mute. But I sat down and began to play. I played the Sonata *Pathétique* of Beethoven; I had never played it like that before. It was not how it sounded—it was how I felt. I was ready to cry, and so was everyone else present.

My small money reserve became dreadfully low. The five golden pounds had already been spent, but I clung tenaciously to the sum I needed for two more weeks of hotel bills. So there was nothing left for real food. For four or five days I ate nothing but the small French grapes which were sold in the street for a few centimes during the season of the wine harvest. I was starving; I was so hungry I couldn't sleep. Those terrible, ravenous days remind me of a tragicomic little interlude: one evening, walking past the Café de la Paix, I noticed in the well-lit restaurant three English officers dining at a table close to the window. One of them was an acquaintance of mine from London. The man, spotting me through the window, made inviting signs and gestures to join them. When I entered the restaurant, he stood up and introduced me to his companions in a flattering way.

"I say, it's good to see you, old chap! Bloody beastly business, this war, ah, what? But, as I say, old boy, we'll beat them, these Jerries!" All this accompanied by loud guffaws.

"Sit down, my dear fellow, and have dinner with us," he said. I answered quickly, without thinking, "No, thank you, I just had my dinner." Something in me couldn't bear the idea of these Englishmen noticing how a ravenously hungry man devours food. He offered me a cup of coffee, which I accepted, but being nervous, I scorched my tongue with the first sip.

A sleepless night with visions of big chunks of beef with *pommes soufflées* and sauce béarnaise was the result of this frustrating experience.

The next afternoon, I walked all the way to the Café de la Rotonde, where my friend, the intern, generously offered me a cup of tea. At a neighboring table a man spoke loudly of a *soupe populaire* for artists. I asked about it and learned there was a place on the Champs-Élysées where bowls of soup and bread were served twice a day by some charitable institution to stranded artists. This time I took a bus and found the place without difficulty, but I was told, "You have to wait an hour before they dish out the precious meal." To kill time, I bought another bunch of grapes and ate them, sitting on a bench. By and by, my colleagues in art and hunger began to assemble, about fifty of them. Some of them looked familiar, but they were reserved and uncommunicative, something I understood perfectly.

A few ladies (the charitable ones) appeared behind a large table and busied themselves piling bowls, cutting up bread, and doing other chores. At last, a man put on the table a large terrine of hot soup with a long ladle. We lined up in front of the table and received our portions from two of the ladies. It was a good vegetable soup with pieces of bread in it, and it tasted to me like just about the best meal I had ever eaten. As I was eating it slowly, with a deep respect for every gulp, I heard a voice calling my first name. Gabriel Astruc in person looked at me in amazement. "Arthur, what are you doing in Paris at a time like this?" I blushed, ashamed of being seen by him at a *soupe populaire*.

"If it interests you, I shall tell you why and also why you see me here," I said.

"Wait for me—I shall be right with you," and he went to talk to the ladies and to some of the "soupers." Astruc himself, as I learned later, was the organizer of the *soupe*. He took me to a nearby café, where I told him of my ill-fated adventure.

"I shall try to arrange something for you," he said, promising to let me know as soon as possible. He also gave me a hundred francs. "This is an advance for some future concert," he said with a smile and left.

Monsieur Astruc managed to find me a job as a translator of letters or documents found on prisoners of war. My knowledge of German, Polish, Russian, French, and English was useful, I was paid a hundred francs a week, and I had my afternoons free. My assignment was not a military one; I was employed as a civilian.

La Rotonde became my headquarters, where now I belonged to the "club." One day Ignacy turned up. He had spent all that time in Tours, having fled with the others when war was declared. We had not seen each other for a long time. Life has separated us ever since, but even if that were not so, we had never had much in common. The Rotonde, however, brought us involuntarily closer together. Two Poles, also new-comers to the café, joined us; one was a painter from Warsaw, Kramsztyk by name; the other, a musician, Morawski, had lived in Paris for years. With these two, we formed an inseparable foursome, meeting daily at the café and spending the rest of the day together.

The war was at a standstill in a way; the terrible war of the trenches had begun, the most cruel of all the wars. The French were determined to hold their lines. "Ils ne passeront pas" became their slogan. The English army was strongly entrenched on the left wing, and the heroic King Albert resisted tenaciously on the outmost corner of his brave country. Italy, originally a member of the Triple Alliance with Germany and Austria, changed her mind and declared war on Austria in the spring.

French papers published horrible stories about crimes committed by the German armies in Belgium, Poland, and northern France. Hundreds of innocent citizens of these countries were shot in cold blood, in retaliation for one soldier killed by a sniper. Wanton killings, rapes, and tortures were luridly reported. The German authorities called these accusations *Greuelpropaganda* (propaganda of horrors), but some of the documents and letters that came into my hands bore out the French reports. A noted composer, Albéric Magnard, had been killed simply because he was not polite enough with the invader. I was deeply humiliated by the thought that our great civilization had degraded itself so abominably following and obeying this evil man, the Kaiser. In a helpless outburst of rage, I swore there and then a sacred oath: "I shall never play in Germany again!"

I have kept this oath up to this day as I write these words—unfortunately for better, and even stronger, reasons.

Morawski* and I became good friends. We used to exchange ideas at the café on many subjects, and we learned to know each other better, not only personally, but also musically. We spent hours at his piano, where he would play his compositions for me, which showed real talent, and I introduced him to the music of Szymanowski.

In those days I assumed still another role; I was posing for a portrait. The painter was an elderly spinster from Poland, Miss Olga Boznanska,

---

* He became many years later the director of the National Conservatory in Warsaw.

who was quite well known in Parisian art circles. She had heard me in Kraków, had liked my playing, and insisted now on painting me. She had a large studio in the Boulevard Montparnasse where I would appear daily at four, sit on an armchair placed on a small dais, and pose for an hour or two.

She was a bit of an eccentric, Olga Boznanska—fiftyish, short and slim, with dark, intense eyes looking out of a small, overpowdered face which made her resemble a Pierrot; she wore always a long black dress, as if she were about to go to church, and a boa around her neck, probably to cover a double chin. At five sharp, every day, Miss Olga would stop painting.

"It's time for tea," she would announce, "and for the visit of my little mice." And out from nowhere, twelve or more mice would run into the middle of the studio to be fed by their painter friend. Some of her lady visitors used to run for the door, shrieking, but I took it rather philosophically. Anyway, my full-length portrait was superb, and she started another one, in half-profile.

Kramsztyk, himself a brilliant portrait painter, asked Miss Olga's permission to paint me in her studio at the same time, which she graciously allowed. I still have in my possession his very fine portrait, but the two by Boznanska disappeared out of my house in Paris during the Second World War.

Coming back to the First World War: Morawski introduced me one evening to a Rumanian family, a widow with two daughters and a son, all three musicians. The son was a very gifted violinist, the elder sister played piano quite well, and the younger one was a good cellist. They were charming, lively people. Morawski taught piano to the girl and became a close friend to the family. On my very first visit the mother kept us for dinner and treated us to some wonderful Rumanian dishes. We discovered we had much in common, these Rumanians and I. After dinner, of course, we made lots of music. The son and I played a sonata, the pianist girl played quite beautifully the *Thème et Variations* by Fauré, and I—I played everything. Morawski and I left at midnight.

I returned often to their hospitable home. The mother was a talkative, clever woman who was planning the careers of her children with great intelligence. It was obvious she favored the son, a good-looking and nice boy, and she was very motherly toward her younger daughter, but Marguerite, the pianist, was treated as a Cinderella. It was incomprehensible to me, because she was lovely, the pure Rumanian type with a beautiful complexion, dark hair, and black velvet eyes. Her melancholic expression touched me; I became in a way her protector, making her play, praising her with emphasis, paying her polite little attentions at table, but also kissing her, when we were alone for a second, or holding her hand under the table.

The French government returned to Paris, and so did all the diplomatic corps. I ventured to go to rue de Grenelle one day and found Count Ignatieff back at the embassy, but I demanded to see Colonel Osnobishin. He received me this time in a small office. He looked a little embarrassed.

"I regret to have let you down," he said, "but there was no time for anything. We received orders to leave immediately. The embassy was in panic. Well, what has become of you since we left?"

I gave him a more or less exact account of my life. He listened with sympathy. When I stood up, he said: "Listen, Roubinshtain, if you need anything, come to see me!"

As a matter of fact, life in the Paris at war was not only tolerable, but had even some advantages. The great capital, abandoned by most of its citizens, had shrunk to the size and character of a very attractive provincial town. In spite of the dangerous proximity of the front, of the incessant movement of troops, we became accustomed to this kind of existence. I believe that for the human race, adaptability to any change of life is limitless.

The maid at the Hotel du Nil woke me up at eight o'clock one morning. "A young girl wants to see you. She is waiting downstairs." I asked who she was. "She didn't care to tell her name." A mystery. I thought that it would have to be someone who had arrived from abroad, because nobody in Paris would wake me up as early as this.

I dressed and went down to the small waiting room next to the entrance. Marguerite, the pianist, sat there quietly with a traveling bag at her feet. She stood up and said simply: "I ran away from home. I came to live with you."

Stupor was my first reaction. Then, I remembered the terrible morning with Pola in Warsaw. I took her hand.

"Marguerite, my dear, what did they do to you?" I asked.

"Nothing. They don't know where I am. Nobody saw me leaving."

This was absurd. I had to find out what was behind it.

"Leave your bag with the concierge," I said, "and let us talk it over."

I took her to a small café on the boulevard where we settled down to coffee and brioches, and I asked her to tell me everything. She had not much to tell.

"Mother does not like me—she never did. She cares only for my brother and my sister. All she wants is to send me back to Rumania to marry some rich old man. But I want to live with you, Arthur! We love each other—it is the only thing that counts."

She sounded pathetic and ludicrous at the same time.

"My dear child," I began, "it would be a lovely dream, but it must remain a dream and nothing else. Reality is often cruel—it seldom allows us to live our dreams." I patted her hands: "You are still a minor, my dear. Your mother has the right to put the police on your trail, to get you back by force, and to sue me for eloping with a minor."

She sat quietly and listened to me with complete indifference, her big eyes drowned in her dream.

This was a difficult day that I shall never forget. We sat and sat in that café until I thought they would throw us out. Then we walked to the Tuileries Gardens and sat down on a bench overlooking the Place de la Concorde. She made me neglect my work, it was past lunchtime, and I kept talking and she kept listening. We were freezing on this cold December day. Finally, exhausted and exasperated, I grabbed her hand and said coldly: "I'll take you to Morawski. We will ask him what to do."

She obeyed, placidly. At the Rotonde, Morawski sat at a table with Ignacy and Kramsztyk. At my urgent request, he followed me out to the street where Marguerite was waiting for us.

Up in his room, Morawski listened to me with growing impatience.

"You silly girl," he shouted angrily at her, "how dare you, trying to mess up your life and Rubinstein's life, too? Come on, I shall take you back to your mother." And she obeyed again, just as placidly. We picked up her bag at my hotel and they left.

A strange girl, this Marguerite. Rather sweet and lovely, but she poisoned the air of Paris for me on that long day.

An Englishman accosted me at the Rotonde: "I hope to hear you in London at your concert in January."

Seeing the expression of incredulity on my face, he produced a London newspaper, the *Daily Telegraph*, where I saw my name announced as the soloist of the London Symphony Orchestra, playing the G major Concerto of Beethoven. Overjoyed at the news, I thanked my Englishman effusively. I longed to leave for London as soon as possible.

A visit to Colonel Osnobishin settled everything. He gave me a signed legal document stating that my artistic work was a useful contribution to the war as propaganda for the Allies. I wrote a short note to Mrs. Bergheim to announce my arrival, and a letter to Muriel explaining the reasons for my return.

I left Paris not without sadness; I had become attached to the Rotonde and its lively "club," and to Olga Boznanska and her mice, and to the passionate Rumanians. Paris in war was tragic and beautiful, and the people of Paris showed heart and courage which I had not seen in them before, or since.

Ignacy, Morawski, and Kramsztyk took me to the Gare du Nord. At our farewell, I promised to meet them at the Rotonde right after the war.

76

London in wartime was a complete contrast to Paris. Instead of a loss in population, which I expected to find, the English capital of early 1915 seemed to have gained a considerable influx of people.

Thousands of Belgians, fleeing the invader, sought refuge in England. Many French families considered the British Isles safer than the Continent. Soldiers and sailors, on leave or on their way to the front, paced the streets. Theaters, music halls, and cinemas were filled every night. Concerts were attracting more people than before the war.

Mrs. Bergheim sent a car to fetch me at Victoria Station and received me with her usual kindness. She was hurt at not hearing from me during my long absence—a quite natural reproach, coming from as great a letter writer as she was.

Muriel, whom I saw the next day, took it more intelligently. She had lost much of her aggressive belligerency, had become more tolerant. Paul, she told me, returned right after war was declared and left for America to see his mother, who was dangerously ill. "He abandoned me to my fate," she said, without a trace of self-pity. "My desk is piled up with unpaid bills from butchers, grocers, milkmen, and what not. But English shopkeepers are the most generous and confident people in the world. They keep up their credit and trust that I will pay my debts one day or another."

And so, Muriel continued to have music, to see her friends, and to pour tea at the studio. On a much smaller scale, of course.

Sylvia Sparrow was back from Lithuania; she had had to travel through the north of Finland and Sweden, from where a ship brought her safely home. She told me wonders of the Mlynarski estate, of their great hospitality, of their guest house, of the beautiful river Niemen, of their charming children.

"The Germans won a big battle in East Prussia and are entering Lithuania," she said. "The whole Mlynarski family is fleeing to Moscow, and Paul and Zosia returned to Warsaw."

That night Sylvia took me to a friend's house, where some Belgian musicians played chamber music. One can well imagine my happy surprise at seeing Eugène Ysaye among them. They played Mozart's G minor Piano Quartet with Mark Hambourg at the keyboard. Hambourg was a pianist of the old virtuoso school; his percussive tone and his freelance treatment of the work was wholly unadaptable for Mozart.

After they finished, Sylvia introduced me to the lady of the house, herself a pianist, and to the Belgians. Ysaye greeted me very warmly and, without transition, invited me graciously to play with him and his colleagues (they were members of the Brussels quartet of his name) the C minor Fauré Quartet. With the kind approval of Hambourg, who had never heard me, I accepted, with my heart beating, and we attacked the work with élan. In the middle of the first movement, the piano has a beautiful phrase which is echoed by the violin. On that occasion, inspired by the master, I played this phrase with a special emotion. Ysaye stopped playing: "C'est beau, c'est beau," he shouted. "Tu es un poète! Recommence!"

I repeated the phrase, blushing, with all the feeling I had. This time, Ysaye continued it so divinely that I, in turn, had a lump in my throat. Strange as it sounds, this Fauré phrase sealed a father and son kind of friendship between us, which lasted until he died.

Sylvia helped me organize a new way of earning money. She rented a studio with a piano, where she gave violin lessons. When I congratulated her on it, she offered to let me share the venture with her.

"Two girls and a young boy asked me if you teach. I told them to come tomorrow at noon and play for you. All three of them can afford to pay; I feel sure that you can find as many pupils as you want."

Her offer appealed to me, and the next day, I became a piano teacher. One of the girls was a hard worker; the other one perspired so profusely that she stopped playing after every five bars to wipe her face and hands. The boy was gifted but lacked coordination.

My staying at Belsize Park became a major problem; it was too far from my daily occupations. I had to find some lodgings somewhere between Kensington and Chelsea, between Sylvia's and Muriel's studios. Mrs. Bergheim was very sweet about it.

"I shall miss you, dear boy, but I understand. Promise, please, to visit me sometime."

After vain attempts at finding something better, I rented a squalid room on Fulham Road (near Edith Grove). Gas-lit, smelly, and unclean, its only virtue was its low price.

Thanks to Eugène Ysaye, whom I saw almost daily, my concert life began to look really exciting. The master and his wife lived in a beautiful town house lent them for the duration of the war by an admirer, an English lord who preferred to stay in the country. Ysaye liked me to come in the afternoon after his siesta, share some strong coffee with him (he abhorred tea!), and play some sonatas or talk concerts. He praised my performance of the G major Beethoven Concerto, when I was very much applauded, and agreed to join me for supper at Edith Grove—a supper consisting of cheddar cheese, crackers, cold ham, and strong coffee. Fortunately, Muriel had some cold beer in the larder. At the first glimpse of the music room, Ysaye exclaimed: "Quelle cave magnifique! Je pourrais passer ma vie la dedans!" Sammons and Sylvia (they were in love), darling Lionel, and Rubio played, in honor of the master, the Quartet of Debussy, which was dedicated to Ysaye. He was delighted with their playing, he kissed Tertis on both cheeks, but said, to our amazement, that he couldn't understand this music, that it was too modern for him.

Ysaye and I gave more than twenty concerts during the season, many for the Red Cross, for the Belgians, for the Poles and other war charities. But I did play sonatas with him at his *own* recital at Queen's Hall, without accepting the fee which he offered; and then he played with me at my recital at Wigmore Hall (the new name for the Bechstein Hall) for my own benefit. And we played, of course, much chamber music at Edith Grove with our old guard and with his new Belgians, and this time we players organized the suppers. It was wonderful! How strange, when I think of it, that the two greatest *violinists* of our time had this all important influence in the development of my career as a *pianist*.

One afternoon, walking through Piccadilly, I was stopped by John Sargent.

"Rubinstein? What a nice surprise. I was talking about you last night with a charming old lady who is terribly anxious to see you. She has tried for years to find your whereabouts and asked me to help her. Do come tomorrow at four to my atelier at Tite Street. She will be there; I am just making a sketch of her."

I was intrigued. "Does she know me personally, or just by hearsay?"

"She knows you very well—she told me."

I tried hard, but couldn't think of any lady of his description. "Thank you," I said. "I shall be at your studio at four."

The next day, I went to his place with great curiosity. There were three other people in the atelier, looking at his pictures, a gray-haired lady and a young couple. The lady exclaimed in several languages when she saw me. "Ah, ah, voilà! Rubinstein, at last—ah, I am so glad, oh, que bien, Juanita! José Antonio! This is Rubinstein." And, smiling at me, "This is my nephew and she is his wife. Ah—"

I still could not make out who she was, and it became clear only after several more of her disconnected little exclamations.

Her name was Eugenia Errazuriz, and she and her daughter had lunch with Armand Gontaut-Biron and me at Romaine Brooks's in Paris in the year 1906. I suddenly remembered how impressed she had been by my performance of the *Après-midi d'un faune*. She told me, in her funny way, that she had never forgotten me, that she tried in vain to locate me ever since that day. Her nephew, José Antonio Gandarillas, who was the most articulate of the three, explained that his aunt was a fanatic admirer of mine as an artist and that she had talked so much about me that he felt as if he had known me all his life.

"Now, since we have found you at last, we will never lose you again."

His aunt approved with her ah's and oh's. The niece, a lovely, very elegant young woman, was silent, but there were stars in her eyes.

I was taken aback and quite embarrassed by this exaggerated talk. John Sargent stood apart, smiling indulgently. Eugenia Errazuriz became excited again.

"Venez, ah, los dos, come to dinner, oh, tonight," she said to Sargent and to me with a bewitching smile.

"With pleasure, thank you," we answered, in chorus. There was something irresistible about her.

I went home to change into a smoking jacket and decided to return and ask Mr. Sargent to take me to that dinner. To be honest, I wanted to find out more about them. He kindly told me all about "Eugenia," as everybody called her. She was the divorced wife of a Chilean diplomat and had lived after her marriage between Paris and London. Celebrated for her beauty, she was known in Paris as "la belle Madame Errazuriz." Having lived away from her country for so many years, she tended to forget her native Spanish a little, and her French and English had never been quite adequate, which accounted for her speaking in this strange gibberish. "And yet," Sargent said, shaking a finger at me emphatically, "I have never known anyone with the unfailing, uncanny taste of this woman. Whether in art, music, literature, or interior decoration, she sees, hears, feels, smells the real value, the real beauty. And so"—he smiled—"her joy in finding you again means that she has seen in you something very special, very precious." I laughed, incredulously.

They lived at the corner of Tite Street and the Embankment, a few houses away from his studio. On the way to their house, John Sargent gave me some additional information: "She lives with her nephew and his wife, who is very rich and is the sister of the Chilean ambassador in London. Eugenia herself never had real money; if she has, she spends it or gives it away to some artist or poet in need."

We entered the house, where a butler showed us the way up to the living room. The three Chileans received us with the same exuberance as before. The large, oak-paneled room contained many beautiful objects, among them a fine Steinway grand. In addition to a Boldini, there was a portrait of Eugenia by Sargent on the wall (and I learned that many other artists, known and unknown, had painted her). The flowers, the furniture, were chosen and distributed with perfect taste. My words of admiration were met by Eugenia's protest: "Too many things, ah, too many little things, ah, ah, il faut peter tout ça, Juanita likes bibelots, hm, hm," and so forth. I finally took a good look at this Eugenia. She must have been once a raving beauty; in her way, she still was, in spite of her fifty or more years. She was nicely plump, the complexion and firmness of her skin was remarkable (the reader must not forget that we still lived before the era of face lifting), and she had an upturned, pert little nose, and a beautiful mouth like a bow. Her hair was gray with streaks of black in it. But what really made her remain beautiful was her irresistible charm and vitality.

At dinner, with a menu which could have pleased Lucullus, we talked excitedly about the war and its tragedy. Eugenia, with all the little defects of her speech, expressed many of my own thoughts, such as her determination not to give in and the conception of an *unconditional* love of life. We spoke of miracles, a delicate subject in the presence of Catholics, but I couldn't refrain from saying what I had on my mind. I always loved the word "miracle" because I always felt that *everything* in the universe without exception is a miracle, and that nothing our brains can conceive of or even dream of is impossible. I said, "If you could look at the world with fresh, unspoiled eyes after a state of amnesia, you would understand what I mean. Can there be a greater miracle than life itself, than music, than flowers, than love? The unfortunate thing is human nature's tendency to become so familiar with the miracle that we develop a vicious way of taking everything for granted."

My often repeated, favorite philosophical credo found a friendly echo in Eugenia. The others, I fear, did not quite understand what I meant, but they liked my passionate conviction. Anyway, I soothed them by playing a few pieces on their lovely Steinway.

Eugenia, José Antonio, and Juanita did certainly not lose me any more. They entered into my life in a strange, surreptitious way. Every day there was a sign of them. A heavy leather traveling bag from Asprey arrived one morning at my lodgings, containing a toilet set in silver with my initials on it and a card from Eugenia, saying: "Thanks for your wonderful music." Another morning a fine satin robe from Harborow's on Bond Street found its way to my room. Juanita, in a letter, explained that she was worried I might get a cold in a lighter one. One night I remarked on a delicate, masculine scent on José Antonio's handkerchief. The next day a large bottle of Penhaligon's Hammam was in my possession—and I must admit that ever since I have never stopped using it. They introduced me at their dinner parties to artists, writers, politicians, ambassadors, treating me always as a guest of honor. But that is not all. One morning, Juanita's butler came to my place.

"To fetch your luggage, sir," he said.

"Why, what for?" I asked, perplexed.

"Madame ordered me to bring you home."

It was Saturday. They intend to take me out of town for a weekend, I thought, but there must be a surprise in store for me. We packed my bags in no time; my big trunk and the rest were still at Mrs. Bergheim's. The chauffeur drove me to a house at the corner of the Royal Hospital Road and Tite Street. The butler opened the door for me, took out the bags, and carried them into the house and up a flight of stairs. I followed him as meekly as a child would follow Santa Claus. We entered a large room with the sun shining through two windows. A Bechstein concert grand stood in a corner. A comfortable couch, two armchairs, and a coffee table made up the furniture. And there were flowers and fruit on the table. The butler showed me a small bedroom and an adjoining bathroom. "This is your apartment, sir," he said with a grin.

I ran to their house, where they were all waiting, knowing that I would come. Such a heartfelt, touching scene took place that I had better not describe it.

Quite naturally, I introduced my Chileans to Muriel, I brought Ysaye to their house, and I acquainted them with "Aunt Clara." They did not get along too well with Muriel. Her badly disguised air of superiority and her shrill laughter were jarring to their innate Latin courtesy. But Eugenia loved the music room. At our next night of music with Ysaye and his quartet, Sylvia, Tertis, Sammons, and Juanita took charge of the supper, which reminded me of the golden horse-winning era.

One night we played chamber music at the house of the Gandarillas when Sargent, Augustus John, the Chilean ambassador and his wife, and the Spanish ambassadress were there.

Ysaye, Désiré Defauw, Tertis, a Belgian cellist, and I were playing the Piano Quintet of Franck when a loud banging against the wall made us stop. José Antonio explained: "Aha, there it goes again. Our neighbor is an old hypochondriac, a retired colonel from service in India. He hates foreigners and annoys us whenever he can." The banging stopped, and we recommenced the Quintet.

Suddenly there was a shouting in the street, just below our opened window. "Stop that confounded noise! There is a war on! Aren't you ashamed to dance at a time like this! Our police should chase all the foreigners out of the country!" We stopped playing; we listened. Gandarillas, indignant at this offensive talk, ran out into the street ready to start a fight, but the man went back to his house. José Antonio refused to give up; he rang his bell. The man did not react. He rang the bell again for a long time; nothing happened. Finally beside himself with rage, Gandarillas smashed the glass of a window near the door and returned to his house with his hand bleeding. While we were all commenting on his courage, two policemen rang the bell and demanded to see the owner of the house. José Antonio went down to talk to them and returned a little embarrassed. "They want all of us to come at once to the police station." This was fun. We began to enjoy it. Our whole party, dressed in elegant evening clothes, the men wearing top hats, entered the police station, where the chauvinistic colonel, with red nose and bulging eyes, waited for us. At the sight of the ambassador, the two great painters, the imposing figure of Ysaye, the dignified ladies, and the rest of us, the magistrate was dumfounded. Then he addressed our accuser angrily: "Is this the company of drunken, riotous disturbers of the peace? Where is that band which plays the disgraceful dance music?"

The man did not answer; he was quite speechless—and a little drunk.

Mr. Sargent explained the affair in a few well-chosen words. We were dismissed by the red-faced magistrate with great apologies for the discomfort he had caused us. Gandarillas offered his choleric neighbor payment for the broken glass, but the man refused proudly to accept it.

One morning I read in the paper that the Russian armies had occupied new fortified lines beyond the river Bug. Poland had been abandoned to the Germans. Later in the day, special bulletins announced: "Warsaw taken by German army."

I beat my head with my fists in helpless rage. I could see my family murdered, Pola raped, Warsaw burning, the world crushed. I was not sure whom I hated more, the Russians or the Germans. Calming down, I hoped only that Pola was at last with her children, that they fled to Russia, that Paul and Zosia were safe, that no harm would be done to my family. We were completely cut off from each other. I sat at home the whole day in brooding despair.

The next morning Muriel sent me a note: "I know how you feel.

Come and have a piece of cheese with me. Love, M." Juanita sent me flowers, as though for a funeral, the dear soul. Ysaye, giving me an extra cup of strong coffee, found the best consolation: "Ne t'en fais pas trop, mon petit. Ils ont pris Bruxelles, aussi. Mais on les aura un jour."

One day Ysaye suggested to Lionel, the Belgian cellist, and myself that we spend the weekend and play chamber music at the estate of Lord Curzon of Kedleston, former viceroy of India. "Queen Elizabeth of Belgium, my faithful and devoted violin pupil," he explained, "entrusted Lord Curzon with the care of her three children for the duration of the war. As an old friend of the royal family I expressed my wish to visit them. Lord Curzon very politely invites the four of us to come to his place for the weekend and to make some music."

We accepted this tempting invitation readily, and the next Saturday afternoon we arrived at Lord Curzon's country seat, near Basingstroke. At the entrance to the stately mansion, Lady Irene, the eldest daughter of the master of the house, received us with characteristic English grace.

"My father is still in town," she informed us, "but he will be back for dinner," and, turning to Ysaye, "Prince Leopold left this morning to join King Albert at the front, and his brother spends his weekend with a school friend. That leaves us only with the little Princess Marie José, but she is the one who really loves music."

After tidying up, we joined Lady Irene and her two sisters at tea. All three were in their teens (they had lost their mother when they were small) and were quite striking. While Irene was pouring tea (coffee for Ysaye), the adorable little Princess entered the room and gave each one of us her tiny hand in the (already) regal manner.

The great violinist asked her with solicitude: "Petite princesse, vous devez être bien triste après le départ de votre frère pour le front, n'est-ce pas?"

She shook her head: "Mais non, pas du tout. Il est parti seulement pour donner l'exemple."

Ysaye played for her some violin pieces she had heard him play before, and she clapped her hands with joy.

We all changed for dinner, but not the maestro, who liked his traditional dark suit with a velvet collar, white shirt, and loose black tie.

Lord Curzon, the last to greet his guests in the large reception room, entered like a supreme judge ready to pronounce a death sentence. His bald head, cold, steel-gray eyes, and thin, tight mouth made his face bland and expressionless, and he walked with pompous dignity. A full-length portrait of him in his regalia as a viceroy and a Knight of the Garter dominated the room.

And yet, at dinner, he was the perfect English host, attending to the wine that was served and seeing that our glasses were refilled, and offering us port and cigars when the ladies had left the dining room.

Later, in the drawing room, we were getting ready to play a quartet when Lord Curzon stopped us.

"Gentlemen, I hope you will give us the pleasure of your music tomorrow in the afternoon. Now, I think, it is time to retire."

In the morning, the butler informed us that breakfast was served in the dining room. "Quite informal, sir," he said.

Lionel and I were the first ready to go down. Lady Irene, who sat at the table, eating, showed us a long service table and invited us to choose what we liked. There were ten or twelve chafing dishes with scrambled eggs and sausages, bacon, kidneys, mushrooms on toast, kippered herrings, and smoked haddock. We served ourselves and joined Irene at the table. After a while the two Belgians made their entrance. Now, a real comedy scene began. Ysaye, looking at all those fish dishes, shouted to his companion, "Mais ce sont des sauvages! Ils mangent du poisson à huit heures du matin!" And he started to complain to poor Irene that there was not an honest piece of bread to be seen, that the coffee smelled like tea, and that the tea smelled like coffee. The young lady had a sense of humor; she laughed tears and so did we. Ysaye regained his calm when he was told that there were some good places for fishing. He was a passionate fisherman.

Lord Curzon did not come down for breakfast. We spent the morning in the company of the young girls. The maestro went fishing, accompanied by a manservant. I played a viola sonata with Lionel, and, alone, I played some Brahms and Chopin. At lunch, Lady Irene said, "My father begs to be excused. He will be back at teatime." He came in at four o'clock, greeted us with a polite bow of his head, drank a cup of tea, and said, "Gentlemen, if you are not tired, it would be delightful to hear some music."

We settled down to play a quartet by Dvořák. The young girls and the little Princess took their seats close to us, and Lord Curzon sat in a comfortable armchair in a corner of the room. At the end of the first movement we saw him peacefully asleep. He woke up brusquely when we finished. "This was quite, quite delightful; thank you very much, gentlemen."

We took a train before dinner and arrived in London a little tired but in good humor. "It was quite, quite delightful, gentlemen," we repeated many times to each other.

José Antonio and Juanita gave a large dinner party. Their guests included two ambassadors and their wives, Harold Nicolson from the

Foreign Office, John Sargent, and a few others whose names I have forgotten. I was seated next to Eugenia. During dinner, among other topics, I let myself go with a panegyrical discourse on the subject of Spain. I spoke to her of my passion for everything Spanish. I told her also of my lost chance of playing in Spain with the Rosé Quartet.

Eugenia listened intently to my long talk. Suddenly, she patted my arm with the mystic air of the Fairy Godmother when she touches Cinderella with her magic wand: "Demain, ah, ah, tomorrow you will go to Spain!"

I kissed her hand for her nice wish.

On the very *next* day, I had a telephone call from a concert manager, not *my* own Daniel Meyer.

"Do you, by any chance, play the D minor Concerto of Brahms?" he asked.

I laughed. "This is the one piece which I have never stopped playing since I was twelve years old."

"Maestro Arbós wired asking if I knew a pianist who could play it with him on such a date [I forget the exact date] in San Sebastián, in Spain. Could you manage to get there in time?"

Eugenia? I asked myself. Was it Eugenia who had arranged it? But it was impossible; she had never met Arbós.

For me, it was the most tempting proposition of my life. But how was it possible? Spain was a neutral country, and I was a Russian subject working for the war. Besides, it had become difficult to pass through France. But I decided not to discourage this manager.

"I shall try," I answered. "Call me again this afternoon."

I ran, wildly excited, to see Eugenia. She heard the news calmly. "Ah, I told you, ah, ah? I felt it, n'est-ce pas?" So it was another *deus ex machina*. When I showed her the terrible complications involved, she smiled, unimpressed. "Why get excited, ah, Arturo, je vais arranger ça, you will go." She went up to her room to telephone a lady, "a close friend of the Russian ambassador," she explained. After a short talk she came back and told me with a triumphant twinkle in her eye: "You will have your visa, ah, ha, just wait!" Her next call was to Harold Nicolson. In spite of her abrupt talk in English or French, he understood perfectly well what she wanted and promised to give her a prompt answer.

Early that afternoon I rang up the manager: "Please wire Arbós that there is a good chance I can arrive on time."

Things moved rapidly. In the evening I received a wire from the Russian ambassador: "Expecting you at the embassy Sunday morning at eleven. Bring passport." Nicolson announced good news. Lord Grey, the Foreign Secretary, would allow me to embark on an English auxiliary warship for Bilbao.

On Sunday morning, Baron Benckendorff, the ambassador, received me in the chancellery of the empty embassy. "I came in from the country especially to sign your document," he said with a vengeance, "and I hope that you deserve it." When he saw my diplomatic passport he changed his tone, however. "Ah, I see that my colleague holds you in high esteem." He signed a declaration, allowing me to visit neutral countries.

I went to see Muriel to say goodbye. "You lucky devil, you!" she laughed. "When you come back you will probably not see me again—I have to return for good to the old country. London can't feed us anymore." I did not quite believe her, but we both became sentimental.

I left with the blessings of the angels from Chile. I could not decide whether Eugenia was a witch or the Queen of all the Good Fairies.

The journey to Bilbao was abominable. The sea was rough, and besides, we were obliged to wear life jackets constantly because of the danger of German submarines. We arrived in Bilbao on the eve of my concert, and a train took me to San Sebastián, where Arbós had reserved a room at the Hotel Continental.

While drinking coffee on the terrace, Arbós gave me some information about the concert. "Spaniards dislike Brahms, just as do the French and the Italians. In order to fight this silly prejudice, I arranged a festival of his music here in San Sebastián. Madrid wouldn't let me do it. But here I can do with my orchestra whatever I want."

On my way to the only rehearsal, next morning, I noticed that the posters had my name written with a pen; they must have been doubtful about my arrival. The concert took place in the small theater of the Casino, which was a legal gambling place, not a very engaging milieu for my beloved D minor Concerto.

However, the Madrid Symphony Orchestra, under Arbós, was well prepared, and it went quite smoothly. The members of the orchestra seemed to be fascinated by my playing; they behaved quite hysterically, shouting bravos in the middle of a phrase, and they gave me a big ovation at the end and kept on hitting me on my back, saying, "Que bien, que bien," in Spanish which I easily understood. Arbós assured me that he had never seen them behaving that way.

The concert was not well attended; the theater was only half-filled. But my personal success, after this monumental and sober work, was absolutely sensational. No Saint-Saëns, no Liszt, no Chopin, had ever excited a public to that extent. They kept me bowing and bowing, until I gave them an encore, against all the rules of the festival. The director of the

Casino, Mr. Dominguez, immediately offered me three more concerts, one with orchestra and two recitals.

María Cristina, the Queen Mother, invited me to her summer palace, Miramar. She received me most graciously, regretting that she did not have a piano at the palace but promising to come to one of the concerts.

The second concert, also with orchestra, was mobbed. The theater was sold out in one hour. The whole city seemed to be eager to hear me. Arbós asked me to play the G minor Saint-Saëns Concerto. During the rehearsal, the theater was full of intruders who, under this or that pretext, had forced their way into the hall.

One hour before the concert, people without tickets occupied the entire staircase, blocking access to the theater. They sat on the steps through the whole concert, trying to catch some sounds of the music coming from the hall.

A delegate of the Spanish Association of Philharmonic Societies offered me a contract for twenty concerts in the most important cities in Spain, beginning in January 1916. I was not sure what the future had in store for me, but I signed, taking the risk. Whatever was to happen, I was humbly grateful to Providence for letting me get this foothold on the country of my dreams.

My next recital was to be in San Sebastián two weeks hence. I jumped at this opportunity. My lifelong desire to see Spain was going to be fulfilled without delay (*vide* my Italian exploits); I was superstitious about postponing any opportunity that presented itself.

Arbós told me about the practical way to travel in his country. "Add up the kilometers you intend to cover and buy a *Kilometrico*. The comptroller will detach from your booklet the number of kilometers you'll use upon each stop on your tour. The advantage is that you travel in first for the price of a third class."

I bought with pride a book of two thousand kilometers which represented Madrid, Toledo, Córdoba, Sevilla, Granada, and the return to San Sebastián.

Without bragging, it was a heroic deed! August in Madrid and Andalusia was hotter than hell; the heat was unbearable even at night. What added greatly to my discomfort was my sartorial unpreparedness for heat waves of this sort. Among the general abandon in clothing by the natives, my autumnal garb cut a conspicuous figure. And yet I never learned to know these cities better than at this very first contact.

Madrid was quite empty. I was told that most of the inhabitants were in San Sebastián (!). And so I spent hours and hours of my two days in the capital at the Prado Museum—in my opinion, the most perfect art gallery in the world. All the paintings you see are supreme masterpieces.

The great art of Velázquez and Goya can be duly appreciated only in Madrid; practically their entire work is confined to the Prado. King Philip IV of Spain, I learned, had been intelligent enough to send Velázquez himself to Rome to acquire the best paintings by the best painters of Italy, a fact which accounts for the wealth of Raphaels, Titians, Tintorettos, and so many other masters one can admire at this unique museum.

Toledo impressed me by its medieval air, by its majestic site on the Tagus River, by its somber, rich cathedral, hidden in a maze of old, narrow streets. What interested me most was to see the large "plaza" in the center of the city, where the autos-da-fé of Jews had taken place at the time of the Spanish Inquisition.

But it was Sevilla, Córdoba, and Granada that I had fallen in love with in Spain; this was the Spain I imagined, the Spain I longed to see. I know that many of my Spanish readers will shake their heads: Another one who sees our country only as the *España de la pandereta*—a derisive term for the flamencos, guitarras, and bullfights, the usual attractions for tourists. From their point of view, they are right. But, pleading my own case only, I admit without shame that my lifelong love of their country grew out of my passion for Mozart's *Don Juan* and *The Marriage of Figaro*, for Bizet's *Carmen*, for *España* of Chabrier, for Rossini's *Barber of Seville*, for the *Iberia* Suite of Albéniz, and so many other scores by great composers of many lands, inspired by the rich Spanish folklore. Most of them evoke the music, life, and customs of Andalusia, centering mainly on Sevilla. The liberation of Granada and the rest of the country by Queen Isabel "la Católica" and her prophetic vision that prompted her to grant Columbus the means for his discovery of America had thrilled my young heart.

What I learned in history about the rest of Spain, and what impressed me most, was the story of the Great Inquisition which cost so many lives of the people of my race, the endless wars of succession to the Spanish throne, and the loss of the Armada in the war with England. The man who opened my heart to the great wonders of Spain, which I learned to know later on so thoroughly and so personally, was Cervantes, when I gained enough knowledge of Spanish to read *Don Quixote* in its original, inimitable language.

I hope that my long *plaidoyer* explains sufficiently my joy when the guide in Sevilla showed me the Barrio de Santa Cruz (the unspoiled seventeenth-century part of the city) and pointed to a bench at a poetic corner: "Doña Elvira waited here for Don Juan." In front of my balcony on the Plaza San Fernando a dozen adorable little girls danced the *sevillana*, passing along the one pair of castanets which each in turn was allowed to use.

The palatial cigarette factory and the suburb of Triana reminded me nostalgically of *Carmen*. The Plaza de Toros looked as though bullfights had started right there.

In spite of the torrid heat, I obliged my guide to climb up with me to the top of the Giralda tower. The poor man took the spiral climb, muttering abominable curses against me.

I loved the lazy cabdrivers with their cocky sombreros and the red carnations in their buttonholes, and the Venta Eritaña, where the flamencos sang and danced. I watched them with delight, sipping *Jerez* (sherry) and devouring *jamón crudo*, that delicious smoked ham. They were glorious, these first days in Sevilla!

Córdoba, on my hot day there, at noon, was aslumber. The streets were abandoned to themselves, guarded here and there by a few stray dogs and cats. My hotel clerk promised me a guide for the afternoon. To kill the time, I wandered around and found by myself the Mezquita with its maze of marble and porphyry columns. I spent two full hours in this huge Moorish cathedral (four stars in Baedeker), not so much for its beauty as for its precious cool air.

After lunch and a siesta, the guide took me for a long walk. He showed me some typical Andalusian houses, with their lovely patios and *rejas,* some more churches, the local bullring, and he made me take, in a café, a dreadful cool drink called *horchata*.

Tired and satisfied, I was ready to pay him off when the man stopped me: "You can't leave Córdoba without visiting the finest bordello in Spain," he made me understand with some words and gestures.

"I have no erotic inclinations tonight," I said, half in French, half in pantomine.

"It does not matter," he gesticulated. "If you offer them one or two bottles of *Jerez*, it will cover your visit."

I was tempted, and he took me into a house which looked just like any other in the neighborhood.

In the cool, pleasant patio refreshed by a small fountain, an elderly couple, seated comfortably in two rocking chairs, moved their wooden fans in a rapid, expert manner. Around the place, eight or nine lovely girls, none over twenty-five, were knitting, looking at pictures in magazines, or just fanning themselves. They were all decently dressed, used no makeup, and behaved as any girls would in a middle-class household. It was the most perfect family picture I have ever seen. Our entrance didn't disturb them in the least.

My guide whispered something to the old man, who clapped his hands and gave a short order. One of the girls left and came back with two bottles of *Jerez*. The couple stood up and invited us to follow them into the reception room. Here, a few red plush sofas, tables with glasses, and some suggestive pictures betrayed the real character of the place. Still, there also hung a Madonna in a corner above an upright piano.

The whole "family" settled down to drink their sherry. The girls, on the pretext of the heat, lifted their skirts up, showing their thighs. At that, the old man tapped my arm and, with a twinkle in his eye, pointed at their pretty legs. The situation became somewhat embarrassing for me. The too-dry sherry, the hot, stifling air, and my linguistic handicap did not inspire in me any sexual desires. My innate vanity, however, could not tolerate the thought of being ridiculed by the girls as a young man afflicted with impotence.

The only means of impressing them was music. I opened the lid of the piano and gave them a concert of Spanish tunes, of *Carmen*, of Viennese valses, and what not. The result was not just a success—one might call it an apocalyptic triumph. The girls fell all over me with kisses and hugs; the old man refused my money for the wine and declared himself ready to offer me any girl I wanted. I refused, of course, all these favors, but I had to sign my name on the piano, which I did, and not without a certain satisfaction. I hope that very piano is still there to bear witness to this lovely hot summer story.

On the morning of my arrival in Granada I asked my cabdriver to take me to the Alhambra Palace hotel, a place which was much recommended by my guidebook. The center of the city, which we passed on the way to the hotel, gave me the impression of a sleepy provincial town with a fine cathedral to account for its importance.

At the end of an indifferent street, an old, narrow portal opened on a beautiful park. Suddenly the whole atmosphere changed, and a mysterious spell took hold of me. I decided to walk, to feel it closer. In this enchanting place, cooled and darkened by the heavy foliage of the trees, I heard a delicate sound of water, of some invisible rills cascading from nowhere to nowhere. As in a dreamland, they were whispering stories of the past, which charmed me by their secrecy. The cabdriver's voice woke me from my hypnotic state; he drove me up the steep alley to the hotel, a red building in a pseudo-Moorish style. Shown to my room, I asked for breakfast. "We serve it on the balcony," I was told. And how right they were. The view from the terrace was unique in its beauty. The part of the city as seen from above gave the illusion of some sacred oasis embedded in a *vega*, the fertile plains of a dazzling green, and protected from far by the majestic mountain range of the Sierra Nevada. Convents with vast open cloisters, churches with their towers, created an air of peace and serenity. I was happy to enjoy the vision of it all by myself, undisturbed. In the afternoon I walked up to the famous Alhambra, the palace of the Moorish caliphs. It stands, in fact, exactly as it was when Boabdil, the last caliph, had to leave it after the reconquest of Granada by Isabel of Castille and Ferdinand of Aragon. It is a vast structure in a pure Moorish style with many domes and towers, loggias and exterior passages, built on a high hill which dominates the whole region. And the interior is enchanting. Outside, a path leads to the most beautiful formal garden, the Generalife, which is a part of the Alhambra. A tender melancholy pervades the whole place, which touched my heart. The great history of the Alhambra dazed and fascinated me.

In the evening, after dinner, a guide persuaded me to visit the Albaicin, the hill opposite the Alhambra, where the gypsies live in caves and entertain tourists with songs and dances. The hotel clerk warned me that it was unsafe to go there with just the guide. "It is better to visit them in the company of other tourists," he said. "The gypsies are apt to create some annoyance." Fond as I was of adventure, I decided to go anyway, but took with me only the amount of money I thought I would spend, leaving the rest with the hotel manager. A cab took us up the hill through some tortuous lanes, and stopped at a terrace where there was a long row of caves instead of houses. I was immediately surrounded by at least a dozen yelling, dark-haired, dark-eyed children who begged shamelessly and insistently for money. It was difficult to get rid of them, but the guide finally succeeded in dispersing them with the help of some older gypsies who, in turn, invited me vociferously to see them perform their dances. The invitation, however, was complicated by the fact that they came from different caves, and pulling me by my sleeves toward this or that place, they immediately started fighting for the privilege of my patronage. Once again, the guide saved me from being torn to pieces by pointing with his cane to one particular cave, and his gesture stopped the ado as if by magic. We entered the whitewashed hole in the hill which was arranged for the show. A few chairs for the guests, two chairs for the guitarists, and a picture of Christ on a corner wall were all the furniture. The dancers and singers were two young, strikingly beautiful girls, a woman in her sixties, and a child (girl) of not more than ten. The two guitarists, who looked like the smugglers in *Carmen*, began to strum their instruments. They delighted me by their strong rhythm and the fine sonority they produced. One of them stopped playing from time to time and sang some strange coloratura cadenzas which I later learned to know as the genuine flamenco *canto jondo*. This music, which has never been written down, is entirely free, improvised. Inherited from the Arabs, it uses Spanish and gypsy folklore rhythms to accompany the singing and dancing. The girls, in their long dresses with trains, red carnations under tall combs in their hair, danced with utmost grace and passion, deadly serious, haughty, never smiling, as if it were a religious rite. The old woman outdid them both with her wild temperament; she seemed to be so obsessed by a demon that she scared me. The little girl, too, was already an accomplished dancer. When the show was over, the six performers began to yell for money, stretching the palms of their hands toward me. The guide had paid the initial fee, but they considered it was not enough. I had a hard time defending myself. When I gave them all the money I carried with me, they still pursued us with their screams until we reached our cab, where the guide raised his stick in a threatening manner. I left with mixed impressions of beauty and horror.

The next morning I took the train to Madrid and San Sebastián, where I arrived completely exhausted. But when Arbós told me happily that both recitals were sold out, I was revived, and I played really quite well. The public received me like an old favorite. Arbós gave me a charming farewell dinner, at which I amused him and his guests with the stories of my adventures in their country.

Fortunately, I was able to return to London through France, thanks to the victory of the Marne. The long, tragic war of the trenches continued.

77

Back in London at my apartment on the Royal Hospital Road I found a leter from Muriel informing me of her departure for America. Her life in London had become utterly intolerable. She had shown, I must admit, a superhuman courage and a stubborn character running for a whole year a large house with children, nurse, and maid, not only without money, but much in debt to various shops and to the Savoy hotel. But frankly I found myself rather relieved by her departure. I had been so unhappy at not being able to be any help to her; it gave me an acute sense of inferiority.

Eugenia, Juanita, and José Antonio received me as a triumphant hero. They had had news from friends in San Sebastián who were at my concerts.

After a few days in London, I left with them for Scotland, where they rented a house for the rest of the summer and part of the autumn.

"We have a good piano for you," they told me. "You can work, ride horses, and shoot grouse."

We arrived in Forres, a small town near Inverness. The house was a regular castle which belonged to Sir William Gordon Cummings, a charming gentleman whom José Antonio invited to be a guest in his own house. I spent a most delightful two months in Scotland, completely carefree, working with pleasure, riding daily with José Antonio, and watching them shoot the poor grouse, which I ate, however, with pleasure in a fabulous dining room to the music of bagpipes played by men in kilts who marched around the table. My room contained a good library which provided me with some fine samples of English literature. There was also a billiard table, my old favorite game. Best of all, I worked with enthusiasm on a fresh repertoire for some concerts with orchestras in Scotland and Leeds, in which I had been asked to perform the Tchaikovski Concerto in B flat and the Second Concerto of Rachmaninoff. An invitation from Glasgow and Edinburgh to play with the Scottish Orchestra conducted by Emil Mlynarski (my future father-in-law) had come as a pleasant surprise.

Sometimes, at night, when I was still playing, my hosts and some of their guests would come down in their dressing gowns and remain listening to me late into the night.

We returned to London by car, driving along the notorious Loch Ness and the beautiful Caledonian Canal, and we stopped in Leeds, where I gave my first concert of the season.

It was there that I experienced the genuine, classical English fog, and I cannot forget it. The car took an hour to get to the entrance of the town hall, a distance less than ten minutes walking. When I tried to find the first step of the invisible staircase, I banged my head hard on the head of one of the two stone lions which "graced" the front of the building, and I had to play the concert with a large bump on my forehead (which the public fortunately could not see). The audience itself was entirely covered by the mist which filled the hall, and so our only communication was made possible by my music and their applause.

The next morning the weather cleared up and we were able to reach London at night.

I shall not describe in detail the months before my return to Spain. Sylvia, assisted generously by Juanita, gave some magnificent parties at Edith Grove, which Muriel had left to her until the lease expired. Ysaye, Tertis, Sammons, Defauw, and a Belgian cellist whose name I forget made some gorgeous music. We played Mozart, Brahms, Fauré, Franck, and twice we were lucky to have some fine players for the Octet of Schubert, my beloved Quintet by him with two cellos, and the Septet of Beethoven. Emil Mlynarski was one of the happy listeners. It was to him that I owed this chance to play the Tchaikovski Concerto for the first time in my life. He told me that his own family was safe in Russia, and that he had come by way of Sweden to fulfill his engagements in Scotland. He also said that he had no news from occupied Poland, and so I remained sadly ignorant about the fate of Pola and my family. As for the Kochanskis and Karol, Sylvia told me that they had stayed in Kiev with Jaroszynski.

After two concerts in London—one with the London Symphony— a Beethoven Festival, conducted by Verbrugghen, and a recital with Ysaye, I left for Glasgow.

At the rehearsal the morning of the concert, my short acquaintance with the difficult Tchaikovski Concerto showed many imperfections. Mr. Mlynarski, instead of getting impatient, was kindness itself.

"Have lunch with me," he said, "and after coffee, I shall take you to my room. There is a piano, so we can talk things over."

His precious advice on how to handle, musically and technically, this exacting score remains in my mind up to this day. He cut the continued fortissimi indicated in the score by a piano and crescendo whenever the phrase allowed it, thus refreshing and heightening the effect of the whole. He proved also how wrong it was to play *too quickly* the valse sequence in the second movement. I never play this work without being conscious of his words. And, thanks to him, I had a real success in Glasgow and Edinburgh.

In London, we had a nice Christmas Eve celebration in the Catholic tradition with my Chileans, and a typical English Christmas dinner, with turkey and a plum pudding flambé, at Mrs. Bergheim's. We greeted the year 1916 at midnight with a great supper given by Juanita for all our friends, musicians, and listeners at Edith Grove.

Right after the New Year I left for Spain. My first three concerts were in Zaragoza, Oviedo, and Bilbao, and I shared them with a brilliant young Spanish cellist, Gaspar Cassadó, each of us playing in turn. After these three quite successful but uneventful concerts, I continued the tour by myself.

Valencia was the city where I experienced again the thrilling, electric contact with the Spanish public which I had felt so keenly in San Sebastián. My engagement called for two concerts on two consecutive days, but during the intermission of the second concert, the Committee of the Philharmonic Society voted by acclamation for two additional recitals on the following two days. And so I played four times in four days for the same public!

I learned on that occasion something about Spanish hospitality. Some painters from the Austrian part of Poland who, as citizens of an enemy country, had had to leave France, had settled in Sagunto, near Valencia. I had known some of them in Poland and in Paris, so naturally I was delighted to find them there. After my last concert I invited them for supper at a good restaurant. About ten of us were talking Polish when a gentleman came up to our table, complimented me on my success, took a chair, and joined us at my table. We were rather shocked by this uncalled-for intrusion—none of us knew enough Spanish, but, being foreigners, we were very polite. I offered him a glass of wine, which he drank to my health. After a few minutes of a futile conversation, he rose to his feet, shook hands with all of us, and left the restaurant. Much later, when I asked for my bill, the waiter told me that everything had been paid by this Spanish gentleman, whose name nobody knew. From what I could understand of the waiter's explanation, the man had declared: "They are guests of my country."

After Valencia, my tour was a real triumph. My debut in Barcelona, Spain's second-largest city, took place in a small hall, but five days later I played in the Palacio de la Música, a very large hall which was not large enough for my public. I played Bach, Beethoven, Schumann, Chopin, Liszt, and also Debussy, Szymanowski, Scriabin, and Medtner, no Brahms and no Spanish music—I was too afraid I would play it with a "foreign accent." What they liked most was Chopin and Liszt. The Madrid Philharmonic Society, I discovered, would not have me because they preferred chamber music to soloists. But my debut in San Sebastián was so well known in Madrid that a theater which usually put on dramas and comedies engaged me for three concerts in the late afternoons—the usual hour for concerts, as one dines so late in Spain.

When I arrived in the capital, all three were sold out and the director proposed two more. Fortunately I found in a piano store an old, much used Bechstein which still had some of its noble qualities. My first recital at the Teatro Lara was such a fantastic success that I was forced to give four or five encores. The audience refused to leave. The Infanta Isabel, the old aunt of the King, Alfonso XIII, was there, and during intermission she called me to her box and invited me for tea the next day.

"I expect you tomorrow at five at my palace. Her Majesty the Queen Victoria Eugenia is coming and hopes to hear you play," she said, very graciously.

This "tea party" was the beginning of my lifelong friendship with the Spanish royal family. I know that the term "friendship" may sound too pretentious; it might be more correct to say that "the royal family bestowed many favors upon me," but I cannot help admitting that my real feelings for them are those of a warm, human friendship, because I have found in each member of that family the most generous, spontaneous enthusiasm and understanding—it has outlasted the revolution, the civil war, and continues now with the third generation of King Alfonso and Queen Victoria Eugenia.

My concerts in Madrid from that day on were honored by the presence of the charming, beautiful, and very musical young Queen, the Infanta Isabel, the Queen Mother María Cristina, and often by the Infantitas Beatriz and María Cristina.

It seemed to be a matter of course that my audiences were made up of the most interesting people in Madrid. Besides the so-called society of the court, musicians, great writers, politicians, and the diplomatic corps were constantly at my concerts. The great Spanish playwright Jacinto Benavente used to listen to my concert on the stage, in a rocking chair, smoking a huge cigar. King Alfonso was quite unmusical, and he attended concerts only when his presence was required, but his friendly feelings toward me were purely personal; he liked to talk to me, and liked to hear me talk.

Eugenia Errazuriz and José Antonio—or Tony as he was called—and Juanita arrived from London to assist at my last recitals. Eugenia was extremely popular with Spanish society, and she introduced me to many families of grandees. Many of them became, thanks to her, my intimate friends for life.

In April, Tony and the Duke and Duchess of Fernán-Núñez organized a great excursion to Sevilla for the Semana Santa and the Feria—Holy Week and the famous Easter fair—a party consisting of the Duke and Duchess of Montellano with their son and daughter, the Duke and Duchess of Aliaga with their daughter, Count Cuevas de Vera, Carlos Salamanca, (whose beautiful sister, Marchioness of Villavieja, was Eugenia's best friend), and Eugenia, Juanita, and myself. Our spectacular "caravan" consisted of four Rolls-Royce cars, and three or more motor wagons for carrying our luggage, food, and all the accessories for picnics. We stopped for a day in Toledo and in Córdoba and traveled leisurely toward our goal. Along the way, we would always have a lovely luncheon under the trees in a picturesque spot. The Duke of Fernán-Núñez would usually decide where we should settle down. Right away the servants would spread a carpet on the grass, bring us comfortable field chairs, and set up a small collapsible table in front of each one of us, and set out dishes, glasses, and silverware. The menu was made up mainly of caviar, smoked salmon, cold duck, salads, cheese, fruit, choice wines, liqueurs, and coffee. Cigars in large humidors were offered to the men, cigarettes in silver boxes to the ladies. This was what my new Spanish friends called a "picnic"!

On one of these occasions an old shepherd who was leading two goats stopped and watched us eating. He wore torn trousers, a faded shirt, and a tattered hat, but his unshaven face had noble features. The Duke of Fernân-Núñez spoke to him: "Compadre, can we offer you something to eat?"

Yes, he would accept it, thank you, said the man. The servants were ordered to give him the same food we were having, including the wine and a cigar. The shepherd ate it all calmly, drank the wine, and lit the cigar. When we finished our picnic and were ready to leave, the old man said to the Duke: "Señor, when you reach the long street of the next village, the second house on the left is where I live. You are welcome to it whenever you choose." With these words, he took leave with a dignified gesture and walked off with his goats.

The Duke was silent for a while. Then he uttered with the hoarse voice of emotion: "They are pretty noble and proud, our Spanish peasants, eh?"

The Semana Santa impressed me in its expression of the deeply rooted faith of the Spanish Catholics mixed with a strong touch of paganism. On Good Friday, pallbearers carried on their shoulders heavy platforms on which were set tableaux from the Passion. There were statues in painted wood of Christ bent under the cross, and some of the Apostles, or the Holy Virgin dressed up all in white, wearing genuine diamond necklaces and brooches lent for good luck by wealthy ladies of the city. The bearers marched the whole day long in slow procession through the main streets of Sevilla. From time to time, they stopped for a drink of wine or to wait for some girl from a balcony to sing a *Saeta*—the imploring improvisation of a prayer to the Virgin. When, perchance, a procession from a rich district church met another from a poorer one, fistfights would break out between the bearers, who by then were heavily drunk. "Your Virgin is nothing but a whore," the men from the poor district would shout. The pious crowd witnessing such scenes rather enjoyed them.

All through Holy Week shops, theaters, banks, and restaurants were closed until Saturday night, the eve of Easter Sunday, when, by a strange tradition, all the theaters in Spain would play the classical *Don Juan Tenorio* by Zorrilla, music halls would open, and a general feasting would take place, not unlike New Year's Eve. On Easter Sunday, and the next two days, the most important bullfights of the year featured the greatest matadors of the time, Gallito, Belmonte, and Gaona. We participated in all the activities of the Feria which followed, we watched and danced the *sevillanas,* we spent whole nights listening to flamencos in the Venta Eritana. Altogether it was a most enjoyable experience, and for years after, I became a part of the Feria.

Our caravan left for Algeciras, where instead of taking a rest, Carlos Cuevas, Manolo Pons (the actual Duke of Montellano), Carlos Salamanca, and I sailed for Tangiers, to get a glimpse of Africa. It was only a two-hour crossing. We roamed the Arab city, stopping at the market, where we bought a few fezzes and Arab babouches, smoking narghiles in a café, and enjoying the exotic local color. When we returned to Algeciras the four of us had a jolly dinner and were in a boisterous mood, drinking a little too much sherry.

A good-looking young lady sat alone at a neighboring table; she was dressed in black and had a sad expression on her face. After dinner, our party scattered in different directions—some went to the casino to gamble, the others went to bed. I remained in the lounge, sipping my coffee, when the lady in black addressed me in French, inquiring about the boat to Tangiers. After I gave her the information, we continued to talk and went out to the lovely garden that runs down to the sea, overlooking the rock of Gibralter. She had lost her husband in the war, she said. I took her hand in sympathy. At that, she grabbed me violently, almost hysterically, and, instantly, we made love on a bench in a dark spot. It was the most unexpected thing in my whole life. She ran back to her room and was gone in the morning. Musing about it later, I realized all of a sudden what the war could do to a broken woman.

The "caravan" returned to Madrid by way of Málaga, Granada, and Ronda, where we were given a wonderful dinner and reception in the palace of the Dukes of Parcent by the Duchess and her lovely daughter, Piedita Iturbe, the haughty and beautiful young girl who had talked to me once in Karlsbad. Back in the capital, Tony and Juanita left by train for London, and Eugenia and I remained in Madrid.

The young Queen used to invite me to play for her and her daughters in her private apartment with only the Duchess San Carlos, her lady-in-waiting, present. Another time, I gave a concert at the Royal Palace for a large gathering of the diplomatic corps, the grandees of Spain, and the various Infantes and Infantas. After each of these appearances I received wonderful presents from both the King and the Queen: a pair of cuff links with small diamonds, a gold watch, a gold cigarette case with the engraved signature "Victoria Eugenia" and the date, and a platinum chain.

The Duke of Alba, the greatest name in Spain after the King, often invited me for dinner. As he also held the Scottish title of Duke of Berwick, he felt it his duty to introduce to Spain the British custom of dining at eight p.m., and not at ten p.m. or later, as is the rule in Spain. Besides, the Duke was pedantically punctual—another un-Spanish characteristic. To my regret, I was a quarter of an hour late for my first dinner. The Palacio do la Liria, the historic palace of the Dukes of Alba, was rather far from my hotel, so I miscalculated the time it takes to get there. As I entered the hall, two men of the ducal livery took my coat and hat and announced sternly that the Duke and his guests were already at table. Not a little abashed, I had to find quickly a plausible excuse. I entered the dining room with catastrophe on my face: "I had a painful accident in the bathroom of my hotel, Señor," I stuttered. "The overheated room and a too hot bath gave me a fainting spell." I closed my eyes. "I had hardly the strength to dress."

My story was received with loud exclamations of sympathy.

"Sit down quietly and relax," said the Duke with genuine concern. "A cup of warm consommé will do you good." A lady gave me a pill. "Take it," she said. "It is for the heart." All through dinner I was treated with solicitude. "Do you feel better? Do you want another pill?" As a matter of fact, I felt quite happy. The palace was a great museum. We had coffee in a room where two portraits by Titian of the Duke of Alba, my host's ancestor, who was the notorious governor of Flanders, hung on the walls. There was another one by Rubens of the same man. I was taken home by a charming couple who insisted on seeing me to my room.

The next time, to my great disgust, I was late again, and not through my fault. Eugenia and some friends detained me too long at a cocktail party. On the way to the Palacio do la Liria I invented a good reason for being late. This time, the Duke rose to greet me with a slight irritation in his voice: "My dear Rubinstein, excuse me for sitting down to dinner without you, but I believe in strict hours for dining."

I replied very calmly: "You are quite right, Señor, but something unforeseen came up. When I entered the taxi, a hotel boy told me there was an urgent telephone call. An American impresario proposed a concert tour in America for the next winter. Our talk made me late; I am terribly sorry."

The Duke's expression changed into a delighted smile: "Oh, oh, congratulations, my dear," he said, and, turning to his guests, he announced: "Rubinstein is engaged for a tour in America."

"Bravo, bravo," and "enhorabuena," shouted the guests. I was duly toasted and became the hero of the evening.

A few weeks later the Duke of Alba invited me for dinner again. For that occasion I was determined to be on time. "I shall kill myself if I am late," I swore. At six thirty I was dressed and at twenty minutes to eight I sat in a taxi. "To the Palacio do la Liria, please," I told the chauffeur. The ride took less than fifteen minutes. We were going along smoothly, there was no traffic, when, passing a darkish square, I heard a loud bang, like a gunshot. The tire of my taxi had been punctured! I was desperate. "Quickly get another taxi," I shouted. My driver smiled, shrugging his shoulders. "There are no taxis hereabouts, but it is not far to walk—just three blocks ahead and one long block to the right and you are there." I started to run as if I was out to win the Olympic championship, and arrived at the palace sweating and out of breath, only ten minutes late. But, fatally, I found them already dining. I was so indignant I was ready to cry.

"A most terrible thing has happened to me," I said with a broken voice, and told the whole tragic story with the taxi. I was ready to leave, I was so unhappy.

The Duke of Alba responded calmly: "Don't be so upset. I quite understand," and with a charming smile, he added: "I enjoyed your little story." This time he had not believed me! The truth was not good enough.

With all my great success, the Philharmonic Societies paid such small fees, and so did the Teatro Lara, that I really needed a good agent. A musician of my acquaintance told me about a man named Daniel, who used to work in Berlin in the office of the great Hermann Wolff, and I made an appointment with him for the next morning.

I discovered that he was a Cuban—his real name was Ernesto de Quesada—and that he had inherited or bought a small printing firm named Daniel, a name which he kept for his concert agency. There was a boyish look about him, belying his thirty or more years, and he was rather shy, but I felt right away that he was the man I needed, a really competent concert agent.

"We can make much more money next season, but it takes some bargaining with the stingy Philharmonic Societies," he said. "In Madrid and Barcelona you ought to give your concerts at your own risk; after expenses the money is yours."

I engaged him as my agent for Spain—and he is still my representative today. We developed a plan for the next season, and he began at once to work out my tour.

Madrid in May was unbearably hot, and life there became equally unpleasant. The war was on everybody's mind. I felt the pulse of the international situation more clearly in this neutral country than in a country at war. Spain was overrun by citizens from both fighting camps who were waging their own little war in Madrid. Spying, intrigues, false alarms, and slanders were their secret weapons. I had a hard time recognizing friend from foe. On one occasion, a Frenchman asked me: "Is it true that you spoke to the counselor of the Austrian Embassy?" "Of course not," I answered. But I was lying; the counselor was a Polish friend of mine. Wherever you went, you kept your eyes wide open: Is this one a spy? Why did he leave so soon? Probably to telephone. Anyway, many of my friends left for the country or for the sea. Eugenia and the Marchioness Villavieja went to visit a friend of theirs near Córdoba, and the court settled for the summer in the Royal Palace of Santander.

78

I arrived in San Sebastián on a warm, sunny morning at the beginning of June 1916. My concerts were scheduled for July, but I needed a rest and fresh air and, mainly, to be away from Madrid.

I settled comfortably at the Hotel Continental in a room overlooking the Concha and enjoyed the view of this pleasant city. In an excellent mood, humming a Spanish tune, I entered the restaurant for lunch. At a table near the window sat the great Sergei Diaghilev in the company of young Léonide Massine, who replaced Nijinsky as first dancer and favorite of this magician of the ballet. Diaghilev, who on previous occasions had taken no notice of me, stood up this time to greet me.

"What a good surprise to see you here," he said with a smile, showing all his teeth. "Please join us at our table." I did, of course (we had *pension complète* at the hotel), and from that time on the three of us shared the same table at meals.

The great man was in deep trouble. For most civilians in Europe the war brought a radical change in their lives, but for Diaghilev it proved a disaster. Here he was in possession of a ballet company of the highest order, and the world, his particular world, was suddenly closed to him. Spain, the only accessible neutral country, became his refuge. But what a precarious refuge it was! True enough, he had a large offer for the coming autumn at the Metropolitan Opera in New York and another one for a long season in Argentina and Uruguay in the summer of 1917, but both so vitally important contracts contained a difficult if not unacceptable clause: neither the Metropolitan Opera nor the Colón of Buenos Aires would agree to take the ballet without Nijinsky. "Our publicity is made on his name," they claimed. And Diaghilev, who had fallen into an uncontrollable jealous rage over Nijinsky's marriage, had dismissed the great dancer and replaced him by the less spectacular Massine. So now the poor man had to compromise; he had to cajole, almost beg, the famous star to join his ballet company for both seasons. He himself and Massine would remain in Europe. But for the present, without adequate means, he was struggling desperately to hold his company together. In addition to the ballet proper, he had two Russian painters and the conductor Ernest Ansermet on his payroll, and he had to provide the money for the Spanish composer Manuel de Falla, whom he had commissioned to write a ballet for the coming season. Picasso was in charge of the decorations and the costumes for this Spanish ballet.

This was the situation when I arrived. Diaghilev had an indomitable spirit, however; he never showed an inkling of his troubles, always kept his sense of humor intact, and so our meals were always graced by lively, witty, and interesting conversations and often by brilliant ideas for new ballets. I became acquainted, of course, with all the members of his company, his stagehands included. De Falla, Lopoukhova,* Adolph Bolm, Lila Kashouba, and the Shabelski sisters became my inseparable companions.

My anticipated "calm retreat" in San Sebastián turned into a wild carousel! It was exciting to watch the morning rehearsals of the lovely dancers in tights. I enjoyed the long sessions with the painters and Ansermet at a café terrace, the lively luncheons at the hotel, and I loved to listen to de Falla playing fragments of his new ballet, *The Three-Cornered Hat.* Late in the evening, Lydia Lopoukhova, Bolm, and other music lovers would drag me into the empty hall of the Casino and make me play for hours, often long past midnight. The whole company showed a remarkable spirit: the dancers went for days without proper food, with unpaid hotel bills, with no money at all, but they never lost their natural gay disposition. They were always ready to have fun, and they wouldn't let their hardships interfere with their work.

Manuel de Falla I found to be an unusual personality. He looked like an ascetic monk in civilian clothes. Always dressed in black, there was something melancholy about his bald head, his penetrating black eyes and bushy eyebrows; even his smile was sad. But his music betrayed a passion so intense that it seemed a complete contrast to the man. Shy and self-conscious about doing a ballet score, he put some old-fashioned minuets and gavottes into the music, but Diaghilev had no use for them.

"I want it all Spanish and none of this outlandish trash," Diaghilev shouted. The next day poor de Falla brought a short sketch of a jota, the

* The future wife of the famous economist John Maynard Keynes.

classical Spanish dance. "This is just what we need," said Diaghilev, and Massine nodded approvingly, "and we want much more of it." So, from day to day, de Falla's jota developed into a long passionate dance for the finale, to the delight of his tormentor. The result was stunning; *The Three-Cornered Hat* became one of the most successful ballets of the repertoire.

Arbós arrived from Madrid for his summer season and gave his first concert with me as soloist. We repeated the Tchaikovski Concerto to a shouting, enthusiastic audience.

Among the most attentive listeners were Diaghilev and a friend of his, Madame Misia Sert. They both loved the Concerto and the way I performed it, and it was on that day that I really won Diaghilev's friendship. Up to then, the many attentions he had shown me had a lot to do with my success in Spain and the possibility of my being useful to him there.

Misia Sert was a remarkable woman with a bewitching charm and vitality rather than beauty. Famous in Paris for having been painted by Manet, Renoir, Toulouse-Lautrec, Vuillard, and Bonnard, and married to José Maria Sert, the Spanish painter, she was influential in the artistic world in Paris. It was she, among others, who helped Diaghilev obtain the funds for his extravagantly expensive seasons from the rich of the international set. Her arrival in San Sebastián brought him much needed relief in the form of a good sum of money. Misia Sert was proud to be the only woman in the world who was not just tolerated by this woman-hater, but actually adored by him.

The Ballet gave two gala performances in the Teatro Victoria Eugenia in San Sebastián with the Madrid Orchestra conducted by Ernest Ansermet. As a sequel, Ansermet kept the orchestra for a concert with me as soloist. We had a packed house and gave all the money to pay off the dancers' hotel bills. Diaghilev, who was in London to raise some funds, brought me two beautiful ties—a charming gesture.

My concert season had started. The tour began in Barcelona and other cities in the province of Catalonia. Everywhere ovations and sold-out halls. In Palma de Mallorca, the widow of Albéniz invited me for dinner, which I readily accepted. She lived in the outskirts of Palma with her two daughters, a married one and Laura, a beautiful young girl. During dinner I amused them with the story of how I met Albéniz without knowing who he was.

"Do you play any of his music?" asked Señora Albéniz.

"Of course," I answered. "I know and love his *Iberia* Suite, but I am afraid to play it in Spain. In Poland the most successful foreign pianists provoke laughter when they play mazurkas of Chopin; they just miss the rhythmical impact of this purely Polish music. And I don't

want to run the risk of being laughed at in Spain, where I am so happy
with my success."

"But, please, play something of Albéniz for us," begged the ladies.

"Señora," I said somewhat ashamed, "I play his music with passion
but in my own way. You see, in my opinion, the texture of the *Iberia*
Suite is a little too thick—it hampers the natural flow of the melody. It
might shock you to hear me leave out many notes in order to project
the essence of the music."

The ladies were not deterred.

"Play the way you feel—it will be so interesting to hear your interpretation."

I began with "Triana," giving it all my innate love for Spanish
rhythms. When I finished, Señora Albeniz said to Laura: "Isn't it amazing?
He plays it exactly as your father used to play it." "Yes, yes," Laura
said. "Papa also left out a lot of the nonessential accompaniment." An
approval coming from the widow and the daughter of the composer,
both pianists, encouraged me considerably. I played three or four other
pieces from *Iberia*, reading them in my way, and my listeners kept
interrupting me with their exclamations: "Papa made this rubato, he
finished it pianissimo, his tempo was exactly the same," and so forth. My
mind was made up.

"Madame," I said, "if you promise to come to Madrid or Barcelona
for its first performance, I shall perform all twelve pieces of the *Iberia*
Suite at my concerts." The ladies promised solemnly. I left Palma to
continue my tour, and I worked wherever I could on this terribly
difficult score.

A month later I announced three special concerts in Madrid, including four of the twelve pieces of *Iberia* in each program. Since
nobody had ever played them before, they were a complete revelation to
the public. I can call these concerts without exaggeration the real turning
point in my career. After every one of the pieces there was a roar. "Bis,
bis, bis," shouted the audience, forcing me to repeat one after another.
At the end they gave me the greatest ovation of my life; I had to bow
a dozen times, I was showered with flowers, and out in the street a
crowd accompanied me to my hotel and continued shouting "Bravo."
Señora Albéniz, Laura, Arbós, de Falla, and other musicians embraced me
and complimented me in the most enthusiastic way. "You played this
music like a born Spaniard," they said. From that day on I was stamped
as the greatest interpreter of Spanish music, and played some of these
pieces in every city with the same success. I also performed a posthumous
piece by Albéniz, *Navarra*, which became the favorite "encore" of my
career. For years, I wasn't allowed to finish a program without playing it.

There was another curious musical incident. Manuel de Falla and I became very friendly. One night he took me to see Pastora Imperio, the famous gypsy singer and dancer, perform his ballet called *El Amor brujo*. It was given late at night in a theater after the regular play. The ballet was about a girl fallen under the spell of witchcraft cast on her by a man (a fine dancer). The music was performed by five or six players, the usual ensemble one hears at nightclubs; the pianist played on an upright piano. But the music fascinated me, especially a dance called the "Fire Dance," magnificently performed by Pastora Imperio. "Could you lend me the score of this dance?" I asked the composer. "I would love to arrange it for the piano and play it in a concert." He laughed. "Of course I will let you have it," he said, "but I doubt if it would make any effect." I did arrange it, just picking it up from the primitive score. When I played it as an encore at my next concert, the public went wild. I *had* to repeat it three times.

Queen Victoria Eugenia used to attend all my concerts and would often invite me to play in her private apartments, as did the old Infanta Isabel and the Queen Mother.

The piano which I used at my concerts began to deteriorate so rapidly that I became ashamed to play on it. One day I complained about it to the young Queen, apologizing for its cold, metallic, and worn-out tone.

"I have noticed it myself," said Her Majesty, and after a short silence, she added: "If you keep the secret carefully, I shall be pleased to send my own Steinway, which you like, for your concerts in Madrid." I laughed, quite confused; this was a very extraordinary offer. "I hope it will not inconvenience Your Majesty."

"Not in the least. I shall have it brought back to the palace after each concert. But I do not want to make it known, not even to the King. He might not approve," she added with a smile. I expressed my deep gratitude inadequately; it was difficult to find the right words.

And so the royal piano was brought to my next concerts and taken back right after I had finished. The Queen was delighted to hear her instrument sound to its best advantage. The public noticed the change, but took for granted that some music lover had lent me his piano.

At one of these concerts something unexpected happened: I was just ready to leave for the theater when the manager called. "Your piano is not here yet. The public is filling the hall—what shall I do?" I became terribly alarmed.

"I shall inquire about it myself," I answered, and called the palace of the Duke of Santo Mauro, the Queen's chamberlain-in-waiting, who knew our secret. "The Duke is out of town," the butler answered. I

rushed to the theater, which was almost full, but the stage was empty—
no piano. At the time to begin the concert there was still no news. I was
frantic. After a quarter of an hour the audience showed their impatience
by clapping and tapping their feet. The manager went out on the stage
and explained that the piano was delayed but it was on its way. After
an hour of agony with the public protesting loudly, the instrument
arrived and was put on the stage in a hurry. Some moments later the
Queen entered the royal box. I gave a huge sigh of relief and began
to play. And the concert turned out to be one of my best—I was determined to appease the audience, and I succeeded in making them
forget the incident.

During intermission I was asked to go up to the royal box, where
I found the Queen flushed with excitement. "I am sorry about your
ordeal waiting for the piano," she said, "but something quite unusual
happened. At luncheon the Queen Mother and the King entered into a
lively political discussion. As a rule, they retire after lunch to rest, but
today their differences of opinion led them to continue their quarrel in
the very apartment where the piano was ready to be taken out. I was on
pins, but I dared not interrupt them. The minute they left the room, my
men rushed the piano to the theater, and we rushed here too, didn't we?"
She smiled at the Duchess San Carlos.

The season of 1916–1917 remains in my memory as the one when
I gave more than a hundred concerts in Spain alone. I can't think of a city
in that country where I had not played. By then I spoke Spanish with
ease. My greatest trouble on that tour was to find adequate pianos fit for
concert performances. More often than not I had to play on weak baby
grands or on very old concert grands lent by some local owners.

I remember a city where the board of directors boasted of having
acquired a *brand-new piano* especially for me. When, to my horror, I
discovered that it was an *upright*, I refused to give the concert and prepared to leave. The mayor of the city caught me at the railway station:
"Please do not humiliate my beloved city," he said, and began to cry!
This broke my heart—and so I played a whole concert on this abominable half-instrument!

In Palma of the Canary Islands I was told that a rich banana grower
owned a genuine Bechstein concert grand. Without losing a second I
went to see him with the hope that he might lend it for my concerts.
The man, a coarse-looking, uneducated fellow, seemed to be flattered by
my request; he had been told that it was an honor for him to let me use it.

"Look," he said proudly, "this piano is the best and the most expensive one in the world—I buy nothing but the best." Showing me a

key, he added, "Nobody has ever touched my piano—I always keep this key in my pocket, and you will be the first one to use it." He solemnly opened the instrument . . . and, lo . . . the inside was a terrible mess. The strings were rusty and partly broken, the wood was eaten by termites— even rats must have made a meal or two of it. I left in a hurry, not having the heart to watch the man's dismay.

Back in Madrid I had the good luck of being present at the first night of Diaghilev's Ballet at the Teatro Real. It was a gala which the royal family attended. I was invited by the Duke and Duchess of Monte- llano to share their box, and for supper after the show. We were en- tranced by the beauty of *Schéhérazade* with Nijinsky again in the role of the slave. During intermission, at the buffet, I noticed a short, dark- haired man in street clothes looking at me; his were the most pene- trating eyes I had ever seen. He addressed me in Spanish: "Es Usted el pianista Rubinstein?" I suddenly knew who he was. "Picasso?" I asked. We both burst out laughing; we recognized each other easily from de- scriptions by our mutual friends. After the ballet, I excused myself from the supper at the Montellanos and joined Picasso at the Café Levante at the Puerta del Sol, a famous meeting place of the artistic and intellectual world. Picasso and I talked for hours about everything; we understood each other perfectly. Our good friendship began that night and is still alive after all these years of fantastic changes in the world and in our own lives.

Eugenia was burning to meet the great men connected with the Ballets Russes. I managed to invite for her Diaghilev, Massine, de Falla, and Picasso for lunch at the Palace Hotel Grill. She was fascinated by all of them but especially by Picasso. Like Gertrude Stein before her, she adopted him for some time to paint her and her daughter's portraits; she made him paint a screen, a brooch, and any paintable object for her. One summer, after the war, she invited him to stay with her in her villa in Biarritz. Picasso, to show his gratitude for her hospitality, had a deli- cate thought. On the last morning of his stay, he painted in secret some frescoes on the wall of his bedroom, and left, kissing her goodbye. When Eugenia entered his room, she gave a shout—out of both delight and dismay! The villa did not belong to her—she had rented it for the sea- son!

The news from Russia was more alarming from day to day. The German armies had been victorious all along the Russian front and were penetrating deep into the country. Events of grave historical conse- quences followed each other in quick succession. The spectacular assas- sination of Rasputin ended the pernicious political interferences of the

Tsarina. After the Tsar's abdication, the new liberal government, presided over by Prince Lvov, elected by the Duma, decided to continue the war against overwhelming odds.

At about that time I was afraid that my passport had become worthless, but the Russian ambassador in Madrid was kind enough to replace it with a new diplomatic document in the name of the Republican government. But politics in Russia suddenly took a dangerous turn.

The Germans conceived a devilish strategic plan. They imported from Switzerland the two famous followers of Marx—Lenin and Trotsky —and planted them in Russia like a germ. They entered St. Petersburg secretly, where Lenin began to harangue the deserters from the army and navy. Soon workers and peasants joined, too, in ever growing numbers. The Duma counteracted by electing a new premier, a socialist, Aleksandr Kerenski. Lenin set up a revolutionary committee in the Smolny Institute, and from there he opposed the decrees of the Duma more and more efficiently; he even tried to establish an armistice with the Germans.

The demoralized army was on the verge of surrendering to the enemy. Treated as cannon fodder by the cynical and unscrupulous governments influenced by the Tsarina under Rasputin's sway, the soldiers joined Lenin's revolution in vast numbers. And there were many mutinies in the naval port of Kronshtadt.

Such was the tragic situation in Russia.

On the western front, the Allied armies held their own, and the war of the trenches continued after the terrible battle of Verdun was won, where hundreds of thousands of brave men fell in defense of the portentous fortress.

The telephone operator of the Palace hotel rang up one morning to say that a gentleman was in the hall who wanted to see me. When I asked him for what purpose, the operator returned with the answer: "He does not want to say it over the telephone, but he insists that it is important."

Slightly intrigued, I went down to the hall, where a fat little man with a round, sweaty face rose to his feet and asked me: "Where can we talk in private?"

"My room would be the best place, I presume," I suggested. We took the elevator and entered my room, whereupon the man made sure that the door was closed. Then, without taking off his coat and hat, he said excitedly: "I want you to come to Argentina."

"What for?" I asked.

"To give concerts."

"Are you an impresario?"

"No," he answered, "but my brother-in-law has a big theater in Buenos Aires."

He looked strange and irresponsible to me, but he was so intent on his purpose that I decided to call Quesada about it.

"Can you come tomorrow at noon?" I said to my visitor. "I must consult my secretary about your proposition. There are other plans in view."

"I shall come, but, please, do not accept other offers before seeing me." I agreed and he left.

Ernesto de Quesada, who had been doing so well for me in Madrid and Barcelona, came in the morning, and I told him about the curious offer of the fellow.

"Don't commit yourself," Quesada advised. "Wait for a serious engagement from Faustino da Rosa, the director of the Teatro Colón, the famous opera house of Buenos Aires, and other theaters. He is the only man who is in the position of introducing you in the proper way in such a rich and important country." Bearing in mind what he had told me, I received the man (I forget his name) with cool indifference and tried to get rid of him, but the fellow was so terribly obstinate he was hard to shake off.

"I am the owner of a great chocolate plant in Buenos Aires," he said, "and I am a rich man. My wish is to help the husband of my only sister in his theatrical enterprises. He asked me to engage the best dramatic company in Madrid for his theater, with the Teatro Lara as preference. The other day I bought a ticket to see the comedy by Benavente which that company was supposed to play. And what did I see when I entered the theater? On the stage sat a man playing the piano; and a full house, with the Queen and the Infantas in the royal box, gave that man ovations I had never witnessed before. So I decided on the spot to get the company *and* this piano player for my brother-in-law's season at his theater."

I couldn't help but laugh at the story as he told it.

"The Lara company might be willing to accept your offer," I said, "but as for myself, I have decided to go to Argentina only under the management of Faustino da Rosa, who has the right organization and the right theater for an artist of my kind, and—"

"You are wrong," he interrupted me. "The Teatro San Martín of my brother-in-law is bigger than da Rosa's Odeon theater, and, besides, his program is all fixed up for this season."

"I am sorry," I said coldly, "but I prefer to wait a year or two rather than be presented in your great country by a man who has never managed a pianist before. And now you must excuse me—I am busy," I said, getting up from my chair. The fellow left angrily, without taking leave.

Quesada enjoyed my story, as did the actors at the theater. A few days later, in the morning, there was a knock at my door. I opened it, and in came my Argentine chocolate maker holding a bag. Without saying a word he opened it, and out spilled a rain of gold sovereigns onto my bed. "This is an advance on your concerts," he said, grinning. "We are ready to guarantee four thousand, five hundred gold pounds* for fifteen concerts in Argentina and Uruguay!" And he counted out five hundred gold pieces on the bed. I was stunned. The gold looked to me like the treasure of Ali Baba. I could not resist the temptation. In the afternoon we signed a contract that would go into effect the beginning of June. Two first-class passages both ways were included. Quesada was pessimistic about the judiciousness of my decision. I suggested he sail with me as my secretary for a good monthly fee and all expenses paid. With him at my side, I would feel more secure about the way these people would present me. To my great relief, Quesada agreed. My only worry was my passport. Mr. Willard, the American ambassador, who befriended me, had doubts that my document would be accepted in South America. For a possible emergency he gave me a letter of introduction to his colleague in Buenos Aires.

At one of the symphony concerts at the Teatro Real I had the opportunity to hear the first performance of de Falla's *Nights in the Gardens of Spain*, conducted by Arbós and played by José Cubiles, a young pianist and friend of the composer. He did not play it by heart, and thus his performance lost much of its bite. But I fell in love with this work, and offered to play it at the last symphony concert of the season. Being constantly on tour, I learned it by reading the score on trains. At the rehearsal I played it by heart. De Falla and Arbós were pleased with my performance at the concert, but the public did not quite respond to it; the work was too complicated for them, and it ended in a dead pianissimo. Nevertheless, Arbós and I were applauded very warmly, and I played the "Fire Dance" as an encore, which produced the usual ovation. The King and the Queen were present at that concert. In the royal box, during intermission, I told Their Majesties about my coming departure for Argentina and complained to the King about the injustice which I, as a Pole, had to suffer over losing my passport because of the political upheavals in Russia! The King, who had close relatives in Poland and who felt a great sympathy for my country, asked me to be at the Royal Palace the next day at noon. "I shall give orders to bring you to my private apartments, and I shall see what can be done."

* A gold sovereign was worth five dollars in gold in those days.

I could hardly sleep that night. At noon sharp, at the palace, an aide-de-camp of the King took me to the royal chambers, where His Majesty received me without delay. The King introduced me to a gentleman who was in the room. "He is my *jefe de seguridad*, my chief of police. He will issue you a legitimate Spanish passport with the indication that you are a citizen of Poland without a diplomatic representation at my court, but with my personal guarantee of your identity. I think that this document will give you the freedom to enter any country." He received my thanks with a charming smile and gave me as a farewell present his photograph in a silver frame with the inscription: "Para Arturo Rubinstein, el gran amigo de España. Alfonso R."

I treasured this picture and the two I had received from the Queen for a long time. Unfortunately, I lost them when the Nazis invaded my house in Paris.

Thanks to my Spanish passport I was recognized by a great nation as the first citizen of a free Poland, which was still far from being an independent country.

In the middle of May 1917, Quesada and I sailed from Cadiz for Buenos Aires on the Spanish steamer *Infanta Isabel*. The long journey, which lasted more than two weeks, gave us a much needed rest. We had on board the charming Lara company and a French comedy company of André Brulé and Regina Badet which was going to Chile and Peru. All these actors were delightful companions; I played often for them, and they loved to listen to me.

Two days before we reached Buenos Aires, I received a cablegram from my impresario (the brother-in-law): "I sold my contract with the Lara Theater and with you to Faustino da Rosa stop he needs you desperately for his Teatro Odeon stop the Guitry Company which he had engaged refuses to sail because of the submarine danger." I called Quesada, gave him a hug, and began to dance and shout. "Ernesto, this one is my best *deus ex machina!*"

Quesada read and reread the telegram.

"It is incredible, it is hard to believe," he said. "This is exactly what we wanted in the first place—you are, indeed, a lucky man!"

"Yes, Ernesto," I said, suddenly becoming serious, "I *am* very lucky, but I have a little theory about this. I have noticed through experience and through my own observations that Providence, Nature, God, or what I would call the Power of Creation seems to favor human beings who accept and love life unconditionally. And I am certainly one who does, with all my heart. So I have discovered as a result of what I can only call miracles that whenever my inner self desires something subconsciously, life will somehow grant it to me."

Afterword

I decided deliberately to draw the curtain here. It was at this point that my young years were over. From then on my life changed color and moved forward at a more steady pace. I had gained the necessary hold on my career—a career that continues, despite many ups and downs, to give me to this very day immeasurable joy.

ARTHUR RUBINSTEIN
New York City
January 1973

Index